IDEAS IN ACTION

Volume II

Other books in American History published by
American Book Company

Leland D. Baldwin,
  *The Flavor of the Past: Readings in American
  Social and Political Portraiture*

Leland D. Baldwin and Robert Kelley,
  The Stream of American History, Third Edition

Leland D. Baldwin and Robert Kelley,
  Survey of American History, Second Edition

IDEAS IN ACTION

Documentary and Interpretive Readings

in American History

VOLUME II — FROM 1877

Compiled and Edited by

Leland D. Baldwin

Emeritus Professor of History
University of Pittsburgh

AMERICAN BOOK COMPANY

Grateful acknowledgment is made to the following publishers and individuals for permission to reprint material which is in copyright or of which they are the authorized publishers:

AMERICAN HERITAGE PUBLISHING CO.: Excerpt from "Daylight in the Swamp," by Stewart Holbrook. © Copyright 1958 by American Heritage Publishing Co., Inc. (October 1958 AMERICAN HERITAGE).

AMERICAN PHILOSOPHICAL SOCIETY: "Social Darwinism and the Businessman," by Irvin G. Wyllie, in PROCEEDINGS of the American Philosophical Society, V. 103 (Oct. 1959), p. 631.

THE AMERICAN SCHOLAR: "The South and the New Freedom: An Interpretation," by Arthur S. Link, reprinted from *The American Scholar*, Volume 20, Number 3, Summer, 1951. Copyright 1951 by the United Chapters of Phi Beta Kappa.

THE ANTIOCH PRESS: Excerpt from *Samuel Gompers*, by Bernard Mandel, and "Neither Ideology Nor Utopia: The New Deal in Retrospect," by Heinz Eulau (*The Antioch Review*, Vol. xix, No. 4).

ATLANTIC-LITTLE, BROWN AND COMPANY: Excerpts from *Memoirs: 1925–1950*, by George F. Kennan, Copyright·© 1967 by George F. Kennan. Excerpt from *The Public Philosophy* by Walter Lippmann, Copyright 1955 by Walter Lippmann.

THE BOBBS-MERRILL COMPANY: Excerpt from *Presidents I've Known*, by Charles Willis Thompson, copyright 1929, 1956 by Charles Willis Thompson. Excerpt from *New Deal Thought*, Howard Zinn, ed., pp. xvi–xvii.

COLUMBIA FORUM: Excerpts from "Sources of the New Deal: Reflections on the Temper of a Time," by Arthur Schlesinger, Fall, 1959, Vol. II, No. 4, Copyright 1959 by the Trustees of Columbia University in the City of New York.

DISSENT: "A Case Against Interventionism," by William Pfaff, Sept.–Oct. 1967.

NORMA MILLAY ELLIS: Excerpt from *Conversation at Midnight*, by Edna St. Vincent Millay, Harper & Row Publishers, Copyright 1937, 1964 by Edna St. Vincent Millay and Norma Millay Ellis.

FOREIGN AFFAIRS: Excerpts from "Origins of the Cold War," by Arthur Schlesinger, Jr., October 1967, from "American Intellectuals and Foreign Policy," by Irving Kristol, July 1967, and from "The Sources of Soviet Conduct," by George F. Kennan, quoted by special permission from FOREIGN AFFAIRS, July 1947, copyright by The Council on Foreign Relations, Inc., New York.

FREEDOM HOUSE PUBLIC AFFAIRS INSTITUTE: Excerpts from report on 1967 Conference on Asian Affairs.

HARCOURT, BRACE & WORLD: Excerpt from *Conquest*, by John Franklin Carter. Excerpt from *Roosevelt: The Lion and the Fox*, © 1956, by James MacGregor Burns. Excerpt from *America's Painless Imperialism*, by John Franklin Carter. Excerpt from *Versailles: Twenty Years After*, by Paul Birdsall, copyright, 1941, by Paul Birdsall. Excerpt from *Views of America*, by Alan F. Westin, © 1966 by Harcourt, Brace & World, Inc.

HARPER & ROW, PUBLISHERS: Excerpts from pp. 26–32, 184 from "Testimony Before the Special House Committee," in *Scientific Management* by Frederick Winslow Taylor, Copyright, 1947 by Harper & Brothers. Excerpt from pp. 340–349 in *Out of Our Past*, by Carl N. Degler, Copyright © 1959 by Carl N. Degler. Abridgment of pp. 44–69 from *The Future of American Politics*, by Samuel Lubell, Copyright © 1965 by Samuel Lubell. Excerpt from pp. 12–13 in *The Ordeal of Change*, by Eric Hoffer (Harper, 1954).

HARPER'S MAGAZINE: Excerpt from "The New Philosophy Comes to Life," by Peter F. Drucker, Copyright © 1957, by Harper's Magazine, Inc., reprinted from the August, 1957 issue of Harper's Magazine by permission of the author. Excerpt from "What's American about America," by John A. Kouwenhoven, Copyright © 1956, by Harper's Magazine, Inc., reprinted from the July, 1956 issue of Harper's Magazine by permission of the author.

HARVARD UNIVERSITY PRESS: Excerpts from *Conservation and the Gospel of Efficiency*, by Samuel P. Hays, Copyright, 1959, by the President and Fellows of Harvard College.

DR. IVES HENDRICK: Extract from *The Life and Letters of Walter Hines Page*, by Burton J. Hendrick.

PREFACE

The primary purpose of this collection of readings is to provide the student with the seminal documents of American history,* interleafing them with more or less recent essays which examine the nation's background and experience in the light of its aims and ideals. It should be recognized that in the allotted space it is impossible to cover all aspects of our development. Indeed, this collection deliberately plays down the descriptive and social side in order to give more attention to intellectual, cultural, and political development. Thus, in connection with the Negro's struggle for equality we reprint a number of documents and essays—but offer no descriptions of Negro life. The latter function is reserved for companion volumes which may be used or not as the student or teacher prefers.

A second object has been to offer some view of historiographical trends, both in fields where relative concensus has been reached and in those where professional opinion is seriously divided. Here again, because of space limitations it is impossible to present each case at length. Thus in covering some of the controversial eras it has seemed best to offer a historiographer's statements of the various views without attempting to judge among them. Somewhat parallel problems are found in presenting the causes of wars and the fame of generals, and I have attempted to pre-

* The Constitution and the Declaration of Independence are readily available in any text, so are omitted to make way for other material.

sent the best thinking in each case—at least the closest attainable thing to con-census.

I am well aware that no two compilers would agree thoroughly on what should be selected for inclusion. Indeed, the task has been made doubly difficult by the tremendous amount of excellent analytical material poured forth in the last twenty years by the younger generation of historians. I have the feeling that frequently, when space limitations dictated that something must go, a critic might say I would have gotten as good results by drawing lots. All I can do is beg for tolerance—or failing that, mercy.

One feature which it is hoped will meet with favor is the frequent use of batteries of quotations—usually short ones—to illuminate the subject being ex-amined, sometimes to present contradictory views.

I have sought to avoid prolixity in the introductions both to chapters and to documents and essays. The temptation is to try to aid the reader by going into devious detail, to introduce events, authors, and books *in extenso*, not only to prove that I am well aware of them, but because they presumably should be a part of the student's education. But I have resisted, with what success the reader must judge. After all, this collection (even taken with its companion volumes) cannot profess to be complete. The serious student can consider it as no more than an introduction to further and more arduous reading.

It is a pleasure to be able to acknowledge here the unfailing courtesy and aid of the library staff at the Santa Barbara Campus of the University of California. Special thanks go to Dr. Donald C. Davidson, the librarian, to Mr. Christian Brun and Mrs. Lorie Ritchie of Special Collections, and to Mrs. Frieda Hagman and her assistants in the Interlibrary Loan service. Thanks are due also to Mr. Roland Harris for his patient and intelligent assistance in research and in the thousand routine chores incident to a work of this kind. Finally, acknowledgment is due my wife for her patient assistance all during the long period since I began this task.

Leland D. Baldwin

CONTENTS

8 CULTURAL FORCES AT THE TURN OF THE CENTURY 155

9 THE POLITICAL WARS OF REFORM 187

18 THE ASIAN FRONT 432

19 THE POSTWAR YEARS: NEW PATTERNS IN POLITICS AND LAW 461

IDEAS IN ACTION

Volume II

TOWARD THE FULFILLMENT OF THE PROMISE OF AMERICA

INTRODUCTION

The promise of America has been defined at length, but the core of the definition is that cultural and material resources shall no longer be the exclusive property of a certain few and shall become of service to all. To be more explicit, the demand was not (as under socialism) to divide up the existing pie equally, but to bake and distribute additional pies. We have seen how this idea lay at the root of many important movements in our history—political, constitutional, social, and economic. Indeed, no strong interest (with the exception of slavocracy) ever denied the goal; quarrels were over the method of reaching the goal and the speed with which it should be attained. As with so many human endeavors, we have approached the goal not so much by intelligent planning as by experiment—that is, by trial and error. Notable instances were the struggle between Hamilton and Jefferson, and the disposition of the public domain; yet to come, in this overview, is—among other things—the struggle over the role of the corporation.

The purpose of this chapter is to sketch a background for an understanding of the nature and techniques of American progress during the last century—a sketch which will be filled in by later chapters. If this initial sketch is largely presented in economic terms, it is not intended to be understood that our progress was solely material. The intimation, rather, is that only the civilization which uses its full ingenuity to overcome and use the material in service to mankind is—or can be—effectively idealistic and spiritual; that is, if it can use the material without worshiping it. Americans have never been able to agree with India that philosophy is a sufficient consolation for an empty belly and that a bed of spikes is somehow more purifying than an inner-spring mattress. As Hu Shih, the Chinese statesman and philosopher pointed out, the Orient has a truly materialistic civilization because it is limited by matter and is incapable of transcending it. Its contentment with little and its fatalistic resignation are more materialistic than its actual hovels and images of the gods.

The evolution of American economic ideas from the heydey of laissez faire to the present state of the affluent society was long and complex, and was marked by bitter infighting among economists, politicians, labor unions, and farmers. The crucial period began after Northern victory in the Civil War turned out to be a victory of industrial capitalists over the locofocos and the aristo-agrarian planters. The dominant Republican Party now found its mission in ensuring Federal complaisance toward rising industry. Enterprisers were permitted to purchase natural resources at low prices, they were granted protective tariffs against foreign competitors, and the laws were tailored to their satisfaction.

Republican policy, be it noted, was in conformity with the effective public will. Since business prosperity lay at the root of national prosperity, it was considered only right and proper for government to lavish natural resources upon it. Attempts to hoard resources were regarded as against the public interest. Suggestions that government regulate private enterprise were considered as obviously socialistic; indeed, it might well be that regulation would have been morally and materially destructive, for after three generations of experiment we are still uncertain about what form regulation should take and how far it should go. The genius of America had risen from the energy of its people and from their insistence that they must be left free from institutional interference in exploiting the vast natural resources of their country. Even the Constitution had been deliberately drawn to prevent governmental interference with the citizen and his enterprises. Employers' guilds and laborers' unions were weak. A vast free domestic market, constantly being expanded as population grew and invention created new needs, beckoned to the manufacturer, and a superb transportation network offered access to remote parts of the country.

Without denying that there were deliberate abuses in industry during this Gilded Age, it is clear that the basic evils of the period rose from economic ignorance. Classical economics was based on the belief that there would always be a scarcity of goods in relation to demand and that competition for the market must be bitter and at times brutal. As a result, a secure place in the market could be held only by the monopolist, who naturally would reduce output and raise prices; our social and mass-production ideal of maximum production for the lowest price would have been regarded as absurd, and doubtless would have been in the context. At any rate, the effect of this "economy of scarcity" ideal was that competition (the basis of laissez-faire doctrine) must logically end when one competitor succeeded in absorbing or ruining the others. Free enterprise meant the right of a man to risk his stake in the competition—and the right of the victor to keep the spoils.

When the risks are great, there is a tendency to ensure success by undercutting the rules of fair play. Laissez-faire theory insists that the market is automatically regulated by the law of supply and demand and that the function of government is merely to serve as an umpire. This has always been more theory than practice, for there are always men who are willing to accept and even demand government intervention when it helps them, though of course they loudly champion laissez faire when government action would hamper them.

The war among competitors frequently resulted in wastefulness and mutual destruction, and this condition was made worse by the rise of a group of reckless financiers and market manipulators—to say nothing of the erratic nature of the business cycle and of the political struggle over a sound currency. Industries and railroads were thus so weakened that the Panic of 1893 hit them hard, and many went bankrupt. The return of the Republicans to power under McKinley in 1897 brought, or at least coincided with, a renewal of business activity, but responsible businessmen were now determined to take steps to see that the debacle was not repeated.

Leadership in this movement was exercised by the great merchant capitalist, John Pierpont Morgan, and by John D. Rockefeller, tremendously successful oil entrepreneur who had gone into banking. These men and their associates, as bankers in a nation with an expanding economy and a serious shortage of credit, were in a position to dictate terms to the chaotic industrialists. The bankers argued that chaos could be forefended only if industrialists and railroaders adopted a live-and-let-live policy which they called "community of interest." To do this it was necessary to form a monopoly or semi-monopoly in each field and dictate common policies. They hoped also to minimize the rise and fall of prices and to pad the disastrous effects of the business cycle; to make savings in buying and manufacturing; to control prices and raise profits; and to block the rising power of labor, which they felt was leading to socialism.

The American revolt against laissez faire was promoted by the studies of American "political economists" in German universities and was marked by the foundation in 1885 of the American Economic Association under the leadership of such men as Simon Patten (1852–1922), Richard T. Ely (1854–1943), and John Bates Clark (1847–1938). The break with classical economics was exemplified in a statement of principles which contained the following: "We regard the State as an agency whose positive assistance is one of the indispensable conditions of human progress." Though the statement was discarded three years later, it remained the motto of a considerable wing of the association, notably Patten, who felt that monopoly was normal and should be regulated by government. Clark, on the other hand, believed in competition as an agent of progress. Here we see the early stages of the struggle between regulationism and atomism, the two wings of Progressivism.

Even before the "community of interest" movement there had arisen a demand that the "trusts" be regulated so as to cut down their power to raise and lower prices at pleasure and to throttle competition. Congress responded reluctantly with the Interstate Commerce Act (1887) and the Sherman Antitrust Act (1890), but both were shorn of power by the Supreme Court. Indeed, the Supreme Court's actions must have encouraged the investment bankers to launch the era of trust formation that coincided with McKinley's administration. Writing in *The Truth about the Trusts* in 1904, John Moody listed 318 principal industrial trusts with a capitalizaion of $7.25 billion—about forty percent of the national total—and 5,288 plants. All together consolidation had brought together capitalizations of $20 billion.

Moody's disclosures had something to do with the swelling of the Progressive Movement—a movement which, however, had many origins and many objectives, and cannot be accurately characterized in a phrase. Some Progressives seemed to apply liberal reformist ideas to the American scene but with the additional faith that they were helping out progress through evolution. Others more closely resembled Jefferson and Jackson, who seemed to believe that they were peeling away unhealthy excrescences and *returning* to the conditions of a purer age. The atavistic survival of this concept split the Progressive movement into two wings—Atomists and Regulationists—and they began to walk warily in each other's presence. The Atomists, who wished to break up the "monopolies"—actually they meant any large corporation—and force the pieces to compete, were (the Regulationists insisted) trying to thwart the economic law which dictated the continual cheapening of goods through the savings of concentration and mass production; continued tampering with the course of nature would bring economic breakdown and chaos. On the other hand, the Regulationists (the Atomists insisted) were building a new Leviathan which must be either the superstate controlling business or superbusiness controlling the state. The Atomists were probably best represented by La Follette and Brandeis, and the Regulationists by Theodore Roosevelt. It is difficult to place Wilson, for he was frequently vague or contradictory.

As perceptive Progressives became fully conscious of their apparent dilemma, the realization angered and embittered some of them. Instead of a glorious sweep straight on to the gates of Paradise, they saw the road fork before them and disaster waiting on both paths. History, instead of being progressive, seemed to be cyclical. Atomism led to economic trouble and brought breakdown or revolution; Regulationism led to something rather resembling what we now call fascism. Apparently we were headed for destruction, either on the horn of dictatorship or on the horn of economic breakdown.

The answer to this dilemma rose from the logic of a pragmatic society which frankly insisted that industry must seek the good of the people as a whole. From this insistence on a better life—with which the American entrepreneur and the engineer fundamentally agreed—there flowed the evolution through mass production, oligopoly, the "new economics," and "countervailing power" to the present "affluent society" and quasi-welfare state. The selections offered in this chapter are intended to follow this evolution. We are less concerned with economic theory *per se* than with the definable historical steps.

The dilemma faced by the progressives in the early years of this century was resolved by the emergence of oligopoly (few sellers), wherein a few giant corporations compete in each field. But their existence was not recognized until after the depression of 1929 was well under way, so theories about their care and feeding had to take second place to the problem of what to do about the Depression.

The problem of depression furnished the arena in which two great economists clashed: John Maynard Keynes (1883–1946), an Englishman, and Joseph Schumpeter (1885–1950), a Czech transplanted to Harvard. Keynes's portrait of an economy subject to collapse at the peak of prosperity and stagnation at the bottom of depression has, after many years, won grudging assent even among conservatives, and is largely responsible for the "new economics" which deprecates thrift, posits government intervention in the economy, and looks on the public debt as fructifying.

On the other hand, Schumpeter held that capitalism's dynamism was perfectly capable of dealing with depressions and indefinitely expanding the economy. Capitalism's problem, rather, rose from its very success, for it created a society which demanded even more goods and services than it could furnish. In the end, the state would have to take over and create a socialist economy.

The problem posed by both Keynes and Schumpeter, then, was how to save capitalism. John Kenneth Galbraith, another Harvard economist, in his book *American Capitalism* (1952) offered at least a partial answer in his portrait of the "countervailing power" which—again like oligopoly, almost unperceived—had set up counter pressures among buyers and sellers, and among competing materials, as glass and tin containers. Prominent among these pressures were not only the great corporations themselves but labor unions, farm cooperatives, chain stores, and, most significantly, the government, which threw its weight from side to side as necessary to maintain a balance among powers.

These developments have helped to create the present economy of the United States, which is far from either being perfect or having built-in stability, but is the best that an industrial society has ever had. But as economists meet around the table with government officials and labor and farm leaders there are also there two unbidden participants, like spectres at a feast. Their names are Poverty and War.

The problem of poverty has become so acute that America is now divided into two nations, each with its own subcultures, and between whom there is almost as little communication as though they spoke different languages. Still, this problem *can* be solved by applying techniques already known and previously used; the question is whether the American public has the intelligence and the will to demand their use, and the persistence to follow through.

The problem of war is worse, for mankind has never really faced up to the sacrifices essential to abolish it. Yes, *sacrifices*, for it has fulfilled certain deep-seated psychological and emotional needs, including what we have chosen to call national and ideological security. One sacrifice that may have to be made is the democratic right to refuse to listen to good advice, and to go mulishly on our merry way making the selfish demands and acting on the insane prejudices which sow the seeds of hatred at home and war abroad.

These are the root causes of modern warfare. There is no doubt that in past ages economic reasons prompted herdsmen and plundering hordes to make war, and even today we see war justified by economic rationalizations; just how sound they are has become a subject of dispute between Lenin's monocausation on one side and the multicausationists on the other (See the selection "Imperialism and

War" by R.N. Carew-Hunt in Chapter 10). Lenin, of course, was trying to prove that a communist state could not be imperialist—a futile and nonsensical exercise. Be that as it may, the experiences of Japan and West Germany since World War II demonstrate that economic imperialism—that is, the annexation of raw materials and markets—is not essential to prosperity.

Though the causes of modern war are primarily psychological and political, a subtle question haunts every thinking man and woman: can we have prosperity without gigantic government expenditures for war? It is notable that the New Deal did not bring economic recovery: World War II did that. And have we been prosperous since that only because of expenditures for wars, past, present, and future? Are we like a bicyclist who remains upright only as long as he maintains momentum? And if so, why have we failed to find a more rational support than war? It is easy, of course, to blame the communist policy of using continuous small wars to sap the democracies' prosperity, but this is no answer for either side; if capitalist prosperity is indeed based on war, then the communists are defeating their own objective by prolonging war. In any case, in this nuclear age it is to the advantage of both sides to take the risk of living without war.

The foregoing presentation is intended to show that, though we have come a long distance toward fulfilling the promise of America, yet internal and external problems remain. Throughout this volume you will examine these problems, considering as many of their aspects as space affords, but do not look for panaceas.

"ONLY THE PRODUCTIVE ARE STRONG, ONLY THE STRONG ARE FREE"

I believe in America because in it we are free—free to choose our government, to speak our minds, to observe our different religions.

Because we are generous with our freedom, we share our rights with those who disagree with us.

Because we hate no people and covet no people's lands.

Because we are blessed with a natural and varied abundance.

Because we have great dreams and because we have the opportunity to make those dreams come true.

.   .   .   .

There are no distant points in the world any longer—our thinking in the future must be world wide. . . .

Freedom is an indivisible word—we must be prepared to extend it to every one, whether they are rich or poor, whether they agree with us or not, no matter what their race or the color of their skin.

The only soil in which liberty can grow is that of a united people—we must have faith that the welfare of one is the welfare of all—we must acknowledge that all are equal before God and before the law.

Only the productive are strong, only the strong are free.

It is inescapably true that to raise the standard of living of any man anywhere in the world is to raise the standard of living by some slight degree of every man, everywhere in the world.

—The words of Wendell Willkie carved on a granite book at his grave in Rushville, Indiana

THE USES OF PHILOSOPHY IN A PRAGMATIC SOCIETY

[The trial-and-error method so prominent in America's political and economic evolution was consistent with its pragmatic way of thinking—or should it be the other way around? The Italian liberal, Mino Vianello, has set forth succinctly the role of pragmatism in democratic society and its contrast with the closed philosophical systems of Europe. The following is taken from Vianello's "Filosofia e società in America," in *Communità*, Anno 13, No. 71 (July 1959), pp. 94–98, translated by Alan F. Westin and printed in his collection *Views of America* (N.Y.: Harcourt, Brace and World, 1966), pp. 7–11.]

In the West the principal requirements for a philosophy are that it be a *critical comprehension* of reality that tends toward a *universal vision* and yet is at the same time endowed with *rigorous logical structure*. . . .

In the course of the nineteenth century this typically Western schema was extended to embrace a third requirement, influenced and confirmed by the development of science, namely, *verifiability*. This, carried over into the domain of action, has given rise, along with the prevalence of democratic ideas, to the growth of a fourth requirement, *positive results*. . . .

The United States was born toward the end of the scientific revolution. A conception of the world oriented to material values was developing to the detriment of the traditional sciences of Western philosophy: metaphysics and formal logic. Faced with an attack from the two characteristic demands of the mental attitudes originating in this new scheme of values, verifiability of theories and positive results for human beings in the moral and political fields, interest in suprasensible reality tended to retreat from the soil in which live ideas are germinated. In America, a continent not burdened with traditions, an intellectual life could be initiated that was closer to the needs of the society being born. . . .

I do not know how much recognition has been given to the fact that it was in America that the physical sciences and then the social sciences were first separated from the bosom of philosophy, which in Europe was still considered "the mother of sciences." It is not remarkable to discover that at Yale the young [Jonathan] Edwards read Newton while he was still alive, whereas at Cambridge, thirty years after Newton's death, the textbook was still Rouhault? And is it not important to repeat here that the democratic system, that is, the system that puts man in the center of political life, became a reality for the first time on the soil of the New World? There is no doubt that the emphasis given from the very beginning to the sciences (or the requirement of verifiability) and to the democratic ideal (or the requirement of positive contribution to human life) is more than sufficient reason for the genesis in America of a profoundly original intellectual universe. . . .

"A better life" is something that cannot exist without the desire for a better life. This desire appears everywhere in human history. But it has become a reality only in America, and a reality so absorbing as to have become the sole reality. It is in relation to this reality that we must seek the requirement of philosophy in America, for it is by this [standard] that the life of individuals and institutions is measured. A society so oriented cannot tolerate anything that leads to withdrawal into self, to the search for satisfaction anywhere else than in visible goods, or to the creation of fixed social bonds. If an idea does not make a contribution in this sense [to a better life], it is worse than a waste of time it; is an obstacle, a social crime. If, on the other hand, it contributes to the betterment of life, it is energetically supported, whatever its theoretical implications.

It is not difficult to show that this position, certainly simplistic to the European eye, contains an inner contradiction. On the one hand it seems that America depends on convictions of a deeply rooted ideal character, and on the other hand that its life is focused on the pursuit of material goods with no consideration for the life of the spirit. But the error here is to take logical activity as the central characteristic, for in America the fusion of principles with the fervor of practical life takes place on the level of individual conscience without any formal systematization, least of all one imposed by an external authority, which is the case in countries with a Catholic tradition.

But neither the assertion that Protestant individualism constitutes a large part of the American tradition, nor the assertion that America, without having produced a philosophy like Hegelianism or Marxism, has been so successful that it now shows the way to the Western world, are fully sufficient to explain what motivates the American thinker. The point is that the triumph of science and democracy has deprived religion of its dogmatic aggressiveness and has transferred its interests to the moral plane. An emphasis on the theoretical aspect of philosophy could not help but revive the great questions of Western thought that, in their turn, would resuscitate religious polemics. Besides involving a departure from the trend they have followed up to now, this would threaten Americans with the risk of breaking up their political unity and, consequently,

their entire way of life. A people cannot change its mental habits unless driven by the force of circumstances, and in America, today as in the past, the circumstances require *tolerance*. The demand for complete liberty of the individual in the realm of ideas is not only a Protestant tradition; it is also enforced by the environment because an ideological struggle would signify paralysis. . . .

The American way of life is the product of environmental circumstances, among which the following three predominate: the immensely vast and virgin territory, industrialism, and the Protestant tradition. American democracy developed in this framework and is inconceivable apart from it. . . . And because these elements necessarily depend upon each other, when one attempts to transplant American pragmatism elsewhere, it very quickly leads to a miscarriage. Since philosophy in America is unlike philosophy anywhere else—that is, *an instrument of life* founded on the requisites of empiricism and practicality—it is inimical to, and in a certain sense even immune from, the excesses of speculation, and is optimistic, progressive, and antitotalitarian. . . .

At the center of pragmatism, as is generally known, is an interest in the future: an idea is valid insofar as it functions in experience. One can even say that our third requirement [of philosophy], namely verifiability, has been subordinated to the last, a situation completely peculiar to American philosophy. . . . At bottom pragmatism is closer to English utilitarianism than to German idealism, and for the motto of the former, "The best idea is that which produces the happiness of the greatest number," it substitutes, "the best action is that which produces the happiness of the greatest number." Its most complete expression on the philosophical level is found in Dewey, for whom ideas are instruments that control the adjustment of the individual to the environment, "mind" being conceived as the expression of organic behavior. And in the socioeconomic sphere its most complete expression is Veblen's masterful analysis of the institutional contradictions in American capitalist society.

In all of this, the center of attention is man in an industrial and democratic society, and the entire emphasis of this movement is essentially a mighty voice in defense of the common man. . . . It can thus be seen that in the last one hundred years Americans have developed systems of thought more adapted to the ends of modern society than have the Europeans, assuming, of course, that the end of society is the constant elevation of man's situation and that the meaning of culture is the knowledge of how to attain harmony between the demands of the individual and those of society.

Some say that this instrumental philosophy is not systematic, and that since it implies, in addition, a denial of God (or perhaps primarily on this account) it is not philosophy at all. But this seems to me a play on words, as if the definition of philosophy were the kind of thing about which argument is possible. . . . The issue that is real because it is founded on reality is that either one wants a democratic society, in which case speculative endeavor ought to be directed to resolving the problem of a common social life, or else one does not, in which case one can undoubtedly continue with the philosophy of the closed system and allow the academic chairs to remain in the power of the rhetoric of the absolute.

THE PROMISE OF SCIENTIFIC MANAGEMENT

The time is fast going by for the great personal or individual achievement of any one man standing alone and without the help of those around him. And the time is coming when all great things will be done by that type of cooperation in which each man performs the function for which he is best suited, each man preserves his own individuality and is supreme in his particular function, and each man at the same time loses none of his originality and proper personal initiative, and yet is controlled by and must work harmoniously with many other men.

—Frederick Winslow Taylor

Effective mass production developed first in the United States because it was promoted by a combination of fundamental and peculiar characteristics which around 1900 existed there and nowhere else. First was American receptivity to new methods, promoted by liberal patent laws, the early application of laboratory tests and research, and by the fact that no restrictions on new processes had been laid down by guilds, labor unions, or hereditary social or economic castes. Second was the intelligence and know-how of American workmen who had been familiar with tools from boyhood—often power-driven tools, at that. Third, the scarcity of labor promoted the invention of labor-saving devices. This meant that power was applied to manufacturing processes wherever possible, that machinery and parts were standardized, that American products were pre-eminently machine-made, and that the bulk of our manufactures made small changes—as in meat packing, flour milling, lumbering, dairying, and oil refining. Fourth was the vast store of natural resources easily and cheaply available to entrepreneurs. Fifth, and as vital as any of the above, was the vast expanding domestic market, unvexed by internal inspection or customs barriers. Lastly was a unique contribution possible (at the moment) only in America: this lay in the American genius for teamwork, on the part of both management and labor. Out of these rose the triumph of mass production.

The evolution toward mass production had gotten well under way before the Civil War. The gunmakers of the Connecticut Valley had introduced the three primary stages: the interchangeable part, machine tools, and the application of power to machinery. These techniques had spread throughout the country, and the demands of the Civil War had accelerated their application. As soon as machine tools began to pour out nuts, bolts, nails, wire, and gadgets, the early stages of mass production were really under way. There remained the fourth step: scientific management and its logical application, the assembly line.

The leader in this advance was Frederick Winslow Taylor (1856–1915), a Philadelphia engineer who in 1893 set himself up as an engineering consultant with "Systematizing Shop Management and Manufacturing Costs a Speciality." Taylor believed that by planning and routing work through the factory and by job and time studies he could set up reasonable and efficient production standards. The slide rule, the stop watch, photography, and Taylor's own development of high-speed tool steel were essential parts of the research of the new school. He was well aware that workmen "soldiered" on the job, and he laid it to the existing antagonism between worker and manager. He hoped to allay this growing antagonism and at the same time increase production by advocating a wage system based on the "differentiated piece rate," which would stimulate and reward the efficient workers and would introduce a new spirit of cooperation—essentially the extension of democracy to industry.

Taylor and the enthusiastic associates who quickly gathered about him saw the industrial problem not only in terms of machines and efficiency but also in terms of human relations. High wages, high standards of safety, and good working conditions entered into their calculations, and they were even aware of the effects upon the job of the social conditions in the community. At first business, rolling luxuriously in profits, hesitated to adopt Taylor's ideas of efficiency, and they actually found a warmer reception in Europe. But by 1911 profits had come down and entrepreneurs were ready to try anything which would reduce costs. Unfortunately management refused at first to adopt Taylor's recommendations for improving labor relations. These had to wait for more enlightened management, and legislative and labor-union pressure.

Taylor summarized his methods in *The Principles of Scientific Management* (1911), but the clearest exposition of his doctrines and their hoped-for effects is in his testimony before a Congressional Committee in January 1912. Herewith we reprint certain passages from the testimony as given in *Scientific Management* (N.Y.: Harper, 1947), pp. 22–33 and 184–185. Taylor used a pen factory as an illustration. Suppose that a workman was turning out ten pens a day for a wage of $2.50, and the foreman puts him on piecework at the rate of ten cents for each pen. Eventually the workman may turn out twenty pens and earn $5.00 a day, thus increasing the output and the profits of the factory at no increase in the price per unit. However, when the directors find out what is happening they complain that the labor market is being spoiled and order that the workmen turn out twenty pens at the old rate of $2.50 per day. The result is discontent and a deliberate slowing down of production. The company has violated the tenets of scientific management and is suffering the consequences in discontented labor, lower production, and increased costs.

Scientific management is not any efficiency device, not a device of any kind for securing efficiency; nor is it any bunch or group of efficiency devices. It is not a new system of figuring costs; it is not a new scheme of paying men; it is not a piecework system; it is not a bonus system; it is not a premium system; it is no scheme for paying men; it is not holding a stop watch on a man and writing things down about him; it is not time study; it is not motion study nor an analysis of the movements of men; it is not the printing and ruling and unloading of a ton or two of blanks on a set of men and saying, "Here's your system; go use it." It is not divided foremanship or functional foremanship; it is not any of the devices which the average man calls to mind when scientific management is spoken of. . . . They are useful adjuncts to scientific management, so are they also useful adjuncts of other systems of management.

Now, in its essence, scientific management involves a complete mental revolution on the part of the workingman engaged in any particular establishment or industry—a complete mental revolution on the part of these men as to their duties toward their work, toward their fellow men, and toward their employers. And it involves the equally complete mental revolution on the part of those on the management's side—the foreman, the superintendent, the owner of the business, the board of directors—a complete mental revolution on their part as to their duties toward their fellow workers in the management, toward their workmen, and toward all of their daily problems. And without this complete mental revolution on both sides scientific management does not exist. . . .

The great revolution that takes place in the mental attitude of the two parties under scientific management is that both sides take their eyes off of the division of the surplus as the all-important matter, and together turn their attention toward increasing the size of the surplus until this surplus becomes so large that it is unnecessary to quarrel over how it shall be divided. They come to see that when they stop pulling against one another, and instead both turn and push shoulder to shoulder in the same direction, the size of the surplus created by their joint efforts is truly astounding. They both realize that when they substitute friendly cooperation and mutual helpfulness for antagonism and strife they are together able to make this surplus so enormously greater than it was in the past that there is ample room for a large increase in wages for the workmen and an equally great increase in profits for the manufacturer. . . .

The substitution of this new outlook—this new viewpoint—is of the very essence of scientific management, and scientific management exists nowhere until after this has become the central idea of both sides; until this new idea of cooperation and peace has been substituted for the old idea of discord and war. . . .

There is, however, one more change in viewpoint which is absolutely essential to the existence of scientific management. Both sides must recognize as essential the substitution of exact scientific investigation and knowledge for the old individual judgment or opinion, either of the workman or the boss, in all matters relating to the work done in the establishment. And this applies both as to the methods to be employed in doing the work and the time in which each job should be done. . . .

What has scientific management accomplished? It has been introduced in a great number and variety of industries in this country, to a greater or less degree, and in those companies which have come under scientific management it is, I think, safe and conservative to say that the output of the individual workman has been, on the average, doubled. This doubling of the output has enabled the manufacturer to earn a larger profit, because it has cheapened the cost of manufacture; and, in addition to enabling the manufacturer to earn a larger profit, it has in many cases—in fact, in most cases—resulted in a very material lowering of the selling price of the article. Through this lowering of the selling price the whole public, the buyer and user, of the joint product of the labor and machinery have profited by getting what they buy cheaper. This is the greatest interest that the general public has in scientific management—that in the end they will get more for their money than they are now getting —in other words, that scientific management will in the end enable us all to live better than we are now living. Through scientific management, then, the manufacturer has already profited, and the general public has also profited.

The greatest gain has come, however, in my judgment, to the workmen who have been working under scientific management. They have received from 30 to 100 per cent higher wages than they received in the past; and, in addition, I do not recall a single case in which they have ever worked longer hours than they did before, but I do recall many instances in which the hours of work where shortened. Perhaps the greatest gain, however,—and I say it without hesitation—is not the increase in wages received by the workmen, but the fact that those who are working under scientific management have come to look upon their employers as their best friends instead of their enemies. They have come to realize that friendship and cooperation are better than war. . . .

The whole world is now, just as it always has been, suffering from underproduction. Underproduction is responsible mainly for low wages; it is responsible for the fact that the poorer people of this world have just so much fewer things to live on (that they have poorer food to eat; pay higher prices for their rents; can buy fewer clothes to wear than they ought to have; in other words, that they lack what I have defined in my direct testimony as true riches); the fact that the poorer people lack in many cases the necessities, and in all cases the luxuries of life which they ought to have, is a justification for the fact that an

increase of output is needed now just as much as it always has been, because absolutely the only way that these necessities and luxuries can be brought into the world is through an increase in output. Now, as I pointed out in my direct testimony, and as an analysis of the testimony presented to this committee will show, a great part of the industrial world is deliberately soldiering. And until we have reached the point where deliberate soldiering has been stopped; and until the normal and proper output per man has been reached, no workman will be asked to work materially harder than he is now working. And, as you know, scientific management is a scheme for greatly increasing the output of the man without materially increasing his effort.

THE CORPORATION AS A SOCIAL INSTITUTION

[The introduction of scientific management brought mass production to its first peak—the assembly line. Another peak—automation—is now being attained, but it is not likely to upset the revolution in economic and social understanding which became clear with the first. This revolution was brilliantly set forth by Peter F. Drucker, an Austrian economist, whose *Concept of the Corporation* (N.Y.: John Day, 1946) was written as an exposition of General Motors, but who brought to his analysis the clear and impartial insight which makes it a remarkable comment on the meaning of America. Drucker's analysis is far too long to reprint, but we can paraphrase parts of it and reprint others.

As Frederick W. Taylor showed at the very outset, there is far more to mass production than careful technical blueprinting and management. It is even more basically a social effort. Now the success of a social effort depends upon the cooperation of the participating individuals. It is perhaps true that machines and many aspects of scientific management could have been developed without the inspiration of democracy. Nevertheless, the ultimate secret of the American know-how lies not in machines, nor in scientific management, nor even in financial and corporation organization. As Taylor pointed out, it depends on the fostering of the spirit of freedom, cooperation, and *esprit de corps* on the part of workers, engineers, management, and capital. This condition may bring an upstanding demand for high wages and miscellaneous benefits (often enforced by strikes), but this demand is only a realization of Taylor's original concept that mass production could be successful only if the workers shared in pride and effort.

The twentieth century's transformation of democracy aided in achieving the desired result not only by forcing the corporations into line but by creating a new atmosphere, in which labor could strive for its rights with more hope of success. Only in so far as this democratization has been achieved can American mass production be said to have succeeded. This idea is something which foreigners usually cannot or will not understand, and it must be admitted that many Americans have fallen short in realization, even Henry Ford himself. On the other hand, it must be recognized that industrial democracy exercised without a proper sense of responsibility and self-restraint on the part of the workers will lead to what we now call "featherbedding" and eventually to breakdown. The purpose of mass production is to raise production, and only then can it raise wages. In the production process it relies chiefly on semiskilled workers, but this is possible only because its preparatory stage utilizes an ever-growing number of skilled men—tool, die, and pattern makers, engineers, chemists, and psychologists.

Experience has shown that the corporation is the most practical agent in working this modern miracle of technical, financial, and social cooperation; and the corporation is useful whether the economy is capitalistic, socialistic, or totalitarian. The more vigorously theorists and politicians have denounced the corporation, the more it has flourished. Internally the corporation is like a planned society. It brings together the factors of production—land, labor, and capital—and adds a fourth, the manager, who makes the whole greater than the sum of its parts. It has proved to be so satisfactory in a number of democratic countries that the theory of socialism has begun to shift away from government ownership of the means of production to government *control* of private producers. Public ownership of production is to be limited to basic industries, and not all socialists agree even on that, for it imposes a burden of debt on the state.

If private control of the corporation is to survive it must meet on three levels the test which any institution must undergo. It must (1) be functionally integrated, that is, have the organization to produce, the leadership to advance, the flexibility to meet new conditions, and the ability to assess realistically how well it is performing its functions; (2) be able to mold its internal policies and relations so as to fulfill society's beliefs and promises; and (3) square its own purpose for existence, the making of profits, with society's view of its purpose for existence, the supplying of cheap goods or services. These three problems must be solved interdependently, for they are equal in importance to survival; failure in any one means death.

Corporations have on the whole successfully met the first test. They have learned that efficiency is best promoted if the organization is neither too big nor too small; hence the halt in the movement toward the unification of steel and of automobile manufacture. This limit still enables the two industries to afford research and pioneering, to take long-term interests into account, and, by amassing adequate reserves and shifting orders among plants, to avoid undue retrenchments and promote company and social stability. Intelligent decentralization within the corporation has promoted flexibility, brought out new leadership, and made more positions for able men.

Corporations have not failed on the second test as dismally as is often claimed. Management has earnestly sought "within the framework imposed by external financial control" to ease the social and psychological problems raised by mass production. Modern economy probably offers a poorer chance to become independent than there was a hundred years ago, but the chances of rising to foreman or into the managerial class would seem to be greater than ever.

There is a common complaint that assembly-line work is monotonous, and so it is. The assembly line, however, employs only part of the men in a factory, nor is it an essential feature of all mass production. Anyhow, there is a tendency among fickle moderns to resent continuous and arduous effort; we forget that monotony is the price not only of security but of knowledge.

Compared with those in other countries American labor-management relations are remarkably successful—even cordial. Nevertheless, many problems remain. Workmen complain that advancement is capricious, or that it is based on formal academic and technical training and there is little chance to develop latent abilities.

It is demonstrable that the managers often fail to give the worker an understanding of the significance of his part in the production process. Instances are told of how morale problems in wartime airplane factories were solved by bringing in bombers with crews to show the worker exactly what he had accomplished.

The corporation, moreover, has failed to raise the workingman's social dignity and status. The result of corporation policies has been that labor unions have copied capital's old tactics and have found their mission in purely negative opposition to any force in business, society, or government that threatens their "rights" and have made the situation worse by their featherbedding, jurisdictional strife, and the initiation fee and other practices. Under the circumstances it is no wonder that labor unions have also failed to win dignity and status for their members.

The third test brings up the problem of balancing the corporation's need for profits against society's need for cheap goods. The human desire for achievement, prestige, and power finds many outlets, of which the profit motive is only one. It is used in our society, which demands material results, as the best way to "co-ordinate individual drives into social purpose and action." Even the U.S.S.R. uses economic incentives and rewards; true enough, it rejects private profit, but it brazenly pumps out of its official monopoly trusts greater profits than capitalistic corporations would dare to demand.

Nineteenth-century men lived in an economy of scarcity, in which it was believed that supply could not overtake demand. The interests of the producer and of society seemed irreconcilable; an industry was sure it must seek monopoly in order to keep from being wrecked by competitors, but society felt it must prevent monopoly in order to keep from being milked. Now we live in an economy made by mass production, in which the supply is prospectively unlimited, but demand is limited only by effective purchasing power. For the first time *maximum profit can be obtained by maximum production at minimum cost*—exactly what society has always wanted. We have not worked out all the details, but the broad outline of the future is clear. Mass production can introduce an economy of plenty, a state which up to our own time only utopian dreamers dared to contemplate. In order to explain this remarkable result we reprint from Drucker's *Concept of the Corporation*, pp. 130–141, 209–210, 219–221.]

In the realm of political beliefs, desires and values we enter a sphere in which the controversies are not merely on methods and techniques but on the goals of social life. Therefore we have to make clear, at the outset, that our concern here is with the particular beliefs, aims and purposes of American society with its roots in the Christian tradition.

It is characteristic of the American tradition that its political philosophy sees social institutions as a means to an end which is beyond society. It has never accepted society as an end in itself; nor has it ever seen social institutions as mere expediency, unconnected with the ultimate ethical ends of individual life. It has, at one and the same time, refused to accept that deification of society which endows the state, the nation or the race with absolute value, omnipotence and omniscience, and that degradation of society which makes the law a mere traffic rule without any ethical significance or reason.

Americans rarely realize how completely their view of society differs from that accepted in Europe where social philosophy for the last three hundred years has fluctuated between regarding society as God and regarding it merely as an expression of brute force. The difference between the American view of the nature and meaning of social organization and the views of modern Europe goes back to the sixteenth and seventeenth centuries. During that period which culminated in the Thirty Years' War (1618–1648) the Continent (and to a lesser degree England) broke with the traditional concept of society as a means to an ethical end—the concept that underlay the great medieval synthesis—and substituted for it either the deification or the degradation of politics. Ever since, the only choice in Europe has been between Hegel and Machiavelli. This country (and that part of English tradition which began with Hooker and led through Locke to Burke) refused to break with the basically Christian view of society as it was developed from the fifth to the fifteenth century and built its society on the re-application of the old principle to new social facts and new social needs.

To this social philosophy the United States owes that character of being at the same time both the most materialistic and the most idealistic society, which has baffled so many observers. This country can be materialistic because it gives an ethical meaning and an importance to the material institutions of social life. This seems outrageous to the European idealist who sees basic beliefs and ethical ends as existing in the realm of pure spirit and as completely detached from the sordid and humdrum human existence. It appears as dangerous nonsense to all those who maintain that society is its own goal and who therefore see in the demand that it justify itself in terms of individual fulfillment a demagogic appeal to the baser instincts of the rabble. At the same time America appears to be unbelievably, at times even childishly, idealistic because to an American material institutions and material gains are never an end in themselves but always a means for the realization of some ideal goal. Hence analysts have fluctuated between describing this country as completely obsessed by the drive for the "almighty dollar" and as quixotically engaged in reforming the world in the search for the

millennium. Undoubtedly either characterization while grossly exaggerated, is essentially correct; but the true picture only emerges if we see the two as complementary. The American who regards social institutions and material goods as ethically valuable *because* they are the means to an ethical goal is neither an idealist nor a naturalist, he is a dualist.

To this philosophy of society this country owes its great political insight. The *Federalist* is a classic of politics precisely because it manages to be profoundly pragmatic and deeply moral at the same time. But to this philosophy America also owes its worst political blind spot: a refusal to see the existence of an irrational, emotional or naturalistic basis of allegiance. Thus the American people have repeatedly failed to see great emotional forces within their own country—the years before the Civil War are a good example—as they often fail to understand the behavior of foreign, especially of European, nations. It was almost impossible for an American to comprehend that, for instance, a German soldier would fight well even though bitterly opposed to Nazism. The proposition—elementary to every European whether German, French or Russian—that you owe allegiance to your country and nation as the permanent facts of human life rather than to the creed adopted by them for the time being, sounds like blasphemy to American ears. To an American too his country is the reality of his social life, but not because it exists but because it is the living embodiment of the American creed which thus receives the emphasis.

It does not concern us here whether this philosophy is a correct or a true statement of political reality. What concerns us is that it is the only concept on which to base a meaningful analysis of American society. For Americans themselves see it that way and judge their society by the degree to which it realizes the basic purposes and beliefs of the individual. Hence Americans can afford to neglect many problems of social and political organization European nations have to face. At the same time this country has to take seriously any question relating to the relationship between American creed and American social performance. It must always ask whether its social institutions carry out the basic promises of American life or not. . . .

Refusal to accept the inevitable shortcomings of any society is responsible for a good deal of what is best in political life. The demand that society be made to live up fully to its promises and beliefs underlies the activity of the reformer and accounts for many social and political advances and improvements. And nothing is more contemptible than the smug resignation to the inevitable imperfections of society which in all ages has characterized the Philistine.

At the same time refusal to understand that society and social institutions cannot be perfect, and that by the very nature of human activity their efficiency is low (though no lower than that of any other man-made thing such as, for instance, a steam engine) accounts for some of the worst mistakes in political analysis and political action. Time and again and in every society there have been men who considered their own society and its institutions doomed and ineffectual because they did not run at a hundred-per-cent efficiency. As long as this leads to nothing worse than premature predictions that this or that institution (capitalism, democracy, the British Empire or Russian communism) are doomed, no real harm is done. But it very often leads to a cynical willingness to give up what we have because it is not perfect. It is, for instance, certainly true that the United States will not be a perfect democracy as long as the American Negro is treated as an outcast. But to conclude therefrom as did a section of the Left that American democracy is nothing but a sham and might as well be scrapped entirely is not only illogical but dangerous. It is political smugness surely as contemptible as that of the Philistine and perhaps more destructive.

Analysis of the degree to which our society and its institutions fulfill our basic beliefs and promises has to start with the realization that without some considerable ethical efficiency no society and no institution can survive. Yet it must also be accepted that not more than partial success can be expected or should be demanded. To paraphrase words of Edmund Burke, it is not enough to prove a society to be less than perfect to justify its overthrow; one must also prove that a new society or new institution is likely to do better.

It will never be possible to obtain anything resembling unanimity on the concrete ways to realize the basic beliefs and promises of American society. But on these beliefs and promises themselves the American people agree apparently with hardly a dissenting voice. Fundamentally, American political philosophy stands on the Christian basis of the uniqueness of the individual. From this follows (a) the promise of justice or, as we usually phrase it, of equal opportunities. From it also follows (b) the promise of individual fulfillment, of the "good life," or, in a perhaps more precise formulation, the promise of status and function as an individual. . . .

Yet they stand in a dialectical contradiction to each other that makes them appear incompatible. One principle demands that each individual have status and function because of his uniqueness as an individual; the other that his status and function depend exclusively on his contribution to society. The first leads to the demand that each member find individual meaning in society—that society be seen as existing exclusively for him. The second leads to the demand that social position be based on individual achievement and ability, that the individual be judged on his social performance alone. The one seems to lead to a hierarchical concept of society, the other to anarchy. . . .

Those two concepts stand in the same relation to each other as the North Pole and the South Pole: neither can be where the other is, yet neither can be without the other. In the American concept of a middle-class society this is clearly recognized; and from this recognition the concept derives much of its strength and all of its appeal. But this recognition also poses for American statesmanship a constant problem of synthesizing and balancing.

If the big-business corporation is America's representative social institution it must realize these basic beliefs of American society—at least enough to satisfy minimum requirements. . . .

The demand for status and function as an individual means that in the modern industrial society the citizen must obtain both standing in his society and individual satisfaction through his membership in the plant, that is, through being an employee. Individual dignity and fulfillment in an industrial society can only be given in and through work. Hence the painful futility of all the brave attempts to give the modern citizen individual fulfillment in "cultural," "recreational" or "leisure-hours" activities. The first demand thus is that our citizens are citizens because they are engaged in industry. This is the problem with which Social Security has tried to grapple. For you are not a citizen if your status in society depends on forces over which you have absolutely no control such as the business cycle. Equally important is that the individual must be able to realize through his work in industry that satisfaction which comes from one's own meaningfulness for society and which expresses the basic conviction of the uniqueness of the person. The industrial society must give its members that sense of importance which cannot be produced by propaganda or by other psychological means, but can only come from the reality of having importance. . . . To attack industrial society, as would the sentimental equalitarian, because it is based on subordination instead of on formal equality, is a misunderstanding of the nature both of industry and of society. Like every other institution which co-ordinates human efforts to a social end, the corporation must be organized on hierarchical lines. But also everybody from the boss to the sweeper must be seen as equally necessary to the success of the common enterprise. . . .

. . . .

We can define the relationship between the corporation and society in several ways. We may say that legally the corporation is a creature of the state, endowed in the interest of society with legal existence, legal rights and privileges. Or we may use the terminology of the political analyst and talk of the corporation as an institution of organized society which has to fulfill basic social tasks. Or, economically, we may talk of the corporation as the unit in which our industrial resources are organized for efficient production. Whatever the terminology, the large corporation is a tool and organ of society. Hence society must demand of the corporation that it be able to discharge the specific economic functions which are its *raison d'être*. This is an absolute, a supreme demand— as absolute and supreme as the demand that the corporation meet the necessities of its own functioning and survival.

How do these two absolute commands relate to each other? Is there conflict or harmony between the demand for efficiency in terms of corporate functioning, and the demand for efficiency in terms of functioning, stability and prosperity of society? Clearly, a functioning free-enterprise society can only exist if the two sets of requirements can be satisfied by one economic policy. If the economic policy needed in the interest of society were in constant conflict with an economic policy needed in the interest of corporate functioning and efficiency, we would have perpetual, paralyzing friction. . . .

It was the essence of the nineteenth century theory of monopoly that maximum profit for the longest period could not be realized by maximum production for the lowest price—the social criterion of efficient production—but only by following the opposite, "monopolistic" policy. If this theory were a correct expression of social reality, industrial society could not exist, at least not in the form in which we know it, as a society of independent, self-governing corporate units. If it were true that the independent business must try to be monopolistic for its own best self-interest, we could not hope to be able to enforce anti-monopoly laws; for no institution can accept rules which go counter to its basic survival interest and purpose. On the other hand, we could not permit business to be monopolistic; for this would deny the basic demands and needs of society. From the classical theory of monopoly no other conclusion is possible than that a free-enterprise economy is impossible once society has become an industrial society. On the basis of the classical theory of monopoly there is no other conclusion but state socialism or a society of compulsory cartels; and in actual practice there is little difference between the two.

This theory of monopoly which is still widely accepted as gospel truth, rests on the assumption—correct in the eighteenth century —that supply will always be limited, whereas demand will always be unlimited. On this assumption, monopolistic behavior will indeed yield the maximum profit. But under modern industrial conditions, it is not supply that is limited, but demand; supply in modern mass-production industry has, by definition, no practical limitations. It is simply not true that contraction of production and artificial maintenance of high prices will always yield the highest profit to the producer. On the contrary, *under conditions of modern technology, the maximum profit is obtained by maximum production at the minimum cost.* To have first realized this was the great achievement and the original contribution of Henry Ford. The essence of the mass-production process is the reversal of the conditions from which the theory of monopoly was deduced. The new assumptions constitute a veritable economic revolution. Like all revolutions, it has created as many problems as it solved; the threat of mass unemployment is very largely a reflection of this change in which supply has become more elastic than demand. But as far as the problem of monopoly is concerned, the new technology can resolve the conflict between social purpose and corporate purpose. For in modern mass-production industry monopolistic

behavior (artificial contraction of production in order to maintain an artificially high price) is uneconomical and unprofitable. Instead, that behavior has become most profitable for the producer which is also most beneficial to society, namely, maximum production at minimum cost.

Under modern mass-production conditions maximum profitability depends on maximum efficiency. In a monopolistic business, competitive market standing is eliminated as a measure of efficiency; and we have seen in the preceding chapter that without the yardstick of the market, the objective checks of efficiency function very poorly, if they function at all. In other words, under modern mass-production conditions, a business will realize the highest rate of profit on its invested capital only if it is subject to that check of the competitive market which a monopolistic business eliminates.

When General Motors in the twenties began to expand rapidly, it was laid down by the top executives that it should not aim at complete control of the automobile market but should in its own best interest keep its market quota low enough to make possible the existence of strong and healthy competitors—not for philanthropic or political reasons, but simply from the point of view of the corporations' efficiency and profitability. It is clear that there is a certain tension between corporate interest in the existence of strong and vigorous competition and the way in which success is measured in terms of a steady tightening of the corporation's hold on the market. In other words, there may be a point where a business may succeed too well for its own good. But this in itself is a complete contradiction of the nineteenth century theory which denied the existence of such a point. According to that theory, the point where a business enterprise begins to lose its social usefulness is the point where it begins to be most profitable. Actually, the point at which a business reaches its maximum social usefulness is also the point of its maximum profitability. *Under conditions of*

modern mass production, there is no con- *ity and social interest in maximum produc-*
flict between corporate interest in profitabil- *tion.*

TRUE AMERICANISM

I, born in a foreign land, pay my tribute to Americanism? Yes, for to me the word
Americanism, *true* Americanism, comprehends the noblest ideas which ever swelled
a human heart with noble pride. . . . You may tell me that these views are vision-
ary, that the destiny of this country is less exalted, that the American people are
less great than I think they are or ought to be. I answer, ideals are like stars; you
will not succeed in touching them with your hands. . . .

We see the vigorous elements of all nations . . . undertaking to commence
a new era in the history of the world, without first destroying the results of the
progress of past periods; undertaking to found a new cosmopolitan nation without
marching over the dead bodies of slain millions. Thus was founded the *great colony
of free humanity,* which has not old England alone, but the *world,* for its mother-
country. . . .

And in this colony of free humanity, whose mother-country is the world, they
established *the Republic of equal rights, where the title of manhood is the title to
citizenship.* . . . This was the dream of the truest friends of man from the beginning. . . . You cannot subvert your neighbor's rights without striking a dangerous
blow at your own. . . . Equality of rights, embodied in general self-government, is
the great moral element of true democracy. . . . There is the solid foundation of
our system of government; there is our mission; there is our greatness; there is our
safety; there, and nowhere else!

This is true Americanism, and to this I pay the tribute of my devotion.

—Carl Schurz, Speech on "True Americanism," Faneuil Hall,
Boston, April 18, 1859, in *Speeches, Correspondence, and
Political Papers* (6v., N.Y.: Putnam's, 1913) 1:49–59

THE PROSPECTS OF AMERICAN CAPITALISM

[For the evolution of American capitalism from oligopoly to countervailing power
and an examination of the "new economics" we turn to the essay with the above
title in Daniel Bell's *The End of Ideology* (N.Y.: The Free Press, 1963), pp. 75–94.
For further enlightenment on oligopoly and countervailing power the student
should read the lengthier popular treatment by John Kenneth Galbraith in his
American Capitalism (1952). An excellent and easily grasped account of Keynesian-
ism is found in Robert L. Heilbroner, *The Worldly Philosophers* (1961).]

It is a striking cultural phenomenon, especially for anyone with a memory of the thirties,
that American capitalism has obtained grudging regard and a new theoretical definition

from critics, especially Keynesian ones, who
once were hostile. The term "American capitalism" points to a necessary distinction, for neo-
classical economics, which marked out the

ground rules for capitalism in general, has never lacked competent intellectual spokesmen. The case for the free market . . . —the proposition that a competitive society is the indispensable *model* to obtain both efficient allocation of resources and free consumer choice—has proved itself a compelling one. . . .

Who, however, was prepared to justify the American capitalist reality, the salient feature of which was an (apparently) paralyzing corporate giantism? By 1940, the majority of the younger economists were convinced that our economy was entering a phase of "secular (in the sense of long-term or permanent) stagnation." The prophet of this new creed was Alvin Hansen of Harvard, but its patristic source was clearly John Maynard Keynes. Although for decades a chorus of Marxian economists had chanted a requiem for the aging capitalist system, in less apocalyptic fashion Keynes located the reasons for degeneration. The system was not functioning, he said, because savings (meaning, on the whole, profits) were not passing over smoothly into investment (particularly in producer's goods), so that the total demand for goods and services would fall short of the capacity of the economy to produce them, resulting thus in unemployment.

Classical economics, it will be remembered, could not admit of crises under capitalism. It repeated Say's Law that every amount of production meant exactly the same amount of consumption, i.e., the money paid out for the production of goods would eventually be used for consumption, so that there could be neither "overproduction" nor "underconsumption." Unemployment, therefore, represented only a temporary dislocation until production and consumption came into balance. (Imbalances would be corrected if prices fell, inducing the consumer to buy, and unemployment would be reduced if wages were lowered, inducing employers to hire. It was all a matter of a free market—and time.) . . .

Keynes had foreshadowed the outlines of the modern "stagnation theory" in his famous *Economic Consequences of the Peace*, written in 1919. The argument, novel then, is familiar now. The compelling social myth that held society together, said Keynes in a metaphor, was the "non-consumption of the cake." Workers were "cajoled by custom, convention, authority" into accepting a small share of the increasing production of the nineteenth century, while the capitalist, free to consume it, made "the duty of 'saving' nine-tenths of virtue, and the growth of the cake the object of true religion." Thus a huge share of production was saved for investment. This tied in with the reality of the nineteenth century: a growing population, which needed food, clothing, shelter, and employment; new sources of foods and raw materials, which demanded exploitation; the development of technology, which permitted new industries. Under these circumstances the entrepreneur could go on baking cakes in order not to eat them.

But this was, after all, said Keynes, only an extraordinary episodic period in economic history. By the 1920's, population growth had slowed down, investment opportunities were vanishing, the spirit of the entrepreneur was flagging. And, perhaps most important of all, savings were losing their social function. The habitual holding-back of large sums from consumption no longer had the useful effect of increasing production; rather it led to economic crises—and stagnation. (Thus Keynes was not concerned with the productivity-increasing aspects of investment: that is something his followers took up. His prognosis was that the economy was close to saturation, and the problem which only the government could undertake was to maintain *effective demand* by spending.)

Keynes's writings in the next fifteen years were a detailed effort to document his analysis. The root evil was the bourgeois "virtue" of thrift ("the penny wisdom of Gladstonian finance"), and the necessary intellectual task of the generation was to exorcise that ghost. Keynes's great work on *The General Theory of Employment, Interest and Money* was not only an economic tract but equally a savage socio-logical polemic against the "puritanism . . . which has neglected the arts of production as well as those of enjoyment."

His aim was the "euthanasia of the *rentier*," enjoying a free and unhampered consumption in a "quasi-stationary" community which, be-cause it had no desire or need to grow, also had little use for savings. But since this psycho-logical revolution against saving was difficult to effect, only one force could effectively guarantee the movement of stored, useless capital into channels that would revive economic activity—and that was the state. With one bold stroke, thus Keynes reintroduced the study of *political* economy, which for him meant a statement of human aims to be defined consciously by an organized consensus (the social interest), as against "*pure* economics" or the "natural laws" of distribution, as determined through the market by the sum total of individual decisions. The political problem of how to reach a con-sensus, and apply its decisions, which for us raises many difficult questions of bureaucrati-zation and power, did not trouble Keynes. Writing in the full stream of English political thought, with its sense of homogeneity and the image of a "common will embodied in the policy of the State," he felt such problems could be solved simply and rationally. His pro-gram, "moderately conservative in its implica-tions," as he put it, excluded any question of the ownership of the instruments of production; all that it required, he wrote blandly, was a "somewhat comprehensive socialization of in-vestment" in order to assure full employ-ment.

The theory of "oversavings," which Keynes had formulated as the key to depression, was picked up enthusiastically by the younger Amer-ican economists and became the guiding con-ception of the Temporary National Economic Committee investigations and monographs of the late thirties. Where Keynes's *General Theory* had been analytical, the American school sought to add a historical dimension as further proof of the impending "secular stag-nation." The lead was taken principally by Alvin Hansen, and the materials summarized in Hansen's major work, *Fiscal Policies and Business Cycles*, in 1941.

His theory . . . stated that the nineteenth century was a unique era wherein a fateful combination of factors had combined to create an industrial explosion. We were, said Hansen, beached at the end of a series of "long waves" whose force was not spent. Mid-nineteenth-century America (1840 to 1870) had been pro-pelled by the age of the railroad; the first part of the twentieth century (1890 to 1930) had been the age of electrification and the automo-bile. But we cannot now "take for granted," Hansen wrote, "the rapid emergence of new industries as rich in investment opportunities . . ." Other factors also tended to create stag-nation: chief of these was a decline in popula-tion growth, the disappearance of new territory, and the growth of monopoly and imperfect competition, which, by protecting prices, inhib-ited the introduction of new machinery which a competitive process would have stimulated.

Within the operational machinery of the capitalist system itself certain internal forces worked to calcify the society. Keynes had not been concerned with industrial organization. Hansen was. He argued that "bigness" was a cause of depression because large corporations tended to accumulate huge depreciation re-serves for replacement of plant and equipment, reserves which remained unspent and also re-duced the need for outside money. In addition, the growth of "capital-saving" (as opposed to labor-saving) machinery, which meant a long-term tendency to lower the ratio of capital to output, added to the piling-up of idle capital. Hansen's conclusions provided a rationale for New Deal policies: state intervention to move the idle capital, attempts to break up "mo-nopolies," and shift to a high-consumption, low-growth economy.

This then was the image of capitalism in the early forties: the capitalist was an old miser sitting on his pile of sterile bullion, which weighed down the economy. Since *he* found it impossible to inject the money into an economy which needed it, if that economy was to provide jobs and the standard of living it was technologically capable of producing, the government would have to force him to disgorge it— or tax it away and spend it on useful projects. . . .

If there was one conservative theoretician who could take the measure of Keynes, and possibly even of Marx, it was Joseph Schumpeter [whose *Capitalism, Socialism and Democracy* was published in 1942.] . . . Schumpeter's defense of capitalism took, as the crucial starting point, the fact that capitalist society was characterized by interrupted but high productive expansion. The contemporary "rediscovery" of productivity (and the consequent ideological use of this concept as a distinguishing element of "American" from static "European" capitalism) is due in great measure to the primary emphasis on productivity in Schumpeter's book. "The capitalist achievement does not typically consist in providing more silk stockings for queens but in bringing them within the reach of factory girls in return for steadily decreasing effort." Using rough computations, Schumpeter pointed out that U.S. national income had been increasing at a compound rate of more than 2 per cent a year. But increase in productivity was possible only through the activity of entrepreneurs, the engineers of social change. By cutting costs, opening new markets, creating new types of production, in short through innovation, the entrepreneur is able to achieve a temporary monopoly position which is the source of *his* profit. Capitalism can continue only if it maintains entrepreneurial rewards whose "short-run inequity" is the price that the masses must pay for the long-run rising living standards that capitalism can achieve.

Schumpeter's iconoclasm extended also to the defense of "bigness." Bigness was a virtue because only big companies could afford the huge and sometimes fruitless outlays for research which were necessary for technical change. Bigness, in that sense, represented the social price for technical change.

But what of the Great Depression? Schumpeter denied that the period from 1929 to 1932 represented a decisive break in the propelling mechanism of capitalist production, as he described it. Contrary to the views of most economists, classical or Keynesian, he calmly accepted depressions as natural, inevitable, and even therapeutic for the growth of the economy. Technological revolutions periodically reshape the existing structure of industry. "The capitalist process, not by coincidence but by virtue of its mechanism, progressively raises the standards of life of the masses. *It does so through a sequence of vicissitudes, the severity of which is proportional to the speed of the advance.*" Any process of change provides disruption; a depression is a normal process of readjustment and displacement, a "shaking out" of the antiquated, the marginal, and inefficient. . . .

Against the pessimism of Hansen and Keynes regarding the possibilities of an expanding economy, Schumpeter projected a vision of new frontiers. "Technological possibilities," he wrote, "are an uncharted sea." It might take the form of great innovations through a new "age of chemicals," which would succeed electricity as a source of investment, or it might be a multiplicity of new products no single one of which might match the impact of, say, the automobile, but which collectively could provide the stimulus toward new growth.

The future, however, rested on the entrepreneur. In his theory of the entrepreneur Schumpeter confronted Marx and Keynes and, in fact, the entire classical school of economics. For Marx, economic growth was a product of the accumulation of capital ever seeking new outlets; Keynes saw that the desire to save became excessive, and he saw effective demand as falling in the absence of government intervention. Schumpeter denied the theoretical basis for chronic oversavings, and his answer to Marx and Keynes rested on a historical foundation. For him, the expansion of industry arises not from the "push" of capital but the "pull" of the entrepreneur. For Schumpeter, industry is financed typically by banks and by the expansion of credit. The entrepreneur works with "other people's money." To collect money from old and unproductive channels, and to command resources, he pays interest. His reward is profit. Economic advance, therefore, is not slowed [as Keynes claimed] by oversavings, or lack of savings, or even the inability of entrepreneurs to tap savings, but simply the lack of opportunities for the entrepreneur to come forth and break new ground—for profit. The function of government, therefore, is not to direct investment, as Keynes saw it, but to encourage the entrepreneur.

And yet, said Schumpeter paradoxically, the *vision* of Marx was correct; capitalism is indeed doomed, but not for the reasons Marx advanced. Capitalism decomposes because its mentality creates a social atmosphere hostile to its functioning, and because, at the same time, the bureaucratization of business atrophies its driving force, the entrepreneurial function.

Paradoxically, capitalism is destroyed by its success. The creation of an open society arouses greater wants and expectations than even capitalism can fulfil. After all, even in the ideal circumstances of America it is still not possible to increase productivity by more than 2 to 3 per cent a year. If the case for capitalism rests on its long-run achievements, in the short run it is the profits and inefficiencies that dominate the picture, and these continually offer ammunition for its critics. And capitalism itself fosters the criticism that threatens it. "The capitalist process," writes Schumpeter, "rationalizes behavior and ideas, and by so doing chases from our minds, along with metaphysical belief, mystic and romantic ideas of all sorts . . ." The critical turn of mind that such rationality creates knows no bounds, and it turns against all institutions, against all accepted tradition and custom, against all authority; it culminates logically in the creation of the "intellectual." The intellectual is both critic and utopian: he needs a hero. The capitalist unheroically estimates rather than gambles, appraises rather than acts. "The stock exchange," as Schumpeter says wryly, "is a poor

substitute for the Holy Grail." And so the intellectual, the product of capitalist rationalism, turns his back on the system and infects the rest of the society with his disappointment. Similarly, the state, responsive to the anticapitalist temper of the society, enacts legislation which is restrictive of the entrepreneurial spirit.

Not only is it menaced from without; the capitalist system is also menaced from within. The entrepreneur, the man who broke "the cake of custom," is replaced by the "executive," and innovation is routinized as technology becomes the business of a team of specialists; thus economic progress tends to become depersonalized and automatized and, without *élan*, must "inevitably" run down. The bureaucratization of capitalism is its undoing.

Schumpeter's appeal for the old "left" intellectual is apparent. Here was a rarity: an economist with a tragic sense of life. Moreover, his doctrine allowed capitalism's critics to have their cake and eat it too: capitalism *was* good, but it had now become depersonalized and bureaucratized—the very charges they had themselves levied against the system. And yet, for the plain and prosaic tasks of understanding the specific problems ahead, Schumpeter's insights are of limited help. In his brilliant book, Schumpeter talks of "capitalism" rather than, like Keynes, of "economies." *He does not talk, however, of concrete capitalist societies.* It was thus not easy to notice that in his analyses he selected the economics of American industry and the sociology of European society and derived his justifications for capitalism from the first and his apocalyptic visions as to its fate from the second. . . . American democracy, with its philosophical roots in Jeffersonianism and its development into a multi-group society, may have very different consequences for capitalism from those of European democracy. But this Schumpeter did not see, or rather did not care to see.

If we are to obtain a realistic picture of what is happening to capitalist society, the inherent contradictions between the visions of

Keynes and Schumpeter will have to be resolved. For while both agree that traditional capitalism is giving way, their theories concerning the reasons for the change are so divergent as to give rise to directly contradictory proposals for policies that might save it. It is one of the virtues of J. K. Galbraith's *American Capitalism* that the problems common to Schumpeter and Keynes are posed in more prosaic yet more manageable terms and some implicit attempt at reconciliation is made.

Galbraith's starting point was the remarkable "failure of nerve" by all strata of American society regarding the future of capitalism at a time when the productive apparatus is actually expanding at a rate as fast as any previous period in United States history. . . . [Liberal and conservative economists, capitalists, workers, and farmers, all expected the economy to collapse with the end of the war expenditures. Why this fixed idea?] Why this high degree of illusion and insecurity? The answer, says Galbraith, is that both camps are "*captives of ideas which cause them to view the world with misgivings or alarm.*" These ideas derive from the system of classical economics and its theory of power.

Classical economists rooted their system in a fear of concentrated power. A liberal society, therefore, was one that diffused power. In the economic realm, no single individual or group should be able to dictate what was to be produced and who would do it. They envisaged a market society in which prices fluctuated readily in response to supply and demand, where producers were free to enter or depart from business, etc. The corollary assumption, operating from economic deterministic premises, is that free markets make free men. If economic power were fragmented, then political power would be atomized as well.

The fact is, of course, that in the major industrial areas of production, oligopoly, i.e., the dominance of a few, is the prevailing feature of the society. Prices are "administered" rather than set in the market; other firms follow this "price leadership," entry into the business

is exceedingly difficult, etc. The liberal, seeing this concentration of economic power, believes it to be dangerous and seeks to break it up.

The singular point that Galbraith makes, following the lead of Schumpeter, is that while oligopoly does exist, few of the consequences the liberals fear actually eventuate. The pattern of oligopoly is natural and almost inevitable in a high-investment economy, and turns out to be not the product of any conspiratorial plot . . . but of the market itself. As an industry grows, the firms already in operation grow, realizing the technical efficiencies gained by large-scale production. The established firms also gain from "the economics of experience." A new firm, when it can mobilize the capital, faces the additional handicaps of lack of personnel, untried executives, etc. So new competition is difficult. Oligopoly in any industry is likely to be achieved in the short space of a few years, and once equilibrium has been achieved the degree of concentration remains remarkably stable.

Against the yardstick of a pure theory of price, the result may be some distortions and inefficiencies in the allocation of resources. But the compensation lies in the technological progress fostered by the large corporation. "It is admirably equipped for financing technical development. Its organization provides strong incentives for undertaking development and for putting it into use. . . . The power that enables the firm to have some influence on price insures that the resulting gains will not be passed on to the public by imitators (who have stood none of the costs of development) before the outlay for development can be recouped. *In this way market power protects the incentive to technical development.*" In agriculture, the principal area where the competitive model still obtains, the farmer does almost no research on his own behalf; the job is left to the state experiment stations and the U.S. Department of Agriculture.

Here is a strong and sophisticated defense of bigness on the criteria of *performance*. But— and this is where Galbraith seeks to explain why businessmen and liberals are captives to the old phantoms—the businessman cannot admit he exercises tremendous power. "This is partly a matter of tradition; it is also an invitation for attention from the public and from the anti-trust section of the Justice Department. Hence, in order to justify his unwillingness to accept federal regulation, he has to deny his exercise of economic power altogether, and maintain the ideology of competition."

The other side of the coin is the phantasm of the liberal: the specter of untrammeled corporate power standing firm on the "commanding heights of the economy." It is against the liberal view, actually, that Galbraith develops his theory of "countervailing powers," a phrase which in its imaginative simplicity crystallizes a feeling a number of observers have had about the society.

In general this feeling was summed up in the image of "functional blocs," such as industry, labor, farmers, that confront and check each other. Galbraith's view is more subtle in its characterization. "Dogmatically stated . . . private economic power is held in check by the countervailing power of those who are subject to it. The first begets the second. The long trend toward concentration of industrial enterprise in the hands of a relatively few firms has brought into existence not only strong sellers, as the economists have supposed, but also strong buyers, as they have failed to see." The self-regulation of the market in America today comes not from the competition of producers, where oligopoly prevails, but the self-generating counter-power of buyers and sellers.

The theory is most evident in the labor-relations field, where strong unions have arisen to check the power of corporations in wage determination. But it operates in other areas as well: great buying chains like Sears Roebuck were able to avoid the oligopolistic domination of rubber prices because of their bulk purchases; A&P, by threatening to go into the processing business, could bring down the price of food supplies. "There are no consumer co-operatives of any importance in the United States," Galbraith writes, "because the chain stores preempted the gains of countervailing power first." The power of the auto companies curbed steel. . . . In some instances, e.g., the building trades, the powers that should oppose each other have entered into collusion, with a consequent loss of economic efficiency.

These economic valences developed in the twenties when buyer combined against seller. Where groups like farmers and workers were unable to generate such balances, the state was forced to step in and help. In the case of the farmers, the effort was begun by Hoover, whose Federal Farm Board undertook to sponsor a system of national co-operatives. In general, however, the New Deal established the countervaling power for competition as the regulator of the disadvantaged groups. From this theory, the substitution of countervailing power for competition as the regulator of private economic power, Galbraith seeks to establish a yardstick for state action, not for regulation, or even "trust-busting," but for the development, where needed, of countervailing power.

In all this, Galbraith has skilfully developed a realistic theory of political economy, more suitable than the old competitive one to a world of economic behemoths. And yet, Galbraith is enough of a Keynesian to know this is not enough. "We have within the economy no mechanism which acts autonomously to insure proper performance; it is sadly evident from experience as well as from theory that the peacetime norm of the American economy is not necessarily stability at a high level of production and employment." The need, therefore, is for some form of centralized government decision, namely, in the area of fiscal policy so as to influence the total demand for goods through taxation or government spending. "If the Keynesian formula is workable, then the last of the major reasons for alarm over American capitalism dissolves."

Yet Galbraith's book fails in a crucial sociological instance. It never answers its own question: *why* are the business community and the Left captives to a description of reality that no longer exists; *why*, in effect, is the myth more compelling than the reality? To reply, as Galbraith does, by supplying a truer picture of the reality is merely like telling a neurotic that his fears are groundless; they may be, but the answer cannot convince the neurotic of the fact until the sources of the fear are laid bare. . . .

Curiously, the problems caused by a permanent war economy Galbraith avoids almost completely. The "creeping socialism" of which the Republicans complain so bitterly is the product not of any willed, ideological plan, but the hardly conscious response of the society to the challenge of war. The most important change in the American economy in the last decade has been the growth of the federal budget. Of every dollar spent in 1953 by the U.S. government, eighty-eight cents went for defense and payment of past wars; social security, health and welfare, education, and housing comprised 4 per cent of the budget. A Republican administration cannot affect appreciably the total magnitude of spending; it can, through tax policy, only affect the distribution of the burden. Thus, the key economic decision—the size of the budget—is, in a cold-war economy, out of the full reach of the business community or of any other single group in the country.

The degree of freedom in a capitalist economy—and the working-out of countervailing power—depends on the degree of mobilization necessary to meet the needs of war. For while individual companies and powerful groups may be able to gain special advantage, the main organizing features of the system impose a technical logic that can only be ignored at peril.

A total war economy involves a detailed co-ordination of diverse items which can only be achieved by requisitioning. It means not only the allocation of basic metals, for example, but the detailed scheduling which controls the literal day-to-day operations of the company. In a modern industrial economy the whole society turns, as the nursery rhyme, on the "want of a nail." . . .

But the defense bedrock apart, the experiences since the end of World War II have demonstrated the increased resilience of the economy to shock. The immediate postwar experience is instructive. From a peak of 135 billions in 1944, government expenditures dropped to only 25 billion dollars in 1946; despite this major contraction of demand, total output in the economy fell only 15 per cent. A large backlog of consumer demand, steady rebuilding of depleted inventories, and new plant expansion had taken up the slack. In early 1947, the economists were again pessimistic, as consumption goods (textiles, shoes, clothing) began to slump. The export market that had held up also began to slip. But the Marshall Plan and a boom in home building created counterpressures.

The sources of this resilience are fairly clear. Firm farm-price supports plus a limited redistribution of income (through veterans' payments, social security, and the like) provide a minimum planking. Structural changes in the corporation are significant: during 1946–48, corporations reinvested 62 per cent of their profits after taxes, as compared with 31 per cent in 1929 and 41 per cent three years before the war. Contrary to the gloomy predictions of the demographers, the American birth rate began rising steadily, and one of the chief factors behind the steady expansion of late nineteenth-century economy has been re-established. (Alvin Hansen based his theory of secular stagnation principally on the falling birthrate.)

These are structural facts on the plus side of the ledger. On the minus side, new instabilities are being introduced into the economy mostly by political countervailing forces. Antiquated industries, like Northern textiles, utilize political pressure to maintain outmoded and dilapidated plants. Wage rates tend to be "sticky," so that prices cannot fall or readjust easily and an employer will tend to cut production instead. The pressure for spending creates a long-run inflationary swell which strands, in the side waters, significant salaried and *rentier* segments of the society.

But the balance, inevitably, will be maintained by government. We seem to be reaching a point where about 20 per cent of gross national product and national income is absorbed and spent by the government. By fairly simple fiscal (i.e., tax and subsidy) payments the government has direct mechanisms to pump money into the economy and (though politically it is more difficult) to suck excess money out of the economic stream. This high federal budget is fixed—for the foreseeable future—by the nature of international tensions and by the indebtedness of the past. It is hard to see how any administration can cut the federal budget below the 20 per cent floor which the permanent mobilization entails. . . .

The key question remains one of *political* economy. On a technical level, economic answers to the organization of production, control of inflation, maintenance of full employment, etc., are available. Political answers, in an interest-group society like ours, are not so easy. But in the long run the problems of the distribution of burdens and the nature of controls cannot be deflected. The "statist" needs of a semi-war economy with its technical imperatives must clash with the restless anti-statist attitudes of the corporate managers. . . . The international situation imposes the same imperatives on Republicans as on Democrats, and the semi-war that is made necessary by it inevitably casts government in the role of controller and dominator of the economy. The real political question in domestic affairs will then become which of the groups will bear the costs of the added burdens.

The intellectual rehabilitation of American capitalism is being completed while the reality itself is rapidly changing; the newest ideologies may become outmoded and require new revisions long before they have had time to get themselves widely understood and accepted.

"We Have Come to Stay."

THE SOUTH AFTER RECONSTRUCTION

INTRODUCTION

The term "New South" was long used to apply rather roughly to the period between Reconstruction and 1915, but has recently fallen into some disrepute because it has been used not only to define a period but also to indicate the ideology of the South's prophets of industry. However that may be, the fact is that the period was one of immense significance. A section which had barely emerged from the frontier stage and still preserved many of its characteristics was now confronted by a galaxy of cruel dilemmas which would have frustrated a more advanced society. Indeed, as we can see now, some of the same problems existant in the North were swept under the carpet, whence they are only now emerging.

Among the problems at the South were education, land ownership, industrialization, urbanization, and of course race relations. U. B. Phillips has called white supremacy the central theme of Southern history (he might with some justification have said *American* history). At any rate, the Negro and his role cannot be separated from the history of the South, and though we shall devote a chapter to the

Negro after Reconstruction, neither that chapter nor this can be regarded as a watertight compartment; they are supplementary.

THE NEO-CALHOUNIAN STRUGGLE IN THE POSTWAR SOUTH

History is singularly barren of instances where a people changed their mind merely because they had lost a war. Indeed, it is almost a psychological law that they will find a way to convince themselves that in reality they won a *moral* victory. This was the case in the South; indeed, the ideal of Southernism continued to evolve so luxuriantly that it did not reach full flower until a generation after Appomattox. If history ever teaches lessons, surely there is one to be learned here.

This being true, no one should be amazed that the South chose to tackle its postwar problems with a body of standards and objectives so like those of its antebellum years that they can only be called Neo-Calhounian. These guidelines did not become clear at first; indeed, it was only Northern pressures that led to their clarification. Nevertheless, by the end of Reconstruction two distinct objectives had emerged. The first was to weld the whites of the South into a single force imbued with all the discipline and desperate courage of a beleaguered garrison. The second was to continue Calhoun's search for a way to impose a Southern veto on any federal policy which endangered white supremacy or the old aristo-agrarian values.

From this distance it is evident that the South won at least a short-term victory regardless of what happens from this time on. It repelled the invasion of Yankee liberalism, welded its whites into one political party, and placed on the throttle of national policy a hand which could at least forbid reform to go full speed ahead. But the victory was gained at fearful cost. The races were divided. Many whites and most Negroes became permanently submerged economically. Vast areas that had once been fruitful were returned to a wilderness scarred by erosion. To regain control of its Negroes, the South had to accept—and on occasion defend—Northern capital; then when the South lifted itself industrially by its bootstraps Northern finance capital moved in and took over. True, this last was also happening in the rest of the country, but the South was peculiarly helpless because it did not possess the institutions that bring together the factors which create a progressive society. Even mechanically it was dependent on the North, for it did not have the tools to make the tools to maintain its productiveness. Worst of all, in the mind of the unreconstructed Southron, was the insidious way in which the nineteenth century was quietly gnawing at the roots of Southernism even while it was in full flower above ground.

The Civil War left the South in ruins, and Reconstruction was a political, not an economic, term. Indeed the South had little with which to build, for it had never had many mechanics nor much liquid capital, but had depended on the North for fabricated goods and credit to move its crops. While some Northern capital moved southward to finance the section's physical plant, it was by no means enough to do the job. The South, therefore, turned to one of the few ways open to it to raise money—cotton. Cultivation of this crop was extended to the lands of yeoman farmers and poor whites, but the more that was produced the lower sank its price until by 1898 it had sunk to five cents a pound.

The war was scarcely over before it was found that Negroes refused to work in gangs as they had in slavery days, so planters divided their land into small tracts, each with a cabin, a mule, and a Negro family, which grew a bale or two of cotton. The tenants were known as sharecroppers because they paid their rent by giving the owner a share of the crop, perhaps a third. In order to maintain the family until the crop was picked, the planter arranged with the neighborhood storekeeper to furnish food, clothing, and fertilizer—or perhaps the planter himself opened a store. At any rate, the furnishing merchant became the middleman between banker and sharecropper. With the price of cotton declining, the sharecropper inevitably became a peon—bound to the soil by the debts which would never be fully paid. No doubt the furnishing merchant took every advantage of the sharecropper's ignorance by shamelessly doctoring his books, but the fact was that he had no alternative. He himself was at the mercy of the banker—and the banker in turn operated on credit manufactured in New York or Chicago and borrowed at as much as twenty percent.

It is easily seen then, that the South was ruining its soil for a scandalously low return, and that planter, sharecropper, yeoman farmer, and poor white were all harassed by a declining standard of living. No doubt those who could, went North or West. Those who remained had no choice but to tighten their belts, squeeze anyone they could, and hope for better times. The Cotton Snob's hope of aristocracy went down the drain, and the South was dotted with the decayed remnants of the aristocratic families that Faulkner was eventually to limn. No less evident was the decline of the yeoman, who before the war had at least eaten well even though he had enjoyed little cash income. Numerous yeomen and planters lost their land and had to depend on day labor—when they could get it—and on the charity of relatives, becoming a class more depressed than even the antebellum poor whites. The price of land dropped to two or three dollars an acre in some areas, or its departing owners merely abandoned it to the eroding effect of the rains which were turning the South into a land of gullies irreclaimable by the techniques of the time.

Strive though they did to save the essence of the old Southern ways of leisure, courtesy, and neighborliness, something had to give. For every man who succeeded, doubtless another became a hard-souled exploiter and yet another escaped by sinking into apathy and defeatism. White men in the Old South had at least been free of direct exploitation and had found ways to bolster the cocky independence which was their trademark. The relation of master and man had applied only to slave owners and slaves; now white men found that their debts and their need of jobs made them as dependent on their more fortunate fellows as were the freedmen. Indeed—ultimate disgrace—white man and black now often worked side by side in the field, at the cotton gin, or on the construction job. Common whites seemed doomed to sink to a level with the freedmen, and perhaps more would have had not their old captains come to the rescue. But that is a later story.

Here was a society in which one would suppose that white men should have been at cross purposes, full of mutual resentments and nascent class consciousness. And yet, paradoxically, exactly the opposite happened. The answer lies in the presence of the Negro and the pressures of the Yankee. Federal policy during Reconstruction and threats of Force Bills thereafter served to confirm Southernism to a degree it had never enjoyed even in the antebellum era. White men were driven into a closer comity than ever, standing together against the Yankee and the Negro. The cachet of being white was a possession so precious that everything else sank into insignificance beside it.

True, some semblance of the old frontier independence was preserved by one means or another. Especially notable was the shared glory of the war which made aristocrats and commoners one in feeling, which infused their daily contacts with camaraderie, and prevented the growth of class consciousness. For their part, the leaders now felt a new sense of responsibility, akin to that of an officer for his men, and this was to become a new phase of the old paternalism which had sprung from the hierarchical values of the South. (See Keith McKean, *Cross Currents in the South*, 1960.)

No doubt also the war had confirmed the South's frontier psychology, especially the individual's picture of himself as dashing and masterful. And the Negro was to play a part in the preservation of this self-portrait. Apparently this was particularly true of the poor whites, who had long hated the Negro but could not touch him so long as he was property; now they could practice on him their yearning for mastery, and could even vent their spite in physical abuse without fear of reprisal.

Finally, and perhaps most important of all to the white man fallen on evil days, was the memory of the time that never was, which lent itself to romantic fancies in which the dreamer or his family had played any role he now chose to portray. The contented darkey, the plantation hoedown, the mint julep, the lavish hunt breakfast, the scholar-planter, the code of chivalry, indeed the whole tradition of lavender and old lace was built up by representing the unusual as the universal condition. The United Confederate Veterans and (from 1894) the United Daughters of the Confederacy became propagandists and were joined by such Southern writers as Thomas Nelson Page, Thomas Dixon, and Stark Young. The whole South joined zealously in the holy crusade, turned every Cotton Snob into an aristocrat, and refurbished its genealogies and where necessary invented them.

W. J. Cash, in his *Mind of the South* (page 124) has poignantly portrayed the rise of the Southern mythus which has become an article of faith, not only in the South but in the envious North.

> Like many another people come upon evil days, the South in its entirety was filled with an immense regret and nostalgia; yearned backward toward its past with passionate longing. And so it happened that, while the actuality of aristocracy was drawing away toward the limbo of aborted and unrealized things, the claim of its possession as an achieved and essentially indefeasible heritage, so far from being abated, was reasserted with a kind of frenzied intensity. . . . Perpetually suspended in the great haze of memory, it hung, as it were, poised, somewhere between earth and sky, colossal, shining, and incomparably lovely—a Cloud-Cuckoo-Land wherein . . . life would move always in stately and noble measure through scenery out of Watteau.

The result of all these factors was the emergence of the firm faith that the Old South had been the acme of civilization, that this had been confirmed in heroic combat and sanctified by the way in which the Redeemers had snatched their country from the postwar "fury of the Northmen." The old Southern values of chivalry, gyneolatry, and hierarchy now became the standards around which Southerners rallied even as they were being subtly eroded by changing circumstances. In a very poignant sense, poignant because there may have been no feasible alternative, outward show became a substitute for reality. Decaying aristocrats sought to give the impression of continuing the old ways in their decaying mansions. Southern womanhood was still worshiped though miscegenation continued. The North was defied even as its capital investment was invited. Emotional harangues on the Lost Cause brought tears to the eyes of listeners but washed away none of the basic problems. Most in evidence—save for a moment during the populist uprising—was the way in which the politician who put on the best show got the most votes.

Reference was made above to the way in which the Southern captains came to the rescue of the submerged whites. These men were, by and large but by no means exclusively, survivors of the antebellum Hamiltonian Whigs. The pressures of war and reconstruction had forced most of the Whigs into the Democratic Party, with the inevitable result that the latter was a patchwork of many political colors, all the way from those old Jacksonians who in some states were willing to cooperate with similar populist elements among the Republicans, to those old Whig Hamiltonians who had much in common with the Northern Republicans that were milking the Treasury to construct public facilities which would benefit private enterprise.

Former Whigs tended to be restless in the Democratic Party, and preferred to be called Conservatives, or at worst, Conservative Democrats. It was this element which in the 1870's threw its support to the milder Republican factions and thus succeeded in regaining control of most of the Southern states. It was this element, also, which made the bargain of 1877 which put Hayes in the White House; circumstances prevented them from obtaining the public facilities for which they had bargained, but at least they had the satisfaction of defeating Tilden, the Jacksonian enemy of public expenditures for the benefit of business. However, the North was so sick of the Carpetbaggers that it left control of the freedmen to the Conservatives, and the latter, in turn, undertook to protect Northern investments—which, of course, they greatly needed.

The Conservatives thus formed the core of the so-called Redeemers—the men who defeated the Carpetbaggers and began the economic reconstruction of the South. They were also the core of the so-called Bourbons, a name properly applied to conservative Democrats everywhere but in actual usage most commonly applied to Southerners. During Reconstruction they fought against the extravagance of the Carpetbaggers, and because the latter introduced many progressive measures the Bourbons seemed to be opposed to progress. This was why they were named Bourbons—because, like the French Bourbon kings, "they never learned and never forgot." Actually this was not quite fair. When they came into power they scaled down the reconstruction debts to reasonable amounts, paid the interest promptly, moderated railroad rates, and appropriated what they could to education.

On the other hand, they promoted peonage by their lien laws and blandly entrenched themselves in office as though it was their natural right—as they undoubtedly believed. Paternalism on their part was natural, for it was only carrying the aristo-agrarian ideal into practice. When they appeared in Congress the Bourbons were known as the "Confederate brigadiers," but they were singularly pacific when compared to their antebellum predecessors. They knew the weakness of their position, whether or not their constituents did. Demagogic Republican politicians regarded them as fair meat and taunted them with being representatives of a shotgun civilization. The brigadiers, in fact, depended on their *quasi* allies, the capitalists, for defense and therefore kept their bargain to protect Northern investments in the South. Bedeviled as they were on one side by their resentful constituents and on the other by Northern demagogues, and seeing their beloved South subjected to alien interests, they must have found it difficult to hold their peace.

Perhaps the realization by Southern captains that the white commoner was sinking to the same level as the freedman led to their resolve to find a way to redraw the old line between the races. It may be they feared that failure to find a way would end by the submerged of both races making common cause in a demand for betterment which would overturn Bourbon primacy. Indeed, there was a threat of this in the Farmers' Alliance movement of the 1880's, a movement in which Negroes shared. The method chosen to lift the fallen was a double one: education and industrialization.

The Bourbons had seen from the first that the North had won because of its overwhelming material might, and they sought to build up similar strength in the South. Honest manual labor was now presented in a different light. It was—they said—the white man of the South more than the Negro who had been freed by the Civil War. It is true that the leading Bourbons reestablished their fortunes with the aid of their Northern contacts and in the 1880's emerged not only as political dictators of the South but as managers or lawyers of Northern enterprise as it began to take over the industries of the South. Still, they may have been right. It is difficult, in looking back, to see how the task of building the New South could have been handled better, for the common Southerner was still averse to being reconstructed and Northern Republican politicos were hostile.

The Bourbons never tired of inviting Northern capitalists to locate industries in the South; they were in effect, as Simkins says, a new generation of economic scalawags beckoning to economic carpetbaggers. They promoted education, industrialization, and diversification of crops, and they rejoiced when their policies blossomed into the Rehabilitation Movement. And yet there was something unrealistic about the program. The iron of defeat had entered into the souls even of the old Whigs and made them one with the sons of Calhoun whenever the interests of the South were involved. They took over Calhoun's struggle to weld the South into a garrison section which could exercise a veto on the nation. Not for a moment did the Bourbon leaders intend by industrialization to do more than give Southernism the power to survive. They believed so thoroughly in cotton, in aristo-agrarianism, and in white supremacy that they could not conceive of scientific truth as having any other basis; they failed to see that the acceptance of material progress might displace cotton and that education might eventually free the mind and spirit and lead to a liberalization of race relations and paternalism.

The South had its phase of the rising agrarian revolt against capitalistic controls in the 1890's. One should never forget that Jefferson and Jackson were

Southerners, and that despite the reactionary earmarks of the doctrine of white supremacy there has always been a strong liberal current in the South. Its pragmatic Jeffersonianism, indeed, has contributed more to American political method than has the transcendental reformism of New England. The Southern agrarian revolt, though it was often led by ambitious men who resented the way in which the Bourbons had sewed up political jobs, was somewhat similar to Jacksonianism. It was directed against railroads and banks and the middleman in cotton and tobacco so far as he represented financial interests, especially from the North. Its backbone was composed of yeoman farmers, and for the most part the mill workers and the poor whites stayed by the Bourbons, along with a considerable part of the yeomen. The reason, of course, was that the commoner feared that the populists' alliances with Negro voters would undermine white supremacy.

The result was that enough white voters rallied to the Democratic Party to save white supremacy and tar the populists with the accusation that they were (says Cash) "traitors and nigger-loving scoundrels, renegade to Southern Womanhood, the Confederate dead, and the God of their fathers; champion of the transformation of the white race into a mongrel breed." Southern populism foundered on the shoals of race conflict and left few furrows in the sea. The orotund Bourbons came back, though now they were forced to adopt the undignified and demagogic electioneering tactics of the populists. The electorate, pretty well contented with rising farm prices after 1900 and indifferent to ideas, came to judge candidates by the show they put on and by the way in which they catered to popular prejudices —particularly negrophobia, Southern romanticism, and a superficial populism.

By about 1900 the old agrarian tradition and the rising industrial interests of the South had worked out a *modus vivendi* which suited them fairly well and which was to survive deep into the new century. Southern Negroes had little choice but to accept their assigned role, whatever secret protests they may have harbored. The rural areas, especially the cotton, rice, and sugar-cane regions, relied largely on Negro labor. The factories, with some exceptions in tobacco, preferred white labor. Negroes were disfranchised by methods previously noted, and wherever possible they were confined to menial work by methods not always free from violence. They could own land, but on the whole it was not wise to show many marks of expertness, prosperity, or self-respect. In the cities Negroes received less pay for the same jobs than white artisans, but the threat of Negro competition was useful in hampering unionization and holding white wages down. Technically the South still held to state rights, but there was a growing readiness to accept federal gifts if there were no strings attached and if they were not intended to benefit the Negro.

Rural and city interests had their clashes, but these were fought out in the white primaries, and when the general election came the interests showed a solid front. After all, they had one common meeting ground: white supremacy. In a general sense, the ruling class succeeded in its original objective of preventing white and black workers from uniting, and the policy of race division suited Northern investors very well. It was not the first nor the last time that local conditions had lent themselves to the illustration of the motto "Divide and rule."

The Southern garrison had won its struggle for the preservation of internal discipline. Meanwhile the battle for the veto on national actions had been progressing on a wider front. This battle for a veto, to which Calhoun devoted his life and which led to secession and war, continued with unabated vigor and still plays its part in nearly every political issue despite the changes wrought by the 1950's and 1960's. Its motivations are the same as with Calhoun: the protection of white supremacy and of the South's economic interests.

The forms taken by the Southern veto are by now familiar. Even before the Civil War the Democratic Party had accepted the Two-thirds Rule in its presidential nominating conventions. This practice meant that after the war the presidential candidate would always be a Northerner but must be satisfactory to the South. The abandonment of the rule in 1936 seemed at first to indicate the healing of old wounds, but it has since led to renewed strife.

The Two-thirds Rule was not the South's only weapon. Its solid allegiance to the Democratic Party meant less reliable states could wield power and furnish candidates in crucial elections, but it also meant that after the election was over the South came into its own. Its Senators and Congressmen were returned with humdrum regularity and so amassed the seniority which made them chairmen of committees and big wheels in the party organization. Each Democratic President learned that to get his program passed, he must win the support of Southern legislators. If he did not, the result was an informal but nonetheless effective alliance with the Republicans to thwart his program. The tactic could be worked at times even when the Republican Party held the Presidency and had a majority in Congress.

With these weapons at its disposal the South has usually been able to enforce its veto. It has blocked or watered down legislation which it feels attacks its interests, such as civil rights bills, election-control bills, antilynching bills, and fair-employment bills. It has been able to fill its basket with federal plums and to bring in federally supported war industries on terms which promote Southern industrialization without seriously violating its concepts of race relations.

Though the North was failing in its effort to control the South politically, it was able to use its financial strength to impose economic controls—and that with the aid of many Southerners. Northern imperial control of the South, therefore, was rooted in the psychological colonialism of Southerners. Basically this was no different from the sentimentalities, the prejudices, the credulities, and the sympathies which laid all Americans open to self-defeat through some form of exploitation. The American paradox is a perpetual puzzle to foreigners; the Southern paradox is a perpetual puzzle to other Americans, and sometimes to Southerners themselves. There was a never-ending clash between Southern individualism and the discipline inculcated by generations of living in a garrison besieged by race and sectional conflicts. Hedonism and puritanism strove for mastery: on one side the appreciation of leisure and its pursuits, of good manners, good conversation, and good whisky; on the other, prohibition of alcoholic liquor in ten states, social conformity as lip service to the aristo-agrarian ideal, political conformity as a defense of white supremacy, and religious conformity to a fervent fundamentalist creed as a bulwark against the infiltration of modern ideas.

The Southern mythus flowered in all its romantic glory in the midst of an economy notable for its hardheadedness in both its industrial and its agricultural aspects. Even in the North the Southern mythus gave a Dixie accent social distinction, and romantic plays about the South were resoundingly successful on Broadway. On the other hand, the North viewed with a certain horror—that can be called hypocritical in the light of some of its own excesses—the lowering of the "threshold of violence" in the South. Anglo-Saxon ideals and civil liberties were emotional guidons to Southerners, but Southerners interpreted the denial of civil liberties to the Negro as the very substance of morality. Long contemplation of the glory of the War for Southern Independence and a deep consciousness of race superiority had made the white South the center of American chauvinism and had loosened the hold of the concept of isolation from foreign affairs.

THE NEW SOUTH

[Henry W. Grady (1850–89), editor of the Atlanta *Constitution* and promoter of the Rehabilitation Movement, was invited to address the New England Society of New York at a banquet on December 21, 1886. His address, called "The New South," immediately became famous and did much to continue the work of rebuilding the South and assuaging sectional animosities after his death almost exactly three years later. It is instructive to note how different was the picture Grady gave of the South and the Negro from that of Cash, Woodward, and the Negro historians. The speech, given here in part, is from J. C. Harris, *Life of Henry W. Grady* (N.Y.: 1890), pp. 83–93.]

Dr. Talmage has drawn for you, with a master's hand, the picture of your returning armies. He has told you how, in the pomp and circumstance of war, they came back to you, marching with proud and victorious tread, reading their glory in a nation's eyes! Will you bear with me while I tell you of another army that sought its home at the close of the late war—an army that marched home in defeat and not in victory—in pathos and not in splendor, but in glory that equaled yours, and to hearts as loving as ever welcomed heroes home! Let me picture to you the footsore Confederate soldier, as buttoning up in his faded gray jacket the parole which was to bear testimony to his children of his fidelity and faith, he turned his face southward from Appomattox in April, 1865. Think of him as ragged, half-starved, heavy-hearted, enfeebled by want and wounds, having fought to exhaustion, he surrenders his gun, wrings the hands of his comrades in silence, and lifting his tear-stained and pallid face for the last time to the graves that dot, old Virginia hills, pulls his gray cap over his brow and begins the slow and painful journey.

What does he find—let me ask you who went to your homes eager to find, in the welcome you had justly earned, full payment for four years' sacrifice—what does he find when, having followed the battle-stained cross against overwhelming odds, dreading death not half so much as surrender, he reaches the home he left so prosperous and beautiful? He finds his house in ruins, his farm devastated, his slaves free, his stock killed, his barns empty, his trade destroyed, his money worthless, his social system, feudal in its magnificence, swept away; his people without law or legal status; his comrades slain, and the burdens of others heavy on his shoulders. Crushed by defeat, his very traditions are gone. Without money, credit, employment, material, or training; and beside all this, confronted with the gravest problem that ever met human intelligence—the establishing of a status for the vast body of his liberated slaves.

What does he do—this hero in gray with a heart of gold? Does he sit down in sullenness and despair? Not for a day. Surely God, who had stripped him of his prosperity, inspired him in his adversity. As ruin was never before so overwhelming, never was restoration swifter. The soldier stepped from the trenches into the furrow; horses that had charged Federal guns marched before the plow, and fields that ran red with human blood in April were green with the harvest in June; women reared in luxury cut up their dresses and made breeches for their husbands, and, with a patience and heroism that fit women always as a garment, gave their hands to work. There was little bitterness in all this. Cheerfulness and frankness prevailed. "Bill Arp" struck the key-note when he said: "Well, I killed as many of them as they did of me, and now I'm going to work." Of the soldier returning home after defeat and roasting some corn on the roadside, who made the remark to his comrades: "You may leave the South if you want to, but I am going to Sandersville, kiss my wife and raise a crop, and if the Yankees fool with me any more, I'll whip 'em again." I want to say to General Sherman, who is considered an able man in our parts, though some people think he is a kind of careless man about fire, that from the ashes he left us in 1864 we have raised a brave and beautiful city; that somehow or other we have caught the sunshine in the bricks and mortar of our homes, and have builded therein not one ignoble prejudice or memory.

But what is the sum of our work? We have found out that in the summing up the free negro counts more than he did as a slave. We have planted the schoolhouse on the hilltop and made it free to white and black. We have sowed towns and cities in the place of theories, and put business above politics. We have challenged your spinners in Massachusetts and your iron-makers in Pennsylvania. We have learned that the $400,000,000 annually received from our cotton crop will make us rich when the supplies that make it are home-raised. . . . We admit that the sun shines as brightly and the moon as softly as it did before the war. We have established thrift in city and country. We have fallen in love with work. We have restored comfort to homes from which culture and elegance never departed. We have let econ-

omy take root and spread among us as rank as the crabgrass which sprung from Sherman's cavalry camps, until we are ready to lay odds on the Georgia Yankee as he manufactures relics of the battlefield in a one-story shanty and squeezes pure olive oil out of his cotton seed, against any down-easter that ever swapped wooden nutmegs for flannel sausage in the valleys of Vermont. Above all, we know that we have achieved in these "piping times of peace" a fuller independence for the South than that which our fathers sought to win in the forum by their eloquence or compel in the field by their swords. . . .

But what of the negro? Have we solved the problem he presents or progressed in honor and equity toward solution? Let the record speak to the point. No section shows a more prosperous laboring population than the negroes of the South, none in fuller sympathy with the employing and land-owning class. He shares our school fund, has the fullest protection of our laws and the friendship of our people. Self-interest, as well as honor, demand that he should have this. Our future, our very existence depend upon our working out this problem in full and exact justice. . . . The relations of the southern people with the negro are close and cordial. We remember with what fidelity for four years he guarded our defenseless women and children, whose husbands and fathers were fighting against his freedom. To his eternal credit be it said that whenever he struck a blow for his own liberty he fought in open battle, and when at last he raised his black and humble hands that the shackles might be struck off, those hands were innocent of wrong against his helpless charges, and worthy to be taken in loving grasp by every man who honors loyalty and devotion. Ruffians have maltreated him, rascals have misled him, philanthropists established a bank for him, but the South, with the North, protests against injustice to this simple and sincere people. To liberty and enfranchisement is as far as law can carry the negro. The rest must be left to conscience and common sense. It must be left to those among whom his lot is cast, with whom he is indissolubly connected, and whose prosperity depends upon their possessing his intelligent sympathy and confidence. Faith has been kept with him, in spite of calumnious assertions to the contrary by those who assume to speak for us or by frank opponents. Faith will be kept with him in the future, if the South holds her reason and integrity.

But have we kept faith with you? In the fullest sense, yes. . . . We fought hard enough to know that we were whipped, and in perfect frankness accept as final the arbitrament of the sword to which we had appealed. The South found her jewel in the toad's head of defeat. The shackles that had held her in narrow limitations fell forever when the shackles of the negro slave were broken. . . .

The old South rested everything on slavery and agriculture, unconscious that these could neither give nor maintain healthy growth. The new South presents a perfect democracy, the oligarchs leading in the popular movement—a social system compact and closely knitted, less splendid on the surface, but stronger at the core—a hundred farms for every plantation, fifty homes for every palace—and a diversified industry that meets the complex need of this complex age.

The new South is enamored of her new work. Her soul is stirred with the breath of a new life. The light of a grander day is falling fair on her face. She is thrilling with the consciousness of growing power and prosperity. As she stands upright, full-statured and equal among the people of the earth, breathing the keen air and looking out upon the expanded horizon, she understands that her emancipation came because through the inscrutable wisdom of God her honest purpose was crossed, and her brave armies were beaten.

This is said in no spirit of time-serving or apology. The South has nothing for which to apologize. She believes that the late struggle between the States was war and not rebellion; revolution and not conspiracy, and that her convictions were as honest as yours. I should be unjust to the dauntless spirit of the South and to my own convictions if I did not make this plain in this presence. The South has nothing to take back. . . . [but] I am glad that the omniscient God held the balance of battle in His Almighty hand and that human slavery was swept forever from American soil, the American Union was saved from the wreck of war. . . .

Now, what answer has New England to this message? . . . If she does not refuse to accept in frankness and sincerity this message of good will and friendship, then will the prophecy of Webster, delivered in this very society forty years ago amid tremendous applause, become true, be verified in its fullest sense, when he said: "Standing hand to hand and clasping hands, we should remain united as we have been for sixty years, citizens of the same country, members of the same government, united, all united now and united forever."

THE "NEW SOUTH" AND THE HISTORIANS

[For a long time the "New South" was characterized as a period of remarkable economic progress in the South, and one in which political and race problems had been pretty well solved. During the last generation, however, this characterization has been radically revised, and that largely by Southern historians. The following examination of the old and new ideas is by Paul M. Gaston, and appeared as "The New South" in A. S. Link and R. W. Patrick, eds., *Writing Southern History* (Louisiana State University Press, 1965), pp. 316–336.]

In 1893, in a pioneer attempt to probe the meaning of the "New South," Amory Dwight Mayo, a northern exponent of new developments below the Potomac, found that there was "a good deal of unnecessary friction in the heated discussion of the question whether there really is a new South." Doubting his own ability to produce a definitive picture, Mayo offered little encouragement to the historians of the future. "Probably the time will never come," he predicted, "when the journalist, or even the average statesman, will be able to take an all-around view of a theme so large that it may be compassed only by many observations of many minds." Since Mayo's time a good many historians, though not so many as one might wish, have set out to "compass" the "New South," but we today are likely to agree that they have yet to produce the "all-around view" with which our guild can be permanently satisfied.

Part of the difficulty—and it is a problem that grows with the passage of time—lies in the extraordinary ambiguity of the term itself. C. Vann Woodward, for example, feels that it has caused so much "mischief" that, if possible, it ought to be abandoned entirely. Most of the confusion stems from the fact that "New South" has customarily implied at least two quite different things. On the one hand, it denotes a particular ideology—thus the "New South School," referring to the Henry Gradys who were prophets of a "New South." On the other hand, it is used with equal, if not greater, frequency to mark off various, and vaguely defined, periods of southern history. It may signify the South since 1865; since 1877; from 1877 to 1913; since 1900, or simply the South of the present. Moreover, many writers who use the term to denote a particular period are not careful to state that "New South" has no connotative meaning. Or, conversely, the term may be implicitly invested with a vague meaning, stemming from the Grady ideology, and the progress of the region measured against achievement of those ideals. In this case one finds, in almost any post-Civil War period one investigates, that

the "New South" is emerging, or must be resisted, or has triumphed, or, as Harry S. Ashmore put it a few years ago, is now "coming to reluctant maturity." Finally, diverse groups have taken the term to describe themselves and their particular periodicals. Among these we find nineteenth-century journals devoted to industrialization and reconciliation, the familiar theme; a twentieth-century communist periodical; and the monthly publication of the Southern Regional Council, advocating a South free of racial discrimination.

Clearly, then, before one can discuss the historiography of the "New South," some definitions and limitations must be established. As for the term itself, the position taken here is that it should be used almost exclusively as an adjective and seldom as a noun; and in its adjectival form it will be restricted largely to modification of the men of the post-Reconstruction years who first worked out in detail an ideology which was enthusiastically preached throughout the region. In addition, it will be used to describe the point of view of historians of a later period whose interpretations reflected the ideas of the original New South crusaders. As for periodization, the discussion will be restricted largely to the period from the end of Reconstruction to the Populist Revolt, the era in which the New South movement had its largest following and made its greatest impact. . . .

There was a time when, under the spell of the New South magic, historians found a central theme for most of the period and developed it with great enthusiasm, conviction, and oftentimes elaborate documentation. If, by a "school" of historians we mean a group of scholars all writing more or less toward the same end, there was in the years between 1900 and the Great Depression a group, composed mostly of Southerners, deserving to be called the New South school of historians.

Albert Bushnell Hart, the Harvard historian, confronted one of the principal characteristics of this group when he wrote, in

1910, that the southern tendency toward exaggeration had to be understood before one could properly evaluate southern writings. In the hands of southern writers, he declared, "the clever but no-wise distinguished professor of Latin is 'Probably the greatest classical scholar in the United States,' the siege of Vicksburg was 'the most terrific contest in the annals of warfare'; the material progress of the South is 'the most marvelous thing in human history.'" Later in the same volume, Hart exposed a critical truth when he explained that the exaggerated statements of southern material growth were widely believed in the region. "In every discussion of Southern affairs," he declared, "an important thing to reckon with is a fixed belief that the South is the most prosperous part of the country, which fits in with the conviction that it has long surpassed all other parts of the world in civilization, in military ardor, and in the power to rise out of the sufferings of a conquered people."

The themes of prosperity and power which Hart noted were rapidly becoming the stock-in-trade of writers on the South's recent history. Guy Carleton Lee, in the preface to Philip Alexander Bruce's *The Rise of the New South*, found the "subject of the South since the Civil War" to be an "inspiring one." Actually, he continued, the years since the war offered "such examples of heroic effort, such persistent struggle, such triumphant results, that the historian finds himself tending to an exaltation of the mind." Bruce's volume, praised by Lee as an authentic and comprehensive study of recent southern history, was "a vital narration of the progress of a mighty people, who, from adversity such as no other section of North America has ever experienced," had brilliantly "won the race with adverse fate and become the pride of the Union."

Bruce's history stands as the capstone of the New South crusade itself; in fact, the New South school of historians, of which Bruce was the first major representative, had its origins in the promotional literature of the New South editors and publicists of the 1880's and 1890's.

During these years the New South propagandists flooded the nation with an insistent literature in which historians of our generation find an astonishing mixture of fact and fancy, wish and reality. Few observers from the North were unimpressed by what they read. To cite a typical example, Charles Dudley Warner, writing in 1886, was persuaded that the South was in the throes of a mighty "economical and political revolution" whose story "will be one of the most marvellous the historian has to deal with."

The marvel lies not so much in the history with which one must deal as in the descriptions that appeared in the eighties and nineties from the pens of the New South promoters. A New South creed, born in the seventies, nurtured in the early eighties, and brought to maturity with Grady's address before the New England Society of New York in 1886, was compounded of two distinct parts, the blending of which by the New South spokesmen accounts for numerous historiographical difficulties. On the one hand was the doctrine that the South was poor, frustrated, and despised because it had, by decree of history, become entangled in wrong policies; the road to the future lay in abandoning one-crop agriculture, militant sectionalism, and outright repression of the Negro, and adopting instead a diversified industrial economy, a spirit of reconciliation, and a program of education providing separate independence for the Negro. The dream which they created was essentially a promise of American life for the South. It proffered all the glitter and glory and freedom from guilt that inhered in the American ideal. Sloughing off those characteristics which had marked him as poor, quarrelsome, unprogressive, guilt-ridden, and unsuccessful, the Southerner would—if he heeded the New South prophets—become a true heir of his heritage: prosperous, successful, confident of the future.

Before long, however, the promotional literature of the New South spokesmen included wondrous descriptions of a people who had already achieved, or were on the verge of achieving, all that had been promised as fruits of long toil. . . . Proclaiming the reality of an affluent and triumphant South, these spokesmen were equally fervent in depicting a South innocent of racial injustice. "Each has his own place," Grady declared of white and black, "and fills it, and is satisfied." The program of paternalism, education, regulated franchise, and increasing segregation was advanced as the final solution to the conundrum presented by the demands of Negro freedom and the American tradition of equality. The New South image thus underwent in a short period a metamorphosis. Emerging from a program of action to save a despondent region from ruin, it evolved into a declaration of triumph. Uncritically it could be assumed that, because "facts" proved it, affluence and power were at hand and that the Negro lived in the best of all possible worlds, righteously separated from, but nurtured by, his white brethren. This was the intellectual tradition which historians of the twentieth century inherited; and with certain exceptions, it was this tradition which dominated southern historical writing until the 1930's when the revisionist erosion set it.

Before that era of devastating reappraisal, however, a pattern of history was established which was comprehensive in scope and appealing in tone. The New South school of historians developed, as the central theme of their works, the concept of triumph over adversity, of steel will and impeccable character overcoming staggering problems, often against what seemed impossible odds. The South that was depicted in most of these early histories rose from the extraordinary devastation of the Reconstruction to a glorious plateau of achievement. Viewed from the plateau, the story was one of hope and inspiration. Holland Thompson [in *The New South*, 1919] the first academic historian to write a general history of the period, opened his work with the declaration that "somehow, somewhere, sometime, a new hopefulness was born and this spirit—evidence of new life— became embodied in 'the New South.'" To optimism and cheerfulness was added the ele-

ment of daring and romance. Broadus Mitchell, in *The Rise of the Cotton Mills in the South*, enticed his readers with the assurance that his story, properly understood, was "not only an industrial chronicle, but a romance, a drama as well." Here, then, were powerful romantic elements to compete with the more popular and more numerous histories of the gallant South that had fallen at Appomattox. And the histories of the new regime had the one virtue denied chronicles of the Old South: they were success stories.

An essential ingredient was the element of strong moral fiber. While the New South historians agreed that the new order differed from the old in innumerable ways, few were willing to concede that the peculiar moral superiority of the Southerner had perished with the Lost Cause. As Bruce put it, the war and Reconstruction had shattered the South's economic structure and visited economic ruin on the region; but they had not destroyed the extraordinary "moral qualities of the people." These, in fact, were strengthened in adversity and were the principal weapons available to Southerners to meet new challenges. Ironically coupled with this sense of moral superiority was the common belief that the war and Reconstruction had emancipated the white South from the shackles of an old order that had barred material progress and prosperity. "The Civil War," Mitchell wrote, "brought into glaring view the absence of Southern economic self-sufficiency," and its outcome freed "not just the slaves, but the South as a whole." The "emancipated" whites, no longer fettered by the economic chains of the past but still endowed with the ancient traits of their forebears, were required to rebuild on new foundations. Driven by "moral incitement" and "civic piety," Southerners undertook the task of creating a prosperous industrial society. In response to a "moral stimulus," their leaders built cotton mills that provided work for impoverished poor whites and, one is almost led to believe, gave little thought to self-enrichment.

It is important to remember that, almost

without exception, New South historians wrote as confirmed nationalists and interpreted southern development within the context of national trends. Reconciliation and conversion to national ways and values were central to their histories. To Paul Herman Buck [in *The Road to Reunion*, 1937] the historian of reconciliation and, in many ways, a characteristic representative of the New South school, "the central theme of American life after the war . . . is not to be found in . . . sectional divergence. It was national integration which marked every important development in the years that followed." This theme of national reconciliation is likely to be deceptive, and one should observe that it was never meant to imply a surrender of southern will to northern superiority. It signified, rather, a recognition in the South that the road to affluence and power led to the adoption of those national patterns which had accounted for American greatness. This is what Edwin Mims meant when he wrote, in his biography of Sidney Lanier that southern progress had been made possible by the "adoption of the national point of view." . . .

New South historians, in stressing the theme of nationalism, were particularly careful to emphasize two complementary aspects. In the first place, they argued that the primary force binding the sections was the adoption by the South of what E. L. Godkin once called "the industrial stage of social progress." To Buck, the South's new departure had brought about an "interlocking of economic dependence" which promoted similarity and destroyed particularism. Broadus and George Mitchell, in *The Industrial Revolution in the South*, argued that the industrialization of the South destroyed "separatism" and invited "national consciousness." In 1908, their historian father, Samuel C. Mitchell, attempted to place the movement toward American nationalism in a universal context, concluding of the South, "We have simply found out God's plan in our generation, and have fallen in line. . . . Whatever tends to equalize economic conditions in different sections of our country," he explained, "promotes

similarity of view and identity of purpose." Bruce also concluded that the industrial revolution in the South was the major factor in producing a republic "united in all its parts," free of debilitating antagonisms.

"HE'S DEAD, BUT HE WON'T LIE DOWN."

In the second place, these historians were convinced that the resurgent southern economy had brought into existence a South of affluence, power, and independence which fully vindicated the New South spokesmen who had called the movement into being. As early as 1885, according to Mims, "factories were prospering, farm products were becoming more diversified, more farmers owned their own places, . . . the national spirit was growing, and . . . [a] day of hope, of freedom, of progress, had dawned." By the end of the century, Mims believed, the South was assured of a "brilliant future." To other historians brilliance did not have to await future developments. Bruce was struck by a "recuperative power in the Southern people" which was "perhaps unsurpassed in history." The Mitchells believed that there "arrived nearly overnight an Industrial Revolution as swift and as vigorous as that in England." Buck pronounced the "economic revolution" to have been both "remarkable" and "sensationally rapid." Reenforcing this sense of material greatness was the common belief that the South had been master of its own destiny, achieving its eminence virtually unaided. Moreover, nothing is so striking to the historian of today as the common absence of suggestions that the region was in any sense a colony of the North. Bruce, for example, noted the prominence of northern financiers in southern railroad development, but his analysis did not lead him to attach any special significance to the fact. Buck, summing up the matter, could declare: "Thirty years after Appomattox there remained no fundamental conflict between the aspirations of North and South. The people of the United States constituted at last a nation integrated and united in sentiment."

It would have been paradoxical in the extreme had these historians coupled their accounts of a pioneering, progressive, and energetic industrial leadership with an interpretation of political development which conceded the truth of the occasional northern charge that "Bourbon" politicians in the South stubbornly held to the past, refusing to adapt to the changing conditions of a new order. . . . On the contrary the early historians believed that the role played by the political leaders of the South was essentially the same as that played by the industrial leaders. Just as the latter had redeemed the South from economic error, so the former had redeemed the region from political error and, in addition, had assured conditions which facilitated sectional reconciliation and material progress.

To understand this favorable interpretation of the "Redeemers," one must recapture something of the perspective from which the New South historians wrote. To them the experience of Reconstruction was a horror unique in American history and for this reason doubly noxious and degrading. Against this background, the Redeemers appeared virtually as knights in shining armor. Their primary task—indeed, their knightly duty—was to cut away the "poisonous growth," as Bruce put it, planted by a band of alien bandits and desecrators.

Thus the image of the Redeemers is a relatively uncomplicated one. They began their careers in glory, especially those who participated in the noble act of securing definitive home rule as a result of the "Wormley House Bargain." They were, in contrast to the "aliens" who had ruled the South before redemption, the "natural" leaders of the region, men who had distinguished themselves during the Civil War. This is not to say that they were the old plantation aristocracy. Several New South historians recognized that many of the leaders came from the new commercial-industrial urban class rather than from the older planter class. In either case, however, they were *natural* leaders, men born to the region.

Their achievement, in the view of the New South historians, amply justified the trust that the masses confided in them. Responsible men, they reversed the corrupt and fraudulent practices of Reconstruction. Holland Thompson pronounced their administrations free from scandal of any kind. "No governments in American history," he wrote, "have been conducted with more economy and more fidelity." Impeccable honesty was coupled with a high sense of fiscal responsibility. The ruinous taxes and extravagant appropriations of the carpetbag regimes were abolished as the Redeemers faced up realistically to the demands of recovery. Expenses were diminished by scaling down dishonest debts, eliminating unnecessary governmental positions, and lowering salaries. A new tax structure released capital for investment. In brief, an atmosphere was created in which business could thrive and men could exercise their initiative without fear of retaliation by a capricious government.

Moreover, none of these achievements would have been secured had the Redeemers not guaranteed freedom from political instability and resumption of Negro-Republican rule. It is in this sense that the New South historians generally applauded the Redeemer creation of a one-party, solid South. Taking the explanations of the political leaders more or less at face value, the historians gave credence to the simple formula that the South's suffering had come as a consequence of Republican domination resulting in "Negro rule." Bruce was convinced that, even after home rule, "an enormous number of black voters" continued to threaten "the stability of Southern institutions." The threat could have become a reality, however, only if the Republican party had found support among native whites, and this could have occurred only if the whites had divided. Patriotism, loyalty to race and region, demanded, then, unswerving support of the Democratic party. The permanence of a "redeemed" South, in short, depended upon the maintenance of a "solid" South.

Thus it was that one-partyism, white supremacy, patriotism, morality in government, and the industrial revolution were all part of one pattern. Finding this connection, the historians of the early part of the century discovered much of which to be proud in the "New South": Reconstruction had been successfully undone, and a superior southern will had charted a prosperous, successful course for the once defeated and occupied land.

Reaction to this felicitous interpretation of the Redeemer era was bound to occur, and signs of dissent began to appear in the 1920's. But it was not until the Depression that full scale revision began to take shape. The glowing picture of a prosperous and triumphant South made little sense to a region soon to be accurately, if somewhat undiplomatically, labeled the nation's "economic problem no. 1." The excruciating plight of the South provided new perspectives that helped to provide new interpretations of the Redeemer era.

The most eloquent and heated, if not the most thoroughly researched, interpretation emanated primarily from Nashville and is associated with the Vanderbilt Agrarian movement. The Nashville Crusaders, in their manifesto, *I'll Take My Stand*, wrote charmingly of an ordered, conservative, soil-oriented style of life, presumably characteristic of the Old South, which had been betrayed by the New South promoters. Lamenting the seduction of younger Southerners by the industrial gospel, the Agrarians called for a critical examination of the "advantages of becoming a 'new South' which," they insisted, would "be only an undistinguished replica of the usual industrial community." Concerned with the present, wishing to launch the counterrevolution which they believed still had chances of success, they charged the New South historians with perpetuating original errors by failing to write genuinely critical history. What should be written, declared Donald Davidson in *The Attack on Leviathan*, was that America's need in 1900 was "to set off the tendencies that were leading the country straight into over-industrialization and social degeneracy." This could have been accomplished most effectively, he concluded, by "strengthening the conservative culture of the South, to the virtues of which [Walter Hines] Page and his followers were blind."

Despite their appeal to traditional values rooted deeply in southern history, the Agrarians produced no historical studies of the Redeemer era, apart from occasional essays such as those by John Donald Wade on Henry Grady and Joel Chandler Harris. Frank Lawrence Owsley, the most distinguished historian in the group, rediscovered the plain people of the Old South, but he did not investigate the social and economic history of this class after the Civil War. The significance of the Agrarians, then, lies primarily in the fact that they heightened awareness of an anti-New South tradition in the region and suggested to historians the profitability of exploring the patterns of conflict and antagonism in modern southern history.

The theme of conflict soon appeared in several works. Benjamin B. Kendrick and Alex M. Arnett, in *The South Looks at Its Past* (1935), found that "the quarter-century that followed the restoration of native white rule in the South was marked by a conflict between those who looked to the past and those who looked to the future." The Redeemer era could be described as a conflict between an Old South party of agrarianism and a New South party of industrialism, with the former fighting a rear-guard action. A similar interpretation was included in William B. Hesseltine's general history of the South, first published in 1936. To him, the South was beset by a conflict between the values of the Old South, embodied in Jefferson Davis, and the New South, embodied in Robert E. Lee, which left a lasting mark on the South. Hesseltine's conflict thesis was developed in more detail in his *Confederate Leaders in the New South*.

However, the new views of conflict between an agrarian and an industrial tradition—a conflict that presumably reached its point of greatest intensity during the Redeemer era—resulted in relatively few serious monographic studies of that period. Commenting on the paucity of such studies, Judson C. Ward suggests that "the slower evolutionary processes of economic and social reconstruction carried on under one-party domination have not possessed for historians the dramatic appeal of the more spectacular period of the Civil War and Restruction which preceded this period or the Populist revolt which followed it." Here Ward raises a point that is crucial in understanding the nature of the revisionism of the 1930's and 1940's. To many scholars of the Depression era, the Populist period held very special attraction. As C. Vann Woodward has pointed out, the two periods had much in common. There was, first of all, the common setting of depression and economic dislocation, coupled with a common antagonism toward the dominant business interests of the country. In addition, a sense of urgency and desperation infected large elements of the population. And, for Southerners, agricultural problems were among the most pressing and agrarian reform was at the center of much political and economic discussion.

Southern scholars began asking themselves why the New South historians had almost uniformly passed over the Populist revolt, as though it were some form of temporary aberration, best neglected and forgotten. Could it be that, in minimizing the significance of southern populism, previous historians had missed a key element in post-Reconstruction history? More important, could it be true that the harmonious structure of New South historiography, based on a general concept of unity, absence of conflict, and progress and reconciliation, might be dismantled by studies that exposed the proportions of the revolt against the New South regimes? Was the seething discontent of the nineties a reflection of agrarians struggling to maintain an old order, or did it represent a much more fundamental and comprehensive indictment of the power structure of the South? These and other questions were raised with increasing frequency in a decade in which thoughtful men found much to condemn in their own generation.

The point here is that the most searching revisionist studies of the Redeemer era—the ones upon which our present view of the period has been built—were primarily studies of Populism and not of the Redeemer era itself. . . . The full impact of the revisionist departure was not apparent until 1951 when Professor Woodward, building on the new monographs and his own extensive research, published his *Origins of the New South*. It was the first general history of the post-Reconstruction South since Holland Thompson's brief volume of 1919 and the first detailed study since Bruce's work of 1905. Resemblances between the new and older works were difficult to find. Not only, of course, had Woodward written from a different perspective, but his skeptical ironic approach to the materials was in direct contrast to the relatively uncomplicated and uncritical studies of the New South school. The results were generally devastating to the old tradition.

A significant clue to Woodward's approach was offered in a shorter book published earlier in the same year, *Reunion and Reaction*, a study of the Compromise of 1877 and the inauguration of the Redeemer regime. Its Beardian interpretation attacked the "Wormley

House Bargain" legend and suggested that re-union was built, in large part, on a community of economic interests, with the Redeemers pledging support of nationalistic economic policies in return for economic aid to the South. Implicit in the settlement was an alliance of capitalists of the South and Northeast to preserve the status quo. Ironically agreeing with the New South historians that reunion was premised on the marriage of southern and northern capitalists, Woodward's revisionism lay in his assertion of the opportunistic and shortsighted motives that underlay the union.

Incorporating this interpretation in *Origins of the New South*, Woodward analyzed in detail the character of the Redeemer leadership, concluding that a high percentage of the new leaders were prewar Whigs, forced into the Democratic party because of the exigencies of white supremacy politics. Few, he found, came from the old planter class; nearly all, including most of those with agrarian connections, were oriented toward the commercial and industrial interests of the region. Redemption, then, was not a restoration of the old order but, rather, "a new phase of the revolutionary process begun in 1865. Only in a limited sense can it be properly called a 'counter-revolution.'"

In describing the policies of the Redeemers, Woodward differed in almost every respect from the New South historians. Retrenchment, hailed by the earlier scholars as an indication of realism, was regarded by Woodward as an abdication of social responsibility. But perhaps a more permanent injury, he wrote, "was the set of values imposed upon the Southern mind by the rationalization of this neglect." Equally devastating to the Redeemer reputation was the lengthy documentation of thievery in official places that marked the careers of many state administrations. Although finding that the stealing was less extensive than during the Reconstruction era, Woodward's history nonetheless tarnished another of the major claims made for the service of the Redeemers to their region.

In dissecting the anatomy of the "Solid South," Woodward cut away the shibboleths of white supremacy to reveal a politics of class and interest that cleverly exploited race and tradition to perpetuate its hold over the region. Detailing the mounting grievances of various anti-Redeemer elements within the South, he attributes the success of the one-party machines to Machiavellian techniques that had been perfected in the fight against the carpetbaggers. The result, at least until the Populist revolt, was political apathy and despair, "a period of political torpor more stultifying, perhaps, than any in . . . [the South's] long history."

But the New South promoters and the historians who followed in their tradition had not built their image of a triumphant South on a basis of political achievement alone. Political leaders, honest and loyal though they might have been, were regarded as benefactors of the region chiefly because they created the order and the atmosphere in which an industrial revolution could take place. Here Woodward does not equivocate in challenging completely the New South point of view. While conceding that the South, in many respects, did hold its own in rates of relative growth, he finds that, in absolute terms, the economic disparity between North and South increased, rather than decreased, during the period 1880–1900. Moreover—and here was the unkindest cut of all—the economy of the South became increasingly controlled by northern and other outside capitalists. The South, Woodward concluded, "was limited largely to the role of a producer of raw materials, a tributary of industrial powers, and an economy dominated by absentee owners." The unhappy result was "low wages, lack of opportunity, and poverty."

By 1951, then, the revisionist movement had found its spokesman in a brilliant work, at once original and yet reflective of two decades of new thought. In conclusion, one ought to ask where we stand today. Have we reached a new consensus? Are counterrevisions of a major nature in progress? Or, is the whole subject being neglected?

There is still much that we do not know.

Woodward was struck by the absence of adequate monographs when he wrote *Origins of the New South,* and anyone who reads his "Critical Essay on Authorities" may find that complaint documented in suggestions for numerous studies. Other periods of southern history, it appears, are more inviting to the profession. Some years ago David Potter made a study of articles appearing in the *Journal of Southern History* from 1935 through 1949. Of those articles which he could classify by period, he found that 48.8 percent had been written on the period 1830–1865 while only 16.3 percent were devoted to the entire period since 1877. During the period 1950–1963, the proportion on the period since 1877 has gone up slightly, to 21.9 percent of the total classifiable by period, but studies of the Redeemer era itself are disappointingly scarce. . . .

For the most part, the work done in recent years has tended to support, rather than to challenge, the principal revisionist findings. There are exceptions. Nash K. Burger and John K. Bettersworth's *South of Appomattox* (New York, 1959) seems blithely unaware of revisionist findings and describes the Redeemers as highly motivated patriots, rescuers of an oppressed people. Thomas B. Alexander's study of Whiggery in the postwar South offers a more serious challenge to Woodward's view of the Redeemers. Examining the Hayes papers, where Woodward located much of the evidence for his economic interpretation of the Compromise of 1877, Alexander found "surprisingly few" items referring to economic matters. He does not press the point but suggests that "a more detailed study of the individual oldline Whigs in Congress might well establish the conclusion that the southern bloc would have acted as it did in 1877 had there been no railroad lobby involved." On the other hand, Alexander's statistical study of former southern Whigs amply confirms the revisionist position that Whiggery was the dominant element in the Democratic party during the Redeemer era.

Alexander's careful study of political backgrounds has been matched by few other studies.

We do not have a major general study of Redeemer politics, such as V. O. Key's pioneer masterpiece on twentieth-century politics, nor do we have sufficient monographs on the structure and process of politics to ease the burden of one undertaking such a task. Two recent interpretive books by T. Harry Williams and Dewey W. Grantham, both quite brief on the period, make stimulating reading but do not depart from the revisionist construction. Indeed, Grantham's excellent account of the forging of the Solid South underscores the extent to which the revisionist position has triumphed. Williams expresses reservations about some parts of the revisionist interpretation, arguing that Woodward erred in describing Redeemer politics as a politics of race and tradition, largely devoid of realistic concerns. Actually, the real difference between the two is slight. The most notable recent advance of political history has resulted from two excellent studies of the Republican party and the South by Vincent P. DeSantis and Stanley P. Hirshson. These works emphasize the continuing influence and importance of the GOP throughout the period, thus correcting occasional careless generalizations about the disappearance of the party in the South after Reconstruction. At the same time, they contribute to a fuller understanding of Redeemer opposition and the perfection of one-party politics.

Studies of race relations . . . were pioneered by Vernon L. Wharton and George B. Tindall. Woodward's *Strange Career of Jim Crow* (New York, 1955) added a new dimension to the subject by advancing the thesis that segregation laws came fairly late and by reemphasizing the degree to which the Redeemers were willing to forestall movements for proscription of Negro rights. Charles E. Wynes and Frenise A. Logan have tested the "Woodward thesis" for Virginia and North Carolina (with positive findings, in the main) and students of other states could follow suit with profit. These recent studies accelerated the dismantling of the image of harmonious racial adjustment, predicated on subordination, given us by the

New South school and, at the same time, revealed greater complexity in the political and economic aspects of race relations.

In the area of economic development one finds occasional echoes of the earlier writings. For example, John S. Ezell, though generally in agreement with Woodward, asserts one older view. He declares that the "crowning glory of the Bourbon era was its sensational success in attracting manufacturing to the South," adding that "the progress of Southern industrialization was little short of a miracle." More commonly, however, scholars have tended to the revisionist position on this as well as on other subjects. . . . Relatively little has been done with the problem of economic colonialism, raised poignantly by Woodward, but studies such as John F. Stover's *The Railroads of the South, 1865–1900* (Chapel Hill, 1955) show how it can be approached through a single industry. Stover's conclusion, in keeping with the revisionist finding, is that northern men and money extended their influence over virtually the entire railroad complex of the South. . . .

Tracing the shifting interpretations of the Redeemer era, as attempted in this essay, raises a number of intriguing questions. Studying the original New South idea leads one to wonder why it had such appeal and persistence, what gave its spokesmen their persuasiveness and ability to deceive others as well as themselves, and why it aroused such enduring partisanship and antagonisms in contemporaries as well as in their descendants.

In trying to understand the New South historians, one feels almost as though they were looking through a powerful telescope. The background against which their histories were written heightened the contrasts and exaggerated the images they saw. They saw southern economic achievements against a scene of grinding poverty, increasing political power and self-determination against an experience of galling powerlessness, attempts at reconciliation against the legacy of hatred and mistrust, and concessions to the Negro against a backdrop of slavery and black codes. It is not surprising that in describing their region's attempt to don the mantle of the American heritage they were lured into admiring the emperor's new clothes. Today, the South's more cosmopolitan historians see the region's history silhouetted against American and world experience; and bitter southern memories are no longer so potent. The most thoroughgoing of the revisionists reveal New South claims in all their factitiousness and find the era that gave birth to them barren and stultifying. Like the child in Andersen's fairy tale, they look at the emperor and exclaim, "But he has got nothing on!"

It is thus clear that New South historians and revisionists alike have shared a fundamental moral concern, a sense of the responsibility to judge, not simply describe, the past. In large measure, the "facts" upon which the changing interpretations have rested have not changed, but values have undergone a revolution. Thus, within the framework of their own value judgments, the earlier historians created an image of inspiration; later historians replaced it with a picture of near degradation. The trend of the future is uncertain. Increasing demand for detailed and impartial testing of current generalizations suggests that the next stage may involve less attention to ultimate meaning. On the other hand, the potent paradoxes and contrasts of the period itself will continue to confront historians with the perennial task of explaining the mentality of the era and the inheritance that it bequeathed.

New York
Historical Society

THE NEGRO AFTER RECONSTRUCTION

3

INTRODUCTION

The generation after the Civil War witnessed a long campaign by the South to undo as nearly as it could the effects of emancipation. The end of Reconstruction saw the North leave the governance of the freedman to the South, but this did not bring internal harmony to the section. The freedmen still voted, and the manipulation of this vote promptly became the object of a political struggle which in the end solved the problem by an agreement to take away the black man's franchise.

In other respects, also, the freedman was the loser. Civil rights were lost even before the franchise. The rural Negro typically became a sharecropper, subject to control by the landowner and the storekeeper—themselves squeezed by economic forces beyond their control. In all too many cases, Negroes who had been skilled handicraftsmen were excluded from their trades by white workers.

On the other hand, a group of Negro leaders was emerging, men like Booker T. Washington and W. E. B. Du Bois, and along with them a number of historians, poets, editors, and other writers. There were a few Negro businessmen, the most successful of them in insurance, largely because most white-controlled companies would not insure Negroes. John Hope Franklin sums up the situation at the turn of the century thus in his *From Slavery to Freedom:*

The end of the century found the Negro in a stronger position in that he had educational institutions in which to develop and social agencies by which he could improve his status. The help which he received from philanthropists did much to make his lot easier, but his experiences in the economic and social world of the whites convinced him more and more that the brunt of the burden of his development would have to be borne by him. He assumed this responsibility without hesitation, and in typically American fashion he sought a larger share of the blessings of liberty. But as he developed his own institutions and, to a considerable extent, his own cultural life, it became clearer that the American melting pot, so far as Negroes were concerned, was not boiling; it was hardly simmering.

Since our emphasis is on ideas rather than social and personal factors, we will stress two significant developments: one of them, the long political and judicial struggle which ended in the triumph of the Jim Crow mentality among whites; the other, the Negro's own search for the means to promote his own advancement.

THE AGE OF BOOKER T. WASHINGTON

[The struggle of the freedmen to improve their educational and economic conditions was led by a remarkable group of men, best known of whom were Booker T. Washington and W. E. B. Du Bois. The work of these two men is ably characterized in the following passage from John Hope Franklin, *From Slavery to Freedom* (N.Y.: Knopf, 1947), pp. 384–390.]

Writing in 1903 Dr. W. E. B. DuBois said, "Easily the most striking thing in the history of the American Negro since 1876 is the ascendancy of Mr. Booker T. Washington." The ascendancy of this man is one of the most dramatic and significant episodes in the history of American education and of race relations. In 1872 Washington, a lad about sixteen years old, arrived at Hampton Institute, a school molded from the ideas of practical education of its founder, General Samuel Chapman Armstrong. Armstrong taught his students that labor was a "spiritual force, that physical work not only increased wage-earning capacity but promoted fidelity, accuracy, honesty, persistence, and intelligence." He emphasized the value of acquiring land and homes, vocations and skills. Washington drank deeply of Armstrong's teachings and, in time, became the most eloquent exponent of the ideals he enunciated. By the time that Washington graduated he was convinced that in order for Negroes to achieve success they must do some useful service that the world wanted. It was his great preoccupation from that point on to find out the ways in which his people could be most useful to the world.

When Washington went to Tuskegee in 1881, he found none of the equipment with which to develop an educational institution; and he found a white community hostile to the idea of a school for Negroes. He, therefore, set about the twofold task of securing the necessary resources with which to conduct a school and of conciliating the whites. It was an ideal situation in which to relate education to life. Students cooperated in doing all the necessary work at Tuskegee, constructing the buildings, producing and cooking the food, and performing innumerable other tasks. The community was given assurances in many ways that the students were there to serve and not to antagonize. Washington believed that Southern whites had to be convinced that the education of the Negroes was in the true interest of the South. The students provided many of the services and much of the produce that the white community needed, and hostility to the new school began to disappear. Washington counseled the Negroes to respect the law and to cooperate with white authorities in maintaining peace. In this way he won the good will of the ruling class.

As Washington saw the salutary effects which his program was having on the white South as well as on his Negro students, he became more and more certain that this was the pattern for strengthening the position of Negroes throughout the area. He became the apostle of a form of industrial education that he saw would not antagonize the South and that would, at the same time, carve out a place of service for Negroes in their communities. Certainly a program of training Negroes to become farmers, mechanics, and domestic servants would be more acceptable to Mississippi's J. K. Vardaman than the program of classical education advocated by many Northern educators. Earlier Vardaman had said, "What the North is sending South is not money but dynamite; this education is ruining our Negroes. They're demanding equality." Washington was not demanding that, and it pleased the Southern whites to hear him say at the Atlanta Exposition in 1895, "In all things that are purely social we can be as separate as the five fingers, yet one as the hand in all things essential to mutual progress." To his own people he uttered this admonition: "To those of my race who depend upon bettering their condition in a foreign land or who underestimate the importance of cultivating friendly relations with the Southern white man . . . I would say 'Cast down your bucket where you are'—cast it down in making friends in every manly way of the people of all races by whom we are surrounded. Cast it down in agriculture, mechanics, in commerce, in domestic service, and in the professions."

Washington never tired of urging Negroes to develop habits and skills that would win for them places in their Southern communities. Intelligent management of farms, ownership of land, habits of thrift, patience, and perseverance, and the cultivation of high morals and good manners were encouraged. He said that the Negro must learn that all races have got on their feet largely by laying an economic foundation and, in general, by beginning in a proper cultivation and ownership of the soil. He was greatly distressed by the mass movement of Negroes from the country to the city, and did what he could to persuade them to return. He did not deprecate the study of such subjects as science, mathematics, and history; but he indicated on many occasions that he regarded them as impractical. He said that he believed that "for years to come the education of the people of my race should be so directed that the greatest proportion of the mental strength of the masses will be brought to bear upon the everyday practical things of life, upon something that is needed to be done, and something which they will be permitted to do in the community in which they reside."

The Washington doctrine of industrial education, or, more properly, vocational education, for the great mass of Negroes was hailed by whites in the North and in the South. Some Northern whites, weary of racial and sectional conflicts, saw in it a formula for peace in the South with the establishment of a satisfactory economic and social equilibrium between the races. Others, skeptical from the beginning, of the capacity of Negroes to become completely assimilated in a highly complex civilization, viewed it as leading the Negro to his proper "place" in American life. Still other Northerners, with an eye on markets and a labor supply in the South, applauded Washington's stand, because it would perhaps make possible the greater economic development of the South. Southerners, on the other hand, liked Washington's relative disinterest in political and civil rights for Negroes. They liked the way in which he placed confidence in the Southern whites regarding their good treatment of Negroes who proved themselves to be useful, law-abiding citizens. They agreed with his advocacy of a type of education which they believed would consign Negroes to an inferior economic and social status in Southern life. Finally, they admired the tact and diplomacy with which he conciliated all groups, North and South. Only twice did he threaten his position among the whites in the South. Speaking on one occasion in Chicago he lashed out at race prejudice and asserted that it was eating away the vitals of the South. On another occasion he visited the White House and had lunch with President Theodore Roosevelt, an incident which was regarded by most Southerners as a serious breach of racial etiquette. After fourteen years of intimate association with Washington, J. L. M. Curry, a leading Southern educator, could say that he had never once known the principal of Tuskegee to say or to do an unwise thing.

Because of their intense interest in the immediate goals of Washington, perhaps few whites saw that this leader looked forward to the complete acceptance and integration of Negroes in American life. On one occasion he said, "I would set no limits to the attainments of the Negro in arts, in letters or statesmanship, but I believe the surest way to reach those ends is by laying the foundation in the little things of life that lie immediately about one's door. I plead for industrial education and development for the Negro not because I want to cramp him, but because I want to free him. I want to see him enter the all-powerful business and commercial world." He always advocated the entrance of the Negro into the professions and other fields; and, it will be recalled, that he urged Negroes to make friends with their white neighbors in every *"manly"* way. Washington believed that the Negro, starting with so little, would have to work up gradually before he could attain a position of power and respectability in the South. The whites, on the other hand, looking at Washington's program of expediency, frequently regarded it as the ultimate solution to the Negro problem and believed that the latter's place would be permanently fixed by the Washington formula.

As Washington's prestige grew to the point where he was regarded not only as the out-standing exponent of industrial education but the spokesman of the millions of Negroes, opposition among his own people increased. Of course, some of it was envy; but a relatively small group of men took serious exception both to the point of view of the Washington philosophy and to the techniques he employed in elevating his people. Foremost among the opponents was W. E. B. DuBois, a young Negro who was trained at Fisk, Harvard (where he received the degree of Doctor of Philosophy), and Berlin. Although born in Massachusetts, DuBois was teaching at Atlanta University; and the series of studies he was making of the conditions of Negroes in the South had furnished him with considerable first-hand information concerning the group for which he undertook to speak. In books, essays, and addresses DuBois opposed what he viewed as the narrow educational program of Washington, which was too predominantly economic in its objectives. His *Souls of Black Folk* (1903) contained several searchingly critical essays on Washington. He accused Washington of preaching a "gospel of Work and Money to such an extent as apparently almost completely to overshadow the higher aims of life." In an essay entitled "The Talented Tenth" DuBois said, "If we make money the object of man-training, we shall develop money-makers but not necessarily men; if we make technical skill the object of education, we may possess artisans but not, in nature, men. Men we shall have only as we make manhood the object of the work of the schools—intelligence, broad sympathy, knowledge of the world that was and is, and of the relation of men to it—this is the curriculum of that Higher Education which must underlie true life." He especially denounced the manner in which Washington deprecated institutions of higher learning, and he insisted that neither the Negro common schools nor Tuskegee could remain open one day were it not for the teachers trained in Negro colleges or trained by their graduates.

DuBois did not approve of the manner in which Washington ignored or winked at the white South's reduction of the Negro's political and civil status. He believed that the extension of the "palm branch" to Southerners had resulted in the disfranchisement of the Negro and the legal creation of a distinct status of civil inferiority of the Negro. DuBois contended that it was not possible, under modern competitive methods, for Negro artisans, business men, and property owners to defend their rights and exist without the suffrage; while the counsel of silent submission to civic inferiority would sap the manhood of any race in the long run. He called Washington's Atlanta Exposition speech the "Atlanta Compromise," "the most notable thing in Mr. Washington's career," and conceded that it made him the most distinguished Southerner since Jefferson Davis. It also made him the leader of his people, not by their own choice, but because of the manner in which he was acclaimed by the whites in the North and in the South. He became "a compromiser between the South, the North, and the Negro" and was consulted whenever any matters arose affecting Negroes anywhere in the United States. As the most eloquent spokesman for a growing number of Negroes, DuBois was alarmed by the ultimate effect of Washington's leadership.

While there was much to be said for the position that Washington took (and DuBois admitted the importance of many of Washington's teachings), his doctrine contained some weaknesses that are perhaps more obvious today than they were 40 years ago. He accepted uncritically the dominant philosophy of American business when he insisted that everyone had his future in his own hands, "that success came to him who was worthy of it, and that the greater the obstacles, the greater the victory over them." It was a doctrine of triumphant commercialism, which was strengthened by his contact with Ogden, Huntington, and other wealthy American business men. The Negro Business League which Washington organized in 1900 to foster business and industry, was based on the philosophy that if a person could make a better article and sell it

cheaper he could command the markets of the world; that if one produced something someone wanted the purchaser would not ask who the seller is. Add to this a generous amount of tact, good manners, resolute will, and a tireless capacity for hard work and success in business would be the reward. As Spero and Harris have pointed out, this philosophy was an adaptation of the theories of free competition and political individualism that had been taught by the school of classical political economy and was becoming more fictitious than ever by 1900. The spread of "vertical and horizontal combinations capitalized in hundreds of millions was discrediting the idea that a man of small capital could raise himself to affluence and power through hard work and thrift." Washington showed little understanding of these realities as he developed a program for the economic salvation of Negroes.

The particular type of industrial education which Washington emphasized, with much attention given to the development of a class of artisans, was outmoded at the time he enunciated it, by the increasing industrialization of the country. He did not seem to grasp fully the effect of the Industrial Revolution upon the tasks that had been performed by the hands of workers for centuries. To be sure, brickmasons, carpenters, blacksmiths, and the like would still be needed, but their tasks were being reduced to a minimum in the industrial age; many of the occupations which Washington was urging Negroes to enter were disappearing almost altogether. As training grounds for industrial workers, the curriculums and the institutions urged by Washington were not at all satisfactory. Neither Washington nor the industrial schools for Negroes took cognizance of the problems peculiar to the wage earner in modern industry. In speaking of organized labor Washington went so far as to say that the Negro did not like an "organization which seems to be founded on a sort of impersonal enmity to the man by whom he is employed." He therefore utterly failed to see the relation of the laboring class to the Industrial Revolution and counseled an approach to the labor problem that had the effect of perpetuating the master-slave tradition.

In counseling Negroes to remain in rural areas Washington not only failed to see that the advent of expensive farm machinery put the impoverished Negro farmer at a serious disadvantage, but also that the industrial urban community was infinitely more attractive to Negroes as well as to whites. There were, on the surface at least, innumerable economic opportunities in the city. Furthermore, the city offered incomparable advantages for cultural and intellectual growth. If Washington wished for his people educational and economic opportunities that would facilitate their assimilation and acceptance, the urban centers seemed to be, by far, the oases in the desert of despair. Indeed, it would seem that nothing represented more vividly the Negro's reflection of a typical American reaction than his inclination to move from the country to the city in the late nineteenth and early twentieth centuries.

Despite the fact that there were Negroes who vigorously opposed Washington's leadership and that there were some valid exceptions to his program for the salvation of the Negro, he was unquestionably the central figure—the dominant personality—in the history of the Negro down to his death in 1915. The vast majority of the Negroes acclaimed him as their leader and few whites ventured into the matter of race relations without his counsel. During his lifetime lynchings decreased only slightly, the Negro was effectively disfranchised, and the black workers were systematically excluded from the major labor organizations; but Washington's influence, sometimes for better and sometimes for worse, was so great that there is considerable justification in calling the period, "The Age of Booker T. Washington."

"The world desires to know what a man can do, not what he knows"

—Booker T. Washington

"CAST DOWN YOUR BUCKET WHERE YOU ARE"

[In September, 1895, at the Cotton States' Exposition in Atlanta, Booker T. Washington delivered the famous "Atlanta Address" which was welcomed by whites as an injunction to the Negro to be content with his role as a manual laborer. It may well be that Washington was yielding to current pressures, but his use of the words "just now" shows that he did not envision the Negro's humble role as permanent.]

A ship lost at sea for many days suddenly sighted a friendly vessel. From the mast of the unfortunate vessel was seen a signal: "Water, water; we die of thirst!" The answer from the friendly vessel at once came back: "Cast down your bucket where you are." A second time the signal, "Water, water; send us water!" ran up from the distressed vessel, and was answered: "Cast down your bucket where you are." The captain of the distressed vessel, at last heeding the injunction, cast down his bucket, and it came up full of fresh, sparkling water from the mouth of the Amazon River. To those of my race who depend upon bettering their condition in a foreign land, or who underestimate the importance of cultivating friendly relations with the Southern white man, who is his next door neighbor, I would say: "Cast down your bucket where you are"— cast it down in making friends in every manly way of the people of all races by whom we are surrounded.

Cast it down in agriculture, mechanics, in commerce, in domestic service, and in the professions. And in this connection it is well to bear in mind that whatever other sins the South may be called to bear, when it comes to business, pure and simple, it is in the South that the Negro is given a man's chance in the commercial world, and in nothing is this Exposition more eloquent than in emphasizing this chance. Our greatest danger is that in the great leap from slavery to freedom we may overlook the fact that the masses of us are to live by the productions of our hands, and fail to keep in mind that we shall prosper in proportion as we learn to dignify and glorify common labor, and put brains and skill into the common occupations of life; shall prosper in proportion as we learn to draw the line between the superficial and the substantial, the ornamental gew-gaws of life and the useful. No race can prosper till it learns that there is as much dignity in tilling a field as in writing a poem. It is at the bottom of life we must begin, and not at the top. Nor should we permit our grievances to overshadow our opportunities.

To those of the white race who look to the incoming of those of foreign birth and strange tongue and habits for the prosperity of the South, were I permitted I would repeat what I say to my own race, "Cast down your bucket where you are." Cast it down among the 8,000,000 Negroes whose habits you know, whose fidelity and love you have tested in days when to have proved treacherous meant the ruin of your firesides. Cast down your bucket among these people who have, without strikes and labor wars, tilled your fields, cleared your forests, builded your railroads and cities, and brought forth treasures from the bowels of the earth, and helped make possible this magnificent representation of the progress of the South. Casting down your bucket among my people, helping and encouraging them as you are doing on these grounds, and, with education of head, hand and heart, you will find that they will buy your surplus land, make blossom the waste places in your fields, and run your

factories. While doing this, you can be sure in the future, as in the past, that you and your families will be surrounded by the most patient, faithful, law-abiding, and unresentful people that the world has seen. As we have proved our loyalty to you in the past, in nursing your children, watching by the sick bed of your mothers and fathers, and often following them with tear-dimmed eyes to their graves, so in the future, in our humble way, we shall stand by you with a devotion that no foreigner can approach, ready to lay down our lives, if need be, in defense of yours, interlacing our industrial, commercial, civil, and religious life with yours in a way that shall make the interests of both races one. In all things that are purely social we can be as separate as the fingers, yet one as the hand in all things essential to mutual progress. . . .

The wisest among my race understand that the agitation of questions of social equality is the extremest folly, and that progress in the enjoyment of all the privileges that will come to us must be the result of severe and constant struggle rather than of artificial forcing. No race that has anything to contribute to the markets of the world is long in any degree ostracized. It is important and right that all privileges of the law be ours, but it is vastly more important that we be prepared for the exercise of those privileges. The opportunity to earn a dollar in a factory just now is worth infinitely more than the opportunity to spend a dollar in an opera house.

In conclusion, may I repeat that nothing in thirty years has given us more hope and encouragement, and drawn us so near to you of the white race, as this opportunity offered by the Exposition; and here bending, as it were, over the altar that represents the results of the struggles of your race and mine, both starting practically empty-handed three decades ago, I pledge that, in your effort to work out the great and intricate problem which God has laid at the doors of the South, you shall have at all times the patient, sympathetic help of my race; only let this be constantly in mind that, while from representations in these buildings of the products of field, of forest, of mine, of factory, letters, and art, much good will come, yet far above and beyond material benefits will be the higher good, that let us pray God will come, in a blotting out of sectional differences and racial animosities and suspicions, in a determination to administer absolute justice, in a willing obedience among all classes to the mandates of law. This, coupled with our material prosperity, will bring into our beloved South a new heaven and a new earth.

THE CIVIL RIGHTS DECISIONS, 1883

United Press International Photo

[The Civil Rights Act of March 1, 1875, aimed to enforce the postbellum amendments by opening all public accommodations to Negroes on equal terms with whites. When the North abandoned the cause of Negro equality, the Supreme Court gladly moved to confirm white supremacy in the South. In *U.S. v. Cruikshank* (1876) Chief Justice Waite asserted that the Fourteenth Amendment "adds nothing to the rights of one citizen as against another. It simply furnishes a federal guaranty against any encroachment by the States upon the fundamental rights which belong to every citizen as a member of society." This ruling was applied in the five *Civil Rights Cases* of 1883 which declared the Civil Rights Act void. Here we give part of Justice Bradley's statement for the majority, and part of Justice Harlan's dissent. These decisions cleared the way for Jim Crow laws and their confirmation by *Plessy v. Ferguson* in 1896.]

Bradley, J. . . . . It is State action of a particular character that is prohibited. Individual invasion of individual rights is not the subject-matter of the amendment. It has a deeper and broader scope. It nullifies and makes void all State legislation, and State action of every kind, which impairs the privileges and immunities of citizens of the United States, or which injures them in life, liberty, or property without due process of law, or which denies to any of them the equal protection of the laws. It not only does this, but, in order that the national will, thus declared, may not be a mere *brutum fulmen*, the last section of the amendment invests Congress with power to enforce it by appropriate legislation. To enforce what? To enforce the prohibition. To adopt appropriate legislation for correcting the effects of such prohibited State laws and State acts, and thus to render them effectually null, void, and innocuous. . . . It does not invest Congress with power to legislate upon subjects which are within the domain of State legislation; but it provides modes of relief against State legislation, or State action, of the kind referred to. It does not authorize Congress to create a code of municipal law for the regulation of private rights; but to provide modes of redress against the operation of State laws, and the action of State officers, executive or judicial, when these are subversive of the fundamental rights specified in the amendment. . . .

Until some State law has been passed, or some State action through its officers or agents has been taken, adverse to the rights of citizens sought to be protected by the fourteenth amendment, no legislation of the United States under said amendment, nor any proceeding under such legislation, can be called into activity: for the prohibitions of the amendment are against State laws and acts done under State authority. . . . In fine, the legislation which Congress is authorized to adopt in this behalf is not general legislation upon the rights of the citizen, but corrective legislation, that is, such as may be necessary and proper for counteracting such laws as the States may adopt or enforce, and which, by the amendment, they are prohibited from making or enforcing, or such acts and proceedings as the States may commit or take, and which, by the amendment, they are prohibited from committing or taking. . . .

On the whole we are of opinion, that no countenance of authority for the passage of the law in question can be found in either the Thirteenth or Fourteenth Amendment of the Constitution; and no other ground of authority for its passage being suggested, it must necessarily be declared void, at least so far as its operation in the several States is concerned.

Harlan, J., dissenting. . . . The opinion in these cases proceeds, it seems to me, upon grounds entirely too narrow and artificial. I cannot resist the conclusion that the substance and spirit of the recent amendments of the Constitution have been sacrificed by a subtle and ingenious verbal criticism. . . . Constitutional provisions, adopted in the interest of liberty, and for the purpose of securing, through national legislation, if need be, rights inhering in a state of freedom, and belonging to American citizenship, have been so construed as to defeat the ends the people desired to accom-

plish, and which they supposed they had accomplished by changes in their fundamental law. . . .

I do not contend that the Thirteenth Amendment invests Congress with authority, by legislation, to define and regulate the entire body of civil rights which citizens enjoy, in the several States. But I hold that since slavery, as the court has repeatedly declared, . . . was the moving or principal cause of the adoption of that amendment, and since that institution rested wholly upon the inferiority, as a race, of those held in bondage, their freedom necessarily involved immunity from, and protection against, all discrimination against them, because of their race, in respect of such civil rights as belong to freemen of other races. Congress, therefore, under its express power to enforce that amendment, by appropriate legislation, may enact laws to protect that people against the deprivation, *because of their race*, of any civil rights granted to other freemen in the same State; and such legislation may be of a direct and primary character, operating upon States, their officers and agents, and, also, upon, at least, such individuals and corporations as exercise public functions and wield power and authority under the State. . . .

No State can sustain her denial to colored citizens of other States, while within her limits, of privileges or immunities, fundamental in republican citizenship, upon the ground that she accords such privileges or immunities only to her white citizens and withholds them from her colored citizens. The colored citizens of other States, within the jurisdiction of that State, could claim . . . every privilege and immunity which that State secures to her white citizens. . . . A colored citizen of Ohio or Indiana, while in the jurisdiction of Tennessee, is entitled to enjoy any privilege or immunity, fundamental in citizenship, which is given to citizens of the white race in the latter State. It is not to be supposed that any one will controvert this proposition. . . .

It was perfectly well known that the great danger to the equal enjoyment by citizens of their rights, as citizens, was to be apprehended not altogether from unfriendly state legislation, but from the hostile action of corporations and individuals in the States. And it is to be pre- sumed that it was intended, by that section, to clothe Congress with power and authority to meet that danger. . . .

PLESSY v. FERGUSON: "SEPARATE BUT EQUAL"

[The sporadic efforts made by Congress to implement the Fourteenth Amend- ment's guarantee to Negroes of equality with whites came to an end in 1896 with the Supreme Court's decision in the case of *Plessy v. Ferguson*. The case arose from the challenge by Plessy, a mulatto, of a Louisiana statute of 1890 which required railroads to provide "equal but separate accommodations" for Negroes and whites. The decision sweepingly opened the door to Jim Crow legislation. A further de- cision in 1899, *Cumming v. County Board of Education* legalized separate schools for whites and blacks. Here we reprint part of the majority opinion in *Plessy v. Ferguson* as delivered by Justice Henry B. Brown and part of the dissenting opin- ion by Justice John Marshall Harlan. Note Brown's acceptance of the current belief that was later to be epitomized by W. G. Sumner as "stateways cannot change folkways." It is clear that court decisions were made on "sociological grounds" long before the charge was levelled at Chief Justice Warren in 1954.]

Brown, J. . . . The object of the amendment was undoubtedly to enforce the absolute equal- ity of the two races before the law, but in the nature of things it could not have been in- tended to abolish distinctions based upon color, or to enforce social, as distinguished from po- litical, equality, or a commingling of the two races upon terms unsatisfactory to either. Laws permitting, and even requiring, their separation in places where they are liable to be brought into contact do not necessarily imply the inferi- ority of either race to the other, and have been generally, if not universally, recognized as within the competency of the state legislatures in the exercise of their police power. The most common instance of this is connected with the establishment of separate schools for white and colored children, which have been held to be a valid exercise of the legislative power even by courts of states where the political rights of the colored race have been longest and most earnestly enforced. . . .

It is claimed by the plaintiff in error that, in any mixed community, the reputation of belonging to the dominant race, in this instance the white race, is *property*, in the same sense that a right of action, or of inheritance, is property. Conceding this to be so, for the pur- poses of this case, we are unable to see how this statute deprives him of, or in any way affects his right to, such property. If he be a white man and assigned to a colored coach, he may have his action for damages against the company for being deprived of his so-called property. Upon the other hand, if he be a colored man and be so assigned, he has been deprived of no property, since he is not lawfully entitled to the reputation of being a white man. . . .

So far, then, as a conflict with the 14th Amendment is concerned, the case reduces itself to the question whether the statute of Louisiana is a reasonable regulation, and with respect to this there must necessarily be a large discretion on the part of the legislature. In de- termining the question of reasonableness it is at liberty to act with reference to the estab- lished usages, customs, and traditions of the people, and with a view to the promotion of their comfort, and the preservation of the public peace and good order. Gauged by this standard, we cannot say that a law which authorizes or even requires the separation of the two races in public conveyances is unreasonable or more obnoxious to the 14th Amendment than the acts of Congress requiring separate schools for colored children in the District of Columbia, the constitutionality of which does not seem to have been questioned, or the corresponding acts of state legislatures.

We consider the underlying fallacy of the plaintiff's argument to consist in the assumption that the enforced separation of the two races stamps the colored race with a badge of inferiority. If this be so, it is not by reason of anything found in the act, but solely because the colored race chooses to put that construction upon it. . . . The argument also assumes that social prejudice may be overcome by legislation, and that equal rights cannot be secured to the Negro except by an enforced commingling of the two races. We cannot accept this proposition. If the two races are to meet on terms of social equality, it must be the result of natural affinities, a mutual appreciation of each other's merits and a voluntary consent of individuals. . . . Legislation is powerless to eradicate racial instincts or to abolish distinctions based upon physical differences, and the attempt to do so can only result in accentuating the difficulties of the present situation. If the civil and political rights of both races be equal, one cannot be inferior to the other civilly or politically. If one race be inferior to the other socially, the Constitution of the United States cannot put them upon the same plane.

Harlan, J., dissenting. . . . In respect of civil rights, common to all citizens, the Constitution of the United States does not, I think, permit any public authority to know the race of those entitled to be protected in the enjoyment of such rights. Every true man has pride of race, and under appropriate circumstances, when the rights of others, his equals before the law, are not to be affected, it is his privilege to express such pride and to take such action based upon

it as to him seems proper. But I deny that any legislative body or judicial tribunal may have regard to the race of citizens when the civil rights of those citizens are involved. Indeed such legislation as that here in question is inconsistent, not only with that equality of rights which pertains to citizenship, national and state, but with the personal liberty enjoyed by everyone within the United States. . . .

In my opinion, the judgment this day rendered will, in time, prove to be quite as pernicious as the decision made by this tribunal in the Dred Scott Case. It was adjudged in that case that the descendants of Africans who were imported into this country and sold as slaves were not included nor intended to be included under the word "citizens" in the Constitution, and could not claim any of the rights and privileges which that instrument provided for and secured to citizens of the United States; that at the time of the adoption of the Constitution they were "considered as a subordinate and inferior class of beings, who had been subjugated by the dominant race, and, whether emancipated or not, yet remained subject to their authority, and had no rights or privileges but such as those who held the power and the government might choose to grant them."

The recent amendments of the Constitution, it was supposed, had eradicated these principles from our institutions. But it seems that we have yet, in some of the states, a dominant race, a superior class of citizens, which assumes to regulate the enjoyment of civil rights, common to all citizens, upon the basis of race. The present decision, it may well be apprehended, will not only stimulate aggressions, more or less brutal and irritating, upon the admitted rights of colored citizens, but will encourage the belief that it is possible, by means of state enactments, to defeat the beneficent purposes which the people of the United States had in view when they adopted the recent amendments of the Constitution, by one of which the blacks of this country were made citizens of the United States and of the states in which they respectively reside and whose privileges and immunities, as citizens, the states are forbidden to abridge. . . .

The destinies of the two races in this country are indissolubly linked together, and the interests of both require that the common government of all shall not permit the seeds of race hate to be planted under the sanction of law. What can more certainly arouse race hate, what more certainly create and perpetuate a feeling of distrust between these races, than state enactments which in fact proceed on the ground that colored citizens are so inferior and degraded that they cannot be allowed to sit in public coaches occupied by white citizens? That, as all will admit, is the real meaning of such legislation as was enacted in Louisiana. . . .

I am of opinion that the statute of Louisiana is inconsistent with the personal liberty of citizens, white and black, in that state, and hostile to both the spirit and letter of the Constitution of the United States. If laws of like character should be enacted in the several states of the Union, the effect would be in the highest degree mischievous. Slavery as an institution tolerated by law would, it is true, have disappeared from our country, but there would remain a power in the states, by sinister legislation, to interfere with the full enjoyment of the blessings of freedom; to regulate civil rights, common to all citizens, upon the basis of race; and to place in a condition of legal inferiority a large body of American citizens, now constituting a part of the political community, called the people of the United States, for whom and by whom, through representatives, our government is administered. Such a system is inconsistent with the guarantee given by the Constitution to each state of a republican form of government, and may be stricken down by Congressional action, or by the courts in the discharge of their solemn duty to maintain the supreme law of the land, anything in the Constitution or laws of any state to the contrary notwithstanding.

For the reasons stated, I am constrained to withhold my assent from the opinion and judgment of the majority.

"LYNCH LAW" AND THE NEGRO

[The brutality of American society toward Negroes may have declined in the items of small routine tortures after emancipation, but it by no means ended the murders. Indeed, these almost took on the character of rituals in which entire communities participated—and that not only in the South. Thomas F. Gossett in his outstanding book, *Race: The History of an Idea in America* (Southern Methodist University Press, 1963), pp. 269–273, has graphically portrayed the tide of lynchings.]

A kind of fever chart in the history of American racism may be discovered by examining the annual statistics on lynching. For a long time, the word *lynch* had no connection with the death penalty or with Negroes. The name goes back to Colonel Charles Lynch of Bedford County, Virginia, who in the uncertain times of the American Revolution organized an informal court to deal with Tories and criminals on the Virginia frontier. The "court" limited itself to fines and whippings and did not hand down death penalties. When times became more peaceful, it was indemnified and exonerated by the Virginia legislature. "Lynch-Law" came to mean extralegal administration of punishment, particularly by whipping. In the 1850's, the term usually referred to the executions of horse-thieves and desperadoes by vigilance committees in the West. But during the Civil War and afterward during Reconstruction, the word *lynch* came to have something approaching its modern meaning—the killing of someone by a mob.

It is a curious fact that in the early years

of the 1880's—when statistics on lynching began to be kept—considerably more whites were lynched than Negroes. Between 1882 and 1888, 595 whites and 440 Negroes were lynched in the United States. But inexorably the figures changed. In 1889, 76 whites and 94 Negroes were lynched. By 1892, lynching reached its highest recorded point, with 69 whites and 162 Negroes suffering this fate. Thereafter the number declined, though for the next twelve years, from 1893 to 1904, an average of more than a hundred Negroes a year were lynched as compared with an average of 29 whites. In the thirty-three year period from 1883 to 1915, the annual toll of Negroes lynched never fell below 50 but once—in 1914, when the number was 49. In nine of these years the figures rose to more than a hundred. During the same period, the number of whites lynched was rapidly declining. In the years from 1906 through 1915, ten times as many Negroes (620) were lynched as whites (61).

What was supposed to explain and justify the horrors of lynching as an instrument of "justice" was the raging urge of Negro men to rape white women. In 1942, a study of lynching disclosed that of the 3,811 Negroes lynched between 1889 and 1941, only 641, or less than 17 per cent, were even accused of rape, either attempted or committed. Negroes were lynched for such "crimes" as threatening to sue a white man, attempting to register to vote, enticing a white man's servant to leave his job, engaging in labor union activities, "being disrespectful to" or "disputing with" a white man, or sometimes for no discoverable reason at all. Mary Turner, in Georgia, was hanged and burned when she was almost at the point of childbirth because she threatened to disclose the names of the men who had killed her husband.

To read the details of lynching is to be reminded of the torture of the Middle Ages. Indeed, the lynchers could sometimes have taught the torturers of that era some lessons. The victims were lucky indeed if they were merely hanged. In Paris, Texas, in 1893 a Negro had his eyes gouged out with a red-hot poker before he was burned to death. In Arkansas in 1921 a crowd of five hundred, including women, watched a Negro slowly burned to death. He was chained to a log and "fairly cooked to death" as small piles of damp leaves were burned under different parts of his body. When the victim would try to hasten his own death by swallowing hot ashes, his tormentors would kick the ashes out of his reach. The victim did not cry out or beg for mercy but answered questions a considerable time after the flesh had fallen away from his bones. A reporter from the *Memphis Press* described the scene in detail and noted how after the victim was dead there was a wild scramble of the mob to secure his bones as souvenirs. W. E. B. DuBois tells of seeing the fingers of a lynched Negro displayed in the windows of a butcher shop in Atlanta. Sometimes victims had their teeth pulled out one by one, their fingers and toes chopped off by axes while they were still alive, and frequently they were castrated or otherwise mutilated. Anyone who is nostalgic for the superior virtue of the past should read a history of lynching in this country. . . .

The Bettmann Archive

As the tide of lynchings rose in the 1890's, Walter Hines Page protested against them and correctly forecast where they would lead. "The gravest significance of this whole matter," he declared in 1893, "lies not in the first violation of the law, nor in the crime of lynching, but in the danger that Southern public sentiment itself under the stress of this new and horrible phase of the race-problem will lose the true perspective of civilization." In 1907, William Graham Sumner—hardly one to be accused of an excessive sensibility—marveled that the country had apparently come to accept as a matter of course lynchings accompanied by torture. "It might have been believed a few years ago," he wrote, "that torture could not be employed under the jurisdiction of the United States, and that, if it was employed, there would be a unanimous outburst of indignant reprobation against those who had so disgraced us." He confessed that he did not understand why the country had been so little moved to protest against lynchings.

Sometimes lynching was condoned or at least explained on the basis of the sexual nature of the Negro man. "The intelligent Negro may understand what social equality truly means," said Thomas Nelson Page in 1904, "but to the ignorant and brutal young Negro, it signifies but one thing: the opportunity to enjoy, equally with white men, the privilege of cohabiting with white women." The South understood the tendency of Negro men, and thus there was among the whites "universal and furious hostility to even the least suggestion of social equality." A number of modern writers have attempted to explain and interpret the relationship between sexual attitudes and race prejudice, especially the violent kind exemplified in lynchings. John Dollard has mentioned the conviction of many southerners that Negro men have exceptionally large genitals and thus their raping of a white woman is a peculiarly horrible and brutal offense. Dollard speculates whether sexual jealousy on the part of white men may be a factor in lynchings. One still hears the idea expressed by white men in the Deep South that they wish they could be Negroes, at least on Saturday nights. Lillian Smith and Oscar Handlin have maintained that the puritanical code of religion in the South has in the minds of the whites invested Negroes with both the attraction and the horror of being completely free sexually. James Baldwin, the Negro author, is convinced that whites generally are obsessed with the Negro as a symbol of sexuality.

A PLEA FOR THE "TALENTED TENTH"

[Booker T. Washington's Atlanta Compromise speech placated whites, but it aroused considerable criticism among Negroes on the ground that he would sacrifice the only guarantees of Negro progress—the vote, civil liberties, and the opportunity to train Negro leaders in institutions of higher education. Criticism finally crystallized in an essay, "The Talented Tenth," written by W. E. B. Du Bois and published in a collection of articles entitled *The Negro Problem* (1903). It was out of this protest that there arose the Niagara Movement and its successor, the National Association for the Advancement of Colored People (N.A.A.C.P.) which has played so large a part in Negro progress. Here we reprint a few of the highlights of the essay.]

The Negro race, like all races, is going to be saved by its exceptional men. The problem of education, then, among Negroes must first of all deal with the Talented Tenth; it is the problem of developing the Best of this race that they may guide the Mass away from the contamination and death of the Worst, in their own and other races. Now the training of men is a difficult and intricate task. Its technique is a matter for educational experts, but its object is for the vision of seers. If we make money the object of man-training, we shall develop money-makers but not necessarily men; if we make technical skill the object of education, we may possess artisans but not, in nature, men. Men we shall have only as we make manhood the object of the work of the schools—intelligence, broad sympathy, knowledge of the world that was and is, and of the relation of men to it—this is the curriculum of that higher Education which must underlie true life. On this foundation we may build bread winning, skill of hand and quickness of brain, with never a fear lest the child and man mistake the means of living for the object of life. . . .

Can the masses of the Negro people be in any possible way more quickly raised than by the effort and example of this aristocracy of talent and character? Was there ever a nation on God's fair earth civilized from the bottom upward? Never; it is, ever was and ever will be from the top downward that culture filters. The Talented Tenth rises and pulls all that are worth the saving up to their vantage ground. This is the history of human progress. . . .

I would not deny, or for a moment seem to deny, the paramount necessity of teaching the Negro to work, and to work steadily and skillfully, or seem to depreciate in the slightest degree the important part industrial schools must play in the accomplishment of these ends, but I *do* say, and insist upon it, that it is industrialism drunk with its vision of success, to imagine that its own work can be accomplished without providing for the training of broadly cultured men and women to teach its own teachers, and to teach the teachers of the public schools.

But I have already said that human education is not simply a matter of schools; it is much more a matter of family and group life—the training of one's home, of one's daily companions, of one's social class. Now the black boy of the South moves in a black world—a world with its own leaders, its own thoughts, its own ideals. In this world he gets by far the larger part of his life training, and through the eyes of this dark world he peers into the veiled world beyond. Who guides and determines the education which he receives in his world? His teachers here are the group-leaders of the Negro people—the physicians and clergymen, the trained fathers and mothers, the influential and forceful men about him of all kinds; here it is, if at all, that the culture of the surrounding world trickles through and is handed on by the graduates of the higher schools. Can such culture training of group leaders be neglected? Can we afford to ignore it? . . . You have no choice; either you must help furnish this race from within its own ranks with thoughtful men of trained leadership, or you must suffer the evil consequences of a headless misguided rabble. . . .

Men of America, the problem is plain before you. Here is a race transplanted through the criminal foolishness of your fathers. Whether you like it or not the millions are here, and here they will remain. If you do not lift them up, they will pull you down. Education and work are the levers to uplift a people. Work alone will not do it unless inspired by the right ideals and guided by intelligence. Education must not simply teach work—it must teach Life. The Talented Tenth of the Negro race must be made leaders of thought and missionaries of culture among their people. No others can do this work and Negro colleges must train men for it. The Negro race, like all other races, is going to be saved by its exceptional men.

THE EMERGENCE OF JIM CROW

Before the extreme racists took over the South around 1900 there were three philosophies of race relations proposed by whites. Liberals like Lewis Blair and G. W. Cable recommended equality—civil, political, and economic—fought against segregation, and ridiculed the belief in Negro inferiority. Very few Southern whites listened to them. The radical philosophy we shall note presently. The remaining philosophy was conservative, and was favored by Southerners who felt that they had a responsibility for the Negro's welfare even though—or because— he was inferior. Conservatives did not, like the poor whites, fear or resent the Negro, were ready to receive the individual on his merits, and were certainly opposed to segregating and humiliating him.

When Northerners lost interest in the freedmen, the latter, though usually remaining Republicans, naturally turned to the conservatives for protection. The alliance bore fruit in the toleration of the Negro franchise in many areas until the 1890's. The Redeemers—the conservatives—had a strong claim on Southern loyalty because they had "redeemed" the South from the Yankees. However, during the 1880's there was a series of financial scandals, and commoners began to resent not only the conservatives' alliance with Negroes but their support of banks, railroads, and other corporations which were blatantly draining the South's economic life blood. The Bourbons justified their economic stand by arguing the South's need of Northern capital. This was true, but it was not an argument calculated to win votes.

The result was the Populist revolt directed against the one-party system, the conservatives, and the financial interests they represented. The Populist radicals appealed to Negro voters on the basis of the camaraderie of misery—"You are in the ditch just like us." Whether they would have advocated social equality is doubtful, but they promised equal civil and political rights. Negroes were given meaningful positions in the inner councils of the party, and in Populist counties they were even called to jury duty. Tom Watson, Populist leader in Georgia, told whites and blacks plainly that race antagonism was being fanned by the financial despots for their own purposes. Lynching was denounced, and when a Negro Populist speaker was threatened with lynching and fled to Watson two thousand armed white farmers surrounded Watson's home to shield the fugitive.

Even with all the flaws that existed in this facade of harmony—and there were many—the condition was too good to last. The Bourbons raised the cry of "Negro domination" against the Populists; at the same time they captured the Gulf States by their control of Negro voters—or at least of the count—in the Black Belt counties. The Populist leaders had taken a calculated risk in wooing Negro voters and had fallen between two stools. At the same time they were appealing to the very Southern commoners who were most negrophobe, and who now refused to abandon their primary allegiance to white supremacy.

Laws disfranchising blacks by any of several shrewd schemes began to operate in the 1890's—grandfather clauses, literacy tests, etc. This was only the beginning, as was seen during the Progressive movement, which in some ways was actually more sweeping and effective than the Northern phase. But it was strictly for whites—indeed, some of the most outstanding Southern Progressives were also propagandists of racism. And it is notable that the Progressive years were the very ones in which white aggression reached its peak in anti-Negro riots and lynchings. It was also the period in which Jim Crow legislation accelerated its attempt to enforce separation of the races in the use of public transportation, waiting rooms, toilets, drinking fountains, restaurants, theaters, and even in industries. Moreover, there was an accentuation of private pressures for segregation in areas not necessarily covered by law. The public memory is short, and a generation later both Southerners and Northerners accepted the claim that Jim Crowism had existed from time immemorial. This was not true, for it was ushered in by the tide of disfranchisement and violence which began in the 1890's.

How can we explain the rising tide of racism? Quite clearly it goes deeper than a mere reaction by the Southern commoner to Negro voting. In his *Strange Career of Jim Crow* (2nd ed., N.Y.: Oxford, 1966), C. Vann Woodward points out that by the 1890's Southern frustrations had "pyramided to a climax of social tensions." The South had not only lost its bid for independence—frustrating enough in itself—but was plunged into what seemed to be a permanent and ever-deepening economic depression. The Populists had sought heroic remedies but failed to find them, or at least failed in their effort to apply them. Under the circumstances, the only possible refuges were psychological. One such refuge was the glorification of the Lost Cause. Another was the venting of frustrations on a helpless scapegoat.

Inevitably, the Negro became this scapegoat as "permissions-to-hate came from sources that had formerly denied such permission." Northern liberals joined the Supreme Court in abandoning the black man to the mercy of the States. Southern populists and conservatives each feared that the other would use the Negro vote, and so agreed on Negro disfranchisement. It was this period that saw the rise of propaganda for empire with its prating about Anglo-Saxon superiority, the White Man's Burden, and Inevitable Destiny. Finally, W. G. Sumner's dictum that "stateways cannot change folkways"—uttered in 1907—buttressed the arguments of certain sociologists and psychologists and became the rock on which the credo of Twentieth-Century Southernism was founded.

This Southern Credo, as expressed by Howard W. Odum in his *Way of the South* (1947), was the belief that the Negro "could not be expected ever to measure up to the white man's standard of character and achievement." Odum went on (page 99) to point out that the North no more than the South envisioned social equality for the Negro.

> What neither the nation nor the South seemed to comprehend . . . was the simple fact . . . that it was all a normal problem of social culture, essentially an American problem, and secondarily a southern problem. The South was different, and it should be different. But it was the normal difference of an important region of a great nation, and should not continue to develop a sectional difference as of one section over against another. It was the southern region within the nation. It was the South, but it was the American South of the United States. What the South did and how it developed were therefore important to the South, but far more important to the nation.

By 1920 the white South had clamped a tight lid on the boiling kettle of black hopes and aspirations and had assured that there would eventually be an explosion. As for the North, since Jim Crowism was a social rather than a legal phenomenon, there was a little more hope. When aspiring blacks from the South crowded into the ghettos of the Northern cities this modicum of hope operated on them in the same way that hope always had affected rising classes in the American democracy, as witness the immigrant masses which had crowded the cities during the past century. Now it was the turn of the blacks.

Free Homesteads

OF 160 ACRES,

FOR

EX-SOLDIERS and SAILORS,

ALONG THE LINES OF RAILROADS,

Under late Act of Congress, April 4th, 1872.

Courtesy of The Old Print Shop, New York

4

THE PUBLIC DOMAIN
AND ITS PROBLEMS

THE HOMESTEAD ACT IN OPERATION

[A recent reexamination of the part the Homestead Act of 1862 played in settlement of the public domain is "The Homestead Act: Free Land Policy in Operation, 1862–1935" by Paul W. Gates. The version given here is from Howard W. Ottoson, ed., *Land Use Policy and Problems in the United States* (University of Nebraska Press, 1963), pp. 28–43.]

Two generations of agitation by land reformers, including workingmen's advocates, Jeffersonian arcadians, and western agrarians, finally produced the Homestead Law of 1862 which offered free a quarter section of public land in the West to citizens or intended citizens who settled upon and improved it. These free-land advocates anticipated Henry George in maintaining that wild, undeveloped land on the frontier had no value until it was improved by the toil of farm makers; the taxes of residents that provided roads and schools; town and county government; subventions that assisted in opening up canals and railroads; and high transportation rates that helped to pay for the railroads. Since it was the investment of the farmer's labor and the public's money that made land valuable, it seemed to the western citizen double taxation to make him pay for government land. The Homestead Act was intended to reward him for his courageous move to the frontier by giving him land, the value of which he and the community would create.

If classical economists found little but sophistry in this reasoning, the western pioneer and the eastern land reformers cared not. Free land, they hoped, would make the life of the pioneer easier, enable him to use his meager capital to purchase farm machinery and livestock, relieve him of debt to the government or to loan sharks (who frequented the land offices to lend their funds at frontier interest rates of 20 to 40 per cent), remove the specter of crushing mortgages, and thereby assure a larger proportion of success among farm makers.

The Homestead Law was the culmination of a series of moves intended to end the policy of using the public lands as a source of revenue for the government. Prior to 1862, the revenue policy had been frequently modified but prices had been reduced only moderately. Now, in one simple act, it seemingly had been replaced by what conservatives regarded as a radical policy of giving land freely to anyone willing to undertake the obligations of farm making.

Not all westerners subscribed to the view that land on the outer fringe of settlement had no value. Some could see that as the western population movement expanded, it shortened the period in which, on successive frontiers land values rose swiftly from little or nothing to a number of dollars an acre. Like speculators from the East, they were prepared to gamble that the land would acquire value with the expected immigration and the improvements the people made. . . .

If conservatives viewed with alarm the social results they foresaw from homesteading, the land reformers were disappointed that the thoroughgoing reconstruction of American land policies they had sought was not achieved. Homesteads were to be alienable, and weak and inadequate safeguards were included to prevent abuse of the law and accumulation of homesteads by capitalists. The privilege of buying public land in unlimited quantities to anticipate settlers' needs was not ended. Huge grants of land were made after the adoption of the Homestead Law to railroads, wagon roads, and states and territories which could make their selections before settlers appeared and thereby acquire the better and more desirable tracts. Indian land, when opened to settlement, was commonly to be sold, not given to settlers, and individual Indian allotments were likewise to be sold. Altogether, between 400 and 500 million acres were selected by states and territories, railroads, and investors and were held for future sales. These were not, therefore, subject to homestead. In fact, the area not open to homestead, though undeveloped, was much greater than the total acreage that homesteaders finally won as free grants. . . .

Free-land policy as embodied in the Homestead Law was then grafted upon a land system to which it was ill-fitted and incongruous. The two systems existed side by side for the next twenty-eight years, indeed longer, during which time the choicer selections of the railroads, states, and speculators were being sold. Hence the amount of homesteading was smaller than otherwise it surely would have been.

That revenue was not abandoned as a basic feature of government land policy is shown by the fact that homesteaders, desiring to expand their holdings beyond the 160 acres they could acquire by right of development, had the choice of buying additional tracts from railroads, states, or territories—or from the federal government if in areas where land had been proclaimed for sale in unlimited amounts. If the land was in unoffered areas, they might secure a preemption, or take a desert-land entry which would cost them $1.25 an acre, or enter a tree claim with its obligation of setting out trees on forty of the 160 acres. Actually, more government land was sold between 1862 and 1891 than was successfully homesteaded and patented between 1862 and 1899. Or, to put it differently, the government derived from the sale of public land in the sixty years following the adoption of the Homestead Act a far greater sum ($223,000,000) than it did in the first sixty years of its land administration ($186,000,-000).

Henceforth, there were two classes of land in official terminology: offered land which was subject to private entry in unlimited amounts and unoffered land which could only be acquired through settlement laws: homestead, preemption, timber culture, timber and stone, and their variations.

Yet it is true that in the unoffered areas large estates were created, such as the bonanza farms of the Dakotas, and the equally large cattle ranches of Wyoming and elsewhere. Some of these holdings, like the bonanza farms, were bought partly from the railroads which placed few limitations on the size of tracts they would sell, and partly from the states. And partly they were acquired through the use of dummy entrymen who took advantage of the loopholes in the settler laws. Others, including some of the large cattle ranches, were not ownerships but enclosures, illegally erected on the public lands which, when the order went out for the removal of the fences, became thereafter open to settlement. These large holdings, together with even larger acquisitions of the timber companies . . . and the discovery that millions of acres of land have passed into private hands by the fraudulent use of the settlement laws, have led historians to misunderstand and underestimate the role of the Homestead Law and related settlement measures. . . .

A reason for the frequency of these misconceptions of homestead is the continued reiteration in the annual reports of the Commissioners of the General Land Office, of the widespread and indeed common violation of the spirit and even the letter of the law by land-hungry settlers, land lookers, petty and large speculators and their agents, and cattle and mining companies. Defective legislation, insufficient staff, poorly paid personnel in the Washington office, the low level of people filling the local land offices, and the practical impossibility of scrutinizing critically the entries made under the various land laws, all combined to make the Commissioners' task of administering the laws most frustrating. Their comments on the amount of perjury, subornation, and misuse of the law became increasingly sharp until finally, the Commissioner [W. A. J. Sparks] under Cleveland, harassed by the degree of maladministration and the widespread dishonesty of people trying to take advantage of the government, took the drastic step of suspending many thousands of land entries moving toward patent to allow time for examination and the cancellation of fraudulent entries. This action led to swift political pressures by western politicians, forcing Cleveland to reverse his subordinate, no matter how just his action. So absorbed were the Commissioners in their efforts to make homestead function as it was intended to, that they devoted the space allowed them for recommendations for future action very largely to the frauds and malfunctionings of the system. Historians have reflected this jaundiced view, relying upon these continued reiterations, and not finding much in the reports about the hundreds of thousands of people successfully making farms for themselves. . . .

In any attempt to appraise the significance of the Homestead Law it should be borne in mind that settlers on unoffered land had more protection for their selections and improvements than they did on offered land. Since speculators could not enter or offer to buy their selections or improvements by falsely swearing at the land office that there were no claims against the land, the settler had less fear, once he had filed his original entry, of being dispossessed.

Having filed his original entry (even though he lacked the means with which to develop his claim), the homesteader had an equity that became increasingly valuable and negotiable as population increased the pressure upon the land supply. In the vanguard of settlement on every frontier were land speculators great and small who spied out choice tracts they wished to hold for the expected rise in value that incoming immigration would bring. The extensive speculator might assemble tracts running of tens of thousands of acres. But of equal importance, possibly, was the small man with no capital for the arduous task of farm making who nevertheless took up a piece of land to which he expected to acquire a preemption right. Frontier custom assured that his claim of one hundred to two hundred acres was his to do with as he wished. With patience and little labor he might improve slightly, sell, and then move to another tract and do the same thing. Government conceded only one preemption right, but that right was almost sacrosanct on the frontier and the same person might make a number of fortunate selections in succession and dispose of them profitably. Some contemporaries were not certain whether the first occupation of pioneers was farm making or land speculation. . . . In addition to the three usual claims it was not unknown for different members of a family to file on adjacent tracts, even though they were violating the spirit if not the letter of the law.

Having established a number of claims which they might be doing little or nothing to develop, settlers had the choice of selling relinquishments to others, borrowing to commute and then skipping the country, attempting to make their improvements with loans until they could get the benefit of rising land values, or holding for long range development. The location, sale, and relinquishment of claims became a major business on the frontier as it proceeded into western Kansas, Nebraska and Dakota. Relinquishments in the middle Eighties sold for $25 to $50 in Kansas, for $50 to $400 in South Dakota and for as little as $5 and a shotgun to $700 in North Dakota. Variations in price partly depended upon the nature of improvements. Undoubtedly, the business of selling relinquishments was carried beyond all justification but it should be emphasized that it permitted persons who lacked the means with which to begin farming to acquire some cash, farm machinery, and stock and after two or three false starts and sale of relinquishments to succeed finally in establishing ownership of a going farm. The process of claim making with the intention of selling was greatly abused, particularly in the Eighties, but despite that abuse it provided opportunities for many settlers to reach their goal of farm ownership.

Land office reports, accounts of the cattle and lumber industry, and other government documents are replete with stories of the use of dummy entrymen by individuals and companies eager to get control of large areas of the public lands. The process was fairly simple. Employees of the cattle, mining, or lumber companies would be induced to file claims under one of the settlement laws, possibly make some slight improvements on their claims, take title by commuting their claims and swear before the land officials that their claims were intended for their own use and that they had entered into no agreement to transfer ownership. Funds for their commutation and a fee for their services that ranged from $50 to $200 were provided by the company. As competition for land intensified, compensation to dummy entrymen reached as high as $1,000 for a quarter section.

A third source of income that the weakly administered public land system made possible to westerners was the practice of mortgaging newly entered land with insurance companies at well beyond its going value and then skipping out with the proceeds of the loan and unloading the property on the credit agency. . . .

Many western settlers had larceny in their hearts when it came to dealing with the government, and it did not stretch their consciences unduly to take advantage of the insurance companies or other absentee sources of capital. . . .

A common error in appraising the Homestead Law has been the assumption that homesteading was only important in the Great Plains and Interior Basin where the unit of farming characteristic of the more humid regions was not suitable. The fact is that 23 per cent (689,000) of all original homestead entries were filed in the states east of the Mississippi and in the first tier west of that river. Twenty-four per cent of the homestead entries that went to final patent were located in this region. . . .

In substantial portions of the second tier of states beyond the Mississippi (extending from Dakota to Oklahoma), the 160-acre unit of farming was not altogether unsuited for farm practices in the late Nineteenth Century. The line of 20-inch rainfall begins roughly just west of the Red River of the North and extends in a gentle southwestward direction. East of that line is perhaps a fifth of North Dakota, a third of South Dakota, more than half of Nebraska, and two-thirds of Kansas. The line of 24-inch rainfall leaves, to the east, a small corner of South Dakota, a fifth of Nebraska, and half of Kansas. To and somewhat beyond the 24-inch rainfall line, corn flourished and the 160-acre unit of agriculture seemed reasonably well adapted to farming. I have conservatively estimated that 150,000 homestead applications were filed in the more humid portions of the Great Plains. This means that, together with the 689,000 entries previously mentioned, 839,-000 homesteads or 28 per cent of the total number of homesteads were commenced in areas generally suitable in the Nineteenth Century for 160-acre farm units. . . .

A second error frequently observed in appraisals of the Homestead Act is forgetting that it took five years, later reduced to three (veterans' military service could be counted), for the original entries to mature. Actually, even more than five years was required for many homesteaders who were driven out by drought, grasshoppers, or other misfortunes, and who had to be allowed extensions of time in which to prove up.

In the land selection process many choices were made by settlers and speculators who were misled by the descriptions on the surveyors' plats; by the land lookers who for fees guided settlers to what soon proved to be questionable locations; and by settlers themselves who may have had little knowledge of the quality of land in the vicinity of the 100th meridian. Some settlers, like those who participated in the great rushes into Oklahoma or who desperately tried to get a claim on the Rosebud Reserva-

tion in South Dakota, had no time to pick and choose but had perforce to take the first vacant land they could find. Inevitably, mistakes were made. Study of the correspondence of the General Land Office and of western congressmen illustrates the frequency with which errors of location were made from the very outset of the public land system, and the disappointments and frustrations of the land locators who sought the privilege of making exchanges. In the absence of land classification, settlers made many errors that resulted in a high rate of failure on homesteads. . . .

Historians have been troubled that the homestead unit was fixed at 160 acres just when, as they say, settlers were preparing to break into the less humid region of the Great Plains where larger farm units were desirable. Paradoxically, they have also been troubled that the Preemption Law which, with homestead, made possible larger farm units, was kept on the statute books. Following the judgment of the Commissioners of the General Land Office who harped on the amount of fraud involved in preemption, they have given undue emphasis to this aspect and insufficient attention to the fact that preemption was consciously retained by Congress surely because of the greater flexibility it allowed settlers in adapting themselves to farming in the dryer portions of America where land was not offered. There is no mention of repeal of preemption in the discussion leading to the adoption of homestead in 1862 and the Law itself carefully provided for saving all preemption rights that may have been established prior to its adoption. Furthermore, just a few days after the adoption of the Homestead Law, Congress, without a word of opposition in either house, enacted a bill that said all lands to which Indian title had been or should thereafter be extinguished should be subject to preemption. We must conclude that Congress had no intention of establishing an inflexible 160-acre unit for settlers in the unoffered areas.

In 1872 and 1873 the two houses of Congress finally came to agreement on a bill to encourage the planting of trees on the Great Plains. An additional quarter section was thereby offered to settlers who would plant and care for forty acres of trees (later reduced to ten acres) for a period of ten years. An effort to limit its benefits to settlers who had not taken up a preemption or homestead, failed. Timber culture was designed further to adapt the post-1862 land system to farming in sub-humid America. The law was not carefully drafted and as with all other land legislation it quickly became subject to abuse and was repealed in 1891. But it had in the meantime, notwithstanding its abuse, served its purpose. With preemption and homestead it provided a flexibility that after its repeal was to be assured by the more direct method of enlarging the homestead unit to 320 and then 640 acres.

How significant was the Homestead Law in enabling settlers to acquire land and to establish themselves on going farms? It is clear that it was most successful in the period from 1863 to 1880 when the greater proportion of homesteads were being established in the states bordering on the Mississippi River. It was successful also in parts of Kansas and Nebraska well east of the 98th meridian where there was abundance of rain, and where commutations, relinquishments, and abandonments were fewer than they were to be in other areas later. In these eighteen years, homesteaders filed on 469,000 tracts and by 1885 had made their final entries and were in process of getting title on 55 per cent. Doubtless some would complete their residence requirements in later years.

The misuse of the Homestead Law was becoming common between 1880 and 1900. As shown, misuse was by persons not primarily interested in farm making but concerned to sell relinquishments to immigrants or to transfer rights to cattle, timber, and mining companies. But the most glaring abuses occurred later. Between 1880 and 1900, approximately half of the homestead entries were filed in the six states and territories extending from Oklahoma to North Dakota and including Minnesota. These all were major farm states and the Homestead Law was contributing largely to the development of farm ownership, notwithstanding its abuses.

In these states and territories, free government land, advertised by the America letters which earlier immigrants had sent back to their families in the Old World, by the government immigration bureaus, by even the colonization departments of the railroads and land companies, provided the lodestone, the directing force, that set in motion continued waves of settlers in search of free land. It was the prospect of disposing of their lands to these settlers and transporting their goods that made possible the financing and construction of the railroads through the Plains, into the Interior Basin and to the Pacific Coast. Homestead, above all other factors, made possible the fast growth of the West and all the problems this rapid growth brought with it.

Altogether, 1,413,513 original homestead entries were filed between 1863 and 1900, but even more were to be filed in the twentieth century for a substantially larger acreage. The great day of farm making with the material aid of Uncle Sam was over, however. True, some twentieth century entries were made with the enlarged units for small stock raising farms or ranches or even wheat farms but the evidence seems strong that the great bulk of the entries filed after 1900 were for large ranching, mining, and lumbering companies. The numbers of original and final homestead entries, when compared with the number of farms in the Rocky Mountain States, provides startling evidence that the homesteads were being assimilated into larger aggregations of land. . . . In six mountain states the original entries came to 848,000, final entries 492,000, and the maximum number of farms 217,000. Thus it seemed to take about four original entries and two final homestead entries to produce a farm, and most of these homesteads were of the enlarged variety.

Major John W. Powell's recommendation of 1879 that the public lands be classified for use and that a 2,560-acre pasturage homestead be established for lands fit only for grazing was somewhat premature, but certainly by 1900, land classification and larger homestead units were essential. Yet the evidence is strong that the enlarged units of 1904, 1909, and 1916 were not altogether wise or successful. The old evils of careless drafting of land legislation, weak and inefficient administrations (inadequately staffed), and the anxiety of interests to take advantage of loopholes in the laws, all brought the Homestead Acts into contempt and censure. But their noble purpose and the great part they played in enabling nearly a million and a half people to acquire farm land, much of which developed into farm homes, far outweigh the misuse to which they were put.

INSTITUTIONS FOR THE ARID LANDS

[John Wesley Powell (1834–1902) lost his right arm at the Battle of Shiloh, but served through the war as an artillery officer, then went on to a remarkable career as geologist and explorer. He was the first to lead a party of whites down the Green and Colorado Rivers and through the Grand Canyon (1869). Presently he entered government service, and from 1880 to 1894 was Director of the Geological Survey. Meanwhile, in 1879, he published his *Report on the Lands of the Arid Region of the United States*, in which he pointed out that 40 percent of the United States was arid and that its value for agriculture depended on whether water could be made available for irrigation. The Homestead Act's allowance of 160 acres was too small for an irrigated farm and even less adequate for a cattleman. Powell proposed that the lands of the public domain be classified on the basis of their usability and that graziers be allowed four square miles. At this time Carl Schurz was President Hayes's Secretary of the Interior, and he joined the advocates of reform in persuading Congress to establish a Land Commission to investigate and make recommendations. The Commission produced a monumental report, but Congress only slowly and reluctantly agreed to some of its milder proposals. Meanwhile, Powell continued to work for reform. His article, "Institutions for the Arid Lands," published in *Century Illustrated Monthly Magazine*, 40: 111–116 (1890), was a factor in encouraging the demand for publicly financed irrigation which culminated in the Newlands Reclamation Act of 1902. Powell pointed out that lands, streams, and forests were interdependent and constituted hydrographic basins which should be treated as units. He introduced his article by spelling out that the East began as a "log-cabin zone" but the West as a miners' zone; the latter was now largely falling into the control of great land engrossers and of groups able to monopolize water rights and afford the capital expense of irrigation. Such a system was dangerous to liberty, for it was difficult for the small farmer to obtain land, and if he did get it he was completely dependent on the water monopolizer. What could be done about this condition?]

It is proposed to present a plan for the solution of these problems, and others connected therewith, in an outline of institutions necessary for the arid lands. Some of these problems have been discussed in former articles, and it may be well to summarize them all once more, as follows:

First. The capital to redeem by irrigation 100,000,000 acres of land is to be obtained, and $1,000,000,000 is necessary.

Second. The lands are to be distributed to the people, and as yet we have no proper system of land laws by which it can be done.

Third. The waters must be divided among the States, and as yet there is no law for it, and the States are now in conflict.

Fourth. The waters are to be divided among the people, so that each man may have the amount necessary to fertilize his farm, each hamlet, town, and city the amount necessary for domestic purposes, and that every thirsty garden may quaff from the crystal waters that come from the mountains.

Fifth. The great forests that clothe the hills, plateaus, and mountains with verdure must be saved from devastation by fire and preserved for the use of man, that the sources of water may be protected, that farms may be fenced and homes built, and that all this wealth of forest may be distributed among the people.

Sixth. The grasses that are to feed the flocks and herds must be protected and utilized.

Seventh. The great mineral deposits—the fuel of the future, the iron for the railroads, and the gold and silver for our money—must be kept ready to the hand of industry and the brain of enterprise.

Eighth. The powers of the factories of that great land are to be created and utilized, that the hum of busy machinery may echo among the mountains—the symphonic music of industry.

A thousand millions of money must be used; who shall furnish it? Great and many industries are to be established; who shall control them? Millions of men are to labor; who shall employ them? This is a great nation, the Government is powerful; shall it engage in this work? So dreamers may dream, and so ambition may dictate, but in the name of the men who labor I demand that the laborers shall employ themselves; that the enterprise shall be controlled by the men who have the genius to organize, and whose homes are in the lands developed, and that the money shall be furnished by the people; and I say to the Government: Hands off! Furnish the people with institutions of justice, and let them do the work for themselves. The solution to be propounded, then, is one of institutions to be organized for the establishment of justice, not of appropriations to be made and offices created by the Government.

In a group of mountains a small river has

its source. A dozen or a score of creeks unite to form the trunk. The creeks higher up divide into brooks. All these streams combined form the drainage system of a hydrographic basin, a unit of country well defined in nature, for it is bounded above and on each side by heights of land that rise as crests to part the waters. Thus hydraulic basin is segregated from hydraulic basin by nature herself, and the landmarks are practically perpetual. In such a basin of the arid region the irrigable lands lie below; not chiefly by the river's side, but on the mesas and low plains that stretch back on each side. Above these lands the pasturage hills and mountains stand, and there the forests and sources of water supply are found. Such a district of country is a commonwealth by itself. The people who live therein are interdependent in all their industries. Every man is interested in the conservation and management of the water supply, for all the waters are needed within the district. The men who control the farming below must also control the upper regions where the waters are gathered from the heavens and stored in the reservoirs. Every farm and garden in the valley below is dependent upon each fountain above.

All of the lands that lie within the basin above the farming districts are the catchment areas for all the waters poured upon the fields below. The waters that control these works all constitute one system, are dependent one upon another, and are independent of all other systems. Not a spring or a creek can be touched without affecting the interests of every man who cultivates the soil in the region. All the waters are common property until they reach the main canal, where they are to be distributed among the people. How these waters are to be caught and the common source of wealth utilized by the individual settlers interested therein is a problem for the men of the district to solve, and for them alone.

But these same people are interested in the forests that crown the heights of the hydrographic basin. If they permit the forests to be destroyed, the source of their water supply is injured and the timber values are wiped out. If the forests are to be guarded, the people directly interested should perform the task. An army of aliens set to watch the forests would need another army of aliens to watch them, and a forestry organization under the hands of the General Government would become a hotbed of corruption; for it would be impossible to fix responsibility and difficult to secure integrity of administration, because ill-defined values in great quantities are involved.

Then the pasturage is to be protected. The men who protect these lands for the water they supply to agriculture can best protect the grasses for the summer pasturage of the cattle and horses and sheep that are to be fed on their farms during the months of winter. Again, the men who create water powers by constructing dams and digging canals should be permitted to utilize these powers for themselves, or to use the income from these powers which they themselves create, for the purpose of constructing and maintaining the works necessary to their agriculture.

Thus it is that there is a body of interdependent and unified interests and values, all collected in one hydrographic basin, and all segregated by well-defined boundary lines from the rest of the world. The people in such a district have common interests, common rights, and common duties, and must necessarily work together for common purposes. Let such a people organize, under national and State laws, a great irrigation district, including an entire hydrographic basin, and let them make their own laws for the division of the waters, for the protection and use of the forests, for the protection of the pasturage on the hills, and for the use of the powers. This, then, is the proposition I make: that the entire arid region be organized into natural hydrographic districts, each one to be a commonwealth within itself for the purpose of controlling and using the great values which have been pointed out. There are some great rivers where the larger trunks would have to be divided into two or more districts, but the majority would be of the character described. Each such community should possess its own irrigation works; it would have to erect diverting dams, dig canals, and construct reservoirs; and such works would have to be maintained from year to year. The plan is to establish local self-government by hydrographic basins.

Let us consider next the part which should be taken by the local governments, the State governments, and the General Government in the establishment and maintenance of these institutions. Let there be established in each district a court to adjudicate questions of water rights, timber rights, pasturage rights, and power rights, in compliance with the special laws of the community and the more general laws of the State and the nation. Let there be appeal from these lower courts to the higher courts. Let the people of the district provide their own officers for the management and control of the waters, for the protection and utilization of the forests, for the protection and management of the pasturage, and for the use of the powers; and with district courts, water masters, foresters, and herders they would be equipped with the local officers necessary for the protection of their own property and the maintenance of individual rights. The interests are theirs, the rights are theirs, the duties are theirs; let them control their own actions. To some extent this can be accomplished by coöperative labor; but ultimately and gradually great capital must be employed in each district. Let them obtain this capital by their own enterprise as a community. Constituting a body corporate, they can tax themselves and they can borrow moneys. They have a basis of land titles, water rights, pasturage rights, forest rights, and power rights; all of these will furnish ample security for the necessary investments; and these district communities, having it in their power to obtain a vast increment by the development of the lands, and to distribute it among the people in severalty, will speedily understand how to attract capital by learning that honesty is the best policy.

Each State should provide courts for the adjudication of litigation between people of different districts, and courts of appeal from the irrigation district courts. It should also establish a general inspection system, and provide that the irrigation reservoirs shall not be constructed in such a manner as to menace the people below and place them in peril from floods. And finally, it should provide general statutes regulating water rights.

But the General Government must bear its part in the establishment of the institutions for the arid region. It is now the owner of most of the lands, and it must provide for the distribution of these lands to the people in part, and in part it must retain possession of them and hold them in trust for the districts. It must also divide the waters of the great rivers among the States. All this can be accomplished in the following manner. Let the General Government make a survey of the lands, segregating and designating the irrigable lands, the timber lands, the pasturage lands, and the mining lands; let the General Government retain possession of all except the irrigable lands, but give these to the people in severalty as homesteads. Then let the General Government declare and provide by statute that the people of each district may control and use the timber, the pasturage, and the water powers, under specific laws enacted by themselves and by the States to which they belong. Then let the General Government further declare and establish by statute how the waters are to be divided among the districts and used on the lands segregated as irrigable lands, and then provide that the waters of each district may be distributed among the people by the authorities of each district under State and national laws. By these means the water would be relegated to the several districts in proper manner, interstate problems would be solved, and the national courts could settle all interstate litigation.

But the mining industries of the country must be considered. Undeveloped mining lands should remain in the possession of the General Government, and titles thereto should pass to individuals, under provisions of statutes already existing, only where such lands are obtained by actual occupation and development, and then in quantities sufficient for mining purposes only. Then mining regions must have mining towns. For these the townsite laws already enacted provide ample resource.

It is thus proposed to divide responsibility for these institutions between the General Government, the State governments, and the local governments. Having done this, it is proposed to allow the people to regulate their own affairs in their own way—borrow money, levy taxes, issue bonds, as they themselves shall determine; construct reservoirs, dig canals, when and how they please; make their own laws and choose their own officers; protect their own forests, utilize their own pasturage, and do as they please with their own powers; and to say to them that "with wisdom you may prosper, but with folly you must fail."

PROGRESSIVISM AND CONSERVATION

The organized conservationists were concerned more with economic justice and democracy in the handling of resources than with mere prevention of waste.

—J. Leonard Bates, 1957

It is from the vantage point of applied science, rather than of democratic protest, that one must understand the historic role of the conservation movement.

—Samuel P. Hays, 1959

[Conservation of natural resources can have two meanings. One would advocate the locking away of resources, presumably for use by future generations. The other would advocate efficient methods of use, and earnest efforts to develop and renew them—as reforestation—by the best scientific techniques. Traditionally, historians have tended to present the movement for conservation as a grand democratic movement to keep "monopolies" from appropriating the public domain and to preserve resources for use by the people—generally meaning the farmer, the small stockman, the hand logger, and the prospector. Recently, however, Samuel P. Hays has presented the conservation movement as basically an attempt by professional scientists, in and out of government, to plan for and promote the efficient development and use of natural resources. The era chiefly in dispute is the Progressive Era, roughly from 1901 to 1916. Here we present samples of the two points of view. The first, by J. Leonard Bates is taken from his article, "Fulfilling Democracy: The Conservation Movement, 1907 to 1921," in the *Mississippi Valley Historical Review*, 44:29–57 (June 1957). The second is from Samuel P. Hays, *Conservation and the Gospel of Efficiency* (Harvard University Press, 1959), pp. 1–3 and 262–276. Perhaps the reader will be moved to speculate that the conservation movement was complex enough to include both views. At any rate, it is clear that neither view was able to completely overshadow the other.]

(1) FULFILLING DEMOCRACY

"Conservation," as related to an evolving government policy in the twentieth century, has not been a clearly defined term. For average citizens it has meant in a general way the prevention of waste. For scholars and government administrators it has frequently meant a little more definitely the careful management of natural resources. Herbert Hoover as food administrator in World War I and as secretary of commerce in the early 1920's helped to popularize such a concept, with emphasis on efficiency of use. There is much to be said for this construction. The acceptance of conservation in a broad sense represents a considerable advance from the nineteenth century when with a few notable exceptions squandering of public and private resources went on recklessly and often cynically. Moreover, its acceptance was a tribute to a group of men whose concept of official responsibility for conservation was not a loose, vague theory, nor a matter of efficiency as such, but a fighting, democratic faith.

Historians of modern reform have given scant attention to a rationale of conservation or to conservation as a democratic movement. In fact the program associated with Theodore Roosevelt and Gifford Pinchot is occasionally disparaged as largely sound and fury. Doubtless the ambiguity and complexity of "conservation" have tended to obscure its democratic implications. Then too, this policy was both a product of and a stimulant to the larger, so-called Progressive Movement; it shared in certain weaknesses of this epoch of reform and has shared in the criticism. The usual interpretation today is that the Progressive Movement was essentially an uprising of the middle class, protesting against monopoly and boss control of politics, stressing heavily the virtues of competition, freedom, and morality. With respect to conservation this view leads to the criticism that there existed a fundamental inconsistency between the ideas of protecting natural resources and the dominant beliefs in individualism and competition with the resultant low prices, heavy consumption, and waste.

There was another side to the Progressive Movement—perhaps the most significant side: the decline of laissez faire, the development of a social conscience, the repudiation of Social Darwinism. Most leaders of progressivism believed in a positive state. Some came to believe in the sort of factory and social legislation, welfare action, utility regulation, and limited government ownership that is associated with the New Deal. A few wished to go farther than the New Deal ever went. While the conservationists, like others progressively inclined, differed among themselves, nevertheless they had a program which may be described as limited socialism in the public interest. Influenced by Henry George, Edward Bellamy, Lester Ward, William James, Arthur Twining Hadley, Thorstein Veblen, Charles A. Beard, and others, these protectors of the public lands were far removed from classical economics.

The organized conservationists were concerned more with economic justice and democracy in the handling of resources than with mere prevention of waste. One aspect of the matter was the price and income situation, the actual monetary rewards from the marvelous wealth of this land. Conservationist believed that somehow the common heritage, the socially created resources and institutions, had passed into the hands of vested interests and that the benefits were siphoned into the hands of a few. There were several ways in which this situation might be remedied, as they saw it: first, to hold on to the remaining public lands, at least temporarily, preventing further monopolization; second, to attempt to give the people a fuller share of opportunities and profits; and finally, in that period of low income to keep prices proportionately low. The monopolists who jacked up prices were anathema, even though their methods might contribute to conservation by reducing consumption. Conservation through penalizing the public was something which democratically motivated leaders were not prepared to accept.

The conservationists' approach was broad. They believed in government studies and safeguards for the preservation of irreplaceable resources such as petroleum; they recognized and struggled with problems which remain today only partially solved. They understood the need for federal leadership in an organic structure based on the unity of nature itself. As early as 1910 Gifford Pinchot proclaimed, "Every river

THE PUBLIC DOMAIN AND ITS PROBLEMS 81

is a unit from its source to its mouth." They made mistakes, of course. Like most progressives, they concluded easily that the opposition on a particular issue consisted of "robber barons," conspirators, and frauds. Yet at times they were capable of a surprising detachment; a key conservationist, for example, referred admiringly to a "very scholarly and fine" argument that the public domain should be turned over to the states.

In a sense the conservation movement was a nonpartisan, statesmanlike cause, winning support from scientists, politicians, and others all over the country. But a fact of long-range significance was its Republican origin; Republicans led by Pinchot and Roosevelt were the main inspiration of this program. These men were proud of their work, many of them almost fanatically devoted to Roosevelt. They did not easily dissociate the Republican party or the "Republican Roosevelt," who had first given them their chance, from the body of their accomplishments. Politics and personalities help appreciably to explain the conservation fight from 1907 to 1921.

In tracing the growth of a new attitude toward public resources it would be inaccurate to give credit only to the Republicans. This enlightenment was evolutionary, like reform in general, and Grover Cleveland, William A. J. Sparks as land commissioner, Hoke Smith as secretary of the interior, and other Democrats in later years made important contributions. Even so, the concern here is with the full-fledged movement to which was given in 1907 the name "conservation." There is no doubt that progressive Republicans were the main actors.

Albert J. Beveridge of Indiana, United States senator, 1899–1911, a Republican and a progressive, was among those who witnessed the beginnings of the conservation policy. In 1921 he wrote to Gifford Pinchot . . .

The whole Conservation system is yours, dear Gifford. I honestly think that you have done more than any other man

for the future well-being of the Republic; and I have said this publicly as well as privately on every appropriate occasion— and I intend to go on saying it.

Pinchot remembered "with keen interest and satisfaction" the beginnings of this movement . . . and in 1937 he recalled . . . "The idea was so new that it did not even have a name. Of course it had to have a name. Our little inside group discussed it a great deal. Finally Overton Price suggested that we should called it 'conservation' and the President said 'O. K.' So we called it the conservation movement.". . .

(2) CONSERVATION AND THE GOSPEL OF EFFICIENCY

The conservation movement has contributed more than its share to the political drama of the twentieth century. A succession of colorful episodes—from the Pinchot-Ballinger controversy, through Teapot Dome, to the Dixon-Yates affair—have embellished the literature of the movement, and called forth fond memories for its later leaders. Cast in the framework of a moral struggle between the virtuous "people," and the evil "interests," these events have provided issues tailor-made to arouse the public to a fighting pitch, and they continue to inspire the historian to recount a tale of noble and stirring enterprise. This crusading quality of the conservation movement has given it an enviable reputation as a defender of spiritual values and national character. He who would battle for conservation fights in a worthy and patriotic cause, and foolhardy, indeed, is he who would sully his reputation by opposition!

Such is the ideological tenor of the present-day conservation movement and of its history as well. But, however much an asset in promoting conservation, this dramatic fervor has constituted a major liability in its careful analysis. For the moral language of conservation battles differed markedly from the course of conservation events. Examining the record, one is forced to distinguish sharply between rhetoric and reality, between the literal meaning of the terminology of the popular struggle and the specific issues of conservation policy at stake. Conservation neither arose from a broad popular outcry, nor centered its fire primarily upon the private corporation. Moreover, corporations often supported conservation policies, while the "people" just as frequently opposed them. In fact, it becomes clear that one must discard completely the struggle against corporations as the setting in which to understand conservation history, and permit an entirely new frame of reference to arise from the evidence itself.

Conservation, above all, was a scientific movement, and its role in history arises from the implications of science and technology in modern society. Conservation leaders sprang from such fields as hydrology, forestry, agrostology, geology, and anthropology. Vigorously active in professional circles in the national capital, these leaders brought the ideals and practices of their crafts into federal resource policy. Loyalty to these professional ideals, not close association with the grass-roots public, set the tone of the Theodore Roosevelt conservation movement. Its essence was rational planning to promote efficient development and use of all natural resources. The idea of efficiency drew these federal scientists from one resource task to another, from specific programs to comprehensive concepts. It molded the policies which they proposed, their administrative techniques, and their relations with Congress and the public. It is from the vantage point of applied science, rather than of democratic protest, that one must understand the historic role of the conservation movement.

The new realms of science and technology, appearing to open up unlimited opportunities for human achievement, filled conservation leaders with intense optimism. They emphasized expansion, not retrenchment; possibilities, not limitations. True, they expressed some fear that diminishing resources would create critical shortages in the future. But they were not Malthusian prophets of despair and gloom. The popular view that in a fit of pessimism they withdrew vast areas of the public lands from present use for future development does not stand examination. In fact, they bitterly opposed those who sought to withdraw resources from commercial development. They displayed that deep sense of hope which pervaded all those at the turn of the century for whom science and technology were revealing visions of an abundant future.

The political implications of conservation, it is particularly important to observe, grew out of the political implications of applied science rather than from conflict over the distribution of wealth. Who should decide the course of resource development? Who should determine the goals and methods of federal resource programs? The correct answer to these questions lay at the heart of the conservation idea. Since resource matters were basically technical in nature, conservationists argued, technicians, rather than legislators, should deal with them. Foresters should determine the desirable annual timber cut; hydraulic engineers should establish the feasible extent of multiple-purpose river development and the specific location of reservoirs; agronomists should decide which forage areas could remain open for grazing without undue damage to water supplies. Conflicts between competing resource users, especially, should not be dealt with through the normal processes of politics. Pressure group action, logrolling in Congress, or partisan debate could not guarantee rational and scientific decisions. Amid such jockeying for advantage with the resulting compromise, concern for efficiency would disappear. Conservationists envisaged, even though they did not realize their aims, a political system guided by the ideal of efficiency and dominated by the technicians who could best determine how to achieve it.

This phase of conservation requires special examination because of its long neglect by historians. Instead of probing the political implications of the technological spirit, they have repeated the political mythology of the "people versus the interests" as the setting for the struggle over resource policy.

.   .   .   .

This point of view correctly describes the ideology of the conservation movement, but fails to analyze its broader meaning. It stresses conservation as a theory of resource ownership when, in fact, the movement was most concerned with resource use. To most historians the amount of exploitation in the nineteenth century varied directly with ownership. Large corporations, they argue, wasted resources lavishly, while small farmers did not. . . .

Resource exploitation, in fact, reflected the attitude not merely of corporations, but of Americans in all walks of life. Small farmers, as well as corporate leaders, helped to establish a wasteful pattern of land use. Everyone in the nineteenth century hoped to make a killing from rising land values and from quickly extracting the cheap, virgin resources of the nation. Corporations often did exploit resources, such as the timber of the Great Lakes forest region. Such examples, however, do not support the general view that corporations by their very nature promoted resource waste, and the larger the corporation and the greater its self-interest, the more destruction it caused. On the contrary, when the conservation movement arose in the early twentieth century, it became clear that larger corporations could more readily afford to undertake conservation practices, that they alone could provide the efficiency, stability of operations, and long-range planning inherent in the conservation idea. Larger owners could best afford to undertake sustained-yield forest and range management, and understood more clearly than did small farmers the requirements for large-scale irrigation and water power development. . . .

The movements for wider land distribution and more efficient land use had entirely separate origins. The first continued after the Forest Reserve Act of 1891, but in a direction diametrically opposed to the spirit of that law. Homesteaders bitterly resented permanent reservation of public land from private entry. To them, forest, range, or mineral reserves differed little from withdrawals for railroad land grants. They fought with equal vigor to abolish both. At the same time, conservation leaders felt closer to the spirit of development, typified by the railroad land grants, than to the reaction against the roads. Both railroads and conservationists promoted large-scale economic development. While the conservation movement emphasized greater efficiency in this process, its goal of planned economic growth and its consolidating tendencies closely approximated the spirit of railroad construction. The transcontinental lines, in fact, cooperated closely with conservationists in developing Western resources, and gave special aid to federal irrigation, forest, and range programs. . . .

The broader significance of the conservation movement stemmed from the role it played in the transformation of a decentralized, nontechnical, loosely organized society, where waste and inefficiency ran rampant, into a highly organized, technical, and centrally planned and directed social organization which could meet a complex world with efficiency and purpose. This spirit of efficiency appeared in many realms of American life, in the professional engineering societies, among forward-looking industrial management leaders, and in municipal government reform, as well as in the resource management concepts of Theodore Roosevelt. The possibilities of applying scientific and technical principles to resource development fired federal officials with enthusiasm for the future and imbued all in the conservation movement with a kindred spirit. These goals required public management, of the nation's streams because private enterprise could not afford to undertake it, of the Western lands to adjust one resource use to another. They also required new administrative methods, utilizing to the fullest extent the latest scientific knowledge and expert, disinterested personnel. This was the gospel of efficiency—efficiency which could be realized only through planning, foresight, and conscious purpose.

The lack of direction in American development appalled Roosevelt and his advisers. They rebelled against a belief in the automatic beneficence of unrestricted economic competition, which, they believed, created only waste, exploitation, and unproductive economic rivalry. To replace competition with economic planning, these new efficiency experts argued, would not only arrest the damage of the past, but could also create new heights of prosperity and material abundance for the future. The conservation movement did not involve a reaction against large-scale corporate business, but, in fact, shared its views in a mutual revulsion against unrestrained competition and undirected economic development. Both groups placed a premium on large-scale capital organization, technology, and industry-wide cooperation and planning to abolish the uncertainties and waste of competitive resource use.

Historians of the Progressive Era have found it increasingly difficult to categorize Theodore Roosevelt. Was he a "liberal" or an "enlightened conservative?" Did he rob the Democrats of their reform proposals and fulfill the aims of late nineteenth-century social revolt, or did he merely mouth their causes and, in practice, betray them? These questions pose difficulties chiefly because they raise the wrong issues. They assume that the significance of Roosevelt's career lies primarily in its role in the social struggle of the late nineteenth and early twentieth centuries between the business community on the one hand and labor and farm groups on the other. On the contrary, Roosevelt was conspicuously aloof from that social struggle. He refused to become identified with it on either side. He was, in fact, predisposed to reject social conflict, in theory and practice, as the greatest danger in American society. His administration and his social and political views are significant primarily for their attempt to supplant this conflict with a "scientific" approach to social and economic questions. . . .

Roosevelt's emphasis on applied science and his conception of the good society as the classless agrarian society were contradictory trends of thought. The one, a faith which looked to the future, accepted wholeheartedly the basic elements of the new technology. The other, essentially backward-looking, longed for the simple agrarian Arcadia which, if it ever existed, could never be revived. He faced two directions at once, accepting the technical requirements of an increasingly organized industrial society, but fearing its social consequences. In this sense, and in this sense alone, Roosevelt sought Jeffersonian ends through Hamiltonian means. He had great respect for both men, each of whom manifested one side of his own contradictory nature. But he admired even more Abraham Lincoln, the spokesman of the "plain people," whose life combined agrarian simplicity and national vigor. By the same token, Roosevelt considered his irrigation program as one of his administration's most important contributions. It expressed in concrete terms his own paradoxical nature: the preservation of American virtues of the past through methods abundantly appropriate to the present.

The contradictory elements of Roosevelt's outlook fused also in an almost mystical approach to the political order best described as "social atomism." Strongly affirming the beneficial role of both expert leadership and the vast mass of humanity, he could not fit into his scheme of things intervening group organization on the middle levels of power. Americans should live, he thought, as individuals rather than as members of "partial" groups, their loyalties should be given not to a class or section but to their national leader. As his administration encountered continued difficulty with Congress, Roosevelt relied more and more on executive commissions, and on action based upon the theory that the executive was the "steward" of the public interest. Feeling that he, rather than Congress, voiced most accurately the popular will, he advocated direct as opposed to representative government. Unable to adjust to a Congress which rejected his gospel of efficiency, Roosevelt took his case to the "people." In doing so he not only bypassed the law-makers but also defied the group demands or organized American society. Growing ever more resentful of the hindrances of a Congress which expressed these demands, Roosevelt drew closer to a conception of the political organization of society wherein representative government would be minimized, and a strong leader, ruling through vigorous purpose, efficiency, and technology, would derive his support from a direct, personal relationship with the people. . . .

In holding these attitudes, Roosevelt personally embodied the popular impulses which swung behind the conservation movement during the years of the great crusade. That crusade found its greatest support among the American urban middle class which shrank in fear from the profound social changes being wrought by the technological age. These people looked backward to individualist agrarian ideals, yet they approved social planning as a means to control their main enemy—group struggle for power. A vigorous and purposeful government became the vehicle by which ideals derived from an individualistic society became adjusted to a new collective age. And the conservation movement provided the most far-reaching opportunity to effect that adjustment. Herein lay much of the social and cultural meaning of the movement for progressive resource planning.

The deepest significance of the conservation movement, however, lay in its political implications: how should resource decisions be made and by whom? Each resource problem involved conflicts. Should they be resolved through partisan politics, through compromise among competing groups, or through judicial decision? To conservationists such methods would defeat the inner spirit of the gospel of efficiency. Instead, experts, using technical and scientific methods, should decide all matters of development and utilization of resources, all problems of allocation of funds. Federal land management agencies should resolve land-use differences among livestock, wildlife, irrigation,

recreation, and settler groups. National commissions should adjust power, irrigation, navigation, and flood control interests to promote the highest multiple-purpose development of river basins. The crux of the gospel of efficiency lay in a rational and scientific method of making basic technological decisions through a single, central authority.

Resource users throughout the country differed sharply from this point of view. They did not share the conservationists' desire for integrated planning and central direction. Instead, each group considered its own particular interest as far more important than any other. Resource users formed their opinions about conservation questions within the limited experience of specific problems faced in their local communities. They understood little and cared less for the needs of the nation as a whole. . . .

Both large and small property owners knew that the conservationists' plans involved methods of decision far beyond their control, and each group feared that a broader program would obscure its own specific needs or minimize its own project. Basin-wide river planning might require a dam in another locality. Multiple-purpose dams might provide less water desperately needed for navigation and more for electric power for some remote industry. Rigid grazing control might benefit the irrigator in the lower basin, but curtail the activities of stockmen on the headwaters. Each group desired financial and technical aid from the federal government, and each supported executive action when favorable to it, but none could feel a deep sense of participation in the process by which technical experts made resource decisions. Experience with the Forest Service and Bureau of Reclamation alienated many groups which found it difficult to influence administrative policy. They opposed plans to establish executive adjustment of conflicting uses and favored methods of decision over which they felt they had some measure of control.

Grass-roots groups utilized a variety of political methods, both judicial and legislative, to protect their interests. Through pressure on federal agencies or influence in selecting personnel, they could even modify the administrative process itself. Western water users, for example, resorted to the courts to counteract a rational state water law and efficient federal water development, both of which they viewed as a menace to their existing rights. . . .

Resource users played a fundamental role in shaping the character of development in a manner contrary to the aims of conservationists. They created a single, rather than a multiple-purpose attack on resource affairs. Economic organizations concerned with single interests—such as navigation, flood control, or irrigation—joined with administrative agencies in charge of individual programs and congressional committees which dealt with specialized subjects to defeat an integrated approach. Through policies devoted to the development of a single resource, Congress found protection against independent executive action, administrative agencies discovered a means to prevent coordination of their work with other bureaus, and local interests created programs of direct benefit to themselves and under their control. Private organizations and their congressional allies established this pattern. Although administrative agencies, such as the Corps of Engineers, took much initiative in preserving their administrative independence, their concern for single-purpose development reflected rather than molded the attitude of Congress. Single-purpose policies, impractical from the point of view of the conservation ideal of maximum development through scientific adjustment of competing uses, became the predominant pattern because they provided opportunities for grass-roots participation in decision-making. They enabled resource users to feel that they had some degree of control over policies that affected them.

The first American conservation movement experimented with the application of the new technology to resource management. Requiring centralized and coordinated decisions, however, this procedure conflicted with American political institutions which drew their vitality from filling local needs. This conflict between the centralizing tendencies of effective economic organization and the decentralizing forces inherent in a multitude of geographical interests presented problems to challenge even the wisest statesman. The Theodore Roosevelt administration, essentially hostile to the wide distribution of decision-making, grappled with this problem but failed to solve it. Instead of recognizing the paradoxes which their own approach raised, conservationists choose merely to identify their opposition as "selfish interests." Yet the conservation movement raised a fundamental question in American life: How can large-scale economic development be effective and at the same time fulfill the desire for significant grass-roots participation? How can the technical requirements of an increasingly complex society be adjusted to the need for the expression of partial and limited aims? This was the basic political problem which a technological age, the spirit of which the conservation movement fully embodied, bequeathed to American society.

New York Public Library Picture Collection

5

THE FAITH OF THE GILDED AGE

INTRODUCTION

Successive generations of rebels have rejected the faith of their elders and sought to represent it either as sham or soulless materialism, but no age has suffered more —often unjustly—at the hands of its successors than the Gilded Age. The name was given to the postwar era by Mark Twain and Charles Dudley Warner in their novel *The Gilded Age* (1873), and has survived to symbolize the entire period between the Civil War and World War I—though obviously the glitter began to fade by the end of the 1890's. It was an age of middle-class ascendance, concerned with the traditional bourgeois pursuits of wealth, respectability, and culture—and ready, if necessary, to settle for the semblance rather than the reality. The inevitable result was to mistake gentility for character—hence the tendency to create pleasing illusions where they did not already exist. And hence the widespread acceptance—at least outwardly—of common standards of morality, of politics, and of the role of wealth. Perhaps no age in American history has been more an age of consensus.

And yet when one probes beneath the surface it becomes evident that Americans were groping for a new sense of identity, for new standards of social, political, and economic behavior. We need mention only the names of such seminal figures as Walt Whitman, Henry George, Simon Patton, Frederick W. Taylor, Jane Addams, and William James to demonstrate this, for out of their work and that of their confreres was to emerge the "big change" of our own century.

Henry F. May in *The End of American Innocence, 1912–1917* (1959) examined American ideas at the very end of the Gilded Age when the old barriers were about to be burst by a wave of philosophical, political, and economic change. He speaks of the Gilded Age as having three articles of faith: moral values, progress, and culture in the sense of cultivated tastes. "We can think of the three," says May, "as a triptych, an altar piece made of three pictures, framed in gold and hinged together. In the center, of course, is moralism, painted in the bold and sure colors used by Roosevelt or Lyman Abbott. On the left, joined to the center by a rivet that keeps coming apart, is progress. On the right, a little smaller and dimmer if one looks closely, is culture. In the revolution we are talking about, when the mob broke in it smashed the right-hand panel most thoroughly. The others did not look the same without it."

It is our purpose to consider the intellectual aspects of the Gilded Age on three levels in separate chapters. First will be an examination of its dominant ideas and ideals, what was spoken of above as consensus. Second will come the currents of protest, the probings for something better. Finally, we shall examine the emergence of the pragmatic spirit and the beginning of its struggle to tread under foot the illusions and brutalities of the Gilded Age.

The present chapter, then, is concerned primarily with the American phase of naturalism—what historians now call Social Darwinism or Spencerianism, and which Andrew Carnegie justified under the rubric "The Gospel of Wealth." We shall present certain of its contemporary religious, economic, and social justifications, and examine—as far as possible—the problem of its influence on American standards.

Social Darwinism reached its zenith in the 1890's, then began to weaken under the attacks of its critics. It did not, however, pass away, for it was the philosophic refuge of the beleaguered standpatters of the Progressive Era, was used to brace up the painted scenery of Normalcy, and became the bible of the Liberty League in the 1930's. Even today it survives in the propaganda of reactionaries, and it constituted the platform of the Republican Party in 1960. All this makes one wonder if Herbert Spencer really invented the doctrine that often went by his name. Isn't it possible that the Roman general seizing Carthaginian ports, the Athenian forcing "allies" to join his league, the Assyrian coming down "like a wolf on the fold," the Pharaoh drafting labor to build his pyramid—isn't it possible that all of them could invoke the survival of the fittest to excuse their actions?

However that may be, there was an opinion even in the Gilded Age that Social Darwinism's ruthless competitiveness would lead to a much higher standard of living and culture. To the amazement of its critics, that proved to be true, as we saw in Chapter 1—possibly from a logic inherent in capitalism, but also from the inherent genius of democracy in molding institutions to serve society.

THE NATURALISTIC PATTERNS OF THOUGHT

[Stow Persons in his brilliant study, *American Minds: A History of Ideas* (N.Y.: Holt, 1958), pp. 217–229, has examined naturalism, the dominant philosophy of the Gilded Age, which owed its wide acceptance to the tremendous changes wrought by industrialism and urbanization.]

The naturalistic mind comprised a fairly well-defined bundle of ideas held by many Americans between the Civil War and the Great Depression of the 1930's. At no time during that period, however, did naturalism completely dominate American thinking. In terms of numbers of adherents, it was probably always in a minority; and since the Depression and the rise of totalitarianism in Europe, its influence has suffered a sharp decline. But the naturalistic mind exerted an influence out of proportion to the number of people who shared its tenets, because it was identified chiefly with articulate groups of the intelligentsia, such as journalists, literary men, business spokesmen, and professors. Certain aspects of naturalism were formulated most clearly in the new universities, especially in the natural sciences and in the newly emancipated disciplines that proudly called themselves "social sciences."

But at no time did the tenets of naturalism hold uncontested sway over American thinking. Throughout its lifespan, naturalism was opposed by the continuing traditions of earlier nineteenth-century democratic thought. The resulting intellectual controversies helped to clarify the issues at the turn of the century. Because of its traditional affiliations and commitments, the democratic mind inevitably resisted certain propositions of naturalism, especially those that bore upon the conditions of human freedom. With the rise of totalitarianism on the international scene during the second quarter of the twentieth century, Americans confronted in practical form issues that they had been debating in the intellectual realm for over half a century. It was inevitable, therefore, that a majority of them should react strongly to totalitarianism on ideological grounds, and that, consequently, certain of the naturalistic ideas should acquire a patriotic as well as a moral stigma. . . .

The naturalistic mind had a peculiar veneration for scientific fact as the most accurate, dependable, and valuable form of knowledge available to man. Scientific knowledge was objective and dispassionate and therefore true. In stressing the truth of scientific fact, the naturalists characteristically contrasted it with the myths, fables, fictions, dreams, or vague impressions of ignorant and selfish men. It was by every right, therefore, that science came to enjoy increasing prestige in the community during the later nineteenth century. Many of the most ardent proponents of this kind of scientism could not themselves be described as scientists in any strict sense of the term; they were merely devotees of a method and a point of view that they believed held the key to a better life.

The earlier naturalists in the years after the Civil War were complacently optimistic because they were confident that scientific truth would gradually replace the accumulated errors and superstitions of the past. Because knowledge was power and power was good and good meant progress, they were under strong compulsion to take an optimistic view of human prospects, even if other aspects of the naturalistic outlook suggested a rather different conclusion. Although science was essentially technique, men had faith in the capacity of these techniques for practical accomplishments. All Americans were conditioned to the activist virtue of practical achievements. Consequently, it was almost inevitable that a scientific outlook should be identified with—or confused with—positive values.

Because they professed to prize verified fact most highly and to distrust speculation, the naturalists tended to be unaware of their underlying assumptions as well as of their debts to the past. Indeed, since the purpose here is to examine the basic postulates of naturalistic thought we shall admittedly do the naturalists some injustice by ignoring their impressive accumulations of data in many fields of thought, accumulations that will substantially remain as permanent monuments to their industry and integrity. Nevertheless, consistency of outlook on the broader questions of life was not one of their virtues. Among their ranks were to be found optimists and pessimists, determinists and believers in free agency, democrats and authoritarians, humanists and theists.

In postulating the primacy of natural law, the naturalists placed themselves in a major American intellectual tradition. But their understanding of this concept and its implications were distinctively modern. Their cosmology was compounded out of the nebular hypothesis of Kant and Laplace, the uniformitarian geology of Lyell, and organic evolution of Darwin. It assumed universal change under natural law. A century earlier enlightened thinkers had also started with natural law, but at least two important differences distinguished these usages. First, the universe of the Enlightenment was a static one, while that of the newer naturalism was dynamic. For the latter, the basic natural

law was the law of evolution. Second, when the enlightened thinker shifted his attention from the physical realm of the social, he transformed his natural laws into natural rights. The modern naturalists, on the other hand, more rigorously carried natural law into the social realm and insisted upon its coercive power over man and society.

The aspects of natural law particularly intriguing to the naturalistic mind was the law of organic evolution, according to which all forms of life were held to be undergoing a gradual transformation or development. The controversies over evolution that for so long occupied the center of attention were in fact only a phase of a much larger conflict of ideas, and they were not always an adequate guide to the nature of that conflict, especially when controversy was precipitated by such an issue as religious fundamentalism.

Naturalists also stressed the universality of natural law as it pertained alike to problems in the physical, biological, and social realms. Since the same law operated in each of these areas, the connections between them were intimate, and transitions were made directly and without difficulty. It was as though the distinction between the social and the biological had been made for some mere practical convenience and was without any basis in fact. Consequently, the naturalist believed it possible to reduce relatively complex social phenomena to relatively simple biological terms, and these, in turn, to even simpler physical and mechanical terms, and by so reducing to understand them. This assumption may be understood by bearing in mind the close affinity between the natural order, the moral order, and the social order in earlier democratic thought. Naturalists perpetuated this assumption, but they subordinated the moral and social orders to the natural.

Whether or not such reductionism contributed to the understanding of human and social problems, it is certain that the coherence of reality assumed by naturalism reinforced the primacy of natural law in its coercive power over the individual. There were no loopholes or interstices in life—or very few. William James, one of the most vigorous critics of naturalism, described the world of the naturalists as a "block universe." Perhaps their major practical problem was to determine the role of the individual in a world governed by natural law. In general, they found very little scope for human freedom. Man was obliged to act out his role in society within the narrow limits of restraints (variously designated as folkways, mores, institutions) over which he had no control. One of their most characteristic contributions was the insistence of naturalists that the individual is the creature of his society. Much of their sociology rested upon this insight. The sociologist William Graham Sumner is sometimes assumed to have espoused moral relativism with his dictum: "the mores make anything right." But this was the scholar's observation; for the practical man it meant that what is, is right because what is, is what has to be.

The very limited freedom man possessed was to be realized in direct proportion to his understanding of the limitations of his situation. Only by knowledge of the social and natural forces impinging upon him did man learn how to maneuver among them and achieve limited objectives, namely, the immediate securities and satisfactions that any solvent society has to offer. In short, there was assumed to be a close correlation between freedom and intelligence. But, unfortunately, the naturalists invented the intelligence test, and they became acutely aware of the abysmal ignorance of the vast mass of humanity. Consequently, their thinking displayed little of that faith in the natural man that had come to characterize

American thought, and they were obliged to stand upon a thoroughgoing repudiation of the traditional doctrine of the free individual.

A characteristic emphasis upon the primacy of natural law was sounded in a book by John W. Draper, *Thoughts on the Future Civil Policy of America*, published in 1865 at the conclusion of the Civil War and the beginning of the naturalistic era. . . . Draper insisted that natural law controlled the social process just as effectively as it governed the bodily growth of the individual organism. The historian, by relying upon the immutable laws of nature, should be able to predict the inevitable course of human affairs as surely as the astronomer predicted the path of a comet. It was especially important at that moment for Americans to grasp this principle, since they were moving rapidly into an era of extensive social changes. Among the natural laws that determined the life courses of nations Draper specified the influence of climate, the effects of immigration, the political force of ideas, and the "natural course" of national development. Then he blandly added that there were also many other laws, which he did not bother to specify.

The analogy between human society and a biological organism was one of the more prominent elements of naturalistic thought. By conceiving of the structure of society as analogous to the parts of an organism, it assumed that a clarification of problems and perspective would be achieved. In fact, however, the organic analogy served a useful purpose only in a form so attenuated as to be practically meaningless. But it did accentuate the strong functional flavor of naturalistic social theory. In historiography, the organic analogy suggested a teleological interpretation of history, a point of view emphasizing the realization of an implicit historical destiny that was already well established in American historical thought by the middle of the nineteenth century. It also suggested the study of the history of institutions as a genetic development rather than as the result of the impingement of causal factors mechanically conceived. Obviously, the genetic approach was welcome in that it freed the historian from much laborious research into causal factors, and historical monographs began to flow from the university presses in abundance.

The theory of the social organism bulked large in early naturalistic social thought, and it is possible that Herbert Spencer was chiefly responsible for it. Spencer's influence and prestige in America during the late nineteenth century was so great that it is difficult to sketch the history of American thought during that time without noticing his leading ideas. Many of the American naturalists attributed their intellectual awakening to his books. William James observed with a mixture of contempt and envy that Spencer was the philosopher of all those who read no other philosopher. Nevertheless, when he organized at Harvard his pioneer course in physiological psychology, James used Spencer's *Psychology* as a text. John R. Commons, the labor economist, recalled that he had been brought up in Indiana on "Hoosierism, Republicanism, Presbyterianism, and Spencerism." William Graham Sumner used Spencer's *Study of Sociology* as a text at Yale in spite of presidential opposition due, apparently, to Spencer's materialism. A whole generation of literary men, including Hamlin Garland, Jack London, Edgar Lee Masters, and Theodore Dreiser, were indoctrinated with Spencer.

Evolution was the central theme that unified Spencer's encyclopedic survey of human knowledge. He was an evolutionist before Darwin, having sketched the outlines of his system in essays published during the 1850's. Although Darwin borrowed from him the phrase "survival of the fittest," Spencer was not a Darwinian natural selectionist. His conception of evolution owed more to the physical principle of the conservation of energy than to the Darwinian principle of random variations. In what has aptly been described as a famous piece of English lexicography, Spencer defined the process as follows: "Evolution is an integration of matter and concomitant dissipation of motion; during which the matter passes from an in-

definite incoherent homogeneity to a definite coherent heterogeneity; and during which the retained motion undergoes a parallel transformation." The definition presupposed a materialistic universe composed of matter and energy.

The evolutionary process as Spencer conceived it had a definite goal: the utmost differentiation of matter into coherent heterogeneous aggregates. At the biological level, including mankind, this differentiation was occurring by means of the struggle for existence and survival of the fittest. Entailing as it did personal hardship and suffering for many, this struggle must nevertheless be accepted as part of an ultimately beneficent process. In his *Social Statics* (1850), Spencer observed sententiously that "the poverty of the incapable, the distresses that come upon the imprudent, the starvation of the idle, and those shoulderings aside of the weak by the strong, which leave so many 'in shallows and in miseries,' are the decrees of a large, farseeing benevolence. . . . It seems hard that widows and orphans should be left to struggle for life or death. Nevertheless, when regarded not separately, but in connection with the interests of universal humanity, these harsh fatalities are seen to be full of the highest beneficence. . . ." Although progress, or social evolution, occurred by means of struggle for survival Spencer did not appear to regard it as any the less certain in its outcome. "Progress is not an accident but a necessity. What we call evil and immortality must disappear. It is certain that man must become perfect."

The naturalistic idea of evolutionary social development accomplished through suffering and death suggests an interesting similarity in the basic patterns of Spencerism and Marxism: an inevitable progression to the good achieved through struggle. Marxism in Europe came eventually to supersede Spencerism as the prevailing naturalistic social philosophy. In America, on the other hand, Marxism never achieved comparable influence.

Since Spencer thought of himself as a scientist rather than as a prophet he did not furnish in any detail the blueprint of the good society of the future that would be appropriate to a perfected humanity. But there were hints of it in his discussion of the social organism. In the twentieth century, his vision would be called totalitarianism. Spencer used the analogy of the biological organism to illuminate his analysis of social problems by indicating appropriate parallels. Human society was like an organism. Its individual members were analogous to the cells of the body. Like the organism, society had specialized functions. Arteries of commerce corresponded to the circulatory system; communications networks were analogous to the nervous system; the processing and consumption of foodstuffs corresponds to the functions of the alimentary tract; the formulation of public policy, to the functions of the brain. While these analogies might not strike a later generation as especially useful or ingenious, it is well to note their implications for social theory. They indicated a new sense of the differentiation of functions in modern society, their interdependence, and a felt need for the subordination of various social processes to the whole. Politically, the organic analogy suggested a repudiation of the traditional compact theory and of natural rights.

Society itself, of course, was evolving along with the rest of the universe. Society in its nineteenth-century condition was most closely analogous to a relatively primitive, undifferentiated type of organism. Spencer himself suggested one of the colonial organisms, such as *volvox*, where specialized cells and functions were beginning to appear but where each cell was still capable of participating in most if not all the life functions. The first requisite of a sound social science was to establish accurately the position of the social organism in the social evolutionary scale at the moment of investigation. Having professed to have done this for his own society, Spencer indicated that the relatively undifferentiated character of the social organism in his own day entailed free competition among individuals as the proper form of social action.

It was of the highest importance that these identifications be made accurately because society was a natural growth, changing according to the universal law of evolution. If ignorant men interfered with its growth, they did so at their peril. Social reformers, do-gooders, and other well-intentioned but ignorant people could do great harm by irresponsibly interfering with social evolutionary processes. Spencer's polemical writings were directed toward this danger. He was particularly exercised over welfare and public-service legislation. But Spencer did not provide precise criteria for the measurement of social evolutionary change, and in their absence his enthusiasm for rugged individualism got the better of him. His only visit to the United States occurred in 1882, when he found competitive enterprise rapidly evolving into monopoly with what might well have seemed appropriate Spencerian spontaneity. Yet he distressed his American disciples profoundly by calling in the reporters and announcing that no such thing would be allowed in England; the state would preserve competitive enterprise by breaking up the monopolies!

In the final analysis, however, in the Spencerian system competitive individualism was clearly but a passing phase of a social evolutionary process. The biological analogy of the struggle for existence was pertinent to the social evolutionary stage in which the naturalists found themselves, and as such it provided a currently authoritative guide for action. But it would be a mistake to assign too inclusive a scope to the principle in reconstructing naturalistic social theory. Students who have recently popularized the term *Social Darwinism* and identified it with the Spencerian school have committed this error by stressing the struggle for existence without indicating clearly the social evolutionary limits within which the concept was restricted. The ultimate anticipations of the naturalists looked toward an integrated society in which there would be no place for competitive individualism as currently understood.

Some of the implications of the organismic theory were developed by John W. Draper. He pointed out that the analogy between the life of the individual organism and that of the nation rested upon a structural similarity. In each, the constituent parts underwent unceasing change. As a physiologist, Draper knew that the death and elimination of cells of the body was the condition of the very life of the organism. A human being weighing 140 pounds took in and discharged some one and a half tons of material annually. Similarly, national survival presupposed the life and death of individuals. The analogy extended to a similarity in the life cycles of individuals and of nations. Each alike must pass through the successive stages of infancy, youth, maturity, and old age. This progression was due, not to the operation of moral laws as an eighteenth-century thinker might have said, but to the physical laws of nature. Life itself was a ceaseless ebb and flow between the organic and the inorganic. One might like to think that the higher organisms were emancipated from the direct control of nature's laws, but this was not to be.

Social evolution, like biological evolution, entailed the increasing differentiation of parts. A growing society was becoming ever more specialized in its various functions and diversified in its requirements of skill and aptitude. Draper insisted, therefore, that equality as a permanent social ideal or objective was absurd. Some must do the menial work, and others, the skilled, responsible, and remunerative work. Given such diversified requirements, true equality was impossible and undesirable. In China, for instance, where the densest population and the most stable government in the world was to be found, intellectual superiority had long conferred the right to rule. Americans, said Draper, in whom the instinct of self-government was strong, were inclined to forget that self-government implied self-restraints voluntarily or spontaneously imposed. Social discipline in Europe was imposed both by moral standards and by force. In America, the force of voluntary self-discipline was exerted chiefly through the appeal to self-interest. In this manner, Americans had, at least momentarily, solved the dilemma of liberty and authority. But however achieved, discipline was mandatory. By thus paying his respects to the economy and efficiency of the current American mode of adjustment, Draper was able to avoid the less palatable compulsive implications of his organic approach to political theory. But these implications were readily apparent in his discussion. They portended a future in which, as population increased and resources dwindled, Americans must inevitably accept increasing measures of regimentation and sharper social distinctions.

THE INFLUENCE OF SOCIAL DARWINISM: THREE VIEWS

[Richard Hofstadter's *Social Darwinism in American Thought* (1944) was an epoch-making study of the influence of Herbert Spencer, the English philosopher, in the Gilded Age. The thesis, however, was not entirely new and, indeed, had appeared in other works, notably in T. C. Cochran and William Miller, *The Age of Enterprise* (1942), which had presented Spencer as "Apostle to the Americans." A frontal attack on the claims made in these two books was made in 1959 by Irvin G. Wyllie in an article "Social Darwinism and the Businessman." Wyllie's objection was based largely on his failure to find much direct evidence of this influence in the correspondence, speeches, and writings of captains of industry, with the notable exception of Carnegie. A riposte was made by Sidney Fine in his

Laissez Faire and the General Welfare State: A Study of Conflict in American Thought, 1865–1901 (1956), where he marshaled evidence to show that if the businessman did not draw his rationalizations directly from Spencer, he at least used the same arguments to justify his acquisitiveness and to stave off government interference—except, of course, in showering down small benefits such as the protective tariff and financing railroads. Certainly the businessman's way of thinking was implicit in the times, and the problem of who influenced whom is perhaps analogous to the old familiar problem of which came first: the chicken or the egg. However all that may be, the spirit of Spencerianism permeated not only business but courts, universities, pulpits, and even to some extent the thinking of the man in the street. Here we offer, in order, excerpts from Hofstadter, Wyllie, and Fine.]

I have said that social Darwinism was a secularist philosophy, but in one important respect this needs qualification. For social Darwinism of the hard-bitten sort represented by men like Sumner embodied a vision of life and, if the phrase will be admitted, expressed a kind of secular piety that commands our attention. Sumner, and no doubt after him all those who at one time or another were impressed by his views, were much concerned to face up to the hardness of life, to the impossibility of finding easy solutions for human ills, to the necessity of labor and self-denial and the inevitability of suffering. Theirs is a kind of naturalistic Calvinism in which man's relation to nature is as hard and demanding as man's relation to God under the Calvinistic system. This secular piety found its practical expression in an economic ethic that seemed to be demanded with special urgency by a growing industrial society which was calling up all the labor and capital it could muster to put to work on its vast unexploited resources. Hard work and hard saving seemed to be called for, while leisure and waste were doubly suspect. The economic ethic engendered by these circumstances puts a premium on those qualities that seemed necessary for the disciplining of a labor force and a force of small investors. In articulating those needs, Sumner expressed an inherited conception of economic life, even today fairly widespread among conservatives in the United States, under which economic activity was considered to be above all a field for the development and encouragement of personal character. Economic life was construed as a set of arrangements that offered inducements to men of good character, while it punished those who were, in Sumner's words, "negligent, shiftless, inefficient, silly, and imprudent."

—Richard Hofstadter, *Social Darwinism in American Thought* (Boston: Beacon Press, 1964), pp. 9–10.

The world has known many businessmen, before Darwin's time as well as after, who were sharp in tooth and claw. To put such men down as social Darwinists, in the absence of evidence that their thinking reflected the influence of Darwin or Spencer, would be to deprive the term of meaning. Those who represent the entrepreneur as a Darwinist portray a man who had a conscious Darwinian perspective on his personal success, his business activities, and his general social role. He was a man who not only recited Spencer's phrases, but understood their implications, and perhaps even their intellectual derivation. He was, in other words, a man of the type of Andrew Carnegie. An avid reader of Spencer, Carnegie was converted to social Darwinism at an early age. . . . Because Carnegie supplied such clear evidence of his intellectual indebtedness he is invariably cited to prove the case for the entrepreneur as a social Darwinist.

What is puzzling, especially in light of the claim that businessmen generally took their cues from Spencer, is that so few others have testified so clearly on this point as Carnegie. If men of affairs explained their personal success and justified their business operations in terms of natural selection and the survival of the fittest we should have abundant evidence on this point. It would be folly to deny that such evidence exists, but it is accurate to say that so far it has not been adduced. The men that historians have called to succeed Carnegie on the witness stand have not only been few in number, but on the whole incompetent as well.

—Irvin G. Wyllie, "Social Darwinism and the Businessman" American Philosophical Society, *Proceedings* (October 1959), 103:631.

Not content merely to be the most influential figure on the American scene, the businessman felt the need for a philosophy to explain and to justify his preeminent position. To a great extent, he found what he sought in the precepts of social Darwinism and laissez-faire economics. The businessman, to be sure, did not accept the doctrines of Spencer and the economists *in toto*: he took from their thought only what suited his needs. His version of laissez faire, unlike theirs, was essentially a rationalization of the *status quo*. The theorists of laissez faire were, after all, reformers in their own manner and were opposed to the use of government for the benefit of any particular class. They denounced evidences of governmental favoritism, such as the protective tariff, that were dear to the heart of the businessman. The businessman, for his part, saw no wrong in government activities that were conducive to his welfare: he did not ordinarily object to the use of state power to promote business enterprise. He tended to become an opponent of the state only when it sought to regulate his economic endeavors or to cater to the needs of other economic groups. Laissez faire to him meant, "Leave things as they now are." "If asked what important law I should change," Andrew Carnegie declared, "I must perforce say none; the laws are perfect."

—Sidney Fine, *Laissez Faire and the General Welfare State* (University of Michigan Press, 1956), pp. 97–98.

SOCIAL DARWINISM

Help the poor and unfortunate *to help themselves*, and elevate them towards human perfection and the divine ideal. . . . [But] adopt all the cunning devices that social science has invented, and you cannot be sure that direct or indirect help of the poor does not undermine their self respect and weaken their independence.

—W. T. Harris, strangely enough a critic of Herbert Spencer

Here, then, is the issue. The gospel of Christ says that progress comes from every individual merging his individuality in sympathy with his neighbors. On the other side, the conviction of the nineteenth century is that progress takes place by virtue of every individual's striving for himself with all his might and trampling his neighbor under foot whenever he gets a chance to do so. This may accurately be called the Gospel of Greed.

—Charles S. Peirce, 1893

If men will not act for themselves, what will they do when the benefit of their effort is for all?

—Elbert Hubbard

Two positive principles lead us. . . . The first is that man, when he is strong, will conquer Nature, open up her resources, and harness them to his service. This is his play, his exercise, his divine mission. . . . Man draws to himself material wealth as surely, as naturally, and as necessarily as the oak draws the elements into itself from the earth. The other principle is that, in the long run, it is only to the man of morality that wealth comes. We believe in the harmony of God's Universe. We know that it is only by working along His laws natural and spiritual that we can work with efficiency. Only by working along the lines of right thinking and right living can the secrets and wealth of Nature be revealed.

—Bishop William Lawrence, 1901

I perceive clearly that the extreme business energy, and this almost maniacal appetite for wealth prevalent in the United States, are parts of amelioration and progress, indispensably needed to prepare the very results I demand. My theory includes riches, and the getting of riches.

—Walt Whitman, *Democratic Vistas*, 1871

THE GOSPEL OF WEALTH

[The Gilded Age saw the rise of the belief that society was benefited by the accumulation of wealth in the hands of the Great Entrepreneurs because they were best fitted to administer it for the public welfare. This philosophy was best expressed—and also given a name—by Andrew Carnegie (1835–1919) in his article "Wealth," published in the *North American Review*, No. 391 (June 1889), pp. 653–664. It is evident that Carnegie was not in agreement with the thesis that high wages stimulate the economy.]

The contrast between the palace of the millionaire and the cottage of the laborer with us to-day measures the change which has come with civilization.

This change, however, is not to be deplored, but welcomed as highly beneficial. It is well, nay, essential for the progress of the race, that the houses of some should be homes for all that is highest and best in literature and the arts, and for all the refinements of civilization, rather than that none should be so. Much better this great irregularity than universal squalor. Without wealth there can be no Mæcenas. The "good old times" were not good old times. Neither master nor servant was as well situated then as to-day. A relapse to old conditions would be disastrous to both—not the least so to him who serves—and would sweep away civilization with it. But whether the change be for good or ill, it is upon us, beyond our power to alter, and therefore to be accepted and made the best of. It is a waste of time to criticise the inevitable.

It is easy to see how the change has come. . . . To-day the world obtains commodities of excellent quality at prices which even the generation preceding this would have deemed incredible. In the commercial world similar causes have produced similar results, and the race is benefited thereby. The poor enjoy what the rich could not before afford. What were the luxuries have become the necessaries of life. . . .

The price we pay for this salutary change is, no doubt, great. We assemble thousands of operatives in the factory, in the mine, and in the counting-house, of whom the employer can know little or nothing, and to whom the employer is little better than a myth. All intercourse between them is at an end. Rigid Castes are formed, and, as usual, mutual ignorance breeds mutual distrust. Each Caste is without sympathy for the other, and ready to credit anything disparaging in regard to it. Under the law of competition, the employer of thousands is forced into the strictest economies, among which the rates paid to labor figure prominently, and often there is friction between the employer and the employed, between capital and labor, between rich and poor. Human society loses homogeneity.

The price which society pays for the law of competition, like the price it pays for cheap comforts and luxuries, is also great; but the advantages of this law are also greater still, for it is to this law that we owe our wonderful material development, which brings improved conditions in its train. But, whether the law be benign or not, we must say of it, as we say of the change in the conditions of men to which we have referred: It is here; we cannot evade it; no substitutes for it have been found; and while the law may be sometimes hard for the individual, it is best for the race, because it insures the survival of the fittest in every department. We accept and welcome, therefore, as conditions to which we must accommodate ourselves, great inequality of environment, the concentration of business, industrial and commercial, in the hands of a few, and the law of competition between these, as being not only beneficial, but essential for the future progress of the race.

Having accepted these, it follows that there must be great scope for the exercise of special ability in the merchant and in the manufacturer who has to conduct affairs upon a great scale. That this talent for organization and management is rare among men is proved by the fact that it invariably secures for its possessor enormous rewards, no matter where or under what laws or conditions. . . . It is a law, as certain as any of the others named, that men possessed of this peculiar talent for affairs, under the free play of economic forces, must, of necessity, soon be in receipt of more revenue than can be judiciously expended upon themselves; and this law is as beneficial for the race as the others.

Objections to the foundations upon which society is based are not in order, because the condition of the race is better with these than it has been with any others which have been tried. Of the effect of any new substitutes proposed we cannot be sure. The Socialist or Anarchist who seeks to overturn present conditions is to be regarded as attacking the foundation upon which civilization itself rests, for civilization took its start from the day that the capable, industrious workman said to his incompetent and lazy fellow, "If thou dost not sow, thou shalt not reap," and thus ended primitive Communism [Socialism] by separating the drones from the bees. One who studies this subject will soon be brought face to face with the conclusion that upon the sacredness of property civilization itself depends—the right of the laborer to his hundred dollars in the savings bank, and equally the legal right of the millionaire to his millions. . . .

We start, then, with a condition of affairs under which the best interests of the race are promoted, but which inevitably gives wealth to the few. Thus far, accepting conditions as they exist, the situation can be surveyed and pronounced good. The question then arises,— and, if the foregoing be correct, it is the only question with which we have to deal,—What is the proper mode of administering wealth after the laws upon which civilization is founded have thrown it into the hands of the few? And it is of this great question that I believe I offer the true solution.

[He deplores the bequeathal of the rich man's holdings to his children or for public uses, and approves the growing tendency to tax away hoarded wealth on the ground that it forces the possessor to devote his money to benefactions of his own choice.]

In this we have the true antidote for the temporary unequal distribution of wealth, the reconciliation of the rich and the poor—a reign of harmony—another ideal, differing, indeed, from that of the Communist in requiring only the further evolution of existing conditions, not the total overthrow of our civilization. It is founded upon the present most intense individualism, and the race is prepared to put it in practice by degrees whenever it pleases. Under its sway we shall have an ideal state, in which the surplus wealth of the few will become, in the best sense, the property of the many, because administered for the common good, and this wealth, passing through the hands of the few, can be made a much more potent force for the elevation of our race than if it had been distributed in small sums to the people themselves. . . .

This, then, is held to be the duty of the man of Wealth: First, to set an example of modest, unostentatious living, shunning display or extravagance; to provide moderately for the legitimate wants of those dependent upon him; and after doing so to consider all surplus revenues which come to him simply as trust funds, which he is called upon to administer, and strictly bound . . . as a matter of duty to administer in the manner which, in his judgment, is best calculated to produce the most beneficial results for the community—the man of wealth thus becoming the mere agent and trustee for his poorer brethren, bringing to their service his superior wisdom, experience, and ability to administer, doing for them better than they would or could do for themselves. . . .

In bestowing charity, the main consideration should be to help those who will help themselves; to provide part of the means by which those who desire to improve may do so; to give those who desire to rise the aids by which they may rise; to assist, but rarely or never to do all. Neither the individual nor the race is improved by alms-giving. Those worthy of assistance, except in rare cases, seldom require assistance. The really valuable men of the race never do, except in cases of accident or sudden change. . . .

The rich man is thus almost restricted to following the examples of Peter Cooper, Enoch Pratt of Baltimore, Mr. Pratt of Brooklyn, Senator Stanford, and others, who know that the best means of benefiting the community is to place within its reach the ladders upon which the aspiring can rise—parks, and means of recreation, by which men are helped in body and mind; works of art, certain to give pleasure and improve the public taste, and public institutions of various kinds, which will improve the general condition of the people—in this manner returning their surplus wealth to the mass of their fellows in the forms best calculated to do them lasting good. . . .

[Of those who do not follow this course] the public verdict will be: "The man who dies thus rich dies disgraced." Such in my opinion is the true Gospel concerning Wealth, obedience to which is destined some day to solve the problem of the Rich and the Poor, and to bring "Peace on earth, among men Good-Will."

"RELIGION PROSPERED WHILE THEOLOGY WENT SLOWLY BANKRUPT"

It would be naïve to suppose that any substantial number of Americans acquiesced in scientific determinism or in those implications and consequences which a Dreiser, a Cabell, a Jeffers logically drew from it. A kindly and amiable people, Americans were not to be impelled by dubious logic to a violence that was foreign to their character, nor did they seek escape from a world which most of them considered unquestionably the best of all possible worlds. For three hundred years Calvinism had taught the depravity of man without any perceptible effect on the cheerfulness, kindliness, or optimism of Americans, and it was scarcely to be expected that a handful of scientists, novelists, and poets would succeed where generations of stout clergymen had failed. American optimism was, in fact, impenetrable and unconquerable.

Few things were more remarkable than the unanimity with which Americans professed a religious faith, for the most part Calvinistic, and the indifference which they displayed to its doctrines. What was remarkable was not the indifference but the persistent profession. Those doctrines had been formulated to explain and, if possible, alleviate the misery of man, to enable him to bear burdens and sorrows otherwise more than he could bear, to sustain him with the assurance that everlasting bliss would be the reward for faith and patience in this vale of wrath and tears. But from the beginning most Americans, except Negro slaves, found this world a paradise rather than a purgatory. Whatever they may have said, or sung, they preferred this life to the next, and when they imagined heaven, they thought of it as operating under an American constitution.

Logically, perhaps, they should have abandoned a religion which, in flagrant contradiction to all experience, taught the depravity of man and the corruption of society and subordinated this life to the next, but Americans were not a logical people. Santayana has observed that in America ideas are abandoned by virtue of a mere change of feeling, without the pressure of new evidence or new arguments: "We do not nowadays refute our predecessors, we pleasantly bid them goodbye." . . .

It is scarcely an exaggeration to say that during the nineteenth century and well into the twentieth, religion prospered while theology went slowly bankrupt.

—Henry Steele Commager, *The American Mind* (Yale
University Press, 1950), pp. 162–163, 165.

ACRES OF DIAMONDS

[Carnegie gave the name to the Gospel of Wealth, but Russell H. Conwell (1843–1925), a Baptist clergyman, was the priest who tended its altar fires. Best known for his lecture "Acres of Diamonds," Conwell delivered it 6,000 times and with the proceeds built Philadelphia's Baptist Temple and founded Temple University. The following excerpts are from the version in T. B. Reed, et al., eds., *Modern Eloquence* (15 v., Philadelphia, 1901–13), 4:307–338.]

. . . The title of this lecture originated away back in 1869. When going down the Tigris River, we hired a guide from Bagdad to show us down to the Arabian Gulf. . . .

He thought it was not only his duty to guide us down the river, but also to entertain us with stories; curious and weird, ancient and modern, strange and familiar. . . . He told me that there once lived near the shore of the River Indus, toward which we were then traveling, an ancient Persian by the name of Al Hafed. He said that Al Hafed owned a large farm, with orchards, grain fields and gardens; that he had money at interest, had a beautiful wife and lovely children, and was a wealthy and contented man. Contented because he was wealthy, and wealthy because he was contented.

One day there visited this old Persian farmer one of those ancient Buddhist priests, one of the wise men of the East, who sat down by Al Hafed's fireside and told the old farmer . . . a very curious thing. He said that a diamond was the last and the highest of God's mineral creations, as a woman is the last and highest of God's animal creations. That is the reason, I suppose, why the two have such a liking for each other.

The old priest told Al Hafed if he had a diamond the size of his thumb, he could purchase a dozen farms like his. "And," said the priest, "if you had a handful of diamonds, you could purchase the county, and if you had a mine of diamonds you could purchase kingdoms, and place your children upon thrones, through the influence of your great wealth."

Al Hafed heard all about the diamonds that night, and went to bed a poor man. He wanted a whole mine of diamonds. Early in the morning he sought the priest and awoke him. Well, I know, by experience, that a priest is very cross when awakened early in the morning.

Al Hafed said: "Will you tell me where I can find diamonds?"

The priest said: "Diamonds? What do you want of diamonds?"

Said Al Hafed: "I want to be immensely rich."

"Well," said the priest, "if you want diamonds, all you have to do is to go and find them, and then you will have them.". . .

So he sold his farm; collected his money that was at interest; left his family in charge of a neighbor, and away he went in search of diamonds.

He began his search, very properly to my mind, at the Mountains of the Moon. Afterwards he came around into Palestine, and then wandered on into Europe. At last, when his money was all gone and he was in rags, poverty and wretchedness, he stood on the shore at Barcelona, in Spain, when a great tidal wave swept through the pillars of Hercules; and the poor, starving, afflicted stranger could not resist the awful temptation to cast himself into that incoming tide; and he sank beneath its foaming crest, never to rise in this life again.

When the old guide had told me that story, he stopped the camel I was riding upon and went back to arrange the baggage on another camel. . . . When he came back and took up the camel's halter once more, I found that was the first story I ever heard wherein the hero was killed in the first chapter. For he went on into the second chapter, just as though there had been no break.

Said he: "The man who purchased Al Hafed's farm, led his camel out into the garden to drink, and as the animal put his nose into the shallow waters of the garden brook, Al Hafed's successor noticed a curious flash of light from the white sands of the stream. Reaching in he pulled out a black stone containing a strange eye of light. He took it into the house as a curious pebble and putting it on the mantel that covered the central fire went his way and forgot all about it.

"But not long after that that same old priest came to visit Al Hafed's successor. The moment he opened the door he noticed the flash of light. He rushed to the mantel and said:—

" 'Here is a diamond! Here is a diamond! Has Al Hafed returned?'

" 'Oh no, Al Hafed has not returned and we have not heard from him since he went away, and that is not a diamond. It is nothing but a stone we found out in our garden.'

" 'But,' said the priest, 'I know a diamond when I see it. I tell you that is a diamond.'

"Then together they rushed out into the garden. They stirred up the white sands with their fingers, and there came up other more beautiful, more valuable gems than the first.

"Thus," said the guide,—and friends it is historically true,—"was discovered the diamond mines of Golconda, the most valuable diamond mines in the history of the ancient world."

Well, when the guide had added the second chapter to his story, he then took off his Turkish red cap, and swung it in the air to call my special attention to the moral; those Arab guides always have morals to their stories, though the stories are not always moral.

He said to me: "Had Al Hafed remained at home, and dug in his own cellar, or underneath his own wheat field, instead of wretchedness, starvation, poverty and death in a strange land, he would have had ACRES OF DIAMONDS."

Acres of Diamonds! For every acre of that old farm, yes, every shovelful, afterwards revealed the gems which since have decorated the crowns of monarchs. . . . Nearly every person here will say: "Oh no, I never had any acres of diamonds or any gold mines or any silver mines."

But I say to you that you did have silver mines, and gold mines, and acres of diamonds, and you have them now. . . .

You had an opportunity to be rich; and to some of you it has been a hardship to purchase a ticket for this lecture. Yet you have no right to be poor. It is all wrong. You have no right to be poor. It is your duty to be rich.

Oh, I know well that there are some things higher, sublimer than money! Ah, yes, there are some things sweeter, holier than gold! Yet I also know that there is not one of those things but is greatly enhanced by the use of money.

"Oh," you will say, "Mr. Conwell, can you, as a Christian teacher, tell the young people to spend their lives making money?"

Yes, I do. Three times I say, I do, I do, I do. You ought to make money. Money is power. Think how much good you could do if you had money now. Money is power and it ought to be in the hands of good men. It would be in the hands of good men if we comply with the Scripture teachings, where God promises prosperity to the righteous man. That means more than being goody-good—it means the all-around righteous man. You should be a righteous man, and if you were, you would be rich. . . .

I say get rich, get rich!

A MESSAGE TO GARCIA

[Elbert Hubbard (1856–1915) was famous in his day as an inspirational writer and a printer of fine books, but is now chiefly remembered as author of the brief tract, "A Message to Garcia." This was written in 1899 in a moment of impatience with inefficient shop help, and was widely accepted as an effective riposte to those who laid poverty and crime at the door of society instead of the individual. Hubbard went down with the *Lusitania* in 1915.]

When war broke out between Spain and the United States, it was very necessary to communicate quickly with the leader of the Insurgents. Garcia was somewhere in the mountain fastnesses of Cuba—no one knew where. No mail nor telegraph message could reach him. The President must secure his co-operation, and quickly.

What to do!

Some one said to the President, "There's a fellow by the name of Rowan will find Garcia for you, if anybody can."

Rowan was sent for and given a letter to be delivered to Garcia. How "the fellow by the name of Rowan" took the letter, sealed it up in an oil-skin pouch, strapped it over his heart, in four days landed by night off the coast of Cuba from an open boat, disappeared into the jungle & in three weeks came out on the other side of the Island, having traversed a hostile country on foot, and delivered his letter to Garcia, are things I have no special desire now to tell in detail.

The point I wish to make is this: McKinley gave Rowan a letter to be delivered to Garcia; Rowan took the letter & did not ask, "Where is he at?"

By the Eternal! there is a man whose form should be cast in deathless bronze and the statue placed in every college of the land. It is not book-learning young men need, nor instruction about this and that, but a stiffening of the vertebrae which will cause them to be loyal to a trust, to act promptly, concentrate their energies: do the thing—"Carry a message to Garcia!". . .

No man, who has endeavored to carry out an enterprise where many hands were needed, but has been well nigh appalled at times by the imbecility of the average man—the inability or unwillingness to concentrate on a thing and do it.

Slip-shod assistance, foolish inattention, dowdy indifference, & half-hearted work seem the rule; and no man succeeds, unless by hook or crook, or threat, he forces or bribes other men to assist him; or mayhap, God in His goodness performs a miracle, & sends him an Angel of Light for an assistant. You, reader, put this matter to a test: You are sitting now in your office—six clerks are within call. Summon any one and make this request: "Please look in the encyclopedia and make a brief memorandum for me concerning the life of Correggio."

Will the clerk quietly say, "Yes sir," and go do the task?

On your life he will not. He will look at you out of a fishy eye and ask one or more of the following questions:

Who was he?

Which Encyclopedia?

Where is the encyclopedia?

Was I hired for that?

Don't you mean Bismarck?

What's the matter with Charlie doing it?

Is he dead?

Is there any hurry?

Shan't I bring you the book and let you look it up yourself?

What do you want to know for?

And I will lay you ten to one that after you have answered the questions, and explained how to find the information, and why you want it, the clerk will go off and get one of the other clerks to help him try to find Garcia—and then come back and tell you there is no such man. Of course I may lose my bet, but according to the Law of Average, I will not. . . .

And this incapacity for independent action, this moral stupidity, this infirmity of the will, this unwillingness to cheerfully catch hold and lift, are the things that put pure Socialism so far into the future. If men will not act for themselves, what will they do when the benefit of their effort is for all? A first-mate with knotted club seems necessary; and the dread of getting "the bounce" Saturday night, holds many a worker to his place. . . .

We have recently been hearing much maudlin sympathy expressed for the "downtrodden denizen of the sweatshop" and the "homeless wanderer searching for honest employment," & with it all often go many hard words for the men in power.

Nothing is said about the employer who grows old before his time in a vain attempt to get frowsy ne'er-do-wells to do intelligent work; and his long, patient striving with "help" that does nothing but loaf when his back is turned. In every store and factory there is a constant weeding-out process going on. . . .

Have I put the matter too strongly? Possibly I have; but when all the world has gone a-slumming I wish to speak a word of sympathy for the man who succeeds—the man who, against great odds, has directed the efforts of others, and having succeeded, finds there's nothing in it: nothing but bare board and clothes. . . .

My heart goes out to the man who does his work when the "boss" is away, as well as when he is at home. And the man, who, when given a letter for Garcia, quietly takes the missive, without asking any idiotic questions, and with no lurking intention of chucking it into the nearest sewer, or of doing aught else but deliver it, never gets "laid off," nor has to go on a strike for higher wages. Civilization is one long anxious search for just such individuals. Anything such a man asks shall be granted; his kind is so rare that no employer can afford to let him go. He is wanted in every city, town and village—in every office, shop, store and factory. The world cries out for such: he is needed, & needed badly—the man who can carry a message to Garcia.

THE ABSURD EFFORT TO MAKE THE WORLD OVER

[William Graham Sumner (1840–1910) began life as a minister but spent most of his mature years as professor of sociology at Yale. A convinced Spencerian, Sumner held that the social and economic orders were subject to natural law and opposed reformers who sought to change them. On the other hand, he defended "the forgotten man" against exploitation by those industrialists who sought to thwart laissez-faire by means of a protective tariff. The result was that the ultra-conservative Sumner became anathema to businessmen and was in perpetual danger of losing his chair. The following excerpt from Sumner's essay of 1894, "The Absurd Effort to Make the World Over," is typical of his defenses of wealth and his innate distrust of democracy. It is drawn from his *War, and Other Essays* (Yale University Press, 1913), pp. 200–210 passim.]

But it is repeated until it has become a commonplace which people are afraid to question, that there is some social danger in the possession of large amounts of wealth by individuals. I ask, Why? . . . Where is the rich man who is oppressing anybody? If there was one, the newspapers would ring with it. The facts about the accumulation of wealth do not constitute a plutocracy, as I will show below. Wealth, in itself considered, is only power, like steam, or electricity, or knowledge. The question of its good or ill turns on the question how it will be used. To prove any harm in aggregations of wealth it must be shown that great wealth is, as a rule, in the ordinary course of social affairs, put to a mischievous use. This cannot be shown beyond the very slightest degree, if at all. . . .

Assuming, however, that the charges against the existing "capitalistic"—that is, industrial—order of things are established, it is proposed to remedy the ill by reconstructing the industrial system on the principles of democracy. Once more we must untangle the snarl of half ideas and muddled facts.

Democracy is, of course, a word to conjure with. We have a democratic-republican political system, and we like it so well that we are prone to take any new step which can be recommended as "democratic" or which will round out some "principle" of democracy to a fuller fulfillment. Everything connected with this domain of political thought is crusted over with false historical traditions, cheap philosophy, and undefined terms, but it is useless to try to criticize it. The whole drift of the world for five hundred years has been toward democracy. That drift, produced by great discoveries and inventions, and by the discovery of a new continent, has raised the middle class out of the servile class. In alliance with the crown they crushed the feudal classes. They made the crown absolute in order to do it. Then they turned against the crown and, with the aid of the handicraftsmen and peasants, conquered it. Now the next conflict which must inevitably come is that between the middle capitalist class and the proletariat, as the word has come to be used. If a certain construction is put on this conflict, it may be called that between democracy and plutocracy, for it seems that industrialism must be developed into plutocracy by the conflict itself. That is the conflict which stands before civilized society to-day. All the signs of the times indicate its commencement, and it is big with fate to mankind and to civilization. . . .

The question, therefore, arises, if it is proposed to reorganize the social system on the principles of American democracy, whether the institutions of industrialism are to be retained. If so, all the virus of capitalism will be retained. It is forgotten, in many schemes of social reformation in which it is proposed to mix what we like with what we do not like, in order to extirpate the latter, that each must undergo a reaction from the other, and that what we like may be extirpated by what we do not like. We may find that instead of democratizing capitalism we have capitalized democracy—that is, have brought in plutocracy. Plutocracy is a political system in which the ruling force is wealth. . . . At present the power of capital is social and industrial, and only in a small degree political. So far as capital is political, it is on account of political abuses, such as tariffs and special legislation on the one hand and legislative strikes on the other.

These conditions exist in the democracy to which it is proposed to transfer the industries. What does that mean except bringing all the power of capital once for all into the political arena and precipitating the conflict of democracy and plutocracy at once? Can anyone imagine that the masterfulness, the overbearing disposition, the greed of gain, and the ruthlessness in methods, which are the faults of the master of industry at his worst, would cease when he was a functionary of the State, which had relieved him of risk and endowed him with authority? Can anyone imagine that politicians would no longer be corruptly fond of money, intriguing, and crafty when they were charged, not only with patronage and government contracts, but also with factories, stores, ships, and railroads? Could we expect anything except that, when the politician and the master of industry were joined in one, we should have the vices of both unchecked by the restraints of either? In any socialistic state there will be one set of positions which will offer chances of wealth beyond the wildest dreams of avarice; viz., on the governing committees. Then there will be rich men whose wealth will indeed be a menace to social interests, and instead of industrial peace there will be such war as no one has dreamed of yet: the war between the political ins and outs—that is, between those who are on the committee and those who want to get on it.

We must not drop the subject of democracy without one word more. The Greeks already had occasion to notice a most serious distinction between two principles of democracy which lie at its roots. Plutarch says that Solon got the archonship in part by promising equality, which some understood of esteem and dignity, others of measure and number. There is one democratic principle which means that each man should be esteemed for his merit and worth, for just what he is, without regard to birth, wealth, rank, or other adventitious circumstances. The other principle is that each one of us ought to be equal to all the others in what he gets and enjoys. The first principle is only partially realizable, but, so far as it goes, it is elevating and socially progressive and profitable. The second is not capable of an intelligible statement. The first is a principle of industrialization. It proceeds from and is intelligible only in a society built on the industrial virtues, free endeavor, security of property, and repression of the baser vices; that is, in a society whose industrial system is built on labor and exchange. The other is only a rule of division for robbers who have to divide plunder or monks who have to divide gifts. If, therefore, we want to democratize industry in the sense of the first principle, we need only perfect what we have now, especially on its political side. If we try to democratize it in the sense of the other principle, we corrupt politics at one stroke; we enter upon an industrial enterprise which will waste capital and bring us all to poverty, and we set loose greed and envy as ruling social passions.

If this poor old world is as bad as they say, one more reflection may check the zeal of the headlong reformer. It is at any rate a tough old world. It has taken its trend and curvature and all its twists and tangles from a long course of formation. All its wry and crooked gnarls and knobs are therefore stiff and stubborn. If we puny men by our arts can do anything at all to straighten them, it will only be by modifying the tendencies of some of the forces at work, so that, after a sufficient time, their action may be changed a little and slowly the lines of movement may be modified. . . .

The things which will change it are the great discoveries and inventions, the new reactions inside the social organism, and the changes in the earth itself on account of changes in the cosmical forces. These causes will make it just what, in fidelity to them, it ought to be.

That is why it is the greatest folly of which a man can be capable, to sit down with a slate and pencil to plan out a new social world.

6

THE COURTS AND THE RIGHTS OF PROPERTY

INTRODUCTION

During the first sesquicentennium of American history the Supreme Court was largely engaged—so it would have asserted—in building and preserving a proper balance among competing forces. As Marshall saw it, he was upholding the federal government against the disruptive actions of the people and the states. As Taney saw it, his contribution was to keep the overweening power of the federal government from crushing the rights of the states, especially as they upheld slavery.

The triumph of industry in the postwar period made it necessary to find a way to adapt to the new age an instrument of government originally intended for an agrarian society. The nation was rapidly becoming urbanized and industrialized, and was in danger of being overwhelmed by complex social and economic problems.

The Supreme Court regarded industry and its vested interests as the primary agents of progress, and after some fumbling during the 1870's, boldly championed them against the "chaotism" of farmers, labor, and even at times the states. Its decision was signaled in 1886 by two epochal decisions. The first, in *Santa Clara County v. Southern Pacific*, accepted the dictum that a corporation, as a legal person, was entitled to the protection of the due process clause of the Fourteenth Amendment. The second, in the *Wabash Case*, denied the right of a state to infringe on the federal commerce power; when later decisions also limited the right of Congress to interfere with business, the result was to set up a "twilight zone" in which business could operate without either state or federal interference.

The effects of these decisions were to set in motion a progression of events which threatened to make the rights of property—that is, the great monopolies—dominant over all other interests. The reaction was not long in appearing, as farmers, labor unions, and finally the middle class, girded for the battle which reached its climax in the New Deal of the 1930's.

THE REVOLUTION IN DUE PROCESS OF LAW

[The decision that the due process of law provision of the Fourteenth Amendment protected corporations revolutionized the old meaning of due process. An excellent account of this revolution is found in Alfred H. Kelly and Winfred A. Harbison, *The American Constitution* (N.Y.: Norton, 1963), pp. 496–542, parts of which are reprinted here.]

In the generation after 1876, the new masters of industry and capital sought little in the way of positive constitutional change. Through the Republican Party they obtained favorable tariff and banking legislation and railroad subsidies in the form of land grants, but these involved no radical alteration in the constitutional system. For the rest, their interests in government were generally negative—they wished protection against the efforts of agrarian and liberal dissident groups to impose governmental controls upon big business. In part this protection could be secured in one way or another through political action. Business leaders influenced party platforms, supported promising candidates, and lobbied against what they considered to be unreasonable and arbitrary state and national legislation. However, these procedures were not always effective. In particular, many of the western states frequently fell into the hands of agrarian radicals who passed laws subjecting railroads and business enterprise to a variety of regulatory measures. Even eastern state legislatures and Congress were not immune to the liberal reformer's zeal. Against such legislation business sought and found protection in the courts.

What business needed was a means whereby the prevailing doctrine of *laissez-faire* economic theory could be written into constitutional law as a positive protection against "unreasonable" legislation. The old doctrine of vested rights, developed by the state and national judiciary between 1790 and 1830, served this purpose to some extent, since in a vague way it guaranteed private property against arbitrary or confiscatory laws. The doctrine had been identified in part with the contract clause, but otherwise it rested upon no specific provision of federal or state constitutions but rather upon the general nature of constitutional government. A more definite identification with the written constitution was highly desirable to the business leaders.

The due process clause in the first section of the Fourteenth Amendment was to serve this purpose. In a series of epoch-making decisions between 1873 and 1898, the Supreme Court revolutionized the historic interpretation of due process of law and thus established the Fourteenth Amendment as the specific constitutional authorization for the doctrine of vested rights.

This constitutional revolution was not a conspiracy. It was a reflection of the prevailing economic philosophy of *laissez faire* and the preoccupation of the country with the rapid development of its natural resources. No group of men sat down together and plotted the changes in constitutional interpretation necessary to extend maximum protection to the property of American industry. The process was a gradual one, in which the decisions responded slowly to the arguments of many different attorneys who came before it and to changes in the point of view of the judges who were appointed to the courts. So involved in legal technicalities was the shift in the meaning of due process that most judges and lawyers seem hardly to have been aware of what was happening. Yet the revolution was no less real because it was gradual and unconscious; and when it was completed, the courts occupied a new position of power and prestige in American life as the guardians of property. . . .

About 1850, the doctrine of vested rights underwent a revival and at the same time became associated to some extent with the guarantee of due process of law in state and federal constitutions. In *Wynehamer v. New York* (1856) the New York Court of Appeals declared unconstitutional a state law regulating the manufacture of liquor and in so doing tied the doctrine of vested rights to the due process clause in the state constitution. It held that this clause constituted a general restriction on the legislature's power to interfere with private property. A year later, in the Dred Scott case, Chief Justice Taney referred incidentally to the due process clause in the Fifth Amendment to the federal Constitution, construing it as pro-

hibiting the federal government from imposing restrictions upon property in slaves within the territories. Again, in *Hepburn v. Griswold* (1870) the Court briefly invoked the due process clause of the Fifth Amendment in holding invalid federal legal tender legislation.

The guarantee of "due process of law" and its counterpart, "the law of the land," were already centuries old in the nineteenth century. In England, the thirty-ninth article of the Great Charter granted by King John to his barons in 1215 contained the pledge that "no freeman shall be taken or imprisoned or disseised or exiled or in any way destroyed . . . except by the lawful judgment of his peers and by the law of the land." Magna Charta from time to time was reaffirmed by successive English monarchs, and in the Statute of Westminster of the Liberties of London, enacted in 1354, the phrase "due process of law" occurred for the first time in English law. According to Sir Edward Coke, "due process of law" and "law of the land" had the same meaning, although no certain definition of either phrase was ever laid down.

The phrase "law of the land" was incorporated in several colonial charters, and thus became a part of the commonly accepted body of liberties of the American colonists. The Massachusetts constitution of 1780 contained the phrase "the law of the land," virtually as it had been originally embodied in Magna Charta. Most of the other early state constitutions contained the same general guarantees. In 1791 due process passed into the federal Constitution with the adoption of the Fifth Amendment, which provided that "no person shall . . . be deprived of life, liberty, or property without due process of law." Thus after some centuries of development "due process of law" found its way into the American constitutional system.

Before 1850 due process was generally assumed to be a procedural rather than a substantive restriction upon governmental authority. That is, it guaranteed certain protective rights to an accused person before he could be deprived of his life, liberty, or property. These rights included protection against arrest without a warrant, the right to counsel, the requirement of indictment by a grand jury before trial, the right of the accused to hear the nature of the evidence against him, the right to an impartial trial by a jury of the accused person's peers, and the requirement of a verdict before any sentence was executed. In other words, due process of law historically was of significance primarily in criminal cases. It promised accused persons that they would not be punished in an arbitrary and indiscriminate fashion and without the protection of long-established criminal procedure. By the same token, due process hitherto had had no relation to the doctrine of vested rights, nor had it constituted any limitation upon the right of legislatures to regulate private property in the interests of the public welfare.

The tentative association between due process of law and the doctrine of vested rights in the Wynehamer, Dred Scott, and Hepburn cases thus represented a radical departure in the historic meaning and content of due process. The new association between due process and vested rights gave due process a substantive content and made it a guarantee against unreasonable legislative interference with private property. Before 1870, the substantive conception of due process was tentative, and had appeared in only a few cases. It remained to be seen whether the due process clause in federal and state constitutions would replace the obligation of contracts clause as the principal constitutional limitation upon legislative capacity to interfere with private property and vested rights.

The Fourteenth Amendment to the federal Constitution, taking effect in 1868, contained in Section 1 the clause: "Nor shall any State deprive any person of life, liberty, or property, without due process of law." Unlike the similar clause in the Fifth Amendment, which guaranteed the individual against the federal government, the due process clause in the Fourteenth Amendment was a federal guar-antee against arbitrary state action interfering with individual rights.

The reader will recall that the entire history of the Fourteenth Amendment prior to passage indicated that it was passed to protect the newly acquired political and legal rights of Negroes against arbitrary state action. There is little evidence that the statesmen who wrote the amendment were interested in bringing about the intervention of the federal government in the protection of vested rights. Certainly there was nothing to indicate in their time that the due process clause of the Fourteenth Amendment was destined to become one of the most important foundation stones of modern constitutional law.

The Supreme Court first ruled upon the meaning of the Fourteenth Amendment in 1873, in the *Slaughterhouse Cases*. The legislature of Louisiana in 1869 had conferred upon one firm what was in effect a monopoly of the slaughterhouse business in New Orleans and had banned all other slaughterhouses already established within the city. Some of the businesses affected brought suit in the Louisiana courts, asserting among other things that the law in question was a violation of the Fourteenth Amendment. The Supreme Court of Louisiana, however, held that the law constituted a legitimate exercise of the police power of the state and thus upheld the constitutionality of the act. An appeal was then taken to the Supreme Court of the United States.

The most insistent claim of the appellant was that the statute in question constituted a violation of the privileges and immunities clause of the Fourteenth Amendment—"no state . . . shall abridge the privileges and immunities of citizens of the United States."

This interpretation of the clause by implication placed all civil rights under the protection of the federal government, but the Court refused to accept this contention. Instead it resorted to the doctrine of dual citizenship. "It is quite clear," said Justice Miller, "that there is a citizenship of the United States and a citizenship of a state, which are distinct from each other."

The consequence of this doctrine of dual citizenship was that the Court was enabled to draw a sharp line between those privileges and immunities which accrued to an individual by virtue of his state citizenship and those which accrued to him by virtue of his citizenship in the national government. Only the latter, said the Court, fell under the protection of the Fourteenth Amendment. . . .

The plaintiffs also asserted that the Louisiana statute in question deprived them of their property without due process of law, again in violation of the Fourteenth Amendment. The Court simply dismissed this contention with the observation that "under no construction of that provision that we have ever seen, or that we deem admissible, can the restraint imposed by the state of Louisiana . . . be held to be a deprivation of property within the meaning of that provision." In other words, the Court accepted without debate the procedural interpretation of due process; it acted as though it had never heard of the substantive interpretations of due process which had been stated briefly by Taney in his Dred Scott opinion and again by the majority in *Hepburn v. Griswold.*

Justice Miller gave the equal protection clause of the Fourteenth Amendment similar summary treatment. The Court simply said that it had reference to state laws discriminating against Negroes. Justice Miller doubted "whether any action of a state not directed by way of discrimination against the Negroes as a class, or on account of their race, will ever be held to come within the purview of this provision." . . .

Why had the Court refused to place the common body of "privileges and immunities" within the protection of the federal government? The answer probably is that it did not care to recognize any profound or fundamental alteration in the relations of state and federal governments as a result of the amendment. And to recognize that all private rights were now entrusted to the specific protection of the federal government would have indeed constituted a radical change in the nature of the American constitutional system. The justices on the bench at the time were political conservatives, interested in seeing the old relationships of state and federal governments maintained with as little disturbance as possible. Hence they advanced the very plausible conception of dual citizenship, which seemed to remove nearly all common private rights from the sphere of federal control.

Furthermore, a majority of the Court were not in sympathy with the argument that the meaning of the amendment extended beyond its immediate purpose—the protection of the Negro. The Court was not impressed by the attempts of counsel to make due process of law a general limitation upon the power of the state to regulate private property. Those lawyers and statesmen who wished to extend the protecting hand of the federal government over vested property rights could draw but cold comfort from the Court's contemptuous rejection of the plea that due process of law was a guarantee of vested property rights against state interference. . . .

Four years later, in 1877, the Court was presented with an opportunity to set forth again its attitude toward due process of law. In *Munn v. Illinois* and in the other *Granger Cases,* the Court again refused to apply a substantive conception of due process. Instead, it reaffirmed at considerable length the right of the states to regulate private property in the public interest.

These cases involved a characteristic example of the way in which the new economic power was clashing with the attempts of the states to subject that power to some degree of regulation. In the seventies a profound movement of agrarian unrest and discontent swept many of the western states. The causes behind the discontent of the farmer were fairly complex. The definition of postwar years had lowered his cash income; he had been left with debts which had been contracted during the period of high farm prices, expansion, and war prosperity; and at the same time he was suffering the more general effects of the great business depression which hung over the entire nation between 1873 and 1880. . . .

Munn v. Illinois arose out of an act passed in 1873 by the Granger-controlled legislature of Illinois fixing the rates for the storage of grain in warehouses located in cities of 100,000 population or more. The only city in Illinois of that size was Chicago, and the law was in reality aimed at preventing abuse of the monopoly which the elevator operators had succeeded in establishing over the grain elevator business at the mouth of the Chicago River. Some nine different elevator firms were engaged in business in this vicinity; yet the uniformity and exorbitancy of their rates indicated clearly that the various firms constituted a near-monopoly.

The elevator operators shortly attacked the constitutionality of the statute in the Illinois courts, asserting that the act constituted an infringement upon the power of Congress to regulate interstate commerce and that it violated the due process clause of the Fourteenth Amendment. The decision of the Illinois Supreme Court was favorable to the constitutionality of the act, and an appeal was then taken to the Supreme Court of the United States.

The other *Granger Cases* had a similar origin. A number of Granger-controlled western legislatures, among them those of Wisconsin, Iowa, and Minnesota, had enacted statutes fixing rail rates within the states. The railroads had attacked the constitutionality of these statutes in the courts of the several states. The issue here was the same as that in *Munn v. Illinois*, and the Court therefore settled these cases by direct reference to the former decision.

The opinion in *Munn v. Illinois*, as presented by Chief Justice Morrison R. Waite, showed that a majority of the Court still clung to the notion of due process of law laid down in the *Slaughterhouse Cases*, though the Court's reasoning showed some evidence that the traditional conception of due process as purely procedural was weakening. Waite began with an analysis of the police power, which he rested

both upon the nature of constitutional government and upon an appeal to history. He quoted the constitution of Massachusetts, which describes the body politic as "a social compact by which the whole people covenants with each citizen, and each citizen with the whole people." From this it followed that the social compact authorized "the establishment of laws requiring each citizen to . . . so use his own property as not unnecessarily to injure another." This was an old common law doctrine which Waite now invoked to support police power. Waite admitted, however, that the state could not control rights which were "purely and exclusively private," an intimation that in certain circumstances the Court might admit due process as a limitation upon police power.

Chief Justice Waite defined the extent of the state's regulatory authority by asserting that when private property is devoted to a public use it is subject to public regulation. "When, therefore," he said, "one devotes his property to a use in which the public has an interest, he, in effect, grants to the public an interest in that use, and must submit to be controlled by the public for the common good." . . .

Field again dissented [as in the *Slaughterhouse Cases*] and this time he based his dissent directly upon the due process clause. He denied specifically that the mere fact that a business was vested with a public interest gave the state any regulatory power. "If this be sound law, if there be no protection, either in the principles upon which our republican government is founded, or in the prohibitions of the Constitution against such invasion of private rights, all property and all business in the State are held at the mercy of a majority of its legislature." Here was an unequivocal demand that the judiciary constitute itself the guardian of property rights against restrictive state legislation under the authority of the federal Constitution. Though only one other justice, Strong, agreed with his dissent, Field was to see his conception of due process triumph completely before he left the Court in 1897.

The Supreme Court had now apparently

placed its approval upon a new era of extensive economic regulation by the states. This dictum, if allowed to stand, would have provided a broad constitutional base for the states to control the mass of powerful propertied interests springing up in the nation. New and powerful corporate interests could have been controlled by law simply because they were "vested with a public interest." State government now had been assigned the right to play an important part in molding the industrial revolution then going on in the nation.

Actually no such thing occurred. . . . [For one thing, the whole spirit of the times was against it. For another, there were] two remedies against restrictive state legislation, and American business availed itself of both of them.

First, business went into politics to protect its interests. It is significant that *Munn v. Illinois* was followed by a perceptible quickening of the interest of industry in politics. Since the state had been confirmed in its power to regulate industry, industrialists now became greatly concerned about the kind of regulation that was to be imposed. Control of a state legislature by a farm group hostile to the railroads, for example, might result in the establishment of rate schedules or warehouse regulations which the railroads would consider altogether inimical to their welfare.

American industry had always been in politics to some degree. After 1880, however, industry and the railroads went into state politics to an extent hitherto unknown. They put forward their own attorneys as candidates for office; they donated funds to political parties; they backed this or that faction in the state legislature. Sometimes less scrupulous industrial leaders resorted to bribery. The eighties and nineties saw a new low in the moral level of the American state legislature. That the seats of assemblymen in Harrisburg or Albany were often for sale was a matter of common knowledge. From the point of view of business these tactics, whether or not they remained within the scope of orthodox political morality, were a matter of practical necessity. State interference with industry might be dangerous. Therefore the state government must be kept out of hostile hands.

Second, business carried the fight against restrictive state legislation into the courts, where after a long fight, it won a substantial victory in the general acceptance of due process as a substantive limitation upon the power of government to regulate private property. The doctrine propounded in *Munn v. Illinois*, that private property vested with a public interest is subject to public regulation, technically was not subsequently overturned, but by 1898 the Court was to strike down statutes imposing "unreasonable" rail rate legislation on the ground that the rates in question were confiscatory and so took property without due process of law. In the next twenty years judicial emphasis was to pass almost completely from the dictum in *Munn v. Illinois* to reiteration of the principle that due process of law offered immunity to private property and vested interest against unreasonable social legislation. In its emphasis upon the capacity of state legislatures to control private property in the interest of the public welfare, *Munn v. Illinois* was at odds with the dominant economic interests of business and industry. And it was big business and industry which, in the generation after 1876, for the most part controlled the formation of national policy in Congress and ultimately in the courts as well.

The judiciary could hardly be expected to remain immune to the "big business" conception of the role of government in society. Judges, then as now, usually reached their positions through the legal profession. The philosophy of the legal profession, as always, was generally colored by the interests and attitudes of the men it most often represented—that is, industrialists, bankers, and railroad men. The path of corporation lawyers to the bench in the two generations after the Civil War was made easier by the fact that the Republican Party controlled the presidency for all but two administrations between 1868 and 1912. The Republican Party was for the most part a party of big business, and the men its Presidents appointed to the bench were most often corporation lawyers by training. Thus, it is not surprising that the attitude of the Supreme Court, as well as that of the federal and state judiciaries in general, began to reflect the economic and social attitudes of big business. Judges of this background might be expected to interpret the Constitution in the light of the *laissez-faire* economic philosophy and to regard the Constitution and the judiciary as bulwarks of property. They did not disappoint these expectations. . . .

In the next dozen years death and retirement depleted the conservative majority on the Court. . . . Most of the new appointees were the product of Reconstruction politics and accustomed to the doctrine of strong national government. Nearly all of them had legal backgrounds calculated to inspire respect for vested interests and property rights. . . . [They] were conservatives, but of a very different kind from the judges who had decided the *Slaughterhouse Cases* and *Munn v. Illinois*. The conservatives of the seventies had been concerned with the protection of the old established state-federal relations against the upheavals of the Civil War and the onslaught of Radical reconstructionism. The conservatism of the new judges, on the other hand, was concerned primarily with protecting the property rights and vested interests of big business and with the defense of the prevailing economic and social order against agrarian and dissident reformers. The new appointees, in short, were extremely receptive to the constitutional theories advanced by Justice

Field and by the brilliant attorneys appearing before the Court.

In 1886, the Court in *Stone v. Farmers Loan and Trust Co.* made its first great concession to the lawyers who were trying to give a substantive meaning to due process and so to link it with the doctrine of vested rights. The case involved a Mississippi statute which had erected a state railroad commission with authority to revise rates, a power which the Mobile and Ohio Railroad Company upon appeal charged was in violation of due process of law.

The Court again said "No," citing *Munn v. Illinois*. Yet the very words of the opinion carried a concession to the argument. "General statutes regulating the use of railroads in a State, or fixing maximum rates of charge for transportation," said Chief Justice Waite, "do not necessarily deprive the corporation owning or operating a railroad within the State of its property, without due process of law within the meaning of the Fourteenth Amendment." But at the same time Waite warned that "it is not to be inferred that this power of limitation or regulation is itself without limit. . . . Under pretense of regulating fares and freights, the State cannot require a railroad corporation to carry persons or property without reward; neither can it do that which in law amounts to a taking of private property for public use without just compensation, or without due process of law."

In other words, the Court now openly admitted that there were conceivable circumstances in which a legislative regulation of private property, a pretended exercise of the

THE COURTS AND THE RIGHTS OF PROPERTY 115

police power, might constitute a violation of due process. All that remained was for the Court to find a specific instance in which legislative regulation denied due process. The emergence of substantive due process would then be virtually complete.

[The decision in the Stone case was announced on January 4th. A few months later, on May 10th, the Supreme Court decided the case of *Santa Clara County v. Southern Pacific Railroad Company,* (along with two similar cases) in which the county sought payment of certain taxes. The significance of the case was in the following terse announcement by Chief Justice Waite:

> The court does not wish to hear argument on the question whether the provisions in the Fourteenth Amendment to the Constitution, which forbids a State to deny to any person within its jurisdiction the equal protection of the laws, applies to these Corporations. We are all of the opinion that it does.]

Four years later the Court, in *Chicago, Milwaukee, and St. Paul Ry. Co. v. Minnesota* (1890), took what was practically the final step in this development, when it declared a Minnesota rail rate statute of 1887 to be in violation of the Fourteenth Amendment. The act in question had set up a rail and warehouse commission with power to examine rail rates and to revise those which it found to be unreasonable or unequal. Justice Blatchford, who wrote the majority opinion, based his argument mainly upon the fact that the law as interpreted by the Minnesota Supreme Court gave the commission final and conclusive rate-fixing powers, with the result that the rates set by it were not subject to any review by the courts as to their equality or reasonableness. Under the statute, said Blatchford, there was "no power in the courts to stay the hands of the Commission, if it chooses to establish rates that are unequal and unreasonable." In other words, he said, the statute "deprives the Company of its right to a judicial

investigation, by due process of law, under the forms and with the machinery provided by the wisdom of successive ages for the investigation judicially of the truth of a matter in controversy." The question of whether a rate was reasonable, he continued, "is eminently a question for judicial investigation, requiring due process of law for its determination. If the company is deprived of the power of charging reasonable rates for the use of its property, and such deprivation takes place in the absence of an investigation by judicial machinery, it is deprived of the lawful use of its property, and thus, in substance and effect, of the property itself, without due process of law and in violation of the Constitution of the United States."

Now on the surface the Court was here concerned merely with a procedural due process and not with a substantive limitation upon the rate-fixing powers of the legislature itself. It merely found a procedural defect in the commission's prescribed method of rate-fixing. In other words, it treated the commission as though it were a court or at least a quasi-judicial body, and it described the determination of the reasonableness of rates as a judicial process. Acting on these assumptions, it found that the commission's mode of fixing rates violated one of the essential elements in procedural due process—the right of appeal.

The commission, however, was more than a quasi-court. Its rate-setting powers had been delegated by the legislature. The Court had said that the commission could not lawfully be given the power to fix rates from which there was no judicial appeal. But what if the legislature itself should set the rate directly and allow no judicial appeal? Here the substantive implication of the decision stood clearly revealed. It would be but a short step for the Court to hold that a rate fixed by the legislature itself, with no appeal to the courts, would violate due process of law. The way was now open for a decision which without seeming to reverse *Munn v. Illinois* would take most of the practical economic significance out of that decision by permitting the courts a general review of all rate-schedules fixed by legislative determination. . . .

To complete the evolution of substantive due process, it remained for the Court only to declare void a statute fixing rates directly through legislative enactment. The Court affirmed its power to do this in 1894 in *Reagan v. Farmers' Loan and Trust Co.*, although no statute was actually declared to be unconstitutional at this time. This step came in 1898 in *Smyth v. Ames*, wherein the Court held void a Nebraska statute setting intrastate freight rates. After protracted inquiry into the earning power of the railroads affected, the opinion concluded that the law imposed rates so low as to be unreasonable and thus to amount to a deprivation of property without due process of law.

Substantive due process was at first concerned only with the protection of vested property rights against the police power of the states. It was property that could not be subjected to unreasonable restrictions. As yet the Court had said nothing of any substantive limitation upon the right of the states to regulate liberty. Yet it was a logical step for the Court to enlarge the substantive limitations of due process to include liberty as well as property. The legal instrument used to bring this about was the doctrine of freedom of contract.

Freedom of contract was a conception introduced into constitutional law directly from *laissez-faire* economics. There is virtually no other explanation for its appearance, for it certainly rested neither upon any specific constitutional principle, nor upon any well-established legal precedent. As we have seen, the old guarantee of liberty in due process had been entirely procedural—it merely threw certain safeguards about accused persons in criminal cases. The new doctrine asserted that when two parties came together to reach an agreement that was not contrary to public policy, the legislature had no right to interfere and to dictate the terms of that agreement or the conditions under which it should be carried out.

In *Allgeyer v. Louisiana* (1897) the Court entered into a comprehensive discussion of the liberty guaranteed by due process of law. Liberty, said the Court, included "not only the right of the citizen to be free from the mere physical restraint of his person, as by incarceration, but the term is deemed to embrace the right of the citizen to be free in the enjoyment of all his faculties; to be free to use them in all lawful ways; to live and work where he will; to earn his livelihood by any lawful calling; to pursue any livelihood or avocation, and for that purpose to enter into all contracts which may be proper, necessary, and essential to his carrying out to a successful conclusion the purposes above mentioned."

In reality, the concept of freedom of contract was to be used after 1900 mainly to invalidate state laws regulating conditions of labor. This became apparent as early as 1898, in *Holden v. Hardy*, when the Court considered whether or not a Utah statute limiting hours of labor in mines to eight hours a day was in violation of freedom of contract.

Although the revolution in due process of law occurred through judicial interpretation of the Fourteenth Amendment, it will be recalled that there was also a due process of law clause in the Fifth Amendment, constituting a guarantee against the federal government. Early Supreme Court opinions, with the exception of the Dred Scott Case and *Hepburn v. Griswold*, interpreted the due process clause in the Fifth Amendment as extending purely procedural safeguards to the individual as against federal action. Presumably it expressed in a general way the same immunities expressed by the other clauses of the Fifth and Sixth Amendments in a specific way.

Once the substantive conception of due process of law had evolved, however, there was every prospect that the idea would be applied to the Fifth Amendment also. Although the federal government had no general police powers except in the territories, it nevertheless possessed extensive regulatory powers over private property within limited spheres of jurisdiction. Congress, in exercising its authority over interstate commerce and taxation, in particular, frequently imposed extensive limitations upon private property rights and vested interests.

After several times suggesting that the due process clauses in the Fifth and Fourteenth Amendments meant substantially the same thing, the Court in *Adair v. United States* (1908) held void a federal statute prohibiting "yellow dog" labor contracts (by which employees agreed not to join labor unions) on the ground that the act impaired freedom of contract and so violated the due process clause of the Fifth Amendment. In a series of cases dealing with the federal commerce power, the Court ruled also that to be within due process, rail rates fixed by the Interstate Commerce Commission must be reasonable and not arbitrary or confiscatory. This was substantially the same conception, applied to federal legislation, as that advanced against state legislation under the Fourteenth Amendment. . . .

In hundreds of cases after 1890, the federal and state judiciaries developed a complex new law of substantive due process controlling state police power and federal legislative capacity. The content of due process underwent constant change and development, so that until 1937, at least, it was not possible at any one time to define absolutely the limits of substantive due process. From the time of the *Slaughterhouse Cases*, the Supreme Court consistently refused to lay down any inclusive definition or set of rules about due process; instead it preferred to develop the concept, as it remarked in 1877, by the method of "inclusion and exclusion." Yet the Court in the generation after 1890 succeeded fairly well in setting forth the fundamental nature of due process in a series of general propositions which remained moderately stable until 1937.

Due process was, broadly speaking, a general substantive limitation upon the police power of the state. Any state statute, ordinance, or administrative act which imposed any kind of limitation upon the right of private property or free contract immediately raised the question of due process of law. And since a majority of statutes of a general public character imposed some limitations upon private property or contractual right, the ramifications of due process were endless. . . .

What constituted a legitimate exercise of the police power now became a judicial question, not merely a legislative question. Whereas formerly the Court had assumed that the decision of the legislature was conclusive as to the limits of the police power, the Court now reserved for itself the right to consider the whole question of whether the statute under review constituted a valid exercise of that power. Theoretically, the will of the legislature was still held in high respect. Actually the Court was often openly contemptuous of the reasons which had impelled legislatures to pass the legislation in question.

To be accepted as within the bounds of due process a statute must in the opinion of the court be "reasonable." This was the general and all-inclusive test that a law under review had to meet and pass. If the purpose for which the statute had been enacted was a reasonable one, if the act employed reasonable means to achieve its ends, if the means employed bore a reasonable and substantial relationship to the purposes of the act, and if the law imposed no unreasonable limitations upon freedom of contract or private vested right, then the Court would accept the law as a legitimate exercise of the police power.

Very closely associated with the concept of reasonableness was the requirement that a statute should not be "arbitrary." On most occasions where a law was found to be unreasonable it was also found to be arbitrary, an arbitrary statute being one "which restricts individual liberty or property right more severely than advantage to the community can possibly justify."

The question of the reasonableness or arbitrariness of a law could not be settled by reference to any specific constitutional provision or any absolute principle of law. A reasonable law was one that seemed sensible, plausible, and intelligent to the judges who passed upon it. What constitutes sensible, plausible, and intelligent public policy, however, is largely a matter of the individual's economic and social philosophy—his standard of values. When the Court applied the test of reasonableness to legislation, therefore, it measured the law against its own economic and social attitudes. If in the light of these attitudes the law seemed intelligent, the justices upheld it; if not, they declared it unreasonable, arbitrary, and a violation of due process of law.

The manner in which the Court used due process as a medium through which to pass upon the constitutionality of state social legislation in the light of the justices' social and economic theories may be illustrated by a consideration of the judicial history of state statutes regulating maximum hours for the employment of labor.

This issue first came before the Court in *Holden v. Hardy* (1898), a case involving the constitutionality of a Utah statute of 1896 prohibiting the employment of workingmen in mines, smelters, or ore refineries for more than eight hours in any one day, except in emergencies. By a vote of 7 to 2 the Court held the statute constitutional. . . .

Holden v. Hardy established no general precedent as to the constitutionality of statutes limiting hours of labor. In *Lochner v. New York* (1905) the Court, by a 5-to-4 majority, declared unconstitutional a New York statute limiting hours of labor in bakeshops to sixty hours in one week or ten hours in any one day. Justice R. W. Peckham, speaking for the majority, first cited the right of free contract as established in *Allgeyer v. Louisiana*, and emphasized further that the right to purchase or sell labor was an important part of the liberty guaranteed by the Fourteenth Amendment. He admitted that state police power might on occasion limit the right of free contract; indeed, he said, the Court had in the past been very liberal in accepting impairment of property or contract rights under state police power. But there were limits to the valid exercise of state police power; otherwise the Fourteenth Amendment would be without meaning. . . . It was

Justice Holmes who made the most effective attack upon the majority for injecting *laissez-faire* social theory into the content of constitutional law and substituting the Court's judgment upon public policy for that of the legislature. He wrote:

> This case is decided upon an economic theory which a large part of the country does not entertain. If it were a question whether I agreed with that theory, I should desire to study it further and long before making up my mind. But I do not conceive that to be my duty, because I strongly believe that my agreement or disagreement has nothing to do with the right of a majority to embody their opinions in law. It is settled by various opinions of this court that state constitutions and state laws may regulate life in many ways which we as legislators might think as injudicious, or if you like as tyrannical, as this, and which, equally with this, interfere with the liberty to contract. . . . The 14th Amendment does not enact Mr. Herbert Spencer's Social Statics . . . a Constitution is not intended to embody a particular economic theory, whether of paternalism and the organic relation of the citizen to the state or of *laissez-faire*. It is made for people of fundamentally differing views, and the accident of our finding certain opinions natural and familiar, or novel and even shocking, ought not to conclude our judgment upon the question whether statutes embodying them conflict with the Constitution of the United States.

It is possible that Holmes' brilliant rebuke in *Lochner v. New York* had some effect upon the other justices. Three years later, in *Muller v. Oregon* (1908), the Court unanimously upheld the constitutionality of an Oregon statute of 1903 prohibiting the employment of women in mechanical establishments, factories, and laundries for more than ten hours in any one day. The Oregon statute was substantially similar to a number of state acts then being enacted for the protection of the health and morals of women, and social workers and liberals generally were exceedingly anxious to secure a favorable judicial verdict on the law. At the request of Florence Kelley and Josephine Goldmark, both prominent social workers, the state of Oregon retained the noted Boston attorney Louis D. Brandeis to defend the constitutionality of the law before the Supreme Court.

Brandeis submitted to the Court a brief which disposed of the constitutional precedents in two pages, but which devoted over a hundred pages to statistics upon hours of labor, American and European factory legislation, and the health and morals of women. The logic behind the brief rested upon the premise that if the Court in fact passed upon legislation of this kind in the light of its reasonable character and plausible relation to the social welfare, then the best possible approach was to overwhelm the justices with direct and specific documentary evidence as to the wisdom and intelligence of the law under review.

The "Brandeis brief," as it was thereafter called, was a spectacular success, and set the precedent for many subsequent appeals to the Court of the same kind. Justice David Brewer in his opinion virtually admitted that Brandeis had succeeded in convincing the Court that the Oregon statute was a reasonable exercise of the state police power. He made the admission with some embarrassment, since it was virtually an open confession that social and economic philosophy and not mere constitutional precedent had been decisive in the Court's decision. . . .

It is clear that the meaning of substantive due process as it developed after 1900 can be expressed by one phrase: "the rule of reason." Reasonableness, however, was not a quality of law specifically defined in the Constitution. It could not be related to any specific legislative limitation which the Constitution imposed upon the states such as that banning *ex post facto* laws. The one source upon which judges could draw when they decided for the first time whether a statute was reasonable was their own social and economic philosophy. If the law appeared to aim at objectives which the justices regarded as socially unwise, then frequently they ruled that it constituted an unrea-

sonable or arbitrary interference with private property rights. If, on the other hand, the law strove for social objectives which the justices thought intelligent, they accepted it as a reasonable exercise of the states' police power.

The result was nothing less than the creation of a new type of judicial review, in which the Court examined the constitutionality of both state and federal legislation in the light of the judges' social and economic ideas. . . . In passing upon the wisdom and desirability of legislation under due process of law, the justices were in reality settling matters of public policy. This was a legislative rather than a judicial function. In democratic states men who decide whether laws are socially wise and desirable ordinarily sit in elective legislative bodies. They are sent there by their constituents to vote for or against measures in accordance with the interests of their constituents and in the light of their convictions as to the wisdom and expediency of the proposals upon which they pass. Legislative issues are commonly political rather than judicial in character, and as such are ordinarily settled in the political arena. But under the new judicial review, the Court, as well as Congress and the various state legislatures, now settled many issues of this kind.

The new judicial review thus made the Supreme Court a kind of "negative third chamber" both to the state legislatures and to Congress. Paralleling this development, the supreme courts of the various states became negative third chambers of their own state legislatures. The judicial chamber, it is true, had only a negative vote. It could not initiate legislation. Though limited in this way, its legislative power was nevertheless real. The judicial veto after 1890 constituted a powerful check upon the policies of every legislative chamber in the nation, a check exercised not only in terms of the requirements of the written constitution but also in terms of the social and economic ideas of the justices concerned. It was this fact which Justice Holmes had in mind when he observed in *Lochner v. New York* that the case was decided in accordance with an economic philosophy with which a large portion of the American people did not agree.

Paradoxically, the early twentieth century witnessed the general acceptance by judges of a theory of jurisprudence which denied the law-making capacities of the judiciary. The prevailing theory of jurisprudence around 1900 was that of "received law." This conception held that judges did not make or formulate law, but simply discovered and applied it. The Constitution, the theory held, was fundamental, absolute, and immutable. It contained, by implication, the answer to every constitutional question which might ever be raised in relation to any state or federal statute. The document was a written expression of certain fundamental principles of eternal right and justice. All that was necessary was for the Court to apply the appropriate word or clause of the Constitution to the law in question. Any constitutional issue could be solved by application of the suitable provisions in the Constitution, and the correct conclusion was presumably self-evident to any competent judge. This concept of jurisprudence Roscoe Pound in 1913 called the "slot-machine theory" of law.

Judges who adhered to the theory of received law were likely to deny strenuously that they were ever influenced by their view of the wisdom of legislation. They would deny even that the "rule of reason" in due process involved judicial discretion in any degree. They would deny also that the realities of social or economic life were any concern of theirs. Constitutional questions were to be settled specifically in accordance with the requirements of the written document. This theory was maintained squarely in the face of the rule of reason, in which it would appear to have been clear to any realistic observer that decisions of the Court were being arrived at in accordance with the social and economic philosophy of the judges who made them. . . .

One important result of the new conception of the judicial function was a great increase in the resort to the judicial veto as applied to both state and national legislation. In the entire seventy-one years between the founding of the national government and secession, the Supreme Court had declared but two acts of Congress unconstitutional—in *Marbury v. Madison* and in *Dred Scot v. Sandford*. While in this same period the Court invalidated state laws with much greater frequency, even this exercise of the judicial veto was attended with considerable restraint. According to Benjamin F. Wright, there were some sixty cases before 1861 in which the Court declared state legislation void. After the Civil War, on the other hand, resort to the judicial veto increased steadily. Professor Wright reports that during the years 1874–1898 there were twelve decisions invalidating acts of Congress and 125 decisions declaring state legislation contrary to the Constitution. After 1898 the Court invalidated acts of Congress with still greater frequency: there were about fifty such decisions between 1898 and 1937, while in the same period the Court invalidated state laws in some four hundred cases. . . .

The rise of substantive due process and the new concept of judicial review were factors in the partial failure of the states to deal adequately with the many social and economic problems growing out of the industrial revolution. Of equal importance in this failure, however, was the fact that most of the problems precipitated by the industrial revolution were regional or even national in scope, so that the area of sovereignty of any one state was not sufficiently broad to make possible the imposition of really effective controls. Rail rate problems, for example, were essentially national in character, and regulation by the various states could result only in a disjointed and confused regional and national rate pattern, or indeed in no pattern at all. The failure of the states to function effectively as the arbiters of American economic life became increasingly clear after 1885. The result was a growing demand for national economic controls and a federal program of regulation on the theory that only the national government could deal effectively with a national economy.

ANTITRUST LAWS AS LIGHTNING RODS FOR DISSENT

My impression would be that looking at the matter from a railroad point of view exclusively it would not be a wise thing to undertake. . . . The attempt would not be likely to succeed; if it did not succeed, and were made on the ground of the inefficiency and uselessness of the Commission, the result would very probably be giving it the power it now lacks. The Commission, as its functions have now been limited by the courts, is, or can be made, of great use to the railroads. It satisfies the popular clamor for a government supervision of railroads, at the same time that that supervision is almost entirely nominal. Further, the older such a commission gets to be, the more inclined it will be found to take the business and railroad view of things. It thus becomes a sort of barrier between the railroad corporations and the people and a sort of protection against hasty and crude legislation hostile to railroad interests. . . . The part of wisdom is not to destroy the Commission, but to utilize it.

> —Richard Olney, prospective Attorney General, early in 1893, speaking to a group of railroad executives who wished to repeal the Interstate Commerce Act

Since the consumers' interest was not emphasized, such enforcement efforts as existed were directed at the punishment of offenses rather than the achievement of economic objectives. . . . In this way the moral aspects of the offense, and that will-o'-the-wisp, corporate intent, became more important considerations than economic results. Antitrust enforcement, not being geared to the idea of consumers' interests, became a hunt for offenders instead of an effort to test the validity of organized power by its performance in aiding or preventing the flow of goods in commerce. The result was that although the economic ideal of a free competitive market as the cornerstone of our economy was kept alive, no adequate enforcement staff was ever provided to make that ideal a reality.

> —Thurman Arnold, *The Bottlenecks of Business* (1940), p. 263

In his more philosophical moods, the businessman might even take a benign view of those who were moved to advocate stronger enforcement of the antitrust laws. Without doubt these laws have performed a notable role in American life as a kind of lightning rod for dissent. Whenever he feels dissatisfied with things as they are, or whenever he is stuck for a program to deal with something he believes to be wrong, the American radical has an unfailing formula. That is to demand that the antitrust laws be more rigorously enforced. For many they have had the standing of a universal cure; in 1947 they were even solemnly invoked as a device for keeping down prices and preventing inflation. No fundamental change in the American economy could or is likely to result from these demands for antitrust enforcement. Thus the businessman has no reason to be alarmed, while the dissident can feel that he has offered a bold and stalwart program. Had the antitrust laws not been available, and had dissent, accordingly, taken other forms in the past, or were it to do so in the future, the challenge might be formidable.

—J. K. Galbraith, *American Capitalism* (Boston: Houghton Mifflin, 1952), pp. 62–63.

THE COURTS AND THE "TWILIGHT ZONE"

Sooner or later deep-seated social and economic problems in a democracy will rise to the political sphere for popular adjudication. After Big Business took over from the Radicals in the Grant Era, the professional politicians of the two political patronage machines had sought diligently to prevent the entry into the political scene of what many dissidents regarded as vital issues. Rising farmer and labor discontent was evidenced by the emergence of third parties and the increasing popularity of the free-silver panacea, and business threw its support first to one old party then to the other in its search for security.

It had long been supposed that, save for federal employees and obvious involvement of conditions of interstate commerce, the states exercised wide police powers. Chief Justice Shaw of Massachusetts had defined police power as "the power vested in the Constitution to make, ordain, and establish all manner of wholesome and reasonable laws, statutes, and ordinances, either with penalties or without, not repugnant to the Constitution, as they shall judge to be for the good and welfare of the Commonwealth and the subjects thereof." The demand for protection against the "invisible government" now led many of the states to pass regulatory laws and to set up regulatory commissions. Such steps brought some encouraging results, and the *Granger Cases* (1877), by confirming the right of the states to regulate grain elevators and railroad rates, seemed to open up a considerable field for state action. However, railroad and industrial combinations were set up under the laws of states which favored their activities, and, since so much of their business was interstate, it soon became evident that it was not possible for state laws seriously to affect them.

The Fifth Amendment had forbidden the federal government to interfere with the rights of persons without due process of law and the Fourteenth Amendment had laid the same injunction on the states. By 1886 the Supreme Court had made it clear that the word "persons" applied not merely to individuals but also to corporations. In that same year in the *Wabash Case* the Supreme Court took advantage of the interstate nature of railroad traffic to limit state control over rate regulations. The result was to spur a demand for federal legislation. Congress was fain to heed the demand, for the old public approval of laissez faire was gradually being displaced by a willingness to accept federal regulation of what were being more and more denounced as economic abuses. Even the railroads themselves went along with the movement, for they were mindful of the advantage of public approval and of the opportunity to shape the inevitable legislation to a harmless mold. The result was the Interstate Commerce Act of 1887. It prohibited the usual rate discriminations, pools, rebates, and long-and-short-haul abuses and insisted that rates must be "reasonable and just"—though it failed to define the term.

It established the Interstate Commerce Commission (the ICC), the first of the long series of independent administrative agencies which now make the federal government so cumbrous. President Cleveland appointed a capable and vigorous commission, and the nation settled back confidently to await reform.

None came. As early as 1892 Richard T. Olney, a Boston corporation lawyer and Cleveland's appointee as Attorney General, was able to point out to the opponents of the act that in its emasculated form it would satisfy the popular clamor at the same time that supervision was almost entirely nominal. With conservative appointments to the commission, it would in time become a barrier between the railroads and the people. "The part of wisdom is not to destroy the Commission, but to utilize it." The ICC was supposed to carry infractions of the law to the courts, and they made it understood that the commission's powers were innocuous. In the *Maximum Freight Rate Case* (1897) the Court sheared the ICC of its presumed power to modify rates and forbade it to seek judicial aid in such cases. It then proceeded in the *Alabama Midland Case* to nullify for all effective purposes its function of judging the facts of the railroads' practices in the long-and-short haul. Of the sixteen cases carried to the Supreme Court by 1906 fifteen were lost, and the railroads defied with impunity the lesser decisions which the commission eventually won. The rate-making power was definitely denied to it in 1897, and the decision only reinforced the growing opinion that the commission was a "useless body for all practical purposes."

The Sherman Antitrust Act of 1890, presumably aimed at monopolies, went through a similar period of frustration. Indeed, the intention of passing a reform law to thwart reform was even more evident. On its face, it made a misdemeanor of monopoly or any attempt to monopolize and declared illegal "every contract, combination in the form of trust or otherwise, or conspiracy, in restraint of trade or commerce among the several States, or with foreign nations." Now the English common law had long sought to discourage *unreasonable* restraints of trade and monopolies which infringed on the public interests. The Sherman Law not only failed to make exceptions but failed to clarify the meaning of its terminology. Enforcement was to be by court decision of cases initiated by aggrieved parties, by district attorneys, or by the Attorney General.

Action was successful in only thirteen of the forty cases involving the Sherman Law and brought into the courts through 1901. Federal law officers moved sluggishly, bringing in only eighteen cases and Olney deliberately threw away the case of *U.S. v. E. C. Knight* (1895) by basing his brief on irrelevant grounds when he appeared before the Supreme Court. The issue hinged on the acquisition of four competing concerns in Philadelphia by the American Sugar Refining Company, which gave the Havemeyers a ninety percent control of the American refining industry. Olney maintained that the *purchase* constituted restraint of interstate commerce but adduced no evidence on its purposes or practices. Under the circumstances the Court was obliged to admit that the purchase was intrastate and perfectly legal.

The federal power to regulate commerce had been restricted or denied by various means: denying the right of the ICC to exercise quasi-judicial functions; the Fifth Amendment's due process clause; carping distinctions between "direct" and "indirect" effects of trusts, and trifling decisions over regulation of contracts;

and, of course, interpreting any desired meaning into—or out of—the loose verbiage of the laws.

Actually, the Supreme Court was occasionally willing to do its share when issues permitted. In the *Trans-Missouri Freight Association Case* (1897) railroads were brought under the act, and in the *Addyston Pipe Case* (1899) it dissolved a pool of cast-iron-pipe manufacturers who were engaging in interstate commerce. Nevertheless, such judicial discouragements to consolidation were so studiously ignored by federal law-enforcement officers that finance capitalists were encouraged to enter upon their heyday. By 1904 John Moody in his *The Truth about the Trusts* claimed that there were 318 manufacturing trusts with a total capital of $7 billion, about forty percent of the manufacturing capital of the United States.

One result of the act, perhaps not unforeseen by insiders, was that the words "or otherwise" included labor unions. Here attorney generals and judges found an issue in which they were interested and proceeded to initiate a hearty campaign for the limitation of those conspirators in restraint of trade. During the period under consideration the courts quite generally deserved the label of being antilabor. In the light of Mr. Dooley's famous dictum that the Supreme Court follows the election returns, their stand is no cause for wonder. Basically the courts reflected, or rather lagged a little behind, the evolution of public opinion. They shared the public's widespread fear of socialism and rather generally searched for means of invalidating labor legislation. Since state legislators had sometimes been thoughtful enough to draw up their bills in vague and sloppy terms, the judges' search was frequently crowned with success. The most fruitful source of power against the states' corporation and labor legislation turned out to be the Fourteenth Amendment, as indicated in the section preceding.

The movement to limit the police power of the states had begun with the *Wabash Case* and was continued in the *Minnesota Rate Case* of 1889 and in *Smyth v. Ames* in 1898; the latter clearly asserted the right of the federal courts to adjudge railroad rates, and it laid down the difficult doctrine that rates must be sufficient to make a fair return upon the cost of replacement of the railroad's property as well as carrying its debts and paying dividends. Through it all the Court carefully avoided any attempt to indicate the point at which protection of the public welfare passed over the line and became confiscation.

The power of the states to regulate wages and conditions of labor was easily limited on the same grounds, though the Supreme Court rather cleverly limited it under color of protecting the Constitutional rights of labor. Thus in *Lochner v. New York* (1905) it threw out a ten-hour law for bakers on the plea that it denied the baker's right to contract to sell his labor on whatever terms he chose. As a result, the Supreme Court was portrayed with deserved sarcasm as the upholder of the God-given right of a three-year-old tenement girl to contract to make artificial flowers for as little as she pleased.

Minimum wage laws, at first opposed by unions on the ground that wages would rise no higher than the minimum stated, were passed by fifteen states but were unexpectedly thrown out in 1923 in the District of Columbia case of *Adkins v. Children's Hospital* and remained out until the New Deal became entrenched in the Supreme Court. Laws governing safety conditions, accident compensation, fire and sanitary inspection, pensions—all have had to be ground out slowly by the mills of the legislative and judicial gods.

But even the Supreme Court learned. Even in its laissez-faire days it was inclined to permit state legislation regulating hours in hazardous occupations (Arizona mines) and hours for women and children. In 1917 it broke precedent by permitting Oregon to enforce a ten-hour law for all factory workers. Congress was mindful of rising protest against using child labor, and twice it tried to do something about it. However, the Keating Law of 1916 prohibiting the passage in interstate commerce of articles made by child labor was thrown out in the case of *Hammer v. Dagenhart* (1918), and an attempt in 1919 to tax such articles was disallowed in the case of *Bailey v. Drexel Furniture Company* (1922). Attempts to get a Constitutional amendment approved by the states did not succeed, but the Supreme Court has since that permitted some limitations.

The courts did not limit themselves to hampering labor legislation but developed interpretations which enabled them to limit or forbid actions by labor unions or individuals. The common-law interpretation of the strike as a conspiracy in restraint of trade had been weakened in Massachusetts by Chief Justice Shaw's decision in 1842 that labor unions and the strike were legal. Other states yielded slowly, until it became evident that the injunction was a more expeditious and thorough weapon against labor. An injunction is a court order requiring a party to do or refrain from doing certain acts; violation of the order entails trial and punishment, not for doing the acts (which may be perfectly lawful) but for contempt of court.

The use of the injunction in labor disputes had begun as early as 1877 in judicial attempts to remedy the lack of legislation against strikes, picketing, and boycotts. But it was the ubiquitous Olney who put the injunction on a firm foundation when, hinging his argument on the Interstate Commerce Act and the Sherman Antitrust Act (both based on federal control of interstate commerce), he carried the Debs injunction case to the Supreme Court under the claim that those acts prohibited collusion among and monopoly by labor unions. Traditionally the injunction had been used to protect real property, but the Court now obliged by declaring that business expectancy of sales and of labor service were properties and were entitled to protection.

Strikes, picketings, and boycotts were legal, and no damages could be recovered for losses due to their exercise, nor at that time could injunctions be issued under *law* to protect these properties in expectancy. The Court now got around this by approving injunctions issued under *equity* on the ground that strikes, picketings, and boycotts constitute malicious conspiracy to injure such properties. It was in this way that the rarely used injunction suddenly came into such frequent use on the initiative of corporations that its critics have bitterly denounced government by injunction. The situation was not remedied until the Norris-La Guardia Act of 1932, and labor is still trying to prevent its use on government initiative.

A long list of interpretive decisions followed. In 1906 in the case of the *Buck Stove and Range Co. v. the American Federation of Labor* the publication of unfair lists was prohibited as a kind of boycott, and Gompers and Mitchell were sentenced to prison though they did not serve. In the *Danbury Hatters' Case*, which ran from 1902 to 1912, a hat company sued 197 members of the United

Hatters' Union for triple damages of $250,000 because of boycott, and in the end it took over the members' homes and bank accounts. In the case of the *United Mine Workers v. Coronado Coal Co.* (1922) it was decided that unincorporated labor unions could be sued for violation of the Sherman Act. On the other hand, employers successfully upheld their right to use the blacklist and the lockout, and to force employees to take the ironclad oath or sign the yellow-dog contract not to join unions. After a long and bloody strike in the West Virginia coal fields in 1906, the companies had forced the workers to sign yellow-dog contracts. When the U.M.W. tried to unionize West Virginia in order to protect their bargaining power in other unionized fields, the organization was successfully prosecuted in the *Hitchman Case* (1917), and the yellow-dog contract was supported. Yellow-dog contracts were prohibited under both the Fifth and Fourteenth Amendments, for the former had been used in the case of *Adair v. United States* (1908) to strike down the federal Erdman Act of 1898 which prohibited employers engaged in interstate commerce to require an employee to agree not to join a union.

It would be caviling to deny that the Supreme Court was convinced that its reasons were soundly Constitutional, even when it reversed itself. Nevertheless, critics found an increasing tendency on the part of the Court to judge expedience as well as constitutionality—a tendency which, carried to its logical conclusion, effectively makes the Supreme Court a third legislative chamber. By the twentieth century a state had been reached where few laws affecting industry could go into effect until they had traveled the long road through the courts and received the imprimatur of the Supreme Court. Just as obvious was the fact that the Supreme Court had skillfully created a "twilight zone" between the powers of the states and those of the federal government—at least by contemporary interpretation—in which corporate "persons" could set their prices and their labor policies with a minimum of interference. This situation was to continue until the judicial revolution of the 1930's.

Donahey, *permission Cleveland* Plain Dealer

7

PROTESTS AND AFFIRMATIONS IN THE GILDED AGE

INTRODUCTION

The dominant spirit of the Gilded Age was to deny or conceal the existence of the problems brought about by social and economic change, or perhaps to offer rationalizations, such as attributing poverty to the laziness or indifference of its victims. Nevertheless, numerous thinkers and doers were engaged in a search for solutions, and, as always in such times, there was a proliferation of panaceas. Americans had long believed that solutions could be imposed by political action, so it is no cause for wonder that a number of these proposed panaceas found their way into the political arena, either in cities, states, or nation.

In this chapter we propose to set forth a few of the many critiques of current conditions and refer to some of the more or less abortive attempts to solve them by political action. It is assumed that the reader is more or less familiar with the basic conditions and problems of agriculture, labor, and urban sprawl.

DEMOCRATIC VISTAS

[Walt Whitman (1819–92), born on Long Island and for many years a wandering printer and newspaper editor, in 1855 published *Leaves of Grass*, a little collection of poetry. It was not until word of English approval found its way back to America that much attention was paid to it, for in its wild and exuberant affirmation it broke all the accepted canons of poetic form and prettiness. This was the introduction of the man who was to become the poet of individualism and democracy, and who saw beneath the callow American surface values which could transform mankind. In 1871, at the beginning of the Gilded Age, Whitman gathered his insights and published them in his greatest prose work, *Democratic Vistas*. The following selection is the key to the work. See *Democratic Vistas* in *Completed Prose Works of Walt Whitman* (Philadelphia: McKay, 1892), pp. 209–227 passim.]

. . . . For, I say, the true nationality of the States, the genuine union, when we come to a mortal crisis, is, and is to be, after all, neither the written law, nor, (as is generally supposed,) either self-interest, or common pecuniary or material objects—but the fervid and tremendous IDEA, melting everything else with resistless heat, and solving all lesser and definite distinctions in vast, indefinite, spiritual, emotional power.

It may be claim'd, (and I admit the weight of the claim,) that common and general worldly prosperity, and a populace well-to-do, and with all life's material comforts, is the main thing, and is enough. It may be argued that our republic is, in performance, really enacting today the grandest arts, poems, &c., by beating up the wilderness into fertile farms, and in her railroads, ships, machinery, &c. And it may be ask'd, Are these not better, indeed, for America, than any utterances even of greatest rhapsode, artist, or literatus?

I too hail those achievements with pride and joy: then answer that the soul of man will not with such only—nay, not with such at all—be finally satisfied; but needs what, (standing on these and on all things, as the feet stand on the ground,) is address'd to the loftiest, to itself alone.

Out of such considerations, such truths, arises for treatment in these Vistas the important question of character, of an American stock-personality, with literatures and arts for outlets and return-expressions, and, of course, to correspond, within outlines common to all. To these, the main affair, the thinkers of the United States, in general so acute, have either given feeblest attention, or have remain'd, and remain, in a state of somnolence.

For my part, I would alarm and caution even the political and business reader, and to the utmost extent, against the prevailing delusion that the establishment of free political institutions, and plentiful intellectual smartness, with general good order, physical plenty, industry, &c., (desirable and precious advantages as they all are,) do, of themselves, determine and yield to our experiment of democracy the fruitage of success. With such advantages at present fully, or almost fully, possess'd—the Union just issued, victorious, from the struggle with the only foes it need ever fear, (namely, those within itself, the interior ones,) and with unprecedented materialistic advancement—society, in these States, is canker'd, crude, superstitious, and rotten. Political, or law-made society is, and private, or voluntary society, is also. In any vigor, the element of the moral conscience, the most important, the verteber to State or man, seems to me either entirely lacking, or seriously enfeebled or ungrown.

I say we had best look our times and lands searchingly in the face, life a physician diagnosing some deep disease. Never was there, perhaps, more hollowness at heart than at present, and here in the United States. Genuine belief seems to have left us. The underlying principles of the States are not honestly believ'd in, (for all this hectic glow, and these melo-dramatic screamings,) nor is humanity itself believ'd in. What penetrating eye does not everywhere see through the mask? The spectacle is appalling. We live in an atmosphere of hypocrisy throughout. The men believe not in the women, nor the women in the men. A scornful superciliousness rules in literature. The aim of all the *littérateurs* is to find something to make fun of. A lot of churches, sects, &c., the most dismal phantasms I know, usurp the name of religion. Conversation is a mass of badinage. From deceit in the spirit, the mother of all false deeds, the offspring is already incalculable. . . .

The depravity of the business classes of our country is not less than has been supposed, but infinitely greater. The official services of America, national, state, and municipal, in all their branches and departments, except, the judiciary, are saturated in corruption, bribery, falsehood, mal-administration; and the judiciary is tainted. The great cities reek with respectable as much as non-respectable robbery and scoundrelism. In fashionable life, flippancy, tepid amours, weak infidelism, small aims, or no aims at all, only to kill time. In business, (this all-devouring modern word, business,) the one sole object is, by any means, pecuniary gain. The magician's serpent in the fable ate up all the other serpents; and money-making is our magician's serpent, remaining to-day sole master of the field. The best class we show, is but a mob of fashionably dress'd speculators and vulgarians. True, indeed, behind this fantastic farce, enacted on the visible stage of society, solid things and stupendous labors are to be discover'd, existing crudely and going on in the background, to advance and tell themselves in time. Yet the truths are none the less terrible. I say that our New World democracy, however great a success in uplifting the masses out of their sloughs, in materialistic development, products, and in a certain highly-deceptive superficial popular intellectuality, is, so far, an almost complete failure in its social aspects, and in really grand religious, moral, literary, and esthetic results. In vain do we march with unprecedented strides to empire so colossal, outvying the antique, beyond Alexander's, beyond the proudest sway of Rome. In vain have we annex'd Texas, California, Alaska, and reach north for Canada and south for Cuba. It is as if we were somehow being endow'd with a vast and more and more thoroughly-appointed body, and then left with little or no soul. . . .

But sternly discarding, shutting our eyes to the glow and grandeur of the general superficial effect, coming down to what is of the only real importance, Personalities, and examining minutely, we question, we ask, Are there, indeed, *men* here worthy the name? Are there athletes? Are there perfect women, to match the generous material luxuriance? Is there a pervading atmosphere of beautiful manners? Are there crops of fine youths, and majestic old persons? Are there arts worthy freedom and a rich people? Is there a great moral and religious civilization—the only justification of a great material one? Confess that to severe eyes, using the moral microscope upon humanity, a sort of dry and flat Sahara appears, these cities, crowded with petty grotesques, malformations, phantoms, playing meaningless antics.

The purpose of democracy . . . is . . . to illustrate, at all hazards, this doctrine or theory that man, properly train'd in sanest, highest freedom, may and must become a law, and series of laws, unto himself, surrounding and providing for, not only his own personal control, but all his relations to other individuals, and to the State; and that, while other theories, as in the past histories of nations, have proved wise enough, and indispensable perhaps for their conditions, *this*, as matters now stand in our civilized world, is the only scheme worth working from, as warranting results like those of Nature's laws, reliable, when once establish'd, to carry on themselves. . . .

As to the political section of Democracy, which introduces and breaks ground for further and vaster sections, few probably are the minds, even in these republican States, that fully comprehend the aptness of that phrase, "THE GOVERNMENT OF THE PEOPLE, BY THE PEOPLE, FOR THE PEOPLE," which we inherit from the lips of Abraham Lincoln; a formula whose verbal shape is homely wit, but whose scope includes both the totality and all minutiæ of the lesson.

The People! Like our huge earth itself, which, to ordinary scansion, is full of vulgar contradictions and offence, man, viewed in the lump, displeases, and is a constant puzzle and affront to the merely educated classes. The rare, cosmical, artist-mind, lit with the Infinite, alone confronts his manifold and oceanic qualities— but taste, intelligence and culture, (so-called,) have been against the masses, and remain so. There is plenty of glamour about the most damnable crimes and hoggish meannesses, special and general, of the feudal and dynastic world over there, with its *personnel* of lords and queens and courts, so well-dress'd and so handsome. But the People are ungrammatical, untidy, and their sins gaunt and ill-bred. . . .

The movements of the late secession war, and their results, to any sense that studies well and comprehends them, show that popular democracy, whatever its faults and dangers, practically justifies itself beyond the proudest claims and wildest hopes of its enthusiasts. Probably no future age can know, but I well know, how the gist of this fiercest and most resolute of the world's warlike contentions resided exclusively in the unnamed, unknown rank and file; and how the brunt of its labor of death was, to all essential purposes, volunteer'd. The People, of their own choice, fighting, dying for their own idea, insolently attack'd by the secession-slave-power, and its very existence imperil'd. Descending to detail, entering any of the armies, and mixing with the private soldiers, we see and have seen august spectacles. We have seen the alacrity with which the American born populace, the peaceablest and most good-natured race in the world, and the most personally independent and intelligent, and the least fitted to submit to the irksomeness and exasperation of regimental discipline, sprang, at the first tap of the drum, to arms—not for gain, nor even glory, nor to repel invasion— but for an emblem, a mere abstraction—for the life, *the safety of the flag.* . . .

What have we here, if not, towering above all talk and argument, the plentifully-supplied, last-needed proof of democracy, in its personalities? Curiously enough, too, the proof on this point comes, I should say, every bit as much from the south, as from the north. Although I have spoken only of the latter, yet I deliberately include all. Grand, common stock! to me the accomplish'd and convincing growth, prophetic of the future. . . .

I say the mission of government, henceforth, in civilized lands, is not repression alone, and not authority alone, not even of law, nor by that favorite standard of the eminent writer, the rule of the best men, the born heroes and captains of the race. . . . but higher than the highest arbitrary rule, to train communities through all their grades, beginning with individuals and ending there again, to rule themselves. What Christ appear'd for in the moral-spiritual field for human-kind. . . . is tallied in like manner, in this other field, by democracy's rule that men, the nation, as a common aggregate of living identities, affording in each a separate and complete subject for freedom, worldly thrift and happiness, and for a fair chance for growth, and for protection in citizenship, &c., must, to the political extent of the suffrage or vote, if no further, be placed, in each and in the whole, on one broad, primary, universal, common platform.

The purpose is not altogether direct; perhaps it is more indirect. For it is not that democracy is of exhaustive account, in itself. Perhaps, indeed, it is, (like Nature,) of no account in itself. It is that, as we see, it is the best, perhaps only, fit and full means, formulater, general caller-forth, trainer, for the million, not for grand material personalities only, but for immortal souls. To be a voter with the rest is not so much; and this, like every institute, will have its imperfections. But to become an enfranchised man, and now, impediments removed, to stand and start without humiliation, and equal with the rest; to commence, or have the road clear'd to commence, the grand experiment of development, whose end, (perhaps requiring several generations,) may be the forming of a full-grown man or woman —that *is* something. To ballast the State is also secured, and in our times is to be secured, in no other way.

We do not, (at any rate I do not,) put it either on the ground that the People, the masses, even the best of them, are, in their latent or exhibited qualities, essentially sensible and good—nor on the ground of their rights; but that good or bad, rights or no rights, the democratic formula is the only safe and preservative one for coming times. We endow the masses with the suffrage for their own sake, no doubt; then, perhaps still more, from another point of view, for community's sake. Leaving the rest to the sentimentalists, we present freedom as sufficient in its scientific aspect, cold as ice, reasoning, deductive, clear and passionless as crystal. . . .

And, topping democracy, this most alluring record, that it alone can bind, and ever seeks to bind, all nations, all men, of however various and distant lands, into a brotherhood, a family. It is the old, yet ever-modern dream of earth, out of her eldest and her youngest, her fond philosophers and poets. Not that half only, individualism, which isolates. There is another half, which is adhesiveness or love, that fuses, ties and aggregates, making the races comrades, and fraternizing all. Both are to be vitalized by religion, (sole worthiest elevator of man or State,) breathing into the proud, material tissues, the breath of life. For I say at the core of democracy, finally, is the religious element. All the religions, old and new, are there. Nor may the scheme step forth, clothed in resplendent beauty and command, till these, bearing the best, the latest fruit, the spiritual, shall fully appear. . . .

Did you, too, O friend, suppose democracy was only for elections, for politics, and for a party name? I say democracy is only of use there that it may pass on and come to its flower and fruits in manners, in the highest forms of interaction between men, and their beliefs. . . . It has been and is carried on by all the moral forces, and by trade, finance, machinery, intercommunications, and, in fact, by all the developments of history, and can no more be stopp'd than the tides, or the earth in its orbit. Doubtless, also, it resides, crude and latent, well down in the hearts of the fair average of the American-born people, mainly in the agricultural regions. But it is not yet, there or anywhere, the fully-receiv'd, the fervid, the absolute faith.

I submit, therefore, that the fruition of democracy, on aught like a grand scale, resides altogether in the future. As, under any profound and comprehensive view of the gorgeous-composite feudal world, we see in it, through the long ages and cycles of ages, the results of a deep, integral, human and divine principle, or fountain, from which issued laws, ecclesia, manners, institutes, costumes, personalities, poems, (hitherto unequall'd,) faithfully partaking of their source, and indeed only arising either to betoken it, or to furnish parts of that varied-flowing display, whose centre was one and absolute—so, long ages hence, shall the due historian or critic make at least an equal retrospect, an equal history for the democratic principle. It too must be adorn'd, credited with its results—then, when it, has fashion'd, systematized, and triumphantly finish'd and carried out, in its own interest, and with un- parallel'd success, a new earth and a new man.

"THE ASSOCIATION OF POVERTY WITH PROGRESS IS THE GREAT ENIGMA OF OUR TIMES"

[Henry George (1839–97), a journalist in the San Francisco area, was struck by the rapidity with which California had moved from frontier to urbanization, and by 1870 was showing many of the marks both of progress and poverty that were found in older states such as New York. As a result he began to search for a cause, and in 1871 in his pamphlet *Our Land and Land Policy* set forth his finding that poverty was due to private preemption (in the form of rent) of the increase in land value which arose from community development; the cure, then, was to abolish all taxes except for a "single tax" which would tax away this increment. The idea was not new, for it had been proposed in Europe, but in 1871 George knew nothing of this. During the following years he read widely and then in 1879 published a more thorough exposition of his theory in *Progress and Poverty*. George's proposed "single tax" was rather widely accepted as a reasonable solution of the problem of poverty, and some cities went so far as to impose double taxation on unused lots. This single tax may have been naïve, but at any rate George's book set its many readers to thinking, and was influential in calling social problems to the attention of such potential reformers and/or intellectuals as Tom L. Johnson, Edward Alsworth Ross, Monsignor John A. Ryan, Clarence Darrow, Hamlin Garland, Richard T. Ely, J. Allen Smith, Walter Rauschenbusch, and John Dewey. Even more profound, if we can believe some, was George's effect abroad, where he was credited by Tolstoy with having much to do with opening the way to the solution of the Russian land problem, and where he was a catalytic influence on George Bernard Shaw. Herewith we give certain highlights of *Progress and Poverty* (N.Y.: Robert Schalkenbach Foundation, 1954), pp. 10, 166–167, 328, and 403– 406. George opened his book with an account of the nineteenth century's inventions and the hopes they raised that humanity would be lifted from poverty, then turned to the actual results. Regardless of the local political or fiscal policies in the ad- vanced nations there was unemployment and distress—and the more advanced the country the greater the distress. Surely, where such results followed so uniformly on material progress, there must be a common cause.]

This association of poverty with progress is the great enigma of our times. It is the central fact from which spring industrial, social, and political difficulties that perplex the world, and with which statesmanship and philan- thropy and education grapple in vain. From it come the clouds that overhang the future of the most progressive and self-reliant nations. It is the riddle which the Sphinx of Fate puts to our civilization and which not to answer is to be destroyed. So long as all the increased wealth which modern progress brings goes but to build up great fortunes, to increase luxury and make sharper the contrast between the House of Have and the House of Want, prog- ress is not real and cannot be permanent. The reaction must come. The tower leans from its foundations, and every new story but hastens the final catastrophe. To educate men who must be condemned to poverty, is but to make them restive; to base on a state of most glaring social inequality political institutions under which men are theoretically equal, is to stand a pyramid on its apex.

.   .   .   .

Rent is also expressed in a selling price. When land is purchased, the payment which is made for the ownership, or right to perpetual use, is rent commuted or capitalized. If I buy land for a small price and hold it until I can sell it for a large price, I have become rich, not by wages for my labor or by interest upon my capital, but by the increase of rent. Rent, in short, is the share in the wealth produced which the exclusive right to the use of natural capabilities gives to the owner. Wherever land has an exchange value there is rent in the economic meaning of the term. Wherever land having a value is used, either by owner or hirer, there is rent actual; wherever it is not used, but still has a value, there is rent potential. It is this capacity of yielding rent which gives value to land. Until its ownership will confer some advantage, land has no value.

Thus rent or land value does not arise from the productiveness or utility of land. It in no wise represents any help or advantage given to production, but simply the power of securing a part of the results of production. No matter what are its capabilities, land can yield no rent and have no value until some one is willing to give labor or the results of labor for the privilege of using it; and what any one will thus give depends not upon the capacity of the land, but upon its capacity as compared with that of land that can be had for nothing. I may have very rich land, but it will yield no rent and have no value so long as there is other land as good to be had without cost. But when this other land is appropriated, and the best land to be had for nothing is inferior, either in fertility, situation, or other quality, my land will begin to have a value and yield rent. And though

the productiveness of my land may decrease, yet if the productiveness of the land to be had without charge decreases in greater proportion, the rent I can get, and consequently the value of my land, will steadily increase. Rent, in short, is the price of monopoly, arising from the reduction to individual ownership of natural elements which human exertion can neither produce nor increase. . . .

.   .   .   .

We have traced the unequal distribution of wealth which is the curse and menace of modern civilization to the institution of private property in land. We have seen that so long as this institution exists no increase in productive power can permanently benefit the masses; but, on the contrary, must tend still further to depress their condition. We have examined all the remedies, short of the abolition of private property in land, which are currently relied on or proposed for the relief of poverty and the better distribution of wealth, and have found them all inefficacious or impracticable.

There is but one way to remove an evil— and that is, to remove its cause. Poverty deepens as wealth increases, and wages are forced down while productive power grows, because land, which is the source of all wealth and the field of all labor, is monopolized. To extirpate poverty, to make wages what justice commands they should be, the full earnings of the laborer, we must therefore substitute for the individual ownership of land a common ownership. Nothing else will go to the cause of the evil—in nothing else is there the slightest hope.

This, then, is the remedy for the unjust and unequal distribution of wealth apparent in modern civilization, and for all the evils which flow from it:

We must make land common property.
.   .   .

.   .   .   .

We have weighed every objection, and seen that neither on the ground of equity or expediency is there anything to deter us from making land common property by confiscating rent.

But a question of method remains. How shall we do it?

We should satisfy the law of justice, we should meet all economic requirements, by at one stroke abolishing all private titles, declaring all land public property, and letting it out to the highest bidders in lots to suit, under such conditions as would sacredly guard the private right to improvements. . . .

But such a plan, though perfectly feasible, does not seem to me the best. Or rather I propose to accomplish the same thing in a simpler, easier, and quieter way, than that of formally confiscating all the land and formally letting it out to the highest bidders.

To do that would involve a needless shock to present customs and habits of thought—which is to be avoided. . . .

To do that would involve a needless extension of governmental machinery—which is to be avoided. . . .

I do not propose either to purchase or to confiscate private property in land. The first would be unjust; the second, needless. Let the individuals who now hold it still retain, if they want to, possession of what they are pleased to call *their* land. Let them continue to call it *their* land. Let them buy and sell, and bequeath and devise it. We may safely leave them the shell, if we take the kernel. *It is not necessary to confiscate land; it is only necessary to confiscate rent. . . .*

We already take some rent in taxation. We have only to make some changes in our modes of taxation to take it all.

What I, therefore, propose, as the simple yet sovereign remedy, which will raise wages, increase the earnings of capital, extirpate pauperism, abolish poverty, give remunerative employment to whoever wishes it, afford free scope to human powers, lessen crime, elevate morals, and taste, and intelligence, purify government and carry civilization to yet nobler heights, is —to appropriate rent by taxation.

In this way the State may become the universal landlord without calling herself so, and without assuming a single new function. In form, the ownership of land would remain just as now. No owner of land need be dispossessed, and no restriction need be placed upon the amount of land any one could hold. For, rent being taken by the State in taxes, land, no matter in whose name it stood, or in what parcels it was held, would be really common property, and every member of the community would participate in the advantages of its ownership.

Now, insomuch as the taxation of rent, or land values, must necessarily be increased just as we abolish other taxes, we may put the proposition into practical form by proposing—

To abolish all taxation save that upon land values.

MARY'S LITTLE LOT

[The following was a doggerel rendition of Henry George's accusation in *Progress and Poverty* that the preemption of rent was the cause of poverty.]

Mary had a little lot,
The soil was very poor;
But still she kept it all the same
And struggled to get more.

She kept the lot until one day
The people settled down;

And where the wilderness had been
Grew up a thriving town.

Then Mary rented out her lot
(She would not sell, you know),
And waited patiently about
For prices still to grow.

They grew, as population came,
And Mary raised the rent;
With common food and raiment now
She could not be content.

She built her up a mansion fine
Had bric-a-brac galore;
And every time the prices rose,
She raised the rent some more.

"What makes the lot keep Mary so?"
The starving people cry;
"Why, Mary keeps the lot, you know,"
The wealthy would reply.

And so each one of you might be
Wealthy, refined, and wise,
If you had only hogged some land
And held it for the rise.

LOOKING BACKWARD

[One evidence of the restiveness that lay beneath the tinselry of the Gilded Age was the publication of a rash of Utopian novels. Among them were Ignatius Donnelly's catastrophic *Caesar's Column* (1891) and William Dean Howells' *A Traveler from Altruria* (1894) and *Through the Eye of the Needle* (1907). The last-named book was a portrayal of the Utopian society of Altruria, but *A Traveler* was such a ruthlessly satirical laying bare of the brutal inconsistency between American ideals and practices that it should destroy the rather common impression that Howells was a smug portrayer of superficialities. The first and most influential of the novels, however, was *Looking Backward*, by Edward Bellamy (1850–98), issued in 1888. Bellamy's hero was a wealthy Bostonian who had been put to sleep by a mesmerist in 1887 and awoke in the year 2000 in a socialist Golden Age. His description of the new order is too long to reprint, but we can give his parable of the coach by which he attempted to describe to his hypothetical readers the exploiters and exploited in 1887. *Looking Backward* led to the formation of numerous socialist organizations called Nationalist Clubs.]

By way of attempting to give the reader some general impression of the way people lived together in those days, and especially of the relations of the rich and poor to one another, perhaps I cannot do better than to compare society as it then was to a prodigious coach which the masses of humanity were harnessed to and dragged toilsomely along a very hilly and sandy road. The driver was hunger, and permitted no lagging, though the pace was necessarily very slow. Despite the difficulty of drawing the coach at all along so hard a road, the top was covered with passengers who never got down, even at the steepest ascents. These seats on top were very breezy and comfortable. Well up out of the dust, their occupants could enjoy the scenery at their leisure, or critically discuss the merits of the straining team. Naturally such places were in great demand and the competition for them was keen, every one seeking as the first end in life to secure a seat on the coach for himself and to leave it to his child after him. By the rule of the coach a man could leave his seat to whom he wished, but on the other hand there were many accidents by which it might at any time be wholly lost. For all that they were so easy, the seats were very insecure, and at every sudden jolt of the coach persons were slipping out of them and falling to the ground, where they were instantly compelled to take hold of the rope and help to drag the coach on which they had before ridden so pleasantly. It was naturally regarded as a terrible misfortune to lose one's seat, and the apprehension that this might happen to them or their friends was a constant cloud upon the happiness of those who rode.

But did they think only of themselves? you ask. Was not their very luxury rendered intolerable to them by comparison with the lot of their brothers and sisters in the harness, and the knowledge that their own weight added to their toil? Had they no compassion for fellow beings from whom fortune only distinguished them? Oh, yes; commiseration was frequently expressed by those who rode for those who had

to pull the coach, especially when the vehicle came to a bad place in the road, as it was constantly doing, or to a particularly steep hill. At such times, the desperate straining of the team, their agonized leaping and plunging under the pitiless lashing of hunger, the many who fainted at the rope and were trampled in the mire, made a very distressing spectacle, which often called forth highly creditable displays of feeling on the top of the coach. At such times the passengers would call down encouragingly to the toilers of the rope, exhorting them to patience, and holding out hopes of possible compensation in another world for the hardness of their lot, while others contributed to buy salves and liniments for the crippled and injured. It was agreed that it was a great pity that the coach should be so hard to pull, and there was a sense of general relief when the specially bad piece of road was gotten over. This relief was not, indeed, wholly on account of the team, for there was always some danger at these bad places of a general overturn in which all would lose their seats.

It must in truth be admitted that the main effect of the spectacle of the misery of the toilers at the rope was to enhance the passengers' sense of the value of their seats upon the coach, and to cause them to hold on to them more desperately than before. If the passengers could only have felt assured that neither they nor their friends would ever fall from the top, it is probable that, beyond contributing to the funds for liniments and bandages, they would have troubled themselves extremely little about those who dragged the coach.

I am well aware that this will appear to the men and women of the twentieth century an incredible inhumanity, but there are two facts, both very curious, which partly explain it. In the first place, it was firmly and sincerely believed that there was no other way in which Society could get along, except the many pulled at the rope and the few rode, and not only this, but that no very radical improvement even was possible, either in the harness, the coach, the roadway, or the distribution of the toil. It had always been as it was, and it always would be so. It was a pity, but it could not be helped, and philosophy forbade wasting compassion on what was beyond remedy.

The other fact is yet more curious, consisting in a singular hallucination which those on the top of the coach generally shared, that they were not exactly like their brothers and sisters who pulled at the rope, but of finer clay, in some way belonging to a higher order of beings who might justly expect to be drawn. This seems unaccountable, but, as I once rode on this very coach and shared that very hallucination, I ought to be believed. The strangest thing about the hallucination was that those who had but just climbed up from the ground, before they had outgrown the marks of the rope upon their hands, began to fall under its influence. As for those whose parents and grand-parents before them had been so fortunate as to keep their seats on the top, the conviction they cherished of the essential difference between their sort of humanity and the common article, was absolute. The effect of such a delusion in moderating fellow feeling for the sufferings of the mass of men into a distant and philosophical compassion, is obvious.

THE SOULLESS CORPORATION

"There is nothing like distance to disinfect dividends."

[The corporation, ran a whimsical complaint of the Progressive Era, had neither a body to be kicked nor a soul to be damned. The case for public control of corporations was stated by Edward Alsworth Ross (1866–1951), a sociologist, in his *Sin and Society* (Boston: Houghton Mifflin, 1907), 105–111, 116, 131.]

Those who contend that men are growing better, and those who insist that matters are growing worse, may both be right. "Look at the amelioration in the lot of women, of children, of blacks, of convicts, of defectives," flute the apologists. "Never were punishments more humane, manners milder, amusements cleaner, gifts larger, the rights of the weak better protected, the lower creatures more considered." "But mark the ruthlessness of industry, the ferocity of business, the friction of classes, the stench of politics," rasp the critics. "Never in our time were children so exploited, workers so driven, consumers so poisoned, passengers so mangled, investors so fleeced, public servants so tempted." The key to the paradox is that while men are improving in their personal relations, the control of industry and business is becoming impersonal.

Take the face-to-face element out of a relation, and any lurking devil in it comes to the surface. . . . It is noteworthy that the strife between employer and employee was never so bitter as it has become since corporations came to be the great employers. So, also, the tension between the railroads and the people has grown with the merging of lines locally owned into huge systems controlled by remote investors in the East or in Europe.

There is nothing like distance to disinfect dividends. Therefore the moral character of the stockholders makes very little difference in the conduct of the affairs of the corporation. Christian or heathen, native or alien, blue blood or plebeian, rich or poor, they all sanction much the same thing, and that is, the policy that promises the biggest dividends in the long run. To the directors their virtual mandate is, "Get results!" The directors pass this mandate to the officers. The officers pass it along to the heads of departments, and these send it on down the line. Take one gas company formed by saints and another formed by sinners. The directors of the two companies will be more alike than the stockholders, the officers will be still more alike, and the men who come into contact with the legislature or the city council, or the gas consumers, will not differ by a shade. The saintly stockholders not only do not know what is going on, but so long as the dividends are comfortable they resent having inconvenient knowledge thrust upon them.

The corporation, to be sure, has certain good points. The corporate owner—of course we are not speaking of one-man corporations, or of those whose officers follow their own sweet will—is not warped by race antipathy or religious prejudice or caste pride. Unlike the individual business man, its course is never shaped by political ambitions or social aspirations or the personal feuds of its wife. It does not exact personal subservience, does not indulge itself in petty tyranny, is not held back from negotiation with its employees by aristocratic haughtiness. It does not feel anger or hold a grudge. If it ruins any one, it does so not from malice, but simply because he stands in the way. Let him meekly creep into the ditch, and it honks by unnoticing. The business man may be swerved by vindictiveness or by generosity, by passion or by conscience, but the genuine corporation responds to but one motive. Toward gain it gravitates with the ruthlessness of a lava stream.

Nevertheless, if the corporate owner is free from the weaknesses of the individual, it escapes also his wholesome limitations. It feels not the restraints that conscience and public sentiment lay on the business man. It fears the law no more, and public indignation far less, than does the individual. You can hiss the bad man, egg him, lampoon him, caricature him, ostracize him and his. Not so with the bad corporation. The corporation, moreover, is not in dread of hell fire. You cannot Christianize it. You may convert its stockholders, animate them with patriotism or public spirit or love of social service; but this will have little or no effect on the tenor of their corporation. In short, it is an entity that transmits the greed of investors, but not their conscience; that returns them profits, but not unpopularity. . . .

Thanks to the magic of limited liability, every years finds a greater distance between the corporate business and its absentee owners. Every year sees these owners more numerous, more scattered, more dominated by the big insiders. Every year sees savings banks, trust companies, and insurance companies coming between the corporate management and the millions who furnish the money, thereby making it harder for their conscience to reach and humanize that management. . . .

Now, the corporation cannot mend itself. More and more it is impersonal and non-moral. More and more the far-away manager is rated as a profit conveyer, and the conduit with the bigger flow is always preferred. It has become a machine, and Mammon is its master. Reform, therefore, will not come from the inside. Those who supply the capital cannot mould it to their better will. But they can change its spirit if they will join with their fellow citizens in restraining the corporation by public opinion and by statute. . . .

Corporations are necessary, yet, through nobody's fault, they tend to become soulless and lawless. By all means let them reap where they have sown. But why let them declare dividends not only on their capital, but also on their power to starve out labor, to wear out litigants, to beat down small competitors, to master the market, to evade taxes, to get the free use of public property? Nothing but the curb of organized society can confine them to their own grist and keep them from grinding into dividends the stamina of children, the health of women, the lives of men, the purity of the ballot, the honor of public servants, and the supremacy of the laws.

"MAN'S LIBERTIES ARE TRAMPLED UNDER FOOT BY CORPORATIONS AND TRUSTS"

[One of the most eloquent defenses of the rights of labor was made by Samuel Gompers (1850–1924), President of the American Federation of Labor during the Pullman strike of 1894. Judge Peter Grosscup was one of the federal judges who issued an injunction against Eugene Debs and his American Railway Union restraining them from interfering with the movement of the mails. When Debs violated the injunction, Grosscup called for federal troops and arraigned Debs before a grand jury. The judge's charge to the jury stated the historic common law thesis that a strike was a restraint of trade and bitterly attacked the efforts of unions to uphold the demands of labor. Debs was sent to prison. Gompers had refused to aid the strikers, but he now came forward with a public letter to Grosscup. See Gompers' "Letter on Labor in Industrial Society," in *American Federationist* (September, 1894), 1:150–152.]

You say that as you stated in your charge to the Grand Jury, you believe in labor organizations within such lawful and reasonable limits as will make them a service to the laboring man, and not a menace to the lawful institutions of the country.

I have . . . only partially been able to discover how far you believe in labor organizations. You would certainly have no objection officially or personally to workingmen organizing, and in their meetings discuss perhaps "the origin of man," benignly smiling upon each other, and declaring that all existing things are right, going to their wretched homes to find some freedom in sleep from gnawing hunger. . . .

You know, or ought to know, that the introduction of machinery is turning into idleness thousands, faster than new industries are founded, and yet, machinery certainly should not be either destroyed or hampered in its full development. The laborer is a man, he is made warm by the same sun and made cold—yes, colder—by the same winter as you are. He has a heart and brain, and feels and knows the human and paternal instinct for those depending upon him as keenly as do you.

What shall the workers do? Sit idly by and see the vast resources of nature and the human mind be utilized and monopolized for the benefit of the comparative few? No. The laborers must learn to think and act, and soon, too, that only by the power of organization, and common concert of action, can either their manhood be maintained, their rights to life (work to sustain it) be recognized, and liberty and rights secured.

Since you say that you favor labor organizations within certain limits, will you kindly give to thousands of your anxious fellow citizens what you believe the workers could and should do in their organizations to solve this great problem? Not what they should not do. You have told us that.

I am not one of those who regards the entire past as a failure. I recognize the progress made and the improved conditions of which nearly the entire civilized world are the beneficiaries. I ask you to explain, however, that if the wealth of the whole world is, as you say, "pre-eminently and beneficially the nation's wealth," how is it that thousands of able-bodied, willing, earnest men and women are suffering the pangs of hunger? We may boast of our wealth and civilization, but to the hungry man and woman and child our progress is a hollow mockery, our civilization a sham, and our "national wealth" a chimera.

You recognize that the industrial forces set in motion by steam and electricity have materially changed the structure of our civilization. You also admit that a system has grown up where the accumulations of the individual have passed from his control into that of representative combinations and trusts, and that the tendency in this direction is on the increase. How, then, can you consistently criticize the workingmen for recognizing that as individuals they can have no influence in deciding what the wages, hours of toil and conditions of employment shall be?

You evidently have observed the growth of corporate wealth and influence. You recognize that wealth, in order to become more highly productive, is concentrated into fewer hands, and controlled by representatives and directors, and yet you sing the old siren song that the workingman should depend entirely upon his own "individual effort."

The school of *laissez faire*, of which you seem to be a pronounced advocate, has produced great men in advocating the theory of each for himself, and his Satanic Majesty taking the hindermost, but the most pronounced advocates of your school of thought in economics have, when practically put to the test, been compelled to admit that combination and organization of the toiling masses are essential both to prevent the deterioration and to secure an improvement in the condition of the wage earners.

If, as you say, the success of commercial society depends upon the full play of competition, why do not you and your confreres turn your attention and direct the shafts of your attacks against the trusts and corporations. . . . Why garland your thoughts in beautiful phrase when speaking of these modern vampires, and steep your pen in gall when writing of the laborers' efforts to secure some of the advantages accruing from the concentrated thought and genius of the ages? . . .

Probably you have not read within the past year of babies dying of starvation at their mothers' breasts. More than likely the thousands of men lying upon the bare stones night after night in the City Hall of Chicago last winter escaped your notice. You may not have heard of the cry for bread that was sounded

through this land of plenty by thousands of honest men and women. But should these and many other painful incidents have passed you by unnoticed, I am fearful that you may learn of them with keener thoughts with the coming sleets and blasts of winter.

You say that "labor cannot afford to attack capital." Let me remind you that labor has no quarrel with capital, as such. It is merely the possessors of capital who refuse to accord to labor the recognition, the right, the justice which is the laborers' due, with whom we contend. . . .

Inquire from the thousands of women and children whose husbands or fathers were suffocated or crushed in the mines through the rapacious greed of stockholders clamoring for more dividends. Investigate the sweating dens of the large cities. Go to the mills, factories, through the country. Visit the modern tenement houses or hovels in which thousands of workers are compelled to eke out an existence. Ask these whether the conqueror (monopoly) cares whether his trophy (the laborers) is destroyed or preserved. Ascertain from employers whether the laborer is not regarded the same as a machine, thrown out as soon as all the work possible has been squeezed out of him.

Are you aware that all the legislation ever secured for the ventilation or safety of mines, factory or workshop is the result of the efforts of organized labor? Do you know that the trade unions were the shield for the seven-year-old children from being the conqueror's trophy until they become somewhat older? And that the reformatory laws now on the statute books, protecting or defending the trophies of both sexes, young and old, from the fond care of the conquerors, were wrested from Congresses, legislatures and parliaments despite the Pullmans, the Jeffries, the Ricks, the Tafts, the Williams, the Woods, or the Grosscups.

By what right, sir, do you assume that the labor organizations do not conduct their affairs within lawful limits, or that they are a menace to the lawful institutions of the country? Is it because some thoughtless or overzealous member at a time of great excitement and smarting under a wrong may violate under a law or commit an improper act? Would you apply the same rule to the churches, the other moral agencies and organizations that you do to the organizations of labor? . . .

Year by year man's liberties are trampled under foot at the bidding of corporations and trusts, rights are invaded and law perverted. In all ages wherever a tyrant has shown himself he has always found some willing judge to clothe that tyranny in the robes of legality, and modern capitalism has proven no exception to the rule.

You may not know that the labor movement as represented by the trades unions, stands for right, for justice, for liberty. You may not imagine that the issuance of an injunction depriving men of a legal as well as a natural right to protect themselves, their wives and

little ones, must fail of its purpose. Repression or oppression never yet succeeded in crushing the truth or redressing a wrong.

In conclusion let me assure you that labor will organize and more compactly than ever and upon practical lines, and despite relentless antagonism, achieve for humanity a nobler manhood, a more beautiful womanhood and a happier childhood.

THE SAVAGE WORLD OF THORSTEIN VEBLEN

[Thorstein Veblen (1857–1929), son of Norwegian immigrants, was the stormy petrel of American economics at the turn of the century. Brilliant, arrogant, and openly contemptuous of colleagues and ever ready—and able—to cuckold them, he never found a comfortable niche in the academic world. And yet he effectively laid the scalpel to the social and economic illusions and pretensions of the Gilded Age. Because it is difficult to gain an understanding of Veblen's concepts from his writings without quoting at impossible length, we turn here to certain excerpts from the brief presentation by Robert L. Heilbroner in *The Worldly Philosophers* (N.Y.: Simon and Schuster, 1961), pp. 180–213 passim. Heilbroner opened with some account of the predatory "robber barons" and the economists who were their official apologists, then turned to Veblen's complex, eccentric, and sometimes unsavory career. Veblen's first book was *The Theory of the Leisure Class*, published in 1899.]

For most people the book appeared to be nothing more than just such a satire on the ways of the aristocratic class, and a telling attack on the follies and foibles of the rich. And so, on the surface, it appeared to be. Veblen, in his brocaded prose, embroidered the thesis that the leisure class advertised its superiority through conspicuous expenditure—blatant or subtle—and that its own hallmark

—leisure itself—was also enjoyed the more fully by being dangled before the eyes of the public. In a thousand examples it held up to acid examination the attitude that "more expensive" necessarily meant "better.". . .

But the descriptions of our penchant for display, however amusing or to the point, were no more than the illustrative material of the book. For as the title made clear, this was an inquiry into the *theory* of the leisure class. Although Veblen might stop along the route to comment on the more striking local scenery, his interest lay at the terminus of his journey, in such questions as What is the nature of economic man? How does it happen that he so builds his community that it will have a leisure class? What is the economic meaning of leisure itself? . . . [Veblen] was not at all sure that the force which bound society together was the interplay of rationally calculated "self-interest" [portrayed by the classical economists] and he was not even wholly convinced that leisure was in and of itself preferable to work. His readings had introduced him to the ways of little-noticed peoples. . . . [some of whom] had well-defined leisure classes. These classes, be it noted, were not idlers. On the contrary, they were among the busiest members of the community. But their "work" was all predatory; they *seized* their riches by force or cunning and took no part in the actual production of wealth by sweat or skill. . . . They did so with the full approval of the community. For these were societies which were rich enough to be able to afford a nonproductive class and aggressive enough in spirit to admire them: far from being regarded as wasters or spoilers, those who rose to the leisured ranks were looked up to as the strong and the able. . . .

And so in modern life Veblen saw the heritage of the past. The leisure class had changed its occupation, it had refined its methods, but its aim was still the same—the predatory seizure of goods without work. . . .

Does this sound farfetched? . . . The notion of man as a thinly civilized barbarian does more than explain the presence of a leisure class and the acceptance of display as the norm of expenditure. It gives a clue to the nature of social cohesion itself. For the earlier economists were not too successful in explaining what bound society together in the face of the powerful divergent interests of its component classes. If Marx's view was right, for example, and the proletariat was irreconcilably and diametrically opposed to the capitalist, what pre-

vented the revolution from breaking out at once? Veblen provides an answer. The lower classes are not at swords' points with the upper; they are bound up with them by the intangible but steely bonds of common attitudes. The workers do not seek to displace their managers; they seek to *emulate* them. They themselves acquiesce in the general judgment that the work they do is somehow less "dignified" than the work of their masters, and their goal is not to rid themselves of a superior class but to climb up to it. In the theory of the leisure class lies the kernel of a theory of social stability. . . .

[His next book, *The Theory of Business Enterprise*] came out in 1904. Factual or not, it was even more coruscating and still more curious than his first. For the point of view which it advocated seemed to fly in the face of common sense itself. Every economist from the days of Adam Smith had made of the capitalist the driving figure in the economic tableau; whether for better or worse, he was generally assumed to be the central generator of economic progress. But with Veblen all this was turned topsy-turvy. The businessman was still the central figure, but no longer the motor force. Now he was portrayed as the *saboteur* of the system!

Needless to say, it was a strange perspective on society which could produce so disconcerting a view. Veblen did not begin, as Ricardo or Marx or the Victorians, with the clash of human interests; he began at a stage below, in the nonhuman substratum of technology. What fascinated him was the machine. He saw society as dominated by the machine, caught up in its standardization, timed to its regular cycle of performance, geared to its insistence on accuracy and precision. More than that, he envisaged the economic process itself as being basically mechanical in character. Economics meant production and production meant the machinelike meshing of society as it turned out goods. Such a social machine would need tenders, of course—technicians and engineers to make whatever adjustments were necessary to ensure the most efficient cooperation of the parts. But from an over-all view, society could best be pictured as a gigantic but purely matter-of-fact mechanism, a highly specialized, highly coordinated human clock-work.

But where would the businessman fit into such a scheme? . . . The machine was not concerned with values and profits; it ground out goods. Hence the businessman would have no function to perform—unless he turned engineer. But as a member of the leisure class he was not interested in engineering; he wanted to accumulate. . . . So the businessman achieved his end, not by working within the framework of the social machine, but by conspiring against it! His function was not to help make goods, but to cause breakdowns in the regular flow of output so that values would fluctuate and he could capitalize on the confusion to reap a profit. And so, on top of the machinelike dependability of the actual production apparatus in the world, the businessman built a superstructure of credit, loans, and make-believe capitalizations. Below, society turned over in its mechanical routine; above, the structure of finance swayed and shifted. And as the financial counterpart to the real world teetered, opportunities for profit constantly appeared, disappeared, and reappeared. But the price of this profit seeking was high; it was the constant disturbing, undoing, even conscious misdirecting of the efforts of society to provision itself.

It is at first blush a rather shocking thesis. That businessmen should work *against* the interests of production seems worse than heretical. It sounds foolish.

But before we dismiss the theory as the product of a strangely warped and bitter mind, let us look again at the scene from which Veblen drew his subject. This was, let us remember, the age of American industry which Matthew Josephson has aptly called the time of the robber barons . . . [and which was characterized all too much by cutthroat competition, stock market rigging, and the creation of great corporations floating on seas of watered stock. The fact was that] *these men were uninterested in producing goods.*

In the light of the times, Veblen's theory does not seem so farfetched. It stung because it described, almost in the terms of a savage ritual, practices which were recognized as the ultimate of sophistication. But his essential thesis was all too well documented by the facts: the function of the great barons of business was indeed very different from the functions of the men who actually ran the productive machine. The blustering bold game of financial chicanery certainly served as much to disturb the flow of goods as to promote it. . . .

But *The Theory of Business Enterprise* was more than an acid treatment of the business system. It was, as well, a theory of social change. For Veblen believed that the days of the business leaders were numbered, that despite their power, there was ranged against them a formidable adversary. It was not the proletariat (for the *Leisure Class* had shown how the underlying population looked up to its leaders), but a still more implacable foe: the machine.

For the machine, thought Veblen, "throws out anthropomorphic habits of thought." It forced men to think in terms of matter-of-fact, in terms precise, measurable, and devoid of superstition and animism. Hence those who came in contact with the machine process found it increasingly difficult to swallow the presumptions of "natural law" and social differentiation which surround the leisure class. And so society divided; not poor against rich, but technician versus businessman, mechanic against war lord, scientist opposed to ritualist.

In a later series of books, principally *The Engineers and the Price System* and *Absentee Ownership and Business Enterprise*, he spelled out the "revolution" in greater detail. Eventually . . . [the engineers] would take counsel among themselves, dispense with the "lieutenants of absentee ownership," and run the economy along the principles of a huge, well-ordered production machine. . . .

What are we to think of this strange figure?

It is hardly necessary to point out that he

went to extremes. His characterization of the leisure class, for example, was a masterpiece of portraiture on one page, but a caricature on the next. . . . Like Marx, Veblen badly underestimated the capacity of a democratic system to correct its own excesses. . . . Veblen seemed to feel that the leisure classes had a monopoly on society's stock of predatoriness and that the engineers and technicians were the sole guardians of its instinct for honest workmanship. But if modern psychology teaches us anything, it is that we are all of us, regardless of social station, the harborers of deep-rooted aggressive tendencies and powerful creative ones. . . .

A final criticism: Veblen's infatuation with the machine is a jarring note in a worldly philosopher otherwise so devoid of lyricism. It is true that machines make us think coldly, but they may end up by making us think too coldly. . . . A corps of engineers might well run our society more efficiently; that it would be more humanely run is a debatable proposition.

But despite these caveats, there is much to be learned from the polite bitterness of this skeptical mind. Certainly his division of America into money-makers and goods-makers is an apt depiction of our economy and more realistic than the stereotype of the Marxian class struggle; and indeed, Veblen's description of the American trait of competitive emulation helps explain why serious class division never materialized in this country. . . .

But most of all, the man gave so much to economics—a new pair of eyes with which to see the world. After Veblen's savage description of the mores of daily life, the classical picture of society as a well-mannered tea party became increasingly difficult to maintain. . . . Man, said Veblen, is not to be comprehended in terms of sophisticated "economic laws" in which his innate ferocity and creativity are both smothered under a cloak of rationalization. He is better dealt with in the less flattering but more fundamental vocabulary of the anthropologist or the psychologist: a creature of strong and irrational drives, credulous, untutored, ritualistic. Leave aside the preconceptions of another age, he asked of the economists, and find out why man actually behaves as he does.

THE SOCIAL GOSPEL

[One of the results of the new climate of opinion being formed toward the end of the Gilded Age was the emergence in the Protestant churches of the Social Gospel. Basically, this was an effort to apply Christ's teachings in an attempt to reform a brutal industrial order, or at least to ameliorate the condition of the working classes. It is often said that the Social Gospel movement was effective in convincing the churches that they had social and material duties to their communities as well as spiritual, and it had a significant influence in enlisting the middle classes in the progressive political crusade. The following account of the Social Gospel is from Carl N. Degler's *Out of Our Past* (N.Y.: Harper and Row, 1959), pp. 340–349.]

Contrary to the opinions of some shortsighted churchmen, the estrangement of the urban working class from Protestantism was something more than a shift in interest or an increase in human depravity. At bottom it stemmed from the failure of the churches to adapt themselves to the altered face of American society. Because, historically, Protestantism in America, like the nation at large, was rural, the Church was bewildered by the city; nothing in its history prepared it for the problems now thrown up by urbanization. Long accustomed to class relations remarkably free of conflict, the Protestant churches, suffused with the Calvinist ethic of individual achievement and responsibility, could not easily understand an era characterized by class warfare, ruthless monopolies, and the squalor of tenement-filled cities. Moreover, many of the urban working-men were immigrants and Catholics and therefore beyond the appeal of the Protestant churches.

The churches were suspicious of, when they were not openly hostile to, the new urban proletariat, who bore slight resemblance to the steady, conservative farmers of an earlier America. . . . The Reverend Washington Gladden was told by one worker in the 1880's that the reason he and his fellows did not attend church was that it seemed to be a place for employers only. "Of course," he admitted, "the manufacturers can and should dress better than the laborer; but when we see them so full of religion on Sunday, and then grinding the faces of the poor on the other six days, we are apt to think they are insincere." Nor was Henry Ward Beecher's remark that any workingman worth his salt could support a family on a dollar a day, providing he did not drink or smoke, conducive to the increase of workingmen in the Protestant churches.

All men of the cloth, however, were not Beechers either in moral obtuseness or income. (Beecher was reputed to have an income in excess of $20,000 a year when he uttered his dictum.) . . . Instinctively almost, leading churchmen appealed to the universal character of Christianity as an antidote to the social cleavage. "Christianity, from the nature of it," Samuel Loomis told the students at Andover Seminary in 1886, "cannot remain the religion of classes; it must be the religion of the whole people or none." The churches will never re-establish contact with the urban masses, Washington Gladden cautioned in the same year, until they recognize that these " 'masses' are composed to a large extent, of . . . wage earners," and the churches must "adjust their theories and their methods" to that fact if they wished "to see daylight shine through this dark problem of church neglect." . . .

As tension between workers and employers was successively built up, discharged, and built again in bitter strikes such as those of 1877, 1886, 1892, and 1894, an increasing number of Protestant clergymen found it difficult to reconcile the doctrines of Jesus with the impersonal and ruthless functioning of a laissez-faire economy. "Jesus Christ knew a great deal more about organizing society," Washington Gladden wryly commented, "than David Ricardo

ever dreamed of knowing, and the application of his law to industrial society will be found to work surprisingly well." The historic alliance between religion and business which began with the Calvinists was coming under searching scrutiny. Many churchmen, Gladden noted, were recognizing that the doctrine of laissez faire not only meant "let well enough alone . . ." but also "let ill enough alone!" . . .

The most obvious and earliest sign that the churches were acting to establish contact with the urban masses was the so-called institutional church—that is, one which performed social services for its members. . . . The institutional church pushed its activities out into the city itself. Volunteer women went out into the streets and into the tenements to seek out the deserving poor; co-operative ventures among several churches were initiated in order to provide church services to those working people who had no nearby churches. It was in these years that youth organizations like Christian Endeavor (Congregational), Epworth League (Methodist), and the Brotherhood of St. Andrew (Episcopal) were started. In short order these organizations undertook projects among the working class.

While the laboring class's lack of interest compelled some Protestant churches to replant their roots in the cities, the urban challenge brought forth a new church, conceived in the city itself. Imported into the United States from England in the 1870's, the Salvation Army by the 1880's was by far the largest Protestant denomination active in the slums and streets of the cities of America. . . .

Pressed by empty churches on the one hand and appalled by the gulf between Christian ethics and social practice on the other, many Protestant clergymen began to listen to academicians like Commons and Ely and ministers like Gladden. As churchmen studied economics, talked with workers, and visited slums, a theological and philosophical basis for a new mission of the Church gradually emerged. The social gospel, as a later generation would call it, was being hammered out on the anvil of social realism. . . .

The doctrine of the social gospel achieved its most eloquent expression in the personality and prolific writings of Walter Rauschenbusch of Rochester Theological Seminary. Over and over again his books appealed for a recognition of the social mission of Christianity. "The chief purpose of the Christian Church in the past has been the salvation of individuals," he wrote in *Christianizing the Social Order* in 1912. "But the most pressing task of the present is not individualistic. Our business is to make over an antiquated and immoral economic system; to get rid of laws, customs, maxims, and philosophies inherited from an evil and despotic past; to create just and brotherly relations between groups and classes of society" and thereby make it possible that men might "live and work in a fashion that will not out-

rage all the better elements in them. Our inherited Christian faith dealt with individuals; our present task deals with society." . . .

Though many rural churches of Protestantism escaped the fire of the new doctrine, and even whole denominations like the Presbyterians were slow to react, the year 1914 found the social gospel permeating the major denominations of Protestantism. The Methodist "Social Creed," setting forth in 1908 a variety of goals for the amelioration of labor conditions, was one of the outstanding fruits of the movement. Included in the Creed were such purposes as "a living wage in every industry," "abolition of child labor," "the highest wage that each industry can afford," and "the recognition of the Golden Rule . . . as the supreme law of society and the sure remedy for all social ills." That same year the Federal Council of Churches of Christ in America was formed by thirty-three Protestant denominations. Since the Council drew its statement of social principles almost verbatim from the Methodist Social Creed, it stood as tangible evidence that the Protestant churches were now willing to commit themselves to the realization of the principal demands of the working people.

The new social outlook of the churches was evident in the report which the Federal Council of Churches issued in 1920 upon completing its investigation into the national steel strike of 1919. The report, for all its endeavor to achieve objectivity, was animated with sympathy for the strikers, as it was heavy with indignation at the callousness of the employers. Protestantism had come a long way since the days of Henry Ward Beecher, half a century before. . . .

With the triumph of the social gospel, Protestantism not only profoundly altered its social outlook but regained much of its lost prestige among the people. There was a period, John Mitchell, president of the United Mine Workers, commented in 1913, "when it was taken for granted that clergymen . . . were unable to comprehend trade unionism." But today, he continued, "many of the denominations as such, and the prevailing opinion among clergymen as individuals, have pronounced for unions. . . ." Under such circumstances, he went on, "it may be regarded as an accepted fact that the church is today emphatically on the side of union labor." Another group, social workers, once critical of the churches' aloofness from the social issues of the day, had returned. In 1905, it was reported that three quarters of the social workers in the American Institute of Social Service were "faithful church members." . . .

In conquering the churches, the social gospel extended its influence through society at large. By helping to heal the widening breach between the working class and the rest of society, by demanding a fair share of American abundance for the worker, the social gospel was instrumental in halting the dangerous drift toward class division so imminent in the 1880's and 1890's. Rather than being an "opiate of the people," as Karl Marx had described religion, the churches in industrial America consciously ranged themselves on the side of the poor and the downtrodden, striving to achieve social justice for all. In doing so they threw a formidable obstacle in the path of socialism in the United States.

On the other hand, a Protestantism shot through with the social gospel is a veritable hothouse of reform movements and social protest; it can no longer be an automatic defender of the *status quo*. Indeed, considering the transcendent standard by which society is judged under the social gospel, those who apply such a yardstick can never be satisfied. After the advent of the social gospel, it was possible to advocate social reform in the language of religion. It is not accidental that reform leaders like Woodrow Wilson and Franklin Roosevelt used religious phrases to clothe their pleas for reform. . . . By broadening the definition of Christianity to include justice for all members of society, the ministers of the social gospel made it possible to harness the long religious heritage of the people in behalf of the realization of the American Dream of justice, equality, and opportunity.

Whereas the urban effect upon Protestantism was at first shattering and only later beneficial, upon Roman Catholicism at first it was not apparent at all. This was true if only because the Catholic Church in America, flourishing largely among the poor immigrants of the cities, required little instruction in the degradation of poverty and the squalor of tenement living. Those Protestant clergymen who were beginning to be concerned over their own churches' alienation from the people were frankly envious of Rome's appeal. "The Catholic Church," remarked Samuel Loomis in 1887, "is emphatically the workingman's church. She rears her edifices in the midst of the densest populations, provides them with many seats and has the seats well filled." Richard Ely, the economist, complained in the middle eighties that Protestant ministers had difficulty being fair to labor, though this was not true of Catholic priests. "It is not a difference of good will," Ely emphasized, "so much as a difference of knowledge. The Catholic revealed an acquaintance with the movements of the masses—the Protestant ignorance." When President Theodore Roosevelt discussed his proposed arbitration commission with union leader John Mitchell during the coal strike of 1902, Mitchell asked, as Roosevelt reported it, that "a Roman Catholic prelate" be put on the body "as the great mass of miners were Roman Catholics." Obviously these Catholic workers trusted their churchmen.

CATHOLICISM AND AMERICANISM

During the Gilded Age the Roman Catholic Church in the United States was growing by leaps and bounds, and in so doing was stirring considerable apprehension among many Americans, not all of them ignorant or insincere. Here we offer several analyses which throw light on the problems of Catholicism and Americanism.

(1) "DEMOCRACY AND CATHOLICISM AGREE"

[DeTocqueville was convinced that, far from there being an inherent contradiction between democracy and Catholicism, they agreed so well that eventually Catholicism would become the dominant—indeed, the only—religion of the United States. See his *Democracy in America* (2v., New York, 1856), 1:328–330, 2:29–30.]

At the present moment more than a million of Christians, professing the truths of the church of Rome, are to be met with in the Union. These catholics are faithful to the observances of their religion; they are fervent and zealous in the support and belief of their doctrines. Nevertheless they constitute the most republican and the most democratic class of citizens which exists in the United States; and although this fact may surprise the observer at first, the cause by which it is occasioned may easily be discovered upon reflection.

I think that the catholic religion has erroneously been looked upon as the natural enemy of democracy. Among the various sects of Christians, catholicism seems to me, on the contrary, to be one of those which are most favourable to the equality of conditions. In the catholic church, the religious community is composed of only two elements; the priest and the people. The priest alone rises above the rank of his flock, and all below him are equal. . . .

It has not unfrequently occurred that the catholic priest has left the service of the altar to mix with the governing powers of society, and to make his place among the civil gradations of men. . . . But no sooner is the priesthood entirely separated from the government, as is the case in the United States, than it is found that no class of men are more naturally disposed than the catholics to transfuse the doctrine of the equality of conditions into the political world. If, then, the catholic citizens of the United States are not forcibly led by the nature of their tenets to adopt democratic and republican principles, at least they are not necessarily opposed to them. . . .

The catholic clergy of the United States has never attempted to oppose this political tendency; but it seeks rather to justify its results. The priests in America have divided the intellectual world into two parts: in the one they place the doctrines of revealed religion, which command their assent; in the other they leave those truths, which they believe to have been freely left open to the researches of political inquiry. Thus the catholics of the United States are at the same time the most faithful believers and the most zealous citizens. . . .

Two things must here be accurately distinguished: equality inclines men to wish to form their own opinions; but, on the other hand, it imbues them with the taste and the idea of unity, simplicity, and impartiality in the power which governs society. . . . The men of our days are naturally little disposed to believe; but, as soon as they have any religion, they immediately find in themselves a latent propensity which urges them unconsciously toward Catholicism. Many of the doctrines and the practices of the Romish church astonish them; but they feel a secret admiration for its discipline, and its great unity attracts them. If Catholicism could at length withdraw itself from the political animosities to which it has given rise, I have hardly any doubt but that the same spirit of the age, which appears to be so opposed to it, would become so favourable as to admit of its great and sudden advancement.

One of the most ordinary weaknesses of the human intellect is to seek to reconcile contrary principles, and to purchase peace at the expense of logic. Thus there have ever been, and will ever be, men who, after having submitted some portion of their religious belief to the principle of authority, will seek to exempt several other parts of their faith from its influence, and to keep their minds floating at random between liberty and obedience. But I am inclined to believe that the number of these thinkers will be less in democratic than in other ages; and that our posterity will tend more and more to a single division into two parts—some relinquishing Christianity entirely, and others returning to the bosom of the Church of Rome.

(2) "MORE AND MORE AMERICA ACCEPTED THE CATHOLIC CHURCH"

[The cogency of DeTocqueville's observations was affirmed over a century later by the Columbia University historian, Henry Steele Commager in his *American Mind* (Yale University Press, 1950), pp. 191–195.]

The question of the harmony of Catholicism with American institutions can be approached logically and theologically or historically and pragmatically. Logically Catholicism would seem to be in conflict with many principles of the American political system, an observation which some may regard as a criticism of that political system rather than of Catholic doctrine. Thus the *Papal Syllabus of Errors* of 1864 pronounced it an error to assert that "it is no longer expedient that the Catholic religion shall be held as the only religion of the State, to the exclusion of all other modes of worship" or "that the church ought to be separated from the state and the state from the church." Thus the encyclical of November 1, 1885, pronounced at variance with Christian and natural law the principle that,

As all men are alike equal by race and nature, so in like manner all are equal in the control of their life; that each one is so far his own master as to be in no sense under the rule of any other individual; that each is free to think on every subject just as he may choose and to do whatever he may like to do; that no man has any right to rule over other men. In a society grounded upon such maxims, all government is nothing more or less than the will of the people, and the people, being under the power of itself alone, is alone its own ruler.

Thus so distinguished a Catholic as Monsignor John A. Ryan insisted that, "According to the Catholic position, the State has no right to make laws affecting the validity of the marriages of baptized persons. . . . She [the church] does not consider that human welfare, or social welfare, is promoted by State recognition of any marriage which she pronounces invalid or by State prohibition of any marriage that she declares valid."

In principle, too, the Catholic church presented a sharp challenge to the American philosophy of the relation of the state to education. Thus the encyclical of Pius XI, *Christian Education of Youth*, stated categorically that "all education belongs pre-eminently to the Church." . . .

Logically these doctrines and expressions spelled hostility to some of the principles and institutions which Americans cherished. . . . [but] there was no basis for any immediate fear that these doctrines would be urged in a doctrinaire manner. The Catholic church was one of the most logical of human institutions, but its logic, unlike that of communism, rejected the doctrinaire approach and adapted itself to realities. These doctrines, Catholic apologists explained, applied only to some ideal situation or to some country completely Catholic and had no present relevance to the United States. . . .

Yet, though Catholicism made itself heard on many matters of domestic and foreign policy, there was seldom convincing evidence that it concerned itself improperly with matters outside the legitimate interest of the church in the spiritual and moral welfare of its communicants, especially as the church itself decided what were its legitimate interests. . . . No method has as yet been found . . . to distinguish the religious from the secular motives that inspire the expression of opinion or to sterilize political opinions of religious origin, nor could any democrat consistently deny voters their right to agitate for policies consistent with their moral convictions even though these happened to coincide with the convictions of their church.

Whatever conclusions might be drawn from a scrutiny of Catholic doctrine, the fact was that Catholicism had flourished as a major religion for three quarters of a century without raising serious difficulties except in the imaginations of men and that democratic institutions seemed as sound when the church numbered twenty-four million members as they had been when it counted its communicants by the hundred thousand. It might, indeed, be maintained that the Catholic church was, during this period, one of the most effective of all agencies for democracy and Americanization. Representing as it did a vast cross section of the American people, it could ignore class, section, and race; peculiarly the church of the newcomers, of those who all too often were regarded as aliens, it could give them not only spiritual refuge but social security. . . . Archbishop Ireland . . . insisted that "the Church of America must be, of course, as Catholic as even in Jerusalem or Rome, but as far as her garments assume color from local atmosphere, she must be American. Let no one dare paint on her brow with a for-

eign tint, or pin to her mantle foreign linings."

Not only did Catholicism accept America but more and more America accepted the Catholic church. This was in part a recognition of its strength, in part the tribute to its historical appeal by a people ever more conscious of their past. . . . It is significant, too, that Catholicism was treated with unvarying respect in the newspapers, magazines, and radio and that Hollywood seemed to prefer Catholic priests to Protestant parsons for its more sentimental religious roles: whether Hollywood's gesture was a tribute to the spiritual authority or to the temporal strength of Catholicism it is unnecessary to determine.

Although Catholicism adapted itself to American democracy, it would be an error to suppose that it was, in any doctrinal sense, Americanized, for a Universal Church, dominated by Italian and French churchmen, could not be expected to accommodate its doctrines to the idiosyncrasies of a people whose contributions to theological thought were so negligible. Indeed it was "those views which . . . are called by some Americanism" that were condemned by the Apostolic Letter, *Testem*

J. Clarence Davies Collection, Museum of the City of New York

Benevolentiae, which Leo XIII addressed to Cardinal Gibbons in 1899. Precisely what those views were is a problem impenetrable to the layman for, when examined, they evaporate into thin air, like the Cheshire cat, leaving nothing but a sardonic—and we may assume a Gallic—grin behind. "Rome had caught something in the air," writes Theodore Maynard, the most recent historian of American Catholicism, "a readiness to yield to the *Zeitgeist* to win souls by accommodation. It was no more than a vague incipience. But it would quite possibly have developed and hardened had not Leo spoke." Just how something which the American Catholic hierarchy declared nonexistent could have hardened is a question best left to theologians, but in any event Leo spoke and "Americanism," if it had ever lived, was dead.

Nor was there any difficulty about modernism in American Catholicism. That heresy, which ravaged the Protestant denominations, was disposed of by a series of encyclicals of 1906–7, notably the great encyclical, *Pascendi Dominici Gregis.* . . . As Theodore Maynard observes, "in America the anti-modernist oath was taken with no recalcitrance." "It has sometimes been suggested," he adds, "that what saved the American Church from these ravages was the fact that American Catholics were not much addicted to speculation." In this, in any event, they were thoroughly American.

(3) "HE LOOKED ON AMERICA AS THE FAIREST CONQUEST FOR DIVINE TRUTH"

[The "Americanism" referred to just above had to do with the controversy over the "Americanism heresy" which became acute in the 1890's. The potential effect of American democracy on the Church was feared in certain conservative European circles, and this fear was fanned by the way in which European liberals portrayed the American Catholic Church as an example of the freedom from papal control that they craved. The accusation rose, at least in part, from a defective French translation of Walter Elliott's *Life of Father Hecker* (N.Y.: Columbus Press, 1891), especially from the introduction contributed by Archbishop John Ireland of St. Paul. Father Isaac Hecker (1819–88), after testing transcendentalism at Brook Farm and Fruitlands, turned in 1844 to Catholicism and in 1858 founded the Paulist order which devoted itself to missionary work in the United States. Here we give Archbishop Ireland's introduction (pp. ix–xi).]

Father Hecker was the typical American priest; his were the gifts of mind and heart that go to do great work for God and for souls in America at the present time. Those qualities, assuredly, were not lacking in him which are the necessary elements of character of the good priest and the great man in any time and place. Those are the subsoil of priestly culture, and with the absence of them no one will succeed in America any more than elsewhere. But suffice they do not. There must be added, over and above, the practical intelligence and the pliability of will to understand one's surroundings, the ground upon which he is to deploy his forces, and to adapt himself to circumstances and opportunities as Providence appoints. I do not expect that my words, as I am here writing, will receive universal approval, and I am not at all sure that their expression would have been countenanced by the priest whose memory brings them to my lips. I write as I think, and the responsibility must be all my own. It is as clear to me as noon-day light that countries and peoples have each their peculiar needs and aspirations as they have their peculiar environments, and that, if we would enter into souls and control them, we must deal with them according to their conditions. . . .

The circumstances of Catholics have been peculiar in the United States, and we have unavoidably suffered on this account. Catholics in largest numbers were Europeans, and so were their priests, many of whom—by no means all —remained in heart and mind and mode of action as alien to America as if they had never been removed from the Shannon, the Loire, or the Rhine. No one need remind me that immigration has brought us inestimable blessings, or that without it the Church in America would be of small stature. The remembrance of a precious fact is not put aside, if I recall an accidental evil attaching to it. Priests foreign in disposition and work were not fitted to make favorable impressions upon the non-Catholic American population, and the American-born children of Catholic immigrants were likely to escape their action. . . . Even priests of American ancestry, ministering to immigrants, not unfrequently fell into the lines of those around them, and did but little to make the Church in America throb with American life. Not so Isaac Thomas Hecker.

Whether consciously or unconsciously I do not know, and it matters not, he looked on America as the fairest conquest for divine truth, and he girded himself with arms shaped and tempered to the American pattern. I think that it may be said that the American current, so plain for the last quarter of a century in the flow of Catholic affairs, is, largely at least, to be traced back to Father Hecker and his early co-workers. It used to be said of them in reproach that they were the "Yankee" Catholic Church; the reproach was their praise. . . . It seems as if Almighty God, intending a great age and a great people, has put here in America a singular development of nature's powers and gifts, both in man and out of man—with the further will, I have the faith, of crowning all with the glory of the supernatural. Father Hecker perceived this, and his mission was to hold in his hands the natural, which Americans extolled and cherished and trusted in, and by properly directing its legitimate tendencies and growth to lead it to the term of its own instincts and aspirations— Catholic truth and Catholic grace.

(4) "ONE FELT THE WIND OF TOMORROW"

[Here follow certain observations of the French liberal Max Leclerc, in *Choses d'Amérique* (Paris 1895), as they appear in John Tracy Ellis, ed., *Documents of American Catholic History* (Milwaukee: Bruce Publishing Co.), pp. 414–419. The presumed "Americanist heresy" apparently was that American churchmen advised flexibility in doctrinal matters in order to win converts. Finally, in 1899, the Vatican took cognizance of it, and in *Testem Benevolentiae* issued a warning carefully phrased to state that the view was in error *if* it was being taught.]

The Church enjoys an absolute freedom, in virtue of common right and within the limits of the nation's laws; she is self-sufficient; she expects nothing from the State which demands nothing of her. She even congratulates herself on being left to her unaided might; she owes to this form of government a vigor, an eternal youthfulness which she certainly does not have elsewhere; she gathers the fruits of independence; she waxes strong under the necessity of making her way in the bright world of competition . . .

The Church is tolerant, she is democratic, she is, in fine, American. . . .

While Europe toils along the well-worn rut of race hatreds, of bloody quarrels between nation and nation, of rivalries between ministers and sovereigns,—an occurrence of capital significance in the history of the world took place on the other side of the ocean and went almost unnoticed: the Catholic Church, the most powerful and most ancient of religious organizations, met up with the youngest and most enterprising of recent societies. The Roman Church, for the first time, found herself at grips with a people of a modern civilization without the interposition of governments, local authorities, intrigues of courts or the schemes of diplomacy. . . . The American nation . . . brings to the Church a contingent of faithful which disturbs the balance in Catholicity, and doubles the hold of the Church of Rome upon the world: one can foresee the day in which the Catholics speaking English will be more numerous than the Catholics speaking any other language.

But at this point several questions arrest us: what is the future of religious opinion on the American continent? . . . The American civilization is profoundly materialistic. When the new settlers, when the sons of the docile recruits of the Catholic Church have been imbued with the American spirit, will there remain a place in their hearts for the precepts of Rome and for the faith?

Be that as it may, the Catholic Church cannot fail to be deeply stirred by this inroad of the Anglo-Saxon race, with its concept of life, its democratic instincts, its relish for action and independence, and a whole long civilization behind it remaining up to then alien to the Church of Rome. The Latin influence will cease to exercise uncontested domination in the Church; the Anglo-Saxon influence will establish for itself a usurping stronghold there, and the history of the world will be swerved by it. Old Europe, shackled by its past, introspective, reduced to helplessness, will cease to attract the constant attention of the Church which will turn toward the new lands with their innumerable inhabitants, for she will recognize that the future is with them. Rome will no longer be in Rome, but in Baltimore or in Carthage.

Already the strong and solemn voice of the Anglo-Saxons has made itself heard and hearkened to in the councils of the Church; it is that voice which thrust upon Rome, by threatening an appeal to the people, the solicitude about social problems, and an inexorably democratic policy. It is by the voice of Cardinal Manning, of Cardinal Gibbons, an English prelate and an American prelate, that modern democracy, the power of tomorrow, has indicated to the Church that she must turn her attention from the powerful of the present in order to bring it to bear on itself. One still remembers the voyage to Rome in June, 1886, of Cardinal Gibbons who came to plead the cause of democracy in the name of the interests of the American Church and to demand the withdrawal of the interdict issued by the Holy See against the powerful secret association of the Knights of Labor. . . . M. de Vogüé said then, and subsequent history has proven him correct: "The term 'revolution' is not excessive. One felt the wind of tomorrow which was blowing, one perceived its force."

"WE ARE CATHOLICS, BUT . . . WE CHANGE WITH A CHANGING WORLD"

The attempt to commit the Catholics of the nineteenth century here in America to all the deeds and utterances of those in the middle ages is futile. We do not hold that the Popes have never been in the wrong; nor are we bound, to quote Cardinal Newman, "to defend the policy or the acts of particular popes, whether before or after the great revolt from their authority in the sixteenth century." If the public law of Europe in the eleventh and twelfth centuries permitted them to declare forfeit the authority of tyrannical princes and emperors, it does not follow that they are permitted to do this now. We are Catholics, but we are also men, and though the essential tenets of the faith are immutable we ourselves change with a changing world. We accept with frank sincerity, with cheerful acquiescence, the principles involved in the rule of the people by the people and for the people, and are content to abide the issue.

—Bishop John L. Spalding, 1894

J. Clarence Davies Collection, Museum of the City of New York

8

CULTURAL FORCES AT THE TURN OF THE CENTURY

INTRODUCTION

It has been the fortune of the United States to arrive at maturity—or at least full growth—on the verge of a century which was to see what have probably been the most profound changes in any comparable time in human history. Moreover, the United States by the very logic inherent in the conditions of its growth was to play a role in these changes—sometimes constructive, sometimes blighting, but always significant.

These readings have sought to present both the good and bad in the American past. Up to the close of the nineteenth century the effect of the United States on the rest of the world was more or less indirect. It presented a scene in which new institutions, new technologies, and news ways of thinking were being worked out, and the result could be judged good or bad only in the eye of the beholder. For the most part, the Old World could, if it wished, shrug its shoulders and pass by on the other side. By 1900 this was no longer possible. American agricultural surpluses were ruining old patterns in Europe, and its gadgets were flooding the European market. Worst of all, American ideas were profoundly disturbing the quietude of peoples all over the world and threatening the old order of classes in Europe and colonial rule abroad.

In this chapter we shall bring together various evidences of the changes occurring in several walks of life and, to a certain extent, show how America and the world interacted. Perhaps the turmoil that marks this century would have come even if there had been no United States, but perhaps it would have been longer in coming—perhaps even less violent. For though America was in many fields a catalyst of change, the fact remains that change was inherent also in Europe. Indeed, Europe was the first to show evidences of the new worlds a-borning in the field of art and the atom.

A PROBLEM IN DYNAMICS: AMERICAN LITERATURE AT THE TURN OF THE CENTURY

[The American literature of the Gilded Age was sometimes disquieting, though by far the most of it sought the prettiness of the standard English product. Still, men like William Dean Howells and Mark Twain offered examples of the realism which was to dominate American fiction and to find imitators in Europe. Henry James fled from America, and yet passed his life in fascinated contemplation of the men and women from whom he had fled. Emily Dickinson pushed back the frontiers of American poetry with subtler meanings and a rare understanding of the link between finite and infinite. With the 1890's there was a further stirring of new ideas, the sense of a new world to be explored. Here we turn to the chapter "A Problem in Dynamics" by Robert E. Spiller in his *The Cycle of American Literature* (N.Y.: Macmillan, 1955), pp. 143–161 passim in the Mentor edition of 1957.]

The decade of the 1890's was one of sudden and swift cultural change. Whether or not there is validity in the superstition that the end of a century actually marks the end of an era in the affairs of men, the rule seems for once to apply. In this *fin de siècle* the forces which had shaped the Continental Nation found their first important literary expression, just as, a century earlier, the surge of nationalism that followed the Revolution had become a literary as well as a political and economic movement. . . .

The literary movement which rose to combat the romanticism [of the dying century] began to play a more vigorous role in the middle nineties than it had in earlier years. Finding its roots in the realism which had attempted to absorb and to portray the expansive forces in the new nation, it gained philosophical depth from the theories of the new evolutionary science, understanding of the human consciousness from the advances in the infant science of psychology, social significance from the makers of systems of society who followed the Industrial Revolution wherever it went, and encouragement from a more intimate knowledge of contemporary French, German, Russian, and other Continental European literatures.

The term "naturalism" is far too limited to describe the new intellectual and literary movements which American writers of the nineties began to share with these Europeans. It was the still fumbling attempt to discover adequate ways of giving expression to views of the universe and of human destiny which were everywhere supplanting the views of the Enlightenment. The Newtonian universe of limited forces and systematic organization, and the Lockean universe of the rational mind, were being hard pushed by concepts of a less logical and less self-determined Man. British and European thinkers like Darwin, Marx, and Freud were formulating theories of nature and human nature which would before long take the place in the general mind of those of Newton, Adam Smith, Rousseau, and Locke. American literature had before this shared with the literatures of other nations a passionate return to Nature; Wordsworth, Goethe, and Emerson were all naturalists in this sense. In the nineties the call for a return to Nature was again sounded, but agreed ideas about Nature were changed. A machine, ruthless and inhuman, had displaced the mountains and ivy-covered ruins upon which a poet could impose his ideas of moral order. Man was being pushed out of the center of the biological world, and his will was being taken from him by such theories as that of natural selection, economic determinism, or subconscious rather than conscious motivation. . . .

Howells, Mark Twain, and other realists

had, by 1890, succeeded in their demand for a fresh and unprejudiced examination of the facts of American life, and a more skeptical and scientific view of personality was appearing in the novels of James and the poems of Emily Dickinson. As literature undertook its normal task of giving expression to life, it was inevitably plunged into an era of experimentation and uncertainty. The literary movement of the nineties was an attempt on the part of a new group of American writers to describe life in general and life in America as it appeared to the dispassionate eye of the new science.

One important by-product of this movement was a close bond between American and Continental European writers and a loosening of the bond with England. Most of the influential popularizers of the new science, like Spencer and Huxley, were British and were early heard and read by impressionable Americans like Mark Twain, Bellamy, Howells, and Garland, but British writers of fiction and poetry like Hardy were not influenced as deeply or as soon by the new ideas as were such Continental writers as Dostoevski, Zola, or Hauptmann. Whereas Longfellow and Lowell read the romantic and idealistic poets and dramatists of France and Spain, Howells, James, and Mark Twain early discovered Turgenev and Tolstoi, Balzac and Zola, Marx and Nietzsche. In his essay on the experimental novel (1880), Zola presented the most germinal single idea to be absorbed by American writers of the *fin de siècle*: the belief that the exact methods of experimental physical science can and should be applied by the writer to the analysis of society and the individual. The essay itself was probably not read by many, if any, Americans, but Zola's attempts to apply his theory to his own fiction were well known to Norris, Crane, Dreiser, and many others. Through this new naturalism American literature was to become an important part of world literature in the next few decades. By supplying a core of fundamental ideas about God, man, society, and nature, it served to focus the second renaissance in American literature as transcendentalism and the romantic philosophy had served the first.

The American response to the ferment of the era was vigorous and practical. To a people accustomed to translating thought into action quickly, the only need was for a working formula once the philosophical doctrine had been made generally known. In William James they were offered a philosopher who laid the foundations of modern psychology by applying a practical methodology to the quest for truth; in Edward Bellamy, a sociologist who devised a system for controlling capitalism through social morality; and in Henry Adams, a historian who sought to explain the American tradition quite scientifically as a phase of cosmic evolution. These were only a few of the many thinkers in all fields of knowledge who appeared between 1885 and 1895 to resolve the dilemma of modern man into a working formula of social behavior. . . .

The philosophy of Pragmatism, as Henry's brother William James developed it, was a revolt against the rationalists. Frankly anti-intellectual, it urged a "looking away from first things, principles, 'categories,' supposed necessities; and of looking toward last things, fruits, consequences, facts." William James defined but did not invent it when he declared that "ideas (which themselves are but part of our experience) become true just in so far as they help us to get into satisfactory relationship with other parts of our experience." The open universe thus proposed gave a sense of release to the open mind; here was the ultimate statement of the right of the individual to push the frontiers of thought as far as they would go. . . .

It would carry this account too far afield to explore other applications of the empirical method to the problems of American living as science moved into scholarship, education, government, religion, and all other departments of American life. In literature it gave immense support to the methods and ideals of the realists at the same time that it presented the problem of human destiny in forms that classic theories of comedy and tragedy could not re-

solve. The times needed a literary man who could at least state the issues of the new order both in human and in cosmic terms.

The historian Henry Adams (1838–1918) inconspicuously offered himself in this role.

History in the hands of the major American historians had become largely a narrative art. Although they made use of documents, the Brahmin Prescott, Motley, Parkman, and Bancroft lacked the philosophical depth and scientific thoroughness of their German contemporaries. The essential difference between them and Adams was that they wished to tell a story in narrative perspective, he to solve a problem in civilization by analyzing it at one point in depth. His problem was to find out just what makes democracy work and to expose its flaws together with its virtues; his point of attack was the period of Jefferson and Madison which lay between that of his grandfather, John Quincy Adams, and that of his great-grandfather, the second President John Adams. . . .

Ostensibly a factual account of the administrations of Jefferson and Madison, it is actually an analysis, on the broadest possible scale, of the rise of a new form of human society to a position of power in the Western world and of the consequences of that shift of power. His speculations on the origins and consequence of democracy reach backward to the earliest colonial times and forward past his own day into the immediate future. . . .

He now became the philosopher of history, the teacher of teachers. From events he turned to causes, from record to meditation. . . . In his presidential address to the American Historical Association in 1894, he made his position clear: historians must renounce their past generalizations as inapplicable to the modern world; if they fail to create a working generalization of their own, they will be forced to accept that of the pessimists whom physical science was already spawning. While warning against the defeatism of contemporary thought, he was calling for what he could not himself produce, a formula by which man could retain his dominant place in the universe.

The human problems which concerned him most had already found expression in the anonymous novels, *Democracy* (1880) and *Esther* (1884), both of them about women whose intuitive curiosity led them to study the sources of human power, the one in the politics and society of democracy, the other in the realms of scientific and religious speculation and of art. When tragedy [in the suicide of his wife], came to him the next year, his reaction was first stoical silence, then a slow beginning of the long preparation for the two great privately printed works, *Mont-Saint-Michel and Chartres* (1904) and *The Education of Henry Adams* (1907), and a lesser work, *A Letter to American Teachers of History* (1910), which was to serve as a binder for the other two. Written in a tone of the elder teacher who had retired from active life and who was now privileged to meditate idly on problems which for him no longer demanded solution, this single work in three parts stated the basic problem of modern man in terms so deep and broad that a new symbolism had to be constructed. Adams laid the foundations for modern literature even more than for modern history by asking questions with which literature alone was competent to deal. He succeeded where others who were more openly committed to literary art, like Hamlin Garland and Frank Norris, were to fail; he translated the new naturalism into meaningful forms of disciplined art. . . .

The secret of Adams's final triumph as a man of letters lay in his ability to reconcile reality and myth by the use of symbols. He had reached the conclusion that "chaos was the law of nature; order the dream of man," but neither law nor dream could be rejected. Unwilling to accept the way of revealed religion, he could nevertheless admit that man had realized his dream of order most successfully in the system and ritual of an organized church. In their worship of the Virgin, the builders of the great cathedrals of Europe had achieved a unity of feeling and thought which the modern world had apparently lost. . . .

The *Education* was written for the young men who might perhaps learn a riper wisdom from the experience of this forgotten historian. If they were to discover the new law of history that would make it a science, they must understand their own time and extract from it a working generalization. All that the physicists themselves could offer was a machine, exhibited at the Chicago Fair in 1893, which could generate power forever, but which, if one were to believe Lord Kelvin, was merely extracting energy from matter in order to dissipate it. The Dynamo offered a kind of unity, but it was the unity of disintegration. Was this the law which the historian must learn to obey and to interpret? . . .

The comic and ironic manner of these twin essays in destiny is deceptive of their depth and wisdom, for the reading of life which they together present is that of tragedy rather than of comedy. All is presented and nothing resolved. When a work of art has taught man again the paradox of life on his earth and in his time without costing him his sense of the value in living, it has won a place among the epics and comedies and tragedies that comprise the literature of the world. Adams's masterwork did just this at the dawn of a new century and of a new era in man's experience. . . .

Whether or not Adams's final works constitute a single literary masterpiece may remain a matter for discussion. . . . But there can be little doubt that their structure of symbols stands at the beginning of the movement in thought and culture which gave force and form to the second American literary renaissance. Through his understanding and acceptance of the description of the universe presented by mathematical physics and evolutionary biology, Adams laid his foundations firmly in the new naturalism which was stirring the literatures of Europe to fresh creative effort. His skepticism helped him to develop what Eliot was later to call the "objective correlative" to his experience and through it to achieve expression for the modern man in art at least a generation before American writers in any numbers succeeded in following him. . . .

The literary movement of the nineties had, at the turn of the century, brought the American face to face with the age of science. As industry herded him from the farms where he was responsible to the weather and the earth into cities where he took his orders from steam and electric power, wheels and cogs, even the average unthinking man was forced to some sort of revaluation of his basic concepts and values.

Twentieth century American literature became a major force in the whole culture of Western Europe because the experience of this change was so much more dramatic in the violence of America's rapid growth than it was elsewhere. Europeans were finally to see in the writings of mid-twentieth century Americans the clear-cut and forceful expression of their own experiences and ideas; but in the 1890's the process of cultural change was not yet completed, the insights for its understanding not yet discovered, and the techniques for its expression in any of the forms of art not yet developed. The *fin de siècle* showed only a hint of what was to come; European literatures—particularly the French and the Russian—were still leading the way.

THE DYNAMO AND THE VIRGIN

[The preceding selection by Robert Spiller was placed first because of his introduction of Henry Adams (1838–1918) as the "literary man who could at least state the issues of the new order both in human and in cosmic terms." Here we offer from *The Education of Henry Adams* (New York: Modern Library, 1931) part of the chapter entitled "The Dynamo and the Virgin" (pages 379–390) in which Adams portrays himself at one of his moments of discovery.

The scene is laid at the Paris Exposition of 1900 where he was fascinated by the new sources of energy, the dynamo and that new discovery, radium. His friend Samuel Langley (1834–1906), the pioneer in aviation, served as interpreter. Another friend, the sculptor Homer St. Gaudens (1848–1907), took him to see the Gothic cathedral at Amiens. Out of these and like experiences Adams drew the inspiration for his study of forces in history.]

Until the Great Exposition of 1900 closed its doors in November, Adams haunted it, aching to absorb knowledge, and helpless to find it. He would have liked to know how much of it could have been grasped by the best-informed man in the world. While he was thus meditating chaos, Langley came by, and showed it to him. At Langley's behest, the Exhibition dropped its superfluous rags and stripped itself to the skin, for Langley knew what to study, and why, and how; while Adams might as well have stood outside in the night, staring at the Milky Way. . . .

Langley, with the ease of a great master of experiment, threw out of the field every exhibit that did not reveal a new application of force, and naturally threw out, to begin with, almost the whole art exhibit. Equally, he ignored almost the whole industrial exhibit. He led his pupil directly to the forces. His chief interest was in new motors to make his airship feasible, and he taught Adams the astonishing complexities of the new Daimler motor, and of the automobile, which, since 1893, had become a nightmare at a hundred kilometers an hour, almost as destructive as the electric tram which was only ten years older; and threatening to become as terrible as the locomotive steam-engine itself, which was almost exactly Adams's own age.

Then he showed his scholar the great hall of dynamos, and explained how little he knew about electricity or force of any kind, even of his own special sun, which spouted heat in inconceivable volume, but which, as far as he knew, might spout less or more, at any time, for all the certainty he felt in it. . . .

Between the dynamo in the gallery of machines and the engine-house outside, the break of continuity amounted to abysmal fracture for a historian's objects. No more relation could he discover between the steam and the electric current than between the Cross and the cathedral. The forces were interchangeable if not reversible, but he could see only an absolute *fiat* in electricity as in faith. Langley could not help him. Indeed, Langley seemed to be worried by the same trouble, for he constantly repeated that the new forces were anarchical, and specially that he was not responsible for the new rays, that were little short of parricidal in their wicked spirit toward science. His own rays, with which he had doubled the solar spectrum, were altogether harmless and beneficent; but Radium denied its God—or, what was to Langley the same thing, denied the truths of his Science. The force was wholly new. . . .

X-rays had played no part whatever in man's consciousness, and the atom itself had figured only as a fiction of thought. In these seven years man had translated himself into a new universe which had no common scale of measurement with the old. He had entered a supersensual world, in which he could measure nothing except by chance collisions of movements imperceptible to his senses, perhaps even imperceptible to his instruments, but perceptible to each other, and so to some known ray at the end of the scale. Langley seemed prepared for anything, even for an indeterminable number of universes interfused—physics stark mad in metaphysics.

Historians undertake to arrange sequences, —called stories, or histories—assuming in silence a relation of cause and effect. . . . Adams, for one, had toiled in vain to find out what [this] meant. He had even published a dozen volumes of American history for no other purpose than to satisfy himself whether, by the severest process of stating, with the least possible comment, such facts as seemed sure, in such order as seemed rigorously consequent, he could fix for a familiar moment a necessary sequence of human movement. . . . Satisfied that the sequence of men led to nothing and that the sequence of their society could lead no further, while the mere sequence of time was artificial, and the sequence of thought was chaos, he turned at last to the sequence of force; and thus it happened that, after ten years' pursuit, he found himself lying in the Gallery of Machines at the Great Exposition of 1900, his historical neck broken by the sudden irruption of forces totally new. . . . The rays that Langley disowned, as well as those which he fathered, were occult, supersensual, irrational; they were a revelation of mysterious energy like that of the Cross; they were what, in terms of mediæval science, were called immediate modes of the divine substance.

The historian was thus reduced to his last resources. Clearly if he was bound to reduce all these forces to a common value, this common value could have no measure but that of their attraction on his own mind. He must treat them as they had been felt; as convertible, reversible, interchangeable attractions on thought. He made up his mind to venture it; he would risk translating rays into faith. Such a reversible process would vastly amuse a chemist, but the chemist could not deny that he, or some of his fellow physicists, could feel the force of both. When Adams was a boy in Boston, the best chemist in the place had probably never heard of Venus except by way of scandal; or of the Virgin except as idolatry; neither had he heard of dynamos or automobiles or radium; yet his mind was ready to feel the force of all, though the rays were unborn and the women were dead. . . . The force of the Virgin was still felt at Lourdes, and seemed to be as potent as X-rays; but in America neither Venus nor Virgin ever had value as force—at most as sentiment. No American had ever been truly afraid of either.

This problem in dynamics gravely perplexed an American historian. The Woman had once been supreme; in France she still seemed potent, not merely as a sentiment, but as a force. Why was she unknown in America? For evidently America was ashamed of her, and she was ashamed of herself, otherwise they would not have strewn fig-leaves so profusely all over her. When she was a true force, she was ignorant of fig-leaves, but the monthly-magazine-made American female had not a feature that would have been recognized by Adam. The trait was notorious, and often humorous, but any one brought up among Puritans knew that sex was sin. In any previous age, sex was strength. Neither art nor beauty was needed. Every one, even among Puritans, knew that neither Diana of the Ephesians nor any of the Oriental goddesses was worshipped for her beauty. She was goddess because of her force; she was the animated dynamo; she was reproduction—the greatest and most mysterious of all energies; all she needed was to be fecund. . . .

Before this historical chasm, a mind like that of Adams felt itself helpless; he turned from the Virgin to the Dynamo as though he were a Branly coherer. On one side, at the Louvre and at Chartres, as he knew by the record of work actually done and still before his eyes, was the highest energy ever known to man, the creator of four-fifths of his noblest art, exercising vastly more attraction over the human mind than all the steam-engines and dynamos ever dreamed of; and yet this energy was unknown to the American mind. An American Virgin would never dare command; an American Venus would never dare exist. . . .

American art, like the American language and American education, was as far as possible sexless. Society regarded this victory over sex as its greatest triumph. . . .

Vaguely seeking a clue, he wandered through the art exhibit, and, in his stroll, stopped almost every day before St. Gaudens's General Sherman, which had been given the central post of honor. St. Gaudens himself was in Paris, putting on the work his usual interminable last touches, and listening to the usual contradictory suggestions of brother sculptors. Of all the American artists who gave to American art whatever life it breathed in the seventies, St. Gaudens was perhaps the most sympathetic, but certainly the most inarticulate. . . .

Once St. Gaudens took him down to Amiens, with a party of Frenchmen, to see the cathedral. Not until they found themselves actually studying the sculpture of the western portal, did it dawn on Adams's mind that, for his purposes, St. Gaudens on that spot had more interest to him than the cathedral itself. Great men before great monuments express great truths, provided they are not taken too solemnly. Adams never tired of quoting the supreme phrase of his idol Gibbon, before the Gothic cathedrals: "I darted a contemptuous look on the stately monuments of superstition." Even in the footnotes of his history, Gibbon had never inserted a bit of humor more human than this. . . .

St. Gaudens liked the stately monuments . . . he loved their dignity; their unity; their scale; their lines; their lights and shadows; their decorative sculpture; but he was even less conscious than they of the force that created it all —the Virgin, the Woman—by whose genius "the stately monuments of superstition" were built, through which she was expressed. . . . The art remained, but the energy was lost even upon the artist. . . . St. Gaudens's art was starved from birth, and Adams's instinct was blighted from babyhood. Each had but half of a nature, and when they came together before the Virgin of Amiens they ought both to have felt in her the force that made them one; but it was not so. To Adams she became more than ever a channel of force; to St. Gaudens she remained as before a channel of taste.

For a symbol of power, St. Gaudens instinctively preferred the horse, as was plain in his horse and Victory of the Sherman monument. Doubtless Sherman also felt it so. The attitude was so American that, for at least forty years, Adams had never realized that any other could be in sound taste. How many years had he taken to admit a notion of what Michael Angelo and Rubens were driving at? He could not say; but he knew that only since 1895 had he begun to feel the Virgin or Venus as force. . . . The idea died out long ago in the German and English stock. St. Gaudens at Amiens was hardly less sensitive to the force of the female energy than Matthew Arnold at the Grande Chartreuse. Neither of them felt goddesses as power—only as reflected emotion, human expression, beauty, purity, taste, scarcely even as sympathy. They felt a railway train as power; yet they, and all other artists, constantly complained that the power embodied in a railway train could never be embodied in art. All the steam in the world could not, like the Virgin, build Chartres.

Yet in mechanics, whatever the mechanicians might think, both energies acted as interchangeable forces on man, and by action on man all known force may be measured. Indeed, few men of science measured force in any other way. After once admitting that a straight line was the shortest distance between two points, no serious mathematician cared to deny anything that suited his convenience, and rejected no symbol, unproved or unprovable, that helped him to accomplish work. The symbol was force, as a compass-needle or a triangle was force, as the mechanist might prove by losing it, and nothing could be gained by ignoring their value. Symbol or energy, the Virgin had acted as the greatest force the Western world ever felt, and had drawn man's activities to herself more strongly than any other power, natural or supernatural, had ever done; the historian's business was to follow the track of the energy; to find where it came from and where it went to; its complex source and shifting channels; its values, equivalents, conversions. It could scarcely be more complex than radium; it could hardly be deflected, diverted, polarized, absorbed more perplexingly than other radiant matter. Adams knew nothing about any of them, but as a mathematical problem of influence on human progress, though all were occult, all reacted on his mind, and he rather inclined to think the Virgin easiest to handle.

It was on this note that Adams began the search which was to lead through cathedrals and mathematical formulas into a seeming blind alley. But of one thing—and perhaps only one—he was convinced: history, to have meaning, must be fused with art, science, and mathematical physics. At the last the skeptical Bostonian bowed his proud head, humbled and despairing, before the Virgin of Chartres, asking if the only meaning of human existence lies in faith.

"FORCES MUST ACT"

But if, in the prodigiously rapid vibration of its last phases, Thought should continue to act as the universal solvent which it is, and should reduce the forces of the molecule, the atom, and the electron to that costless servitude to which it has reduced the old elements of earth and air, fire and water; if man should continue to set free the infinite forces of nature, and attain the control of cosmic forces on a cosmic scale, the consequences may be as surprising as the change of water to vapor, of the worm to the butterfly, of radium to electrons. At a given volume and velocity, the forces that are concentrated on his head must act.

—Henry Adams, "The Rule of Phase Applied to History,"
in *The Tendency of History* (N.Y.: Macmillan, 1928),
p. 173

"FORM FOLLOWS FUNCTION"

[Louis Henri Sullivan (1856–1924), born of Irish, French, and German stock, was an architect in Chicago, the original home of the skyscraper, a form in which he was to excel. At the time American architects, with few exceptions, were bound by the European cultivated tradition—as witness the elaborate chateaux of millionaires' row on New York's Fifth Avenue. Sullivan's cleansing influence on the new age of architecture was profound, and it was his pupil, Frank Lloyd Wright, who was to become the doyen of modernists. Sullivan saw his career as exemplifying the unfolding of his central idea—Form follows Function—and wrote of it in his *Autobiography of an Idea* (1924). The following excerpts are taken from the Dover Publications, Inc., reprint of 1956, passim, and they refer to the time when Sullivan had, at the age of twenty-five, attained some reputation and entered a lucrative partnership. It should be recognized that Sullivan was applying to architecture the same principles that American mechanics were applying to machinery and that Frederick W. Taylor was applying to production.]

Now Louis felt he had arrived at a point where he had a foothold, where he could make a *beginning* in the open world. Having come into its responsibilities, he would face it boldly. He could now, undisturbed, start on the course of practical experimentation he long had in mind, which was to make an architecture that fitted its functions—a realistic architecture based on well defined utilitarian needs—that all practical demands of utility should be paramount as basis of planning and design; that no architectural dictum, or tradition, or superstition, or habit, should stand in the way. He would brush them all aside, regardless of commentators. For his view, his conviction was this: That the architectural art to be of contemporary immediate value must be *plastic*; all senseless conventional rigidity must be taken out of it; it must intelligently serve—it must not suppress. In this wise the forms under his hand would grow naturally out of the needs and express them frankly, and freshly. This

meant in his courageous mind that he would put to the test a formula he had evolved, through long contemplation of living things, namely that *form follows function*, which would mean, in practice, that architecture might again become a living art, if this formula were but adhered to.

The building business was again under full swing, and a series of important mercantile structures came into the office, each one of which he treated experimentally, feeling his way toward a basic process, a grammar of his own. The immediate problem was increased daylight, the maximum of daylight. This led him to use slender piers, tending toward a masonry and iron combination, the beginnings of a vertical system. This method upset all precedent, and led Louis's contemporaries to regard him as an iconoclast, a revolutionary, which was true enough—yet into the work was slowly infiltrated a corresponding system of artistic expression, which appeared in these structures as novel and to some repellent, in its total disregard of accepted notions. But to all objections Louis turned a deaf ear. If a thousand proclaimed him wrong, the thousand could not change his course. As buildings varying in character came under his hand, he extended to them his system of form and function, and as he did so his conviction increased that architectural manipulation, as a homely art or a fine art must be rendered completely plastic to the mind and the hand of the designer; that materials and forms must yield to the mastery of his imagination and his will; through this alone could modern conditions be met and faithfully expressed. This meant the casting aside of all pedantry, of all the artificial teachings of the schools, of the thoughtless acceptance of inane traditions, of puerile habits of uninquiring minds; that all this mess, devoid of a center of gravity of thought, and vacant of sympathy and understanding, must be superseded by a sane philosophy of a living architecture, good for all time, founded on the only possible foundation—Man and his powers. Such philosophy Louis had already developed in broad outline in the course of his many dissatisfactions and contemplations. He wished now to test it out in the broad daylight of action, and to perfect its form and content. This philosophy developed will be set forth in these closing chapters.

It is not to be supposed that Louis arrived directly at results as though by magic. Quite the contrary, he arrived slowly though boldly through the years, by means of incessant thought, self correction, hard work and dogged perseverance. For it was his fascinating task to build up a system of technique, a mastery of technique. And such a system could scarcely be expected to reach its fullness of development, short of maturity, assuming it would reach its fullness then, or could ever reach it; for the world of expression is limitless; the theory so deep in idea, so rich in content, as to preclude any ending of its beneficent, all-inclusive power. And we may here recall Monsieur Clopet, the book of descriptive geometry that went into the waste basket, and the thunderclap admonition: "Our demonstrations shall be such as to admit of no exception." . . .

So he kept on with his innocent studies, becoming more and more enamoured of the sciences, particularly those dealing with forms of life and the aspects of life's urging, called functions. And amid the immense number and variety of living forms, he noted that invariably the form expressed the function, as, for instance, the oak tree expressed the function oak, the pine tree the function pine, and so on through the amazing series. And, inquiring more deeply, he discovered that in truth it was not simply a matter of form expressing function, but the vital idea was this: That the function *created* or organized its form. Discernment of this idea threw a vast light upon all things within the universe, and condensed with astounding impressiveness upon mankind, upon all civilizations, all institutions, every form and aspect of society, every mass-thought and mass-result, every individual thought and individual result. Hence, Louis began to regard all functions in nature as powers, manifestations of the all-power of Life, and thus man's power came into direct relationship with all other powers. The application of the idea to the Architectural art was manifest enough, namely, that the function of a building must predetermine and organize its form. But it was the application to man's thought and deeds; to his inherent powers and the results of the application of these powers, mental, moral, physical, that thrilled Louis to the depths as he realized that, as one stumbling upon a treasure, he has found that of which he had dreamed in Paris, and had promised himself to discover,—a universal law admitting of no exception in any phase or application whatsoever.

Thus Louis believed he had found the open sesame, and that his industry would do the rest. But this innocent and credulous young person was not yet cynical in inquiry; he was too much of an enthusiastic boy to suspect that within the social organism were mask-forms, counterfeit forms, forms with protective coloration, forms invisible except to those in the know. Surely, he was an innocent with his heart wrapped up in the arts, in the philosophies, in the religions, in the beatitudes of nature's loveliness, in his search for the reality of man, in his profound faith in the beneficence of power. So he lived in his world, which, to be sure, was a very active world indeed. And yet, withal, he had a marked ability to interpret the physiognomy of things, to read character, to enter into personalities. He knew a dishonest man as readily as he knew a snake if he came in contact with him. *Per contra* he knew an honest man—and there were many. What delighted him was to observe the ins and outs of personality—wherein he was especially sensitive and keen to the slightest rhythms.

ART AND NON-ART

[The individualism of the Progressive Era produced not only rebels in politics and literature, but rebels in art. The modern period of American art is frequently dated from 1908 when Robert Henri withdrew his paintings from exhibition at the National Academy of Design and organized an exhibition for the works of such experimenters as Glackens, Luks, and Shinn. This was the origin of the "Ash Can School," so called because its members deliberately selected unconventional subjects to which the Gilded Age had preferred to close its eyes. Then in 1913 came the Armory Show, which introduced the art-viewing public to the contemporary painting and sculpture of Europe as well as America. The shock was profound, and made it clear that the artist no longer created for the masses, but for a coterie or perhaps only for himself. The artistic world faced a long period of experimentation and—like the political and economic worlds—still does. In the social and economic turmoil of the turn of the century, and soon in the clash and fall of empires and the march of new ideologies, the artist saw the justification of his alienation from the masses. Oliver W. Larkin, Professor of Art at Smith College, describes this alienation and its reasons in *Art and Life in America* (N.Y.: Rinehart, 1949), pp. 347–353.]

This sense of alienation from the world's people was to permeate the modern effort. The very terms the artists and their spokesmen used—terms like "plastic equivalent" and "significant form"—drove artist and layman further apart. A multitude of "isms" developed as numerous branches and shoots put forth from the trunk of this modern tree, sect warred upon sect, and manifestoes became wordy skirmishes on the battleground of aesthetic theories.

Half a century later one can see a common effort and a pervasive character in all this pioneering. In peculiarly bleak circumstances the painter and architect, the sculptor and stage designer can be seen struggling to regain lost ground and to re-establish what had always been their function in the world. Since time began, the artist's emotions have run deeper than the average, his imagination has ranged further, his eye has seen more clearly, his brain and hand have been capable of perceiving and of setting forth relationships of which most men were oblivious. His special act has been the making of forms through which others shared with him the meaning of experiences common to all. Such was Giotto, summing up all that religious men once believed, and Goya making the *Disasters of War* to chastise men for being barbarians; such was Daumier, going blind in his sixties over the lithographic stones which bore his passionate belief in justice and the essential decency of the small citizen.

In the mind of the true artist there has been a tension when the traditional and familiar forms of art, which have been socially shaped and are persistent, meet the changing experiences of the present moment. From this tension he creates a synthesis; he must make new forms because old ones are inadequate for new content. To ask that he do anything less is to ask that he cease to be an artist. . . .

The fruitful continuity between art and the normal experience of mankind had broken down, though philosophers differed on when, how, and why. Henry Adams concluded it had happened when the Virgin ceased to be a power and became a picture; Tolstoy said it was when the artist forgot his fraternity with suffering men; Veblen, when art became a showy index of superfluous wealth.

Faced with the dislocation between art and non-art, a man could move into the more comfortable past and stay there. He could rebuild the Parthenon as the First National Bank, place a mortarboard on Athena's head and call her the Spirit of Education, or attempt nothing less than the rehabilitation of the artist as a maker of forms of and for his time. In the latter case he would claim certain drastic freedoms, personal and artistic, in the teeth of convention and of visual habit.

First of all, the modern would reject the so-called "imitation of nature." For roughly five hundred years artists had objectified their vision in forms which corresponded more or less with what every man saw about him. The worst of them had been content with painted equivalents of this "nature"; the best of them sought something more, knowing that no artist can literally imitate nature even if he wishes, and that nature and art may overlap but never coincide. When the modern compared Rembrandt, Poussin, and Veronese with the "naturalism" of his own day, he found in the latter a transcription of observed fact into which the artist had put no thought, feeling, or personal conviction, and from which the layman derived only the lazy pleasures of recognition.

Once more the balance would have to shift toward those elements in a work of art which result directly from the play of the artist's intellect, his emotions, his human sympathies upon his visual material. This revolution would bring gain and loss; it would restore to the artist his reason for being but it would make shapes and colors so new and unfamiliar as to provide small ground for mutual understanding between artist and public. The consequent estrangement could be charged to modern society itself, or it could be rationalized by the notion that art by its nature can never appeal to the many. The artist could be socially hopeful though independent or he could deny his responsibility to any but himself.

If Van Gogh and Gauguin, Cézanne, Seurat, and Renoir were the patron saints of the moderns it was because each of them managed to be in his own way a fully creative artist. None of them was content with a passive reflection of the external world; each of them used the impressionist freedoms to gain still greater freedoms. . . .

The modern movement, however, was not simply a pendulum swing from the conventional to the personal, from the descriptive to the expressive; its history cannot be told as a series of individual rebellions. Those rebellions and their theoretical justifications followed logically enough one from another. But art like other forms of living does not develop in a vacuum; in the first decade and a half of the new century its inconsistencies were no more blatant than those of Europe as a whole. In that Europe reformers and scientists promised a better world, and belligerent nationalisms threatened to destroy it. Alfred Dreyfus made racial hatred a world issue and British policemen wrestled with suffragettes while the French occupied Morocco and the Italians fought the Turks over Tripoli. Briand broke the French railway strike; Nicolle announced that typhus could be controlled; and Norman Angell wrote *The Great Illusion*.

In such a world the artist, unless a complete anarchist, asked himself how his forms could be used for more humane living and for enlightened social purposes. The problem of the designed community, for instance, absorbed Englishmen and Continentals; the garden cities of the former remained dreams unless a wealthy individual was on hand to build them; the German liberals faced the fact that only the municipality or the state could instrument such planning. Just as the painters had to free themselves from the bond of literal imitation, so the designers and craftsmen had to break with the historic "styles." John Ruskin and William Morris had taught them that art's function is

WALL PAPER. "DAISY". REPRINTED FROM WOODBLOCKS BY WILLIAM MORRIS (1834-1896)

New York Public Library Picture Collection

to serve man, but since the nineties it had been clear that no revival of the guild system could provide an honest three-dimensional environment for more than a few men, nor could the handmade article defy the machine-turned piece. . . .

The new leaven was soon at work through the whole complacent mass in London, Paris, Berlin, Vienna, Rome, and Moscow, and new content burst old forms in every one of the arts. Resistance to change came from two sources: from the vested interests of the academies and schools, and from the disinclination of the vast public to new ways of seeing. The

needs of defense and offense drew rebellious individuals into groups which formed, dissolved, and re-formed in the twenty years before the first World War; and as the painters, architects, writers, and musicians perceived their common aims, their exchange of ideas became international.

The modernists now made no concessions to their opponents, and in 1914 Clive Bell published his book *Art*. . . . Discarding the art of the Renaissance and most of what intervened between it and postimpressionism, Bell asked: "What quality is common to Sta. Sophia and the windows at Chartres, Mexican sculpture, a Persian bowl, Chinese carpets, Giotto's frescoes at Padua, and the masterpieces of Poussin, Piero della Francesca, and Cézanne?" His answer was "Significant Form"—the relations of lines and colors which stir our aesthetic emotions when those emotions are free from all associations. "The representative element in a work of art may or may not be harmful; always it is irrelevant. For, to appreciate a work of art we need bring with us nothing from life, no knowledge of its ideas and affairs, no familiarity with its emotions. Art transports us from the world of man's activity to a world of aesthetic exaltation. . . . It is a world with emotions of its own."

At Florence in 1913 the futurist Soffici spoke in the same vein, declaring that pure painting derives from the study of forms alone, is regulated by its own laws, and exists for its own sake. In Paris in 1913 Apollinaire published *The Cubist Painters: Aesthetic Meditations*, in which he declared that the world was moving toward a new and a pure art which would stand, with respect to painting, as music stands to literature.

And finally, in 1914 came the English translation of Kandinsky's *Art of Spiritual Harmony*. In his own painted improvisations this expressionist had externalized his "inner need" in absolute patterns. Now he explained that the psychic and spiritual vibration of color has nothing to do with the colors we see with our eyes. All outer supports having failed mankind

—religious dogma, scientific laws, and moral precepts—man turns in upon himself; Maeterlinck and Debussy, Picasso and Matisse move toward the nonmaterial, the abstract, raising a spiritual pyramid which shall reach toward heaven.

The base of the pyramid had now been laid, and the modern theory of form and content, art and society, present and past, would not henceforth be greatly changed. The nations went to war, and in the brutality and the illogic of the conflict more than one modern saw proof of the arguments by which he had rationalized his alienation from the common aims and his contempt for man in the mass.

THE REFORMERS CALL ON DARWIN

Few of the progressives showed any desire for an entirely new system of thinking. They too were sons of the nineteenth century, entranced by science, confirmed Darwinians. Like the conservatives, and quite as unconsciously, they adapted to their own needs ideological possibilities already at hand.

Conservative Darwinism itself suggested the reform reply. After all, Conservative Darwinism was supposedly Darwinism, and the heart of the Darwinian doctrine was continuous evolution in relation to the environment. Conservative Darwinians had recognized evolution up to the present, and then, for all practical purposes, they had called a halt. In the name of environmentalism, they advocated ideas which they called timeless and which were therefore independent of any environment, past or present. Accepting a doctrine that inevitably suggested a relationship between ideas and material things, the Conservative Darwinians nevertheless talked as if truth were absolute.

Each of these phases of Conservative Darwinism pointed to its own obvious question. Why not insist on thoroughgoing evolution and argue that contemporary institutions could and should change rapidly? Why not call for thoroughgoing evolution and argue that contemporary institutions could and should change rapidly? Why not call for thoroughgoing environmentalism and explain away any apparent superiority of a Rockefeller or an Anglo-Saxon by arguing that they had enjoyed favorable environments? Why not consider Conservative Darwinism itself nothing more than an ideology that had developed in an environment of political bosses and trust magnates in order to justify that environment? Why not, in short, work out a Reform Darwinism that would dissolve away conservatism's steel chain of ideas while leaving Darwinism itself intact? Why not—if you were a Darwinian who disliked Conservative Darwinism, if you wanted to replace dreary inevitabilities with a philosophy of flux that justified experiment and change? The attraction of Reform Darwinism was the greater because it could use all the cosmetics of science by which Conservative Darwinism made itself so alluring. As a matter of fact, Reform Darwinism could claim to be, and was claimed to be, a good deal more scientific than Conservative Darwinism because it related more things more continuously to environment.

—Eric Goldman, *Rendezvous with Destiny*, (N.Y.: Knopf, 1952), Vintage edition of 1956, pp. 72–73.

PRAGMATISM AND AMERICAN CHARACTER

[As early as 1867 William T. Harris had founded his *Journal of Speculative Philosophy* and was gathering around him the St. Louis School as agents of protest. In Cambridge, Chauncey Wright and Charles S. Peirce were beating out the ideas which (perhaps in misunderstood and misapplied form) were to give rise to pragmatism. One of their associates was William James (1842–1910), brother of the novelist Henry James and lifelong Harvard professor, first as biologist, then psychologist, and finally as philosopher. Unlike his brother, he reveled in the challenge of raw, tough-minded America and felt that despite its plutocratic abuses (the worship of "the bitch goddess SUCCESS"), it held more promise for the human race than venal and effete Europe. He believed that man is by instinct a fighting animal, but he sought to utilize this pugnacity in socially useful ways by finding in concerted constructive efforts a "moral equivalent of war." However much pragmatism may have fallen short of being a philosophical system, it consisted so well with American traditional (and democratic) methods of arriving at conclusions that it weakened many of the tenets of the Gilded Age and introduced the more typically American Progressive Era. The following is taken from Henry Steele Commager, *The American Mind* (Yale University Press, 1950), pp. 93–98.]

Mark Twain once observed that he had never known a real seeker after truth: sooner or later everyone engaged in that search found what he was looking for and gave up the quest. It was a pity that he did not know William James. For James believed, passionately, that truth was not something that was found, once and for all, but was forever in the making, that it was not single and absolute but plural and contingent. It was not only that he was tolerant and hospitable to a degree heretofore unknown in modern philosophy but that tolerance and hospitality were an essential ingredient in his philosophical system. Philosophy had for him, as his colleague and critic, Santayana, observed, "a Polish constitution; so long as a single vote was cast against the majority, nothing could pass. . . . It would have depressed him," he added, "if he had had to confess that any important question was finally settled."

This was an exaggeration. One important question was settled, with irrevocable finality: the question of the relative validity of dogma and skepticism. For, almost from the beginning, James confronted all dogma with skepticism and made skepticism itself a dogma. He turned his countenance from all absolutes, causes, finalities, fixed principles, abstractions, and rigidities, and embraced instead pluralism, uncertainty, practicality, common sense, adventure, and flexibility. To the philosophy of first causes he opposed one of consequences; to the philosophy of ultimates he opposed one of expediency; to the philosophy of determinism he opposed one of free will. To the concept that truth could be found either by the exercise of pure reason or by the scientific observation of nature, he opposed the concept that truth was not in fact to be found but to be made, that it was not something that was inert and static but something that happened to an idea or a course of conduct:

> The truth of an idea is not a stagnant property inherent in it. Truth *happens* to an idea. It *becomes* true, is *made* true by events: its verity *is* in fact an event, a process: the process namely of its verifying itself, its veri-*fication*. Its validity is the process of its valid-*ation*. . . . The true is the name of whatever proves itself to be good in the way of belief, and good, too, for definite assignable reasons.

To this attitude toward truth, James applied first the name "practicalism" and then pragmatism. Pragmatism was not in itself a philosophy but a philosophical method; to Giovanni Papini's observation that it was a method of doing without a philosophy, James made no objection, for he was willing enough to dispense with most of the formal philosophies of the past in so far as they required adherence to some established orthodoxy. As he could not reconcile the conflicting monisms of the reigning philosophical systems, he submitted pragmatism as "a method of settling metaphysical disputes that might otherwise be interminable." Confronted by questions which, for the most part, merely raised other and more profound questions, James asked instead what the practical consequences of any answer would be and accepted or rejected that answer as its consequences were profitable or unprofitable, useful or useless, good or bad. . . . In short, "the true is only the expedient in the way of our thinking, just as 'the right' is only the expedient in the way of our behaving."

Pragmatism was a philosophy of expedience. It put ideas to work and judged them by their results. It accepted "any idea upon which we can ride" as "true instrumentally," and instrumentalism came to be its preferred name. It rejected theories and abstractions and established the single standard of workability. It was as practical as the patent office—or the Declaration of Independence. Its expediency was individual; it came, increasingly, to be social, to require that men work together to establish the truth of their hopes.

It was a democratic philosophy, held every man a philosopher, gave every man a vote, and counted the votes of the simple and the humble equal to those of the learned and the proud. It took its truths where it found them, sometimes in the unlikeliest places. It made philosophy a servant, not a master, an instrument, not an end. It assumed that men could direct their spiritual as they did their political destinies; it overthrew the tyranny of philosophical authoritarianism and substituted the democracy of popular representation.

It was an individualistic philosophy. It assigned to each individual, as it were, a leading role in the drama of salvation, gave him a share and a responsibility in making what he held good come true. It denied him the consolation of unconditional reliance on God or on Nature and decreed that he succeed or fail through his own efforts. It emphasized his uniqueness rather than his conformity, and it encouraged him to put his own faith to the test. It was voluntaristic and raised its armies by enlistment, not by conscription. It was impatient with authority—the authority of history or science or theology—and preferred the teachings of experience to the dictates of logic. It stood for home rule in the realm of ideas. It celebrated the perceptions of the average man rather than the subtleties of metaphysicians, for "it is only the minds debauched of learning," said James, "who have ever suspected common sense of not being absolutely true."

It was a humane and optimistic philosophy. It subscribed readily enough to the doctrine of progress, but made that doctrine contingent rather than absolute—contingent upon the contributions which men were willing to risk for its realization. It held that man's fate was not determined by mechanical powers but by man himself, and it insisted that man could create as well as succumb to environment. It accepted evolution, but emphasized its flexibility and submitted that the mind and spirit of man was as much a part of the evolutionary process as his body. It assured to every man the dignity of active participation in the drama of the cosmos. Because it taught that men held the future in their own hands, it was drenched with optimism.

It was an adventurous philosophy. It asserted that truth was prospective as well as retrospective. Rejecting any guarantee of ultimate salvation, it gambled instead on the virtue, the intelligence, and the courage of men. It was willing to try any hypothesis and would not discriminate against novelty, originality, or even eccentricity. It assumed that "the universe is still pursuing its adventures" and joined gaily in the pursuit. It repudiated any system of moral security and voted instead for free enterprise in the moral realm. The challenge was familiar:

> Suppose that the world's author put the case to you before creation, saying: "I am going to make a world not certain to be saved, a world the perfection of which shall be conditional merely, the condition being that each several agent does its own level best. I offer you the chance of taking part in such a world. Its safety, you see, is unwarranted. It is a real adventure, with real danger, yet it may win through. It is a social scheme of cooperative work genuinely to be done. Will you join the procession? Will you trust yourself and trust the other agents enough to face the risk?"

That there was a risk was clear enough to James, for men might guess wrong, or the attempt might fail. Yet it was the effort, the fight, that exhilarated him. Nor did he, in fact, ever dream though right were worsted wrong would triumph; he held we fall to rise, are baffled to fight better, sleep to wake.

That these qualities in pragmatism reflected qualities in the American character has been too often remarked to justify elaboration. Practical, democratic, individualistic, opportunistic, spontaneous, hopeful, pragmatism was wonderfully adapted to the temperament of the average American. It cleared away the jungle of theology and metaphysics and deterministic science and allowed the warm sun of common sense to quicken the American spirit as the pioneer cleared the forests and the underbrush and allowed the sun to quicken the soil of the American West. In a sense, the whole of American experience had prepared for it and now seemed to validate and justify it. For America had been a gamble that had paid off, an experiment that had succeeded; it had enlisted the average man, had required him to play his part in a common enterprise, and had rewarded his courage and audacity with boundless generosity. In practice, Americans had always been instrumentalists. They

had assumed that their faiths were true and had so acted as to make them true. They had assumed the worth of democracy, of equality, of freedom, assessed the practical consequences of these assumptions, and committed themselves to their realization. When they had pledged their lives, their fortunes, and their sacred honor to the triumph of the doctrines of the Declaration, they had acted pragmatically. Every American knew that the world in which he lived was, in part, of his own making, that he had bent Nature to his will and won Providence over to his side, and the sublimation of this long experience to a philosophical theory could not startle him. Pragmatism's willingness to break with the past, reject traditional habits, try new methods, put beliefs to a vote, make a future to order, excited not only sympathy but a feeling of familiarity. No wonder that, despite the broadsides of more formidable philosophers, pragmatism caught on until it came to be almost the official philosophy of America. To Americans it seemed the common sense of the matter, and the average American rejoiced that the logicians and metaphysicians who had long plagued him were at last confounded.

Not only was pragmatism sympathetic to the American character, its implications and conclusions were no less harmonious with the most authentic American thought. For though James rejected the sentimentality and the monism of the Transcendentalists and accepted evolution, he was nevertheless closer to Emerson and the Transcendentalists than he ever admitted. "Why should we not also enjoy an original relation to the universe?" Emerson had asked, and James had but echoed the question. The methods of the two philosophies—if either can be called that—were dramatically different, but the inspiration and the consequences were much the same. Both expressed the optimism and the practical idealism of the American character; both were individualistic and democratic. The Transcendentalists, even with their faith in a priori truths, had the sporting instinct; they took a chance that the heart knew better than the head, they gambled on what their intuitions told them was good, even against the findings of the laboratory, and labored heroically to make that good come true. Nor, on the other hand, was pragmatism without its intuitive elements. James, who had been trained in the laboratory, revered the factual, the concrete, statistical evidence and sensational proof, but his faith in an open universe, in a pluralistic cosmos, in the notion that truth could be tested by its consequences, was no less an assumption than the faith of the Transcendentalists that their intuitions would lead them to God was an assumption. By any pragmatic test, too, these different ways of thinking had much in common, for they led to much the same consequences—to a tender interest in the underprivileged, a deep respect for the integrity of the individual, a fighting confidence in the possibility of reform. Between Thoreau's opposition to the Mexican and James's to the Philippine War there was not much to choose, nor in their open-mindedness toward social and political experiments. The comparison must not be pressed too far. Pragmatism expressed the individualism of the pioneer who felled the forests of Indiana rather than of the visionaries who ploughed the fields of Brook Farm; it was closer to the opportunism of the Progressive movement than to the fanaticism of the abolitionist crusade.

WHAT PRAGMATISM MEANS

[William James graphically explained the meaning of his philosophy in *Pragmatism* (London: Longmans, Green, 1907), pp. 43–81, from which the following excerpts are taken.]

Some years ago, being with a camping party in the mountains, I returned from a solitary ramble to find every one engaged in a ferocious metaphysical dispute. The *corpus* of the dispute was a squirrel—a live squirrel supposed to be clinging to one side of a tree-trunk; while over against the tree's opposite side a human being was imagined to stand. This human witness tries to get sight of the squirrel by moving rapidly round the tree, but no matter how fast he goes, the squirrel moves as fast in the opposite direction, and always keeps the tree between himself and the man, so that never a glimpse of him is caught. The resultant metaphysical problem now is this: *Does the man go round the squirrel or not?* He goes round the tree, sure enough, and the squirrel is on the tree; but does he go round the squirrel? In the unlimited leisure of the wilderness, discussion had been worn threadbare. Every one had taken sides, and was obstinate; and the numbers on both sides were even. Each side, when I appeared therefore appealed to me to make it a majority. Mindful of the scholastic adage that whenever you meet a contradiction you must make a distinction, I immediately sought and found one, as follows: "Which party is right," I said, "depends on what you *practically mean* by 'going round' the squirrel. If you mean passing from the north of him to the east, then to the south, then to the west, and then to the north of him again, obviously the man does go round him, for he occupies these successive positions. But if on the contrary you mean being first in front of him, then on the right of him, then behind him, then on his left, and finally in front again, it is quite as obvious that the man fails to go round him, for by the compensating movements the squirrel makes, he keeps his belly turned towards the man all the time, and his back turned away. Make the distinction, and there is no occasion for any farther dispute. You are both right and both wrong according as you conceive the verb 'to go round' in one practical fashion or the other."

Although one or two of the hotter disputants called my speech a shuffling evasion, saying they wanted no quibbling or scholastic hair-splitting, but meant just plain honest English "round," the majority seemed to think that the distinction had assuaged the dispute.

I tell this trivial anecdote because it is a peculiarly simple example of what I wish now to speak of as *the pragmatic method*. The pragmatic method is primarily a method of settling metaphysical disputes that otherwise might be interminable. Is the world one or many?—fated or free?—material or spiritual?—here are notions either of which may or may not hold good of the world; and disputes over such notions are unending. The pragmatic method in such cases is to try to interpret each notion by tracing its respective practical consequences. What difference would it practically make to any one if this notion rather than that notion were true? If no practical difference whatever can be traced, then the alternatives mean practically the same thing, and all dispute is idle. Whenever a dispute is serious, we ought to be able to show some practical difference that must follow from one side or the other's being right. . . .

It is astonishing to see how many philosophical disputes collapse into insignificance the moment you subject them to this simple test of tracing a concrete consequence. There can *be* no difference anywhere that doesn't *make* a difference elsewhere—no difference in abstract truth that doesn't express itself in a difference in concrete fact and in conduct consequent upon that fact, imposed on somebody, somehow, somewhere, and somewhen. The whole function of philosophy ought to be to find out what definite difference it will make to you and me, at definite instants of our life, if this world-formula or that world-formula be the true one. . . .

Theories thus become instruments, not answers to enigmas, in which we can rest. We don't lie back upon them, we move forward, and, on occasion, make nature over again by their aid. Pragmatism unstiffens all our theories, limbers them up and sets each one at work. Being nothing essentially new, it harmonizes with many ancient philosophic tendencies. It

agrees with nominalism for instance, in always appealing to particulars; with utilitarianism in emphasizing practical aspects; with positivism in its disdain for verbal solutions, useless questions and metaphysical abstractions.

All these, you see, are *anti-intellectualist* tendencies. Against rationalism as a pretension and a method pragmatism is fully armed and militant. But, at the outset, at least, it stands for no particular results. It has no dogmas, and no doctrines save its method. As the young Italian pragmatist Papini has well said, it lies in the midst of our theories, like a corridor in a hotel. Innumerable chambers open out of it. In one you may find a man writing an atheistic volume; in the next some one on his knees praying for faith and strength; in a third a chemist investigating a body's properties. In a fourth a system of idealistic metaphysics is being excogitated; in a fifth the impossibility of metaphysics is being shown. But they all own the corridor, and all must pass through it if they want a practicable way of getting into or out of their respective rooms.

No particular results then, so far, but only an attitude of orientation, is what the pragmatic method means. *The attitude of looking away from first things, principles, "categories," supposed necessities; and of looking towards last things, fruits, consequences, facts.*

So much for the pragmatic method! You may say that I have been praising it rather than explaining it to you, but I shall presently explain it abundantly enough by showing how it works on some familiar problems. Meanwhile the word pragmatism has come to be used in a still wider sense, as meaning also a certain *theory of truth.* . . . *Ideas (which themselves are but parts of our experience) become true just in so far as they help us to get into satisfactory relation with other parts of our experience,* to summarize them and get about among them by conceptual short-cuts instead of following the interminable succession of particular phenomena. Any idea upon which we can ride, so to speak; any idea that will carry us prosperously from any one part of our experience to any other part, linking things satisfactorily, working securely, simplifying, saving labor; is true for just so much, true in so far forth, true *instrumentally*. This is the "instrumental" view of truth taught so successfully at Chicago [by John Dewey].

The observable process which Schiller and Dewey particularly singled out for generalization is the familiar one by which any individual settles into *new opinions*. The process here is always the same. The individual has a stock of old opinions already, but he meets a new experience that puts them to a strain. Somebody contradicts them; or in a reflective moment he discovers that they contradict each other; or he hears of facts with which they are incompatible; or desires arise in him which they cease to satisfy. The result is an inward trouble to which his mind till then had been a stranger, and from which he seeks to escape by modifying his previous mass of opinions. He saves as much of it as he can, for in this matter of belief we are all extreme conservatives. So he tries to change first this opinion, and then that (for they resist change very variously), until at last some new idea comes up which he can graft upon the ancient stock with a minimum of disturbance of the latter, some idea that mediates between the stock and the new experience and runs them into one another most felicitously and expediently.

This new idea is then adopted as the true one. It preserves the older stock of truths with a minimum of modification, stretching them just enough to make them admit the novelty, but conceiving that in ways as familiar as the case leaves possible. An *outrée* explanation, violating all our preconceptions, would never pass for a true account of novelty. We should scratch round industriously till we found something less excentric. The most violent revolutions in an individual's beliefs leave most of his old order standing. Time and space, cause and effect, nature and history, and one's own biography remain untouched. New truth is always a go-between, a smoother-over of transitions. It marries old opinion to new fact so as ever

to show a minimum of jolt, a maximum of continuity. We hold a theory true just in proportion to its success in solving this "problem of maxima and minima." But success in solving this problem is eminently a matter of approximation. We say this theory solves it on the whole more satisfactorily than that theory; but that means more satisfactorily to ourselves, and individuals will emphasize their points of satisfaction differently. To a certain degree, therefore, everything here is plastic. . . .

Pragmatism is uncomfortable away from facts. Rationalism is comfortable only in the presence of abstractions. This pragmatist talk about truths in the plural, about their utility and satisfactoriness, about the success with which they "work," etc., suggests to the typical intellectualist mind a sort of coarse lame second-rate makeshift article of truth. Such truths are not real truth. Such tests are merely subjective. As against this, objective truth must be something non-utilitarian, haughty, refined, remote, august, exalted. It must be an absolute correspondence of our thoughts with an equally absolute reality. It must be what we *ought* to think unconditionally. The conditioned ways in which we *do* think are so much irrelevance and matter for psychology. Down with psychology, up with logic, in all this question!

See the exquisite contrast of the types of mind! The pragmatist clings to facts and concreteness, observes truth at its work in particular cases, and generalizes. Truth, for him, becomes a class-name for all sorts of definite working-values in experience. For the rationalist it remains a pure abstraction, to the bare name of which we must defer. When the pragmatist undertakes to show in detail just *why* we must defer, the rationalist is unable to recognize the concretes from which his own abstraction is taken. He accuses us of *denying* truth; whereas we have only sought to trace exactly why people follow it and always ought to follow it. Your typical ultra-abstractionist fairly shudders at concreteness: other things equal, he positively prefers the pale and spectral. If the two universes were offered, he would always choose the skinny outline rather than the rich thicket of reality. It is so much purer, clearer, nobler. . . .

Now pragmatism, devoted though she be to facts, has no such materialistic bias as ordinary empiricism labors under. Moreover, she has no objection whatever to the realizing of abstractions, so long as you get about among particulars with their aid and they actually carry you somewhere. Interested in no conclusions but those which our minds and our experiences work out together, she has no *a priori* prejudices against theology. *If theological ideas prove to have a value for concrete life, they will be true, for pragmatism, in the sense of being good for so much. . . .* [The same with the Absolute.] What do believers in the Absolute mean by saying that their belief affords them comfort? They mean that since, in the Absolute finite evil is "overruled" already, we may, therefore, whenever we wish, treat the temporal as if it were potentially the eternal, be sure that we can trust its outcome, and, without sin, dismiss our fear and drop the worry of our finite responsibility. In short, they mean that we have a right ever and anon to take a moral holiday, to let the world wag in its own way, feeling that its issues are in better hands than ours and are none of our business. . . .

If the Absolute means this, and means no more than this, who can possibly deny the truth of it? To deny it would be to insist that men should never relax, and that holidays are never in order. . . .

Truth is *one species of good*, and not, as is usually supposed, a category distinct from good, and co-ordinate with it. *The true is the name of whatever proves itself to be good in the way of belief, and good, too, for definite, assignable reasons. . . .* Certain ideas are not only agreeable to think about, or agreeable as supporting other ideas that we are fond of, but they are also helpful in life's practical struggles. If there be any life that it is really better we should lead, and if there be any idea which, if believed in, would help us to lead that life, then it would be really *better for us* to believe in that idea, *unless, indeed, belief in it incidentally clashed with other greater vital benefits. . . .*

[Pragmatism] has in fact no prejudices whatever, no obstructive dogmas, no rigid canons of what shall count as proof. She is completely genial. She will entertain any hypothesis, she will consider any evidence. It follows that in the religious field she is at a great advantage both over positivistic empiricism, with its anti-theological bias, and over religious rationalism, with its exclusive interest in the remote, the noble, the simple, and the abstract in the way of conception.

In short, she widens the field of search for God. Rationalism sticks to logic and the empyrean. Empiricism sticks to the external senses. Pragmatism is willing to take anything, to follow either logic or the senses and to count the humblest and most personal experiences. She will count mystical experiences if they have practical consequences. She will take a God who lives in the very dirt of private fact—if that should seem a likely place to find him.

Her only test of probable truth is what works best in the way of leading us, what fits every part of life best and combines with the collectivity of experience's demands, nothing being omitted.

"THE LIFE OF THE LAW IS NOT LOGIC, BUT EXPERIENCE"

[Oliver Wendell Holmes, Jr. (1841–1935) was one of those dissidents that Brahmin Boston produces from time to time. After service in the Civil War, he took up the law, and in 1881 published *The Common Law*, an assertion that the life of the law was not logic but experience. In effect, it was an attack on the traditional view that law was an expression of natural moral law and that its growth was merely the process of finding new moral meanings. Holmes asserted that law was *made* not found, that it grew by a process analogous to the growth of an organism. This was venturesome doctrine, but like his friend, William James, Holmes reveled in conflict and experiment. From the Supreme bench of Massachusetts, Holmes moved in 1902 to the Supreme Court and there until his retirement in 1932 he served as a legal catalyst, defending the evolutionary view of law against the conservative majority. One would probably be mistaken to list Holmes as a reformer; more likely he was swayed by a pragmatic sense of what was possible and a willingness to see legislatures and courts experiment with efforts to promote social welfare. The following is taken from Holmes's "The Path of the Law," in *Harvard Law Review*, vol. 10 (March 25, 1897).]

When we study law we are not studying a mystery but a well-known profession. We are studying what we shall want in order to appear before judges, or to advise people in such a way as to keep them out of court. The reason why it is a profession, why people will pay lawyers to argue for them or to advise them, is that in societies like ours the command of the public force is intrusted to the judges in certain cases, and the whole power of the state will be put forth, if necessary, to carry out their judgments and decrees. People want to know under what circumstances and how far they will run the risk of coming against what is so much stronger than themselves, and hence it becomes a business to find out when this danger is to be feared. The object of our study, then, is prediction, the prediction of the incidence of the public force through the instrumentality of the courts. . . .

I wish, if I can, to lay down some first principles for the study of this body of dogma or systematized prediction which we call the law, for men who want to use it as the instrument of their business to enable them to prophesy in their turn, and, as bearing upon the study, I wish to point out an ideal which as yet our law has not attained.

The first thing for a business-like understanding of the matter is to understand its limits, and therefore I think it desirable at once to point out and dispel a confusion between morality and law, which sometimes rises to the height of conscious theory, and more often

and indeed constantly is making trouble in detail without reaching the point of consciousness. You can see very plainly that a bad man has as much reason as a good one for wishing to avoid an encounter with the public force, and therefore you can see the practical importance of the distinction between morality and law. A man who cares nothing for an ethical rule which is believed and practised by his neighbors is likely nevertheless to care a good deal to avoid being made to pay money, and will want to keep out of jail if he can. . . .

The confusion with which I am dealing besets confessedly legal conceptions. Take the fundamental question, What constitutes the law? You will find some text writers telling you that it is . . . a system of reason, that it is a deduction from principles of ethics or admitted axioms or what not, which may or may not coincide with the decisions. But if we take the view of our friend the bad man we shall find that he does not care two straws for the axioms or deductions, but that he does want to know what the Massachusetts or English courts are likely to do in fact. I am much of this mind. The prophecies of what the courts will do in fact, and nothing more pretentious, are what I mean by the law. . . . For my own part, I often doubt whether it would not be a gain if every word of moral significance could be banished from the law altogether, and other words adopted which should convey legal ideas uncolored by anything outside the law. We should lose the fossil records of a good deal of history and the majesty got from ethical associations, but by ridding ourselves of an unnecessary confusion we should gain very much in the clearness of our thought.

So much for the limits of the law. The next thing which I wish to consider is what are the forces which determine its content and its growth. . . . It is with regard to them that a second fallacy comes in, which I think it important to expose.

The fallacy to which I refer is the notion that the only force at work in the development of the law is logic. . . . The condition of our thinking about the universe is that it is capable of being thought about rationally, or, in other words, that every part of it is effect and cause in the same sense in which those parts are with which we are most familiar. So in the broadest sense it is true that the law is a logical development, like everything else. The danger of which I speak is not the admission that the principles governing other phenomena also govern the law, but the notion that a given system, ours, for instance, can be worked out like mathematics from some general axioms of conduct. . . .

This mode of thinking is entirely natural. The training of lawyers is a training in logic. The processes of analogy, discrimination, and deduction are those in which they are most at home. The language of judicial decision is mainly the language of logic. And the logical method and form flatter that longing for certainty and for repose which is in every human mind. But certainty generally is illusion, and repose is not the destiny of man. Behind the logical form lies a judgment as to the relative worth and importance of competing legislative grounds, often an inarticulate and unconscious judgment, it is true, and yet the very root and nerve of the whole proceeding. You can give any conclusion a logical form. You always can imply a condition in a contract. But why do you imply it? It is because of some belief as to the practice of the community or of a class, or because of some opinion as to policy, or, in short, because of some attitude of yours upon a matter not capable of exact quantitative measurement, and therefore not capable of founding exact logical conclusions. Such matters really are battle grounds where the means do not exist for determinations that shall be good for all time, and where the decision can do no more than embody the preference of a given body in a given time and place. We do not realize how large a part of our law is open to reconsideration upon a slight change in the habit of the public mind. No concrete proposition is self evident, no matter how ready we may be to accept it. . . .

I think that the judges themselves have failed adequately to recognize their duty of weighing considerations of social advantage. The duty is inevitable, and the result of the often proclaimed judicial aversion to deal with such considerations is simply to leave the very ground and foundation of judgments inarticulate, and often unconscious, as I have said. When socialism first began to be talked about, the comfortable classes of the community were a good deal frightened. I suspect that this fear has influenced judicial action both here and in England, yet it is certain that it is not a conscious factor in the decisions to which I refer. I think that something similar has led people who no longer hope to control the legislatures to look to the courts as expounders of the Constitutions, and that in some courts new principles have been discovered outside the bodies of those instruments, which may be generalized into acceptance of the economic doctrines which prevailed about fifty years ago, and a wholesale prohibition of what a tribunal of lawyers does not think about right. I cannot but believe that if the training of lawyers led them habitually to consider more definitely and explicitly the social advantage on which the rule they lay down must be justified, they sometimes would hesitate where now they are confident, and see that really they were taking sides upon debatable and often burning questions.

So much for the fallacy of logical form. Now let us consider the present condition of the law as a subject for study, and the ideal toward which it tends. . . . The development of our law has gone on for nearly a thousand years, like the development of a plant, each generation taking the inevitable next step, mind, like matter, simply obeying a law of spontaneous growth. . . . The rational study of law is still to a large extent the study of history. History must be a part of the study, because without it we cannot know the precise scope of rules which it is our business to know. It is a part of the rational study, because it is the first step toward an enlightened scepticism, that is, toward a deliberate reconsideration of the worth of those rules. . . . For the rational study of the law the black-letter man may be the man of the present, but the man of the future is the man of statistics and the master of economics. . . .

There is another study which sometimes is undervalued by the practical minded, for which I wish to say a good word, although I think a good deal of pretty poor stuff goes under that name. I mean the study of what is called jurisprudence. Jurisprudence, as I look at it, is simply law in its most generalized part. Every effort to reduce a case to a rule is an effort of jurisprudence, although the name as used in English is confined to the broadest rules and most fundamental conceptions. One mark of a great lawyer is that he sees the application of the broadest rules. . . . The way to gain a liberal view of your subject is not to read something else, but to get to the bottom of the subject itself. The means of doing that are, in the first place, to follow the existing body of dogma into its highest generalizations by the help of jurisprudence; next, to discover from history how it has come to be what it is; and, finally, so far as you can, to consider the ends which the several rules seek to accomplish, the reasons why those ends are desired, what is given up to gain them, and whether they are worth the price.

JUSTICE HOLMES ON LIFE AND THE LAW

The life of the law has not been logic: it has been experience. The felt necessities of the time, the prevalent moral and political theories, intuitions of public policy, avowed or unconscious, even the prejudices which judges share with their fellow-men, have had a good deal more to do than the syllogism in determining the rules by which men should be governed. The law embodies the story of a nation's development through many centuries, and it cannot be dealt with as if it contained only the axioms and corollaries of a book of mathematics.

—*The Common Law,* 1881

[Men have come to believe] that the ultimate good desired is better reached by free trade in ideas—that the best test of truth is the power of the thought to get itself accepted in the competition of the market; and that truth is the only ground upon which their wishes safely can be carried out. That, at any rate, is the theory of our Constitution. It is an experiment, as all life is an experiment. Every year, if not every day, we have to wager our salvation upon some prophecy based upon imperfect knowledge. While that experiment is part of our system I think that we should be eternally vigilant against attempts to check the expression of opinions that we loathe and believe to be fraught with death, unless they so imminently threaten immediate interference with the lawful and pressing purposes of the law that an immediate check is required to save the country.

—Dissenting Opinion in *Abrams v. U.S.*, 1919

The end of life is life. Life is action, the use of one's powers. As to use them to their height is our joy and duty, so it is the one end that justifies itself.

. . . Life is a roar of bargain and battle; but in the very heart of it there rises a mystic spiritual tone that gives meaning to the whole, and transmutes the dull details into romance.

. . . Man is born a predestined idealist, for he is born to act. To act is to affirm the worth of an end, and to persist in affirming the worth of an end is to make an ideal.

—*Speeches* (Boston: Little, Brown, 1913), pp. 85, 97, 96 seriatim

ROSCOE POUND AND SOCIOLOGICAL JURISPRUDENCE

[The natural outcome of the pragmatic climate was the growing tendency to judge legal problems in the light of society's welfare. The key role of Dean Roscoe Pound (1870–1964) of the Harvard Law School in this development is described by Henry Steele Commager in *The American Mind* (Yale University Press, 1950), pp. 377–381.]

To make law an efficient instrument for social reconstruction was the task which Pound set himself. It was no simple task. It required not only the repudiation and discrediting of those concepts which had for so long dominated legal thought and paralyzed legal progress but, more important, the formulation and vindication of new legal concepts and of new techniques to translate those concepts into practices. To the philosophy of law which Pound formulated for these purposes he gave the name "sociological jurisprudence." It was a mouthfilling word, but its meaning was clear enough. Pound himself put it succinctly:

The sociological movement in jurisprudence is a movement for pragmatism as a philosophy of law; for the adjustment of principles and doctrines to the human conditions they are to govern rather than to assume first principles; for putting the human factor in the central place and relegating logic to its true position as an instrument.

Elsewhere he has spoken of it as a method of social engineering, stressing emphatically its constructive aspects. It is, he has said,

a process, an activity, not merely a body of knowledge or a fixed order of construction. It is a doing of things, not a serving as passive instruments through which mathematical formulas and mechanical laws realize themselves in the eternally appointed way. The engineer is judged by what he does. His work is judged by its adequacy to the purposes for which it is done, not by its conformity to some ideal form of a traditional plan. We are beginning . . . to think of jurist and judge and lawmaker in the same way. We are coming to study the legal order instead of debating as to the nature of law. We are thinking of interests, claims, demands, not of rights; of what we have to secure or satisfy, not exclusively of the institutions by which we have sought to secure or satisfy them, as if those institutions were ultimate things existing for themselves. (*Interpretations of Legal History*, p. 152)

Sociological jurisprudence was, like pragmatism, a method—a new way of thinking about law and of applying it. It was a shift from absolutes to relatives, from doctrines to practices, from passive—and therefore pessimistic—determinism to creative—and therefore optimistic—freedom. How revolutionary that method was, how sharply it broke with the methods of natural and historical and analytical law, is best explained by Pound himself. Speaking in the year Holmes warned against the use of the Fourteenth Amendment "to prevent the making of experiments that an important part of the community desires," he said:

> In the last century we studied law from within. The jurists of today are studying it from without. The past century sought to develop completely and harmoniously the fundamental principles which jurists discovered by metaphysics or by history. The jurists of today seek to enable and to compel lawmaking and also the interpretation and application of legal rules, to take more account and more intelligent account, of the social facts upon which law must proceed and to which it is to be applied. Where the last century studied law in the abstract, they insist upon study of the actual social effects of legal institutions and legal doctrines. Where the last century prepared for legislation by study of other legislation analytically, they insist upon sociological study in connection with legal study in preparation for legislation. Where the last century held comparative law the best foundation for wise lawmaking, they hold it not enough to compare the laws themselves, but that even more their social operation must be studied and the effects which they produce, if any, when put in action. Where the last century studied only the making of law, they hold it necessary to study as well the means of making legal rules effective. (*The Spirit of the Common Law*, pp. 212–213)

Sociological jurisprudence was, however, more than a method. It had substance, as well, and an affirmative program. It held that the truth of law, like truth in general, was something to be found through experience, that it was relative, and that it could be created. It asserted that good law was what worked best for society, that law was functional and to be understood in terms of ends rather than origins, and that the actual workings of the law were more important than its abstract legal content. It insisted that law was a social science, dependent upon rather than independent of society, that it should be required to conform to social needs and judged by the degree to which it filled those needs. It pointed out that the life of the law was in its administration and enforcement, that law was not only a prediction of what judges would say but what officers would do, and that administration could be studied empirically. It affirmed that the past had exhausted neither the law nor the inventive and creative capacity of men, that law was a continuous social product, that it was susceptible to continuous improvement and a proper subject for social engineering. It confessed that in the making of law judges played a decisive part, but promised to legal scholars and commentators, to statesmen and administrators, a role scarcely less significant. It maintained, finally, that law was as concerned with the collective social good as with the individual good, that the whole range of social interests, needs, and wants came legitimately within its scope, and that it could not protect personal liberty except as part of a larger social security and liberty.

Sociological jurisprudence was pragmatism, and—for all Pound's generous tributes to his Harvard colleague—it was a pragmatism that owed more to Dewey than to James. It had less tolerance for dissent than had James's version of pragmatism, less room, perhaps, for idiosyncrasy, eccentricity, and nonconformity. It saw law not primarily as a concise body of principles regulating the relationship between the individual and his government but as a sprawling body of practices conditioning the conduct of the individual in his society. It used law not as a shield to safeguard personal rights and liberties but as a cooperative instrument to satisfy social needs. It was a legal philosophy fitted to the realities of social life in an urban order, of economic life in an industrial order, and of political life in an egalitarian order.

The impact of sociological jurisprudence was immediate and far reaching and, it should be added, triumphant. It could be traced in the realm of criminal law, where it shifted attention from the criminal to the crime and ultimately to the social background of crime. It could be seen in the field of administration, where it directed attention to the enforcement rather than the making of law. It could be read in the domain of legal scholarship, which for a generation dedicated itself largely to the elaboration of Roscoe Pound's insights. Its most dramatic, and perhaps its most consequential, results were to be found, however, in the arena of constitutional law, and thus of public policy.

There were, to be sure, anticipations and precedents, for Pound was not the first to protest against mechanical, nor did he invent sociological, jurisprudence. What he did, rather, was to create, especially in the legal profession, a climate of opinion favorable to the reception of sociological doctrines. For, notwithstanding the earlier contributions of Miller, Harlan, Bradley, Moody, and even Holmes himself, it is no great exaggeration to say that sociological jurisprudence was formally introduced to the Supreme Court in 1908, when Louis Brandeis submitted his brief in the case of *Muller* vs. *Oregon,* and that it was officially recognized as part of constitutional law when the Senate reluctantly confirmed Mr. Brandeis' nomination to that Court. That it was, for many years, a minor part, is confessed by the frequency and vigor of Brandeis' dissents; that in the end it became acceptable and even respectable is clear to anyone familiar with the history of the Court, and of constitutional law, in the decades of the thirties and the forties. Illustrations would require us to thread our way through the labyrinths of constitutional law. It is sufficient, perhaps, to refer to the . . . willingness to make the due process clause of the Fourteenth Amendment an instrument for the protection of personal and social liberties rather than for conferring exemptions from social responsibility upon property.

Anticipated by Holmes, championed unceasingly by Brandeis, supported by the muscular Harlan Stone and the eloquent Benjamin Cardozo and the learned Felix Frankfurter, sociological jurisprudence became, after the great struggle of 1937, the all but official doctrine of the Court. Responsibility for what may, fairly enough, be called a constitutional revolution is widespread, but only those blind to the realization that ideas are weapons would deny that Roscoe Pound shares with such men as Holmes, Brandeis, and Franklin Roosevelt responsibility for that revolution.

PROGRESSIVE EDUCATION: THE OBJECT AND THE IRONY

[Pragmatism was applied to education under the name of Instrumentalism by John Dewey (1859–1952), philosopher of the University of Chicago and Columbia. Dewey wrote voluminously but with unvarying turbidity, and this may help to explain why (to his dismay) his educational ideas were bowdlerized by pseudo-disciples and by conservatives desirous of substituting technical training for intellectual training. The method of Instrumentalism and its debasement are set forth by Stow Persons in *American Minds* (N.Y.: Holt, 1958), pp. 305–308.]

As an educational philosophy, progressivism rested squarely on certain psychological assumptions. Man's primary experience, like that of all other animals, is an active process of doing and undergoing. This experience is ultimately tangible, and not primarily cognitive in character. Knowledge is, in fact, only one form of experience, and secondary and derived at that, no matter how important may be its contributions. Also, the qualities of primary experience are esthetic; they are feelings, directly connected with sensory experiences. In these terms, the good life consists in the richness and variety of the satisfactions that primary experience yields. The function of knowledge is thus instrumental; its object is to regulate the events of primary experience. To "know" an object is to understand its possible consequences for experience. Activity directed by anticipated consequences is behavior controlled by meanings. Thinking arises out of problems. It is simply an attempt to resolve ambiguous situations into experiences the consequences of which have been foreseen. Thus in the largest sense, education is life, and vice versa. The key to successful living is the capacity to solve problems, and to this end the scientific method provides the educator with a central inspiration.

Dewey had been among the first to insist upon the modern genetic theory of the relationship between the organism and its environment. This relationship is one of interaction between the primary elements of experience. It is the given condition of life, with which analysis must start. The implications of this view for educational theory are readily apparent. The self develops out of its experiences, and not simply out of the unfolding of inborn capacities. Education may thus be defined as learning from experience. It must proceed in terms of the specific needs and interests of each child—that is, his current experience. If the student is to learn anything of value from his educational activity, it must be connected with his current experience; otherwise his schooling will become artificial because divorced from the stream of life as he experiences it. Motives as an incentive to learning are very important, and motives come from the child's reactions to concrete situations.

Progressive educators were proudly conscious of the fact that their pedagogical theory constituted a revolutionary departure from traditional American educational theory and practice. They insisted that, in divorcing its concept of knowledge from experience and from physical activity, the older educational philosophy was perpetuating an abstract and artificial concept of knowledge. It was, in fact, perpetuating the ancient dualism of mind and body. Dewey acknowledged, however, that in the fervor of their rebellion against the traditional point of view, his disciples sometimes went to the opposite extreme and failed to maintain contact between expressional activities and the intellectual possibilities of these activities. So keen was their awareness of change that they insisted that the object of education was not to transmit fixed beliefs or to build habits which might dominate behavior. Rather, its objective was to facilitate the reconstruction of experience by equipping the child to cope with novel situations by means of self-controlled behavior. In order that the individual might deal successfully with unique occasions, much importance was attached to the training of the intellect not merely as an adapting mechanism but as a creative force capable of fashioning new adjustments.

Since the time of Horace Mann, American philosophies of public education have been firmly rooted in the democratic ideology. But no educators have insisted more strenuously on the relevance of their theories to a democratic society than the progressive pedagogues. The unique needs of each child must receive individual attention. The progressives found this ideal difficult to reconcile with a rigid and prescribed curriculum. Properly conceived, the results of education should be freedom, initiative, and activity. To secure these outcomes, the teacher should think of himself as a partner of the pupil, since authority in another person was clearly undesirable. The facts of the situation were the only authority to be acknowledged. The old-fashioned classroom with its rigid discipline, rote learning, and authoritative dispensation of truth was palpably incompatible with the nurture of mature, self-disciplined, and intelligent adults. The best hope of democracy, said Dewey, is the school. Here must be developed emotionally mature and self-reliant individuals if democracy is to survive.

Like certain religious modernists who diluted their religion to the point where they could identify religion with life itself, progressive educators made the mistake of identifying education with the whole of life. John Childs declared education to be its own end, co-extensive with experience itself. Education as preparation for the future was thus supplanted by education focused on "rich and vital living *now*." From this point of view, formal schooling merely accentuated a perpetual process during important years of individual development. Nevertheless, rich and vital though the *now* of childhood might be, the progressives did insist, if in a roundabout way, on preparation for the future. The school, they said, must be in vital contact with the activities of the community and not be isolated from them. But these activities were for the most part the activities of adults and not of children. The one day of the year in which a school boy sits behind the governor's desk hardly accomplishes the effective fusion of child and adult. The community, in short, continued to insist upon the distinction between childhood and adulthood even if the educators did not. And yet John Childs was prepared to assess the value of a school in terms of the quality of interaction with the wider social life of which the school is part. In learning to cope with living issues, children do not require mechanical drill or compulsory learning. They will be found to acquire naturally the necessary skills as these are needed.

The older America had clearly been an adult's world. Its schools had effectively functioned to mold each generation of youth in the image of its forebears. It had regarded adolescence as a period of training to be passed through as quickly as possible. Progressive educators rejected this paternalism. Not the least revolutionary of their accomplishments was the liberation of the young from the old by dissolving the differences between them. The activities of the young were to be regarded as equally important to those of adults. At the same time, school was to be a place where children "grew up" by learning to cope with problems of the real world under controlled conditions of optimum desirability.

Dewey's educational philosophy suffered an ironic fate. The prime object of his theory was to develop in individuals the capacity to reconstruct reality in order to achieve more enduring satisfactions. His emphasis upon reconstruction was strongly intellectualist in character. He repeatedly stressed reliance on the scientific method of observation, hypothesis, and experiment. Such traditional educational objectives as the memorizing of an established body of knowledge, the inculcation of discipline, of patriotism, or of conformity were all discarded in favor of a mental cultivation calculated to equip the student with the most difficult of attainments, namely, the capacity to cope with novel situations. Yet the progressive ideal was curiously perverted by the obvious prolongation of youth that characterizes twentieth-century America. It became increasingly evident that the schools and even the colleges were places where children, instead of growing up, retained the privilege of remaining children. The progressive education movement came under vigorous attack for abandoning the traditional intellectual content of the curriculum in favor of such things as personality development and "life adjustment." Complaints were heard that the products of progressive schools, although presumably well-adjusted, frequently did not know the multiplication table or the elements of grammar—both of which might be justified as useful aids in the reconstruction of experience.

PRAGMATISM AND RELATIVISM

Pragmatism dissolves dogmas into beliefs, eternities and necessities into change and chance, conclusions and finalities into processes. Men have invented philosophy precisely because they find change, chance and process too much for them, and desire infallible security and certainty. Pragmatism . . . calls for too complete a disillusion.

—Horace Kallen

The real trouble with us reformers is that we made reform a crusade against standards. Well, we smashed them all and now neither we nor anybody else have anything left.

—J. Allen Smith

Fictions served to guide and control many rebellious generations, but they could do so only because they were not known to be fictions, and they lose their power as soon as we recognize them as such.

—Joseph Wood Krutch

The trap in pragmatism, as we have long since realized, is that its relativism may deteriorate into brutal expediency—not but what a moral order based on an absolute may do the same, as history so amply shows. This is not the only problem, for the relative and the absolute are eternally at war, and the conflict has become more bitter as the century grows older. William James insisted that the practical consequence of pragmatism "is the well-known democratic respect for the sacredness of individuality—is, at any rate, the outward tolerance of whatever itself is not intolerant." But progressivism, which drew its origin and its method from pragmatism, all too often claimed to be based on morality—that is, on an allegiance to an absolute.

And there the battle joined between tender-minded, mystical believers in an eternally revealed absolute, and the no less absolutist tough-minded skeptics who demanded scientific proof. James found his answer in neither, but advocated—to oversimplify—an adventurous testing of both viewpoints and the acceptance of the attitude that worked best under the circumstances, a pragmatic search which would lead step by step to the truth-for-the-day. The relativism thus championed called for a superb moral balance which might tip over into either enemy's camp, and frequently did. The fundamental question then and now is this: can humanity ever reach the stage where it can know an axiom is false yet recognize its value and use it? Einstein proved the falsity of Euclid's simple geometric axioms, and yet they are useful in our day-to-day pursuits.

Perhaps this century's unrest rises in some part from this battle, which has pinned the workaday world between two moral rigidities of communism and revealed divine law. Must the democratic leader sometimes violate the moral code in order to make democracy work—accept damnation that the people may live? Early in this century, Lincoln Steffens, the demon muckraker, posed this question to W. S. U'Ren, the Oregon reformer, and wrote of the result in *The Upbuilders* (N.Y.: Doubleday, Page, 1909), pp. 325–326. After devoting a chapter to U'Ren's bargaining and conniving he closed with this anecdote:

I've told the worst of it—yes, practically all of it; and it may not be considered as very bad; certainly it never was selfish; but it was corruption. So I ask:

"Isn't U'Ren only *our* damned rascal?"

I put the question to U'Ren himself one day. I was at his home, a small cottage on a point of land that looks up the Willamette River to the famous Falls. One afternoon, when the country lawyer was telling me his story, the "wrong as well as the right of it," and we were in the midst of one of his deals, his wife looked into the parlour and asked him if he wouldn't get her some wood. He rose and we went out to the wood-shed; and, as he chopped, I said:

"How well off are you, U'Ren?"

He rested his axe to answer: "I think," he said, "that I am one of the richest men in Oregon."

"How is that? Have you made money?"

"My earnings average about $1,800 a year. But that isn't what I mean. I haven't any money, but I haven't any wants either, not for myself."

"What about your conscience?" I persisted. "What have those compromises with corruption cost you?"

"Nothing," he said. "I never have done a dishonest or a dishonourable thing."

"No, but you have made bargains with the devil to get him to pass your laws. You remember Moses? He also broke the covenants of the Lord, and you know what happened to him. He was taken up where he could see the Land of Promise, but he wasn't allowed to go over into it. Why won't it be so with you? You may have saved the people of Oregon, but haven't you lost your own soul? Won't you go to hell?"

He was looking down while I spoke, and he didn't see that I was speaking half in fun. Evidently he considered the prospect seriously, for after a moment, he looked up steadily at me, and in even tones answered out of his deliberation.

"Well," he said, "I would *go* to hell for the people of Oregon!"

New York Press

9

THE POLITICAL WARS OF REFORM

INTRODUCTION

A reformer seeks to purify the existing process of government in order to effect more completely its traditional aims. A progressive favors the gradual introduction of wholly new processes of government intended to achieve novel aims.

—Allan Nevins

The Progressive Era is usually roughly defined as lasting from the accession of Theodore Roosevelt to the Presidency in 1901 to the entry of the United States into World War I in 1917. During the period the tumultuous progressives occupied the center of the political stage and they won some victories, especially in the cities and states, but on the national scene their legislative reforms were by no means sweeping.

The progressives sought to institute "direct democracy"—that is, give the people a greater voice by means of the primary, the short ballot, and the initiative and referendum. They renovated state and municipal governments, passed social and labor legislation, began to conserve natural resources, and, finally, brought to a head the struggle between atomism and regulationism described in Chapter 1. The fact is that at least in the battle over the trusts conservative solutions won. Indeed, the enactments of the New Freedom were tailored as much to the measure of the conservative small businessman and Southern Hamiltonians as to that of progressive reformers. Wilson's later legislation, accused of resembling TR's New Nationalism, was aimed at placating farmers and workers, and by no means instituted a bright new day of reform.

The clue to all this is simply that the faith of the Gilded Age still ruled, even though it had to back up a step or two. The proof was seen in the next decade when progressivism, though far from dead, entered a period of dormancy.

What then was the significance of progressivism? For one thing, it continued the current of reform from the mugwumps of 1872 and the populists of the 1890's, even though in some different terms. For another thing, it shifted the base of reform from the "wild asses" of populism to the urban middle class (and perhaps also the working class) and in so doing not only made it respectable but created a climate in which big business also wished to be respectable. Finally, it trained reformers in the use of political organization and introduced the use of experts, the forerunners of the modern brain trusts. It is significant that many—not all— of the New Dealers of the 1930's were "blooded" in the progressive wars.

ON THE PROSPECTS OF POLITICAL REFORM

When Doctor Johnson said that patriotism was the last refuge of a scoundrel, he ignored the enormous possibilities of the word reform.

—Senator Roscoe Conkling of New York

A reformer is one who gives to the capitalist for nothing that which the real politician holds for a price.

—Anonymous, about 1888

We not only want a man who is a pronounced Republican, thoroughly tried in the crucial tests of experience, but we want also a man whose very name will allay instead of exciting the distrust that disturbs the industrial interests of this country. He must, of course . . . be a friend to human liberty, to equality of rights . . . but there is one thing in which our platform reminded us today he must not believe, and that is a substantial reduction of the duties on iron and steel and wool.

—Joseph B. Foraker, 1884

The purification of politics is an iridescent dream. Government is force. Politics is a battle for supremacy. Parties are the armies. The Decalogue and the Golden Rule have no place in a political campaign. . . . The commander who lost the battle through the activity of his moral nature would be the derision and jest of history. To defeat the antagonist and expel the party in power is the purpose.

—Senator J. J. Ingalls of Kansas, 1890

THE PEOPLE'S PARTY PLATFORM OF 1892

[The groundswell of protest against the way in which the two "old" parties were engaged in a sham battle, and were refusing to deal with the issues which reformers regarded as vital, found expression in the Populist Platform of 1892. It was written largely by Ignatius Donnelly and was adopted by a convention meeting in Omaha. The platform as given below is from John D. Hicks, *The Populist Revolt* (University of Minnesota, 1931), pp. 439–444.]

We meet in the midst of a nation brought to the verge of moral, political, and material ruin. Corruption dominates the ballot-box, the legislatures, the Congress, and touches even the ermine of the bench. The people are demoralized; most of the States have been compelled to isolate the voters at the polling-places to prevent universal intimidation or bribery. The newspapers are largely subsidized or muzzled; public opinion silenced; business prostrated; our homes covered with mortgages; labor impoverished; and the land concentrating in the hands of the capitalists. The urban workmen are denied the right of organization for self-protection; imported pauperized labor beats down their wages; a hireling standing army, unrecognized by our laws, is established to shoot them down, and they are rapidly degenerating into European conditions. The fruits of the toil of millions are boldly stolen to build up colossal fortunes for a few, unprecedented in the history of mankind; and the possessors of these, in turn, despise the republic and endanger liberty. From the same prolific womb of governmental in-justice we breed the two great classes—tramps and millionaires.

The national power to create money is appropriated to enrich bondholders; a vast public debt, payable in legal tender currency, has been funded into gold-bearing bonds, thereby adding millions to the burdens of the people. Silver, which has been accepted as coin since the dawn of history, has been demonetized to add to the purchasing power of gold by decreasing the value of all forms of property as well as human labor; and the supply of currency is purposely abridged to fatten usurers, bankrupt enterprise, and enslave industry. A vast conspiracy against mankind has been organized on two continents, and it is rapidly taking possession of the world. If not met and overthrown at once, it forebodes terrible social convulsions, the destruction of civilization, or the establishment of an absolute despotism.

We have witnessed for more than a quarter of a century the struggles of the two great political parties for power and plunder, while grievous wrongs have been inflicted upon the suffering people. We charge that the controlling influences dominating both these parties have permitted the existing dreadful conditions to develop without serious effort to prevent or restrain them. Neither do they now promise us any substantial reform. They have agreed together to ignore in the coming campaign every issue but one. They propose to drown the outcries of a plundered people with the uproar of a sham battle over the tariff, so that capitalists, corporations, national banks, rings, trusts, watered stock, the demonetization of silver, and the oppressions of the usurers may all be lost sight of. They propose to sacrifice our homes, lives and children on the altar of mammon; to destroy the multitude in order to secure corruption funds from the millionaires. . . .

We declare, therefore,—

First. That the union of the labor forces of the United States this day consummated shall be permanent and perpetual; may its spirit enter all hearts for the salvation of the republic and the uplifting of mankind!

Second. Wealth belongs to him who creates it, and every dollar taken from industry without an equivalent is robbery. "If any will not work, neither shall he eat." The interests of rural and civic labor are the same; their enemies are identical.

Third. We believe that the time has come when the railroad corporations will either own the people or the people must own the railroads. . . .

[Here follow three demands.]

First, *Money.* We demand a national currency, safe, sound, and flexible, issued by the general government only, a full legal tender for all debts, public and private, and that, without the use of banking corporations, a just, equitable, and efficient means of distribution direct to the people, at a tax not to exceed two per cent per annum, to be provided as set forth in the sub-treasury plan of the Farmers' Alliance, or a better system; also, by payments in discharge of its obligations for public improvements.

(a) We demand free and unlimited coinage of silver and gold at the present legal ratio of sixteen to one.

(b) We demand that the amount of circulating medium be speedily increased to not less than fifty dollars per capita.

(c) We demand a graduated income tax.

(d) We believe that the money of the country should be kept as much as possible in the hands of the people, and hence we demand that all state and national revenues shall be limited to the necessary expenses of the government economically and honestly administered.

(e) We demand that postal savings banks be established by the government for the safe deposit of the earnings of the people and to facilitate exchange.

Second, *Transportation.* Transportation being a means of exchange and a public necessity, the government should own and operate the railroads in the interest of the people.

(a) The telegraph and telephone, like the post-office system, being a necessity for the transmission of news, should be owned and operated by the government in the interest of the people.

Third, *Land.* The land, including all the natural sources of wealth, is the heritage of the people, and should not be monopolized for speculative purposes, and alien ownership of land should be prohibited. All land now held by railroads and other corporations in excess of their actual needs, and all lands now owned by aliens, should be reclaimed by the government and held for actual settlers only.

GROVER CLEVELAND (1837–1908)

A public office is a public trust.

> —Slogan drawn from Cleveland's speeches
> and used in the Campaign of 1884

They love him most for the enemies he has made.

> —Governor E. S. Bragg of Wisconsin, 1884

Your every voter, as surely as your chief magistrate, under the same high sanction, though in a different sphere, exercises a public trust.

> —Inaugural Address, 1885

When more of the people's sustenance is exacted through the form of taxation than is necessary to meet the just obligations of the Government and expenses of its economical administration, such taxation becomes ruthless extortion and a violation of the fundamental principles of a free Government.

> —Second Annual Message, 1886

It is a condition which confronts us, not a theory.

> —Protesting the protective tariff, 1887

Communism is a hateful thing and a menace to peace and organized government; but the communism of combined wealth and capital, the outgrowth of overweening cupidity and selfishness, which insidiously undermines the justice and integrity of free institutions, is not less dangerous than the communism of oppressed poverty and toil, which, exasperated by injustice and discontent, attacks with wild disorder the citadel of rule.

> —Fourth Annual Message, Dec. 3, 1888

No harm shall come to any business interest as the result of administrative policy so long as I am President. . . . A transfer of executive control from one party to another does not mean any serious disturbance of existing conditions.

> —Grover Cleveland, 1892

The lessons of paternalism ought to be unlearned and the better lesson taught that while the people should patriotically and cheerfully support their Government, its functions do not include the support of the people.

> —Second Inaugural Address, 1893

He restored honesty and impartiality to government at a time when the service had become indispensable to the health of the republic. . . . To have bequeathed a nation such an example of iron fortitude is better than to have swayed parliaments or to have won battles or to have annexed provinces.

—Allan Nevins

I have tried so hard to do right.

—Cleveland's dying words, 1910

"YOU SHALL NOT CRUCIFY MANKIND UPON A CROSS OF GOLD"

[Next to some of the orations of Webster, Bryan's "Cross of Gold Speech" on July 8, 1896, to the Chicago Convention of the Democratic Party ranks as most famous. Actually, the speech was made up of the most effective portions of the free-silver speeches Bryan had been delivering for years, and was artfully calculated to stampede the convention into nominating him for the Presidency. See W. J. Bryan, *The First Battle* (Chicago, 1896).]

We say to you [gold men] that you have made the definition of a business man too limited in its application. The man who is employed for wages is as much a business man as his employer; the attorney in a country town is as much a business man as the corporation counsel in a great metropolis; the merchant at the cross-roads store is as much a business man as the merchant of New York; the farmer who goes forth in the morning and toils all day, who begins in the spring and toils all summer, and who by the application of brain and muscle to the natural resources of the country creates wealth, is as much a business man as the man who goes upon the Board of Trade and bets upon the price of grain; the miners who go down a thousand feet into the earth, or climb two thousand feet upon the cliffs, and bring forth from their hiding places the precious metals to be poured into the channels of trade are as much business men as the few financial magnates who, in a back room, corner the money of the world. We come to speak of this broader class of business men.

Ah, my friends, we say not one word against those who live upon the Atlantic Coast, but the hardy pioneers who have braved all the dangers of the wilderness. . . . It is for these that we speak. We do not come as aggressors. Our war is not a war of conquest; we are fighting in the defense of our homes, our families, and posterity. We have petitioned, and our petitions have been scorned; we have entreated, and our entreaties have been disregarded; we have begged, and they have mocked when our calamity came. We beg no longer; we entreat no more; we petition no more. We defy them! . . .

If they ask us why it is that we say more on the money question than we say upon the tariff question, I reply that, if protection has slain its thousands, the gold standard has slain its tens of thousands. If they ask us why we do not embody in our platform all the things that we believe in, we reply that when we have restored the money of the Constitution, all other necessary reform will be possible; but that until this is done, there is no other reform that can be accomplished. . . .

The sympathies of the Democratic party,

as shown by the platform, are on the side of the struggling masses who have ever been the foundation of the Democratic party. There are two ideas of government. There are those who believe that if you will only legislate to make the well-to-do prosperous, their prosperity will leak through on those below. The Democratic idea, however, has been that if you legislate to make the masses prosperous, their prosperity will find its way up through every class which rests upon them.

You come to us and tell us that the great cities are in favor of the gold standard; we reply that the great cities rest upon our broad and fertile prairies. Burn down your cities and leave our farms, and your cities will spring up again as if by magic; but destroy our farms and the grass will grow in the streets of every city in the country.

My friends, we declare that this nation is able to legislate for its own people on every question, without waiting for the aid or consent of any other nation on earth; and upon that issue we expect to carry every state in the Union. . . . Our ancestors, when but three millions in number, had the courage to declare their political independence of every other nation; shall we, their descendants, when we have grown to seventy millions, declare that we are less independent than our forefathers?

No, my friends, that will never be the verdict of our people. Therefore, we care not upon what lines the battle is fought. If they say bimetallism is good, but that we cannot have it until other nations help us, we reply, that instead of having a gold standard because England has, we will restore bimetallism, and then let England have bimetallism because the United States has it. If they dare to come out in the open field and defend the gold standard as a good thing, we will fight them to the uttermost. Having behind us the producing masses of this nation and the world, supported by the commercial interests, the laboring interests and the toilers everywhere, we will answer their demand for a gold standard by saying to them: You shall not press down upon the brow of labor this crown of thorns, you shall not crucify mankind upon a cross of gold.

THE BATTLE OF THE STANDARDS

The people have a right to make their own mistakes.

You shall not press down upon the brow of labor this crown of thorns; you shall not crucify mankind upon a cross of gold.

—William Jennings Bryan

Like the Platte—six inches deep and six miles wide at the mouth.

—Joseph B. Foraker, speaking of Bryan

We put him to school and he wound up stealing the school books.

—Populist Ignatius Donnelly, speaking of Bryan's preemption of the silver issue

I brag and chant of Bryan, Bryan, Bryan,
Candidate for president who sketched a silver Zion. . . .

> In a coat like a deacon, in a black Stetson hat
> He scourged the elephant plutocrats
> With barbed wire from the Platte
>
> —Vachel Lindsay

[McKinley] had the art . . . of throwing a moral gloss over policies which were dubious, if not actually immoral, and this he did with a sort of self-deceiving sincerity.

—William R. Thayer

The Free Silver movement is a fake. Free silver is the cow-bird of the reform movement. It waited until the nest had been built by the sacrifices and labor of others, and then it laid its eggs in it, pushing out the others which it smashed on the ground. . . . The People's Party has been betrayed. No party that does not lead its leaders will ever succeed.

—Henry Demarest Lloyd

[This was the first great] struggle of the masses in our country against the privileged classes. It was not free silver that frightened the plutocratic leaders. What they feared then, what they fear now, is free men.

—Tom Johnson, 1912

NEW DIRECTIONS FOR REFORM

[Herbert Croly (1869–1930) in *The Promise of American Life* (N.Y.: Macmillan, 1909) attributed the ineffectiveness of reformers to their embrace of moral rather than realistic standards. As a remedy he proposed that they recognize that the great corporations were legitimate evidences of efficiency and instruments for improving the standard of living, and that they boldly use the federal government to regulate them when necessary. This would necessitate the repeal or drastic amendment of the Sherman Antitrust Law. Here we give certain points in Croly's argument, taken from pages 144–150 and 357–371. Note how Croly seemed to forecast oligopoly, but failed to see how corporate mass production could reconcile the interests of producer and consumer. (See again the selection from Drucker in Chapter 1.)]

Reformers are sufficiently united upon their statement of fundamental principles. They all of them agree to conceive of reform as at bottom a moral protest and awakening, which seeks to enforce the violated laws and to restore the American political and economic system to its pristine purity and vigor. From their point of view certain abuses have become unwholesomely conspicuous, because the average American citizen has been a little lethargic, and allowed a few of his more energetic and unscrupulous fellow-citizens to exploit for selfish purposes the opportunities of American business and politics. The function of reform, consequently, is to deprive these parasites of their peculiar opportunities. . . . But the point is the agreement among practical reformers that reform means at bottom no more than moral and political purification.

The plain fact is that the traditional American political system, which so many good reformers wish to restore by some sort of reforming revivalism, is just as much responsible for the existing political and economic abuses as the Constitution was responsible for the evil of slavery. As long, consequently, as reform is considered to be a species of higher conservatism, the existing abuses can no more be frankly faced and fully understood than the Whig leaders were able to face and understand the full meaning and consequences of any attempt on the part of a democracy to keep house with slavery. The first condition of a better understanding and a more efficient coöperation among the reforming leaders is a better understanding of the meaning of reform and the function of reformers. They will never be united on the basis of allegiance to the traditional American political creed, because that creed itself is overflowing with inconsistencies and ambiguities, which afford a footing for almost every extreme of radicalism and conservatism; and in case they persist in the attempt to reform political and economic abuses merely by a restoration of earlier conditions and methods, they will be compromising much that is good in the present economic and political organization without recovering that which was good in the past. . . .

Reform exclusively as a moral protest and awakening is condemned to sterility. Reformers exclusively as moral protestants and purifiers are condemned to misdirected effort, to an illiberal puritanism, and to personal self-stultification. Reform must necessarily mean an intellectual as well as a moral challenge; and its higher purposes will never be accomplished unless it is accompanied by a masterful and jubilant intellectual awakening. . . .

. . . .

The central government in its policy toward the large corporations must adopt one of two courses. Either it must discriminate in their favor or it must discriminate against them. The third alternative—that of being what is called "impartial"—has no real existence; and it is essential that the illusory nature of a policy of impartiality should in the beginning be clearly understood. . . . Such a policy has unquestionably a great deal to recommend it as a transitional means of dealing with the problem of corporate aggrandizement, but let there be no mistake: it is not really a policy of strict neutrality between the small and the large industrial agent. Any recognition of the large corporations, any successful attempt to give them a legal standing as authentic as their economic efficiency, amounts substantially to a discrimination in their favor. . . .

Thus the recognition of the large corporation is equivalent to the perpetuation of its existing advantages. It is not an explicit discrimination against their smaller competitors, but it amounts to such discrimination. If the small competitor is to be allowed a chance of regaining his former economic importance, he must receive the active assistance of the government. Its policy must become, not one of recognition, but one of recognition under conditions which would impair the efficiency of the large industrial organizations.

The huge corporations have contributed to American economic efficiency. They constitute an important step in the direction of the better organization of industry and commerce. They have not, except in certain exceptional cases, suppressed competition; but they have regulated it; and it should be the effort of all civilized societies to substitute coöperative for competitive methods, wherever coöperation can prove its efficiency. Deliberately to undo this work of industrial and commercial organization would constitute a logical application of the principle of equal rights, but it would also constitute a step backward in the process of economic and social advance. The process of industrial organization should be allowed to work itself out. Whenever the smaller competitor of the large corporation is unable to keep his head above water with his own exertions, he should be allowed to drown. That the smaller business man will entirely be displaced by the large corporation is wholly improbable. There are certain industries and lines of trade in which he will be able to hold his own; but where he is not able to hold his own, there is no public interest promoted by any expensive attempt to save his life.

The Sherman Anti-Trust Law constitutes

THE WAR CHANT
Every time I come to town
The boys keep a-kickin' my dawg aroun'.
Makes no diff'rence if he is a houn'—
They gotta quit kickin' my dawg aroun'!

Mrs. Helen Turner Johnson

The "common people" show rising resentment against the trusts during the Taft era.

precisely such an attempt to save the life of the small competitor; and in case the Roosevelt-Taft policy of recognition tempered by regulation is to prevail, the first step to be taken is the repeal or the revision of that law. As long as it remains on the statute books in its existing form, it constitutes an announcement that the national interest of the American people demands active discrimination in favor of the small industrial and commercial agent. It denies the desirability of recognizing what has already been accomplished in the way of industrial and commercial organization; and according to prevalent interpretations, it makes the legal standing of all large industrial combinations insecure—no matter how conducive to economic efficiency their business policy may be. . . .

The only sound point of departure for a national economic policy is . . . the acceptance by the state of certain of the results of corporate industrial organization. Such state recognition is equivalent to discrimination in their favor, because it leaves them in possession of those fundamental economic advantages, dependent on terminals, large capital, and natural resources, which place them beyond effective competition; and the state has good reason to suffer this discrimination, because a wise government can always make more social capital out of a coöperative industrial organization than it can out of an extremely competitive one.

It is extremely improbable that, even when officially recognized in this way, the process of corporate combination would go beyond a certain point. It might result in a condition similar to that which now prevails in the steel industry or that of sugar refining; but it should be added that in industries organized to that extent there is not very much competition in prices. Prices are usually regulated by agreement among the leading producers; and competition among the several producers turns upon quickness of delivery and the quality of the service or product. Whether or not this restriction of competition works badly depends usually upon the enlightened shrewdness with which the schedule of rates and prices is fixed. A corporation management which was thoroughly alive to its own interest would endeavor to arrange a scale of prices, which, while affording a sufficient profit, would encourage the increased use of the product, and that is precisely the policy which has been adopted by the best managed American railroad and industrial corporations.

But it must always be kept in mind that, in the absence of a certain amount of competition, such a policy cannot be taken wholly for granted. A short-sighted management may prefer to reap large profits for a short time and at the expense of the increased use of its product or service. Moreover, the margin between the cost of production and the particular price at which the product or service can be sold consistent with its largely increasing use may enable the producer to gather enormous profits; and such profits may not stimulate competition to any effective extent, precisely because they depend upon advantages in production which cannot be duplicated. No state desirous of promoting the economic welfare of its citizens can remain indifferent to the chance thus afforded of earnings disproportionately large to the economic service actually rendered.

In dealing with this question of possibly excessive profits under such a method of economic organization, the state has many resources at its disposal besides the most obvious one of incessant official interference with the essentials of corporation management. Of these the most useful consists unquestionably in its power of taxation. It can constitute a system of taxation, in respect to the semi-monopolistic corporations, which would deprive them of the fruits of an excessively large margin between the cost of production and the price at which the product or service could be increasingly sold. . . .

The objection will, no doubt, be immediately urged that a system of this kind would prevent any improvement of service from going beyond a certain point, just because it would cease to be profitable beyond a certain point. But such an objection would not be valid, provided the scale of taxation were properly graduated. . . .

The foregoing plan, however, is not suggested as a final and entirely satisfactory method of incorporating semi-monopolistic business organizations into the economic system of a nationalizing democracy. I do not believe that any formula can be framed which will by the magic of some chemical process convert a purely selfish economic motive into an unqualified public economic benefit. But some such plan as that proposed above may enable an industrial democracy to get over the period of transition between the partial and the complete adaptation of these companies to their place in a system of national economy. They can never be completely incorporated so long as the interest of their owners is different from that of the community as a whole, but in the meantime they can be encouraged to grow and perhaps to become more efficient, while at the same time they can be prevented from becoming a source of undesirable or dangerous individual economic inequalities.

THEODORE ROOSEVELT SPEAKS

The bravest man I ever knew was one that followed me up San Juan Hill.

My problems are moral problems, and my teaching has been plain morality.

I have let up in every case where I have had any possible excuse for so doing.

      —Protest against being called a trust buster

I wish to preach, not the doctrine of ignoble ease, but the doctrine of the strenuous life.

Far better it is to dare mighty things, to win glorious triumphs, even though check-ered by failure, than to take rank with those poor spirits who neither enjoy much nor suffer much, because they live in the gray twilight that knows not victory nor defeat.

We demand that big business give the people a square deal; in return we must insist that when anyone engaged in big business honestly endeavors to do right he shall himself be given a square deal.

The men with the muck-rake are often indispensable to the well-being of society; but only if they know when to stop raking the muck.

Nothing is more true than that excess of every kind is followed by reaction; a fact which should be pondered by reformer and reactionary alike. We are face to face with new conceptions of the relations of property to human welfare, chiefly because certain advocates of the rights of property as against the rights of men have been pushing their claims too far. The man who wrongly holds that every human right is secondary to his profit must now give way to the advocate of human welfare, who rightly maintains that every man holds his property subject to the general right of the community to regulate its use to whatever degree the public welfare may re-quire it. But I think we may go still further. . . . Let us admit also the right to regulate the terms and conditions of labor, which is the chief element of wealth, directly in the interest of the common good. The fundamental thing to do for every man is to give him a chance to reach a place in which he will make the greatest possible contribution to the public welfare.

—Speech at Osawatomie, Kansas, Aug. 31, 1910,
launching the New Nationalism

THE TRUSTS, THE PEOPLE, AND THE SQUARE DEAL

[Theodore Roosevelt's clearest expression of his Regulationist doctrine and of his impatience with the accusation that he had been a "trust buster" is found in an article, "The Trusts, the People, and the Square Deal," in *The Outlook* of Nov. 18, 1911 (99:649–656), of which magazine he became contributing editor on leav-ing the Presidency. Here we reprint a few highlights from the long article. He opened with the criticism that the Sherman Antitrust Law took the wrong ap-proach, though he approved of the action of the Supreme Court in breaking up the Standard Oil and Tobacco Trusts because they had been guilty of "immoral and anti-social practices," but then went on to criticize the Atomists.]

Sincere zealots who believed that all com-binations could be destroyed and the old-time conditions of unregulated competition restored, insincere politicians who knew better but made believe that they thought whatever their con-stituents wished them to think, crafty reaction-aries who wished to see on the statute-books laws which they believed unenforceable, and the almost solid "Wall Street crowd" or representatives of "big business" who at that time opposed with equal violence both wise and necessary and unwise and improper regulation of business—all fought against the adoption of a sane, effective, and far-reaching policy. . . .

To attempt to meet the whole problem not by administrative governmental action but by a succession of lawsuits is hopeless from the standpoint of working out a permanently satisfactory solution. . . .

The Anti-Trust Law cannot meet the whole situation, nor can any modification of the principle of the Anti-Trust Law avail to meet the whole situation. The fact is that many of the men who have called themselves Progressives, and who certainly believe that they are Progressives, represent in reality in this matter not progress at all but a kind of sincere rural toryism. These men believe that it is possible by strengthening the Anti-Trust Law to restore business to the competitive conditions of the middle of the last century. Any such effort is foredoomed to end in failure, and, if successful, would be mischievous to the last degree. Business cannot be successfully conducted in accordance with the practices and theories of sixty years ago unless we abolish steam, electricity, big cities, and, in short, not only all modern business and modern industrial conditions, but all the modern conditions of our civilization.

The effort to restore competition as it was sixty years ago, and to trust for justice solely to this proposed restoration of competition, is just as foolish as if we should go back to the flintlocks of Washington's Continentals as a substitute for modern weapons of precision. The effort to prohibit all combinations, good or bad, is bound to fail, and ought to fail; when made, it merely means that some of the worst combinations are not checked and that honest business is checked. Our purpose should be, not to strangle business as an incident of strangling combinations, but to regulate big corporations in thoroughgoing and effective

fashion, so as to help legitimate business as an incident to thoroughly and completely safeguarding the interests of the people as a whole. . . .

Nor can action be effectively taken by any one State. Congress alone has power under the Constitution effectively and thoroughly and at all points to deal with inter-State commerce . . . although until Congress does act affirmatively and thoroughly it is idle to expect that the States will or ought to rest content with non-action on the part of both Federal and State authorities. This statement, by the way, applies also to the question of "usurpation" by any one branch of our Government of the rights of another branch. It is contended that in these recent decisions the Supreme Court legislated; so it did; and it had to; because Congress had signally failed to do *its* duty by legislating. For the Supreme Court to nullify an act of the Legislature as unconstitutional except on the clearest grounds is usurpation; to interpret such an act in an obviously wrong sense is usurpation; but where the legislative body persistently leaves open a field which it is absolutely imperative, from the public standpoint, to fill, then no possible blame attaches to the official or officials who step in because they have to, and who then do the needed work in the interest of the people. The blame in such cases lies with the body which has been derelict, and not with the body which reluctantly makes good the dereliction. . . .

We demand that big business give the people a square deal; in return we must insist that when any one engaged in big business honestly endeavors to do right he shall himself be given a square deal; and the first, and most elementary, kind of square deal is to give him in advance full information as to just what he can, and what he cannot, legally and properly do. It is absurd, and much worse than absurd, to treat the deliberate lawbreaker as on an exact par with the man eager to obey the law, whose only desire is to find out from some competent Governmental authority what the law is, and then to live up to it. Moreover, it is absurd to treat the size of a corporation as in itself a crime. . . .

Not only should any huge corporation which has gained its position by unfair methods, and by interference with the rights of others, by demoralizing and corrupt practices, in short, by sheer baseness and wrong-doing, be broken up, but it should be made the business of some administrative governmental body, by constant supervision, to see that it does not come together again, save under such strict control as shall insure the community against all repetition of the bad conduct. . . . But nothing of importance is gained by breaking up a huge inter-State and international industrial organization *which has not offended otherwise than by its size*, into a number of small concerns without any attempt to regulate the way in which those concerns as a whole shall do business.

"WE STAND AT ARMAGEDDON, AND WE BATTLE FOR THE LORD"

[TR's address to the national convention of the Progressive Party on August 6, 1912, was formally entitled "A Confession of Faith," but its closing words became the rallying cry of the party and gave a name to the three-cornered Presidential Campaign. The excerpts given here are from TR's *Works* 17:254–299. His long recital of proposed reforms is omitted.]

To you, men and women who have come here to this great city of this great State formally to launch a new party, a party of the people of the whole Union, the National Progressive party, I extend my hearty greeting. You are taking a bold and a greatly needed step for the service of our beloved country. The old parties are husks, with no real soul within either, divided on artificial lines, boss-ridden and privilege-controlled, each a jumble of incongruous elements, and neither daring to speak out wisely and fearlessly what should be said on the vital issues of the day. This new movement is a movement of truth, sincerity, and wisdom, a movement which proposes to put at the service of all our people the collective power of the people, through their governmental agencies, alike in the nation and in the several States. We propose boldly to face the real and great questions of the day, and not skilfully to evade them as do the old parties. We propose to raise aloft a standard to which all honest men can repair, and under which all can fight, no matter what their past political differences, if they are content to face the future and no longer to dwell among the dead issues of the past. We propose to put forth a platform which shall not be a platform of the ordinary and insincere kind, but shall be a contract with the people; and, if the people accept this contract by putting us in power, we shall hold ourselves under honorable obligation to fulfil every promise it contains as loyally as if it were actually enforceable under the penalties of the law.

The prime need to-day is to face the fact that we are now in the midst of a great economic evolution. There is urgent necessity of applying both common sense and the highest ethical standard to this movement for better economic conditions among the mass of our people if we are to make it one of healthy evolution and not one of revolution. . . .

It is utterly hopeless to attempt to control the trusts merely by the antitrust law, or by any law the same in principle, no matter what the modifications may be in detail. In the first place, these great corporations cannot possibly be controlled merely by a succession of lawsuits. The administrative branch of the government must exercise such control. . . . The antitrust law should be kept on the statute-books and strengthened so as to make it genuinely and thoroughly effective against every big concern tending to monopoly or guilty of antisocial practices. At the same time, a national industrial commission should be created which should have complete power to regulate and control all the great industrial concerns engaged in interstate business—which practically means all of them in this country. . . .

Surely there never was a fight better worth making than the one in which we are engaged. It little matters what befalls any one of us who for the time being stands in the forefront of the battle. I hope we shall win, and I believe that if we can wake the people to what the fight really means we shall win. But, win or lose, we shall not falter. Whatever fate may at the moment overtake any of us, the movement itself will not stop. Our cause is based on the eternal principle of righteousness; and even though we who now lead may for the time fail, in the end the cause itself shall triumph. Six weeks ago, here in Chicago, I spoke to the honest representatives of a convention which was not dominated by honest men. . . . Now to you men, who, in your turn, have come together to spend and be spent in the endless crusade against wrong, to you who face the future resolute and confident, to you who strive in a spirit of brotherhood for the betterment of our nation, to you who gird yourselves for this great new fight in the never-ending warfare for the good of humankind, I say in closing what in that speech I said in closing: We stand at Armageddon, and we battle for the Lord.

TAFT AT ARMAGEDDON

Whether I win or lose is not the important thing. But I am in this fight to perform a great public duty—the duty of keeping Theodore Roosevelt out of the White House.

—Taft, speaking to Charles W. Thompson, 1912

The Republican party needs the discipline of defeat, and the great object that I have in carrying on this campaign is saving the parts of the party which can be saved, and making a solid disciplined force which will be ready to take advantage of our old-time enemy the Democrats.

—Taft, writing in July, 1912

Taft felt that he ought to make some explanation of his course in breaking the precedent set by every President from Washington to Roosevelt and appealing to mass meetings for votes. Even in his long list of luckless experiments in the art of expression, this one shines out as a pearl of great price. "Even a rat will fight when driven into a corner," he said gloomily—and thus vanished the last lingering chance he had of getting a look-in in the Presidential primary States.

—C. W. Thompson, *Presidents I've Known* (1929), p. 222

T.R. TO W.H.T.

Or ever the knightly fight was on,
The skirmish of smear and smudge,
I was a king in Washington
And you were a circuit judge.

I saw, I took, I made you great,
Friendly I called you "Will."
And back in Nineteen Hundred and Eight,
Out in Chicago, Ill.
I made the convention nominate,
And now—the terrible chill.

For many a sun has set and shone
On the path we used to trudge
When I was a king in Washington
And you were a circuit judge.

I passed the lie and you passed it back;
You said I was all untruth;
I said that honesty was your lack;
You said I'd not reck nor ruth;
You called me a megalomaniac—
I called you a Serpent's Tooth. . . .

—F. P. Adams in the *New York World* parodying Henley's "I Was
a King in Babylon." The labeling of Taft as a circuit judge was
poetic license, as he had held many offices since his judicial days.

Mrs. Helen Turner Johnson

TR glares while Taft pleads for tariff reduction and Senator Aldrich says, "Aw, hang the consumer!"

WHAT WAS THE NEW FREEDOM?

[Wilson's ignorance of economics was probably even greater than that of the average progressive leader, and as a result he sometimes uttered vague or conflicting statements which—as King Mongkut would have put it—made the definition of the New Freedom "a puzzlement." William E. Leuchtenburg in his introduction to the reprint of Wilson's *The New Freedom* (Englewood Cliffs: Prentice-Hall, 1961), pp. 6–17, gives some idea of how Wilson's mastery of words sometimes tended to give dazzling light but little heat.]

In the 1912 campaign, Wilson transmuted the trust question into "a second struggle for emancipation." At stake were no longer pecuniary matters like markets and profits but the eternal truths by which men live. Wilson identified the plight of the man seeking enough capital to start a small business with the ageless struggle of men for liberty. "Are you not eager for the time when the genius and initiative of all the people shall be called into the service of business? when newcomers with new ideas, new entries with new enthusiasm, independent men, shall be welcomed? when your sons shall be able to look forward to becoming, not employees, but heads of some small, it may be, but hopeful, business, where their best energies shall be inspired by the knowledge that they are their own masters, with the paths of the world open before them?" Wilson asked. "Surely you must feel the inspiration of such a new dawn of liberty." . . .

Wilson had an unusual capacity for making mundane issues seem like moral questions of transcendent importance. Some men regarded this gift as a blessing, others as an annoyance. He could make men see the spiritual possibilities of matters to which they had been blind before, but he could also make of political issues more than was actually there. Even the short ballot could be made to seem an evidence of Divine Providence. "His mind," a contemporary critic remarked, "is like a light which destroys the outlines of what it plays upon; there is much illumination, but you see very little." He gave to the trust question in 1912 a spirit of elevated thought and action men had rarely heard before, but he left both many of his contemporaries and two generations of historians bewildered about precisely what he did propose to do about the trusts.

It is sometimes said that the distinction between the New Nationalism and the New Freedom is that Roosevelt wanted to permit the trusts to grow and regulate them, while Wilson wanted to break them up. This would be a logical distinction, but it does not seem to be an accurate one. Much of Wilson's rhetoric makes little sense unless one supposes he was advocating the dissolution of the trusts, yet on more than one occasion he made clear that he did not favor dismemberment. In 1912, Wilson declared: "I am not one of those who think that competition can be established by law against the drift of a world-wide economic tendency." If his faith in competition drove him in the direction of dissecting the trusts, his organic conception of society restrained him. . . . In his first inaugural address, Wil-

son stated: "We shall deal with our economic system as it is and as it may be modified, not as it might be if we had a clean sheet of paper to write upon."

While, on occasion, Wilson adopted Brandeis' view that bigness was, in itself, a curse, more often he insisted that he did not oppose bigness as such, so long as this great size had been acquired fairly. "I am not afraid of anything that is normal," Wilson asserted, and if trusts were the product of natural growth, he had no quarrel with them. There was no little casuistry in Wilson's distinction between big business and the trusts, and, in fact, he did almost nothing, either as governor or as president, to disturb existing agglomerations. He aimed rather at halting the process of concentration before it went any further. While he was worried about the tendency toward monopoly in particular industries, he was most alarmed by the "community of interest" created by "the combination of the combinations," and he wanted to use the power of government to insure intercorporate competition. "It has been said that you cannot 'unscramble eggs,' and I am perfectly willing to admit it," Wilson declared in 1912, "but I can see in all cases before they are scrambled that they are not put in the same basket and entrusted to the same groups of persons."

Wilson believed that only in a society of free enterprise could men be free. In 1910, he observed that in the modern business world, men were no longer individuals but "fractions." Having lost their independence of choice in business, they had "lost also their individual choice within the field of morals." In a truly competitive society, on the other hand, each man's rewards would be determined by his character. A believer in progress who was at the same time deeply aware of the sinfulness of man, he distrusted concentrating power in the hands of corporations or of governments which would determine a man's lot in life for him. If each man were free to follow his own self-interest, aware of his need to answer to his Maker, the interests of society would be best advanced. Only in such a society could each man be a "distinct moral agent," responsible for his own destiny and living his life with an almost overpowering sense of the presence of God. Man, observed Wilson, was "not the creature of the drawing room or the stock exchange, but a lonely, awful soul confronted by the Source of all souls."

Nothing distressed Wilson more than the fear that the middle class, the class which originated new enterprises, was "being crushed between the upper and nether millstones." He hoped he would never see an America which consisted only "of masters and employees," where the opportunities for the man who would take risks had been snuffed out. . . . By using the power of government to restore competition, Wilson hoped he could arrest the change from the old middle class of the independent professional and businessman to the new middle class of the white collar worker and the salaried professional.

He wanted to help not the established businessman, but the new entrepreneur. The real division in the country, he said in 1908, was not between capital and labor, but rather between large, concentrated capital and more dispersed economic forces. . . . If the government denied special privileges, Wilson thought, these "artificial" creations of the trusts, stripped of their unfair advantage, would not be able to stand up in competition with businesses that had grown naturally.

Wilson charged that government had been rigged against the small entrepreneur not only because it had granted special privileges to trusts but because both governments and political parties were controlled by machines. The objection to the machine was the same as the objection to the trust: it used government for private purposes. Wilson sought to free government from its tie with any one class, and to divorce government from its association either with trusts or with machine bosses. His main disagreement with the Bull Moose Party of 1912 arose from his conviction that Theodore Roosevelt, instead of destroying

these evil cabals, aimed to institutionalize the alliance of politics and business under the aegis of the super-trusts.

He believed that politics must be purified. The government had been defiled by its association with privileged monopolists and he would wash it clean. Repeatedly Wislon returned to the imagery of light, air, and sun; government had been besmirched and had to be cleansed. By removing tariff privileges, he would "let the sun shine through the clouds again as once it shone." "We are going into this garden and give the little plants air and light in which to grow," Wilson explained. "We are going to pull up every root that has so spread itself as to draw the nutriment of the soil from other roots." The energies of free men would then be able to find expression. To purify politics, he would break the nexus of government and special interests and arouse the citizenry to a moral awakening. . . .

The core of Wilson's thought was a protest against paternalism, and he disliked the paternalism of the welfare state almost as much as he objected to the egregiousness of the trusts. To be sure, he had come by 1912 to favor a number of welfare measures, although he did not go nearly so far as Roosevelt in this direction; yet his emphasis differed quite sharply from that of the statist progressives. He no more wished to grant special privileges to workers or farmers than to business corporations. He saw the state not as an agency to help direct society, but rather as an instrument to remove the shackles preventing men from having the same opportunity to compete. As Walter Lippmann put it: Wilson's political beliefs were "a fusion of Jeffersonian democracy with a kind of British Cobdenism. This meant in practical life a conviction that the world needs not so much to be administered as to be released from control."

Curiously, for a man who is taken as the exemplar of the intellectual in government, Wilson distrusted the new class of experts, and viewed with alarm the growth of commissions, which would provide the intellectuals with their home in government. He appeared to have for experts the tolerant disdain with which a university president views the claims to omniscience of his faculty. "I have lived with experts all my life," he observed, "and I know that experts . . . don't even perceive what is under their nose." His chief adviser, Brandeis, had the same suspicion of the planners, but he came to see more quickly than Wilson the need for expertise, and it was, of course, Brandeis who, by his brief in *Muller v. Oregon*, had given the intellectual new stature and a new role in securing progressive legislation. Under Brandeis's tutelage, Wilson modified some of his views. Yet even at the end of the campaign, he still remained suspicious of government commissions and arrogant intellectuals.

Nevertheless, no one who understood Wilson could have supposed that he wished to preside over an impotent government. . . . He quickly demonstrated that he had the power to command, and it was not long before he recognized that the ideology of Cobdenism had little relevance to America in the second decade of the twentieth century. Before he had ended his first term of office, he had jettisoned almost every one of the New Freedom doctrines. Even in his first months as president, when he adhered with reasonable faith to the philosophy of the New Freedom, he felt compelled to concede a good deal to the advocates of a positive state. By the end of 1916, he had gone virtually all the way. He had approved welfare legislation like the Child Labor Law and the La Follette Seamen's Act; he had fought for special interest measures like the Adamson Act and the Rural Credits Act; and he had surrendered to business demands for a tariff commission, protection against "dumping," and government sanction of export cartels. With scarcely a backward glance at the crusade for a New Freedom, he claimed in 1916 to have enacted the program of the Bull Moose Party as well as his own.

By 1916, Wilson's campaign of four years before already seemed curiously antiquated.

When he had run for president for the first time, he had spoken to a nation that stood at a great divide, looking longingly at the nineteenth-century world it was leaving, peering, half-hopefully, half-anxiously, at the twentieth-century world it was about to enter. Wilson's campaign of 1912 caught perfectly the mood of America that year, a nation captivated by the new and yearning for the old. In the same sentence, he could say that he wanted "to express the *new* spirit of our politics and *restore* our politics to their full spiritual vigor again." He identified himself with progress, spoke of "the presence of a new organization of society," and in a year when America was excited by the New Theater and the New Poetry, called his political program the New Freedom. Yet at the same time he exploited the resentment at the impersonal nature of the modern world and the disappearance of the village. He talked of "restoration" and "return"; celebrated the "America of the fathers"; and resorted repeatedly to images of a pristine rural life: "voting populations of the countryside, men tramping over the mountains, men going to the general store up in the village, men moving in little talking groups to the corner grocery to cast their ballots." Never did he try to evoke a similar urban idyll. "You know what the vitality of America consists of," Wilson declared. "Its vitality does not lie in New York, nor in Chicago; it will not be sapped by anything that happens in St. Louis." Precisely at the point in time when the city was beginning to overtake the rural town, Wilson warned that "if America discourages the locality, the community, the self-contained town, she will kill the nation."

By 1916, America had already taken several long strides from the village world Wilson had held up as an ideal. Today, we have travelled so far from that world that much of *The New Freedom* no longer seems usable. "If America is not to have free enterprise," Wilson told a crowd in Denver in October 1912, "then she can have freedom of no sort whatever." A statement of this sort—one which pays such homage to "free enterprise"—has a curious ring for the modern liberal, and it is here that much of the difficulty of the usability of Wilson's words for the liberal of the 1960's lies. Wilson's New Freedom was a progressive response, but it was a special brand of progressivism. It was deeply rooted in nineteenth-century British liberalism. . . .

In only one important respect does *The New Freedom* speak directly to the liberal of today. In warning of the perils of "corporate philanthropy," Wilson anticipated the modern-day concern with the Organization Man. Wilson feared that the corporation might not only do economic mischief, but, more important, that it would swallow up the individual.

The vast impersonality of modern business, Wilson warned, was destroying the independence of men. The country doctor was devoured by the city hospital, the village attorney by the mammoth law firm, the small businessman by the corporation. The menace came not simply from the malevolent corporation, but, perhaps even more, from the well-intentioned corporation which, through its profit-sharing and bonus plans, subtly destroyed men's wills by offering them security and contentment. In his alarm at the permeation of the values of the large organization through all of American culture, he expressed fears which a half-century later would be even more keenly felt.

ATOMISM VERSUS REGULATIONISM

You have asked me to state what the essential difference is between the Democratic Party's solution of the Trust Problem and that of the New Party; and how to propose to "regulate competition." My answer is this:

The two parties differ fundamentally regarding the economic policy which the country should pursue. The Democratic Party insists that competition can be and should be maintained in every branch of private industry; that competition can be and should be restored in those branches of industry in which it has been suppressed by the trusts; and that, if at any future time monopoly should appear to be desirable in any branch of industry, the monopoly should be a public one—a monopoly owned by the people and not by the capitalists. The New Party, on the other hand, insists that private monopoly may be desirable in some branches of industry, or at all events, is inevitable; and that existing trusts should not be dismembered or forcibly dislodged from those branches of industry in which they have already acquired a monopoly, but should be made 'good' by regulation. In other words, the New Party declares that private monopoly in industry is not necessarily evil, but may do evil; and that legislation should be limited to such laws and regulations as should attempt merely to prevent the doing of evil. The New Party does not fear commercial power, however great, if only methods for regulation are provided. We believe that no methods of regulation ever have been or can be devised to remove the menace inherent in private monopoly and overweening commercial power.

This difference in the economic policy of the two parties is fundamental and irreconcilable. It is the difference between industrial liberty and industrial absolutism, tempered by governmental (that is, party) supervision.

—Louis Brandeis to Woodrow Wilson, Sept. 30, 1912, in Arthur S. Link, *Wilson: The Road to the White House* (Princeton Univ. Press, 1947), p. 492. It was this letter, defining the difference between Atomism and Regulationism which set the tone of Wilson's antitrust proposals in the Campaign of 1912. The "New Party" refers, of course, to the Progressives.

FROM THE NEW FREEDOM TO THE NEW NATIONALISM

[Wilson's program had been almost naïvely simple: revise the tariff to deny special privileges to industries; coordinate the national banks; and restore competition among the great corporations. Indeed, he had denounced the elaborate proposals of Roosevelt's New Nationalism as being cures that might well be worse than the disease. Nevertheless, within a few months Wilson found himself under implacable political pressures which actually threatened to give him little or nothing unless he consented to move toward the New Nationalism. Practically the only item of his program that he got was the Underwood Tariff.

Northern and Western Democrats had moved beyond the simple agrarianism of 1896, but the majority of Southern Congressmen knew but little about the terrible urban and industrial problems of the Northeast, and still thought in populist terms. What they wanted was rural credits and effective government control on the top level of the proposed Federal Reserve System. Now that the Democrats controlled Congress, the more important committees were chaired by Southerners, and they used their power to get what they wanted for the South.

This was only the beginning. Wilson had believed that the trust problem could be solved by a few simple definitions of restraint of trade and tighter enforcement by the Justice Department and the courts. Instead, when the Clayton Bill emerged it was much more pretentious, and an additional bill set up a Federal Trade Commission with considerable supervisory powers—just what Roosevelt had proposed.

Here we turn to Arthur S. Link's perceptive article "The South and the New Freedom: An Interpretation," in *The American Scholar* 20:314–324 (Summer 1951), taking it up on page 319.]

The Southern leaders in Congress had nothing to do with bringing about this profound change in Wilson's antitrust policy. The Southern and Western Agrarian radicals, acting with a small Labor bloc in the House, worked hard, however, to have a provision inserted in the Clayton bill exempting farm and labor unions from the operation and application of the antitrust laws. This had been one of the major objectives of the American Federation of Labor since 1906 and had been given Democratic approval in the platforms of 1908 and 1912. Although Wilson was rapidly abandoning his New Freedom assumptions, he was not yet ready to go so far as to approve what

was obviously legislation in the interest of particular classes. Since the first days of his administration he had resisted bitterly this move, and a bill specifically exempting farm and labor unions from antitrust prosecutions, which had been passed by the House in the previous session, was blocked by administration pressure. When the Clayton bill was under discussion in the House committee, however, the Agrarian and Labor bloc declared that they would guarantee its defeat unless Wilson gave in to their demands.

Thus faced with another major revolt within his party, Wilson resolved his dilemma by resorting, it must be admitted, to one of the most artful dodges in the history of American politics. . . . On the face of it, the new provision did indeed seem to give the exemption and immunity from antitrust prosecutions that the farm and labor spokesmen were demanding. Actually, this was not the case at all. Farm and labor organizations were not to be construed by the courts as being, *per se*, combinations in restraint of trade, but they were in no way freed from the threat of prosecution if they violated the antitrust laws.

Wilson had completed his program of domestic reform by the fall of 1914. In his letters and public statements at the time, he made it clear that he thought everything had been done that was necessary to clear away special privilege and put all classes on an equal footing. Under the operation of the beneficent new laws, Wilson was sure that the nation would enjoy a long period of prosperity and economic freedom. As we have seen, he had been forced partially to abandon his earlier position and to make important concessions in order to get his program across. He was reconciled to the concessions he had been compelled to make, but he was absolutely determined to draw the line at the point it had reached by the fall of 1914. . . .

There were, however, several great political forces at work which were so strong that Wilson would be compelled to accommodate his program to satisfy their demands. One was the well-organized Agrarian movement for the establishment of a federal system of long-term rural credits. Another was the movement in behalf of federal social legislation, which was rapidly gaining momentum during this period. Another was the movement for women's suffrage, which was becoming so powerful that it would soon be dangerous for any politician to oppose it. Finally, there was the fact that the Progressive party was obviously disintegrating after 1914 and that the only hope the Democrats had of obtaining a national majority in 1916 was in winning a large minority of the former Bull Moosers to the Democratic side. . . . When it became evident that the Demo-

crats could win the election of 1916 only by adopting the New Nationalism, lock, stock and barrel, Wilson capitulated and supported the very demands he had so long opposed, as strongly as if he had been their originator. . . .

The main objective of the Southern Agrarian progressives after 1914 was the adoption of a federal rural credits bill. The first nationwide movement for long-term federal rural credit facilities had been inaugurated by the Southern Commercial Congress in 1913, and during the next year or two there was widespread discussion of the subject all over the country. In the spring of 1914 a joint subcommittee drew up the bill which was finally passed in 1916 and which would have passed in 1914 had not Wilson let it be known that he would veto the bill if Congress enacted it. Both Wilson and the Agrarian leaders proclaimed themselves advocates of a rural credits measure. What, therefore, was the root of the difference between them? Wilson would not agree to the establishment of a system involving direct subsidies or financial support by the government, and Wilson, Secretary of Agriculture Houston, and Carter Glass were insistent that the government should do no more than provide for the structure of a rural credits system, with capital and management to be provided by private sources. The Agrarian spokesmen, on the other hand, contended that any system which was not operated and financed by the government was bound to fail. But as this involved the direct intervention by the government in behalf of a special class, Wilson was absolutely adamant against it. The result was an impasse, with both sides holding out stubbornly for their own proposals until 1916, when Wilson accepted the Agrarian proposal for reasons of political expediency.

It was, in fact, in agricultural legislation that the Southern Agrarians had the greatest influence in the shaping of the later Wilsonian program. Their greatest contribution was undoubtedly the forcing of the Rural Credits Act of 1916, but they were also able to obtain the adoption of the Lever Warehouse Act in

1914, the Smith-Lever Act for rural extension work of the same year, the Smith-Hughes Act for vocational education, and the program of federal subsidies for highway improvement in 1916.

Southern influence was practically negligible, however, in the formulation of the remaining great social and economic legislation of 1961—the federal Workmen's Compensation Act, the Child Labor Law, the Adamson Act, and the act establishing the Federal Tariff Commission. But there still remain three other areas of legislation in which the influence of the Southern Agrarians was decisive. . . .

With the opening of Congress in December, 1915, the Southern progressives found themselves virtually in control of the House Ways and Means Committee. Long before the new session convened, a majority of the committee declared in writing to the new chairman, Claude Kitchin of North Carolina, their determination to overhaul the tax structure and make it more democratic. The result was that during the winter and spring of 1916 the control of federal tax policy was literally taken out of the hands of the administration leaders and assumed by these Southern Agrarians and their Western allies. It was obvious by this time that some kind of preparedness measures would be adopted, and that either the government would have to find new sources of revenue or else resort to borrowing. The Republicans proposed a bond issue; the administration proposed new consumption and excise and increased income taxes. The Ways and Means Committee, however, replied with one of the most startling and significant tax bills in the history of the country. The Southern Agrarians, who had bitterly resisted the preparedness movement, saw now that new

defense measures were inevitable; but they were determined that the people of the East, who had been most vociferous in support of preparedness, should pay for it. Kitchin said as much, in fact, before the House caucus when he explained the new tax bill, which greatly increased the income tax, levied the first federal inheritance tax in our history, and placed an excess profits tax on munitions manufacturers.

The last area in which Southern influence was decisive in determining the policies of the Wilson administration was the federal government's policy toward Negroes. Here the Southern contribution was definitely retrogressive and proved that it was impossible for white Southerners of all shades of opinion to get much beyond the rationale of slavery. Suffice it to say that Wilson practically sacrificed the Negroes on the altar of political expediency, by allowing segregation in the government departments, dismissal and downgrading of Negro civil servants in the South, and the like, in order to win Southern support for his program.

Yet in spite of this and other blind spots in the Southern progressive program, it must be concluded that the contributions of the Southern Agrarians were undoubtedly in many ways decisive in moving the Wilson administration away from a static laissez-faire program, to which it was originally dedicated, toward a dynamic, positive program of federal action. Although their program was limited in scope and motivated largely by class interests, the Southern progressives could claim as much credit as could several other major groups for the amazing metamorphosis in Democratic policy that occurred from 1913 to 1916. That is the real significance of their contribution.

AFTER-THOUGHTS ON PROGRESSIVISM

The clash over the nature and meaning of progressivism continues, and instead of a consensus being in sight seems to be becoming more complicated. Here we will offer in chronological order a number of critiques.

(1) DEWEY'S CRITIQUE OF PROGRESSIVISM

In the bleak light of normalcy in the early 1920's, after World War I had ended Progressivism, Dewey undertook a postmortem examination of the Progressive Era. The spirit of the times suggested a more critical analysis of American history than he might have made earlier. His central problem was to explain why political liberalism in America was so fragile a flower. He found the answer in the peculiar character of American democracy. The Enlightenment had nurtured a revolutionary point of view in science and philosophy that had found its social expression in nineteenth-century democracy, with its ideal of freedom and equality of opportunity. While this ideal remained the genuinely spiritual element of the American tradition, it had never been fully realized.

Rather, during the nineteenth century, democracy had become closely identified with evangelical Protestantism. In Dewey's opinion, the fusion of democracy and religion had produced results at once admirable and deplorable. The heart of democracy was the American middle class, a fairly prosperous and well-disposed people, moderate in outlook, sympathetic to reform, pacifism, and public education but largely devoid of taste or discrimination. . . . Dewey readily conceded that the churches had performed an important social function in maintaining a basic decency and order in an expanding society. But their concept of cultural life had been narrow; they grasped power in the form of moral authority; and they perpetuated a reign of mediocrity. It was to such degrading influences that Dewey ascribed the failure of democracy to find the kind of leadership to which eighteenth-century Republicanism had proudly resorted. Democracy had no place among its leaders for such intellectuals as Jefferson, Franklin, or Adams; its dislike of privilege focused itself with special resentment upon the cultivated and the expert. In the twentieth century, William Jennings Bryan best represented this spirit. Bryan's anti-evolution crusade reflected the popular fear of whatever seemed to threaten the security and order of a precariously held civilization. The fundamentalist insistence upon uniformity of belief revealed the need of the insecure for conformity.

Progressivism, as Dewey now sadly realized, had been a kind of moral crusade. Bryan, Theodore Roosevelt, and Wilson had been revivalists whose activities had expressed "moral emotions rather than the insight and policy of intelligence." . . . A temper of mind began to emerge with the preparedness movement of 1916, which in the end proved fatal to Progressivism. The events of the war years showed many Americans to be "social fundamentalists," enlightened in scientific or religious matters but prejudiced, emotional, and ignorant of political and economic affairs. The effect of the war upon such an immature people was to render them unwilling and unable to recapture the mood of prewar Progressivism.

—Stow Persons, *American Minds* (N.Y.: Holt, 1958), pp. 403–404.

(2) THE CEREMONIAL SOLUTION TO THE TRUST PROBLEM

We have seen that the growth of great organization in America occurred in the face of a religion which officially was dedicated to the preservation of the economic independence of individuals. In such a situation it was inevitable that a ceremony should be evolved which reconciled current mental pictures of what men thought society ought to be with reality. The learned mythology of the time insisted that American industry was made up of small competing concerns which, if they were not individuals, nevertheless approach that ideal. "Bigness" was regarded as a curse because it led to monopoly and interfered with the operation of the laws of supply and demand. At the same time specialized techniques made bigness essential to producing goods in large enough quantities and at a price low enough so that they could be made part of the American standard of living. In order to reconcile the ideal with the practical necessity, it became necessary to develop a procedure which constantly attacked bigness on rational legal and economic grounds, and at the same time never really interfered with combinations. Such pressures gave rise to the antitrust laws which appeared to be a complete prohibition of large combinations. The same pressures made the enforcement of the antitrust laws a pure ritual. The effect of this statement of the ideal and its lack of actual enforcement was to convince reformers either that large combinations did not actually exist, or else that if they did exist, they were about to be done away with just as soon as right-thinking men were elected to office. Trust busting therefore became one of the great moral issues of the day, while at the same time great combinations thrived and escaped regulation. . . .

Since the organizations were demanded, attempts to stop their growth necessarily became purely ceremonial. As fast as one cloak was stripped off and declared illegal by the courts, other cloaks were manufactured and put on. The antitrust laws, being a preaching device, naturally performed only the functions of preaching. The actual result of the antitrust laws was to promote the growth of great industrial organizations by deflecting the attack on them into purely moral and ceremonial channels. . . .

One great change, however, did come over corporate activity because of the philosophy which produced the antitrust laws. Since everyone thought of these great enterprises as individuals which should be moral and gentlemanly in their dealings, they came gradually to conform to those standards. This is in accordance with the principle of political dynamics which makes it inevitable that an institution will, in the long run, conform to the character which men give it. The antitrust laws were based on a popular conception that great corporations *could* be made respectable. Following that ideal, great corporations *did* become respectable.

—Thurman Arnold, *The Folklore of Capitalism* (Yale Univ. Press, 1937), pp. 207–208, 211–212, 221.

(3) A LIBERAL-COLLECTIVIST PHILOSOPHY

Only a gifted few progressives understood that they were helping to create a new political philosophy. It is easy for us now to see that their era was the crucible where, by the classic Hegelian process, a new political philosophy was in the making. From the time of the Founders there had been two attitudes toward the state: the Jeffersonian, relying upon a minimal state, decentralized institutions and the good sense of the local yeomanry; and the Hamiltonian, at home with vigorous government and a national outlook, but interested before all else in the welfare of the managers and owners of the commercial, banking, and industrial enterprises of the country. By the beginning of this century there was emerging a third, the liberal-collectivist, sharing with the first its democratic sympathies and with the second its national and statist focus.

—Otis L. Graham, *An Encore for Reform* (1967), p. 185

(4) MEN OF GOOD HOPE

What needs to be emphasized now is that these men were radicals, in the sense that we use that term today. Their demands for a real social equality and a more equitable distribution of the national wealth belong in the category of those simple but overwhelming requests that require a drastic overhauling of our economic system and a transformation in our social ethic—one might almost say a religious revival —if they are to be realized. They hoped and expected to achieve what we should call their utopian goal by appealing to the good sense and justice of their fellow Americans. They envisaged a Christian society where all would have a comfortable sufficiency, where the atmosphere would be wholesome and polite, where perfect equality woud exist as a matter of course, and where the citizen would not be offended, either by the vulgar plutocrat or the rude proletarian.

There is something naïve and strait-laced in many of their proposals, and we in the twentieth century who have become wiser and more cynical about human perversity may smile at the simplicity of the progressive paradise. And yet it has been demonstrated that the progressives were less timid and cautious, less hypothetical, than their modern counterparts, and less sentimental too. The open society may be an anachronism, but it is a valid and a sensible ideal. And for all their lapses, the progressives, although completely absorbed in the cause of the underprivileged, seldom romanticized "Labor" or the "Little People" or degenerated into the sloppy and maudlin rhetoric of which so many of our present-day liberals are guilty.

Today progressivism, properly interpreted, provides a philosophy for America that is deeply radical in its implications, thoroughly rooted in the American experience, and irreconcilably antitotalitarian. It is a humanist philosophy, undisguisedly ethical, riveted to principles. It is not a creed for opportunists, for the politically ambitious (although it has inadvertently brought fame and popularity to its seers and expounders), but it is a very satisfactory faith, as Charles Russell said, for a person who wants to stay on good terms with himself. . . .

The progressive tradition thus provides the foundations for an indigenous radicalism peculiarly tuned to the American historical experience. It undercuts the contentions of the superpatriots, with their curious and erroneous notions of "Americanism" and "un-Americanism," by showing that a stand against privilege and monopoly has been characteristically American and that forms of socialism are not incompatible with democracy. Progressivism is preeminently the philosophy of social experimentation, of the mixed economy. It is neither for nor against the government; it is against faction, special interests, monopoly, and privilege. Instead of pretending that class bitterness is some kind of foreign poison and that it is indecent even to suggest the possibility of one class or group exploiting another, progressivism proposes to eliminate the conditions that aggravate this tendency and to re-establish a classless or open society. It attempts to carry out this program not through a temporary dictatorship of the working class, not by autocratic fiat, but by abolishing special privileges and by restoring in greater measure the equality of opportunity.

—Daniel Aaron, *Men of Good Hope* (N.Y.: Oxford, 1951), pp. 307–308. Aaron is concerned not only with the Progressive era but with reformers from Emerson onward.

10

INEVITABLE DESTINY

INTRODUCTION

In this chapter and the next two we shall examine some of the main streams of American foreign and colonial policy from the 1890's to the 1930's, and also some of the world conditions in which they operated. The subject, in so far as it is amenable to organization, can be comprehended under three heads—which, however, are by no means exclusive. The most inclusive topic is the emergence of the United States from isolation in the 1890's and its retreat thereto (at least politically) in the 1920's. The other topics are the evolution of the Monroe Doctrine in the Western Hemisphere and the evolution of the Open Door Policy in the Far East. Since it is impossible to do full justice to these topics in a work of this kind, the serious student is referred to Norman Graebner's *Ideas and Diplomacy* (N.Y.: Oxford, 1964) for an extended and masterly combination of documents and commentary on the entire sweep of American foreign and colonial policy.

IMPERIALISM AND WAR

[John Hobson was an English economist who in 1905 published *Imperialism: A Study*, which became one of the seminal books of this century. As he saw it, imperialism rose chiefly from economic greed, and the reasons usually given were cited by imperialists to deceive the public. Lenin seized on Hobson's thesis and wrested it to paper over certain cracks in Marxist ideology. His *Imperialism,* printed in Zurich in 1916, became the blueprint of communist international policy. The subject of imperialism is very complex and its bibliography is immense, but see Parker T. Moon, *Imperialism and World Politics* (1926), which leans to the economic interpretation, and E. M. Winslow, *The Pattern of Imperialism* (1948), which sets the balance straight by stressing the noneconomic. A brief introduction to an understanding of the way in which Lenin and later communists use the word communism is given by R. N. Carew-Hunt in his *A Guide to Communist Jargon* (N.Y.: Macmillan, 1957), pp. 82–88.)

The term imperialism has largely replaced capitalism in the Communist vocabulary. It is also used as a synonym for colonialism, which, oddly enough, is not to be found in any Russian dictionary of foreign words, and was first given currency by Khrushchev and Bulganin during their Asian tour in 1955. Since then it has been the subject of numerous articles in Russian periodicals which describe conditions in territories under British administration with the usual irresponsible mendacity.

The concept of imperialism derives from Lenin's *Imperialism: The Highest Stage of Capitalism* (1916), the most revolutionary writing of this century, as communist policy has been largely based on its conclusions, and of all the Marxist-Leninist texts the most important for an understanding of the present communist world-view. Lenin's immediate object was to explain why the capitalist system still persisted in spite of its contradictions, and why the conditions of the European workers, or at least of a section of them, had greatly improved, although Marx had declared that they must inevitably worsen. He did this by asserting that there had entered into the situation a new factor which had not existed in Marx's day, and that this was imperialism, the emergence of which he dates precisely from 1898–1900.

Briefly, the essential features of imperialism are the concentration of capital, the merging of industrial and banking capital into "finance capital" and the division of the world between national and international monopolies. Lenin called this "moribund capitalism," as it repre-

sented, in his view the last stage of the capitalist system which precedes its final collapse and the victory of the proletariat. It should be observed that imperialism thus denotes the predominance of a certain form of capital. It does not signify the direct domination over foreign lands, though such domination usually takes place. But Lenin does not seem to have regarded the actual possession of an empire as essential to it, so that, according to his theory, the United States is an imperialist Power, as communist propaganda daily represents it.

How then did imperialism come about? Because the more developed countries had reached a point at which they were producing more goods than their home markets could absorb, and were therefore driven to find markets in backward countries, which were then annexed, to which they could sell these surplus products in exchange for cheap raw materials. Thus the development of the capitalist system rendered the possession of colonies essential. But Lenin held that there were now no more of them to be had, and that a country could thus satisfy its needs only by seizing those of another. This scramble operated in accordance with the so-called Law of the Uneven Development of Capitalism; that is, success depended on the relative strength of the contending parties, which was a variable factor, since as that of one country increased, that of another declined. Hence Lenin concluded that imperialism must lead to war, as the great Powers would be forever falling out among themselves, the less fortunate being discontented with their share of the colonial market, which they would seek to extend as soon as they were strong enough to do so. This theory of the inevitability of war in the period of imperialist capitalism was modified by the Twentieth Congress, partly because it was useless for the Communists to organize world-wide peace campaigns if wars could not be prevented, and partly because the greater part of the colonial world had regained its independence during the last ten years, though without the capitalist countries collapsing as they should have done. But the theory enabled Lenin to declare that the First World War was an imperialist one; that is, that it was fundamentally a struggle between the imperialist Powers for markets; and the Second World War was pronounced to be the same until Hitler attacked the Soviet Union, when its character immediately changed.

The theory led to other conclusions also. Investment abroad at higher rates of interest than were obtainable at home increased the numbers of the parasitic rentier class, and thus sharpened the class struggle. Yet Lenin none the less argued, not altogether consistently, that the "super-profits" obtained by exploiting backward peoples enabled the capitalists of the metropolitan countries to weaken the revolutionary zeal of the workers, particularly those in the upper strata, by bribing them with higher wages and better conditions at the expense of the new proletariat of the exploited countries.

Again, the theory provided a justification of the October Revolution. According to the Marxist analysis, the proletarian revolution should take place in the most highly industrialized country, because it would be in such a country that the contradictions inherent in capitalism would be most fully developed. The introduction of this new factor of imperialism made it possible to evade this conclusion, as industrially backward countries could now be represented as simply appendages of the metropolitan countries. Thus the revolution might well take place in one that was only partially developed, as it had done in Russia because

that country was "the weakest link in the capitalist chain." A rider to the above was Lenin's statement that "Socialism is possible . . . even in one country," which was to be the basis of Stalin's policy from 1924 onwards.

Thus the doctrine could be used to serve the following purposes:

(1) To provide an explanation of why Marx's Law of Increasing Misery had not been fulfilled, at least in the imperialist countries.

(2) To account for why the proletarian revolution had occurred in a country which did not satisfy Marx's requirements.

(3) To demonstrate that all wars between imperialist countries could be explained in economic terms.

(4) To emphasize that the best way to promote the world revolutionary struggle was to stir up the peoples of the backward countries, thus cutting the tap-roots of the prosperity of the metropolitan countries, which would then have to reduce wages and cut down social services, thus proving that reforms were no substitute for revolution, as Marx had always contended.

Lenin's doctrine illustrates the weakness of monocausal explanations of highly complex phenomena, and is open to criticism at many points. Thus the Austrian economist Joseph Schumpeter has pointed out that a State is not imperialist if it pursues a concrete interest and abandons its aggressive attitude once this has been secured. What characterizes imperialism is that it is aggression which is objectless and irrational. It first appears in history with peoples whose circumstances led them to acquire a predatory disposition and a corresponding social organization before they settled permanently, so that the urge to conquer and subdue became an atavism, persisting long after the need to do so had disappeared. Certainly it is not a reflex of the capitalist system, which engenders, particularly among the workers, an attitude of mind which is strongly anti-imperialist, so that, as Schumpeter says, "modern pacifism is unquestionably a phenomenon of the capitalist world." He adduces the example of the United States, which had no lack of opportunities, and even of excuses, for pursuing an imperialist policy which it did not in fact adopt. As for Britain, he maintains that the greater part of its colonial empire was acquired in the pre-capitalist period, the conquerors being either adventurers unable to find a foothold at home, or men who had been driven into exile. The State had little to do with the matter, and only interfered, generally with extreme reluctance, when a colony was in existence. It was indeed the Conservative Disraeli who first introduced the notion of imperialism into British politics at the general election of 1874, though it was he who had declared in 1852 that "These wretched colonies . . . are a millstone round our necks." Yet his "Imperial Federation" did not extend beyond welding the existing empire into a closer union under the Crown. Once this idea had caught the popular imagination as according with the growing wealth and power of the country, it had served its purpose, and he did not attempt to harness it to an expansionist policy, nor would he have carried the electorate with him had he done so. It was not indeed until the middle 'nineties that the British Government, under Chamberlain, embarked upon a policy which can fairly be described as imperialist.

Again, Raymond Aron has pointed out that neither of the two World Wars was imperialist in the Leninist sense that they were due to economic rivalry, that this rivalry was the result of a struggle for colonies and that millions of men were thus sent to their deaths to open up new markets. In the twenty years before the first war the capitalist system had never been so flourishing, and the wealth of Germany had doubled. England and Germany were each other's best customers, and although there was friction, it was never remotely to the interest of the capitalists of either country to go to war on this account. The Leninist theory is based upon the myth that there existed an entity called "German (or alternatively British) capitalism," pursuing in full awareness long-range objectives, and manipulating governments to serve its economic interests. It is true that once such interests have been created, the banks and big business will use pressure to maintain them. But their creation has rarely been due to the pursuit of capitalist profits, but rather to the political ambition of governments, which is then camouflaged by invoking economic motives, seeing that every epoch finds its own formula for dissimulating the will to power. These motives are then accepted at their face value, and become transformed into real causes of conflict.

What therefore vitiates Lenin's theory is the false association he makes between imperialism and capitalism, and his assumption that there is a direct causal relationship between the two—a view which reflects the fundamental Marxist axiom that every phenomenon must have an economic explanation. At the same time, his theory is of value to Communists, since if imperialism can be predicated only of capitalism, it follows that colonial exploitation by a country which is not capitalist cannot be imperialist.

THE RISE OF INEVITABLE DESTINY

The century from 1815 to 1914 was a period of peace and progress such as had not been known since the palmy days of Rome. There were, of course, many reasons for this happy state of affairs, but most important was the world balance of power maintained largely by the mild ascendance of Great Britain in international councils, the economic strength of her bankers, her manufacturers, and her traders, and the rule of her navy over the paths of commerce. Hence this period is called the *Pax Britannica*—the British Peace.

British rule had its faults, but in retrospect its virtues shine brighter. Where the Union Jack flew, there were trade and good order, there were schools and local assemblies of the people, there were missionaries and technicians bringing the arts of Western Civilization. Britain's power was based (among other things) upon her realistic acceptance of the commercial standard of success which, after the first years, promoted the welfare of both rulers and ruled; upon a certain flexibility, which made it possible to meet special situations with special measures; and upon "a sense of the limits of power," which meant that those who struggled for self-rule would sooner or later be accepted as equals and partners. Here were the blessed reasons why the British Empire was self-liquidating, why its rule was doomed from the day its flag was run up an alien pole.

The British economic empire was even more important than its political empire. The Union Jack did not wave over the vast stretches of China and South America, but they were nevertheless British to all intents and purposes and at the same time fairly free to experiment with revolutions, war lords, and constitutions. The United States was also a part of this empire, led by loose financial strings which were not severed until World War I. Even the Dutch and French empires were strongly influenced by the financial enterprise of the British.

Imperialism, says William L. Langer,* is "the rule or control, political or economic, direct or indirect, of one state, nation or people over similar groups—or perhaps one might better say the disposition, urge or striving to establish such rule or control." Actually imperialism is not confined to capitalist countries: the Soviet Union (leaving aside the question of whether it is socialistic) is the most ruthless imperialism since Rome.

Imperialism, after all, can be nationalism projected beyond the national border. Nationalism is the community of basic ways and beliefs within a political entity. It carries with it a worship of those ways and, oftentimes, a belief in the nation's mission to rule over lesser peoples, or at least to give them the benefit of superior culture and institutions. The nation is not necessarily the creation of blood, but of history, geography, ideas, and usually culture and language. Nationalism finds expression in several ways: ideologies, the cultural, political, and institutional beliefs and way of life—of which democracy is one; militarism, by which everything is subordinated to the military search for strength; navalism, in which the navy is the weapon of might; irredentism, the propaganda for the recovery of "lost" provinces; and, of course, the active thrust of imperialism.

Soon after 1870 it became evident that a resurgence of imperialism was under way. Nationalism was making strides with the unification of Germany and Italy and the stirring of national consciousness among the Slavic peoples. The kings and nobles of Europe had seen how the Industrial Revolution and rising democracy had destroyed the old political order in England and France, and how the logical result of their influence would be to break down economic and eventually political barriers between nations.

The counterattack is seen most clearly in Germany. The junkers sought there to bind the Industrial Revolution and the rising bourgeois to their own interests. They succeeded. The internationalizing influence of the Industrial Revolution was thwarted by restoring a modern version of mercantilism, that is, making it depend-

* William L. Langer, *Diplomacy of Imperialism* (2v., 1925) 1: 67.

ent on government favors such as tariffs and trade blocks and by using its strength primarily to build up military power rather than to raise the standard of living. Popular discontent was allayed by measures of state socialism. A subtle propaganda was begun about the mystic ties of blood and *Volk*. Then presently the search for power began to take on imperialist color as the Pan-German movement attempted to unite all Germans politically and sought to bolster economic power and prestige by acquiring overseas colonies.

The rise of neo-mercantilism was fostered by a series of economic changes which stemmed primarily from technological development. Manufactures were now much less expensive, especially the textiles and metals desired by less advanced areas. The revolution in transportation and communication had also cheapened the processes of collection and transportation so much that colonies could afford European goods, and European workers could afford colonial goods. Business became more efficient and began to pile up surpluses of goods and capital. Now we know that in such a case the pressure can be relieved by raising wages, reducing interest rates, developing new processes and industries which will employ more men, or by investing abroad. All of these relief valves found some favor, but the last most of all; the difference between three-per-cent income on French railway bonds and ten to twenty-per-cent on Indo-Chinese railway bonds was a persuasive argument. Investors demanded overseas investments for their surplus capital, then demanded political control in order to protect it and to exclude foreign competitors. Industrialists with surpluses made similar demands.

Another economic change that became evident to the observing after 1870 was the decline in Britain's proportion of world manufacture and commerce. In 1870 Britain made one third of the world's goods; by 1900 it made one fifth. In the same period the United States jumped from a quarter to a third. In 1870 Britain controlled about 22 per cent of the world's trade; in 1913 this had fallen to 15 per cent. Great Britain was clearly losing out to younger and more vigorous rivals and was being forced to live more and more off its fat—that is, existing investments. It was not mere desire to maintain prestige that led to its participation in the resurgence of imperialism after 1870; it was dire necessity. By 1890 British statesmen began to feel that the Empire was like an old stag that lives in continual danger of being pulled down by wolves. The logical step, then, was to look around for friends. We shall return later to this search.

Imperialism was impelled to action not by the nation as a whole but by certain interests which obtained an "effective majority" and utilized the collective power of the nation despite some compromises made to satisfy dissidents. It is the fashion to blame business altogether for imperialism; this indictment is too sweeping, for certain business interests were among its most inveterate enemies. Wisconsin dairymen and Southern cotton-seed-oil men would naturally oppose the acquisition of copra for making margarine and soap. Louisiana sugar growers opposed the acquisition of new sugar sources in Hawaii, the Philippines, and Puerto Rico. Both interests would support Philippine independence.

However, business supporters of imperialism would include importers and exporters, and importers and users of colonial raw materials. Shipping interests would welcome enterprises likely to furnish cargo and would demand coaling stations, naval bases, subsidized immigration, and sometimes protection from foreign shipping. Bankers would be involved in all of the above interests and would prosper with them, and would therefore naturally do everything possible to promote them.

The pressure of nonbusiness interests, however, was probably even more effective. Explorers and adventurers were always calling the attention of governments and businessmen to golden opportunities. Military and naval men took pride in their conquests and did everything to justify them and to retain and defend them. Diplomatic and colonial officials naturally defended their profession of manipulating or governing "backward" races. Politicians advanced their own interests by promoting the public dither which the cable enabled the penny press to make over colonial affairs. Then there were the missionaries. Their very promotion of order enabled white traders and other exploiters to make entry, bringing with them the vices and contentions of Christendom. In desperation the missionaries then sought annexation to the countries of their origin in order to impose restrictions on vicious whites.

Propaganda for empire was usually based upon certain dynamic ideas. The appeal to national honor and prestige at times made the home taxpayers consent to wage war to seize colonies or to support vigorous action in defense of compatriots' lives and property. There was fear of aggression, to which the natural response was the aggressive defense: the seizure of naval bases, coaling stations, and colonies as posts for defending trade routes by ensuring naval supremacy. The American demand for control of the Caribbean and for the digging of the Panama Canal was more for strategic than economic reasons. Then there were the arguments that an industrial nation must control colonies for their trade and raw materials and as outlets for surplus population. Actually, trade and emigrants stubbornly go where they please, while overseas raw materials are utterly useless without absolute command of the ocean highways.

The most popular defense of imperialism, however, was "aggressive altruism." Imperialism was exploitative and therefore inconsistent with Christian morality, which had made great progress during the nineteenth century; so it was necessary to find good moral reasons whenever it was proposed to do something immoral. Kipling made the point in 1899 when he admonished the United States to "Take up the White Man's Burden" and retain the Philippines. Hence we had in Britain and the United States the White Man's Burden, in France the *mission civilisatrice*, and in Germany the mission to spread *Kultur*. It was the use of "brutal force to impose on unwilling peoples the blessings" of one's own civilization: the willingness to fight other civilized nations on behalf of the imposition of one's own superior civilization.

How stand the balance sheets of imperialism, now that its heyday is past? Critics have almost invariably judged colonial administration not by the historic norm but by the *best* Christian standards. By and large, Western imperialism has governed less harshly than the old native régimes; moreover, whether or not for altruistic reasons, it has sought to raise the local sanitary, technical, and educational standards. On the whole it has succeeded, and the proof, paradoxically, lies in the ability of the rebels against imperialism to use the arguments, the ideals, and the methods of the West against their Western rulers. Actually this is why the West has yielded—it recognizes its spiritual kinship with those who take their own part. After all, good government is no substitute for self-government, and the peoples of the colonial world are demanding and receiving the right to work out their own institutions. But the stamp of Western Civilization has been placed irrevocably upon Africa and Asia, whatever compromises they may adopt in the end. Nowhere does history show such tremendous cultural changes (progress, perhaps) in such a short time and with such relatively small expenditure in blood and human misery.

The old imperialism of the sixteenth to eighteenth centuries was primarily aimed at building up trade and acquiring settlement colonies. That of the nineteenth century, especially after 1870, was aimed primarily at the exploitation of native resources and man power. Not only did the United States begin its imperialistic adventure later than other powers, but it was not pushed by any dire necessity to obtain raw materials or to dispose of surplus goods and capital. It was animated by the *hope* of trade, by the desire for prestige, by a sense of moral responsibility, and most of all by strategy. Its imperialism was more like the earlier phase than the latter; indeed, when it began its great adventure, it was still heavily in debt to Europe and had less than half a billion dollars invested abroad—and two thirds of that in Canada and Mexico.

American ideology presented a clash between the democratic doctrine of equality and the heritage of a people who had been accustomed to regard Indians and Negroes as inferiors. Thus it did not need the rising racism of Europe to implant the concept of a master race in America, but many Americans welcomed the "scientific" demonstration of the master-race theory. This demonstration stemmed from two sources: the idea of natural selection as expressed in Social Darwinism; and the racism of Gobineau and Houston Stewart Chamberlain, brought back from Germany by American graduate students. The first was most likely to take the form of an Anglo-Saxon mythus; the second expanded the master race to include the Teutons, whose purest representatives were found in Germany but who (it was claimed) had carried their blood and their genius for mastery to surrounding nations. Popularizers in the United States did not always clearly distinguish between the two ideas, but Anglo-Saxonism was the stronger because it was reinforced by a common language and by long familiarity with English literature and institutions. The publicists of expansion may have had their private quarrels with British snobbery, but in other things they were Anglophile.

The first prominent American to adopt Anglo-Saxonism was John Fiske, Harvard historian and popularizer of the theory of evolution and Social Darwinism. He taught that industrialism would win over barbaric militancy, that Anglo-Saxons would multiply and spread over the world (comprising four fifths of the human race!) carrying industry, order, and democracy. Meanwhile, at Johns Hopkins, the German-trained historian Herbert Baxter Adams was presiding over a seminar which found the origin of democracy and the Anglo-Saxon genius for self-government in the primitive village institutions of the German tribes. Among his students were Woodrow Wilson, Frederick Jackson Turner, Albert Shaw, Thorstein Veblen, Richard T. Ely, and J. Franklin Jameson, all to become formative influences in American scholarly or public life—though they did not all accept his extreme views. At Columbia another German-trained man, John W. Burgess, was laying the foundations of political science. Of Tennessee slave-owning Unionist stock, Burgess taught that Teutons possessed superior mental and political gifts. Among those who sat under his tutelage were Theodore Roosevelt, strenuous advocate of Anglo-

Saxon superiority, and William A. Dunning, who sponsored the negrophobe view of reconstruction.

Anglo-Saxonism found champions among a group of influential publicists: Albert Shaw, editor of the *Review of Reviews* from 1891 to 1937; Whitelaw Reid, a power in the Republican Party and editor of Greeley's old *Tribune*; James H. Bridge, former secretary to Carnegie and then editor of California's *Overland Monthly*; and Murat Halstead, editor, prolific hack writer, and political critic. In 1885 there appeared *Our Country: Its Possible Future and Its Present Crisis* by the Rev. Josiah Strong. Intended to raise money for missions, the book received enormous public attention because it contained a chapter on "The Anglo-Saxon and the World's Future," which proclaimed this race as its brother's keeper. With their "unequaled energy" and "peculiarly aggressive traits" the Anglo-Saxons were destined to inundate the world, carrying with them superior civil and religious institutions—provided they were not first devitalized by tobacco and alcohol.

Closely associated with the survival-of-the-fittest doctrine was a group of men who saw in the decline of Anglo-Saxon militancy the opportunity of the "dark races," especially of the yellow. There was some difference of opinion as to whether the menace would come from China or Japan, but Jack London solved the difficulty by warning that Japan might find a way to control and use the immense capacities of China for the conquest of the world. A picturesque prophet of the Yellow Peril was the Californian, General Homer Lea, who despite the handicap of being a hunchback became an adjutant to Sun Yat-sen and a significant figure in the Chinese Revolution. His principal books were *The Valor of Ignorance* (1909), a warning that Japan intended to invade the United States, and *The Day of the Saxon* (1912), which foretold the destruction of the British Empire by Germany and the Orient. The Yellow Peril propaganda was strengthened by Japan's victory over Russia and dignified by Theodore Roosevelt's support. After World War I it received a new lease on life in the racist writings of Madison Grant and Lothrop Stoddard.

The outstanding advocate of American expansion in the 1890's was Admiral Alfred Thayer Mahan. The publication in 1890 of his *Influence of Sea Power Upon History* launched him into a career as the historian and protagonist of sea power; before the decade was out, he was to add a powerful impetus to the navalism already growing up not only in the United States but in other nations. Mahan's thesis was that sea power had been the chief factor in making and breaking nations and empires, and he drew chiefly on England for proof. The significance of sea power was that it fostered and protected commerce; hence a navy, merchant marine, bases, and coaling stations were essentials of national greatness. In 1890 the United States was lacking in all of these, and Mahan demanded that it supply the realistic basis for its destined expansion. Not only must it build up the navy and merchant marine, but it must dig an isthmian canal and acquire bases and colonies in the Caribbean and the Pacific. He believed that the United States and Britain were agents of the divine will, and that they must prepare for the coming struggle with the Yellow Peril.

Despite this pious obeisance to Providence, Mahan approached his problems in a notably realistic manner, basing his recommendations upon power rather than sentiment. He recognized that England's naval power rose from the facts that it was an island, rich in coal and timber, and situated so as to block the Atlantic entrances to France and Germany. His disciples in Germany ignored these factors and confidently counted on beating England at its own game; actually, the United States and Japan more nearly met the requirements of the Mahan strategic concept. While he analyzed correctly the reasons for the rise of England, there is wide argument that Mahan's glorification of sea power has not stood the test of time as a historical generalization. Not only have commentators pointed out historical inaccuracies in his thesis, but geopolitical extremists have tried to show that the land mass of Eurasia cannot be dominated by sea power. Certainly the growth of the land-sea-air team (not to mention pushbutton warfare) has put a different face on the power picture.

Whatever history's decision may be on the validity of Mahan's thesis, the fact remains that it had tremendous effect upon succeeding thought and action. Propaganda for an isthmian canal and for the annexation of Cuba and Hawaii was stepped up; and there was talk that, while Cuba was being taken from decadent Spain, the Philippines might as well be taken also as a foothold in the Far East. The effect upon politicians was notable. His ideas were adopted by a group of Republican Senators, including Henry Teller of Colorado, Orville Platt of Connecticut, William E. Chandler of New Hampshire, William P. Frye of Maine, and above all Henry Cabot Lodge of Massachusetts. A young Indiana politician named Albert Beveridge was gaining national attention by his word-pictures of American destiny.

Not least was Theodore Roosevelt. Expansion suited his gospel of the strenuous life and his opinion that war was a beneficial stimulant of the national glands, so he poured out articles and reviews urging America to seek a place in the sun. Before long, as Assistant Secretary of the Navy, he was going to be in a situation where he could do something about it. These men, all Republicans, and most of them alarmed by the populist movement, not only favored expansion for its own sake but expected to make it a counter to the swelling chorus of radical and popular protest. That it had possibilities was shown by the fact that the Trans-Mississippi Congress held in 1897 at Salt Lake City to promote Western interests passed a resolution favoring an isthmian canal and the annexation of Hawaii. The president of the congress was none other than the populist idol, William Jennings Bryan.

In the light of the usual accusations that businessmen lead in imperialism, it is interesting to note that in the United States they violently opposed it, at least up to May 1898. It was the scholars, the publicists, the strategists, and the politicians who espoused it. They (especially Mahan and Beveridge) sometimes spoke of the commercial advantages of imperialism, but when it came down to actual argument they stressed the White Man's Burden and the historic American mission to spread democracy. Even Anglo-Saxonism, though it had certainly helped to form their attitudes, was not primarily invoked. The New Manifest Destiny, it was claimed, had about it a certain fatefulness which could be resisted successfully neither by the aggressors nor by their victims. America, they said, had an "inevitable destiny" to expand and bring light to the world, then quite without humor beat the alarum lest we come short of that destiny. In the Calvinist tradition that the elect must strive to fulfill the will of God, they devoted themselves unstintingly to helping "destiny" fulfill itself.

It is difficult to conceive of a nation with the power and dynamism of the United States remaining permanently aloof from world affairs in any case; nevertheless it was the Spanish-American War which saddled the country with the two specific responsibilities which were to mold future American foreign policy. First, the expansion of American strategic and economic interests to the Philippines brought us into vital contact with imperial Europe and Japan; the effect in the long run was to place our western frontier on the China coast. Second, the expansion of our strategic and economic interests into the Caribbean made another vital contact with imperial Europe, especially Germany, which was edging toward a strong position in Latin America; the effect in the long run was to place our eastern frontier on the Rhine. These assumptions of responsibility, unfortunately, were not understood by the people at large nor even by Congress, and the Executive was left to handle them as best he could without their comprehension or support. Therein lies much of the reason for the ridiculous inconsistencies and the repeated and resounding failures of American foreign policy between that time and this.

"THE FATAL DREAM OF SOUTHERN DOMINION"

[On January 11, 1871, Carl Schurz (1829–1906), then Senator from Missouri, made a speech opposing Grant's proposed annexation of Santo Domingo. He insisted that, once annexation had begun, the Anglo-Saxon race, "notorious for its land hunger" would grasp the entire Caribbean area. In such "a romantic longing for the south" Schurz saw the ruin of the free institutions of the republic even as the Holy Roman Empire had been ruined by its fatal dream of dominating Italy. The speech appears in Schurz's *Speeches, Correspondence, and Political Papers* (6v., N.Y.: Putnam's, 1913), 2:71–122.]

We may be asked, why should we not have all this? Are not those countries rich, fertile and beautiful? Do they not offer all the magnificence of tropical production? Are not their mountains full of precious ore? Yes, they are rich; I do not deny it; they are fertile; they may be considered as possessing magnificent resources; and yet I would ask every Senator before me, before he lays his hand upon that seductive portion of the globe for the purpose of incorporating it in this Republic, and fusing it with our political system, is there not a voice speaking within him telling him to consider it well, to pause, to ponder and to beware? Consider: if you incorporate those tropical countries with the Republic of the United States, you will have to incorporate their people too. If you do that, you will have to accept them as a component and cooperative element in that system of Government, the blessing of which we now enjoy. . . .

And who are they? People who have nothing in common with us; neither language, nor habits, nor institutions, nor traditions, nor opinions nor ways of thinking; nay, not even a code of morals—people who cannot even be reached by our teachings, for they will not understand or appreciate them; all the good lessons we may try to impart to them will evaporate into nothing under the hot rays of the tropical sun. How will you fit them into our political system? Have you thought of it?

It is said that our free institutions exhibit a wonderful power in blending and assimilating the most heterogeneous elements of population living under their beneficent influence. So they do. Under the influences of our northern clime we certainly find such effects produced. The most stubborn prejudices are melted, the most inveterate habits are gradually changed; the best faculties resting in the various races of men congregating here are drawn to light and developed, and finally those heterogeneous elements are fitted for the great duties and responsibilities of republican citizenship. . . . Assimilation here, therefore, is assimilation upward.

But it must not be forgotten that Anglo-Saxon vigor stands here upon its own congenial ground; from the very atmosphere its energies receive their inspiration, and by the very necessity of things Anglo-Saxon vigor is here the absorbing element, the assimilating force.

But how is it in the American tropics? The Anglo-Saxon invading them meets there the mixed Latin, Indian and African races upon *their* own congenial ground. There *they* receive their characteristic inspirations from the atmosphere; there they develop their characteristic qualities under the influences of tropical nature; there *they* are the natural growth of the soil, and the Anglo-Saxon appearing as a mere exotic plant, *they* will not be the assimilating force. And what will be the consequence? Inevitably this: that in the course of time and by the process of assimilation the Anglo-Saxon will lose more than the Africo-Indo-Latin mixture will gain. This will be assimilation indeed, but it will be assimilation downward. . . .

Fancy ten or twelve tropical States added to the Southern States we already possess; fancy the Senators and Representatives of ten or twelve millions of tropical people, people of the Latin race mixed with Indian and African blood; people who, as I already have stated, have neither language nor traditions nor habits nor political institutions nor morals in common with us; fancy them sitting in the Halls of Congress, throwing the weight of their intelligence, their morality, their political notions and habits, their prejudices and passions, into the scale of the destinies of this Republic; and, what is more, fancy the Government of this Republic making itself responsible for order and security and republican institutions in such

States, inhabited by such people; fancy this, and then tell me, does not your imagination recoil from the picture? . . .

What else, then, is urged? "Manifest destiny." "Manifest destiny" is a great cry; and that cry has played a sinister part in the history of the world before this. "Manifest destiny" is written upon some of the saddest pages of the history of nations. And I might here recall some of the memories which will crowd upon the minds of those who have sprung from the nation of which I am a son. It is one of the most remarkable pathological phenomena in the history of the world that northern nations are so frequently haunted by a romantic longing for the south. And how often has that vague dream brought forth deplorable disaster! You have read the history of Germany in the Middle Ages. There was the great power of what might then be called the civilized world; and that power abandoning itself to the fatal dream of southern dominion. It was on the beautiful plains of Italy that the German empire spent its strength. It was in hunting after southern shadows that it frittered away its great opportunities of home consolidation. It was, so to say, in the embraces of that beautiful southern siren that the German empire lost its manhood.

That was "manifest destiny," if you will call it so. And here now stands the American Republic; so vigorous, so beautiful, so great, so hopeful on the ground of her strength; and she, too, is to be seduced with the treacherous charm! And the cry of "manifest destiny" is raised by the thoughtless spirit of adventure hurrying her on to take the fatal leap into a region far more dangerous than Italy, where her very vitality, perhaps, would meet with deadly contamination.

Sir, if that were manifest destiny, then I should be seriously tempted to call it manifest doom. But is it, indeed, manifest destiny? What is destiny for a country and a people like this? Sir, the reason, the good sense, the conscience, the enlightened will of the American people is their destiny. Let them acknowledge no other. And I fondly trust that reason, that sound sense, that conscience, that enlightened will, can never be seduced by the deceptive allurements of tropical splendor! Away, then, with the wild cry for tropical possession. . . . Beware of every addition in that quarter where the very sun hatches out the serpent's eggs of danger to our republican institutions.

THE ANGLO-SAXON AND THE WORLD'S FUTURE

It seems to me that God, with infinite wisdom and skill, is training the Anglo-Saxon race for an hour sure to come in the world's future. Heretofore there has always been in the history of the world a comparatively unoccupied land westward, into which the crowded countries of the East have poured their surplus populations. But the widening waves of migration, which millenniums ago rolled east and west from the valley of the Euphrates, meet to-day on our Pacific coast. There are no more new worlds. The unoccupied arable lands of the earth are limited, and will soon be taken. The time is coming when the pressure of population on the means of subsistence will be felt here as it is now felt in Europe and Asia. Then will the world enter upon a new stage of its history—*the final competition of races, for which the Anglo-Saxon is being schooled.* Long before the thousand millions are here, the mighty *centrifugal* tendency, inherent in this stock and strengthened in the United States, will assert itself. Then this race of unequaled energy, with all the majesty of numbers and the might of wealth behind it—the representative, let us hope, of the largest liberty, the purest Christianity, the highest civilization—having developed peculiarly aggressive traits calculated to impress its institutions upon mankind, will spread itself over the earth. If I read not amiss, this powerful race will move down upon Mexico, down upon Central and South America, out upon the islands of the sea, over upon Africa and beyond. And can any one doubt that the result of this competition of races will be the "survival of the fittest"? . . .

Is there room for reasonable doubt that this race, unless devitalized by alcohol and tobacco, is destined to dispossess many weaker races, assimilate others, and mold the remainder, until, in a very true and important sense, it has Anglo-Saxonized mankind? . . .

—Rev. Josiah Strong, *Our Country* (1885)

"THE UNITED STATES IS PRACTICALLY SOVEREIGN ON THIS CONTINENT"

[The quarrel between Great Britain and Venezuela over the boundary between the latter country and Guiana reached the acute stage when Cleveland's Secretary of State, Richard Olney, demanded that the issue be submitted to arbitration. Olney's note (July 20, 1895) to Lord Salisbury, British Prime Minister and Foreign Secretary, stirred a furor in Britain and America, and created ineradicable resentments in Latin America by its arrogant claim to sovereignty in the Western Hemisphere. Salisbury's reply was long delayed, and then refused arbitration and coolly read a lecture to Cleveland on the meaning of the Monroe Doctrine. Cleveland's message to Congress (Dec. 17, 1895) reiterated the American interpretation of the

Monroe Doctrine and asked for a commission whose decision would be enforced on Britain. Suddenly war seemed imminent, and the startled Salisbury, embroiled in troubles with the Boers and Germany, backed down and accepted arbitration—which in the end gave Britain most of what it had claimed. The accusation has been made that the actions of Cleveland and Olney were motivated by the hope of furnishing a counterirritant to the current free-silver agitation. At any rate, the episode marked a rapprochement in Anglo-American relations and foreshadowed American emergence from isolation. Herewith we give excerpts from Olney's note and from Cleveland's message.]

That America is in no part open to colonization, though the proposition was not universally admitted at the time of its first enunciation, has long been universally conceded. We are now concerned, therefore, only with that other practical application of the Monroe doctrine the disregard of which by an European power is to be deemed an act of unfriendliness towards the United States. . . . It is that no European power or combination of European powers shall forcibly deprive an American state of the right and power of self-government and of shaping for itself its own political fortunes and destinies. . . . The states of America, South as well as North, by geographical proximity, by natural sympathy, by similarity of governmental constitutions, are friends and allies, commercially and politically, of the United States. To allow the subjugation of any of them by an European power is, of course, to completely reverse that situation and signifies the loss of all the advantages incident to their natural relations to us.

But that is not all. The people of the United States have a vital interest in the cause of popular self-government. They have secured the right for themselves and their posterity at the cost of infinite blood and treasure. They have realized and exemplified its beneficent operation by a career unexampled in point of national greatness or individual felicity. They believe it to be for the healing of all nations, and that civilization must either advance or retrograde accordingly as its supremacy is extended or curtailed. . . .

They believe it not to be tolerated that the political control of an American state shall be forcibly assumed by an European power. . . . Today the United States is practically sovereign on this continent, and its fiat is law upon the subjects to which it confines its interposition. Why? It is not because of the pure friendship or good will felt for it. It is not simply by reason of its high character as a civilized state, nor because wisdom and justice and equity are the invariable characteristics of the dealings of the United States. It is because, in addition to all other grounds, its infinite resources combined with its isolated position render it master of the situation and practically invulnerable as against any or all other powers.

—Secretary of State Olney, July 1895

The disputed frontier of Venezuela has nothing to do with any of the questions dealt with by President Monroe. It is not a question of the colonization of a European Power of any portion of America. It is not a question of the imposition upon the communities of South America of any system of government devised in Europe. It is simply the determination of the frontier of a British possession which belonged to the Throne of England long before the Republic of Venezuela came into existence.

—Lord Salisbury's reply to Olney, November 1895

It will be seen from the correspondence herewith submitted that this proposition has been declined by the British Government upon grounds which in the circumstances seem to me to be far from satisfactory. . . .

The dispute has reached such a stage as to make it now incumbent upon the United States to take measures to determine with sufficient certainty for its justification what is the true divisional line between the Republic of Venezuela and British Guiana. The inquiry to that end should of course be conducted carefully and judicially, and due weight should be given to all available evidence, records, and facts in support of the claims of both parties.

In order that such an examination should be prosecuted in a thorough and satisfactory manner, I suggest that the Congress make an adequate appropriation for the expenses of a commission, to be appointed by the Executive, who shall make the necessary investigation and report upon the matter with the least possible delay. When such report is made and accepted it will, in my opinion, be the duty of the United States to resist by every means in its power, as a wilful aggression upon its rights and interests, the appropriation by Great Britain of any lands or the exercise of governmental jurisdiction over any territory which after investigation we have determined of right belongs to Venezuela.

In making these recommendations I am fully alive to the responsibility incurred and keenly realize all the consequences that may follow.

I am, nevertheless, firm in my conviction that while it is a grievous thing to contemplate the two great English-speaking peoples of the world as being otherwise than friendly competitors in the onward march of civilization and strenuous and worthy rivals in all the arts of peace, there is no calamity which a great nation can invite which equals that which follows a supine submission to wrong and injustice and the consequent loss of national self-respect and honor, beneath which are shielded and defended a people's safety and greatness.

—President Cleveland's Message to Congress, December 1895

In English eyes the United States was then so completely a negligible quantity that it was believed only words the equivalent of blows would be really effective.

—Richard Olney, 1912

THE ANGLO-AMERICAN RAPPROCHEMENT

The same tendency is shown in the undeniable disposition of the British people and of British statesmen to cultivate the good-will of the United States, and to draw closer the relations between the two countries. For the disposition underlying such a tendency Mr. Balfour has used an expression, "race patriotism." . . . That there is a lukewarm response in the United States is due to that narrow conception which grew up with the middle of the century. . . . When we begin really to look abroad, and to busy ourselves with our duties to the world at large in our generation—and not before—we shall stretch out our hands to Great Britain, realizing that in unity of heart among the English-speaking races lies the best hope of humanity in the doubtful days ahead.

—A. T. Mahan, *The Interest of America in Sea Power* (1897)

The good understanding between us is based on something deeper than mere expediency. All who think cannot but see there is a sanction like that of religion which binds us in partnership in the serious work of the world. . . . We are joint ministers in the same sacred missions of freedom and progress, charged with duties we cannot evade by the imposition of irresistible hands.

—John Hay, at Lord Mayor's banquet, April 21, 1898

Nothing can be more obvious, therefore, than that the conditions for which Washington made his rule [of isolation] no longer exist. . . . There is a patriotism of race as well as of country—and the Anglo-American is as little likely to be indifferent to the one as to the other. . . . That they would be found standing together against any alien foe by whom either was menaced with destruction or irreparable calamity, it is not permissible to doubt. Nothing less could be expected of the close community between them in origin, speech, thought, literature, institutions, ideals and in the kind and degree of the civilization enjoyed by both.

—Richard Olney, *Atlantic Monthly*, May 1898, pp. 582, 588

[Who can say] that the occasion may not arise . . . in the future that Anglo-Saxon liberty and Anglo-Saxon interests may hereafter be menaced by a great combination of other Powers? Yes, Sir, I think that such a thing is possible, and, in that case, whether it be America or whether it be England that is menaced, I hope that blood will be found to be thicker than water.

—Joseph Chamberlain, speaking in the House of Commons, June 1898

One of the five clauses in the British draft for a treaty [with Germany] stipulated: "It is agreed that this Convention shall not apply to questions on the American Continent, nor bind either High Contracting Party to join in hostilities against the United States of America." Despite that fact, the failure of the negotiations seem to have been ascribed by Landsdowne primarily to "the risk of entangling ourselves in a policy which might be hostile to America. With our knowledge of the German Emperor's views in regard to the United States, this is to my mind a formidable obstacle."

—Abortive Anglo-German treaty of alliance, 1901, H. C. Allen, *Great Britain and the United States* (London: Odhams Press, 1954), p. 559

The welfare of the United States and its immunity from entanglements with other powers is greatly strengthened by strong ties of friendship and by unanimity of action with Great Britain.

—Statement by the General Board of the U.S. Navy, 1906

McKINLEY'S WAR MESSAGE

[The blowing up of the *Maine* in Havana harbor brought a crisis in American relations with Spain. A Naval Court of Inquiry decided that the explosion was the result of an external cause, and public opinion leaped to the conclusion that it had been set by Spanish agents. Actually, the Cuban rebels had more to gain by setting the explosion, for they could hope to draw the United States into war. A long and involved diplomatic interchange followed between Spain and the United States. Finally, though McKinley seems to have opposed war, he was unable to withstand

Congressional pressure and on April 11, 1898, sent a message to Congress recommending war.]

The grounds for such intervention may be briefly summarized as follows:

First. In the cause of humanity and to put an end to the barbarities, bloodshed, starvation, and horrible miseries now existing there, and which the parties to the conflict are either unable or unwilling to stop or mitigate. It is no answer to say this is all in another country, belonging to another nation, and is therefore none of our business. It is specially our duty, for it is right at our door.

Second. We owe it to our citizens in Cuba to afford them that protection and indemnity for life and property which no government there can or will afford, and to that end to terminate the conditions that deprive them of legal protection.

Third. The right to intervene may be justified by the very serious injury to the commerce, trade, and business of our people and by the wanton destruction of property and devastation of the island.

Fourth, and which is of the utmost importance. The present condition of affairs in Cuba is a constant menace to our peace, and entails upon this government an enormous expense. With such a conflict waged for years in an island so near us and with which our people have such trade and business relations; when the lives and liberty of our citizens are in constant danger and their property destroyed and themselves ruined; where our trading vessels are liable to seizure and are seized at our very door by warships of a foreign nation; the expeditions of filibustering [freebooting] that we are powerless to prevent altogether, and the irritating questions and entanglements thus arising—all these and others that I need not mention, with the resulting strained relations, are a constant menace to our peace and compel us to keep on a semi-war footing with a nation with which we are at peace.

These elements of danger and disorder already pointed out have been strikingly illustrated by a tragic event which has deeply and justly moved the American people. I have already transmitted to Congress the report of the Naval Court of Inquiry on the destruction of the battleship *Maine* in the harbor of Havana during the night of the 15th of February. The destruction of that noble vessel has filled the national heart with inexpressible horror. Two hundred and fifty-eight brave sailors and marines and two officers of our Navy, reposing in the fancied security of a friendly harbor, have been hurled to death, grief and want brought to their homes and sorrow to the nation. . . .

The long trial has proved that the object for which Spain has waged the war cannot be attained. The fire of insurrection may flame or may smolder with varying seasons, but it has not been, and it is plain that it cannot be, extinguished by present methods. The only hope of relief and repose from a condition which can no longer be endured is the enforced pacification of Cuba. In the name of humanity, in the name of civilization, in behalf of endangered American interests which give us the right and the duty to speak and to act, the war in Cuba must stop. . . .

The issue is now with the Congress. It is a solemn responsibility. I have exhausted every effort to relieve the intolerable condition of affairs which is at our doors. Prepared to execute every obligation imposed upon me by the Constitution and the law, I await your action.

[In order to allow time for American citizens to get out of Cuba, McKinley held up delivery of the message for some days. Then, on the 11th, he received cablegrams advising him that Spain had met every demand, including the granting of an armistice in Cuba and disbandment of concentration camps. Thereupon McKinley added the following paragraphs, leaving the whole matter to Congress.]

Yesterday, and since the preparation of the foregoing message, official information was received by me that the latest decree of the Queen Regent of Spain directs General Blanco, in order to prepare and facilitate peace, to proclaim a suspension of hostilities, the duration and details of which have not yet been communicated to me.

This fact, with every other pertinent consideration, will, I am sure, have your just and careful attention in the solemn deliberations upon which you are about to enter. If this measure attains a successful result, then our aspirations as a Christian, peace-loving people will be realized. If it fails, it will be only another justification for our contemplated action.

"WHAT SHALL HISTORY SAY OF US?"

[Albert J. Beveridge (1862–1927), the young Senator-elect from Indiana, visited the Philippines in 1899 to view the situation. On his return he championed the cause of annexation, and in a speech delivered before the Senate on January 9, 1900, summarized the principal reasons for building an empire. In one respect, at least, he may have been right—in his belief that "the power that rules the Pacific" would be "the power that rules the world."]

Mr. President, the times call for candor. The Philippines are ours forever, "territory belonging to the United States," as the Constitution calls them. And just beyond the Philippines are China's illimitable markets. We will not retreat from either. We will not repudiate our duty in the archipelago. We will not abandon our opportunity in the Orient. We will not renounce our part in the mission of our race, trustee, under God, of the civilization of the world. And we will move forward to our work, not howling out regrets like slaves whipped to their burdens, but with gratitude for a task worthy of our strength, and thanksgiving to Almighty God that He has marked us as His chosen people, henceforth to lead in the regeneration of the world.

This island empire is the last land left in all the oceans. If it should prove a mistake to abandon it, the blunder once made would be irretrievable. If it proves a mistake to hold it, the error can be corrected when we will. Every other progressive nation stands ready to relieve us.

But to hold it will be no mistake. Our largest trade henceforth must be with Asia. The Pacific is our ocean. More and more Europe will manufacture the most it needs, secure from its colonies the most it consumes. Where shall we turn for consumers of our surplus? Geography answers the question. China is our natural customer. She is nearer to us than to England, Germany, or Russia, the commercial powers of the present and the future. They have moved nearer to China by securing permanent bases on her borders. The Philippines give us a base at the door of all the East.

Lines of navigation from our ports to the Orient and Australia; from the Isthmian Canal to Asia; from all Oriental ports to Australia, converge at and separate from the Philippines. They are a self-supporting, dividend-paying fleet, permanently anchored at a spot selected by the strategy of Providence, commanding the Pacific. And the Pacific is the ocean of the commerce of the future. Most future wars will be conflicts for commerce. The power that rules the Pacific, therefore, is the power that rules the world. And, with the Philippines, that power is and will forever be the American Republic. . . .

But, Senators, it would be better to abandon this combined garden and Gibraltar of the Pacific, and count our blood and treasure already spent a profitable loss, than to apply any academic arrangement of self-government to these children. They are not capable of self-government. How could they be? They are not of a self-governing race. . . . How shall they, in the twinkling of an eye, be exalted to the heights of self-governing peoples which required a thousand years for us to reach, Anglo-Saxon though we are? . . .

Mr. President, this question is deeper than any question of party politics; deeper than any question of the isolated policy of our country even; deeper even than any question of constitutional power. It is elemental. It is racial. God has not been preparing the English-speaking and Teutonic peoples for a thousand years for nothing but vain and idle self-contemplation and self-admiration. No! He has made us the master organizers of the world to establish system where chaos reigns. He has given us the spirit of progress to overwhelm the forces of reaction throughout the earth. He has made us adepts in government that we may administer government among savage and senile peoples. Were it not for such a force as this the world would relapse into barbarism and night. And of all our race He has marked the American people as His chosen nation to finally lead in the regeneration of the world. This is the divine mission of America, and it holds for us all the profit, all the glory, all the happiness possible to man. We are trustees of the world's progress, guardians of its righteous peace. The judgment of the Master is upon us: "Ye have been faithful over a few things; I will make you ruler over many things."

What shall history say of us? Shall it say that we renounced that holy trust, left the savage to his base condition, the wilderness to the reign of waste, deserted duty, abandoned glory, forget our sordid profit even, because we feared our strength and read the charter of our powers with the doubter's eye and the quibbler's mind? Shall it say that, called by events to captain and command the proudest, ablest, purest race of history in history's noblest work, we declined that great commission? Our fathers would not have had it so. No! They founded no paralytic government, incapable of the simplest acts of administration. They planted no sluggard people, passive while the world's work calls them. They established no reactionary nation. They unfurled no retreating flag.

That flag has never paused in its onward march. Who dares halt it now—now, when history's largest events are carrying it forward; now, when we are at last one people, strong enough for any task, great enough for any glory destiny can bestow? How comes it that our first century closes with the process of consolidating the American people into a unit just accomplished, and quick upon the stroke of that great hour presses upon us our world opportunity, world duty, and world glory, which none but a people welded into an indivisible nation can achieve or perform?

Blind indeed is he who sees not the hand of God in events so vast, so harmonious, so benign. Reactionary indeed is the mind that perceives not that this vital people is the strongest of the saving forces of the world; that our place, therefore, is at the head of the constructing and redeeming nations of the earth; and that to stand aside while events march on is a surrender of our interests, a betrayal of our duty as blind as it is base. Craven indeed is the heart that fears to perform a work so golden and so noble; that dares not win a glory so immortal.

HOW McKINLEY DECIDED TO ANNEX THE PHILIPPINES

How the President came to the decision [to annex the entire Philippine Archipelago] was told in a well-authenticated interview at the White House, November 21, 1899. He was receiving a committee representing the General Missionary Committee of the Methodist Episcopal Church, then in session in Washington. . . . [When] they turned to leave, the President said, earnestly:—

"Hold a moment longer! Not quite yet, gentlemen! Before you go I would like to say just a word about the Philippine business. I have been criticized a good deal about the Philippines, but don't deserve it. The truth is I didn't want the Philippines, and when they came to us, as a gift from the gods, I did not know what to do with them. . . . I sought counsel from all sides—Democrats as well as Republicans—but got little help. I thought first we would take only Manila; then Luzon; then other islands, perhaps, also. I walked the floor of the White House night after night until midnight; and I am not ashamed to tell you, gentlemen, that I went down on my knees and prayed Almighty God for light and guidance more than one night. And one night late it came to me this way—I don't know how it was, but it came: (1) That we could not give them back to Spain—that would be cowardly and dishonorable; (2) that we could not turn them over to France or Germany—our commercial rivals in the Orient—that would be bad business and discreditable; (3) that we could not leave them to themselves—they were unfit for self-government—and they would soon have anarchy and misrule over there worse than Spain's was; and (4) that there was nothing left for us to do but to take them all, and to educate the Filipinos, and uplift and civilize and Christianize them, and by God's grace do the very best we could by them, as our fellow-men for whom Christ also died. And then I went to bed, and went to sleep, and slept soundly.

—Charles S. Olcott, *Life of William McKinley* (2v., N.Y.: Houghton Mifflin, 1916), 2:109–111

THE CONQUEST OF THE UNITED STATES BY SPAIN

[We will never know the relative strengths of expansionist and anti-expansionist sentiment. It may be that the former was a little the stronger during and immediately after the Spanish-American War; if so, the latter soon rallied sufficient strength to moderate the tide but not enough to reverse it. William Graham Sumner's "The Conquest of the United States by Spain," delivered in 1898, was a long and closely reasoned philippic against imperialism and a prescient and detailed warning of its results. Here we can give only certain highlights from his main theme that imperialism would doom liberty. The material is taken from Sumner's collection of essays published in 1911 under the same title by Yale University Press, pp. 297–334 passim.]

During the last year the public has been familiarized with descriptions of Spain and of Spanish methods of doing things until the name of Spain has become a symbol for a certain well-defined set of notions and policies. On the other hand, the name of the United States has always been, for all of us, a symbol for a state of things, a set of ideas and traditions, a group of views about social and political affairs. Spain was the first, for a long time the greatest, of the modern imperialistic states. The United States, by its historical origin, its traditions, and its principles, is the chief representative of the revolt and reaction against that kind of a state. I intend to show that, by the line of action now proposed to us, which we call expansion and imperialism, we are throwing away some of the most important elements of the American symbol and are adopting some of the most important elements of the Spanish symbol. We have beaten Spain in a military conflict, but we are submitting to be conquered by her on the field of ideas and policies. . . .

Let us be well assured that self-government is not a matter of flags and Fourth of July orations, nor yet of strife to get offices. Eternal vigilance is the price of that as of every other political good. The perpetuity of self-government depends on the sound political sense of the people, and sound political sense is a matter of habit and practice. We can give it up and we can take instead pomp and glory. That is what Spain did. She had as much self-government as any country in Europe at the beginning of the sixteenth century. The union of the smaller states into one big one gave an impulse to her national feeling and national develop-

ment. The discovery of America put into her hands the control of immense territories. National pride and ambition were stimulated. Then came the struggle with France for world-dominion, which resulted in absolute monarchy and bankruptcy for Spain. She lost self-government and saw her resources spent on interests which were foreign to her, but she could talk about an empire on which the sun never set and boast of her colonies, her gold-mines, her fleets and armies and debts. She had glory and pride, mixed, of course, with defeat and disaster, such as must be experienced by any nation on that course of policy; and she grew weaker in her industry and commerce and poorer in the status of the population all the time. She has never been able to recover real self-government yet.

If we Americans believe in self-government, why do we let it slip away from us? Why do we barter it away for military glory as Spain did? . . . [Our] protected position is sure to pass away. As the country fills up with population, and the task of getting a living out of the ground becomes more difficult, the struggle for existence will become harder and the competition of life more severe. Then liberty and de-

mocracy will cost something, if they are to be maintained.

Now what will hasten the day when our present advantages will wear out and when we shall come down to the conditions of the older and densely populated nations? The answer is: war, debt, taxation, diplomacy, a grand governmental system, pomp, glory, a big army and navy, lavish expenditures, political jobbery—in a word, imperialism. . . . The laws of nature and of human nature are just as valid for Americans as for anybody else, and if we com-

mit acts we shall have to take consequences, just like other people. Therefore prudence demands that we look ahead to see what we are about to do, and that we gauge the means at our disposal, if we do not want to bring calamity on ourselves and our children.

We see that the peculiarities of our system of government set limitations on us. We cannot do things which a great centralized monarchy could do. The very blessings and special advantages which we enjoy, as compared with others, bring disabilities with them. . . . We cannot govern dependencies consistently with our political system, and . . . if we try it, the State which our fathers founded will suffer a reaction which will transform it into another empire just after the fashion of all the old ones. That is what imperialism means. That is what it will be; and the democratic republic, which has been, will stand in history, like the colonial organization of earlier days, as a mere transition form.

PLATFORM OF THE ANTI-IMPERIALIST LEAGUE

[Opposition to the annexations that followed the Spanish-American War resulted in the formation of opposition groups, and in October, 1899, they came together to form the American Anti-Imperialist League. The platform given below was adopted on October 18, and is reprinted from *The Speeches, Correspondence, and Political Papers of Carl Schurz* (6v., N.Y.: Putnam's, 1913), 6:77–79. Schurz, who had been active in thwarting the annexation of Santo Domingo, was now one of the leaders of the League. It endorsed Bryan in 1900, but did not save him—and itself—from disastrous defeat.]

We hold that the policy known as imperialism is hostile to liberty and tends toward militarism, an evil from which it has been our glory to be free. . . . We demand the immediate cessation of the war against liberty, begun by Spain and continued by us. We urge that Congress be promptly convened to announce to the Filipinos our purpose to concede to them the independence for which they have so long fought and which of right is theirs. . . . Much as we abhor the war of "criminal aggression" in the Philippines, . . . the real firing line is not

in the suburbs of Manila. The foe is of our own household. The attempt of 1861 was to divide the country. That of 1899 is to destroy its fundamental principles and noblest ideals. . . .

We deny that the obligation of all citizens to support their Government in times of grave National peril applies to the present situation. If an Administration may with impunity ignore the issues upon which it was chosen, deliberately create a condition of war anywhere on the face of the globe, debauch the civil service for spoils to promote the adventure, organize a truth-repressing censorship and demand of all citizens a suspension of judgment and their unanimous support while it chooses to continue the fighting, representative government itself is imperiled.

We propose to contribute to the defeat of any person or party that stands for the forcible subjugation of any people. We shall oppose for reëlection all who in the White House or in Congress betray American liberty in pursuit of un-American ends. We still hope that both of our great political parties will support and defend the Declaration of Independence in the closing campaign of the century.

We hold, with Abraham Lincoln, that "no man is good enough to govern another without that man's consent. When the white man governs himself, that is self-government, but when he governs himself and also governs another man, that is more than self-government—this is despotism." "Our reliance is in the love of liberty which God has planted in us. Our defense is in the spirit which prizes liberty as the heritage of all men in all lands. Those who deny freedom to others deserve it not for themselves, and under a just God cannot long retain it."

We cordially invite the coöperation of all men and women who remain loyal to the Declaration of Independence and the Constitution of the United States.

SECOND THOUGHTS

A splendid little war.

—John Hay

If old Dewey had just sailed away when he smashed that Spanish fleet, what a lot of trouble he would have saved us.

—President McKinley, late in 1898

Destiny is not as manifest as it was a few weeks ago.

—Bryan, referring to the outbreak of the Philippine War

Dishyer White Man's Burden ain't what it's cracked up to be.

—Black trooper in the Philippines

President McKinley confessed that he had not known the location of the Philippines, and had to search for them on a globe. At that he was better informed than many of his compatriots. Some people were amazed to find that they were a group of islands in the Far East, having been under the impression that they were somehow connected with one of St. Paul's epistles.

—Anonymous

I'm only a common soldier-man, in the blasted Philippines;
They say I've got Brown Brothers here, but I dunno what it means.
I like the word Fraternity, but still I draw the line;
He *may* be a brother of William H. Taft, but he ain't no brother of
    mine.

—Robert F. Morrison in the *Manila Sunday Sun*

Honest Friendship with All Nations, Entangling Alliances with None.—THOMAS JEFFERSON.

From the New York World

11

PROBLEMS OF AMERICAN EMPIRE

VIEWS OF AMERICAN EMPIRE

The mission of the United States is one of benevolent assimilation, substituting the mild sway of justice and right for arbitrary rule.

—William McKinley, 1898

We have bought ten million Malays at two dollars a head unpicked, and nobody knows what it will cost to pick them.

—Thomas B. Reed, on the purchase of the Philippine Islands

Poor Mexico! So far from God and so close to the United States.

—President Porfirio Díaz, ironically the man who opened up Mexico to U.S. business

The marines have landed and have the situation well in hand.

—Common news bulletin from the Caribbean

In these smaller countries of the South, controlled by our soldiers, our bankers, and our oil kings, we are developing our Irelands, our Egypts, and our Indias. So far they are weak and we have been able to hide them from others. But at the rate the world is moving they can hardly be expected to remain always powerless and isolated. Our North American Christian civilization will find its final test in the way we treat our next-door neighbors. We are piling up hatreds, suspicions, records for exploitation and destruction of sovereignty in Latin America, such as have never failed in all history to react in war, suffering, and defeat of high moral and spiritual ideals. How can the United States expect to be the one exception to the rule?

—Samuel Guy Inman, in *The Atlantic Monthly*, July 1924

PROBLEMS OF EAST AND WEST

When we consider in detail the impact of the West upon the Far East prior to World War I, it becomes evident that by far the greatest influence was wielded by Great Britain. The United States ranked a poor second, making its contributions chiefly in the fields of technology and education. Nevertheless, it is true that the United States was a factor in the "awakening" of Asia (not simply the Far East), and that as Europe's attention was diverted to its internal affairs the Asian nations turned to America for financial and technical aid. The Soviet Union was engaged with internal problems and was not to become a serious power factor in the Far East until the 1930's. The United States government made a colossal blunder (and a fateful one) when in the early 1920's it remained deaf to Sun Yat-sen's appeals for help and forced him to turn to Russia.

The West had for a century or more been under the impression that the Far East was dripping with wealth and that its trade was destined to rival that of India. We know now that Japan and China are relatively poor in resources, and that such riches as the Far East offers are pretty well concentrated in Manchuria and in Indonesia and the southeast projection of Asia. Western interest in the Far East was based more on the hope of a vast trade than on actual accomplishments. The hope of trade, however, was reinforced by a struggle for power which might have occurred in any case. Russia and Japan both had their eyes on Manchuria, which was definitely worth having, and their struggle affected all those powers which had territory or interests in the Far East. Prestige as well as trade was at stake. Just as important in the long run was missionary interest. The Open Door was in Britain and America as much the creation of missionaries as of businessmen, and, indeed, the missionaries (who were part and parcel of their pragmatic civilization) had been partly responsible for the false hopes of the businessmen.

Westerners, whether traders, colonial administrators, or missionaries, were frequently prevented by ignorance, prejudice, or laziness from forming a just understanding of the people among whom they lived, and so they carried home fables and snap judgments which crucially influenced Western political and economic decisions. One needs only to refer to Kipling's "East is East, and West is West, and never the twain shall meet" as an illustration. Actually, it is a defensible thesis that the distinction between East and West is one of time, that is, of stage of development. Up until 1400 there was a striking resemblance between Europe and Asia psychologically and culturally, with the latter having the cultural advantage. The chief significant differences lay in certain Westerners' restlessness under the rigid social and psychological controls which were necessary to keep a reasonable degree of balance in Nature; out of this were to come experimental science and religious and political liberties. There is no reason to suppose that this development was inevitable in the West; indeed, it is now in great danger of being wiped out. It is safe to say that any fundamental institution or idea which we regard as Western had its parallel in the East—and that includes activism, individualism, pragmatism, and experimental science.

Just what was this Western Civilization which traders, missionaries, colonial administrators, and Asiatic students carried to the Far East? Basically it was an attempt to master Nature by learning her secrets ("truth") through the use of experimental science. Its material object was to harness power to industry and transportation in order to utilize land and resources efficiently; at the same time it attempted to war against disease through medicine and sanitation. Its social object was the search for greater security and a higher standard of living for the masses as well as the classes. Its political object was to entrust the masses with their own government at the same time that it attempted to promote equal justice and freedom of opportunity and a high standard of public morality. Its intellectual object was to strike off the bonds of superstition through education and the search for truth, and to use popular enlightenment as a means of advance and of preserving a balance in politics and economics. Its moral object was to preserve and extend human freedom and dignity, which it regarded as the applicable-on-earth part of eternal moral values.

Western Civilization was not solely nor (said many) essentially connected with Christianity, materialism, imperialism, or the white race. Yet there had always been a stiff conflict within Western Civilization as to its true meaning, and its intolerant aspects have frequently impressed the Oriental observer more than its virtues. The two aspects of human nature have long struggled over whether Western Civilization shall be authoritarian or democratic, dominating or compromising. There has been a widespread opposition to science, because the truths it finds are frequently unpleasant or menacing to things as they are. There have been differences over how widely truth should be known and applied, for those who take a pessimistic view of human nature feel that the masses are not fitted to be trusted with knowledge, which, as we know, is power. Then of course there are honest, as well as dishonest and selfish, conflicts over the meaning and interpretation of scientific facts as found, or supposedly found.

Asians naturally resent the idea that the West is superior and the East inferior. They point out truly that Western Civilization in its origins vitally depended on Eastern contributions; that it has no consistent meaning or acceptance in the West —a statement which is not quite accurate; that it has no characteristic altogether confined to the West; and that it is the creation of yesterday in what we smugly call its home. In short, they prefer to call it Modern Civilization, and they are probably right. At any rate, certain limits must be borne in mind:

(1) Its roots are universal and its nourishment also.

(2) It has been a method and process rather than a structure.

(3) Its characteristics are not unique to the West, nor are they nontransferable.

(4) It is of recent growth; probably a man from Mars would not have recognized it as a separate civilization before the Fifteenth Century.

(5) Its shoots are being scattered and grafted everywhere. The result will not be Western Civilization but something or some things more universal.

Asia had chosen to get along with Nature rather than to conquer and exploit her. The Easterner understood the value of psychological satisfaction, the importance of being wanted, appreciated, and understood by those around him. Hence his stress on courtesy as lubrication for the social wheels; his desire to have time to enjoy living; and his refusal to work harder than was necessary to furnish the minimum means for simple enjoyment—a sort of materialism in itself. But this did not mean that Asians became alike. Quite the contrary, as we can see by looking at the three principal civilizations before the coming of Westerners. India was a congeries of independent states ruled by a military aristocracy and socially organized in castes; its outlook on life was otherworldly, metaphysical, pessimistic, quietist, and docile. China was historically united, ruled by an aristocracy of learning, and socially organized in clans or families; its outlook on life was this-worldly, ethical, and optimistic; its people held a nice balance between submission to fate and a practical belief in taking their own part—a close approach to the Greek ideal of moderation. Japan was technically a centralized state ruled by a descendant of the gods but actually a feudal state ruled by a military aristocracy and socially organized in clans; its outlook on life was this-worldly, opportunistic, and aggressive, but it acted as a rigid unit which brutally inhibited individual action or responsibility and was in consequence continually in danger of blowing up.

The above is necessarily an oversimplification and ignores the numerous exceptions in national character as well as the nuances of thought and behavior; so also does what follows. The impact of Western ideas and methods was bound to strike Easterners differently. The Indians, absorbed in eternal values, were troubled and resentful at the intrusion of the practical and material West. It took two centuries of British example and education to prepare them to live in the modern world. On the other hand, the Japanese, alive to facts, saw that they must at least adopt modern technology if they expected to survive; accordingly they took it in suddenly and as a national unit, but they tried to reconcile it with the preservation of their rigid social order and their concepts of divine origin and destiny to rule the world. The result was heightened frustration and an increase of internal turmoil in the individual. The Chinese, arrogantly sure of their values, saw no reason to substitute efficiency for learning, law for custom, brusqeness for manners, haste for leisure, force for reason, factories for handicrafts, or Christianity for the ethics of moderation. As for democracy, they already had something resembling it in village life, where democracy really mattered; moreover, in *yin* and *yang* they had a satisfactory philosophy of change and compromise far older than the democracy of the

West. Therefore China balked at change and for a hundred years fought a stubborn rear-guard action against it.

Asian conquerors had seldom attempted to make the conquered over in their own image; they had been content to collect tribute and bask in power and glory; usually they in the end were absorbed by the conquered. The irruption of the West into Asia was explosive because of the demand that the *status quo* be broken up and centuries of evolution suddenly by-passed. It is the Oriental belief that Western imperialism rose from greed and violence and from a feeling of inferiority and uncertainty, as witnessed by our intolerance and the self-defensive, crusading fervor of Christianity. Certainly Western imperialism was accompanied by use of military force; seizure of territory; humiliation of native governments; political domination, however concealed or indirect; economic exploitation with its control of tariffs, markets, and prices, and its forced labor; the deliberate destruction of indigenous and sometimes superior civilizations; and an intense racial arrogance, which was all the worse because it struck at the self-respect of the conquered.

The last was doubtless the most fateful of all. Certain idealists have tried to assert that arrogance is a monopoly of whites; this assertion is far from accurate, though other peoples are less concerned with the color of the skin than with differences in caste, culture, and religion. Moslems spat on the infidel dog; Brahmins were contaminated if a European cast his shadow on them; Chinese regarded foreigners as barbarians and devils and would have no diplomatic relations with them unless they came bearing tribute; while Japanese were convinced of their divine origin and of their destiny to rule a world inhabited by inferior races. When Europeans came into the Orient they were regarded as hollow-eyed ghosts, disgustingly hairy, and clearly primitive in their culture.

A stranger's vices are the most disgusting and naturally make a greater impression than one's own; even his mannerisms and blunders evoke distaste and ridicule. This reaction operated both ways when white men settled in the Orient. Then there was also the radical difference in climate, food, and tempo, and the effects of strange diseases, and of filth, misery, and apparent shiftlessness. The difference in living standards meant that the white man typically lived in ease surrounded by native servants, and he tended to judge the country by these servants since his contacts were otherwise pretty well limited to business associates. Often he became captious and even brutal in his treatment of servants; white women were the worst offenders, for with little to occupy their time they became subject to nervous strain and paranoia, and consequently to unreasonable outbursts and devastating rages. The Britisher was a natural-born snob, and when a member of the lower class was placed on top he became insufferable; the American likewise, though he was more a financial than a social snob.

At any rate, there developed an attitude among Westerners in the East known as the Shanghai Mind—or Manila, or Singapore, or Calcutta Mind. The Shanghai Mind carried in virulent form the usual Western concepts of the East: that the East understands only force; that cruel and unjust punishments are universal; that consciences and elections are for sale; and that faction and intrigue are the normal order. These ideas may or may not be correct (quite often they are), but they corrupted the Western administrator and businessman as he practiced them and lessened the chances of introducing better standards. Hence the policy of the iron fist, which has promoted the native belief that *whites* understood only force. To remain a ruler, the foreigner (he believed) must be consistently merciless; every concession would be interpreted only as a sign of weakness, and more concessions would be demanded until in the end the foreigner would be expelled. Now that is exactly what happened, so the Shanghai Mind was right. It failed to grasp what the people at home realized: that the democratic process must result in the gradual abandonment of imperialism. The Shanghai Mind, being on the spot and personally involved, could see nothing less than perpetual control.

The manifestations of the Shanghai Mind were frequently more evident to the East than the goodwill of democracy. People were pushed off the sidewalks, servants abused, the cultured higher classes were snubbed and excluded from clubs, hotels, and reserved boxes at race tracks. Religious and social rivalries were used to divide and rule; news was censored and writers subsidized to write favorably or to manufacture lies. Most of us are saved by our sense of humor from thrusting our cosmogonies on others, but the average missionary was a man with little knowledge, understanding, or tolerance, who saw the East as plunged in darkness and waiting to be saved. Nathaniel Peffer speaks of the shock of seeing temples invaded by a foreign missionary "shouting to men bent in prayer to turn from the vain worship of idols and give ear unto the truth." Among Westerners racism was most evident in British and Americans, even though they gave the most reasonable government, promoted welfare programs most zealously, and indulged in fewer economic abuses. The impact of the Shanghai Mind on the East was worse than open abuse, and British and Americans earned a kind of hatred which the French and Japanese largely escaped—until later.

The inevitable result was that resentment grew and festered under the continual charge of the Oriental's unfitness to manage his own affairs. There was a growing cynicism toward Western professions and institutions; the treatment of Chinese and Japanese in California was apt proof. When Westerners did good in the Orient there was immediately a search for the hidden joker. Christianity was denounced as an opening wedge for exploitation, as unfortunately it often was. Arrogance and oppression became the special province of the Westerner. If only he would leave, Asians would be be like brothers; and Indian communal riots and Japanese sharp practices were excused as having been stirred up or made necessary by Westerners. They emphasized the horrors of Western history and romanticized their own past. There had been no greed, cruelty, disease, superstition, economic oppression, no plural societies with caste, color, religious and economic rivalries—indeed, no death or taxes until the Westerner introduced them!

The Westernization of Asia was imposed either by foreign powers or by the ruling classes in control of wealth and political power. There was little intention to raise the standard of living of the masses; indeed, the foreigners were more concerned with this than were the local innovators aside from some Western-schooled idealists. It was, however, the masses whose toil yielded the profits upon which foreign and local entrepreneurs battened. Now your common man is the greatest conservative in the world in his stubborn determination to cling to the old; so the restlessness among the masses was at first an expression of resentment at the changes being imposed upon them. In time, however, they came to see their ancient lot as the victims in the East's compromise with Nature, a fact called to their attention by the way in which the West had wrung from Nature the means for a high standard of living for its masses. Western methods were now coming in but served only to reduce the Eastern commoner's standard of living further and to quicken his pace and steal from him the ability to savor living. Why then, he asked, was he doomed to toil at starvation wages in factories and on plantations when there was a way to better his standard? Simple enough, replied the local entrepreneur, it is Western imperialism that is to blame; cast out the West and everything will be wonderful. This he said knowing that he as well as the West was to blame, but hoping to succeed to the political and economic controls and investments abandoned by the departing West.

Now of course there is the argument that a "backward" country has no right to sit on its resources and that, if it does, a more "progressive" country has the right to force their development. The Oriental view was that the West should have accepted such trade as the East cared to allow and encouraged Asians to seek education in the West. Probably the Orient was right, but that was not the way it happened. Power breeds resentment regardless of whether it is used well or ill— or not at all. The West was doomed to be damned, no matter what it did. It was criticized because it was not always altruistic, because it was altruistic with a motive, or because its altruism did not take proper cognizance of all the warring creeds and interests of the East—an impossible task. Western administrators were criticized because they ignored local tyranny, because they permitted or supported it, and because they overthrew it.

There were three opinions among Orientals as to how Western Civilization should be utilized. Some wished to adopt it entire; some favored adopting its science and technology only; while others wished to reject mechanization but to accept nationalism and democracy. Those who studied the West with honest intent to learn were struck by its political concepts and stirred by the orations of men like Edmund Burke and Patrick Henry. Nevertheless, they either failed to understand the delicate balance necessary to make democracy work or those to whom they taught it thought that the democratic method could be applied without training. The result was that the Orient came to interpret democracy, not as government by the people but as independence from foreign control. From that point it was easy to go on to aping the nondemocratic wing of Western Civilization; as when Japan modeled its constitution on that of Prussia, and when China adopted one-party government.

The Orient may have misinterpreted the actual nature of the vital principle of Western Civilization and have adopted the authoritarianism which is destructive of that principle. However, what happens in the Orient may depend in the long run on the outcome of the struggle within Western Civilization itself. Certainly the evidences of transition in the Orient are overwhelming, and not merely in the rise of Western-educated leaders, in the growth of mechanized industry, and in the creation of unified governments either by local or by imperial powers. More fundamental are (1) the growth of the spirit of critical judgment and experimental accuracy, along with the decline of religion as a determining factor in all questions; and (2) the growth of the "consciously fostered personality of the individual and of groups under objective laws," along with its accompaniments of feminism, labor consciousness, and a public responsibility for promoting the economic changes which Western capital can no longer assume.

THE WHITE MAN'S BURDEN

Take up the White Man's burden—
    Send forth the best ye breed—
Go bind your sons to exile
    To serve your captives' need;
To wait in heavy harness
    On fluttered folk and wild—
Your new-caught, sullen peoples,
    Half devil and half child.

Take up the White Man's burden—
    The savage wars of peace—
Fill full the mouth of Famine
    And bid the sickness cease;
And when your goal is nearest
    The end for others sought,
Watch Sloth and heathen Folly
    Bring all your hope to naught.

Take up the White Man's burden—
    And reap his old reward:
The blame of those ye better,
    The hate of those ye guard—
The cry of hosts ye humour
    (Ah, slowly!) toward the light;—
"Why brought ye us from bondage,
    "Our loved Egyptian night?

Take up the White Man's burden—
    Ye dare not stoop to less—
Nor call too loud on Freedom
    To cloak your weariness;
By all ye cry or whisper,
    By all ye leave or do,
The silent, sullen peoples
    Shall weigh your Gods and you.

—Rudyard Kipling, 1899, written to help persuade the
United States to annex the Philippines

OPEN DOOR DOCUMENTS

(1) HAY PROPOSES THE OPEN DOOR

[Secretary of State John Hay, in his desire to protect American commercial interests in East Asia, sought to get the great powers to stop carving out "spheres of interest" and to open to others the spheres they had already set up. The following sent to Ambassador Joseph Choate in London (Sept. 6, 1899) states Hay's intentions. See *Papers Relating to the Foreign Relations of the U.S., 1899* (1901), pp. 131–133.]

This Government is animated by a sincere desire that the interests of our citizens may not be prejudiced through exclusive treatment by any of the controlling powers within their so-called "spheres of interest" in China, and hopes also to retain there an open market for the commerce of the world, remove dangerous sources of international irritation, and hasten thereby united or concerted action of the powers at Pekin in favor of the administrative reforms so urgently needed for strengthening the Imperial Government and maintaining the integrity of China in which the whole western world is alike concerned. It believes that such a result may be greatly assisted by a declaration by the various powers claiming "spheres of interest" in China of their intentions as regards treatment of foreign trade therein. The present moment seems a particularly opportune one for informing Her Britannic Majesty's Government of the desire of the United States to see it make a formal declaration and to lend its support in obtaining similar declarations from the various powers claiming "spheres of influence" in China, to the effect that each in its respective spheres of interest or influence.

First. Will in no wise interfere with any treaty port or any vested interest within any so-called "sphere of interest" or leased territory it may have in China.

Second. That the Chinese treaty tariff of the time being shall apply to all merchandise landed or shipped to all such ports as are within said "sphere of interest" (unless they be "free ports"), no matter to what nationality it may belong, and that duties so leviable shall be collected by the Chinese Government.

Third. That it will levy no higher harbor dues on vessels of another nationality frequenting any port in such "sphere" than shall be levied on vessels of its own nationality, and no higher railroad charges over lines built, controlled, or operated within its "sphere" on merchandise belonging to citizens or subjects of other nationalities transported through such "sphere" than shall be levied on similar merchandise belonging to its own nationals transported over equal distances.

(2) ASSENT IS "FINAL AND DEFINITIVE"

[Only Italy, which had no spheres of influence, agreed to Hay's proposals. Russia declined, and the others hedged. Nevertheless, Hay blandly instructed U.S. ministers to the various countries to announce that the policy was in effect by mutual consent. The form used appears in *Foreign Relations, 1899*, p. 142, dated March 20, 1900.]

Sir: The_____Government having accepted the declaration suggested by the United States concerning foreign trade in China, the terms of which I transmitted to you in my instruction No. ____ of ____, and like action having been taken by all the various powers having leased territory or so-called "spheres of interest" in the Chinese Empire, as shown by the notes which I herewith transmit to you, you will please inform the Government to which you are accredited that the condition originally attached to its acceptance—that all other powers concerned should likewise accept the proposals of the United States—having been complied with, this Government will therefore consider the assent given to it by ____ ____ as final and definitive.

You will also transmit to the minister for foreign affairs copies of the present inclosures, and by the same occasion convey to him the expression of the sincere gratification which the President feels at the successful termination of these negotiations, in which he sees proof of the friendly spirit which animates the various powers interested in the untrammeled development of commerce and industry in the Chinese Empire, and a source of vast benefit to the whole commercial world.

(3) HAY EXPANDS THE MEANING OF THE OPEN DOOR

[When the various powers sent troops to relieve the foreign residents besieged by the Boxers in Tientsin and Peking, Hay seized the opportunity to assert that Chinese territorial integrity must be preserved. See his note to French ambassador Thiébaut, July 3, 1900, in *Foreign Relations, 1900* (1902), pp. 318–319. Evidently Hay was continuing the bluff begun a few months before.]

SIR: I have the honor to acknowledge the receipt of your note of yesterday's date, in which you present more fully the considerations you expressed to me in the course of our conversation yesterday afternoon respecting the policy of the powers in the treatment of the existing crisis in China and the steps to be taken by them to insure the safety of their national representatives and citizens in Pekin and throughout the Empire, to maintain the territorial status quo, and, through substantial guaranties, to prevent a recurrence of the recent deplorable events. . . .

To attain these objects the Government of the United States is now, as heretofore, ready to act concurrently with the other powers in opening up communication with Pekin and rescuing the imperiled Americans and foreigners there, to afford all possible protection every-

where in China to American life and property, to guard all legitimate American interests in the Empire, and to aid in preventing a spread of the disorders to other provinces, and in securing future immunity from a recurrence of such disasters—seeking to these ends a solution which may bring about permanent peace and safety to China, preserve Chinese territorial and administrative entity, protect all rights guaranteed to friendly powers by treaty, and safeguard for the world the principle of equal and impartial trade with all parts of the Chinese Empire.

I am communicating these views to all the governments represented diplomatically at Pekin, substantially as herein outlined; and it gives me much pleasure to advise you of their purport, in view of their virtual accord with the policy independently formulated by the Government of the French Republic.

(4) THE ROOT-TAKAHIRA AGREEMENT

[Japan felt that it had been sold out by Roosevelt at the Portsmouth Conference, in his desire to ensure a balance of power in the Far East. Japan was bent on annexing Korea, and Roosevelt, seeing that he could not prevent it, traded for a Japanese promise not to aggress on the Philippines—the Taft-Katsura Agreement; another interpretation is that it was merely an agreement to disagree. Three years later he finally got Japan to agree to the Open Door in an exchange of notes between Ambassador Takahira and Secretary of State Root, on November 30, 1908. See *Foreign Relations, 1908* (1912), pp. 510–512.]

1. It is the wish of the two Governments to encourage the free and peaceful development of their commerce on the Pacific Ocean.

2. The policy of both Governments, uninfluenced by any aggressive tendencies, is directed to the maintenance of the existing status quo in the region above mentioned and to the defense of the principle of equal opportunity for commerce and industry in China.

3. They are accordingly firmly resolved reciprocally to respect the territorial possessions belonging to each other in said region.

4. They are also determined to preserve the common interest of all powers in China by supporting by all pacific means at their disposal the independence and integrity of China and the principle of equal opportunity for commerce and industry of all nations in that Empire.

5. Should any event occur threatening the status quo as above described or the principle of equal opportunity as above defined, it remains for the two Governments to communicate with each other in order to arrive at an understanding as to what measures they may consider it useful to take.

(5) THE LANSING-ISHII AGREEMENT

[World War I presented Japan with a golden opportunity to make itself dominant in East Asia, and early in 1915 it presented China with the famous Twenty-One Demands. If agreed to, they would have slammed shut the Open Door and made China a Japanese protectorate. Secretary of State Bryan protested vigorously, and Japan withdrew the most onerous of the demands. As for the others, China delayed and argued until at last the war was over and Japan did not dare to act. Meanwhile, however, Japan demanded that the United States recognize her paramount interest in China, under threat of leaving the war—perhaps even going over to the side of Germany. Secretary of State Lansing grudgingly agreed (Nov. 2, 1917) to a document intended to be ambiguous, though "special interest" is a well-understood diplomatic term for political and economic priority. At least Japan remained in the war. See *Foreign Relations, 1917* (1926), p. 264.]

EXCELLENCY: I have the honor to communicate herein my understanding of the agreement reached by us in our recent conversations touching the questions of mutual interest to our Governments relating to the Republic of China.

In order to silence mischievous reports that have from time to time been circulated, it is believed by us that a public announcement once more of the desires and intentions shared by our two Governments with regard to China is advisable.

The Governments of the United States and Japan recognize that territorial propinquity creates special relations between countries, and, consequently, the Government of the United States recognizes that Japan has special interests in China, particularly in the part to which her possessions are contiguous.

The territorial sovereignty of China, nevertheless, remains unimpaired and the Government of the United States has every confidence in the repeated assurances of the Imperial Japanese Government that while geographical position gives Japan such special interests they have no desire to discriminate against the trade of other nations or to disregard the commercial rights heretofore granted by China in treaties with other powers.

The Governments of the United States and Japan deny that they have any purpose to infringe in any way the independence or territorial integrity of China and they declare, furthermore, that they always adhere to the principle of the so-called "open door" or equal opportunity for commerce and industry in China.

Moreover, they mutually declare that they are opposed to the acquisition by any Government of any special rights or privileges that would affect the independence or territorial integrity of China or that would deny to the subjects or citizens of any country the full enjoyment of equal opportunity in the commerce and industry of China.

(6) THE NINE-POWER PACT GUARANTEES THE OPEN DOOR

[Japan regarded the Lansing-Ishii passage as a victory, but it was far from satisfied, and in April 1918 began moving 72,000 troops into Vladivostok, which was defenseless because of the Bolshevik Revolution. Wilson's desire to counter this move was one of the reasons why he sent troops to Eastern Siberia some months later, and they apparently clashed more often with the Japanese than with the Russians. The Washington Conference of 1921–22 was motivated not only by the desire for naval limitation but also by the objections of Canada to the Anglo-Japanese Alliance and by the Japanese threat to the Open Door. The Anglo-Japanese Alliance was supplanted by the Four-Power Pact, binding Britain, Japan, France, and the United States to "respect" one another's rights in the Pacific and to consult in case of threat by a fifth power. The Nine-Power Pact quietly abrogated the Lansing-Ishii Agreement by binding all the signatories to respect the Open Door; on the other hand, it pointedly omitted any obligation to fight for its validity. See *Foreign Relations, 1922* (1938), 1:278–280. Of course, this was not the end of the controversy over the Open Door, and we shall return to it in a later chapter.]

ARTICLE I   The Contracting Powers, other than China, agree:

(1) To respect the sovereignty, the independence, and the territorial and administrative integrity of China;

(2) To provide the fullest and most unembarrassed opportunity to China to develop and maintain for herself an effective and stable government;

(3) To use their influence for the purpose of effectually establishing and maintaining the principle of equal opportunity for the commerce and industry of all nations throughout the territory of China;

(4) To refrain from taking advantage of conditions in China in order to seek special rights or privileges which would abridge the rights of subjects or citizens of friendly States, and from countenancing action inimical to the security of such States.

ARTICLE II   The Contracting Powers agree not to enter into any treaty, agreement, arrangement, or understanding, either with one another, or, individually or collectively, with any Power or Powers, which would infringe or impair the principles stated in Article I.

ARTICLE III   With a view to applying more effectually the principles of the Open Door or equality of opportunity in China for the trade and industry of all nations, the Contracting Powers, other than China, agree that they will not seek, nor support their respective nationals in seeking—

(a) any arrangement which might purport to establish in favour of their interests any general superiority of rights with respect to commercial or economic development in any designated region of China;

(b) any such monopoly or preference as would deprive the nationals of any other Power of the right of undertaking any legitimate trade or industry in China, or of participating with the Chinese Government, or with any local authority, in any category of public enterprise, or which by reason of its scope, duration or geographical extent is calculated to frustrate the practical application of the principle of equal opportunity.

It is understood that the foregoing stipulations of this Article are not to be so construed as to prohibit the acquisition of such properties or rights as may be necessary to the conduct of a particular commercial, industrial, or financial undertaking or to the encouragement of invention and research.

China undertakes to be guided by the principles stated in the foregoing stipulations of this Article in dealing with applications for economic rights and privileges from Governments and nationals of all foreign countries, whether parties to the present Treaty or not.

ARTICLE IV   The Contracting Powers agree not to support any agreements by their respective nationals with each other designed to create Spheres of Influence or to provide for the enjoyment of mutually exclusive opportunities in designated parts of Chinese territory.

ARTICLE V   China agrees that, throughout the whole of the railways in China, she will not exercise or permit unfair discrimination of any kind. In particular there shall be no discrimination whatever, direct or indirect, in respect of charges or of facilities on the ground of the nationality of passengers or the countries from which or to which they are proceeding, or the origin or ownership of goods or the country from which or to which they are consigned, or the nationality or ownership of the ship or other means of conveying such passengers or goods before or after their transport on the Chinese Railways.

The Contracting Powers, other than China, assume a corresponding obligation in respect of any of the aforesaid railways over which they or their nationals are in a position to exercise any control in virtue of any concession, special agreement or otherwise.

ARTICLE VI   The Contracting Powers, other than China, agree fully to respect China's rights as a neutral in time of war to which China is not a party; and China declares that when she is a neutral she will observe the obligations of neutrality.

ARTICLE VII   The Contracting Powers agree that, whenever a situation arises which in the opinion of any one of them involves the application of the stipulations of the present Treaty, and renders desirable discussion of such application, there shall be full and frank communication between the Contracting Powers concerned. . . .

THE WATER CURE

Q. Please tell the committee what you actually saw?—A. That is, you want me to describe one individual case of a man being put through the water cure?

Q. Yes; I would like you to do that, sir.—A. Very good, sir. A man is thrown down on his back and three or four men sit or stand on his arms and legs and hold him down, and either a gun barrel or a rifle barrel or a carbine barrel or a stick as big as a belaying pin—that is, with an inch circumference——

Senator Beveridge. As big in its diameter?

A. (Continued.) Yes; is simply thrust into his jaws and his jaws are thrust back, and, if possible, a wooden log or stone is put under his head——

Senator Patterson. Under his head or neck?

A. (Continued.) Under his neck, so he can be held firmly.

Senator Burrows. His jaws are forced open, you say? How do you mean, crosswise?

The Witness. Yes, sir; as a gag. In the case of very old men I have seen their teeth fall out—I mean when it was done a little roughly. He is simply held down, and then water is poured onto his face, down his throat and nose from a jar, and that is kept up until the man gives some sign of giving in or becomes unconscious, and when he becomes unconscious he is simply rolled aside and he is allowed to come to. That is as near a description as I think I can give. All the cases were alike I saw on that occasion.

By Senator Culberson:

Q. Is the water allowed to remain in the man or is it any way expelled from him, by any method?—A. Well, I know that in a great many cases, in almost every case, the men have been a little roughly handled; they were rolled aside rudely, so that water was expelled. A man suffers tremendously; there is no doubt about it. His suffering must be that of a man who is drowning, but who can not drown.

> —Lt. Grover Flint, testifying before a Senate committee, 1902, on the method of forcing prisoners to give information in the Philippines

PROBLEMS OF THE CARIBBEAN FRONTIER

The greatest weakness of the Caribbean countries then and now lies in their dependence on one crop—usually sugar or coffee—or at the most two or three. This makes Caribbean prosperity dependent on outside countries, especially the United States, which even before World War I was taking half the exports of these countries and now takes three quarters. The danger lies not only in their dependence upon the American economic situation but in the ease with which they and other tropical countries can glut the market. The condition has been only partly remedied by the guarantees to them of a certain percentage of the American market. The practice of democracy is partly dependent upon a rather widespread ownership of property among a country's citizens, a condition which has never existed in Caribbean states except, significantly, in Costa Rica. Moreover, national incomes are low; all nine states have only about one percent of that of the United States. The effect upon government budgets, education, welfare, and internal development is obvious.

Caribbean development of mines, railways, and even of plantations has therefore largely depended upon foreign loans and investments. This practice has meant that the Caribbean dictators, called *caudillos*, have been in a position to treat their countries as private possessions, to spend borrowings as they please, and to force investors to purchase justice in addition to their physical assets. Foreign investors were frequently (they felt) compelled to finance revolutions in order to put into power governments which were benevolent toward their interests. Investors, it must be acknowledged, did not always seek to benefit the countries in which they operated. They sometimes imported Jamaican Negro labor, evaded their welfare responsibilities, exploited the soil, and sought special legal privileges and tax exemptions. Between them investors and bankers were draining away the economic life of the state without making adequate return, and few local patriots were ready to acknowledge that the *caudillo* was at least as much to blame as the foreigners.

It was quite usual for European governments to back up their nationals who were jockeying for Caribbean perquisites, and sometimes this interference extended to the use of force. The United States now looked upon these activities with disfavor lest they lead to permanent occupation, and there was pressure on Roosevelt to forbid them. England and other countries pointed out to him that, if he forbade foreign intervention, he must undertake himself to protect their rights and collect debts owed to their nationals. Roosevelt substantially accepted the argument and put into effect what has come to be known as the Roosevelt Corollary of the Monroe Doctrine. When the Dominican Republic defaulted and European intervention seemed imminent, TR installed (1905) an American customs collector who was to turn over part of the receipts to the republic and pay the rest to creditors, mostly European bankers.

Taft and his Secretary of State, Philander Chase Knox, took the next step in the form of so-called Dollar Diplomacy. Under threat of intervention they forced Nicaragua to refund its foreign-held debt with New York money. Their purpose was to reduce the chances of foreign intervention and at the same time give warning to American investors that the government would back only such loans as were approved by the State Department. The idea was sound, and it served to remove the bankers' power to make risky loans in confidence that the government would collect them. Nevertheless, Dollar Diplomacy itself had to be forced upon the unwilling "banana republics" with marines.

Jefferson had laid down the "will of the nation" test for deciding whether to receive envoys from revolutionary governments; the result had been that *de facto* governments were recognized, regardless of the crimes which had brought them into power. Wilson, however, was nothing if not moral, and he sharply reversed the historic policy of recognition by holding that the United States had a moral duty to look after the morals of its neighbors. He could not, he said, recognize "government by murder." When he sought to lessen Caribbean chaos by prohibiting revolutions—the so-called Wilson Corollary to the Monroe Doctrine—the curious result was that the marines were busier than ever, both as bill-collecting agents and as discouragers of revolution. The situation certainly was not one to make a Caribbean patriot happy, for revolution was literally his only way of cleaning house. Wilson's toughest problem arose, however, from Mexico, and two interventions occurred, one at Vera Cruz in 1914 and another in Chihuahua in 1916. The only result was to add to the mounting chorus of Latin-American protest.

Pan-American Conferences begun by Blaine in 1889 were followed intermittently by others, but they were always plagued by an attitude of suspicion on the part of the Latin members, especially after the Spanish-American War and TR's arrogant action in Panama. Nevertheless, progress was made and special conferences to deal with finances, trade, transportation, sanitation, intercultural relations, etc. succeeded in ironing out many difficult problems. On the whole, strange as it may seem, Wilson's administration saw an improvement in our psychological relations with Latin America. True, he intervened more frequently than his predecessors, but he never agreed with them that intervention was desirable. Indeed, he had promised that "the United States will never again seek one additional foot of territory by conquest," and his withdrawals from Mexico (when apparently American public opinion urged conquest) convinced thoughtful Latin Americans that he had meant what he said.

A retrospect of American imperialism in the Caribbean brings to light certain facts which were not clear to contemporaries. True enough, Cuba, Panama, Haiti, the Dominican Republic, and Nicaragua had treaties of protection forced upon them, and all the Central American republics had been subjected to the pressure of Dollar Diplomacy or had unwillingly entertained marines. But these protectorates were nothing like the pattern set up by European empires. They were limited in duration, their citizens could not be drafted to fight the protector's wars, and they conducted their own foreign affairs even though certain rules were laid down by Washington. Even in domestic affairs American control was usually confined to the fiscal administration and to supervision of elections. The era of political and fiscal protectorates was ephemeral and passed away as the Caribbean states became more orderly and as the overwhelming power of the United States made it useless for Europe to threaten its strategic security. Such control as survives is based upon economic treaties and common strategic interests.

American influence on South America was up to World War I more institutional than economic. The framers of the Latin-American constitutions found that the Constitution of the United States was a handy pattern, particularly because their local diversities frequently necessitated the adoption of federalism. While the United States wielded few cultural and literary influences, its educational contributions were large. In their Latin-American economic interests Americans lagged far behind the British. Still, they provided a number of significant builders. The Panama Railway was constructed in the 1850's by an American syndicate, and it was largely Americans who financed, built, and operated the Mexican railways. Submarine cables, telegraphs, and of course mines were included among American enterprise. The National City Bank had from its early years financed trade with Cuba, and eventually it became a power in financing Cuban economic enterprise and government. During and after World War I its control displaced British capital in the island and secured what many asserted was an economic and political throttlehold. At the same time its branches spread all over Latin America and led in exchange, securities, and the supervision of American investments. Minor C. Keith covered Central America with railroads, built up the banana business, and organized the United Fruit Company. Though he certainly did much for Central America, he was also accused of heartless exploitation.

Nevertheless, Latin America became economically complementary to Europe rather than the United States because the latter could furnish most of its own raw materials. Latin America was culturally closer to Europe than to the United States, with Hispanic and French cultures ascendant. It was basically Catholic, even though much of the thinking element was strongly tinged by French liberalism and Freemasonry, which were regarded as connected. European ideals of aristocratic and authoritarian ascendancy were honored, at least in practice. Only in democratic *aspirations* and in a common suspicion of European imperialism were the United States and Latin America drawn together. Thus long before the United States had any considerable economic stake south of the Caribbean it had become apparent that there was a deep, though possibly exaggerated, psychological abyss between North America and Latin America.

Latin-American suspicions of the United States found their origin in the long series of seizures and enforced purchases by which the latter had expanded its territory. The war of literary propaganda was waged by a group of poets, historians, and publicists, some of them the undoubted intellectual leaders of Latin America. The basis of their challenge was the contrast between American materialism and Hispanic spirituality. Outstanding among these critics was José Enrique Rodó, the literary philosopher of Uruguay. In his *Ariel* (1900) he drew, on one hand, a striking analogy between Shakespeare's airy sprite Ariel and the graceful, imaginative, and idealistic Hispanic peoples and, on the other hand, between the brute-like, malevolent Caliban and the vulgar, sordid, materialistic Anglo-Saxons. True, he was willing to award to the latter energy, enthusiasm, the urge to action, and a sort of blundering moral capacity. But, and only the Latin American could perceive how damning was the judgment, they had no poetic sense. The menace of Americanization struck panic to the hearts of the thoughtful, for they loved Hispanic culture and naturally regarded it as the acme of civilization. It was not conquest they feared so much as infiltration.

High-minded men like Rodó had a host of less restrained imitators who embarked upon a campaign of hate which cut loose from the anchors of truth and consistency. Xenophobia afforded a fruitful field for the designing commercial and political propagandists of Europe. Spain sought to promote a Pan-Hispanic bloc, and France a Pan-Latin bloc. Even English commercial interests were not above whispering campaigns. Some of the European-inspired propaganda was so ridiculous that it should have been transparent. A Frenchman, for example, wrote that the United States was about to prohibit music without words on the ground that pure melody was morally enervating! The sensationalism of American newspapers and moving pictures, the crass materialism of the business scene (to the casual observer), the intolerance and sterility of orthodox Protestants and the spiritual aridity of the modernists, the violations of civil liberties, the mythus of white supremacy, the divorce and murder and insanity rates, the publicity given to sex crimes and bathing beauties—all these things lent themselves to the literary Yankee-phobes. American domestic wrangles with their false charges and recriminations were rich sources of Latin propaganda about imperialism and Wall Street domination. Some American tourists and even some Americans resident in Latin America seemed strangely released from polite inhibitions. They occasionally were unreliable and overbearing in business, drank excessively, and made little attempt to conceal their contempt for those among whom they lived.

Now, of course, Latin America has rivalries of its own. Brazil and Argentina have long struggled for the control of the area between them, and Uruguay owes its creation and Paraguay its continuance to their values as buffer states. Argentineans are a vigorous mixture of Spanish and Italian blood. Brazil's Amazon jungle is largely inhabited by Indians and its Bulge by Negroes, but its South compares in vigor with the Argentine since its people are a mixture of the old mestizo Paulistas and newer German and Italian immigrants. The rivalry between Chile on one side and Peru and Bolivia on the other led to the Pacific War and to wounds that still rankle. Brazil has had boundary disputes with all of its neighbors. Colombia's multiplying peasantry, based on small coffee farms, are spreading over the country and building a solid industrial basis as well. In time they may well provide a northern rival to Argentine influence.

Latin-American countries have developed psychological diversities which separate them from each other and give to each, in the eyes of their neighbors, a reputation for typical characteristics. The typical Brazilians are gay, gentle, and carefree; the typical Argentines have the surface stolidity and coldness of the Castilians and a moroseness and inordinate egotism which casts the Castilian into the shade. The Chileans are cold, energetic, and practical. The Peruvians—the Limeños, at least—are gay, proud, and ambitious. Not only are there differences among Spaniards and Portuguese, but the great Indian races lend their characters to the complex. The intrepid Guarani give Paraguay an unsurpassed military reputation, and the submissive Incas have molded much of Ecuador, Peru, and Bolivia. . . . The Mexican is given to opposite drives which lead to contradictory moods and actions (*vacilada*), or in other words, "to the Sancho Panzan jollity and the quixotic delirium is united in our hearts the sadness of the Indian." The Negro influences Brazil and the littoral of Peru; and Haiti, though tinged at the top with French culture, is permeated with the African spirit. The Cuban is an inveterate gambler, full of gay defiance and a persistent sense of disproportion (*choteo*). Slavs, Germans, and especially Italians have profoundly changed the basic Spanish stocks in southern Brazil, and in Uruguay and Argentina.

Thus the Latin-American nations each have their own characteristics and some of them have been vitally influenced by the Indian and the Negro. Yet the inescapable fact is that Hispanic culture reigns more or less completely from the Rio Grande to Cape Horn. More than this, Hispanic psychology has given to those nations their one most outstanding common characteristic: intense individualism. Only recently has it been altered as modern influences have begun to break down the old self-contained ways. It is noteworthy that a somewhat similar psychology once ruled over northwestern Europe; the Englishman of the Elizabethan Renascence would perhaps recognize more of his own ways in modern Hispanic America than in North America.

When one looks at the typical middle- and upper-class Latin-American family as it existed around 1900 (and does still to a considerable extent), he finds that it was a little republic of relatives. It had all the problems of power politics, touchy family honor, alliances offensive and defensive, diplomatic punctilio, tiresome circumlocutions, and elaborate machinery for saving face. It battled as a unit, shared in the gains or glory of one member or hung its collective head at his disgrace. This state of affairs promoted an elaborate punctilio, for no one could afford to insult rivals or friends when the least slip might make an enemy for life. Underneath the charm and courtesy there was in process a combat far more deadly than the social strife of the English-speaking peoples, for it recognized no philosophy of compromise, no permanent middle ground between absolute domination and abject submission—no middle ground between dignity and ridiculousness. The struggle was for prestige, for personal domination, even more than for wealth and achievements.

Once the premise of complete individualism was established, there followed a stream of practical deductions. Since not everyone could rule, it was necessary to find ways of saving face, to give the appearance of belonging to the ascendant group. Many a man remained contented in a subordinate clerkship because he could wear a white collar and shuffle papers rather than wear a black shirt and wield a shovel. Contempt for manual labor was a blighting heritage from Spain which was reinforced by the exploitation of Indian and Negro labor. Life was spent primarily in laying wires and only secondarily in performing one's job. Administrators were chosen for their acceptability, not their ability. Charm, tact, personal services, political acceptability, and family connections were the true virtues rewarded in the Horatio Alger literature of the South.

The existence of this rabid individualism lay at the basis of caudillism, for general order could be brought only by a man who was strong enough to force submission and yet knew how to enable his countrymen to save face by preserving their individual dignity and the appearance of sharing the trappings of power. The result was a sentimental regard for liberty and democracy, but their growth was hampered because the method of change through successive social and political compromises was unknown. But change has made inroads as science and industry and modern influences began to break down the old self-contained ways. The gradual rise of mass purchasing power has had a profound effect in awakening individuals to the fact that each has a stake in the welfare of all. Industrial and agricultural progress carried with it the requirement of literacy. Even the *caudillos* strove to promote national wealth and knowledge. Perhaps they did not wish to promote popular control, but the very necessities of modern life forced them to take the steps to that goal one by one.

The persistence of Hispanic psychology has served to give an air of unreality even in recent decades to relations between the United States and the countries to the South, though the weakening of the psychology of extreme individualism may have brought more respect for the method of compromise. The North American concept of the good neighbor—the *buen vecino*—is of people who live in adjacent houses and who visit back and forth, play gin rummy together, borrow flour and sugar, and take turns at baby-sitting. The Hispanic concept of the fortress family envisions a relationship between rich and poor acquaintances, much like the relation between patron and client inherited from the Romans; essentially it is a hangover of the age of aristocracy. The patron gives his client odd jobs, makes little loans never intended to be repaid, and stands godfather to his children. The poor neighbor votes as he is instructed, performs distasteful but necessary business, and sings his patron's praises exactly as the rich man's generosity warrants. A palace with no poor at the door is no palace, says a Spanish adage. The poor, therefore, are essential to the ego of the rich, and they can save their own egos by the many subterfuges well known to men of Mediterranean blood. Even the beggar can look upon himself as exploiting the rich patron who throws him a coin; the patron can feed his vanity upon the music of the beggar's praise.

This, then, was the Hispanic concept of the Good Neighbor Policy that was announced in 1933. The Hispanic nations accepted their role enthusiastically, expecting that the stream of loans, christening gifts, and distasteful but lucrative assignments would soon begin. Everyone in Hispanic America knew that a gentleman is marked by his generosity, but it was presently found that the Yanqui expected to keep his purse strings drawn and yet be regarded as a true hidalgo. He expected to collect from his debtors and yet have them like and respect him—a hard thing in any society. By Hispanic standards Mr. Franklin D. Roosevelt apparently did not mean what he said. He did not admit Argentine beef, he haggled over oil expropriations, and with ungentlemanly persistence he continued to present bills that were long overdue. Nothing, it seemed, was to be allowed to the poor man who sat in the palace gate and whose very presence served to make it a palace. We shall see in good time how Roosevelt learned his lesson and opened the federal purse to the clamoring Good Neighbors to the South.

THE CONSTITUTION DOES NOT FOLLOW THE FLAG

[Whether or not because of anti-imperialist pressure, Congress failed to erect a Cabinet department for the administration of new possessions, but farmed them out among existing departments. It also dealt legislatively with them piecemeal. The result was that a number of problems were laid before the Supreme Court from 1901 to 1922 in the so-called *Insular Cases*. The Supreme Court felt its way through existing legislation and emerged with a peculiarly illogical system, somewhat like that which had led to the rebellion of the Thirteen Colonies. It was decided that there are two kinds of possessions: incorporated and unincorporated. The former (Alaska and Hawaii) were presumably destined for statehood and were entitled to the guarantees of the federal Constitution. The latter (Puerto Rico; the Philippines, later granted independence; Samoa; etc.) were not destined for statehood and were not entitled by right to Constitutional guarantees. That is, the Constitution did not follow the flag. However, unincorporated territories were entitled to certain "fundamental" Constitutional rights as contrasted to "formal" or "procedural" rights. Fundamental rights included the guarantee against deprivation of life, liberty, and property without due process of law; jury trial and uniform tariff rates were formal. One of the early *Insular Cases* was *Downes v. Bid-*

well (1901), which upheld the constitutionality of the Foraker Act of 1900 setting up a government for Puerto Rico and laid down the rule that the Constitution did not necessarily follow the flag—therefore duties could be laid on goods brought from that island to the United States.]

Mr. Justice Brown announced the conclusion and judgment of the court . . . :

We are also of opinion that the power to acquire territory by treaty implies, not only the power to govern such territory, but to prescribe upon what terms the United States will receive its inhabitants, and what their status shall be in what Chief Justice Marshall termed the "American empire." There seems to be no middle ground between this position and the doctrine that if their inhabitants do not become, immediately upon annexation, citizens of the United States, their children thereafter born, whether savages or civilized, are such, and entitled to all the rights, privileges, and immunities of citizens. If such be their status, the consequences will be extremely serious. Indeed, it is doubtful if Congress would ever assent to the annexation of territory upon the condition that its inhabitants, however foreign they may be to our habits, traditions, and modes of life, shall become at once citizens of the United States. . . .

It is obvious that in the annexation of outlying and distant possessions grave questions will arise from differences of race, habits, laws, and customs of the people, and from differences of soil, climate, and production, which may require action on the part of Congress that would be quite unnecessary in the annexation of contiguous territory inhabited only by people of the same race, or by scattered bodies of native Indians.

We suggest, without intending to decide, that there may be a distinction between certain natural rights enforced in the Constitution by prohibitions against interference with them, and what may be termed artificial or remedial rights which are peculiar to our own system of jurisprudence. Of the former class are the rights to one's own religious opinions and to a public expression of them, or, as sometimes said, to worship God according to the dictates of one's own conscience; the right to personal liberty and individual property; to freedom of speech and of the press; to free access to courts of justice, to due process of law, and to an equal protection of the laws; to immunities from unreasonable searches and seizures, as well as cruel and unusual punishments; and to such other immunities as are indispensable to a free government. Of the latter class are the rights to citizenship, to suffrage, . . . and to the particular methods of procedure pointed out in the Constitution, which are peculiar to Anglo-Saxon jurisprudence, and some of which have already been held by the states to be unnecessary to the proper protection of individuals.

Whatever may be finally decided by the American people as to the status of these islands and their inhabitants,—whether they shall be introduced into the sisterhood of states or be permitted to form independent governments,—it does not follow that in the meantime, awaiting that decision, the people are in the matter of personal rights unprotected by the provisions of our Constitution and subject to the merely arbitrary control of Congress. Even if regarded as aliens, they are entitled under the principles of the Constitution to be protected in life, liberty, and property. This has been frequently held by this court in respect to the Chinese, even when aliens, not possessed of the political rights of citizens of the United States. . . .

We do not desire, however, to anticipate the difficulties which would naturally arise in this connection, but merely to disclaim any intention to hold that the inhabitants of these territories are subject to an unrestrained power on the part of Congress to deal with them upon the theory that they have no rights which it is bound to respect. . . .

Choice in some cases, the natural gravitation of small bodies towards large ones in others, the result of a successful war in still others, may bring about conditions which would render the annexation of distant possessions desirable. If those possessions are inhabited by alien races, differing from us in religion, customs, laws, methods of taxation, and modes of thought, the administration of government and justice, according to Anglo-Saxon principles, may for a time be impossible; and the question at once arises whether large concessions ought not to be made for a time, that ultimately our own theories may be carried out, and the blessings of a free government under the Constitution extended to them. We decline to hold that there is anything in the Constitution to forbid such action.

We are therefore of opinion that the island of Porto Rico is a territory appurtenant and belonging to the United States, but not a part of the United States within the revenue clauses of the Constitution; that the Foraker act is constitutional, so far as it imposes duties upon imports from such island, and that the plaintiff cannot recover back the duties exacted in this case.

TR'S BIG STICK DIPLOMACY

I have always been fond of the West African proverb: "Speak softly and carry a big stick, and you will go far."

The above statement by Theodore Roosevelt gave the name to his vigorous diplomacy. Though perhaps properly applied to the entire sweep of his foreign relations, it came to be applied primarily to the relations with the Caribbean republics.

(1) SHAKING THE BIG STICK AT THE KAISER

[An early use of the Big Stick was against Germany and on behalf of Venezuela. When Cipriano Castro, the Venezuelan caudillo, refused to pay claims against him, Germany, Britain, and Italy joined in a blockade and Castro agreed to arbitration. Kaiser Wilhelm II was slow in accepting. The American press and public suspected that Germany intended to grab territory, and became so aroused that Roosevelt brought the Kaiser sharply to book early in 1903. Roosevelt told of the affair in a letter of August 21, 1916, to William R. Thayer. For years it was supposed that in his account TR was simply indulging in a juvenile wish fulfillment, but in 1956 Howard K. Beale demonstrated that his story was substantially accurate. The following version of the letter is taken from Beale, *Theodore Roosevelt and the Rise of America to World Power* (Johns Hopkins University Press, 1956), pp. 399–401.]

I speedily became convinced that Germany was the . . . really formidable party, in the transaction. . . . I became convinced that England would not back Germany in the event of a clash over the matter between Germany and the United States, but would remain neutral. . . . I also became convinced that Germany intended to seize some Venezuelan harbor and turn it into a strongly fortified place of arms, on the model of Kiaochow, with a view to exercising some measure of control over the future Isthmian Canal, and over South American affairs generally. . . . Germany declined to agree to arbitrate . . . and declined to say that she would not take possession of Venezuelan territory, merely saying that such possession would be "temporary"—which might mean anything. I finally decided that no useful purpose would be served by further delay, and I took action accordingly. I assembled our battle fleet, under Admiral Dewey, near Porto Rico, for "maneuvres," with instructions that the fleet should be kept in hand and in fighting trim, and should be ready to sail at an hour's notice. . . .

I saw the [German] Ambassador, and explained that in view of the presence of the German squadron on the Venezuelan coast I could not permit longer delay in answering my request for an arbitration, and that I could not acquiesce in any seizure of Venezuelan territory. The Ambassador responded that his Government could not agree to arbitrate, and that there was no intention to take "permanent" possession of Venezuelan territory. I answered that Kiaochow was not a "permanent" possession of Germany's—that . . . I did not intend to have another Kiaochow, held by similar tenure, on the approach to the Isthmian Canal. The Ambassador repeated that his Government would not agree to arbitrate. I then asked him to inform his Government that if no notification for arbitration came during the next ten days I would be obliged to order Dewey to take his fleet to the Venezuelan coast and see that the German forces did not take possession of any territory. He expressed very grave concern and asked me if I realized the serious consequences that would follow such action; consequences so serious to both countries that he dreaded to give them a name. I answered that I had thoroughly counted the cost before I decided on the step, and asked him to look at the map, as a glance would show him that there was no spot in the world where Germany in the event of conflict with the United States would be at a greater disadvantage than in the Caribbean sea.

A week later the Ambassador came to see me, talked pleasantly on several subjects, and rose to go. I asked him if he had any answer to make from his Government to my request, and when he said no, I informed him that in such event it was useless to wait as long as I had intended, and that Dewey would be ordered to sail twenty four hours in advance of the time I had set. He expressed deep apprehension, and said that his Government would not arbitrate. However, less than twenty four hours before the time I had appointed for calling the order to Dewey, the Ambassador notified me that His Imperial Majesty the German Emperor had directed him to request me to undertake arbitration myself.

(2) THE PLATT AMENDMENT AND THE TREATY OF 1903 WITH CUBA

[The United States desired to retain some hold over Cuba, not merely for economic reasons but because it was a focal point for yellow fever infection, because of the fear that Germany might get a foothold, and because of the fear that the island would fall into anarchy—as it did repeatedly. Cuba's reluctance to accept the status of a protectorate of the United States delayed American withdrawal from the island. Finally, in March 1901 Congress added to a military supply bill an amendment, named for Senator Orville Platt of Connecticut, providing for withdrawal if certain provisions would be incorporated in the Cuban constitution. Cuba reluctantly agreed. Two years later the provisions were confirmed by a treaty between the two powers, and it remained in force until 1934. The following text of the Treaty is from W. M. Malloy, *Treaties*, etc. (1910), 1:362–364.]

ARTICLE I   The Government of Cuba shall never enter into any treaty or other compact with any foreign power or powers which will impair or tend to impair the independence of Cuba, nor in any manner authorize or permit any foreign power or powers to obtain by colonization or for military or naval purposes, or otherwise, lodgment in or control over any portion of said island.

ARTICLE II   The Government of Cuba shall not assume or contract any public debt to pay the interest upon which, and to make reasonable sinking-fund provision for the ultimate discharge of which, the ordinary revenues of the Island of Cuba, after defraying the current expenses of the Government, shall be inadequate.

ARTICLE III   The Government of Cuba consents that the United States may exercise the right to intervene for the preservation of Cuban independence, the maintenance of a government adequate for the protection of life, property, and individual liberty, and for discharging the obligations with respect to Cuba imposed by the Treaty of Paris on the United States, now to be assumed and undertaken by the Government of Cuba.

ARTICLE IV   All acts of the United States in Cuba during its military occupancy thereof are ratified and validated, and all lawful rights acquired thereunder shall be maintained and protected.

ARTICLE V   The Government of Cuba will execute, and, as far as necessary, extend the plans already devised, or other plans to be mutually agreed upon, for the sanitation of the cities of the island, to the end that a recurrence of epidemic and infectious diseases may be prevented, thereby assuring protection to the people and commerce of Cuba, as well as to the commerce of the Southern ports of the United States and the people residing therein.

ARTICLE VI   The Island of Pines shall be omitted from the boundaries of Cuba specified in the Constitution, the title thereto being left to future adjustment by treaty.

ARTICLE VII   To enable the United States to maintain the independence of Cuba, and to protect the people thereof, as well as for its own defense, the Government of Cuba will sell or lease to the United States lands necessary for coaling or naval stations, at certain specified points, to be agreed upon with the President of the United States.

ARTICLE VIII   The present Convention shall be ratified by each party in conformity with the respective Constitutions of the two countries, and the ratifications shall be exchanged in the City of Washington within eight months from this date.

(3) "I TOOK THE ISTHMUS"

[The righteousness of TR's action in acquiring the Panama Canal Zone has been bitterly debated, and so far as abstract justice is concerned may or may not be a draw. At any rate, in 1921, after TR passed away and oil was discovered in Colombia, Congress voted to pay that country $25 billion in what was plainly an indemnity. Roosevelt had stoutly maintained that his actions had been legal under the Bidlack Treaty of 1846, and to his dying day vituperated Colombia for attempting to block progress. On May 4, 1912, in Baltimore he delivered one of several defenses. See his *Works*, 19:280–282.]

When I became President I found the negotiations for the Panama Canal going on with great dignity, as they had gone on for the previous seventy years. The Isthmus had been discovered four centuries before by the Spaniards, and they at once said that it would be a splendid thing to put a canal across it. There had been four centuries of conversation upon the subject, and I came to the conclusion it had better be translated into action.

I did my level best to get Colombia to agree with us. I tried to treat her more than justly, more than generously. I tried to do everything I could for her, but I was not going to have any one hold up Uncle Sam. Finally I came to the conclusion that to negotiate further with Colombia was about like trying to nail currant jelly to the wall. You cannot do it. And it is not the fault of the nail, it is the fault of the jelly!

So then two courses were open to me. If I had followed the precedent, say, of President Buchanan, I would have sent an able report to Congress. Congress would have held a series of masterly debates on the able report and we would have had half a century more of conversation. And the Canal would be fifty years in the future. Instead of doing that, I took the Isthmus and started the Canal, and I let Congress debate me instead of the Canal. And it proved a first-class working compromise! We got the Canal and Congress got the debate, and instead of debating the Canal, which would have been a calamity, they debated me, which did not make any difference to anybody and least of all to me. The Canal will be finished in a couple of years, and the debate about me goes fitfully on and I do not think it will be finished until long after I am dead.

(4) THE ROOSEVELT COROLLARY

[When in 1904 the Dominican Republic defaulted in payment of certain debts to European creditors, certain powers threatened intervention. To prevent this Roosevelt agreed to collect for them, and installed an American collector of customs in the country. This action, supplementing the "no-coercion" principle of the Monroe Doctrine was explained in his Message of December 5, 1905. See *Foreign Relations, 1905* (1906) pp. xxxiv–xxv.]

It must be understood that under no circumstances will the United States use the Monroe Doctrine as a cloak for territorial aggression. We desire peace with all the world, but perhaps most of all with the other peoples of the American Continent. There are of course limits to the wrongs which any self-respecting nation can endure. It is always possible that wrong actions toward this Nation, or toward citizens of this Nation, in some State unable to keep order among its own people, unable to secure justice from outsiders, and unwilling to do justice to those outsiders who treat it well, may result in our having to take action to protect our rights; but such action will not be taken with a view to territorial aggression, and it will be taken at all only with extreme reluctance and when it has become evident that every other resource has been exhausted.

Moreover, we must make it evident that we do not intend to permit the Monroe Doctrine to be used by any nation on this Continent as a shield to protect it from the consequences of its own misdeeds against foreign nations. If a republic to the south of us commits a tort against a foreign nation, such as an outrage against a citizen of that nation, then the Monroe Doctrine does not force us to interfere to prevent punishment of the tort, save to see that the punishment does not assume the form of territorial occupation in any shape. The case is more difficult when it refers to a contractual obligation. Our own Government has always refused to enforce such contractual obligations on behalf of its citizens by an appeal to arms. It is much to be wished that all foreign governments would take the same view. But they do not; and in consequence we are liable at any time to be brought face to face with disagreeable alternatives. On the one hand, this country would certainly decline to go to war to prevent a foreign government from collecting a just debt; on the other hand, it is very inadvisable to permit any foreign power to take possession, even temporarily, of the customhouses of an American Republic in order to enforce the payment of its obligations; for such temporary occupation might turn into a permanent occupation. The only escape from these alternatives may at any time be that we must ourselves undertake to bring about some arrangement by which so much as possible of a just obligation shall be paid. It is far better that this country should put through such an arrangement, rather than allow any foreign country to undertake it. To do so insures the defaulting republic from having to pay debts of an improper character under duress, while it also insures honest creditors of the republic from being passed by in the interest of dishonest or grasping creditors. Moreover, for the United States to take such a position offers the only possible way of insuring us against a clash with some foreign power. The position is, therefore, in the interest of peace as well as in the interest of justice. It is of benefit to our people; it is of benefit to foreign peoples; and most of all it is really of benefit to the people of the country concerned.

TAKE CARE, ROOSEVELT!

The United States are powerful and huge;
When they stir, an earthquake
Shakes the enormous vertebrae of the Andes.
Your shout is like the roar of a lion.
   . . . You are rich;
You add to the worship of Hercules the worship of Mammon,
And lighting the path of your easy conquests
Liberty raises her torch in New York.

But our America, . . .
Men with Saxon eyes and barbarous souls, lives,

And dreams, and loves, and is the child of the Sun.
Take care: Long live Hispanic America!
The Spanish lion has a thousand cubs.
You would need, Roosevelt, to be the terrible Rifleman
And the mighty hunter of God Himself
To hold us in your iron claws.

> —Rubén Darío, Nicaraguan poet, protesting to Theodore Roosevelt. Quoted from Laurence Duggan, *The Americas: The Search for Hemisphere Security* (N.Y.: Holt, 1949), p. 53

TAFT'S DOLLAR DIPLOMACY

[Philander C. Knox, Taft's Secretary of State, launched what was to become a long series of military interventions in the Caribbean, justifying them by what he called Dollar Diplomacy. The term was applied to both China and Latin America, but it had little success in the former, for there was little room for American investment. The application was far more vigorous in Latin America. As noted, the intention was to forefend any excuse for European intervention by having the Caribbean nations refund their foreign debts with New York money; any further borrowing had to be done in the United States, and unless it officially approved of the loan the State Department would not back efforts to collect in case of default. In his Message of December 3, 1912, Taft explained the policy.]

The diplomacy of the present administration has sought to respond to modern ideas of commercial intercourse. This policy has been characterized as substituting dollars for bullets. It is one that appeals alike to idealistic humanitarian sentiments, to the dictates of sound policy and strategy, and to legitimate commercial aims. It is an effort frankly directed to the increase of American trade upon the axiomatic principle that the Government of the United States shall extend all proper support to every legitimate and beneficial American enterprise abroad. How great have been the results of this diplomacy, coupled with the maximum and minimum provision of the tariff law, will be seen by some consideration of the wonderful increase in the export trade of the United States. Because modern diplomacy is commercial, there has been a disposition in some quarters to attribute to it none but materialistic aims. How strikingly erroneous is such an impression may be seen from a study of the results

by which the diplomacy of the United States can be judged. . . .

In China the policy of encouraging financial investment to enable that country to help itself has had the result of giving new life and practical application to the open-door policy. The consistent purpose of the present administration has been to encourage the use of American capital in the development of China by the promotion of those essential reforms to which China is pledged by treaties with the United States and other powers. . . .

In Central America the aim has been to help such countries as Nicaragua and Honduras to help themselves. They are the immediate beneficiaries. The national benefit to the United States is twofold. First, it is obvious that the Monroe doctrine is more vital in the neighborhood of the Panama Canal and the zone of the Caribbean than anywhere else. There, too, the maintenance of that doctrine falls most heavily upon the United States. It is therefore essential that the countries within that sphere shall be removed from the jeopardy involved by heavy foreign debt and chaotic national finances and from the ever-present danger of international complications due to disorder at home. Hence the United States has been glad to encourage and support American bankers who were willing to lend a helping hand to the financial rehabilitation of such countries because this financial rehabilitation and the protection of their customhouses from being the prey of would-be dictators would remove at one stroke the menace of foreign creditors and the menace of revolutionary disorder.

The second advantage of the United States is one affecting chiefly all the southern and Gulf ports and the business and industry of the South. The Republics of Central America and the Caribbean possess great natural wealth. They need only a measure of stability and the means of financial regeneration to enter upon an era of peace and prosperity, bringing profit and happiness to themselves and at the same time creating conditions sure to lead to a flourishing interchange of trade with this country.

WILSON'S MORAL DIPLOMACY

[As we have seen, Wilson insisted that, to obtain recognition, a government must have come into power by means that met his moral approval—that is, by democratic means. This was, in effect, a Wilson Corollary to the Monroe Doctrine, and as a result Wilson was in continual trouble with Mexico and the Caribbean nations. The problem survived under Harding and Coolidge, who continued the policy at least to some extent. The Wilson Corollary, of course, was secretly welcomed by dictators, for it guaranteed their tenure against housecleaning by revolution.]

(1) RECOGNITION AS AN ACT OF MORAL APPROVAL

[As Wilson once put it, he could not recognize government by murder. The following letter to Bryan, dated July 23, 1918, and written after Bryan left the State Department, expressed Wilson's refusal to recognize the revolutionary government of Tinoco in Costa Rica. See R. S. Baker, *Woodrow Wilson: Life and Letters* (8v., Garden City: Doubleday, Doran, 1939), 8:291–292.]

I value your long letter about the Costa Rican situation but beg to assure you in reply that no item of foreign policy has received more frequent or careful consideration by me or has been looked at from more angles, and I feel obliged to retain immovably my position that I will not and cannot recognize a government which originated in individual unconstitutional action. This is a test case and I am sure that my yielding in it would break down the whole morale of our relations, particularly with Central America.

I cannot tell you how many persons have been to me and laid the various aspects of this matter before me. The latest was Mr. Samuel Untermyer, who very earnestly urged the same course upon me that you are urging. But behind it all, my dear Mr. Bryan, there are contending business interests in the United States which we ought to be very careful to disappoint in what is nothing less than an attempt on their part to use the Government of Costa Rica for their own benefit.

I am always sorry to differ from you in any matter of importance, but this is a matter in which I feel bound both by principle and expediency.

(2) "SHOOTING MEN INTO SELF-GOVERNMENT"

[The British, with their long imperial experience, looked upon Wilson's grandiloquent pronouncements about forcing democracy on Mexico as ridiculously naïve. Walter Hines Page, Ambassador to St. James's, described the difference in British and American attitudes in a letter to Wilson, given in Burton J. Hendricks, *The Life and Letters of Walter H. Page* (Garden City: Doubleday, 1922), p. 188. Perhaps a present-day American can understand better why Sir Edward Grey was dissolved in laughter!]

To the President

. . . The foregoing I wrote before this Mexican business took its present place. I can't get away from the feeling that the English simply do not and will not believe in any unselfish public action—further than the keeping of order. They have a mania for order, sheer order, order for the sake of order. They can't see how anything can come in any one's thought before order or how anything need come afterward. Even Sir Edward Grey jocularly ran me across our history with questions like this:

"Suppose you have to intervene, what then?"

"Make 'em vote and live by their decisions."

"But suppose they will not so live?"

"We'll go in again and make 'em vote again."

"And keep this up 200 years?" asked he.

"Yes," said I. "The United States will be here two hundred years and it can continue to shoot men for that little space till they learn to vote and to rule themselves."

I have never seen him laugh so heartily. Shooting men into self-government! Shooting them into orderliness—he comprehends that; and that's all right. But that's as far as his habit of mind goes. At Sheffield last night, when I had to make a speech, I explained "idealism" (they always quote it) in Government. They listened attentively and even eagerly. Then they came up and asked if I really meant that Government should concern itself with idealistic things—beyond keeping order. Ought they to do so in India?—I assure you they don't think beyond order. A nigger lynched in Mississippi offends them more than a tyrant in Mexico.

(3) THE MEANING OF CARRIZAL

[On June 21, 1916, during Pershing's pursuit of Villa in Chihuahua, a detachment of U.S. cavalry was defeated by Carranzistas at Carrizal with the loss of 45 men killed, wounded, and captured. This defeat was widely greeted by Latin Americans as a stunning check to American prestige, a disgrace which a Latin country would have had to wipe out at any cost. Nevertheless, the next February, Wilson withdrew Pershing's troops even though Villa was uncaught and Mexico refused to guarantee American lives and property. Manuel Ugarte, an Argentine, in his analysis of the episode graphically portrayed Latin-American contempt for *norteamericano* realism and at the same time the inability of a Latin-American country to rally the material and spiritual forces necessary to uphold its rights and ideals. See his *The Destiny of a Continent* (N.Y.: Knopf, 1925), pp. 253–255.]

. . . [T]he significance of Carrizal goes beyond that of a little skirmish in the War. The battle, which lasted two hours and engaged only a few hundred men, had only a relative importance from the military point of view, but it marked the first time since 1848 that our Latin America had spoken out effectively against that gradual invasion which was crushing her resistance little by little. It was the first shot fired at that uniform which seemed to have the privilege of going about in neighbouring countries as if frontiers and autonomy had been abolished. It was not a handful of soldiers who fell at Carrizal, but the superstitious respect surrounding the agents of imperialism. What all the presidents of Latin America had not dared to attempt by means of peaceful diplomacy was effected, rifle in hand, by a mere colonel, and those tragic penalties which our governments allude to whenever they are opposed, did not make themselves felt in any form. The invading army gathered up its dead and retired from the country. But does this mean that one bloody fray is enough to change our destiny? Must we deduce as a conclusion, that a military effort can save us?

Nothing would be more puerile than to suppose that imperialism timidly gave up the struggle. It would have been easy for the United States to pour 200,000 men over the frontier, and reach the capital in a fortnight. Why did they not do so? To Latin-American ideas it would have been by no means a brilliant feat.

We should have gone on, appealing to military honour and all our principles. The psychology of the great nation in the North is different. Faced with the resistance which seemed probable, involving a series of ambushes and interminable guerilla warfare in the mountains, it calculated the advantages and disadvantages, stated the problem in practical terms, taking into account the circumstances of the moment, the sacrifices demanded by the enterprise, the benefits which it might bring them, and the possibility of achieving the same end by other means. With regard to its timeliness, the events which were revolutionising Europe obliged the United States to reserve all their strength for a decisive intervention, which was already appearing before the mind's eye of their clear-sighted rulers. As regards the cost of the enterprise and the effort which it would be necessary to put forth, an expert general drew up a statement of the subject with figures. As to the possible benefits, they appeared insufficient compared to the risks. The mental balance, the sense of reality, the most obvious characteristics of this people, declined the adventure. The favourite plan of Germany was to immobilise the United States by means of Mexico. A reflected light from Europe played upon the frontier. And besides, given the mentality of the age, was the effort useful or necessary? From the economic point of view, did not the United States hold the future of the country in their hands?

(4) "AN INTERCHANGE OF VIEWS CHARMING AND HOPEFUL"

[Why Wilson's naïve Moral Diplomacy and his frequent military interventions received approval in Latin America may lie in his scintillating use of words, a gift always valued in Latin America. The following address, given to the Pan-American Scientific Congress on January 6, 1916, is a case in point. See Baker, *Wilson*, 3:443–445.]

The Monroe Doctrine was proclaimed by the United States on her own authority. It always has been maintained and always will be maintained upon her own responsibility. But the Monroe Doctrine demanded merely that European Governments should not attempt to extend their political systems to this side of the Atlantic. It did not disclose the use which the United States intended to make of her power on this side of the Atlantic. It was a hand held up in warning, but there was no promise in it of what America was going to do with the implied and partial protectorate which she apparently was trying to set up on this side of the water; and I believe you will sustain me in the statement that it has been fears and suspicions on this score which have hitherto prevented the greater intimacy and confidence and trust between the Americas. The States of America have not been certain what the United States would do with her power. That doubt must be removed. And latterly there has been a very frank interchange of views between the authorities in Washington and those who represented the other States of this hemisphere, an interchange of views charming and hopeful, because based upon an increasingly sure appreciation of the spirit in which they were undertaken. These gentlemen have seen that if America is to come into her own, into her legitimate own, in a world of peace and order, she must establish the foundations of amity so that no one will hereafter doubt them.

I hope and I believe that this can be accomplished. These conferences have enabled me to forsee how it will be accomplished. It will be accomplished in the first place, by the States of America uniting in guaranteeing to each other absolutely political independence and territorial integrity. In the second place, and as a necessary corollary to that, guaranteeing the agreement to settle all pending boundary disputes as soon as possible and by amicable process; by agreeing that all disputes among themselves, should they unhappily arise, will be handled by patient, impartial investigation, and settled by arbitration; and the agreement necessary to the peace of the Americas, that no State of either continent will permit revolutionary expeditions against another State to be fitted out on its territory, and that they will prohibit the exportation of the munitions of war for the purpose of supplying revolutionists against neighboring Governments.

You see what our thought is, gentlemen, not only the international peace of America but the domestic peace of America. If American States are constantly in ferment, if any of them are constantly in ferment, there will be a standing threat to their relations with one another. It is just as much to our interest to assist each other to the orderly processes within our own borders as it is to orderly processes in our controversies with one another. These are very practical suggestions which have sprung up in the minds of thoughtful men, and I, for my part, believe that they are going to lead the way to something that America has prayed for for many a generation. For they are based, in the first place, so far as the stronger States are concerned, upon the handsome principle of self-restraint and respect for the rights of everybody. They are based upon the principles of absolute political equality among the States, equality of right, not equality of indulgence. They are based, in short, upon the solid eternal foundations of justice and humanity. No man can turn away from these things without turning away from the hope of the world. These are things, ladies and gentlemen, for which the world has hoped and waited with prayerful heart. God grant that it may be granted to America to lift this light on high for the illumination of the world.

MR. DOOLEY ON IMPERIALISM

Hands across the sea and into someone's pockets.

Take up the white man's burden and hand it to the coons.

To most people a savage nation is one that doesn't wear uncomfortable clothes.

There's one consolation—if the American people can govern themselves, they can govern anything that walks.

To the Filipinos:

We can't give you any votes because we haven't more than enough to go around now, but we'll treat you the way a father should treat his children if we have to break every bone in your bodies. So come to our arms.

On the Yellow Peril:

A subject race is only funny when it's really subject. About three years ago I stopped laughing at Japanese jokes. You have to feel superior to laugh, and I'm getting over that feeling.

—Finley Peter Dunne

12

WORLD WAR I: CRUSADE AND RETREAT

THE MALADY OF THE DEMOCRATIC STATES

As the century advanced and the evidence mounted of the democracies' paralysis of will, Walter Lippmann, long-time journalist and political analyst, sought the reason in his *Essays in the Public Philosophy* (Boston: Little, Brown, 1955). As he saw it, the reason lay fundamentally in the fact that the masses had gained a veto over executive action, and so had laid the world open to alternate appeasement and holocaust.

In 1884 Sir Henry Maine had warned that democratic government, to survive, must meet the same hard tests as monarchy—it must protect the national interests at home and abroad by severe taxation, the enforcement of unpopular laws, and by choosing between war on one side and unsatisfactory diplomatic arrangements on the other. However, during the latter part of the nineteenth century dire crises had been few and this had confirmed liberals in their belief that weak government was practicable and that there was no harm in yielding to the onward march of democracy.

It had long been supposed that a bankrupt nation could not carry on war. Now it became evident that war could be prosecuted as long as raw materials held out and the industrial and military organizations could be preserved. Indeed, World War I demonstrated that so far as these factors were concerned war could be carried—and was being carried—to and beyond the point of irrationality. The only drawback was that the people would not stand for it. Hitherto foreign affairs had been shaped by the heads of states and political leaders and representative parliaments had usually followed their judgment. Now the governments of the democracies faced the test of whether they could actually continue on the course they had begun. Here we reprint the highlights of Lippmann's analysis from page 17 to page 29 of the Mentor edition of 1956.

The strain of the war worked up a menacing popular pressure upon the weak governments. We can, I think, point to 1917 as the year when the pressure became so strong that the institutional framework of the stablished governments broke under it.

The strain became unbearable. 1917 was the year of the two Russian revolutions. It was the year of the American involvement which brought with it the declaration of the Wilsonian principles. For Italy it was the year of Caporetto. For Austria-Hungary it was the beginning of the end under the successor of Francis Joseph. For Germany it was the year of the July crisis and of the need of the Prussian monarchy to listen to the Reichstag and its demand for a negotiated peace. For France it was the year of the mutinies, and for Britain the year of mortal peril from the submarine. In eastern and central Europe tortured and infuriated masses brought down the historic states and the institutions of the old regime. In western Europe and in North America the breakthrough took the form—if I may use the term—of a deep and pervasive infiltration. Behind the facade, which was little changed, the old structure of executive government with the consent of a representative assembly was dismantled—not everywhere and not in all fields, but where it mattered the most—in the making of high policy for war and peace.

The existing governments had exhausted

their imperium—their authority to bind and their power to command. With their traditional means they were no longer able to carry on the hyperbolic war; yet they were unable to negotiate peace. They had, therefore, to turn to the people. They had to ask still greater exertions and sacrifices. They obtained them by "democratizing" the conduct and the aims of the war: by pursuing total victory and by promising total peace.

In substance they ceded the executive power of decision over the strategical and the political conditions for concluding the war. In effect they lost control of the war. This revolution appeared to be a cession of power to the representative assemblies, and when it happened it was acclaimed as promising the end of the evils of secret diplomacy and the undemocratic conduct of unpopular wars. In fact, the powers which were ceded by the executive passed through the assemblies, which could not exercise them, to the mass of voters who, though unable also to exercise them, passed them on to the party bosses, the agents of pressure groups, and the magnates of the new media of mass communications.

The consequences were disastrous and revolutionary. The democracies became incapacitated to wage war for rational ends and to make a peace which would be observed or could be enforced. . . .

If I am right in what I have been saying,

there has developed in this century a functional derangement of the relationship between the mass of the people and the government. The people have acquired power which they are incapable of exercising, and the governments they elect have lost powers which they must recover if they are to govern. . . . A mass cannot govern. The people, as Jefferson said, are not "qualified to exercise themselves the Executive Department; but they are qualified to name the person who shall exercise it. . . . They are not qualified to legislate; with us therefore they only choose the legislators."

Where mass opinion dominates the government, there is a morbid derangement of the true functions of power. The derangement brings about the enfeeblement, verging on paralysis, of the capacity to govern. This breakdown in the constitutional order is the cause of the precipitate and catastrophic decline of Western society. It may, if it cannot be arrested and reversed, bring about the fall of the West. . . .

In the winter of 1918–1919, for example, Lloyd George, Clemenceau, Wilson and Orlando were at a critical juncture of modern history. The Germans were defeated, their government was overthrown, their troops disarmed and disbanded. The Allies were called upon to decide whether they would dictate a punitive peace or would negotiate a peace of reconciliation.

In the Thirties the British and the French governments had to decide whether to rearm and to take concerted measures to contain Hitler and Mussolini or whether to remain unarmed and to appease them. The United States had to decide whether to arm in order to contain the Japanese or to negotiate with them at the expense of China.

During the Second World War the British and the American governments had again to make the choice between total victory with unconditional surrender and negotiated settlements whose end was reconciliation.

These were momentous issues, like choosing at the fork of the road a way from which there is no turning back: whether to arm or not to arm—whether, as a conflict blows up, to intervene or to withdraw—whether in war to fight for the unconditional surrender of the adversary or for his reconciliation. The issues are so momentous that public feeling quickly becomes incandescent to them. But they can be answered with the only words that a great mass *qua* mass can speak—with a Yes or a No.

Experience since 1917 indicates that in matters of war and peace the popular answer in the democracies is likely to be No. For everything connected with war has become dangerous, painful, disagreeable and exhausting to very nearly everyone. The rule to which there are few exceptions—the acceptance of the Marshall Plan is one of them—is that at the critical junctures, when the stakes are high, the prevailing mass opinion will impose what amounts to a veto upon changing the course on which the government is at the time proceeding. Prepare for war in time of peace? No. It is bad to raise taxes, to unbalance the budget, to take men away from their schools or their jobs, to provoke the enemy. Intervene in a developing conflict? No. Avoid the risk of war. Withdraw from the area of the conflict? No. The adversary must not be appeased. Reduce your claims on the area? No. Righteousness cannot be compromised. Negotiate a compromise peace as soon as the opportunity presents itself? No. The aggressor must be punished. Remain armed to enforce the dictated settlement? No. The war is over.

The unhappy truth is that the prevailing public opinion has been destructively wrong at the critical junctures. The people have imposed a veto upon the judgments of informed and responsible officials. They have compelled the governments, which usually knew what would have been wiser, or was necessary, or was more expedient, to be too late with too little, or too long with too much, too pacifist in peace and too bellicose in war, too neutralist or appeasing in negotiation or too intransigent. Mass opinion has acquired mounting power in this century. It has shown itself to be a dangerous master of decisions when the stakes are life and death.

The errors of public opinion in these matters have a common characteristic. The movement of opinion is slower than the movement of events. Because of that, the cycle of subjective sentiments on war and peace is usually out of gear with the cycle of objective developments. Just because they are mass opinions there is an inertia in them. It takes much longer to change many minds than to change a few. It takes time to inform and to persuade and to arouse large scattered varied multitudes of persons. So before the multitude have caught up with the old events there are likely to be new ones coming up over the horizon with which the government should be preparing to deal. But the majority will be more aware of what they have just caught up with near at hand than with what is still distant and in the future. For these reasons the propensity to say No to a change of course sets up a compulsion to make mistakes. The opinion deals with a situation which no longer exists.

When the world wars came, the people of the liberal democracies could not be aroused to the exertions and the sacrifices of the struggle until they had been frightened by the opening disasters, had been incited to passionate hatred, and had become intoxicated with unlimited hope. To overcome this inertia the enemy had to be portrayed as evil incarnate, as absolute and congenital wickedness. The people wanted to be told that when this particular enemy had been forced to unconditional surrender, they would re-enter the golden age. This unique war would end all wars. This last war would make the world safe for democracy. This crusade would make the whole world a democracy.

As a result of this impassioned nonsense public opinion became so envenomed that the people would not countenance a workable peace. . . .

It was not for want of power but for want of statesmanship that the liberal democracies failed. They failed to restore order in that great part of the world which—outside of revolutionary Russia—was still within the orbit of their influence, still amenable to their leadership, still subject to their decisions, still working within the same economy, still living in the same international community, still thinking in the same universe of discourse. In this failure to make peace there was generated the cycle of wars in which the West has suffered so sudden and so spectacular a decline.

Public opinion, having vetoed reconciliation, had made the settlement unworkable. And so when a new generation of Germans grew up, they rebelled. But by that time the Western democracies, so recently too warlike to make peace with the unarmed German Republic, had become too pacifist to take the risks which could have prevented the war Hitler was announcing he would wage against Europe. Having refused the risk of trying to prevent war, they would not now prepare for the war. The European democracies chose to rely on the double negative of unarmed appeasement, and the American democracy chose to rely on unarmed isolation.

When the unprevented war came, the fatal cycle was repeated. Western Europe was defeated and occupied before the British people began seriously to wage the war. And after the catastrophe in Western Europe eighteen agonizing months of indecision elapsed before the surprise and shock of Pearl Harbor did for the American people what no amount of argument and evidence and reason had been able to do.

Once again it seemed impossible to wage the war energetically except by inciting the people to paroxysms of hatred and to utopian dreams. So they were told that the Four Freedoms would be established everywhere, once the incurably bad Germans and the incurably bad Japanese had been forced to surrender unconditionally. The war could be popular only if the enemy was altogether evil and the Allies very nearly perfect. This mixture of envenomed hatred and furious righteousness made a public opinion which would not tolerate the calculated compromises that durable settlements demand. Once again the people were drugged by the propaganda which had aroused them to fight the war and to endure its miseries. Once again they would not think, once again they would not allow their leaders to think, about an eventual peace with their enemies, or about the differences that must arise among the Allies in this coalition, as in all earlier ones. How well this popular diplomacy worked is attested by the fact that less than five years after the democracies had disarmed their enemies, they were imploring their former enemies, Germany and Japan, to rearm.

The record shows that the people of the democracies, having become sovereign in this century, have made it increasingly difficult for their governments to prepare properly for war or to make peace. Their responsible officials have been like the ministers of an opinionated and willful despot. Between the critical junctures, when public opinion has been inattentive or not vehemently aroused, responsible officials have often been able to circumvent extremist popular opinions and to wheedle their way towards moderation and good sense. In the crises, however, democratic officials—over and above their own human propensity to err—have been compelled to make the big mistakes that public opinion has insisted upon. Even the greatest men have not been able to turn back the massive tides of opinion and of sentiment.

There is no mystery about why there is such a tendency for popular opinion to be wrong in judging war and peace. Strategic and diplomatic decisions call for a kind of knowledge—not to speak of an experience and a seasoned judgment—which cannot be had by glancing at newspapers, listening to snatches of radio comment, watching politicians perform on television, hearing occasional lectures, and reading a few books. It would not be enough to make a man competent to decide whether to amputate a leg, and it is not enough to qualify him to choose war or peace, to arm or not to arm, to intervene or to withdraw, to fight on or to negotiate.

Usually, moreover, when the decision is critical and urgent, the public will not be told the whole truth. What can be told to the great public it will not hear in the complicated and qualified concreteness that is needed for a practical decision. When distant and unfamiliar and complex things are communicated to great masses of people, the truth suffers a considerable and often a radical distortion. The complex is made over into the simple, the hypothetical into the dogmatic, and the relative into an absolute. Even when there is no deliberate distortion by censorship and propaganda, which is unlikely in time of war, the public opinion of masses cannot be counted upon to apprehend regularly and promptly the reality of things. There is an inherent tendency in opinion to feed upon rumors excited by our own wishes and fears.

At the critical moments in this sad history, there have been men, worth listening to, who warned the people against their mistakes. Always, too, there have been men inside the governments who judged correctly, because they were permitted to know in time, the uncensored and unvarnished truth. But the climate of modern democracy does not usually inspire them to speak out. . . . With exceptions so rare that they are regarded as miracles and freaks of nature, successful democratic politicians are insecure and intimidated men. They advance politically only as they placate, appease, bribe, seduce, bamboozle, or otherwise manage to manipulate the demanding and threatening elements in their constituencies. The decisive consideration is not whether the proposition is good but whether it is popular—not whether it will work well and prove itself but whether the active talking constituents like it immediately. Politicians rationalize this servitude by saying that in a democracy public men are the servants of the people.

This devitalization of the governing power is the malady of democratic states. As the malady grows the executives become highly susceptible to encroachment and usurpation by elected assemblies; they are pressed and harassed by the higgling of parties, by the agents of organized interests, and by the spokesmen of sectarians and ideologues. The malady can be fatal. It can be deadly to the very survival of the state as a free society if, when the great and hard issues of war and peace, of security and solvency, of revolution and order are up for decision, the executive and judicial departments, with their civil servants and technicians, have lost their power to decide.

"HISTORY DOES NOT FORGIVE US OUR NATIONAL MISTAKES"

[The dire meaning of American isolation before 1914 has been eloquently portrayed by George F. Kennan in the fourth lecture of his *American Diplomacy: 1900–1950* (University of Chicago Press, 1950), pp. 65–73. Kennan believes that World War I was the fatal act which destroyed the delicate balance of power and seemed to predetermine World War II. But the sole responsibility was not Europe's. The tremendous power of the United States thrust upon it a share of this responsibility whether or not it recognized the fact, and to the United States must go a share—perhaps the biggest share—of responsibility for not having acted to prevent the war or, once it started, not having moderated its course and consequences. Unfortunately, the United States did not recognize that its welfare hinged on peace and stability as vitally as did the welfare of Europe. Kennan thus brings home to the United States the same accusation that Walter Lippmann made against democracies in general.]

Once in the war, we had no difficulty in discovering—and lost no time in doing so—that the issues involved in it were of the greatest significance to us.

It is surely a curious characteristic of democracy: this amazing ability to shift gears overnight in one's ideological attitudes, depending on whether one considers one's self at war or at peace. Day before yesterday, let us say, the issues at stake between ourselves and another power were not worth the life of a single American boy. Today, nothing else counts at all; our cause is holy; the cost is no consideration; violence must know no limitations short of unconditional surrender.

Now I know the answer to this one. A democracy is peace-loving. It does not like to go to war. It is slow to rise to provocation. When it has once been provoked to the point where it must grasp the sword, it does not easily forgive its adversary for having produced this situation. The fact of the provocation then becomes itself the issue. Democracy fights in anger—it fights for the very reason that it was forced to go to war. It fights to punish the power that was rash enough and hostile enough to provoke it—to teach that power a lesson it will not forget, to prevent the thing from happening again. Such a war must be carried to the bitter end.

This is true enough, and, if nations could afford to operate in the moral climate of individual ethics, it would be understandable and acceptable. But I sometimes wonder whether in this respect a democracy is not uncomfortably similar to one of those prehistoric monsters with a body as long as this room and a brain the size of a pin: he lies there in his comfortable primeval mud and pays little attention to his environment; he is slow to wrath—in fact, you practically have to whack his tail off to make him aware that his interests are being disturbed; but, once he grasps this, he lays about him with such blind determination that he not only destroys his adversary but largely wrecks his native habitat. You wonder whether it would not have been wiser for him to have taken a little more interest in what was going on at an earlier date and to have seen whether he could not have

McCutcheon, The Chicago Tribune

Wilson said, could guarantee equilibrium under such a system? It would be based this time on a "community of power," on "an organized common peace," on a League of Nations which would mobilize the conscience and power of mankind against aggression. Autocratic government would be done away with. Peoples would themselves choose the sovereignty under which they wished to reside. . . . There would be open diplomacy this time; peoples, not governments, would run things. Armaments would be reduced by mutual agreement. The peace would be just and secure.

In the name of such principles you could fight a war to the end. A future so brilliant would surely wash away the follies and brutalities of the war, redress its injuries, heal the wounds it had left. This theory gave us justification both for continuing the war to its bitter and terrible end . . . the same time for refusing to preoccupy ourselves with the practical problems and maladjustments to which the course of hostilities was leading. Under the protecting shadow of this theory, the guns continued their terrible work for a final year and a half after our entry. Under the shadow of this theory Wilson went to Versailles unprepared to face the sordid but all-important details of the day of reckoning. Under this theory he suffered his tragic and historic failure. Under this theory things advanced with a deadly logic and precision to a peace which was indeed "forced upon the loser, a victor's terms imposed upon the vanquished, accepted in humiliation, under duress"—a peace that did indeed leave a sting, a resentment, a bitter memory, and upon which its own terms came later to rest "as upon quicksand."

And the tragedy of this outcome was not substantially mitigated by the fact that we were not signatories to the Treaty of Versailles and kept ourselves aloof from its punitive provisions. The damage had been done. The equilibrium of Europe had been shattered. Austria-Hungary was gone. There was nothing effective to take its place. Germany, smarting from the sting of defeat and plunged into profound so-

prevented some of these situations from arising instead of proceeding from an undiscriminating indifference to a holy wrath equally undiscriminating. . . .

Considerations of the power balance argued against total victory. Perhaps it was for this very reason that people in this country rejected them so emphatically and sought more sweeping and grandiose objectives, for the accomplishment of which total victory could plausibly be represented as absolutely essential. In any case, a line of thought grew up, under Wilson's leadership, which provided both rationale and objective for our part in fighting the war to a bitter end. Germany was militaristic and antidemocratic. The Allies were fighting to make the world safe for democracy. Prussian militarism had to be destroyed to make way for the sort of peace we wanted. This peace would not be based on the old balance of power. Who, as

cial unrest by the breakup of her traditional institutions, was left nevertheless as the only great united state in Central Europe. Russia was no longer there, as a possible reliable ally, to help France contain German power. From the Russian plain there leered a single hostile eye, skeptical of Europe's values, rejoicing at all Europe's misfortunes, ready to collaborate solely for the final destruction of her spirit and her pride. Between Russia and Germany were only the pathetic new states of eastern and Central Europe, lacking in domestic stability and the traditions of statesmanship—their peoples bewildered, uncertain, vacillating between brashness and timidity in the exercise of the unaccustomed responsibilities of independence. And to the other side of Germany were France and England, reeling, themselves, from the vicissitudes of the war, wounded far more deeply than they themselves realized, the plume of their manhood gone, their world positions shaken.

Truly, this was a peace which had the tragedies of the future written into it as by the devil's own hand. It was a peace, as the French historian Bainville said, which was too mild for the hardships it contained. And this was the sort of peace you got when you allowed war hysteria and impractical idealism to lie down together in your mind, like the lion and the lamb; when you indulged yourself in the colossal conceit of thinking that you could suddenly make international life over into what you believed to be your own image; when you dismissed the past with contempt, rejected the relevance of the past to the future, and refused to occupy yourself with the real problems that a study of the past would suggest.

But suppose you hadn't taken this line. Would things have been different? Was there another line you could take?

It does seem to me there was.

[Here Kennan introduces the warnings published in 1913 by Lewis Einstein, an American diplomat, and suggests that if the United States had reacted intelligently to them it would have armed itself enough to have made its word carry weight and have striven to prevent war or, once it had started, to moderate its course.]

But I think I hear one great, and even indignant, objection to what I have suggested; and I must speak to it before I close. People will say to me: You know that what you have suggested was totally impossible from the standpoint of public opinion; that people in general had no idea that our interests were affected by what was going on in Europe in 1913; that they would never have dreamed of spending real money for armaments in time of peace; that they would never have gone into a war deliberately, as a result of cold calculation about the balance of power elsewhere; that they would have made war only upon direct provocation; that they could never have been brought to forgive such provocation and to refrain from pressing such a war to its final conclusion. And you know that they would not have been happy unless they had been able to clothe their military effort in the language of idealism and to persuade themselves that anything so important as Americans fighting on foreign soil had to end with a basic alteration of the terms of life among nations and a settlement of this business for once and for all. You—these people will say to me—hold yourself out as a realist, and yet none of these things you are talking about were even ever within the realm of practical possibility from the standpoint of domestic realities in our own country.

I have no quarrel with this argument. I am even going to concede it. I do think that political leaders might have made greater efforts than they did, from time to time, to inform themselves and to tell people the true facts, and I think people might even have understood them and been grateful to them if they had. But let us let that go and say that basically the argument is sound. I still have one thing to say about it.

I am not talking here about the behavior of Woodrow Wilson or Colonel House or Robert Lansing. I am talking about the behavior of the United States of America. History does not forgive us our national mistakes because they are explicable in terms of our domestic politics. If you say that mistakes of the past were unavoidable because of our domestic predilections and habits of thought, you are saying that what stopped us from being more effective than we were was democracy, as practiced in this country. And, if that is true, let us recognize it and measure the full seriousness of it—and find something to do about it. A nation which excuses its own failures by the sacred untouchableness of its own habits can excuse itself into complete disaster. I said in the first of these lectures that the margin in which it is given to us to commit blunders has been drastically narrowed in the last fifty years. If it was the workings of our democracy that were inadequate in the past, let us say so. Whoever thinks the future is going to be easier than the past is certainly mad. And the system under which we are going to have to continue to conduct foreign policy is, I hope and pray, the system of democracy.

AMERICAN INTERVENTION: 1917

[The literature on American intervention in World War I is simply too diverse to permit us to give a decent representation to each point of view. As the next best thing we give here part of the little summary, *American Intervention: 1917 and 1941* (Washington: Service Center for Teachers of History, rev. ed., 1968), pp. 1–20 of manuscript version. It is the work of Ernest R. May, one of the younger writers on the subject who has done much to clarify thinking on the issue.]

For Marxists, only socialist states can be "peace-loving." "Aggressive capitalist-imperialist" countries cannot. On the historical record, however, the American people deserve such a label at least as much as any other. Having led most modern peace movements, including those for arbitration and disarmament, and insisted until very recently that their governments pursue isolationist foreign policies and maintain only minimal military forces, Americans could be said not only to love peace but to have been infatuated with it.

Not least among evidences of this romance is their remorse over departures from peaceful ways. Bitter self-recrimination followed the Mexican War, the Civil War, the Spanish-American War, and especially the two World Wars.

In historical writing, it is true, the reaction usually developed slowly. After World War I, according to most observers, disillusionment quickly settled over the public. Books dealing with the war continued nevertheless to express pride and satisfaction in American intervention.

The most widely read were two semi-autobiographies: *The Life and Letters of Walter H. Page* (3 volumes; Garden City, 1922–26), edited by Burton J. Hendrick, and *The Intimate Papers of Colonel House* (4 volumes; Boston, 1926–28), edited by Charles Seymour. According to the extracts from diaries and letters published in these volumes, Page, who had been American ambassador in London, and House, who had been President Wilson's confidant and unofficial ambassador-at-large, had both advocated intervention and rejoiced that it had taken place. Though the collections consisted more of raw materials for history than of narrative and analysis, they set forth one interpretation of Wilson's diplomacy.

Both works divided the 1914–17 years into two periods, broken by the "Lusitania" crisis of May–June, 1915. In the first period, according to both Page-Hendrick and House-Seymour, the United States did not yet face a moral imperative to intervene. The issue was simply whether or not to obstruct the Allies. Wilson and his official aides, Secretary of State William Jennings Bryan and State Department Counselor Robert Lansing, inclined to be overly legalistic. In particular, they pressed for acceptance by the belligerents of the unratified Declaration of London of 1909, a code of rules for naval warfare which, by protecting American trade with continental Europe, would seriously limit the Allies' ability to cut off food and supplies for Germany. Page fought such a policy with all his resources. On one occasion he visited the foreign secretary, Sir Edward Grey, read him a formal note from the State Department, and then said, "I have now read the dispatch, but I do not agree with it; let us consider how it should be answered!" House meanwhile carried on the same battle in Washington, quietly advising Wilson and going behind the back of the State Department to work out a compromise with the British ambassador. The United States eventually gave up the Declaration of London. Both Page-Hendrick and House-Seymour celebrate this victory as the first among many that kept the United States from getting in the way of the Allies.

In the second phase, after the "Lusitania" sinking, according to both works, benevolent neutrality ceased to be enough. Page had actually become convinced earlier that German militarism represented a threat to American democracy; House had had twinges of the same conviction. After the spring of 1915, Page rarely doubted that it was his country's duty to get into the war as soon as possible. House urged breaking relations with Germany. When Wilson allowed the "Lusitania" issue to cool, House advised that the next submarine incident, the sinking of the "Arabic" in August, 1915, be made occasion for the break. He made the same plea after an attack on the Channel steamer, "Sussex," in the spring of 1916. At moments of crisis, House and Page stood together in urging that opportunity be seized for a rupture in relations or a declaration of war.

House meanwhile recommended that Wilson plan for possible intervention. In the winter of 1915–16 he induced the President to send him to Europe on an extraordinary mis-

sion. He sought an agreement with the Allies under which Wilson would make a public appeal for peace negotiations. If the Germans either refused or, accepting, declined to meet conditions satisfactory to the Allies, the United States would then intervene. Though actually initialled by House and Grey in February, 1916, and endorsed conditionally by Wilson, this agreement never went into effect. When Wilson made a public peace appeal in December, 1916, he regarded the understanding out of date. To House, this appeal seemed a mistake which happily came to nought. And in 1917 the President finally yielded, broke relations, and asked Congress to declare war on Germany.

Through both the Page and House accounts ran a contention that American intervention had been the right course, at least after the "Lusitania" sinking. This contention rested in part on an assumption that the Allies had had morality on their side and that Germany, absolutist and aggressively militarist, represented principles antithetic to those of the United States and the western Allies. The war had tested which code, which set of political abstractions, would prevail, and the United States had had to join in preventing a German victory in order to defend representative government, individual freedom, and the bourgeois virtues. Indeed, defeat of Imperial Germany, a malignant survival of feudalism, had been necessary if the world were to be made safe for democracy.

But the Page-Hendrick and House-Seymour view drew on another line of reasoning, occasionally in evidence at the time but best articulated later by Walter Lippmann in U. S. Foreign Policy: Shield of the Republic (Boston: Little, Brown, 1943). In this argument the security of the United States depended on there being no dominant power in Europe. Wilhelminian Germany, like Napoleonic France, threatened to master all the continent's immense war potential. If that occurred, the United States would confront an enemy stronger than itself, not only capable of challenging its hemispheric supremacy but of jeopardizing its very existence. As Page and House hinted and Lippmann, among others, said explicitly, the United States had a vital security interest in helping the Allies to prevent German triumph.

Only toward the end of the 1920's did another version of American intervention begin to gain currency. It grew out of the "revisionism" of Americans, Englishmen, and Germans who reexamined the wartime assumption that Germany had been responsible for starting the war. Drawing on the forty volumes of *Diplomatischen Akten des Auswärtigen Amtes, 1871–1914*, better known as *Die Grosse Politik*, these writers portrayed Imperial Germany as no worse than her opponents. Meanwhile, bickering among erstwhile allies, coupled with the consolidation of Soviet power and the rise of Fascism in Italy, made it seem doubtful if the war had in fact made democracy safer. As Warren I. Cohen describes in *The American Revisionists* (Chicago: University of Chicago Press, 1967), these new perceptions led to questioning of the moral premises so confidently accepted by Page and House.

In 1929 C. Hartley Grattan published in New York a detailed indictment of Wilson's diplomacy entitled *Why We Fought*. Contending that neither the United States nor the world had gained anything from the war, he asked how and why America had given up neutrality. Wilson's abandonment of the Declaration of London and retreat from an initial ban on private loans to belligerent governments, he found explicable only as reflecting first the sentimental Anglophilism of Page, House, and Wilson and, second, the influence of capitalists, financiers, and munitions makers who profited from supplying the Allies. Wilson had taken a stand against German submarine warfare more because it menaced trade than because it threatened neutral rights, Grattan argued, and had pressed his case to the point of war in order to protect America's investment in the Allied cause. Citing tendentious testimony from a senile congressman that Wilson had called a "sunrise conference" early in 1916 to tell congressional leaders that he wanted war, Grattan charged the President with having meditated this step long in advance. The final prod to action he found in a 1917 telegram from Page warning that Britain faced economic collapse if America did not come in. And the public followed, Grattan reasoned, because it had been barraged with English propaganda and frightened by administration-contrived tales of German espionage and sabotage. Though this crude summary does not do justice to Grattan's skillfully argued indictment, it suffices to indicate his themes—that the administration worked in the interest of munition makers and bankers and that the people had been tricked into an irrational and almost hysterical frame of mind.

Such views won wide credence during the Great Depression. In 1936 and 1937, Ray Stannard Baker, who had worked with Wilson at Versailles and later, reached the neutrality years in volumes V and VI of his eight-volume authorized biography. Despite his continuing reverence for Wilson, Baker assailed the follies of Page and House, deplored the dropping of the Declaration of London, ridiculed the House-Grey understanding, and lamented the final decision to intervene. Walter Millis of the *New York Herald Tribune* meanwhile devoted his lively pen and studious mind to a one volume account of the background of intervention, *Road to War, 1914–1917* (Boston: Houghton Mifflin, 1935). A popular best-seller, Millis's book also poked sardonic fun at the illusions of the interventionists and suggested that the event itself had been due to a combination of folly, sentimentalism, and greed. In 1936 the United States Senate set up a special committee under the chairmanship of Senator Gerald P. Nye of North Dakota to investigate the influence of munitions makers on foreign policy. The committee interrogated representatives of such firms as J. P. Morgan and Company and the National City Bank of New York and ransacked the files of the State and Treasury Departments. Meanwhile, international lawyers, such as Edwin M. Borchard of Yale and the elderly John Bassett Moore, assailed the legal theories upon which Wilson had acted. Borchard and William P. Lage published *Neutrality for the United States* (New Haven: Yale U. Press, 1937), denouncing any and all efforts to safeguard "freedom of the seas." Amid this climate, Congress passed Neutrality Acts designed, as someone said, to prevent any future President from getting the United States into the 1914–1918 war.

Scholars also joined in the hue and cry. Joseph V. Fuller, a historian for the Department of State and author of a monograph on Bismarckian diplomacy, published an article in the *Journal of Modern History* for 1934. He asked why the Germans had not abandoned submarine warfare and thus deprived Wilson of his excuse for intervention. He answered that Germany had to stop munitions from reaching the Allies and that the provocation was therefore Wilson's refusal to heed pleas for an arms embargo. He stressed this policy of Wilson's over others. In 1939, H. C. Peterson of the University of Oklahoma authored *Propaganda for War* (Norman: U. of Okla. Press, 1939), a lengthy monograph on how Sir Gilbert Parker and agencies in Wellington House entrapped the American public. Among other such articles and monographs, Charles Callan Tansill's *America Goes to War* (Boston: Little, Brown, 1938), stood foremost. Eventually a professor at Fordham University and then at Georgetown University, Tansill had previously published monographs on American relations with Santo Domingo and on the acquisition of the Virgin Islands. Though not allowed to use the Wilson manuscripts, which Baker still hoarded, he had seen parts of the unpublished House diaries and had been given free rein among the gatherings of the Nye Committee. Correspondence from an obliging officer in the Berlin Marine-Archiv enabled him to sketch the German side. His bibliography, though including some items not actually used, was full and impressive.

Tansill's volume stressed the enormous growth of American trade in munitions and other war supplies and the extent of American private loans to the Allies. Portraying House, Page, and even Lansing as influenced by these interests and moved by blind hatred for Germany, he showed how they frustrated true neutrality, as he conceived it, persuading the President to abandon the Declaration of London, give up his early opposition to loans, resist pressure for an arms embargo, and take an unjustifiable stand against German submarine warfare. Some of the chapter titles indicate the thread of argument: "III. War Profits Beckon to 'Big Business',""VI. England Looks Upon the Declaration of London as a 'Mere Scrap of Paper'," "XI. Mr. Lansing Leads the President Along the Road to War," "XV. Colonel House Blocks a Path to Peace," "XVIII. The Kaiser Chooses Peace with America Rather Than Victory at Verdun." Though reviewers in scholarly journals did not call his book dispassionate, most found it solid and convincing.

The interpretation popularized by Grattan and Millis and footnoted by Tansill had, of course, its own foundation in faith. It rested on the premise that the United States had had no reason, moral or material, for opposing Germany or helping the Allies. Some members of this school assumed that if the United States had remained neutral a negotiated peace would have resulted, with happier results than those of the Versailles *Diktat*. Even if Germany had been absolutist, militaristic, and imperialistic, which these writers doubted, and even if it had been on the edge of triumph, still they felt that the outcome of the war should have remained a matter of indifference to Americans. As many writers asserted, among them Charles A. Beard in his eloquent *Open Door at Home* (New York: Macmillan, 1934), the United States was strong precisely because it did not involve itself in European diplomatic chicanery and waste its substance in preparations for war. From this premise it followed as night the day that the intervention of 1917 had been at least a blunder and probably a crime.

Though most writing on 1914–17 in the twenty years after Versailles resembled either that in Page's *Letters* and the House *Papers* or Grattan and Tansill, a third approach had already been discovered. In 1923 Malbone W. Graham published a University of Texas Ph.D. thesis entitled *The Controversy Between the United States and Allied Governments Respecting Neutral Rights and Commerce During the Period of American Neutrality, 1914–1917* (Austin: U. of Texas, 1923). It neither glorified American policy nor recriminated against its architects. Graham found that with slight departures in one direction or another the United States had tried to follow the applicable rules of international law. Another scholar, Richard Van Alstyne, writing in the *Journal of Modern History* for 1935 reached much the same conclusion about the abandonment of the Declaration of London. But, curiously enough, it was Charles Seymour, the editor of the House *Papers*, who published the first book-length study dealing with intervention as a historical episode rather than a question of moral doctrine.

In *American Diplomacy during the World War* (Baltimore: Johns Hopkins U. Press, 1934), the Albert Shaw lectures for 1933, and in supplementary essays published as *American Neutrality, 1914–1917* (New Haven: Yale U. Press, 1935), Seymour analyzed Wilson's policies toward the Allies, his efforts to mediate, and his opposition to the submarine. He reported that the President and his advisers, while influenced by belief in the moral superiority of the English and French, had adhered to international law as they understood it and, indeed, taken risks to prevent inroads upon it. In the interval between the "Sussex" pledge and the coming of war, when German submarines were under control, Seymour pointed out, American relations with Britain had become so troubled that Wilson talked vexedly of employing economic sanctions against the Allies.

The submarine issue alone, Seymour contended, brought intervention. Wilson saw German undersea warfare as a challenge that could not be ignored. If a belligerent could extend its operations anywhere, interfere with the trade of neutral states, and imperil the lives of neutral citizens, then neither neutrality nor international law possessed meaning. In conscience, the President felt compelled to oppose the Germans on this issue and, paradoxically, to risk neutrality for the sake of neutrality. He was not entirely altruistic, for American lives and property were at stake. Though the German government respected Wilson's wishes for a time, it eventually ceased to do so. At Spa on January 7, 1917, the Kaiser and his advisers decided to launch an unrestricted submarine campaign in defiance of the United States and in conscious certainty that war would result. The decisive roles were played by these German leaders, not by Page, House, Lansing, or even Wilson.

Much the same view of intervention appeared in a bulkier study, Harley F. Notter's *The Origins of the Foreign Policy of Woodrow Wilson* (Baltimore: Johns Hopkins U. Press, 1937). Setting Wilson's diplomacy in the context of his earlier life and thought, Notter's volume tended to highlight Wilson's preoccupation with moral issues. But it was more diffuse, less studied, and less incisive than Seymour's volumes.

When World War II forced thought to more immediate problems of neutrality, debate tended to lapse. After Pearl Harbor, the parallels of 1919 seemed more relevant than those of 1917, and scholarly work centered on the armistice, the peace conference, and the fight over the League of Nations.

After World War II a generation with different attitudes and preoccupations began to restudy problems of World War I. Lippmann had already provided one new point of departure by suggesting that intervention had been necessary for the rescue of the balance of power and the protection of American security. In various popular and scholarly periodicals and in a book, *In Defense of the National Interest* (New York: Knopf, 1951), a University of Chicago political scientist, Hans J. Morgenthau, attacked the Wilson administration for having failed to concentrate on realistic goals. In 1950, in lectures printed as *American Diplomacy, 1900–1950* (Chicago: U. of Chicago

Press, 1950), the erudite and sophisticated career diplomat, George Frost Kennan, put the same charge into captivating phrases. He accused Wilson and other American leaders of excessive moralism and legalism. Taking a position halfway between the major prewar schools, he argued that while intervention might have been justified by the national interest, the overlay of other excuses had ruined its purpose. As a result, the United States became "uncomfortably similar to one of those prehistoric monsters with a body as long as this room and a brain the size of a pin; he lies there in his comfortable primeval mud and pays little attention to his environment; he is slow to wrath—in fact, you practically have to whack his tail off to make him aware that his interests are being disturbed; but, once he grasps this, he lays about him with such blind determination that he not only destroys his adversary but largely wrecks his native habitat." While prewar writers had argued over whether intervention had been right or wrong, Morgenthau and Kennan suggested instead that it had been right, but for the wrong reasons.

This hypothesis intrigued a number of young scholars. Robert E. Osgood, a political scientist in Morgenthau's Chicago Center for the Study of American Foreign Policy, investigated it in *Ideals and Self-Interest in America's Foreign Relations* (Chicago: U. of Chicago Press, 1953). In several chapters devoted to World War I, he amplified the theses that Morgenthau and Kennan had sketched. Another political scientist, Edward H. Buehrig of the University of Indiana, in *Woodrow Wilson and the Balance of Power* (Bloomington: Indiana U. Press, 1955), assessed these criticisms as not altogether fair. The submarine issue symbolized a clash of national interests, he said, and while American leaders did concern themselves with legal and moral issues, Wilson, House, and especially Lansing showed acute awareness of the balance of power. Daniel M. Smith in *Robert Lansing and American Neutrality, 1914–1917* (Berkeley and Los Angeles: U. of California Press, 1958), detailed the evidence regarding Lansing, stressing that Lansing's opinions derived from a mixture of political, economic, and moral considerations. In a subsequent article, "National Interest and American Intervention, 1917: An Historiographical Appraisal," in the *Journal of American History* for June, 1965, Smith carefully weighed up the support for the balance-of-power thesis to be found in known evidence. He concluded that it left much out of account and therefore belonged among the "more simplistic" interpretations.

Meanwhile, like the tortoise competing with the hare, the separate line of scholarship started by Graham, Van Alstyne, and Seymour kept up its plodding pace. Arthur S. Link, Professor of History at Princeton, Northwestern, and then Princeton again, launched a magisterial biography of Wilson. In a shorter work, *Woodrow Wilson and the Progressive Era* (New York: Harper, 1954), and in *Wilson, the Diplomatist* (Baltimore: Johns Hopkins U. Press, 1957), the Albert Shaw lectures for 1956, Link sketched his tentative findings about the 1914–1917 period. By 1965, he had finally completed the fifth volume of *Wilson* (Princeton, N.J., Princeton U. Press, 1947–   ) carrying the narrative to the declaration of war. By that time, my own *The World War and American Isolation* (Cambridge: Harvard U. Press, 1959) had appeared. In that book, I argued that in nearly every case requiring a decision by the President, considerations of law, morality, power, national prestige, and domestic politics all had to be taken into account. Neither Wilson nor his advisers could ever see very clearly the probable results of their decisions. In each instance, the weight of argument seemed to command the course finally adopted. Each time, however, the decision tended to close out one or more alternatives until in 1917 there seemed no real option except war. The Germans, whom I tried to study in some detail, found themselves similarly driven into a corner from which they too could see no exit. Karl E. Birnbaum, a Swedish scholar, in *Peace Moves and U-Boat Warfare, 1916–1917* (Stockholm:

Almquist and Wiksell, 1958) described more fully German diplomatic maneuvers in the crucial final stage, suggesting that there might have been moments when better communications between Berlin and Washington could have altered the outcome. But the necessary understanding of the other side simply did not exist within the Kaiser's councils or, equally importantly, among leaders in the Reichstag. The German decision to force a crisis, compelling Wilson either to make war or to concede that he had bluffed, therefore had about it a quality of tragic inevitability.

The central themes of Link's vast and nearly definitive biographical volumes proved not to differ markedly from those foreshadowed in his shorter works and set forth in my own book. By meticulous analysis of data, some of which was uniquely available to him (notably, French diplomatic archives which remain officially closed), he set the record straight on a number of points where others, including myself, had been in doubt or in error. Thus, for example, he proved that the House-Grey agreement merited less attention than it had received. Playing a devious game, House had misled Wilson as to what he was seeking, misrepresented the President's views when speaking to the Allies, and then misrepresented their views to Washington. In accepting the document, Wilson had no sense of committing himself to intervention. Also, Link showed that a public letter sent to Senator Stone by Wilson in 1916, seemingly stating a dogmatic moral position with regard to submarine warfare, was actually a hastily drafted document tailored to fit a particular challenge to presidential leadership of the legislative branch. It neither expressed Wilson's private thoughts nor mirrored the policy he was pursuing. Link showed what a flexible and conciliatory course Wilson actually followed, backing away between 1915 and 1917 from the perilous ground taken in the "Lusitania" correspondence and standing instead on the proposition that submarine operations would become cause for war only in the event of willful attacks on American citizens or

ships. Better than anyone else, Link described the domestic problems that Wilson faced, the difficulties made for him by, on the one hand, near-pacifist Democrats, German-Americans, and Irish-Americans, who opposed any resolute defense of American interests or rights against Germany, and, on the other hand, by Roosevelt Republicans, Anglophiles, Francophiles, and chauvinists who clamored against any compromises whatever. The Wilson one sees in Link's biography is many-sided, moved by conscience and by deeply-felt religious ideas, by a sense of responsibility for the economic welfare of his country and for its international standing, credit, and influence, and by an additional sense of responsibility as leader of a party and sponsor of domestic reforms, the success of which seemed to depend on his party's continuance in power. The range of alternatives open to him in regard to the European war appears narrower than either the Page-House, the isolationist, or the Morgenthau-Kennan school would concede; the choices made by him seem the best that, in the circumstances, any prudent man could have made.

It is perhaps significant that most who continue to debate whether intervention in World War I was right or wrong describe themselves as political scientists. Historians by and large now deal with World War I much as with the Punic or Napoleonic wars, seeking rather to achieve some kind of empathy than to deliver praise or blame. The chief exceptions, as yet few in number, have some association with what is called "the New Left."

Because the New Left accords a great deal of attention to businessmen and bankers, it is sometimes confused with an older school of "economic" interpretation. In fact, it is quite different. The older group took the view that businessmen constituted a special class. Through force, corruption, and chicanery, this class used government to serve its special interests at the expense of the interests of other classes. Thus, bankers and munitions makers brought about American intervention in order to protect their investments and profits. Although New Left thought owes much to Marxist class-struggle analysis, from which most "economic" interpretation derived, it also has a debt to Louis Hartz, John Higham, and others who challenged traditional assumptions by marshalling evidence that American history had been characterized less by conflict among interest groups or ideologies than by broad consensus. The New Left argues that, from the late nineteenth century onward, America has had a single dominant value system, in which the protection of private property, opportunity for individual enrichment, increase in production, and expansion of markets have been goals above all others. This capitalist value system, the New Left regards as wrong, and as productive of evil. It leads inevitably, they contend, to varieties of imperialism designed to ensure access to markets and, as a corollary, to conflict with revolutionary movements that espouse other than free-market forms of economic and political organization. But the New Left does not, like the old Left, charge these outcomes to conspiracies. Instead, its members blame the whole society's failure to stand back and think critically about fundamental assumptions. Those who have touched on American intervention in World War I, notably William Appleman Williams in *The Tragedy of American Diplomacy* (revised and enlarged ed., New York: Dell, 1962) and N. Gordon Levin, Jr., in *Woodrow Wilson and World Politics* (New York: Oxford U. Press, 1968), concede that each move by the American government was, in the circumstances, logical and understandable. Indeed, they agree that Wilson's actions had a quality of inevitability, given the values accepted by him and by the largest part of the American public. They raise the philosophical question—one that might be raised with regard to Republican Rome or Napoleonic France— of whether the results might not have been otherwise if these values had been radically different.

THE ANGLO-AMERICAN UNDERSTANDING

If Great Britain failed . . . The United States would have to step in, at least temporarily, in order to re-establish the balance of power in Europe, never mind against which country, or group of countries, our efforts may have to be directed. . . . In fact, we are ourselves becoming, owing to our strength and geographical situation, more and more the balance of power of the whole globe.

—Theodore Roosevelt, 1911

A certain intimacy, if it may be called so, of attraction and repulsion, which has made the relations between Britain and the United States at once more easy and more difficult, more cordial and more intractable, than those between any two other countries.

—Sir Edward Grey, British Foreign Minister

I should like to impress upon you that it is extremely important to be able to yield on certain questions where vital interests are not at stake. Don't forget that George III lost the United States through lawyers and by pressing a legal point.

—Cecil Spring-Rice to Sir Edward Grey

I knew that you believed the hope and salvation of the world lay in a close and cordial understanding between the free nations, more especially between those who were of the household of our language. I said [to President Wilson] that we could almost endure with equanimity all the horrors of this terrible struggle if they led in the end to a close, sure and permanent understanding between the English-speaking peoples. If we stood together we were safe. If we did not stand together nothing was safe.

—Cecil Spring-Rice to Foreign Minister Arthur Balfour

Let the neutrals complain about our blockade and other measures taken as much as they may, the fact remains that no neutral national has ever lost his life as the result of it.

—Prime Minister Asquith

I saw with apprehension the tide of resentment against Great Britain rising higher and higher in this country. . . . I did all that I could to prolong the disputes by preparing . . . long and detailed replies, and introducing technical and contro-versial matters in the hope that before the extended interchange of arguments came to an end something would happen to change the current of American public opin-ion or to make the American people perceive that German absolutism was a menace to their liberties and to democratic institutions everywhere.

—Robert Lansing, Counsellor of the State Department

We are face to face with something they are going to do, and they are going to do it no matter what representations we make. We cannot convince them or change them, we can only show them very clearly . . . that we mean to hold them to a strict responsibility for every invasion of our rights as neutrals.

—Wilson to Bryan, March 25, 1915

Blockade of Germany was essential to the victory of the Allies, but the ill-will of the United States meant their certain defeat. After Paris had been saved by the battle of the Marne, the Allies could do no more than hold their own against Germany; sometimes they did not even do that. Germany and Austria were self-supporting in the huge supply of munitions. The Allies soon became dependent for an adequate supply on the United States. If we quarrelled with the United States we could not get that supply. It was better therefore to carry on the war without blockade, if need be, than to incur a break with the United States about contra-band and thereby deprive the Allies of the resources necessary to carry on the war at all or with any chance of success. The object of diplomacy, therefore, was to secure the maximum of blockade that could be enforced without a rupture with the United States. . . .

There was one mistake in diplomacy that, if it had been made, would have been fatal to the cause of the Allies. It was carefully avoided. This cardinal mistake would have been a breach with the United States, not necessarily a rupture, but a state of things that would have provoked American interference with the blockade, or led to an embargo on exports of munitions from the United States.

Germany, on the other hand, did make this cardinal mistake.

—Sir Edward Grey, *Twenty-Five Years, 1892–1916*
(2v., N.Y.: Stokes, 1925), 2:107, 170

Now the relations I have established with Sir Edward Grey have been built up on frankness, fairness and friendship. I can't have relations of any other sort.

—Walter Hines Page

"I am instructed," [Page] said, "to read this dispatch to you." He read and I listened. He then said: "I have now read the dispatch, but I do not agree with it: let us consider how it should be answered."

—Sir Edward Grey

House left me in no doubt from the first that he held German militarism responsible for the war, and that he regarded the struggle as one between democracy and something that was undemocratic and antipathetic to American ideals. It was not necessary to spend much time in putting our case to him. He had a way of saying "I know it" in a tone and manner that carried conviction both of his sympathy with, and understanding of, what was said to him.

—Sir Edward Grey

America had better look out after this war. . . . I shall stand no nonsense from America after the war.

—Kaiser William II, speaking to U.S. Ambassador Gerard

It has always been my dream that the two English-speaking nations should some day be united in a great cause, and today my dream is realized. Together we are fighting for the greatest cause that peoples can fight. The Anglo-Saxon race must save civilization.

—George V, to Pershing's staff, 1917

WOODROW WILSON SPEAKS

(1) "PEACE WITHOUT VICTORY"

[Wilson was convinced that the war if carried to the dire extent of victory for either side would disastrously affect the future of the world. Accordingly, on January 22,

Permission Chicago Daily News

Wilson and preparedness

1917, he laid before the Senate and the world his plea for "peace without victory" guaranteed by a League of Nations. The following is from Wilson's *Public Papers*, 4:410–414.]

The present war must first be ended; but we owe it to candour and to a just regard for the opinion of mankind to say that, so far as our participation in guarantees of future peace is concerned, it makes a great deal of difference in what way and upon what terms it is ended. The treaties and agreements which bring it to an end must embody terms which will create a peace that will win the approval of mankind, not merely a peace that will serve the several interests and immediate aims of the nations engaged. . . .

Mere agreements may not make peace secure. It will be absolutely necessary that a force be created as a guarantor of the permanency of the settlement so much greater than the force of any nation now engaged or any alliance hitherto formed or projected that no nation, no probable combination of nations could face or withstand it. If the peace presently to be made is to endure, it must be a

peace made secure by the organized major force of mankind. . . .

There must be, not a balance of power, but a community of power; not organized rivalries, but an organized common peace.

Fortunately we have received very explicit assurances on this point. The statesmen of both of the groups of nations now arrayed against one another have said, in terms that could not be misinterpreted, that it was no part of the purpose they had in mind to crush their antagonists. But the implications of these assurances may not be equally clear to all,—may not be the same on both sides of the water. I think it will be serviceable if I attempt to set forth what we understand them to be.

They imply, first of all, that . . . it must be a peace without victory . . . Victory would mean peace forced upon the loser, a victor's terms imposed upon the vanquished. It would be accepted in humiliation, under duress, at an intolerable sacrifice, and would have a sting, a resentment, a bitter memory upon which terms of peace would rest, not permanently, but only as upon quicksand. Only a peace between equals can last. Only a peace the very principle of which is equality and a common participation in a common benefit. The right state of mind, the right feeling between nations, is as necessary for a lasting peace as is the just settlement of vexed questions of territory or of racial and national allegiance.

The equality of nations upon which peace must be founded if it is to last must be an equality of rights; the guarantees exchanged must neither recognize nor imply a difference between big nations and small, between those that are powerful and those that are weak. Right must be based upon the common strength, not upon the individual strength, of the nations upon whose concert peace will depend. . . .

And there is a deeper thing involved than even equality of right among organized nations. No peace can last, or ought to last, which does not recognize and accept the principle that governments derive all their just powers from the consent of the governed, and that no right anywhere exists to hand peoples about from sovereignty to sovereignty as if they were property. . . . Any peace which does not recognize and accept this principle will inevitably be upset. It will not rest upon the affections or the convictions of mankind. The ferment of spirit of whole populations will fight subtly and constantly against it, and all the world will sympathize. The world can be at peace only if its life is stable, and there can be no stability where the will is in rebellion, where there is not tranquility of spirit and a sense of justice, of freedom, and of right. . . .

I would fain believe that I am speaking for the silent mass of mankind everywhere who have as yet had no place or opportunity to speak their real hearts out concerning the death and ruin they see to have come already upon the persons and the homes they hold most dear. . . .

I am proposing, as it were, that the nations should with one accord adopt the doctrine of President Monroe as the doctrine of the world: that no nation should seek to extend its polity over any other nation or people, but that every people should be left free to determine its own polity, its own way of development, unhindered, unthreatened, unafraid, the little along with the great and powerful.

I am proposing that all nations henceforth avoid entangling alliances which would draw them into competitions of power; catch them in a net of intrigue and selfish rivalry, and disturb their own affairs with influences intruded from without. There is no entangling alliance in a concert of power. When all unite to act in the same sense and with the same purpose all act in the common interest and are free to live their own lives under a common protection.

I am proposing government by the consent of the governed; that freedom of the seas which in international conference after conference representatives of the United States have urged with the eloquence of those who are the convinced disciples of liberty; and that moderation of armaments which makes of armies and navies a power for order merely, not an instrument of aggression or of selfish violence.

These are American principles, American policies. We could stand for no others. And they are also the principles and policies of forward looking men and women everywhere, of every modern nation, of every enlightened community. They are the principles of mankind and must prevail.

(2) WILSON ASKS FOR WAR

[On April 2, 1917, Wilson appeared before Congress and in a moving address recommended a declaration of war on Germany. Parts of the address follow, taken from Woodrow Wilson, *War and Peace: Presidential Messages, Addresses, and Public Papers* (2v., N.Y.: Harper, 1927), 1:6–16.]

While we do these things, these deeply momentous things, let us be very clear, and make very clear to all the world what our motives and our objects are. . . . to vindicate the principles of peace and justice in the life of the world as against selfish and autocratic power and to set up amongst the really free and self-governed peoples of the world such a concert of purpose and of action as will henceforth insure the observance of those principles. Neutrality is no longer feasible or desirable where the peace of the world is involved and the freedom of its peoples, and the menace to that peace and freedom lies in the existence of autocratic governments backed by organized force which is controlled wholly by their will, not by the will of their people. We have seen the last of neutrality in such circumstances. We are at the beginning of an age in which it will be insisted that the same standards of conduct and of responsibility for wrong done shall be observed among nations and their governments that are observed among the individual citizens of civilized states.

We have no quarrel with the German people. We have no feeling towards them but one of sympathy and friendship. It was not upon their impulse that their government acted in entering this war. It was not with their previous knowledge or approval. . . . We are glad, now that we see the facts with no veil of false pretense about them, to fight thus for the ultimate peace of the world and for the liberation of its peoples, the German peoples included: for the rights of nations great and small and the privilege of men everywhere to choose their way of life and of obedi-

ence. The world must be made safe for democracy. Its peace must be planted upon the tested foundations of political liberty. We have no selfish ends to serve. We desire no conquest, no dominion. We seek no indemnities for ourselves, no material compensation for the sacrifices we shall freely make. We are but one of the champions of the rights of mankind. We shall be satisfied when those rights have been made as secure as the faith and the freedom of nations can make them. . . .

It is a distressing and oppressive duty, Gentlemen of the Congress, which I have performed in thus addressing you. There are, it may be, many months of fiery trial and sacrifice ahead of us. It is a fearful thing to lead this great peaceful people into war, into the most terrible and disastrous of all wars, civilization itself seeming to be in the balance. But the right is more precious than peace, and we shall fight for the things which we have always carried nearest our hearts,—for democracy, for the right of those who submit to authority to have a voice in their own Governments, for the rights and liberties of small nations, for a universal dominion of right by such a concert of free peoples as shall bring peace and safety to all nations and make the world itself at last free. To such a task we can dedicate our lives and our fortunes, everything that we are and everything that we have, with the pride of those who know that the day has come when America is privileged to spend her blood and her might for the principles that gave her birth and happiness and the peace which she has treasured. God helping her, she can do no other.

(3) PEACE WITH JUSTICE: THE FOURTEEN POINTS

[Wilson's appeal for "peace without victory" had failed, and the United States had gone to war. Now the best he could get would be a peace with justice, and he sought earnestly to find ways to define its provisions. On January 8, 1918, Wilson laid before Congress his proposed terms for peace, the so-called Fourteen Points.

The following is taken from *War and Peace*, 1:158–162. Unfortunately, Wilson spoke with minimal regard for the wishes of the Allies, and the terms—some of them—far from being "too concrete to admit of any further doubt or question" were contradictory and unrealistic. When Wilson opened this Pandora's Box, far more than fourteen points flew out.]

It will be our wish and purpose that the processes of peace, when they are begun, shall be absolutely open and that they shall involve and permit henceforth no secret understandings of any kind. The day of conquest and aggrandizement is gone by; so is also the day of secret covenants entered into in the interest of particular governments and likely at some unlooked-for moment to upset the peace of the world. . . .

We entered this war because violations of right had occurred which touched us to the quick and made the life of our own people impossible unless they were corrected and the world secured once for all against their recurrence. What we demand in this war, therefore, is nothing peculiar to ourselves. It is that the world be made fit and safe to live in; and particularly that it be made safe for every peace-loving nation which, like our own, wishes to live its own life, determine its own institutions, be assured of justice and fair dealing by the other peoples of the world as against force and selfish aggression, All the peoples of the world are in effect partners in this interest, and for our own part we see very clearly that unless justice be done to others it will not be done to us. The program of the world's peace, therefore, is our program; and that program, the only possible program, as we see it, is this:

I. Open covenants of peace, openly arrived at, after which there shall be no private international understandings of any kind but diplomacy shall proceed always frankly and in the public view.

II. Absolute freedom of navigation upon the seas, outside territorial waters, alike in peace and in war, except as the seas may be closed in whole or in part by international action for the enforcement of international covenants.

III. The removal, so far as possible, of all economic barriers and the establishment of an equality of trade conditions among all the nations consenting to the peace and associating themselves for its maintenance.

IV. Adequate guarantees given and taken that national armaments will be reduced to the lowest point consistent with domestic safety.

V. A free, open-minded, and absolutely impartial adjustment of all colonial claims, based upon a strict observance of the principle that in determining all such questions of sovereignty the interests of the populations concerned must have equal weight with the equitable claims of the government whose title is to be determined.

VI. The evacuation of all Russian territory and such a settlement of all questions affecting Russia as will secure the best and freest coöperation of the other nations of the world in obtaining for her an unhampered and unembarrassed opportunity for the independent determination of her own political development and national policy and assure her of a sincere welcome into the society of free nations under institutions of her own choosing; and, more than a welcome, assistance also of every kind that she may need and may herself desire. The treatment accorded Russia by her sister nations in the months to come will be the acid test of their good will, of their comprehension of her needs as distinguished from their own interests, and of their intelligent and unselfish sympathy.

VII. Belgium, the whole world will agree, must be evacuated and restored, without any attempt to limit the sovereignty which she enjoys in common with all other free nations. No other single act will serve as this will serve to restore confidence among the nations in the laws which they have themselves set and determined for the government of their relations with one another. Without this healing act the whole structure and validity of international law is forever impaired.

VIII. All French territory should be freed and the invaded portions restored, and the wrong done to France by Prussia in 1871 in the matter of Alsace-Lorraine, which has unsettled the peace of the world for nearly fifty years, should be righted, in order that peace may once more be made secure in the interest of all.

IX. A readjustment of the frontiers of Italy should be effected along clearly recognizable lines of nationality.

X. The peoples of Austria-Hungary, whose place among the nations we wish to see safeguarded and assured, should be accorded the freest opportunity of autonomous development.

XI. Rumania, Serbia, and Montenegro should be evacuated; occupied territories restored; Serbia accorded free and secure access to the sea; and the relations of the several Balkan states to one another determined by friendly counsel along historically established lines of allegiance and nationality; and international guarantees of the political and economic independence and territorial integrity of the several Balkan states should be entered into.

XII. The Turkish portions of the present Ottoman Empire should be assured a secure sovereignty, but the other nationalities which are now under Turkish rule should be assured an undoubted security of life and an absolutely unmolested opportunity of autonomous development, and the Dardanelles should be permanently opened as a free passage to the ships and commerce of all nations under international guarantees.

XIII. An independent Polish state should be erected which should include the territories inhabited by indisputably Polish populations, which should be assured a free and secure access to the sea, and whose political and economic independence and territorial integrity should be guaranteed by international covenant.

XIV. A general association of nations must be formed under specific covenants for the purpose of affording mutual guarantees of political independence and territorial integrity to great and small states alike.

In regard to these essential rectifications of wrong and assertions of right we feel ourselves to be intimate partners of all the governments and peoples associated together against the Imperialists. We cannot be separated in interest or divided in purpose. We stand together until the end.

For such arrangements and covenants we are willing to fight and to continue to fight until they are achieved; but only because we wish the right to prevail and desire a just and stable peace such as can be secured only by removing the chief provocations to war, which this program does remove. . . .

We have spoken now, surely, in terms too concrete to admit of any further doubt or question. An evident principle runs through the whole program I have outlined. It is the principle of justice to all peoples and nationalities, and their right to live on equal terms of liberty and safety with one another, whether they be strong or weak. Unless this principle be made its foundation no part of the structure of international justice can stand. The people of the United States could act upon no other principle; and to the vindication of this principle they are ready to devote their lives, their honor, and everything that they possess. The moral climax of this the culminating and final war for human liberty has come, and they are ready to put their own strength, their own highest purpose, their own integrity and devotion to the test.

VERSAILLES: TWENTY YEARS AFTER

[The Williams College historian, Paul Birdsall, in his book of the above title (N.Y.: Reynal and Hitchcock, 1941) gave a temperate and, in the main, approving account of Wilson's "stands on principle" at Versailles, and asserted that "he emerges as the only man of real stature at Paris." The concluding pages, 289–295, are reprinted here.]

The intellectual nihilism of the twenty years since Versailles has destroyed faith in the Wilsonian program at Paris. By misrepresenting the character of the treaty, the motives that inspired it, above all by denial of any genuine American stake in European settlement, it has provided the strongest moral force by which Hitler "softens" his victims before striking them down with physical force. The disillusioned liberal has been the unwitting ally of the cynical advocate of physical force as the only conceivable basis for world politics.

In such an atmosphere, any constructive effort like Wilson's is bound to appear silly and unrealistic. The romantic liberal must see the immediate realization of his hopes or turn on the author of his hopes with charges of betrayal, and those who have thoroughly cynical reasons for opposing a new order will welcome the charges. The statesman who labors for the best constructive results obtainable in a chaotic world starts under the terrible handicap of a war on two fronts: against cynical opposition, and equally against his sentimental and perfectionist supporters. At Paris the situation was complicated by the fact that the American Delegation contained not merely representatives of the Simon-pure liberal school, but advocates of the opposition itself, not in any cynical sense, but because they were so profoundly impressed with political realities as they existed that instinctively they thought in terms of compromise beyond the limits of any real necessity.

In this welter of conflicting viewpoints it has recently become fashionable to eschew all standards of judgment and to resort to the methods of social psychology in describing the mêlée. The result has the pleasingly remote, detached, and scientific atmosphere of a study in anthropology. It becomes a study in abstraction and determinism, and involves no issues or principles with which any reader need concern himself. It is both the realistic and the scientific method applied to the writing of history, and it reinforces the intellectual nihilism of the disillusioned liberal.

Is it really scientific in taking account of all the data within the particular field of its concern? The only thing this method leaves out is the set of standards and principles which men themselves accepted as the basis upon which they agreed to work, and thereby accepted as the standards by which they might legitimately be judged. The only element which gives coherence and significance to the study of the Paris Peace Conference is the set of principles with reference to which it acted, the degree to which it embodied them in the treaties, the extent to which it departed from them, and the reasons—personal and political —for the result. No account which ignores or pre-judges that frame of reference can claim to be scientific.

To assume at the outset that the Fourteen Points were unreal and impractical, incapable of being translated into concrete terms of peace, ignores the simple fact that they constituted a legal contract between the Allied and Associated Powers and Germany to govern the terms of peace. It is just as unrealistic to impugn the intelligence and integrity of the Peace Commissioners who took the contract seriously in the first place as to denounce them all indiscriminately as hypocrites who systematically violated principles in which they never believed, or as fools who could not recognize the violation of a principle when they committed it. The contract was there as the basis of all their efforts. It was a reasonably ascertainable contract, the details of application admittedly difficult, but by no means so impossible as many writers have alleged. It is quite as possible to distinguish between the degrees of good faith and intelligence brought to the task by the different national delegations at Paris, as it is possible to distinguish the degrees of intelligence and good faith within the personnel of any one of these delegations. Such treatment must, obviously, take account of the real political pressures upon men by national tradition and public opinion. To ignore the necessity of reasonable compromise in political affairs is just as fatal to realism as to assume that, all politics being of the essence of compromise, there are no rules at all and no standards of judgments but those of immediate political success.

It is an extraordinary fact that as yet there has been no balanced interpretation of Peace Conference diplomacy to take the measure of all the factors involved. When a penetrating critic like Harold Nicolson undertakes to recall the discussion to a firm basis of reality by emphasizing the fundamental conflict of principle, he does so only to go off the deep end of romantic-liberal disillusionment, and produces a spiritual autobiography of his loss of faith in Wilson. In his reaction against the prophets and dreamers of the world, he embraces the realists who at least know the rules of the balance of power in Europe—for example, Eyre Crowe of the British Foreign Office and Colonel House, "the best diplomatic brain America has yet produced."

The issue of realism at Paris is mainly the question of the short-term as against the long-range view. The pressures of national demands, made effective and menacing through diplomatic strategy in the League of Nations Commission, made immediate and pressing by the danger of delay in pacifying a turbulent and disintegrating Europe, necessitated a degree of compromise. The realists of the American Delegation lost their perspective under such pressure and were ready to throw away all their cargo in the scramble for the lifeboats. The cargo consisted of the Fourteen Points, the substance of the Pre-Armistice Agreement, the contract with Germany. Colonel House felt that if the boat were lightened sufficiently, it would still carry the League of Nations, but Harold Nicolson's description of a general *sauve qui peut* attitude in the later phases of the Peace Conference applies well to elements within the American delegation. In this atmosphere, one concession was an argument for the next.

Mezes could not see why the American delegation should "stand up so much straighter" on the Fiume question against the Italians than in other questions involving other Powers; Colonel House advocated extreme concessions to the Japanese on the ground that, although clearly a violation of principle, it was no worse than many other concessions which had already been made. There was little attempt to discriminate between detail and principle, between the relative merits of national demands, between the varying degrees of diplomatic strength which supported the demands. Above all, there was no thought save for the immediate future—make peace quickly and start the League of Nations. The realism of these men consisted in an abdication of sheer nerve and intelligence.

Naturally, President Wilson looked stiff and unrealistic when viewed through the eyes of such men, at the very time when William Bullitt was resigning from the American Delegation in protest at Wilson's sacrifice of principle, and others were grumbling that the treaty was thoroughly bad. To the former group he seemed rigid and uncompromising, to the latter weak and uncertain in his stand on principle. A careful study of the record reveals an extraordinary consistency in Wilson's fight for his program under overwhelming difficulties, as well as a high degree of political intelligence in translating the abstract principle of his program into concrete details of application.

The President's understanding of the real issues involved in the Saar case was superior to that of his own experts, and that was the only issue where he stood completely alone against everyone in Paris. In the Polish case, he was convinced by the arguments of Lloyd George as to the long-term results of a settlement based on the Polish Commission's report and loyally supported Lloyd George's efforts to modify that settlement in the face of the Polish sympathies of the American experts. He withstood steadfastly Colonel House's pressure to compromise on the Colonial question, the Rhineland, the Saar, the Adriatic. His worst defeats were the Reparations settlement and Shantung; the first occurred while Wilson was ill, when Colonel House abandoned the American program; the second, because of an impregnable political and diplomatic position held by the Japanese.

Throughout the conference Wilson maintained his stand on principle as the only safe guide in a welter of conflicting interests, as the sole safeguard against laying foundations for future conflict. That was the meaning of his attempt to force an admission from Colonel House that the pro-French proposals of the American experts for the Saar valley were a violation of the Fourteen Points. The record for the crucial April period is eloquent testimony to the President's perspective and force, and Fiume is the final symbol. In the nature of the case, Wilson's role—aside from the arduous work in the League of Nations Commission—had to be negative rather than constructive, to concern itself with prevention rather than cure. Consequently the failure of his curative and constructive work, as the result primarily of American refusal to ratify the treaty and enter the League of Nations, has obscured the real nature of his achievement at Paris. It is so much easier to record failures than to carry through the laborious task of assessing a man's work by careful measurement of what he prevented, as well as by study of positive achievements.

Perhaps the most general criticism President Wilson has encountered, at the time and since, has been on the score of his decision to attend the Peace Conference in person. The decision itself was attributed to excessive vanity, and the effect has generally been described as the degradation of the remote and lofty, almost godlike arbiter to a bloody and battered contestant in the European prize ring. The assumption is that Wilson in Washington could have retained his detachment with an ultimate power of decision while delegating the rough-and-tumble of negotiation to Colonel House in Paris. It is interesting that Secretary Lansing and Colonel House, who agreed upon practically nothing else, should have consistently concurred on the unwisdom of the President's coming to Paris. Independently, they tried in advance to prevent it; subsequently, they communed over the misfortune of the event. Yet, in view of Lansing's attitude toward Colonel House, it is difficult to imagine his acquiescing in the Colonel's primacy in Paris. It is possible that each man in the assurance of his own superior wisdom felt confident of exercising greater influence in Wilson's absence.

The present book affords the most positive answer on this point. The record clearly shows that on every major question but that of Reparation, the Treaty of Versailles would have been a worse treaty had Wilson remained in Washington. With all his mistakes, he emerges as the only man of real stature at Paris.

WOODROW WILSON: PRO AND CONTRA

He is standing at the throne of a God whose approval he won and has received. As he looks down from there, I say to him: "I did my best. I am doing it now. You are still the captain of my soul."

—Newton D. Baker, speaking at the Democratic National Convention, 1924

It was the human spirit itself that failed at Paris. . . . It was not Wilson who failed there, but humanity itself. It was not the statesmen that failed, so much as the spirit of the peoples behind them.

—General Jan Smuts, 1921

God gave him a great vision.
The Devil gave him an imperious heart.
The proud heart is still.
The vision lives.

—William Allen White

In fact arguments, however soundly reasoned, did not appeal to him if they were opposed to his feeling of what was the right thing to do. Even established facts were ignored if they did not fit in with this intuitive sense, this semi-divine power to select the right. Such an attitude of mind is essentially feminine.

—Robert Lansing

Byzantine Logothete

—Theodore Roosevelt, harking back to the Byzantine officials who wrote notes to the barbarians instead of resisting them

Edouard Réquin, Musée de la Guerre

Left to right: Clemenceau, Wilson, Lloyd George, Orlando

I had to deal in the peace conference with two men, one of whom thought he was Napoleon and the other Jesus Christ.

—Clemenceau, referring to Lloyd George and Wilson

Mr. Wilson and his dynasty, his heirs and assigns, or anybody that is his, anybody who with bent knee has served his purpose, must be driven from all control, from all influence upon the government of the United States.

—Henry Cabot Lodge at the Republican National Convention, 1920

THE OPEN DOOR VERSUS THE RISING TIDE OF REVOLUTION

Walter Lippmann's analysis of "The Malady of Democratic States" is a gloomy forecast of the passing of democracy, at least as we have understood it, through the weakening of will and the destructive effects of war. These conditions, more than intelligent self-interest or humane instincts, have led to the collapse of the West's colonial empires, but the old antagonisms remain and are grist to the mill of those heretical Westerners, the communists. Indeed, the enemies of the West insist that its science, its prosperity, and its democracy would have been impossible without the resources of the colonial world. Moreover, they continue, the West has by no means surrendered real control but uses its financial power and its corporate efficiency to hold the former colonies as economic tributaries.

They point to the United States as the incontrovertible proof of their claim. Now it is certainly true that the United States has been the most dynamic force in this century. There have been two sides to this. It has regarded itself as spreading the creative urge and a willingness to experiment with the new and to trust the common people with political power and a high standard of living. Its critics challenge every point and portray it as a juggernaut crushing all aspirations to political and cultural self-determination and economic independence. A historian might reason that extremes rarely represent truth, and we do not intend here to try to prove either.

There is, however, a view of the origins and nature of American dynamism which does much to explain the course of events in this century and which must be treated with respect. William Appleman Williams of the University of Wisconsin has offered an interpretation of American history in which the key word is *expansion*, sometimes territorial but always economic. Essentially, he says, democracy has worked because America has been able to engage in continuous expansion, and the reason it has developed such a psychopathic fear of revolutions in this century is that they threaten to block the further expansion of private enterprise.

As Williams sees it, the United States (imitating Britain) chose to evade socialism by assuring an Open Door to private exploitation of its vast resources and internal market, and as the need arose expanded this exploitation to the Pacific. Expansion then took the form of an Open Door for American trade, with the intention to "stabilize the world in a pro-American equilibrium." Actually, as

Williams acknowledges, certain elements in this thesis have been stated by Brooks Adams, Turner, Beard, Potter, and anti-expansionists from the 1830's onward, though they were not thinking in terms of evading socialism but rather of equalizing opportunity. See, for example, David Potter's *People of Plenty*, first published in 1954. Certainly Williams is correct in asserting that as a nation we have sought to escape the necessity of getting down to basics and tackling our problems with the materials at hand.

What is new is the light that Williams casts on the entire course of American history as economically determined, probably (though he does not say that) an equation with monocausal Marxism—which, of course, is by no means the same as communism. At any rate, without intrusive moralizing, he rests his critique of American history on the thesis that the expansion necessary to shore up private property has led from one mishap to another and finally to the brink of destruction. With the most honest and benevolent intentions the United States has exploited the world and bottled up its legitimate aspirations until now it may well be on the verge of an explosion.

Williams proposes a regime primarily dependent on internal construction; trading with other nations freely but without financial pressures; and standing ready to help them to help themselves. Hitherto Americans have usually rejected economic determinism as the key to their history, but there is, nevertheless; a certain credibility to the thesis that economic expansionism has made our foreign policy something less than the beneficent influence we have supposed it to be. It may be that after three decades of struggle Americans would welcome an Open Door at home—the state of the world permitting.

Williams' thesis is set forth in *The Contours of American History* (Reprint, Chicago: Quadrangle, 1966), and the foreign policy aspects are treated more fully in *The Tragedy of American Diplomacy*, rev. ed. (N.Y.: Delta, 1962). Here we will offer from the latter book part of Chapter 3 (pp. 86–102) in which Williams gives his explanation of why Wilson and his successors went astray.

Woodrow Wilson's attempt to use America's great power to make the world safe for democracy, and to establish an international order to maintain that security, was an essentially conservative effort. His definition of democracy, his emphasis on preserving that particular society, and the means he proposed to accomplish the task were rooted in the nineteenth-century liberal conception of the world. . . .

American liberalism was a philosophy derived from the axiom and belief that a harmony of interests actually existed and could be secured. Such an underlying community of interest was held to eventuate in community well-being if it was not distorted or thwarted. . . . Founded on a simple (if not crude) concept of natural law, its theory was as neat a circle as ever was drawn freehand. Conflicts of interest were asserted to be mere appearances, or the result of misguided action by others, because the doctrine of a harmony of interests defined them in that fashion. Hence intervention in the social process was necessary and justified only to remove the obstacles placed there by others who did not understand or honor the truth.

Though negative in form, such intervention became very positive in practice, for the theory defined every opponent of the United States as being misadvised about the nature of the world. In a way that John Locke had tended to do in his own philosophical writings which provided the master text for liberalism,

Americans became very prone to define such rivals as unnatural men. They were thus beyond the pale and almost, if not wholly, beyond redemption. Reinforced by an expansionist, or frontier, interpretation of history that explained nationalistic expansion as a necessary and justified part of natural law, the theory was further supported by ethnic and religious prejudices. The final result was that domestic problems became international problems, for it was necessary to remove the restrictions upon America's natural right to resolve its domestic difficulties by natural expansion. . . . [Americans] were neither hypocrites nor sophists; they simply accepted and believed the idea that American expansion naturally improved the world—as well as being necessary for their own democracy and prosperity. . . .

Wilson . . . transferred his approach to domestic affairs to the problems of foreign policy. His conception of the League of Nations, for example, was clearly evolved in that fashion. And for Wilson, as for his predecessors and successors, the Open Door Policy was

ORGIE MANIACLE

ALL FOR DEMOCRACY

ALL FOR HONOR

ALL FOR WORLD PEACE

ALL FOR JESUS

EDITOR   CAPITALIST   POLITICIAN   MINISTER

Permission of Dr. Robert L. Leslie

A caustic socialist criticism of World War I

America's version of the liberal policy of informal empire or free-trade imperialism. None of them had the slightest idea of organizing the co-operative, planned, balanced economic development of world resources. Wilson aimed to use American power, inside and outside the League of Nations, merely to order the world so that such classical competition could proceed in peace. If this could be done, he was confident that American economic power could take care of the United States—and of the world. . . .

The convergence of the reformist and economic expansionism generated enthusiasm for America's mission in the world. The frontier interpretation of American history, having been modernized to fit an industrial society, was once again becoming an article of faith—just as its agrarian version had done in the 1830's and 1840's. Americans increasingly considered themselves once more on the move to "extend the area of freedom."

But this new enthusiasm in the United States developed at a time when classical liberalism was coming under heavy criticism in much of the world. Thus there were many doubts about the *kind* of freedom that America was extending, as well as above the morality of doing so. In addition to questions about the economic effects of such overseas expansion, there was also skepticism about some of its political and social characteristics. An increasing number of foreigners was aware, for example, that political and social democracy in the United States were largely limited to white Anglo-Saxons.

When transferred to the world scene, those color and ethnic restrictions became even more apparent. Democracy tended in practice to be replaced by an outlook summarized in the familiar phrase about the white man's burden. That approach was based on the quite different thesis that colored people were somehow never ready for democracy and self-government. It was possible, of course, to defend various limitations on democracy and representative government on logical as well as historical and practical grounds. Indeed, a very great deal of intellectual and emotional energy was invested in that effort by Americans, as well as by Europeans with colonial empires to defend.

Such arguments were not very strong, however, because political democracy had begun, even in the white Western countries, as a process in which only a small segment of the adult population participated. Colored peoples pointed out, quite plausibly, that their societies were already structured for such a form of democracy. And when, as was the case with American liberalism, it was further implied, if not vehemently asserted, that democracy *really* worked only for white, Anglo-Saxon, Protestant Christians, the appeal of democracy suffered even more. For this argument led rather rapidly to the conclusion that even at best democracy meant little more than the modification of colonialism in the direction of less harsh protectorates or open-door imperialism.

For these reasons, American liberalism's definition of democracy as it pertained to self-determination and colonialism lost much of its democratic content once it moved beyond Western Europe. Colonial societies began to realize that America's anticolonialism neither implied nor offered freedom from extensive and intensive foreign influence. . . .

At best, Wilson's actions were in keeping with the principles of a moralistic and paternalistic open-door imperialism. At worst, he intervened with force in the affairs of other nations. America's verbal support for the principle of self-determination became in practice the reordering of national boundaries in Europe on the basis of ethnic and linguistic criteria. Though it had considerable relevance for Western Europe, this principle and practice of nationality had less meaning in Eastern Europe —and still less throughout the rest of the world. But it was not even applied to many areas. Japan was treated as an inferior, for example, and the colonial empires were hardly touched. They were most certainly not broken up into independent states according to the principle of self-determination. And even though some im-

provements did result from the mandate system where it was applied, that approach was characterized by minimum changes in the existing pattern of colonialism.

Taken seriously, a commitment to the principle of self-determination means a policy of standing aside for peoples to make their own choices, economic as well as political and cultural. It is based on a willingness to live and let live—a broad tolerance for other peoples' preferences and a willingness, if the opportunity is offered, to help them achieve their own goals in their own fashion. It is the philosophy of an integrated personality, and it might be defined as the foreign policy of a mature society. Though it avowed this principle, the actions of America in the realm of foreign affairs did not follow this pattern. Hence it was not surprising, as Wilson's actions became apparent, that many peoples of the world felt misled by Wilson's slogans about self-determination. It was one thing to shape one's own culture, but quite another to be pushed aside while others haggled over ethnic statistics and then drew lines on a map.

As suggested by many of his actions in Mexico, and by his call for war without quarter until Germany erected a government that "we can trust," Wilson's liberal practice was not in keeping with his liberal principles. This became even more apparent as he began to reveal his ideals about a League of Nations. That program amounted to a direct and almost literal application of the principles of America's domestic liberalism to the world at large. The League of Nations became the state, and its function was to maintain order and enforce the rules of the game at the international level. Given such security, the national pursuit of self-interest would, according to the doctrine of a harmony of interests, produce peace and prosperity throughout the world.

Beyond that point, however, the attempt to formulate an international system on the principles of such liberalism encountered a difficult issue. It was simple to say that the League corresponded to the state, but it was not at all easy to specify the power structure of the international state. The logical answer defined it as a Parliament of Man, but that did not answer the question; it only asked it in a different way. It was still necessary to specify such mundane but vital things as the nature of the franchise and the institutional structure of the government. Wilson answered such questions by combining his concept of America's supremacy with the political theory of classical liberalism. Every nation could vote, but nothing could be done without the prior existence of a concert of power (or harmony of interests) among the big nations. That was as weighted a franchise as ever proposed under the name of liberalism, particularly since Wilson assumed that America (in association with Great Britain) would lead the concert of major powers.

Considered on its own merits, the idea of a concert of power among the strongest nations had much to recommend it on the grounds that it assigned responsibility to those with the ability to make basic decisions. But when judged against the rhetoric and principles of classical liberalism it was quite clearly a contradiction in terms. For by the key tenet of liberalism, namely the existence of a harmony of interests, it was possible to produce the general welfare only under conditions of free competition. Yet by establishing an oligopoly of power, and formalizing it in an unconditional guarantee of "the territorial integrity and existing political independence" of the nations admitted to the League (on criteria prescribed by the oligopoly itself), Wilson's proposal destroyed the possibility of free competition. And it was precisely on this point that the League of Nations was attacked by some American liberals themselves, as well as by radicals and conservatives in the United States and throughout the world. . . .

[Wilson thus refused to alter the status quo save by the "slow process of reform," and alienated many liberals who wished to alter certain institutions—particularly private property—which were throttling liberalism's "natural harmony of interests." Radicals, notably the communists, rejected all the assumptions of liberalism and proposed to turn management of production and consumption of goods and services over to the state, and thus assure their equitable distribution.]

As for color or ethnic origins, they denied the validity of such criteria as the basis of any decision, an attitude that enabled them to avoid Wilson's contradiction between self-determination and nationality and the exclusiveness of his Protestant Christianity and Anglo-Saxonism. In this way, radicals appealed to all men across all existing—or proposed—boundaries.

Their approach to self-determination gave the radicals a double-edged weapon against colonialism and the less overt forms of imperial expansion such as the Open Door Policy. For by asserting the right of self-determination, they identified themselves with anticolonialism, which was the lowest common denominator of nationalism, yet also aligned themselves with the more developed and specific expressions of nationalism. Thus they offered leadership to those who wished to end formal colonialism, as well as to others who sought to assert their full sovereignty against spheres of influence and similar restrictions established under the Open Door Policy.

In the broadest sense, therefore, the radicals offered the peoples of the world an explanation of their existing hardships, a program to end such difficulties and build a better world, and leadership in that common effort. This radical assault on classical liberalism and conservatism was a direct challenge to Wilson and to the United States. And through the communist victory of November 1917, in Russia, all those separate revolutions—in economics, politics, social values, and international affairs—seemed to become institutionalized in a nation of tremendous potential.

Though obviously of great importance to an understanding of American diplomacy in the twentieth century, the Bolshevik Revolution and the subsequent rise of the Soviet Union as a thermonuclear power can nevertheless be overemphasized to the point of creating serious errors of analysis and interpretation. Indeed, that very preoccupation (and the warped perspective that it created) does a great deal to explain many otherwise perplexing actions by American leaders. It helps tremendously, for example, to account for the near-panic manifested by otherwise perceptive, intelligent, and sober men when Castro sustained his power in Cuba. And in a broader sense, it offers considerable insight into the way that American leaders persistently interpreted political and social unrest throughout the world as a consequence of the Bolshevik Revolution, and also into the way that they steadily expanded the nation's commitments beyond a rational calculation (even by the axioms of their expansionist *Weltanschauung*) of the country's resources.

This myopic and self-defeating preoccupation with the Bolshevik Revolution existed long before the Soviet Union orbited a man in space. Fundamentally, and from the outset, American leaders were for many, many years more afraid of the implicit and indirect challenge of the revolution than they were of the actual power of the Soviet Union. . . . From 1917 to 1950, the United States had, *and knew it had*, a preponderance of power as compared to the Soviet Union. . . .

It thus seems clear that the great majority of American leaders were—like President Wilson—concerned so deeply with the Bolshevik Revolution because at bottom they were so uneasy about what Wilson called the "general feeling of revolt" against the existing order, and about the increasing intensity of that dissatisfaction. From this it follows that the Bolshevik Revolution was only the symbol of all the revolutions that grew out of that discontent. And that is perhaps the crucial insight into the tragedy of American diplomacy.

Those other specific and general revolutions would have continued and come to their climaxes even if the Bolsheviks had never seized power in Russia. They were revolutions that had been fed and sustained by the policies of the West itself for more than a century. American policy was fundamentally no more than a sophisticated version of those same policies.

The underlying nature of the tragedy is defined by the confrontation between those two elements, not just or primarily by the conflict between the United States and the Soviet Union. The tragedy was of course dramatized, and unquestionably made more intense, by the way that American leaders reduced all such revolutions to the Bolshevik Revolution. Indeed, their behavior could be offered as a textbook example of the reductionist fallacy. Or, to use a metaphor from daily life, they blinded themselves at the outset of their search for an answer to the "general feeling of revolt" that disturbed them so much.

It is vital to realize, therefore, that the radical and revolutionary impact was not limited—even between 1917 and 1921—to events in Russia. On the European scene, communists came to power in Hungary and showed strength in Germany; and the heretical liberals attacked the status quo in England and other countries. The Arab Revolution in the Middle East, while it was predominantly anticolonial and nationalistic and was led by liberals and conservatives, nevertheless represented the international elements of the broad radical movement. A similar pattern emerged in the Far East. Chinese revolutionaries, some of whom did look to Russia for advice and leadership, asserted their rapport with the radical challenge —on domestic as well as international issues. And Japanese conservatives (and liberals), who asserted their nationalistic and ethnic equality with the West, pre-empted certain radical policies as weapons for their own purposes. All of these developments, considered individually and en masse, posed serious problems for American leadership at the end of World War I.

Confronted directly by the opposition overseas, Wilson faced still other difficulties. His original hope to establish a concert of power with Great Britain and France was weakened by their initial opposition to certain of his proposals. The revolutionary ferment in Europe, Asia, and the Middle East only intensified the determination of the imperial powers to retain and strengthen their existing empires. A similar reaction occurred in America, and Wilson's coalition for the crusade to make the world safe for democracy disintegrated into a great internal struggle over what policy would enable America to assert its power most effectively in dealing with Japanese and European competitors and the wave of revolutions engulfing the world.

Wilson's personal dilemma symbolized the broader difficulties faced by classical liberalism. According to the basic principles of natural law, he should have accepted the revolutions as competing units which would contribute their share to a broader and deeper harmony of interests. But his expansionist philosophy of his-

tory, his Calvinism, and his nationalism—which also were integral parts of his liberalism—prompted him to oppose the revolutions as barricades on America's road to domestic well-being and world leadership. The tragedy was defined by his attempt to resolve the dilemma by preserving and extending democracy through a policy of open-door expansion.

His approach satisfied neither his own followers nor the foreigners who looked to America (and to Wilson in particular) for a creative alternative to the revolutionaries. Instead, it left the battleground to the conservatives and the radicals. By attempting to achieve security through the traditional policy of the open door, America's conservatives emphasized the weakest aspects of Wilson's own program. And the liberals, having failed to offer a positive and effective alternative of their own, had in the end no place to go but into a bipartisan alignment with the conservatives.

13

NORMALCY AND ABNORMALCY

INTRODUCTION

America's present need is not heroics but healing; not nostrums but normalcy; not revolution but restoration; not surgery but serenity; not the dramatic but the dispassionate; not experiment but equipoise; not submergence in internationality but sustainment in triumphant nationality.

> —Senator Warren G. Harding of Ohio, speaking in Boston, May 14, 1920. The speech was written by Professor Jacob Hollander of Johns Hopkins, and Harding misread "normality" as "normalcy."

Progressivism and World War I had seen the culmination of a surge toward fulfillment of Wilson's interpretation of the American mission. It was a magnificent effort, but it carried penalties. By 1920 the people had been under a quarter-century of moral tension, a tension too great to support. They looked about them and saw the promises of the progressive leaders failing to materialize, but on the contrary saw prices shooting up with inflation, and war profiteers riding in limousines and living in mansions. The old ambivalence toward Europe was revived as people listened to the sly tales told by returning soldiers of the European civilization to which Americans had long looked for cultural guidance. Worst of all, Europe had turned Versailles into a struggle, not for peace or democracy, but for spoils, and had tried to shame the United States into underwriting their booty. There was a growing conviction that moral ideals had been betrayed by a cynical Europe, and many Americans in turn became cynical about any hope of international justice or cooperation.

The plain fact was that the nation had relapsed into normalcy as soon as the war was over (in certain respects even before that), and the election of 1920 only regularized the decision. The "normalcy" which the Old Guard preached meant two things: retreat from all foreign obligations which might hamper complete freedom of action in the international political sphere; and the cleansing away of a number of the domestic reforms of the Progressive Era. The Old Guard's strategy was to read new meanings into antimonopoly legislation both by administrative decisions and by packed courts. The architects of the new day might have admitted that they were being clever, but they would have indignantly denied any imputation of dishonesty. "It is not that the courts flout statutory law," said one of them, "but that they interpret it in harmony with economic law. They are changing with the people and the times."

That the reaction first took the form of nativist opposition to Old World ideas and interests is not strange, for distrust of Europe was a traditional part of the ambivalent American pattern. One may question, however, the honesty of the attempt made in certain quarters to blame Europe. Rather, it may be that, having looked into the great world of responsibility, Americans preferred to retreat to the playland of adolescent irresponsibility. Still, it was not the moral thing to do, so they sought to excuse their conduct by interpreting it as an attempt to remain pure and undefiled. Quite clearly the country had once more—as after the Civil War—entered a period when democracy was overshadowed. Having rejected the moral course, people denied that it was the moral course; the transition to a rather general acceptance of materialist standards was then easy and natural. The *status quo* gave them material prosperity or the chance to acquire it; hence anything that questioned the *status quo* was suspect. Democracy by its very definition questions things as they are; so there was a mounting distrust of it, and a surge of fear and intolerance which sought human sacrifices—and found them. Liberals were persecuted as Reds; Negroes, Jews, and Catholics were hounded because they were *different* in color or religious mores; and for a moment the clock was set back by a new attempt to censor and direct personal thinking and morals.

The confusion which followed the retreat from the American mission was of course not all due to the fact of retreat. It may well be that it would have come even had there been no war. The technological revolution with its new social techniques would have occurred in any case, and the clash which it brought between new and old standards would have introduced an age of uncertainty, frustration, and social disintegration. But the 1920's were too complex to be described in simple terms. There was another side. In Chapter 1 we examined expositions of oligopoly and countervailing power, developments which were changing the economic complexion of America—we can hope for the better. True enough, the times were also in the grip of a speculative craze, and presently we shall turn to Galbraith for an account of its results. True also, agriculture and a number of industries were in depression long before 1929 with results that were almost revolutionary among many farmers and workers. The fact was that the economy was overdue for an overhaul, and these very conditions were to bring on the crisis which led to reform.

Normalcy was not only a time of social transition but of social improvement. Psychiatrists and professional social workers were learning to deal with the maladjusted and the poverty-stricken with understanding. The public was learning about economic and social fundamentals, a fact which presently began to affect public institutions and services, and to promote laws regulating corporations, the tariff, and the stock market. The citizen learned more about the world at large and this was reflected in the difference in his attitudes after World War I and World War II. It was this generation, as we shall see, which rose to the crisis of Depression and to a new challenge to world responsibility.

DISCONTENT UNDER NORMALCY

[The New Deal was not something new and strange to America, but it grew out of pragmatic experience and the discontents of the 1920's. This was the thesis of Arthur M. Schlesinger, Jr., in his article "Sources of the New Deal: Reflections on the Temper of a Time" in *Columbia University Forum*, 2:4–12 (Fall 1959). The following is that portion of the larger essay which describes the discontents of the 1920's.]

The official order in the Twenties presented perhaps the nearest we ever came in our history to the identification of the national interest with the interests, values and goals of a specific class—in this case, of course, the American business community. During the generation before Harding, the political leaders who had commanded the loyalties and the energies of the American people—Theodore Roosevelt and Woodrow Wilson—expressed strains in American life distinct from and often opposed to the dominant values of business. They represented a fusion of patrician and intellectual attitudes which saw in public policy an outlet for creative energy—in Lippmann's phrase, they stood for mastery as against drift. In the service of this conception, they led the people into great national efforts of various sorts, culminating in the convulsive and terrible experience of war. Two decades of this—two decades under the glittering eyes of such leaders as Roosevelt

and Wilson, Bryan and La Follette—left the nation in a state of exhaustion.

By 1920 the nation was tired of public crisis. It was tired of discipline and sacrifice. It was tired of abstract and intangible objectives. It could gird itself no longer for heroic moral or intellectual effort. Its instinct for idealism was spent. "It is only once in a generation," Wilson himself had said, "that a people can be lifted above material things. That is why conservative government is in the saddle two-thirds of the time." And the junior official to whom he made this remark, the young Assistant Secretary of the Navy, also noted soon after his unsuccessful try for the Vice-Presidency in 1920, "Every war brings after it a period of materialism and conservatism; people tire quickly of ideals and we are now repeating history." . . .

Yet, for all the material contentment of the Twenties, the decade was also marked by mounting spiritual and psychological discontent. One could detect abundant and multiplying symptoms of what Josiah Royce, after Hegel, used to call a self-estranged social order. The official creed began to encounter growing skepticism, and even opposition and ridicule, in the community at large. Able and ambitious groups, denied what they considered fitting recognition or opportunity, began to turn against the Establishment.

If the economic crash of 1929 astonished the experts, a spiritual crash was diagnosed well in advance. "By 1927," reported Scott Fitzgerald, "a widespread neurosis began to be evident, faintly signalled, like a nervous beating of the feet, by the popularity of crossword puzzles." In the same year Walter Lippmann pointed more soberly to the growing discrepancy between the nominal political issues of the day and the actual emotions of the people. If politics took up these real issues, Lippmann said, it would revolutionize the existing party system. "It is not surprising, then, that our political leaders are greatly occupied in dampening down interest, in obscuring issues, and in attempting to distract attention from the realities of American life."

What was wrong with the New Era was not (as yet) evidence of incompetence or stupidity in public policy. Rather, there was a profound discontent with the monopoly of power and prestige by a single class and the resulting indifference of the national government to deeper tensions. Those excluded from the magic circle suffered boredom, resentment, irritation and eventually indignation over what seemed the intolerable pretensions and irrelevances of their masters. Now it is the gravest error to underrate the power of boredom as a factor in social change. Our political scientists have pointed out convincingly how the human tendency toward inertia sets limits on liberalism; I wish they would spend equal time showing how the human capacity for boredom sets limits on conservatism. The dominant official society—the Establishment—of the Twenties was an exceedingly boring one, neither bright

nor witty nor picturesque nor even handsome, and this prodded the human impulse to redress the balance by kicking up heels in back streets.

All this encouraged the defection of specific groups from a social order which ignored their needs and snubbed their ambitions. Within the business community itself there were dissident individuals, especially in the underdeveloped areas of the country, who considered that opportunities for local growth were unduly restrained by Wall Street's control of the money market. The farmers felt themselves shut out from the prevailing prosperity. Elements in the labor movement resented their evident second-class citizenship. Members of foreign nationality groups, especially the newer immigration and its children, chafed under the prevalent assumption that the real America was Anglo-Saxon, Protestant, middle-class and white. In time some of the younger people of the nation began to grow restless before the ideals held out to them; while others, in accepting these ideals, acquired a smug mediocrity which even depressed some of their elders.

Gravest among the symptoms was the defection of the intellectuals: writers, educators, newspapermen, editors—those who manned the machinery of opinion and who transmitted ideas. The fact of their particular estrangement and discontent guaranteed the articulation, and thus, to a degree, the coordination of the larger unrest. The intellectuals put the ruling class in its place by substituting for its own admiring picture of itself a set of disrespectful images, which an increasing number of people found delightful and persuasive; the insiders, who had before been seen in the reverent terms of Bruce Barton and the *American Magazine*, were now to be seen less reverently through the eyes of H. L. Mencken and Sinclair Lewis. Satire liberated people from the illusion of business infallibility and opened their minds to other visions of American possibility. The next function of the intellectuals was precisely to explore and substantiate those other visions. They did so with zest and ingenuity; and the result was that, beneath the official crust, the

Twenties billowed with agitation, criticism and hope. Dewey affirmed man's capability for social invention and management; Beard argued that intelligent national planning was the irresistible next phase in history; Parrington insisted that Jeffersonian idealism had a sound basis in the American past, and indeed, expressed a truer Americanism than did materialism. Together the satirists and the prophets drew a new portrait of America—both of the American present and of the American promise—and the increasingly visible discrepancy between what was and what might be in America armed the spreading discontent.

The well of idealism was rising again; energies were being replenished, batteries recharged. Outsiders were preparing to hammer on the gates of the citadel. The 1928 election, in which an Irish Catholic challenged Yankee Protestant supremacy, illustrated the gathering revolt against the Establishment. And, though Hoover won the election, Samuel Lubell has pointed out that "Smith split not only the Solid South but the Republican North as well.". . . A Democratic victory would surely have meant the discharge into public life of able and ambitious people denied preference under a business administration—much the same sort of people, indeed, who eventually came to power with the New Deal; and it would have meant new opportunities for groups that had seen the door slammed in their faces in the Twenties—labor, the farmers, the ethnic minorities, the intellectuals.

FAMOUS WORDS IN THE TWENTIES

We won the war!

> —American boast, some distance from being a fact

Only saps work!

> —Stock exchange slogan

Every day in every way, I'm getting better and better.

> —Dr. Coué solemnly guaranteed that if one repeated this several times a day it would guarantee success.

All I ever did was supply a demand. They talk about me not being on the legitimate. Nobody's on the legit. You know that and so do they.

> —"Scarface Al" Capone, feeling sorry for himself

You can't teach an Old Guard new tricks.

Our country has deliberately undertaken a great social and economic experiment, noble in motive and far-reaching in purpose.

> —Candidate Hoover, 1928, on Prohibition

One can imagine the pious chagrin of a patent medicine advertiser who supposed that he had been lying to 100,000 readers, when he was lying to only half the number because the publisher was lying to him.

—John T. Flynn

Keep Cool with Coolidge.

—Republican slogan in 1924

They hired the money, didn't they?

—Calvin Coolidge, referring to the Allied war debts

I do not choose to run for President in 1928.

—Calvin Coolidge

We in America today are nearer to the final triumph over poverty than ever before in the history of any land.

—Herbert Hoover, 1928

THE ECONOMIC BATTLE AMONG THE DEMOCRACIES

The postwar period was to show in tragic detail the seeming determination of the democracies to pull down the pillars of the temple of Western Civilization they had built with such toil during the last few centuries. No one knows whether if the United States had joined the League it would have become the effective instrument Wilson envisioned for the solution of world problems. As it was, the League was handicapped by the Covenant's provision for unanimity of decisions, and this became a fatal weakness in view of the way in which the great powers promptly fell to quarreling. The result was to weaken and divide the democracies, encourage the growth of predatory totalitarianism, and finally to precipitate a conflict which on several occasions could have been nipped in the bud had the democracies stood together. Until almost the eve of the final explosion they had the power. What they lacked was the foresight and the will.

In a sense the war had been fought to defend laissez faire against German regimentation, and there was some relief at being able to renew the old game of cutthroat competition after having been hampered by obligations to allies. Neo-mercantilism, which had come in with the resurgence of imperialism, was now bolstered by tariffs, subsidies, quotas, trade blocks, and barter agreements. The tariff policy and the marketing methods of the United States were partly to blame, but there were also the rivalries among the powers and the succession states. In their attempts to make themselves self-sufficient, largely for military reasons, the flow of trade was hampered and the standard of living was frequently lowered.

The succession states broke up the traditional trading areas. Indeed, the continent was so broken up by self-determination that it would have been almost impossible to introduce the savings of mass production, even had the élite been willing to abandon its ideal of service to the few.

By what has already been said, it is clear that the United States had its share in the democracies' failure to meet the developing world crisis. It had retreated into political isolation, but economically it entered on a course of conquest, encouraged quite often by Secretary of Commerce Herbert Hoover. The State Department did all it could to foster the Open Door all over the world for American finance and trade, but the policy of conquest was essentially set by the great corporations and was based on the same ruthless and cold-blooded laissez faire doctrines as were being followed by the financial interests of the European democracies.

The American economic invasion of the world began long before World War I, but its most serious phase followed upon the war. This fact is explained primarily by three factors. First, the war had grievously weakened the European economy, but it had filled American coffers with surplus capital which needed an outlet. Second, American technology (again partly because of the war) had stepped up the rhythm of production to the point where a surplus of goods existed and had to be gotten rid of.

Third, the new technology of the United States needed a number of raw materials which the country did not produce in satisfactory quantities, but which foreigners manipulated so as to create an artificial scarcity and raise the prices; among these may be named rubber, tin, tungsten, vanadium, and jute. Fourth, the United States had to face the fact that it was approaching the end of the more easily exploited supplies of some of its own raw materials, especially petroleum, copper, nickel, and aluminum. Both petroleum and metals had become the bases of powerful industries which were determined to gain access to foreign sources. Last, businessmen partook of the dynamism of their young and vigorous country and delighted in the creativeness of the factory and the excitement of the marketplace.

War itself does not increase wealth, but it shifts bases and brings into play new technologies and opens new markets. It is quite true that the war slowed the American rate of increase of wealth, but it almost ruined Europe. The war had all but stripped Europe of liquid capital, and Europe had to depend upon the United States for much of the machinery and fertilizer essential to restore production in factories and on the farms. A coordinated international economic effort would probably have forestalled the coming age of crisis, but the American people had turned their back on "foreign entanglements," and the Harding administration was jittery over any act which could be interpreted as an entanglement. American business was merrily engaged in scuttling even the mild controls of the New Freedom, and it would certainly have vetoed any American effort to aid Europe on a no-return basis as a misuse of public funds and a violation of the businessman's right to make a profit. On the other hand, Europe would certainly have protested with one voice against American gifts accompanied by any coordinated plan of recovery.

The Fordney-McCumber Tariff was the Old Guard's response to the primary postwar depression. Even while the United States was denying its markets to foreign goods, its industrialists were demanding access to the markets of other nations. The American tariff stimulated a world movement toward the erection of trade barriers and tariff walls, but Americans found ways to get under, over, or around them. One way was to purchase or erect factories in foreign countries and make goods designed in America. Another way was to make big loans to foreign governments and enterprises in return for the opening of new markets.

The advantages which the United States now enjoyed in production made it wish to get access to all markets where it could undersell European goods, though it still did not wish to lower its own tariff wall, and the Hawley-Smoot Tariff of 1930 actually raised it again. Change had to wait for the New Deal, when the United States began to negotiate a long series of tariff-reduction agreements under the influence of Cordell Hull. On the other hand, Europe was now raising tariff barriers, and so it resented American attempts to tear them down and blamed these for world economic deterioration. Certainly economic decline had already set in, and the Hull treaties, though intended to counteract it, came too late. At any rate, by 1942 the Hull treaties had lowered tariff rates almost 30 percent under those of 1933. The United States was to make this attack on neomercantilism a condition of the lend-lease aid which it granted to co-belligerents during World War II.

As American business began to look abroad for a market for its surplus goods and capital, its salesmen, engineers, and bank representatives began to establish themselves in foreign cities. Hoover's Department of Commerce men invaded the world with their slide rules and statistical abstracts and probed shrewdly for openings into which goods and capital could be poured. Then, of course, there were the American tourists, who were the backbone of the resort business almost everywhere.

But it was the machine that was the real invader, either actually or by its products and methods. It revolutionized marketing, for it refused to be impressed by international boundaries but regarded the world as an integral market. It found ways to suit product and advertising to each race and climate, not even forgetting to picture the American car as driven by a blonde in Sweden and by a brunette in the Mediterranean. American corporations crept under national barriers by buying or building factories in the desired marketing area. They had abundant capital for repairs and modernization, or could plunge in initial construction costs. They could profit by a backlog of expensive research, designing, and business and production techniques which could have been worked out only in a mass-production country. They could pay higher wages and could wait for profits.

The superiority of American goods in quality, attractiveness, or cheapness forced European competitors to adopt American methods or face ruin. But the European countries did not have the capital, resources, or market to build up native mass-production industries. They could not and would not accept higher labor costs, which alone could build a market. When labor demanded higher wages and shorter hours, industrialists answered that such things were against the laws of economics. The rebuttal that they were being given in America only turned the wrath of the industrialists against the United States. Quite clearly it was menacing the foundations of the European order, where the élite—the social, economic, and intellectual leaders and their families—had exercised the greater share of control.

True enough, Europeans sought to learn from the United States. Engineers, especially Germans, streamed across the Atlantic, and hundreds of their reports appeared in book form. Ford's *My Life and Work* sold 300,000 copies in Germany alone. There was a lively movement to adapt American machinery to European conditions. Automobiles and agricultural implements had to be lightened, while coal cutters had to be redesigned for the thinner European coal seams. Cartels were formed to unite nations into profitable mass-production and marketing areas. As it was, the adoption of American business, marketing, and production methods was more striking than the changes in the product.

Europe could not go all the way toward mass production, either for economic or for psychological reasons. Germany, the industrial heart of the continent and industrially the most forward-looking, recognized the advantages of mass production and seriously sought to introduce it as a means of restoring its old hegemony. Though the government devoted a quarter of the national income to the change-over, all it did was to create labor dislocations, lose foreign trade, and hasten the coming of Hitler. It is true that the Nazis were able to clear away some obstacles to production, but complete success was hampered by several factors. There was the German petty official's affinity for red tape and ritual. There was the thriftiness which made it impossible to throw away a fairly new but still obsolete machine and replace it by a better one. But most important of all was the failure to put into effect the spirit of freedom on the part of workers and engineers, which is the core of the American know-how. The result was that German industry did not success-fully introduce American machine methods (with a few exceptions) but remained based on the skilled worker. German engineers saw that they were blocked and warned that in case of a second conflict with America, Germany was doomed to defeat. If Germany failed to implement mass production, it was not likely that any other nation could succeed. Britain was even less successful than Germany in adopting American methods, but it reacted with a "confident over-conservatism." The habit of winning had bred an optimism which took too little note of realities.

The new Russia was in its technological aspects peculiarly the child of Amer-ica. Throughout the 1920's American engineers, either hired singly or representing engineering or manufacturing firms, swarmed into Russia, and some of them remained through the 1930's. "Fordism" was carried to Russia by Ford engineers, and the word entered the language to denote the ruthless speed-up and stretch-out more usually called Stakhanovism. Curiously enough, this phenomenon was on the increase in the boasted "workers' state" while it was decreasing in capitalist Amer-ica. This is one reason why the Russians failed to profit fully by American teaching. In the United States the worker and engineer retained the spirit of freedom; it brought discontent and strikes, but it also brought a cure to abuses and a certain pride in sharing in production. In Russia all decisions had to be made in conformity with rigid ideological principles which destroyed the spirit of freedom.

American culture and institutions were regarded by Europeans as mere exten-sions of the machine; certainly America owed much of its ability to develop social services and activities to the surplus afforded by the machine. The European accusation was that American society was the slave of the machine. Nevertheless, Europe was fascinated by ways and things American. American slang came into use, often amusingly warped out of its true meaning. Bars, cocktails, dances, food, clothes, bobbed-hair styles, and card games imported from America became the mode, and the slim American woman replaced the plump Viennese woman as the standard of Paris fashion. American competitive sports, particularly basketball, found considerable vogue over the world. The art and serious music of America received little attention until after World War II, but "le jazz hot" swept Europe and was being widely though somewhat mechanically imitated. Free clinics and dispensaries, community settlements, free libraries, and the practice of sending out visiting nurses, all were started or stimulated by the American example. John Dewey's Instrumentalism made headway, and wider and better educational facilities were provided, often on the American model. Hollywood motion pictures had the cachet of showing American scenes, fashions, dances, and living conditions. It was not intended as propaganda, but European politicians and businessmen rightly regarded it as that. Not only did the American movie sell American sewing machines, kitchen gadgets, athletic equipment, and intercom sets, but it spread dissatisfaction with living and working conditions—which perhaps was all to the good. At one time in the 1920's, as high as 90 percent of the moving pictures shown in Europe were of American origin.

The leaven of America was adding to the ferment already under way in the world. It was destroying Europe's colonial prestige and was ruining the snug berths of the social and economic élite. This was not merely a matter of economic rivalry. The élite view was that the masses were incapable of absorbing culture and that it must be preserved as the precious heritage of a select few. Europe's workers may or may not have been capable of enjoying the physical or cultural advantages which the élite regarded as their own perquisites, but they nonetheless resented the arrogant assertion that they could not or should not. Most frightening of all to Europe's dominators was an uneasy feeling that sooner or later economic power would result in passing the leadership in the arts and sciences to America.

The European movement to restore its position of world preeminence or at least to stave off further American encroachment took on two principal forms, one propagandistic and the other financial. Propaganda was carried on in Europe itself, in the United States, and in the traditional colonial and other marketing areas. The arguments presented to Europeans stemmed chiefly from the assertion that American government and capital were engaged in a deliberate plot to conquer the world economically and culturally. Germans had given the name *Amerikanismus* to the process of Americanization; to Europeans it meant (as Eric Fischer has expressed it) the "conversion of the world into a purely materialistic state, where economic interests and power prevail." Americans admitted the fact of the Americanization of the world, but they saw it as the spread of the creative urge and a willingness to experiment with the new and to trust the people with political power and with a high economic standard.

When hostile European critics analyze American "ideals," they are not likely to select the ones noted above which *we* regard as most characteristic. Rather, they are inclined to take three others, which they insist are dominant if not all-inclusive: materialism, standardization, and quantitativeness. It is difficult for Americans to realize that in the eyes of many intelligent Europeans we are as much "faceless men" as the subjects of any dictator. Standardization, they say, not only prevents the preservation of precious diversities and the discovery of new values but promotes mediocrity and shoddiness; not only did our ruthless efficiency promote the standardization of goods, but it arose from a standardization of soul which was evident well over a century ago. There is some proof for this, however directly it may contradict the mythus of the pioneer individualist. On the other hand, the purchasing power provided by standardization is boosting the American market for specialty goods to the point where it has become a mainstay not only of importers but of domestic manufactures.

The third accusation, that the United States possesses a quantitative civilization in comparison to Europe's qualitative civilization, has considerable truth. Critics assert that this rises from democracy's gospel of equality, which has been forced to sacrifice the esthetic because the masses cannot understand or appreciate the fine and the beautiful; therefore the fine and the beautiful will perish unless there is an aristocracy to cherish them. This is the accusation that hurts the most because it conceivably could turn out to be true. America is built upon a splendid faith that, given time, the masses can become aristocrats in the best sense of the word. If we fail, all that can be said is that at least it was worth trying once in history.

European propagandists against America frequently used the same arguments in their imperial possessions, and because they were appealing to a native élite of nobility or education they had considerable success. It was possible also to use the argument there that squeezing of wages and inflation of prices were due to American economic imperialism. The argument had some success and may have helped to delay the crest of the wave of native revolt until after World War II. The native élite who then came into control found the argument useful in hushing the murmurs of the masses. The bogy of American imperialism was also invoked in the Latin-American nations, which had a long history of political independence and economic dependence.

The European propaganda directed at the United States had considerable success not only because it was aided by many gaggling Americans but by the American's inner uncertainty and his usual respect (willing or not) for the old centers of Western Civilization. Abusive literature poured from the press and was reprinted and eagerly read in America. André Siegfried's *America Comes of Age* (1927) may well stand for this whole liturgy of abuse which surely must have been inspired by fear. Siegfried saw civilization as the sole possession of France. The United States was placed outside; so were Britain and Germany, though they were permitted a place closer to the fence where they could peer longingly through the pickets. Siegfried's was only one of a flood of anti-American books, which one commentator estimated at about five hundred.

Anyone who studies the domestic history of the 1920's must recognize that the United States forged many of the propaganda weapons used against it, by the ill-advised policies which laid it open to criticism and ridicule. The Fordney-McCumber Tariff led to the accusation that the United States was hogging the world's economic resources, and it doubtless had much to do with the naval race that ensued. Backing down on the League and the added refusal to join the World Court led to charges of hypocrisy. Violation of civil liberties was a vulnerable Achilles' heel; the day of the executions of Sacco and Vanzetti was observed as a day of world mourning, and not only by communists. Years later, in some parts of the world Americans had to stay indoors on the anniversaries of the executions lest they be subject to mob violence. The highhandedness of some American capitalists and their employees gave grounds for agitation in Mexico and the Caribbean, and the Soviet took up the issue with relish. Prohibition, the war debts, and the literature of futility were other handles for anti-American propaganda.

Europe's propaganda posited a gigantic conspiracy between American government and business to conquer and rule the world's economy; the not-too-subtle implication was that America's materialism made it regard economic rule as all that was worth having, for of course it carried with it all necessary power over political action without assuming detailed political responsibility. Actually the American businessman was suspicious of government activities which were not strictly subordinated to business wishes, and this suspicion forbade the centralized planning and direction which would have been essential in carrying out such a plot. True, private business was ready to use the State Department in muscling into foreign control of raw materials, notably petroleum, but there was no suggestion of government control—as there was in Great Britain, where government exercised an influence tantamount to control over banking, communications, shipping, and petroleum. Private business availed itself of Hoover's Department of Commerce studies of foreign conditions and opportunities, but thereafter with a few exceptions it was on its own. American corporations which were producing abroad did not carry with them even the live-and-let-live arrangements which obtained at home; they were competitors, not cooperative conquerors. Most significant of all, Americans failed utterly to see World War I as a step in the development of empire but quite simply and profanely called it a naïve and aberrant moral crusade, whose outcome should have been plain as a pikestaff to anyone not blinded by Wilson's utopian idealism. The view may have been mistaken, but there it was.

Europe's economic struggle against the United States was inextricably connected with government action, for it depended upon government fostering of cartels and upon government subsidization of shipping, support of prices, and erection of tariffs, quotas, barter agreements, and trade blocks. Crux of the struggle and a powerful psychological factor on both sides of the Atlantic was the problem of the war debts. The United States had extended credit in exchange for simple notes bearing interest at five percent but with no specification as to time or conditions of repayment. Including the succession states, the United States had loaned to at least sixteen countries about $7 billion before the Armistice and $3.25 billion thereafter. The issue of the war debts depends on so many intangibles that it is useless to pass judgment on their justice or injustice. On the other hand, it is difficult to defend the economics of the American demand for repayment. The debts had been contracted in the form of credits which were largely expended for American goods and were partly used by Europe to lay the basis for the postwar economic battle. At any rate, the debts could not be repaid in gold; for one thing there was not at the time that much gold in the world, and half of it was already in America. They could conceivably have been paid in goods, but American industry and labor would have united to veto that.

Regardless of the war-debts situation, Europe's economy showed unexpected recuperative ability. Perhaps it is fair to say that it was the psychological factors which in the long run blocked recovery. Most prominent of these was the French fear of Germany. Actually western Germany was the production center of Europe, and the continent could not prosper until Germany recovered. Nevertheless, as German steel masters organized cartels and made them the basis for German economic recovery, France became panicky and early in 1923 occupied the Ruhr industrial area with the clear intention of hampering German steel production. The Weimar Republic (the Second Reich) retaliated by an inflation which reached the point where the gibe was made that marks were worth more as waste paper than as money. France ruined German steel production, at least for a decade, but the effect on the French franc and on the French industrial set-up was to prove disastrous.

Given the French state of mind, it is a question whether even a Marshall Plan would have been of permanent help, but there was little or no disposition in the United States to offer government aid. This was a job for bankers. Accordingly in 1924 an international commission recommended the Dawes Plan for the rehabilitation of Germany, and this was supplemented in 1929 by the Young Plan. They were based upon the granting of British and American loans to counter the damage worked by the occupation of the Ruhr and the inflation of German currency. The Dawes and Young Plans marked the fact that American capital was venturing abroad in competition with Britain. The latter was now under serious handicaps. Its supply of liquid capital was small and was needed at home to modernize old and start new industries. On the other hand, it needed to make foreign investments to stimulate foreign trade. In this dilemma Britain resorted to earmarking, that is, loans were made abroad on condition that the recipients buy British. Washington discouraged such tactics by American bankers, but the bankers often got the same result by such subterfuges as installment selling. Meanwhile British capital feared losing control of its own industries to American investors. British General Electric sought to prevent this by prohibiting American stockholders from voting; this practice had to be abandoned lest it provoke an American capital boycott and lead to retaliation against British investors abroad. Actually, the various European corporations sought to limit control by foreigners of any nationality; thus the Swedish Match Trust limited foreigners to 1/1000 of a vote per share.

The American people and the American government may have been short-sighted in their economic policies, but the latter did encourage loans to foreign states and corporations. All together, up through 1929 about $12 billion of private capital went abroad, though of course not all of it was owing at one time. In all governments, officials are frequently interchangeable with finance and industry, but the State Department did not go as far toward an amalgamation of government and business policies as did the administration in general. In 1921 the State Department undertook an informal supervision of bankers' loans with the purpose of discouraging loans to countries which were defaulting or which were fighting American trade "unfairly." The department therefore frequently refused to authenticate loans to foreign monopolies, though it seemed to have no prejudice against granting loans in countries ruled by dictators.

Let us now turn to Europe's attempt to save itself by controlling raw materials and the markets for finished goods. The principal instrument used for this purpose was the cartel. In its simplest form the cartel is merely a pool, an agreement to divide materials, production, or markets, or to maintain prices; from this it ranges through various complex forms, but most typically it is a binding intercorporate arrangement which serves the same purpose as a holding company. The cartel on the European continent was often formed with governmental backing and was intended to balance the resources and mass market which gave American industries unrivaled competitive bases.

German cartels hoped to dominate their fields, and some of their rivals in smaller countries were sucked into cooperation by a desperate desire to save what they could. Germany's inflation had given a few industrialists a chance to concentrate industry to an extent unprecedented in their country, and the Dawes and Young Plans had provided funds to bring the German industrial plant up to date. Germany's new plant and its patent controls put it in the position to dominate many cartels, and presently Hitler found in Hjalmar Schacht a financial genius who could manipulate these to build up Germany's national power.

Steel and munitions had been under the control of cartels even before World War I, and the postwar years saw an extension of the system into numerous other fields, especially chemicals. These cartels were able to force British and American industries to cooperate or else to form rival cartels. Inducements to those ends were persuasive, for the cartels' division of markets enabled American members of cartels to do as they pleased at home or gave them a part of the domestic or foreign market safe from foreign interference. American competitors frequently allied with competing cartels; thus the Rockefeller and Ford interests allied with Germany's I. G. Farben, while Morgan and Du Pont allied with British Imperial Chemical Industries. American corporations were able to enter into these agreements because the Webb-Pomerene Act of 1918 permitted combination in selling agencies for purposes of foreign trade, and this act was in 1924 expanded by the Federal Trade Commission to permit price fixing and allotting export orders.

European governments frequently backed their national cartels, and such articles as rubber, coffee, nitrates, potash, tin, camphor, sisal, iodine, mercury, and Egyptian long-staple cotton had their prices artificially pegged at high levels. Favorite devices were to exclude foreign ownership of sources or means of production, and to lay embargoes and export restrictions. Whether or not foreign controls were aimed at the United States, they bore hardest upon it. Though this country used one half of the mineral production of the world, it was deficient in thirty materials of vital importance in industry and warfare. The conflict over control of raw materials and markets literally covered the earth, outside of the Soviet Union. It was particularly vicious in the struggle over rubber, petroleum, tin, copper, and nickel. Rivalry was extended to cables, radio channels, aviation lines, and merchant shipping. In some fields, notably in petroleum, compromises were eventually made for joint exploitation by rival companies.

It is difficult to assess the actual extent or success of the American invasion of Europe and of the world. Financially, private citizens of the United States had no more invested in the world during the interwar years than had Britain, nor did they have as much invested in Europe (outside of the war debts) as did Europe in the United States. American technology and know-how made great strides in Europe, but they did not remake European industry in the American image. American cultural and institutional standards also made headway, but it is even more clear that they did not remake Europe even though their prestige excited much superficial imitation. Perhaps wiser economic, political, and military policies on the part of the United States would have forestalled World War II—but so they might have, also, if exercised by the nations of Europe.

Perhaps in the long run the principal effects of America may be seen to have been its disturbance of the patterns of élite control of economic and political power. In both respects the American example (despite the Depression of the 1930's) remained a menace to the old élite and a symbol of hope for the struggling masses. No doubt this was an element in the political struggle between classes—certainly in Britain and France—which paralyzed government in the 1930's and which encouraged the totalitarians to take their fatal risks. But in looking back it becomes evident that a principal cause of the war lay in the cutthroat rivalries of the democracies. Like the Babylonian monarchy, they had been weighed in the balances and found wanting.

THE COLOSSUS OF ECONOMIC EMPIRE

Why, if we are an Empire, have we failed to demand the slightest extension of our national sovereignty? If we are imperialistic, why have we not annexed the Caribbean and Central American States when it has been within our powers to do so? Why, if we are in quest of world-power, do we advocate naval disarmament, limit our ability to defend our Pacific possessions, and seek to outlaw war as an instrument of policy? The world is puzzled and irritated by our ambiguous attitude. We are not playing the game in the conventional way. That we are not adverse to wealth and power is obvious. It is not yet obvious that we prefer to acquire wealth and power through indirect, non-political methods. By its annual trade-balances, its foreign loans, its domestic prosperity, and the huge volumes of its imports and exports, the United States is creating an economic empire over most of the planet. In the conventional Old World sense, it is not an empire at all and is unlikely to become one. It involves no political expansion, menaces the sovereignty of no foreign nation, displaces existing allegiances, languages, flags, and loyalties in no quarter of the globe. Yet year by year, our economic power, operating within the accepted limits of American policy, has grown until the United States now bestrides the Western Hemisphere like a Colossus and casts long shadows over Europe and Asia. While Europe and Asia invoke their policies and their armaments to obtain for them a place in the economic sun, the American empire is intangible, invulnerable, an influence over the minds and customs of mankind which is confirmed every time the world installs an adding-machine, dances to jazz, buys a bale of cotton, sells a pound of rubber, or borrows an American dollar.

—John Franklin Carter, *America's Painless Imperialism*
(N.Y.: Harcourt, Brace, 1928), pp. 3–4

THE GREAT CRASH

[The Harvard economist, John K. Galbraith, has analyzed the basic causes of the stock market collapse and of the ensuing Great Depression in a readable book, *The Great Crash: 1929* (N.Y.: Houghton Mifflin, 1961). Here we give part of his summary, found between pages 173–193, and which can profitably be read in connection with the section in Chapter 1, "The Prospects of American Capitalism," by Daniel Bell. Professor Galbraith first pointed out the existence of a great speculative orgy, then examined the reasons why economic activity turned down in 1929, and why once started down it continued to decline for a decade. We begin at this point.]

There seems little question that in 1929, modifying a famous cliché, the economy was fundamentally unsound. This is a circumstance of first-rate importance. Many things were wrong, but five weaknesses seem to have had an especially intimate bearing on the ensuing disaster. They are:

1) The bad distribution of income. In 1929 the rich were indubitably rich. The figures are not entirely satisfactory, but it seems certain that the 5 per cent of the population with the highest incomes in that year received approximately one third of all personal income. . . .

This highly unequal income distribution meant that the economy was dependent on a high level of investment or a high level of luxury consumer spending or both. The rich cannot buy great quantities of bread. If they are to dispose of what they receive it must be on luxuries or by way of investment in new plants and new projects. Both investment and luxury spending are subject, inevitably, to more erratic influences and to wider fluctuations than the bread and rent outlays of the $25-a-week workman. This high-bracket spending and investment was especially susceptible, one may assume, to the crushing news from the stock market in October of 1929.

2) The bad corporate structure. . . . American enterprise in the twenties had opened its hospitable arms to an exceptional number of promoters, grafters, swindlers, impostors, and frauds. This, in the long history of such activities, was a kind of flood tide of corporate larceny.

The most important corporate weakness was inherent in the vast new structure of holding companies and investment trusts. . . . Dividends from the operating companies paid the interest on the bonds of upstream holding companies. The interruption of the dividends meant default on the bonds, bankruptcy, and the collapse of the structure. Under these circumstances, the temptation to curtail investment in operating plant in order to continue dividends was obviously strong. This added to deflationary pressures. The latter, in turn, curtailed earnings and helped bring down the corporate pyramids. . . . It would be hard to imagine a corporate system better designed to continue and accentuate a deflationary spiral.

3) The bad banking structure. . . . Although the bankers were not unusually foolish in 1929, the banking structure was inherently weak. The weakness was implicit in the large numbers of independent units. When one bank failed, the assets of others were frozen while depositors elsewhere had a pregnant warning to go and ask for their money. Thus one failure led to other failures, and these spread with a domino effect. . . . This happened after 1929. Again it would be hard to imagine a better arrangement for magnifying the effects of fear. . . .

4) The dubious state of the foreign balance. This is a familiar story. During the First World War, the United States became a creditor on international account. In the decade following, the surplus of exports over imports which once had paid the interest and principal

on loans from Europe continued. The high tariffs, which restricted imports and helped to create this surplus of exports remained. However, history and traditional trading habits also accounted for the persistence of the favorable balance, so called.

Before, payments on interest and principal had in effect been deducted from the trade balance. Now that the United States was a creditor, they were added to this balance. . . . Other countries which were buying more than they sold, and had debt payments to make in addition, had somehow to find the means for making up the deficit in their transactions with the United States.

During most of the twenties the difference was covered by cash—i.e., gold payments to the United States—and by new private loans by the United States to other countries. Most of the loans were to governments—national, state, or municipal bodies—and a large proportion were to Germany and Central and South America. The underwriters' margins in handling these loans were generous; the public took them up with enthusiasm; competition for the business was keen. . . .

[But eventually the borrowers were faced with the consequences of borrowing beyond their means to repay.] This meant that they had either to increase their exports to the United States or reduce their imports or default on their past loans. President Hoover and the Congress moved promptly to eliminate the first possibility—that the accounts would be balanced by larger imports—by sharply increasing the tariff. Accordingly, debts, including war debts, went into default and there was a precipitate fall in American exports. The reduction was not vast in relation to total output of the American economy, but it contributed to the general distress and was especially hard on farmers.

5) The poor state of economic intelligence. To regard the people of any time as particularly obtuse seems vaguely improper, and it also establishes a precedent which members of this generation might regret. Yet it seems certain that the economists and those who offered economic counsel in the late twenties and early thirties were almost uniquely perverse. In the months and years following the stock market crash, the burden of reputable economic advice was invariably on the side of measures that would make things worse. . . . Asked how the government could best advance recovery, the sound and responsible adviser urged that the budget be balanced. Both parties agreed on this. . . .

There was also the bogey of "going off" the gold standard and, most surprisingly, of risking inflation. Until 1932 the United States added formidably to its gold reserves, and instead of inflation the country was experiencing the most violent deflation in the nation's history. Yet every sober adviser saw dangers here, including the danger of runaway price increases. . . .

The rejection of both fiscal (tax and expenditure) and monetary policy amounted precisely to a rejection of all affirmative government economic policy. The economic advisers of the day had both the unanimity and the authority to force the leaders of both parties to disavow all the available steps to check deflation and depression. In its own way this was a marked achievement—a triumph of dogma over thought. The consequences were profound. . . .

It is in light of the above weaknesses of the economy that the role of the stock market crash in the great tragedy of the thirties must be seen. . . . The collapse in securities values affected in the first instance the wealthy and the well-to-do. But we see that in the world of 1929 this was a vital group. The members disposed of a large proportion of the consumer income; they were the source of a lion's share of personal saving and investment. Anything that struck at the spending or investment by this group would of necessity have broad effects on expenditure and income in the economy at large. Precisely such a blow was struck by the stock market crash. In addition, the crash promptly removed from the economy the support that it had been deriving from the spending of stock market gains.

The stock market crash was also an exceptionally effective way of exploiting the weaknesses of the corporate structure. Operating companies at the end of the holding-company chain were forced by the crash to retrench. The subsequent collapse of these systems and also of the investment trusts effectively destroyed both the ability to borrow and the willingness to lend for investment. What have long looked like purely fiduciary effects were, in fact, quickly translated into declining orders and increasing unemployment.

The crash was also effective in bringing to an end the foreign lending by which the international accounts had been balanced. Now the accounts had, in the main, to be balanced by reduced exports. This put prompt and heavy pressure on export markets for wheat, cotton, and tobacco. Perhaps the foreign loans had only delayed an adjustment in the balance which had one day to come. The stock market crash served nonetheless to precipitate the adjustment with great suddenness at a most unpropitious time. The instinct of farmers who traced their troubles to the stock market was not totally misguided.

Finally, when the misfortune had struck,

the attitudes of the time kept anything from being done about it. This, perhaps, was the most disconcerting feature of all. Some people were hungry in 1930 and 1931 and 1932. Others were tortured by the fear that they might go hungry. Yet others suffered the agony of the descent from the honor and respectability that goes with income into poverty. And still others feared that they would be next. Meanwhile everyone suffered from a sense of utter hopelessness. Nothing, it seemed, could be done. And given the ideas which controlled policy, nothing could be done.

Had the economy been fundamentally sound in 1929 the effect of the great stock market crash might have been small. Alternatively, the shock to confidence and the loss of spending by those who were caught in the market might soon have worn off. But business in 1929 was not sound; on the contrary it was exceedingly fragile. It was vulnerable to the kind of blow it received from Wall Street. Those who have emphasized this vulnerability are obviously on strong ground. Yet when a greenhouse succumbs to a hailstorm something more than a purely passive role is normally attributed to the storm. One must accord similar significance to the typhoon which blew out of lower Manhattan in October 1929.

PROTEST BY A THOUSAND ECONOMISTS

[A striking illustration of Republican indifference to expert advice was shown in May, 1930, when 1,028 professional economists signed a plea asking Hoover to veto the unprecedentedly steep Hawley-Smoot Tariff Bill on the ground that it would reduce foreign trade, deepen the depression, and anger foreign nations—all of which it promptly did. The protest was organized by Paul H. Douglas of the University of Chicago, later a Senator.]

Our export trade, in general, would suffer. Countries cannot permanently buy from us unless they are permitted to sell to us, and the more we restrict the importation of goods from them by means [of] ever higher tariffs, the more we reduce the possibility of our exporting to them. . . .

There are already many evidences that such action would inevitably provoke other countries to pay us back in kind by levying retaliatory duties against our goods. There are few more ironical spectacles than that of the American Government as it seeks, on the one hand, to promote exports through the activity

Permission of New York World-Telegram. Copyright

Talburt warns Congress that the proposed Hawley-Smoot Tariff will upset business.

markets to absorb the increasing output of their machines.

Further barriers to trade will serve them not well, but ill.

Many of our citizens have invested their money in foreign enterprises. . . . These investors, too, would suffer if restrictive duties were to be increased, since such action would make it still more difficult for their foreign debtors to pay them the interest due them.

America is now facing the problem of unemployment. The proponents of higher tariffs claim that an increase in rates will give work to the idle. This is not true. We cannot increase employment by restricting trade. American industry, in the present crisis, might well be spared the burden of adjusting itself to higher schedules of duties.

Finally, we would urge our government to consider the bitterness which a policy of higher tariffs would inevitably inject into our international relations. The United States was ably represented at the world economic conference which was held under the auspices of the League of Nations in 1927. This conference adopted a resolution announcing that "the time has come to put an end to the increase in tariffs and to move in the opposite direction."

The higher duties proposed in our pending legislation violate the spirit of this agreement and plainly invite other nations to compete with us in raising further barriers to trade. A tariff war does not furnish good soil for the growth of world peace.

of the Bureau of Foreign and Domestic Commerce, while, on the other hand, by increasing tariffs it makes exportation ever more difficult.

We do not believe that American manufacturers, in general, need higher tariffs. The report of the President's Committee on Recent Economic Changes has shown that industrial efficiency has increased, that costs have fallen, that profits have grown with amazing rapidity since the end of the World War. Already our factories supply our people with over 96 per cent of the manufactured goods which they consume, and our producers look to foreign

THE ORDEAL OF HERBERT HOOVER

[Herbert Hoover, as Secretary of Commerce, had been one of the spokesmen for a moderate, and responsible version of laissez faire, and in 1922 had published a book entitled *American Individualism* which in essentials expressed the faith of the businessman in the decade of the 1920's. The pressures of politics during the Depression forced him sometimes to take positions he might have preferred to avoid, but he was by no means the callous figure his numerous critics portrayed. Carl N. Degler in an article under the above title in *The Yale Review*, 52:563–583 (Summer 1963) cogently analyzes the strengths and weaknesses of Hoover and

makes the point that he was a "transitional figure in the development of the government as an active force in the economy in times of depression." Only the last few pages are reprinted here, but they summarize very cogently the true role of Hoover.]

As one reviews the actions which Hoover took it is impossible to describe him as a do-nothing president. He was unquestionably one of the truly activist presidents of our history. But he was an activist within a very rigid framework of ideology. Of all American presidents, Herbert Hoover was probably the most singlemindedly committed to a system of beliefs. His pragmatism was well hidden and what there was of it emerged only after great prodding from events. To a remarkable degree, one can observe in his acts as president those principles of individualism which he set forth so simply in his book ten years before. The very same principle, for example, which prevented his sanctioning federal relief to the unemployed, dictated the tone and content of his veto of the bill to create a government corporation to operate Muscle Shoals. The government, he said, should not compete with private enterprise. Moreover, such a project, by being run by the federal government, abrogated the basic principle that all such enterprises should be "administered by the people upon the ground, responsible to their own communities, directing them solely for the benefit of their communities and not for the purposes of social theories or national politics. Any other course deprives them of liberty." It was this same belief in individual freedom and cooperation which kept him from accepting a governmental system of old age and unemployment insurance. He advocated such measures only when undertaken voluntarily and through private insurance companies.

Even the Reconstruction Finance Corporation, perhaps his most enduring anti-depression agency, was created to assist private business, not to supplant it. True, it was a credit agency in competition with private enterprise, but it was designed to perform tasks which no private institution dared risk; the competition was

therefore minimal if not nonexistent. Moreover, although it has been frequently alleged that the RFC lent money to corporations while the Administration denied relief to the unemployed, in Hoover's mind the distinction was crucial and real. The RFC was making loans which would be repaid—and most were—when the banks got back on their feet; it was not making grants. Even when Hoover did permit the RFC to lend money to the states for relief purposes he still insisted that no grants of federal funds be made.

But there was an even more important social justification for agencies like the RFC and the Federal Home Loan Board, which Congress created in July 1932 at the President's request. Hoover recognized as no president had before that the welfare of society was dependent upon business and that government, therefore, must step in. He did this, not because, as some critics said, he favored business over the common people, but because he recognized that if the banks failed the economy would collapse, savings would be lost, and jobs destroyed. The RFC and the Federal Home Loan Board, in effect, socialized the losses of financial institutions by using government to spread their obligations through society. Hoover was not prepared, though, to socialize the losses of the unemployed. That step in ameliorating the impact of the Depression was undertaken by the New Deal through the WPA and other relief agencies. In this respect Hoover was a transitional figure in the development of the government as an active force in the economy in times of depression. He was the first to smash the old shibboleth of government unconcern and impotence.

Perhaps his long-term role was even greater. In the face of great opposition and much outright hostility, he made a determined and even courageous effort to give the business community and voluntary private agencies a chance to show whether they could bring the nation out of a depression. Their failure to do so gave a moral as well as a political impetus to the New Deal. . . . After Hoover's Administration no one could say that government had rushed in before other social or economic agencies had been given a try. That this was so goes a long way toward explaining the remarkable consensus among Americans ever since the 1930's that government has the prime responsibility for averting or cushioning the effects of a depression.

A second principle which stopped Hoover from permitting the federal government to provide relief was his conviction that the budget must not be unbalanced. As early as February 1930 he warned the Congress against extravagance and told of his own efforts to economize. Economy was essential, he emphasized, in order to avoid increasing taxes. But as decreasing revenues began to fall behind expenditures, Hoover's concern to keep the budget in balance overcame his reluctance to increase taxes. On July 1, 1931 the deficit was almost $500 million—an astronomical figure in those days when the total federal budget was less than $4 billion. In December of that same year Hoover recommended an increase in taxes. . . . [After considerable delay Congress passed] one of the largest peacetime tax increases in American history.

Today it seems incredible that in a time of economic slump when consumer purchasing power was the principal requirement for recovery, the nation should elect to take money out of the hands of consumers. Yet this was precisely what the bill, recommended and signed by the Republican President and passed by the Democratic House, entailed. . . .

From the record, then, it is evident that Democrats were in no better theoretical position to deal with the Depression than Hoover. Leaders of both parties thought of the government as a large household whose accounts must be balanced if national bankruptcy were to be avoided. Neither party could conceive of the central role which government must play in the economy in an industrial society in time of depression. It would take the whole decade of the New Deal and the continuance of the Depression before that fact would be learned by leaders and people alike.

Despite his fixation on the question of the budget, Hoover's conception of the Depression was sophisticated, rational, and coherent; the remedies he suggested were equally so, given his assumptions. In trying to find a way out, Hoover placed most reliance on what modern economists would call the "expectations" of businessmen. If businessmen feel that times are good or at least that they are getting better, they will invest in new plant and equipment, which in turn will employ men and create purchasing power. In substance, the remedies Hoover offered were designed to raise the expectations of businessmen and to maintain purchasing power until the economy picked up again. His first step was securing agreement among businessmen to hold the line on wages in order to keep purchasing power from falling. (And, by and large, as a result of his efforts, wage rates did not fall until the middle of 1931, but employment did, with, unfortunately, the same effect.) A second step in his program was to use government to help out with public work projects and, when private agencies proved inadequate, to provide credit through agencies like the RFC and the Home Loan Board. Finally, as a third arrow in his anti-depression quiver, Hoover sought, through the prestige of his office, to create that sense of confidence and approaching good times which would encourage businessmen to invest. As it turned out, though, he gambled and lost. For with each successive ineffectual statement, the value of his words dropped, until, like the worthless coins of a profligate monarch who debases his own coinage, they were hurled back at his head by a disenchanted press and people.

The Hoover recovery program failed, but probably no government program then thought permissible could have been any more successful. Certainly the New Deal with its more massive injection of government money into the economy succeeded little better. It ended the decade with 9.5 million still unemployed, and industrial production remained below the 1929 level throughout the 1930's except for a brief period in late 1936 and early 1937. On the other hand, most of the countries of Western and Central Europe regained the 1929 level of production by early 1935. . . .

All through the Depression, Hoover's unvarying theme was that all this would pass and the essential vigor of the American economy would reassert itself. Undoubtedly he counted too heavily on the influence of his words to overcome the lack of business confidence, but there is no question of his optimistic outlook. One measure of it was the shock he received when he read Roosevelt's address to the Commonwealth Club in San Francisco. That was the speech in which Roosevelt talked about the frontier being ended and opportunities for economic growth being limited. Hoover took up the challenge, denying "the whole idea that we have ended the advance of America, that this country has reached the zenith of its power, the height of its development. That is the counsel of despair for the future of America. That is not the spirit by which we shall emerge from this depression." The important point is that such pessimism was really not expressive of Roosevelt's thought, either. . . . The speech belied his abundant enthusiasm for the future, and his deep faith in the country and its capacities. Moreover, he soon contradicted its import in his Inaugural Address, when he electrified the country with the cry, "All we have to fear is fear itself."

How ironical that these words of Roosevelt should be so well known, when it was Herbert Hoover who all along had been saying the same thing—in less graphic and less credible language, to be sure—but saying it nonetheless. That fact, too, contributed to the ordeal of Herbert Hoover.

THE GREATEST INNOCENT BYSTANDER IN HISTORY

[Hoover] suppressed the drama which another man, with a politician's instinct for heroizing himself in any crisis, might have turned to his own advantage. If he had any illusions, and certainly the President had few, . . . one was a blind faith that some way democracy in the end would be able to see with its own eyes the truth. He believed that the people could see it clearly and logically without drama, without a hero in whose struggles they could see a story, and so feel their way to the truth. But, alas, the President was wrong in attributing a logical habit of mind to men in the mass. They must emotionalize their thinking. They need a story. They learn their truth in parables. He will be known as the greatest innocent bystander in history. But history will also write him down an earnest, honest, intelligent man, full of courage and patriotism, undaunted to the last.

—William Allen White, *Autobiography*, pp. 634–635

THE SWOPE PLAN FOR THE STABILIZATION OF INDUSTRY

[On September 16, 1931, Gerard Swope, President of General Electric Company, brought before the public a plan for bringing back prosperity by setting aside the antitrust laws and enabling industry to minimize wasteful competition. Much of the plan was devoted to extending "welfare capitalism" to almost the entire population of wage earners, but nothing was said about workmen protecting their interests by unionization. When business leaders laid the Swope Plan before the presidential candidates in 1932 Hoover rejected it as fascistic; Roosevelt accepted it, and later made it the basis of the National Industrial Recovery Act. The following excerpts from the Plan are taken from the version that appeared in *Monthly Labor Review*, 33:1049–1057 (Nov. 1931).]

In the situation that confronts us at the present, the most disturbing aspect is that men who are able to work, who are competent workers, who above all things desire work, can not find work to do. That this condition has ever been present in such periods detracts nothing from its wrongness. That industry must evolve and make effective those measures which will first ameliorate and ultimately eliminate it, must be the reaction of everyone who gives thought to what is taking place. I say that industry must do this thing, because it will surely be done. . . .

Coordination of production is impossible under our present laws, and it is vain to think of their amendment or repeal unless the public is assured of the constructive nature of the steps industry will take, and that the interests of the public will be adequately safeguarded.

The general principles underlying what I am going to say are as follows:

1. Every effort should be made to stabilize industry and thereby stabilize employment to give to the worker regularity and continuity of employment, and when this is impracticable, unemployment insurance should be provided.

2. Organized industry should take the lead, recognizing its responsibility to its employees, to the public, and to its stockholders—rather than that democratic society should act through its government. . . .

If either the individual States or the Federal Government act, the power of taxation has no economic restraints.

3. There should be standardized forms of reports. . . .

4. Production and consumption should be coordinated on a broader and more intelligent basis thus tending to regularize employment and thereby removing fear from the minds of the workers as to continuity of employment; as to their surviving dependents in case of death; and as to old age. This should be done preferably by the joint participation and joint administration of management and employees. These things can not be done by an individual unit—organized industry must do them.

5. If organized industry is to undertake this work, every effort should be made to preserve the benefits of individual originality, initiative, and enterprise, and to see that the public is assured that its interests will be protected, and this can be done most effectively by working through the agency of the Federal Government.

There is nothing new or original in what I am proposing. I am merely bringing together well-considered propositions that have found support, including some that have been put into actual practice.

The following plan is offered as a means to correlate into a comprehensive whole the at present undirected efforts of forward-looking business enterprises toward stabilization; for the further development of industry and commerce; for the protection of employees and stockholders; for the best service to the public and in general the best interests of society. Legislation will be required to make such a plan possible, including the probable modification of some existing laws.

An outline of the more important features follows:

1. All industrial and commercial companies (including subsidiaries) with 50 or more employees, and doing an interstate business, may form a trade association which shall be under the supervision of a Federal body referred to later.

2. These trade associations may outline trade practices, business ethics, methods of

standard accounting and cost practice, standard forms of balance sheet and earnings statement, etc., and may collect and distribute information on volume of business transacted, inventories of merchandise on hand, simplification and standardization of products, stabilization of prices, and all matters which may arise from time to time relating to the growth and development of industry and commerce in order to promote stabilization of employment and give the best service to the public. Much of this sort of exchange of information and data is already being carried on by trade associations now in existence. A great deal more valuable work of this character is possible.

3. The public interests shall be protected by the supervision of companies and trade associations by the Federal Trade Commission or by a bureau of the Department of Commerce or by some Federal supervisory body specially constituted. . . .

8. For the protection of employees, the following plans shall be adopted by all of these companies:

[Here follow detailed proposals for pensions, life and disability insurance, workmen's compensation, and unemployment insurance, financed and administered jointly by employers and employees.]

It's all part of a great big plan.

Hutton, permission The Philadelphia Enquirer

14

TOWARD AN UNDERSTANDING OF THE NEW DEAL

INTRODUCTION

Doubtless it will be many generations before the last word is said on the origins, nature, and effects of the New Deal, so what is given hereafter must be by way of an interim report. For a couple of decades, historians tended to present it as probably the most far-reaching change since the Civil War, but it remained moot whether it was revolution or accelerated evolution.

Recently the purists of the New Left have come forward with their "presentist" bias and severe moral judgments. They criticize the New Deal because it did not boldly strike out in new directions—as socializing the means of production and frankly organizing the underprivileged as a new political base to supplant the smugly sterile middle class. The criticism was also made in the 1930's by a number of New Dealers (not to mention the chronically dissatisfied radicals), but they yielded to what they conceived to be political necessities. Certainly the New Deal failed (for whatever reasons) to solve the fundamental problems of American society, and its economic solutions are far from being fully tested. Still, it is well to bear in mind Solon's maxim: A lawgiver should attempt only as much good as the people can bear.

THE OLD PROGRESSIVES AND THE NEW DEAL

[The moot problem of whether the New Deal was the continuation and fulfillment of progressivism is examined by Otis L. Graham in *An Encore for Reform: The Old Progressives and the New Deal* (N.Y.: Oxford, 1967), of which we give extracts taken from pages 180–186. As Graham sees it, most of the surviving Old Progressives were dismayed by the New Deal's reliance on big government, its class legislation, and its concern with economic security.]

Progressivism, in its larger aspect individualistic and oriented toward freedom from both the conditions and the sensation of restraint, was not to be fulfilled in a movement that increased the power of the meddling state. Focusing always on what was morally right, and finding that invariably in a state of mind that looked beyond self and class, the progressives felt defeated by any "reform" that accepted special claims and honored them. Aimed at unifying the American people, progressivism would produce few men who, even after the social education acquired during lengthy careers in public affairs, could accept frank class legislation.

With such goals as they had, in fact, they could hardly have met with any substantial success. Centralization was the forecast for America, in industry, in government, in demography. Only those progressives who limited their hopes to a more humane treatment of the poor were able to find satisfaction in the achievement of Roosevelt's general welfare state. A short time before he died in 1933, George Record, speaking for those progressives whose original and sustaining impulse had been to restore the small-town synthesis their fathers had presumably enjoyed, was able to sum up their efforts in a sentence: "I think if you are going to write the history of that movement you ought to write it from the standpoint that it was a failure."

The student of history sees in a longer perspective what any American observes in his lifetime, the inexorable democratization of our common life—the enlargement of political rights, material security, meaningful freedom. Liberalism is the name of the movement that, through ideas and political action, has sought to hasten this process. In an era when institutions and social patterns are transformed in every generation, it is not just the ordinary, conservative citizen who finds himself and his standards outmoded by the arrival of the next generation with its new problems and its inevitable irreverence. Such is the pace of change that the greatest losses of liberalism are by defection. There are men whose function it is at one phase of history to announce new social imperatives to a reluctant community and to demolish the resisting barriers of habit and self-interest; but who, lingering too long, cannot find it in themselves to abandon the issues and techniques of their great campaigns, and all too often become gradually identified with views and social classes which are either irrelevant or reactionary. This was in fact the fate of a great number of the progressives. . . .

Most progressives . . . were troubled by the interventionist state of the 1930's, and went reluctantly, often unwillingly, into a future where the state took on such powers, where the individual counted for so little. It may seem odd that they proved in the end to have such a distrust for a democratic government, since their generation is remembered chiefly for its use of national power. But only a gifted few progressives understood that they were helping to create a new political philosophy. It is easy for us now to see that their era was the crucible where, by the classic Hegelian process, a new political philosophy was in the making. From the time of the Founders there had been two attitudes toward the state: the Jeffersonian, relying upon a minimal state, decentralized institutions and the good sense of the local yeomanry; and the Hamiltonian, at home with vigorous government and a national outlook, but interested before all else in the welfare of the managers and owners of the commercial, banking, and industrial enterprises of the country. By the beginning of this century there was emerging a third, the liberal-collectivist, sharing with the first its democratic sympathies and with the second its national and statist focus. The progressives may have played an important part in this intellectual transition, but they did not do so consciously in most instances.

The progressives may have played an important part in this intellectual transition, but they did not do so consciously in most instances. They had not moved as far from the Founders' fear of political power as their practice suggested. With the example of Italy and Germany before them in the 1930's, they were not convinced that the confident democratic planners of the new school could avoid falling, along with their enlarged state, into the hands of the Hamiltonian plutocrats who knew a few tricks of their own about governing. The progressives were fated to live and act in the age when the tactics and political philosophy of democrats were being altered to take into account the fantastic private governments being erected all around them. They shared in that alteration, but they did not find it intellectually or emotionally easy. The New Deal in part actually mirrored their confusions, and the unreconciled state of American political ideas, but it was less concerned with polity than politics, afraid not of rash action but of not acting at all. It, therefore, despite its apparent good intentions (in which only a minority of them consistently believed), threatened rashly to deliver the hopes of liberalism into the hands of those who wished nothing more than to be handed the instruments of tyranny.

With the American future as the stakes, their crippling apprehensions and confusions are readily forgivable. To accept what Roosevelt and the New Dealers had done and wished to do demanded more openness to experiment with political institutions, more trust in the tractability of the state to democratic purposes, more willingness to turn the cumulated rancor of the lower third against the upper, than most progressives could produce, although these had been the very qualities that had marked them as reformers, sometimes as radicals, in their own day.

TUGWELL'S DREAM

[Anti-New Dealers got a lot of fun out of this bit of free verse written in 1915 by Rexford Guy Tugwell (b. 1891), one of FDR's Brain Trust, and an important architect of reform. Tugwell has lived to have the last laugh, for the New Deal did "make America over."]

I am strong,
I am big and well made,
I am muscled and lean and nervous,

I am frank and sure and incisive.
I bend the forces untamable;
I harness the powers irresistible—
All this I do; but I shall do more
I am sick of a nation's stenches,
I am sick of propertied czars
I have dreamed my great dream of their passing,
I have gathered my tools and my charts;
My plans are fashioned and practical;
I shall roll up my sleeves—make America over!

THE REVOLT OF THE CITIES

[Samuel Lubell is universally recognized as a penetrating analyst of the American political scene. His *The Future of American Politics* (N.Y.: Harper, 1951) did much to explain the "Roosevelt Revolution" by pointing out the spurs to change felt by the cities, the South, the Negroes, and Western farmers. Lubell then examined the role of the new middle class created by the New Deal and the effects of the changing world situation and concluded that the nation has moved into a new political era in which the old rules no longer apply; and that a realignment of parties is under way—thus far benefiting the Democrats, though there is no assurance that this will continue.

Here we will offer a part of his analysis of urban discontents and their effects. By 1930 there had been a great increase in urban population, due in part to the movement from poverty-stricken rural areas, but even more to the foreign-born and their children. The foreign element lived under conditions which they came to resent as they learned about the potentialities of America and as the children acquired schooling. These newcomers had no basic loyalty to either party but their resentments made them ripe for plucking by whichever would satisfy their aspirations.

The Republican Party, coasting on past prestige and devoted to rural and business conservatism, was not attractive. The Democrats were more accustomed to working with urban immigrants and their problems and also could lay some claim to the allegiance of white migrants from the South. Neither party seemed to realize the opportunity, though the evidence was before them in Smith's poll in the cities in 1928, where economic, racial, religious, and cultural differences with the white, Anglo-Saxon, Protestant majority were sharpest.

The following excerpts are taken from the edition of 1965 from pp. 44 to 68 passim.]

The real revolutionary surge behind the New Deal lay in the coupling of the depression with the rise of a new generation, which had been malnourished on the congestion of our cities and the abuses of industrialism.

Roosevelt did not start this revolt of the city. What he did do was to awaken the climbing urban masses to a consciousness of the power in their numbers. He extended to them the warming hand of recognition, through patronage and protective legislation. In the New Deal he supplied the leveling philosophy required by their sheer numbers and by the hungers stimulated by advertising. In turn, the big-city masses furnished the votes which re-elected Roosevelt again and again—and, in the process, ended the traditional Republican majority in this country.

In the elections that followed this same big-city generation would stand like a human wall between the Republicans and their past dominance. It was this generation—now grown to parenthood and in many cases to home-owning, but still bound by common underdog attitudes—which the Republicans had to crack to win and hold the Presidency. . . .

So overwhelming was Roosevelt's 1936 victory, that its political decisiveness is often overlooked. With only Maine and Vermont remaining Republican, Roosevelt's re-election seemed primarily a vote of gratitude for lifting the country out of a desperate economic crisis. Certainly many people favored him for that reason. But 1936 was also the year of realignment in which the Democrats became the nation's normal majority party. The traditional dominance which the Republicans had enjoyed since the Civil War was washed away and a new era in American politics began.

The depression vote of 1932 still mirrored the orbit of conflict of the old Republican order. The G.O.P. cleavage had been mainly a struggle between the "progressives" of the Midwest and Far West against the industrial East. Roosevelt's first campaign was directed primarily toward splitting off this "progressive" vote. His best showing came in the Western and Mountain states. All six states he lost— Pennsylvania, Delaware, Connecticut, Vermont, New Hampshire and Maine—were in the East.

The shift in the basis of Roosevelt's appeal "from acreage to population," to use Raymond Moley's phrase, occurred in 1935. . . . Not only in Washington but throughout the country 1935 was the year of decision. To go back to the old order or to move forward to something different? That was the question posed

for decision in 1935, in countless different ways, in every phase of life.

In the early New Deal days how things were done had been less important than getting the stalled economy going again. By 1935 recovery had progressed to the point where there no longer was any question that the country would be saved. The new issue was: Would the "good old days" of unchallenged business dominance be restored? Or was America to be reshaped? . . .

The formation of the CIO marked the fusing of the interests of the immigrant and native-stock workers, both Negro and white. That, I believe, is perhaps the most telling accomplishment of the CIO. Its political importance can hardly be exaggerated. The mass production industries had been the ones in which racial and religious antagonisms among the workers, were most divisive. . . .

By 1935, of course, the immigrants had made considerable progress toward Americanization. But the key to the change was the rise of a common class consciousness among all workers. The depression, in making all workers more aware of their economic interests, suppressed their racial and religious antagonisms. Put crudely, the hatred of bankers among the native American workers had become greater than their hatred of the Pope or even of the Negro.

This struggle between the old nativist prejudices and the newer class consciousness still remains one of the crucial behind-the-scenes battles in the mass production unions. Class feeling or racial-religious feeling? The future of American labor rests largely on which holds the ascendancy. . . .

Negroes were another voting element which was determined to go forward rather than back. In some cities as many as four out of five Negro families were on relief. "Don't Buy Where You Can't Work" campaigns were being pressed to force white storeowners to hire Negroes. In Harlem the accumulated tensions of the depression years were exploded suddenly by a [destructive riot which]. . . . set off a series of far-reaching changes. Harlem's shopowners hastily put on Negro employees. Before the year was out Tammany Hall had named its first Negro district leader. Mayor Fiorello La Guardia had appointed the first Negro magistrate. In 1932 most Negro voters in the country were still Republican. In 1936, in many cities two of every three Negro voters were for Roosevelt. . . .

A new nationalizing force had clearly been injected into American politics. In the past American political realignments have always followed sectional lines. The Revolt of the City, however, had drawn the same class-conscious line of economic interest across the entire country, overriding not only regional distinctions but equally strong cultural differences.

This development was not without its irony. In drawing the line of cleavage between worker and "economic royalists," Roosevelt unquestionably sharpened the sense of class division in American society. Yet, in doing so, he subordinated the old nativistic prejudices of race and religion, which had divided the lower half of American society for so long, bringing to these lower income elements a greater degree of social unity than they had ever shared before. Was Roosevelt dividing or unifying the country? . . . .

If the 1936 vote marked the emergence of the new Roosevelt coalition, the third-term election brought the crucial trial by fire and water which demonstrated the coalition's durability.

In both 1932 and 1936 Roosevelt would still have been elected without his heavy urban pluralities. In 1940, however, with the war and the third-term issue cutting heavily into his rural strength, the margin of victory that accounted for at least 212 electoral votes was supplied by the dozen largest cities in the country.

In every city I visited while doing a post-election survey I found that the Roosevelt vote broke at virtually the same economic level, between $45 and $60 a month rent. Below that line his pluralities were overwhelming. Above it, they faded away. . . .

In every city one could see the same inexorable spread of numbers and the same leveling pressures. Almost it seemed, in fact, that the Republicans had decided to abandon the cities to the Democratic masses, taking refuge in the suburbs. . . .

As a reporter in Washington I had shared the general belief that the New Deal was hastily improvised and animated by no coherent philosophy. When one translated its benefits down to what they meant to the families I was interviewing in 1940, the whole Roosevelt program took on a new consistency.

The depression had thrown grave strains upon lower income families. Many family heads had lost their jobs, never to be employed regularly again. In some instances, the children were old enough to take over the bread-winning, which often robbed the deposed patriarch of his self-respect. In other families the parents had to struggle along until the children grew of age and took over.

In varied ways the New Deal eased these family strains. Through the HOLC a million homes were saved. Many home-owners were too old to have been able to buy a new home, if they had lost their old ones. With their children grown older, I found, many were renting out part of the house, often to a married son or daughter.

Into the CCC camps went 2,750,000 sons of the cities. No longer a drain on the family larder, they even sent some money back home. Children in high school might get NYA aid. Those who went to work usually did so in low-wage industries where the effects of the wage-hour law were most noticeable.

These and other New Deal benefits did not solve all the family problems by any means. They did ease the adjustments that had to be made as the unfortunates of one generation grew unemployable and another generation finally found its opportunity in defense employment.

The recovery from the depression low helped Roosevelt politically with all groups. It was particularly important in the cities because that recovery coincided with the hatching out of the birth rates of 1910 to 1920 and the rise of a new generation. The very size of the Democratically inclined families helped knit them to the New Deal. Even persons who had done rather well for themselves were likely to have a less fortunate family member lower down the economic ladder being benefited by the New Deal. Old-age pensions and other aid eased the burden of having to care for parents too old to work. Instead of being dragged by family burdens, the rising generation was able to solidify its gains. . . .

Paradoxically, the New Deal also appears to have grown stronger politically after it was abandoned. The outbreak of the war put an end to social reform. But the war boom made unnecessary any additional New Deal measures. In fact, the war succeeded in doing what the New Deal never could accomplish; it brought the country out of the depression. . . .

The defense boom sparked anew the migration from farm to city. It also sparked new vigor into the marriage rate. In the middle 1930's one of four youths in their late teens and early twenties had never had regular work. By 1939 the marriage rate had risen from the depression low of eight to nearly eleven per thousand population. In 1941 it leaped to almost thirteen per thousand.

Economically speaking, then, the defense boom was the happy ending which saved the New Deal and made it a success story. The years of full employment which followed the outbreak of Hitler's War solved the economic problem of the Roosevelt generation, solidifying them in the Democratic party. But in the process this generation changed markedly. Not only had it aged and taken on new responsibilities, but much of this generation had climbed from poverty into the middle class. The rise of this new middle class—whose significance was only dimly sensed even by professional politicians—is worth examining.

SIDELIGHTS OF THE THIRTIES

By God, I never thought I'd live to see this. Why this is a second honeymoon.

—Harold Ickes, FDR's Secretary of the Interior
and a veteran of TR's crusade

We will tax and tax, and spend and spend, and elect and elect.

> —Attributed to Harry Hopkins, 1938, by Frank R. Kent
> and formally denied

For quite a while I have lived in a commuter community that is rabidly anti-Roosevelt and I am convinced that the heart of their hatred is not economic. The real source of the venom is that Rooseveltism challenged their feeling that they were superior people, occupying by right a privileged position in the world. I am convinced that a lot of them would even have backed many of his economic measures if they had been permitted to believe the laws represented the fulfillment of their responsibility as "superior people." They were not permitted that belief. Instead, as the New Deal went on, it chipped away more and more at their sense of superiority. By the second term, it was pressing hard on a vital spot and the conservatives were screaming.

> —Quoted in Eric Goldman, *Rendezvous with Destiny* (1956), p. 289

In the twenties, America hailed Lindbergh as the Lone Eagle; in the thirties, when word arrived that Amelia Earhart was lost at sea, the *New Republic* asked the government to prohibit citizens from engaging in such "useless" exploits.

> —William E. Leuchtenburg

If the archetypical progressive was Jane Addams singing "Onward, Christian Soldiers," the representative New Dealer was Harry Hopkins betting on the horses at Laurel Race Track.

> —William E. Leuchtenburg

The socialistic movement of the 1930's, the socialism of Norman Thomas, could not afford the luxury of the earlier belief in the inevitable course of history. It was forced to take stands on the particular issues of the day. But it too rejected completely the premises of the society which shaped these issues. In effect, the Socialist Party acknowledged the fact that it lived "in" the world, but refused the responsibility of becoming a part "of" it. But such a straddle is impossible for a *political* movement. It was as if it consented to a duel, with no choice as to weapons, place, amount of preparation, etc. Politically, the consequences were disastrous. Each issue could only be met by an ambiguous political formula which would satisfy neither the purists, nor the activist who lived with the daily problem of choice.

> —Daniel Bell, "Socialism: The Dream and the Reality,"
> *Antioch Review*, March 1952

ROOSEVELT'S FAILURE AS A PARTY LEADER

[There is no doubt that the election of 1936 saw the rallying to the Democrats of a grand coalition of elements that had hitherto been politically indifferent or had supported the Republicans. Thenceforth the Democrats took the role of majority party, but it remained a coalition; it never became a tightly bound party, and perhaps could not because of its diverse elements. In later years it lost, at times, the allegiance of the new middle class created by the New Deal, for apparently this element voted for Eisenhower twice, pretty much went for Nixon in 1960, and was split on race issues and the Vietnam War. James MacGregor Burns in *Roosevelt: The Lion and the Fox* (N.Y.: Harcourt, Brace, 1956), pp. 370–380, argues that the failure was largely due to Roosevelt's own shortcomings as a party leader. For one thing, he refused to interfere in state politics until the famous Purge of 1938—and then it was too late. He had not cultivated the loyalty of local candidates and party groups, nor even of the more obscure members of Congress. State leaders were left to build their own organizations free of White House control, with the result that many states were racked by internal feuds and their politicos held bitter resentments against the White House. The Court-packing bill and the Purge gave them opportunities to express their hostilities.]

"If our beloved leader," wrote William Allen White to Farley early in the second term, "cannot find the least common multiple between John Lewis and Carter Glass he will have to take a maul and crack the monolith, forget that he had a party and build his policy with the pieces which fall under his hammer." The perceptive old Kansan's comment was typical of the hopes of many liberals of the day. The President had pulled so many rabbits out of his hat. Could he not produce just one more?

The purge indicated that he could not. The hat was empty. But White's suggestion posed the cardinal test of Roosevelt as party leader. How much leeway did the President have? Was it ever possible for him to build a stronger party? Or did the nature of the American party system, and especially the Democratic party, preclude the basic changes that would have been necessary to carry through the broader New Deal that the President proclaimed in his second-term inaugural?

On the face of it the forces of inertia were impressive. The American party system does not lend itself easily to change. In its major respects the national party is a holding company for complex and interlacing clusters of local groups revolving around men holding or contending for innumerable state and local offices—governors, sheriffs, state legislators, mayors, district attorneys, United States senators, county commissioners, city councilmen, and so on, all strung loosely together by party tradition, presidential leadership, and, to some extent, common ideas. As long as the American constitutional system creates electoral prizes to hold and contend for in the states and localities, the party is likely to remain undisciplined and decentralized.

Long immersed in the local undergrowth of American politics, Roosevelt was wholly familiar with the obstacles to party change. His refusal to break with some of the more unsavory local bosses like Hague and Kelly is clear evidence that he had no disposition to undertake the most obvious kind of reform. Perhaps, though, the President underestimated the possibility of party invigoration from the top.

Some New Dealers, worried by the decay of the Democratic party as a bulwark for progressive government, wanted to build up "presidential" factions pledged to the New Deal, factions that could lift the party out of the ruck of local bickering and orient it toward its national program. Attempts to build such presidential factions were abortive. They might have succeeded, however, had the President given them direction and backing. The New Deal had stimulated vigorous new elements in the party that put programs before local patronage, that were chiefly concerned with national policies of reform and recovery. By joining hands with these elements, by exploiting his own popularity and his control over the national party machinery, the President could have challenged anti-New Deal factions and tried to convert neutralists into backers of the New Deal.

Whether such an attempt would have succeeded cannot be answered because the attempt was never made. Paradoxically enough, however, the purge itself indicates that a long-run, well-organized effort might have worked in many states. For the purge did succeed under two conditions—in a Northern urban area, where there was some planning rather than total improvisation, and in those Southern states where the White House was helping a well-entrenched incumbent rather than trying to oust a well-entrenched opponent. The first was the case of O'Connor, the second the cases of Pepper and of Barkley. Indeed, the results of the purge charted a rough line between the area within the presidential reach and the area beyond it. Undoubtedly the former area would have been much bigger had Roosevelt systematically nourished New Deal strength within the party during his first term.

But he did not. The reasons that the President ignored the potentialities of the great political organization he headed were manifold. He was something of a prisoner of the great concessions he had made to gain the 1932 nomination, including the admission of Garner and other conservatives to the inner circle. His first-term successes had made his method of personal leadership look workable; overcoming crisis after crisis through his limitless resource-

fulness and magnetism, Roosevelt did not bother to organize the party for the long run. As a politician eager to win, Roosevelt was concerned with his own political and electoral standing at whatever expense to the party. It was much easier to exploit his own political skill than try to improve the rickety, sprawling party organization.

The main reason, however, for Roosevelt's failure to build up the party lay in his unwillingness to commit himself to the full implications of party leadership, in his eternal desire to keep open alternative tactical lines of action, including a line of retreat. The personal traits that made Roosevelt a brilliant tactician—his dexterity, his command of a variety of roles, his skill in attack and defense, above all his personal magnetism and *charisma*—were not the best traits for hard, long-range purposeful building of a strong popular movement behind a coherent political program. The latter would have demanded a continuing intellectual and political commitment to a set strategy—and this kind of commitment Roosevelt would not make.

He never forgot the great lesson of Woodrow Wilson, who got too far ahead of his followers. Perhaps, though, he never appreciated enough Wlison's injunction that "if the President leads the way, his party can hardly resist him." If Roosevelt had led and organized the party toward well-drawn goals, if he had aroused and tied into the party the masses of farmers and workers and reliefers and white-collar workers and minority religious and racial groups, if he had met the massed power of group interests with an organized movement of his own, the story of the New Deal on the domestic front during the second term might have been quite different.

Thus Roosevelt can be described as a great party leader only if the term is rigidly defined. On the one hand he tied the party, loosely perhaps, to a program; he brought it glorious victories; he helped point it in new ideological directions. On the other hand, he subordinated the party to his own political needs; he failed to exploit its full possibilities as a source of liberal thought and action; and he left the party, at least at its base, little stronger than when he became its leader.

Yet in an assessment of his party leadership there is a final argument in Roosevelt's defense. Even while the New Deal was running out domestically, new problems and new forces were coming into national and world focus. Whatever the weaknesses of his shiftiness and improvising, these same qualities gave him a flexibility of maneuver to meet new conditions. That flexibility was desperately needed as 1938 and 1939 brought crisis after crisis in world affairs.

Berryman, permission The Star, *Washington, D.C.*

Sancho Panza Garner protests against Don Quixote Roosevelt's attempted purge of Democrats who disagree with him.

"IF IT'S IN THE CONSTITUTION, IT'S THE LAW"

We're nine judicial gentlemen who shun the common herd,
Nine official mental men who speak the final word.
We do not issue postage stamps or face the microphones,
Or osculate with infants, or preside at corner-stones.
But we're the court of last resort in litigation legal.
(See: Case of Brooklyn Chicken *versus* Washington Blue Eagle.)
We never heed the demagogues, their millions and their minions,
But use *this* handy yard-stick when in doubt about opinions:

Chorus
If it's In The Constitution, it's the law,
For The Constitution hasn't got a flaw.
If it's In The Constitution, it's okay,
Whether yesterday, tomorrow, or today—
Hooray!
If it's In The Constitution, it must stay!

Like oysters in our cloisters, we avoid the storm and strife.
Some President appoints us, and we're put away for life.
When Congress passes laws that lack historical foundation,
We hasten from a huddle and reverse the legislation.
The sainted Constitution, that great document for students,
Provides an air-tight alibi for all our jurisprudence.
So don't blame us if now and then we seem to act like bounders;
Blame Hamilton and Franklin and the patriotic founders.

Chorus
If it's In The Constitution, it's the law, *etc.*

—Arthur L. Lippmann, *Life Magazine*, August 1935. A satirical view of a Supreme Court whose rigidity was to bring on the Court-packing fight less than two years later.

FRANKLIN D. ROOSEVELT SPEAKS

The country needs and, unless I mistake its temper, the country demands bold, persistent experimentation. It is common sense to take a method and try it: If it fails, admit it frankly and try another. But above all, try something. The millions who are in want will not stand by silently forever while the things to satisfy their needs are within easy reach.

—Address at Oglethorpe University, May 22, 1932

These unhappy times call for the building of plans that rest upon the forgotten, the unorganized but the indispensable units of economic power, for plans like those of 1917 that build from the bottom up and not from the top down, that put their faith once more in the forgotten man at the bottom of the economic pyramid.

—The "Forgotten Man" Radio Speech, April 8, 1932

What do the people of America want more than anything else? In my mind, two things: Work; work, with all the moral and spiritual values that go with work. And with work, a reasonable measure of security—security for themselves and for their wives and children. Work and security—these are more than words. They are more than facts. They are the spiritual values, the true goal toward which our efforts of reconstruction should lead. These are the values that this program is intended to gain; these are the values we have failed to achieve by the leadership we now have.

Our Republican leaders tell us economic laws—sacred, inviolable, unchangeable—that these laws cause panics which no one could prevent. But while they prate of economic laws, men and women are starving. We must lay hold of the fact that economic laws are not made by nature. They are made by human beings. . . .

Throughout the nation, men and women, forgotten in the political philosophy of the government of the last years look to us here for guidance and for more equitable opportunity to share in the distribution of national wealth.

On the farms, in the large metropolitan areas, in the smaller cities and in the villages, millions of our citizens cherish the hope that their old standards of living and of thought have not gone forever. Those millions cannot and shall not hope in vain.

I pledge you—I pledge myself to a new deal for the American people. Let us all here assembled constitute ourselves prophets of a new order of competence and of courage. This is more than a political campaign; it is a call to arms. Give me your help, not to win votes alone, but to win in this crusade to restore America to its own people.

—The "New Deal" Acceptance Speech, Chicago, July 2, 1932

A glance at the situation today only too clearly indicates that equality of opportunity as we have known it no longer exists. Our industrial plant is built; the problem just now is whether under existing conditions it is not overbuilt. Our last frontier has long since been reached, and there is practically no more free land. More than half of our people do not live on the farms or on lands and cannot derive a living by cultivating their own property. There is no safety valve in the form of a Western prairie to which those thrown out of work by the Eastern economic machines can go for a new start. We are not able to invite the immigration from Europe to share our endless plenty. We are now providing a drab living for our own people.

Our system of constantly rising tariffs has at last reacted against us. . . . This has resulted in the reduction of the operation of . . . American plants, and opportunity for employment.

Just as freedom to farm has ceased, so also the opportunity in business has narrowed. It still is true that men can start small enterprises, trusting to native shrewdness and ability to keep abreast of competitors; but area after area has been preempted altogether by the great corporations, and even in the fields which still have no great concerns, the small man starts under a handicap. . . . Put plainly, we are steering a steady course toward economic oligarchy, if we are not there already.

Clearly, all this calls for a re-appraisal of values. A mere builder of more industrial plants, a creator of more railroad systems, an organizer of more corporations, is as likely to be a danger as a help. The day of the great promoter or the financial Titan, to whom we granted anything if only he would build, or develop, is over. Our task now is not discovery or exploitation of natural resources, or necessarily producing more goods. It is the soberer, less dramatic business of administering resources and plants already in hand, of seeking to reestablish foreign markets for our surplus production, of meeting the problem of underconsumption, of adjusting production to consumption, of distributing wealth, and products more equitably, of adapting existing economic organizations to the service of the people. The day of enlightened administration has come.

—"Commonwealth Club" Speech, San Francisco, Sept. 23, 1932. This was interpreted as the acceptance by FDR that the economy had reached a permanent level.

I am certain that my fellow Americans expect that on my induction into the Presidency I will address them with a candor and a decision which the present situation of our Nation impels. This is preeminently the time to speak the truth, the whole truth, frankly and boldly. Nor need we shrink from honestly facing conditions in our country today. This great Nation will endure as it has endured, will revive and will prosper. So, first of all, let me assert my firm belief that the only thing we have to fear is fear itself—nameless, unreasoning, unjustified terror which paralyzes needed efforts to convert retreat into advance. In every dark hour of our national life a leadership of frankness and vigor has met with that understanding and support of the people themselves which is essential to victory. I am convinced that you will again give that support to leadership in these critical days. . . .

This Nation asks for action, and action now. Our greatest primary task is to put people to work. This is no unsolvable problem if we face it wisely and courageously. It can be accomplished in part by direct recruiting by the Government itself, treating the task as we would treat the emergency of a war, but at the same time, through this employment, accomplishing greatly needed projects to stimulate and reorganize the use of our natural resources. . . .

Through this program of action we address ourselves to putting our own national house in order and making income balance outgo. Our international trade relations, though vastly important, are in point of time and necessity secondary to the establishment of a sound national economy. I favor as a practical policy the putting of first things first. I shall spare no effort to restore world trade by international economic readjustment, but the emergency at home cannot wait on that accomplishment. . . .

With this pledge taken, I assume unhesitatingly the leadership of this great army of our people dedicated to a disciplined attack upon our common problems. . . .

For the trust reposed in me I will return the courage and the devotion that befit the time. I can do no less.

We face the arduous days that lie before us in the warm courage of national unity; with the clear consciousness of seeking old and precious moral values; with the clean satisfaction that comes from the stern performance of duty by old and young alike. We aim at the assurance of a rounded and permanent national life.

We do not distrust the future of essential democracy. The people of the United States have not failed. In their need they have registered a mandate that they want direct, vigorous action. They have asked for discipline and direction under leadership. They have made me the present instrument of their wishes. In the spirit of the gift I take it.

In this dedication of a Nation we humbly ask the blessing of God. May He protect each and every one of us. May He guide me in the days to come.

—First Inaugural Address, Washington, March 4, 1933

We find our population suffering from old inequalities, little changed by past sporadic remedies. In spite of our efforts and in spite of our talk, we have not weeded out the over-privileged and we have not effectively lifted up the under-privileged. Both of these manifestations of injustice have retarded happiness. No wise man has any intention of destroying what is known as the profit motive: because by the profit motive we mean the right by work to earn a decent livelihood for ourselves and for our families.

We have, however, a clear mandate from the people, that Americans must foreswear that conception of the acquisition of wealth which, through excessive profits, creates undue private power over private affairs and, to our misfortune, over public affairs as well. In building toward this end we do not destroy ambition nor do we seek to divide our wealth into equal shares on stated occasions. We continue to recognize the greater ability of some to earn more than others. But we do assert that the ambition of the individual to obtain for him and his a proper security, a reasonable leisure, and a decent living throughout life, is an ambition to be preferred to the appetite for great wealth and great power. . . .

In defining immediate factors which enter into our quest, I have spoken to the Congress and the people of three great divisions:

1. The security of a livelihood through the better use of the national resources of the land in which we live.
2. The security against the major hazards and vicissitudes of life.
3. The security of decent homes.

I am now ready to submit to the Congress a broad program designed ultimately to establish all three of these factors of security—a program which because of many lost years will take many future years to fulfill.

—Annual Message to Congress, Jan. 4, 1935, launching
what is now called the Second New Deal.

I can realize that gentlemen in well-warmed and well-stocked clubs will discourse on the expenses of Government and the suffering that they are going through because their Government is spending money for work relief. I wish I could take some of these men out on the battle-line of human necessity, and show them the facts that we in the Government are facing. If these more fortunate Americans will come with me, I will not only show them the necessity for the expenditures of this Government, but I will show them, as well, the definite and beneficial results we have attained with the dollars we have spent. Some of these same gentlemen tell me that a dole would be more economical than work relief. That is true. But the men who tell me that have, unfortunately, too little contact with the true America to realize that in this business of relief we are dealing with properly self-respecting Americans to whom a mere dole outrages every instinct of individual independence. Most Americans want to give something for what they get. That something, which in this case is honest work, is the saving barrier between them and moral disintegration. I propose to build that barrier high and keep it high.

—Address at Atlanta, Nov. 29, 1935

Philadelphia is a good city in which to write American history. This is fitting ground on which to reaffirm the faith of our fathers; to pledge ourselves to restore to the people a wider freedom—to give to 1936 as the founders gave to 1776—an American way of life. . . .

Political tyranny was wiped out at Philadelphia on July 4, 1776. But, since that struggle, man's inventive genius released new forces in our land which reordered the lives of our people. The age of machinery, of railroads, of steam and electricity; the telegraph and the radio; mass production, mass distribution—all of these combined to bring forward a new civilization and with it a problem for those who sought to remain free.

For out of this modern civilization economic royalists carved new dynasties. New Kingdoms were built upon concentration of control over material things. Through new uses of corporations, banks and securities, new machinery of industry and agriculture, of labor and capital—all undreamed of by the fathers—the whole structure of modern life was impressed into this royal service. . . .

These economic royalists complain that we seek to overthrow the institutions of America. What they really complain of is that we seek to take away their power. Our allegiance to American institutions requires the overthrow of this kind of power. In vain they seek to hide behind the Flag and the Constitution. In their blindness they forget what the Flag and the Constitution stand for. Now, as always, for over a century and a half, the Flag, the Constitution, stand against a dictatorship by mob rule and the over-privileged alike, and the Flag and the Constitution stand for democracy, not tyranny; for freedom, but not subjection. . . .

We do not see faith, hope and charity as unattainable ideals, but we use them as stout supports of a Nation fighting the fight for freedom in a modern civilization.

Faith—in the soundness of democracy in the midst of dictatorships.

Hope—renewed because we know so well the progress we have made.

Charity—in the true spirit of that grand old word. For charity . . . means love . . . that does not merely share the wealth of the giver, but in true sympathy and wisdom helps men to help themselves.

We seek not merely to make Government a mechanical implement, but to give it the vibrant personal character that is the very embodiment of human charity. . . .

Better the occasional faults of a Government that lives in a spirit of charity than the consistent omissions of a Government frozen in the ice of its own indifference.

There is a mysterious cycle in human events. To some generations much is given. Of other generations much is expected. This generation of Americans has a rendezvous with destiny.

—Acceptance Speech, Philadelphia, June 27, 1936

In the summer of 1933, a nice old gentleman wearing a silk hat fell off the end of a pier. A friend ran down the pier, dived overboard and pulled him out; but the silk hat floated off with the tide. After the old gentleman had been revived, he was effusive in his thanks. He praised his friend for saving his life. Today, three years later, the old gentleman is berating his friend because the silk hat was lost.

—Parable during Campaign of 1936 on the ingratitude of businessmen

In this nation I see tens of millions of its citizens—a substantial part of its whole population—who at this very moment are denied the greater part of what the very lowest standards of today call the necessities of life.

I see millions of families trying to live on income so meager that the pall of family disaster hangs over them day by day.

I see millions whose daily lives in city and on farm continue under conditions labeled indecent by a so-called polite society half a century ago.

I see millions denied education, recreation, and the opportunity to better their lot and the lot of their children.

I see millions lacking the means to buy the products of farm and factory and by their poverty denying work and productiveness to many other millions.

I see one-third of a nation ill-housed, ill-clad, ill-nourished.

It is not in despair that I paint you that picture. I paint it for you in hope— because the Nation, seeing and understanding the injustice in it, propose to paint it out. . . .

To maintain a democracy of effort requires a vast amount of patience in dealing with differing methods, a vast amount of humility. But out of the confusion of many voices rises an understanding of dominant public need. Then political leadership can voice common ideals, and aid in their realization.

—Second Inaugural Address, Jan. 20, 1937

FRANKLIN DELANO ROOSEVELT: PRO AND CONTRA

A second class intellect, but a first class temperament.

—Justice Oliver Wendell Holmes

Roosevelt is the only man we ever had in the White House who would understand that my boss is a sonofabitch.

—Mill worker quoted in Eric Goldman, *Rendezvous with Destiny* (1956), p. 268

As I said near the beginning of this book, I could never really understand what was going on in Roosevelt's heavily forested interior. But, as a result of my observation of him and the time that I have had to digest that observation and the opinions of others, I am sure of one thing: although crippled physically and prey to various infections, he was spiritually the healthiest man I have ever known. He was gloriously and happily free of the various forms of psychic maladjustment which are called by such names as inhibition, complex, phobia. His mind, if not always orderly, bore no traces of paralysis and neither did his emotional constitution; and his heart was certainly in the right place. Furthermore, he was entirely conscious of these extraordinary advantages that he enjoyed, and this consciousness gave him the power to soar above circumstances which would have held other men earthbound.

—Robert Sherwood, *Roosevelt and Hopkins* (N.Y.: Harper, 1948), p. 882

The hitch came with Roosevelt's failure to follow through. Pragmatism requires the application of the test of utility or workableness for success. And by this Roosevelt refused to abide. He would launch an idea as an experiment, but, once it had been launched, he would not subject it to the pragmatic test. It became, in his mind, an expression of settled conviction, an indispensable element in a great, unified plan.

That Roosevelt could look back over the vast aggregation of policies adopted between March, 1933, and November, 1936, and see it as the result of a single, predetermined plan was a tribute to his imagination. But not to his grasp of economics. One had only to review the heterogeneous origins of the policies he had embraced by the time of his re-election, the varying circumstances, impulses, beliefs that had produced them, to guess at their substantive conflict and contradiction. . . .

If this aggregation of policies springing from circumstances, motives, purposes, and situations so various gave the observer the sense of a certain rugged grandeur, it arose chiefly from the wonder that one man could have been so flexible as to permit himself to believe so many things in so short a time. But to look upon these policies as the result of a unified plan was to believe that the accumulation of stuffed snakes, baseball pictures, school flags, old tennis shoes, carpenter's tools, geometry books, and chemistry sets in a boy's bedroom could have been put there by an interior decorator.

—Raymond Moley in *After Seven Years* (N.Y.: Harper and Row, 1939).

NEITHER IDEOLOGY NOR UTOPIA

[Heinz Eulau in his essay "Neither Ideology Nor Utopia: The New Deal in Retrospect" in *Antioch Review* 19:523–537 (Winter 1959–60) accepts the New Deal on its own terms. Rather than criticizing it as a perfunctory ceremonial gesture, Eulau regards it as an exhibition of political maturity and a step in the pragmatic evolution of American institutions.]

The New Deal of Franklin D. Roosevelt, just as the New Freedom of Woodrow Wilson before, and the Fair Deal of Harry Truman later, had its quota of ideologues, but was not an ideology; it had its following of true believers but was not a chiliastic faith; it produced far-ranging reforms, but was not a crusade; it was rich in inventions, but was not an experiment; it mobilized huge majorities, but was not a revolt of the masses; it generated forceful national leadership, but was not a charismatic surrender. It is possible to see the New Deal as the fulfillment of the promise of American life

—Herbert Croly's dream in the years before the first World War; or as an exercise in instrumental pragmatism which John Dewey had celebrated in the years following that war. But if it was the realization of the liberal promise or the application of the pragmatic philosophy, it was so by way of improvisation rather than design. All of these elements were present, but they do not express the dynamics of the New Deal. If it was anything, the New Deal between 1932 and 1940 was, simply and foremost, evidence of the viability of democratic politics in an age of crisis. . . .

Though the New Deal was non-ideological, this does not mean that it was anti-ideological. In fact, it was shot through with ideologies, or utopias, whichever emphasis one may prefer. Total planners and piecemeal planners, budget-balancers and deficit-spenders, trust-regulators and trust-busters, protectionists and free traders, "sound money" proponents and inflationists—all vied with each other under the hospitable tent that was the New Deal. Wall Street bankers, Midwest farmers, Harvard economists, Columbia lawyers, labor intellectuals, old-time progressives, new liberals, social workers—men of the Right, Left, and Middle—supplied ideas and programs, if not panaceas. Theories were welcome as they had never been welcome before; and never before, or thereafter, did so many blueprints of a better order reach the citadel of influence. Ideas were, indeed, the true coins of the realm.

But, for precisely these reasons, there was little of the ideological in the New Deal—if by ideology one means a coherent and consistent set of beliefs, values, opinions, and aspirations. To attempt to construct out of the welter of these beliefs and values, opinions and aspirations an internally congruent system of thought is to do violence to history and to the meaning of the New Deal. . . . In fact, insofar as it responded to ideological pressures at all, the New Deal was engaged in a continuous effort to disengage itself from ideological commitments. . . .

All this does not mean that the New Deal was not anchored in a cultural milieu of attitudes and predispositions which was congenial to its operation. This milieu was the liberal tradition in America. As Louis Hartz has suggested, in one sense the whole American political tradition is liberal. In this perspective, the New Deal, non-ideological though it was, was clearly an indication, if not a vindication, of liberalism. Without this tradition, there would have been no New Deal. But, in the American context, the liberal tradition as such has rarely been experienced as an ideology. Rather, it appears as a cultural fact which, like the air we breathe, is so close, so natural, so much a part of our daily life that we fail to notice it. The liberal tradition explains, I suspect, why its many contradictions and inconsistencies were "built in" New Deal programs, plans, and policies. For liberalism, unlike other isms, has never been a set of dogmas, but a state of mind. It represents an attitude which insists on questioning self-evident propositions, partly to find out what evidence there is to support them, partly to discover possible alternatives. It follows that liberalism is not bound to any particular social or economic system. No wonder that so many different ideologues, theoreticians, administrators, and politicians could find the New Deal a congenial environment in which to work. Indeed, they shaped that environment. And the New Deal reflected, in varying degrees and at varying times, the varying enthusiasms and different approaches to the national problems.

That the New Deal gave new hope to millions, that it brought new confidence into government, that it ultimately became a testament of national courage, there is little doubt. Where there had been drift, the New Deal offered mastery. . . . It generated fresh expectations in the hearts of people who had recently experienced little but misery, and a new spirit came about the land. But it was a hope and a spirit nourished not by promises and good intentions, but by governmental action. The New Deal was a reconfirmation of the old American assumption that action is its own reward. What the New Deal articulated was not a faith in a better morrow, but a call for action now.

And the people were captivated, not because they were asked to be true believers, but because action gave them a new sense of dignity. The dole had given them the minimum means of subsistence, and charity had made them loathe a humility to which they were not accustomed. Now they found their way into public works, conservation corps, rural settlements, and, as the economy began to grind again, back into jobs in industry, transportation, and commerce. They were grateful. But even if the New Deal had tried to take the role of the savior, it is doubtful that it could have saved many souls. What generated the new spirit that made the thirties so exciting was not government action alone. True, the government played a role it had never played in the lives of Americans before. But what sustained the popular drive and confidence that came with the New Deal was the old faith that man can control his destiny—given the conditions that make action and self-help possible. . . .

The New Deal, then, was not an "escape from freedom," a surrender of the intellectual faculties. Rather than calling for faith, it was an enormous educational effort. Perhaps never before in the history of the republic was it necessary to re-educate the preferences and redirect the energies of the people. Whatever one may wish to call it—propaganda or education—the American people were exposed to a flow of information about the activities of the government unexcelled in the past. And the people responded. There was new understanding of the difficulties besetting the nation, a new tolerance of innovations, and a new commitment to creative intelligence in politics. Rarely has there been so much knowledgeable participation of the people in public affairs. . . . The New Deal was what it was and became what it became precisely because it did not promise a millennium, but confronted the American people with the harsh realities of the present, first at home, and then abroad.

To think of the New Deal as a unified program, a plan, or a policy is as mistaken as to think of it as a movement or a crusade. There were many programs and policies, and there was more than a movement. What made the New Deal the phenomenon it was—a new deal in American life, a fresh start—was not a zest for reform, but the need to respond to national problems as they were dictated by the exigencies of the moment, not as they may have been preconceived by reformers. Whatever preferences for reform may have motivated individual New Dealers as they found themselves in the seats of power and influence after the politically lean years of normalcy, the task at hand was to

revive the economy, not to translate long-cherished proposals for reform into reality.

Reforms, of course, there were. Some were successful and became permanent features of American life. Industrial violence, long the scourge of labor-management relations, gave way to the peaceful method of collective bargaining. Unemployment and old-age insurance programs remedied long-standing ills among the socially and economically most disadvantaged sector of the population. Securities legislation brought discipline and responsibility into the disorderly state of banking and investment practices. But other reforms were doomed to failure. Rural resettlement was a temporary stopgap and fell victim to its own idealism. The National Resources Planning Board never got off the ground. Other programs were conceived as self-liquidating and were liquidated, though some of them, like the Civilian Conservation Corps or Public Works Administration, left a rich heritage of national accomplishment. Still other programs represented *ad hoc* inventions to cope with pressing problems which had hardly been envisaged by the reformers. They were, in fact, determined efforts by the government to maintain the *status quo*. Programs such as agricultural adjustment or bank deposit insurance were acts not so much of reform as of preservation.

The one attempt made to conduct a crusade—the National Recovery Administration under Hugh Johnson—resembled more an Alice-in-Wonderland grotesque than a viable governmental structure and policy. NRA had important successes—abolishing child labor, setting maximum hours and minimum wages, removing unfair trade practices, and so forth—which, once re-enacted after NRA's demise, became monuments of social progress. But, on the whole, NRA was a fiasco because it tried to do too much in too little time within a single institutional setting which, at its roots, sought to reconcile business regulation by business itself with protection of free-market mechanisms by the government. The effort often led to an atmosphere of histrionics much at variance with that kind of earnestness that is the hallmark of reform. The Blue Eagle campaign was more a circus, really, than a crusade, and few tears were shed when the whole enterprise was declared unconstitutional.

It is only in the perspective of history that the New Deal can possibly be conceived as a political or social movement. But even in this perspective, it was only a new phase, a most intensive phase, perhaps, forced by the great depression to heroic exertion, in the long-range national development which is the promise of American life. It was directly related—not only in ideas it shared, but also in some of its older personnel—to both the Square Deal and the New Freedom, to the historical trend to achieve Jeffersonian ends by Hamiltonian means. That the Square Deal had been Republican and the New Freedom Democratic made the national character of the New Deal all the more poignant. Of all the movements, so-called, in American history, the New Deal was truly national in scope, liberal in purpose, and effective in action.

The New Deal has come to be cited as the prize exhibit of the success of the experimental method in the making of public policy and the development of administrative techniques. The New Deal's willingness and capacity to chart new social and political paths is seen as an expression of John Dewey's philosophy of instrumentalism. But this interpretation represents a tendency to over-intellectualize the political process. It is more often in the nature of an apologia than of analysis. By calling anything new an "experiment," success of the experiment is heralded as proof of the uses of experimentation, while failure is explained away as inconsequential. The analogy between social efforts to create new alternatives and scientific experimentation ignores more than it explains. In fact, when the metaphor becomes a myth, it may be detrimental to a genuine understanding of the New Deal.

Roosevelt himself gave credence to the experimental metaphor when he declared that what the country needed was "bold, persistent experimentation." Yet one may doubt that his call for experimentation was intended to make experimental pragmatism into a political formula. . . . Quite clearly, Roosevelt's accent was less on the nature of the method used than on the injunction to "try something." . . .

Though the New Deal was not an experiment or a series of experiments, it was admittedly an experience in social inventiveness. There was, again in Roosevelt's words, no room for "foolish traditions." Innovation, not experiment, was the trade-mark of the New Deal. The proliferation of administrative agencies came with the suspicion that the old-line departments would not or could not aggressively pursue the new policies; balancing the budget no longer meant what it had traditionally meant— social values defied accounting in terms of dollars and cents, and it was the national economy, not the government budget, that was thought to be at stake; an agriculture of abundance was to be realized, paradoxically, through promoting programs of scarcity, like killing pigs and plowing under the crops which could not be marketed at adequate prices; and on the political front, from Roosevelt's personal appearance at the 1932 Chicago convention to his breaking of the two-term tradition eight years later, the New Deal defied conventions. Yet, it is interesting to note that in politics proper this proved most difficult, as the ill-fated "court-packing plan" or the President's aborted attempt to influence the 1938 Democratic primaries demonstrated.

But, paradoxically too, the New Deal with all its inventions was in the great American political and social tradition. For that tradition meant innovation: free public lands, free religious worship, free public education, a chance at economic betterment and social mobility, a broad democratic franchise, and many other social gains had at first been innovations—inventions which at one time had made the difference between the Old World and the New. The New Deal was in the mainstream of that tradition, but again with a difference. . . . The New Deal elections were not plebiscites, but hard-fought, free battles of the ballot. Even in the landslide election of 1936, almost seventeen million people, or about 38 per cent of the total electorate, voted for the Republican candidate. In spite of the personal attractiveness of the Democratic candidate, few campaigns in twentieth century America have been as genuinely democratic as the early New Deal elections. Although the press was predominantly anti-New Deal, rarely has there been so much discussion of the real issues facing the nation. What moved the New Deal majorities was not a sense of revolt, but a renewed spirit of confidence in the willingness and ability of the government to carry out the popular mandate.

In organizing its electoral majorities, the New Deal restructured the political map. Its political techniques were anything but the contrived plebiscitarian technology of mass manipulation. That the New Deal succeeded in harnessing to its wagon the forces of labor, the young as well as the old, the socially underprivileged ethnic groups, farmers as well as urbanites, former Republicans as well as former Socialists, was not the result of hidden persuasion or silent threat, but of its sensitivity to popular needs and demands. In doing so, the New Deal was an almost perfect system of political feedback. Rarely in a modern democracy has the politics of democracy been equally conducive to the strengthening of democracy as a viable political system. . . .

The New Deal majority was, above all, a product of the political process as it had developed its particular flavor in the American culture. . . . To assume that the New Deal majorities were united in purposes and goals is not only naive, but incorrect. The New Deal majorities were, in reality, only evidence of the complex processes of group adjustment and compromise that had preceded the electoral majorities; proof that these processes were reasonably efficient in generating the electoral power that was needed to continue the processes of adjustment and compromise. Like all American majorities, the New Deal majorities were the products of a salient coalition politics, only more so. No ideological or militant poli-

tics, no revolt of the masses, could have been equally successful—at least not in a free democracy.

If ever the right man came to occupy the right office at the right time, Franklin D. Roosevelt was that man. . . . But to acknowledge that FDR was the chief architect of the New Deal, its most convincing spokesman, its forceful leader and also its most tangible target, is not to imply that he was a charismatic personality. Undoubtedly, there were people who ascribed to him the qualities of charisma—infallibility, omniscience, omnipotence. . . . but to the vast majority of the American people he was Mr. President—the legally chosen head of a government whose function it was to represent and execute the power of the nation in time of crisis. This role FDR was superbly fitted and able to carry out. . . . The President's personality and the character of the New Deal, if it is permissible to speak of character, were admirably blended to produce the kind of strong governmental leadership which the nation required in the moment of crisis. But this makes it all the more necessary not to exaggerate, yet also not to minimize, the role of the President in the total configuration of the New Deal. Because the tendency to exaggerate has probably been the dominant one, it seems desirable to point to some less frequently noticed features of the New Deal's personnel. . . .

While Roosevelt never allowed the impression to prevail that he was not boss and master of the situation, his effectiveness as a leader derived from his ability to allow his lieutenants enough free-wheeling initiative to work out programs and policies—and it was one of his favorite images to see himself as the quarterback who was merely called upon to call the signals. . . .

Moreover, the spirit of leadership under the New Deal was not only pervasive in the executive branch, but also in the legislative branch, and, after the mandate of 1936, in the judicial branch as well. There has been a tendency to neglect the part played by Congress in providing political leadership. There were the

"Hundred Days," it is true, when the new Congress had little choice but to go along with the President's "must" programs. But the New Deal Congresses were not simply "rubber-stamp" legislatures. They included men of vision, wisdom, and sagacity, progressives who often succeeded in moving the White House in directions in which it would not have moved on its own initiative. Similarly, once the Supreme Court—or rather two of its members, including the Chief Justice—had realized that it could not set itself up against the wishes of the great majority of the people and the popular President, it produced decisions which themselves were important ingredients of New Deal policies. . . .

If the New Deal was not an ideology, a faith, a crusade, an experiment, a revolt, or a charisma, what was it? In retrospect, what makes the New Deal so memorable, so significant an event in the history of the United States is that it is both a symbol and evidence of the nation's political maturity: its ability to solve its problems through politics rather than through ideology or violence. Politicians though they were, the Founding Fathers essentially distrusted politics. Whatever their real commitments, they believed in the cult of reason and natural law. In the Civil War, ideological intransigence— Lincoln, who came too late and passed away too early, excepted—underlined the poverty of politics, so largely responsible for both the violence and its unfortunate aftermath. By way of contrast, the New Deal was neither distrustful of politics nor poor in political strategies. If a commitment there was, it was a commitment to a mature politics.

A mature politics cannot afford to be either ideological or utopian. Ideologists and utopians are essentially apolitical. They are, in many respects, like children who are preoccupied almost exclusively with what they want when they want it, for whom their little selves are the center of the cosmos. Preoccupied with their own diagnoses and therapies, ideologists and utopians are, paradoxically, "thoughtless" in the literal sense of the word—blind to the needs of others and unconcerned with the consequences of their self-centered aspirations for others. Responsibility is a concept alien to both children and ideologues alike. Maturity, on the other hand, is the capacity to respond to others without making the demands of the self the sole criterion of perception or behavior. Real and necessary as the demands of the mature person are, maturity involves recognition of the legitimate interests of others. A mature politics involves adjustment, compromise, integration. It can never be a purely ideological politics which exaggerates the importance of the self at the expense of the other, or which may even mean the destruction of the other.

The New Deal was a politics of maturity in this sense, for it brought to the problems it faced political, not ideological, solutions. This is often not understood by its ideological critics or ideological defenders. The very debate which the New Deal aroused, and continues to arouse, is the best evidence. The New Deal is "incomprehensible" to the ideologues of the Right and Left because it was so unideological, because it was not a "scheme" but a "deal" so different from the political solitaire which the ideologue likes to play. The New Deal was a search for acceptable solutions to problems rather than an imposition of preconceived solutions on problems. The ideologues and theoreticians were necessary to the New Deal, vital in its growth and development, but they could not be its conductors. Some were disgusted, others despaired, unable to fathom the rationale of a program which was no program and had no rationale that fitted their ideological preconceptions. Those who stayed with the New Deal—men as different in their interests as Harold Ickes, the old progressive, or Jesse Jones, the financier, or Henry Wallace, the Republican farmer—served the New Deal for what it was: not a return to an ideological yesteryear, or a road to a utopian tomorrow, but a political enterprise which harnessed political forces in the spirit of political maturity.

It was not so much a characteristic of the

New Deal's political maturity that many ideas and interests found expression in the hurly-burly of politics, but that politics took these ideas and interests seriously, that it encouraged their expression, that it took it for granted that these ideas and interests would clash, and that it was ready to give, but also to take away. The New Deal represented, on the level of national politics, a tough-mindedness that allowed for little ideological self-indulgence. Ideological thinking, however camouflaged, is tender-minded because it is self-indulgent. But in politics self-indulgence means bargaining from a position of weakness rather than strength. It represents an escape from a politics of maturity, not a recognition of the potentialities as well as limitations of political life. The New Deal was politically tough and mature, for it accepted the limits of the possible. . . .

Only when the shadow of war had become a spectre worse than depression, and when the New Deal had remedied much of what sickened American life, did politics give way to defense and apologia as well as to surrender of the political imagination. There appeared the bandwagon mentality—what Morris Cohen has called "the vile habit of thinking that the latest is always the best"—and the convenient belief that present trends will continue indefinitely into the future. It was then that the New Deal tended to become an affair of pronunciamento and magic formula. But this, in fact, meant the end of the New Deal. Yet it is against this later phase that the New Deal can be best assessed—as a flowering of sensitivity to the paradoxes, ambiguities, complications, compromises, and adventures of politics. To live with these characteristics, not only to tolerate them but to thrive on them, was the mark of that political maturity which distinguished the New Deal as a national event.

WHEN THE NEW DEAL WAS OVER THE FUNDAMENTAL PROBLEMS REMAINED

Yet, when [the New Deal] was over, the fundamental problem remained—and still remains—unsolved: how to bring the blessings of immense natural wealth and staggering productive potential to every person in the land. Also unsolved was the political corollary of that problem; how to organize ordinary people to convey to national leadership something more subtle than the wail of crisis (which speaks for itself); how to communicate the day-to-day pains felt, between emergencies, in garbage-strewn slums, crowded schools, grimy bus stations, inadequate hospital wards, Negro ghettos, and rural shacks—the environment of millions of Americans clawing for subsistence in the richest country in the world.

When the reform energies of the New Deal began to wane around 1939 and the depression was over, the nation was back to its normal state: a permanent army of unemployed; twenty or thirty million poverty-ridden people effectively blocked from public view by a huge, prosperous, and fervently consuming middle class; a tremendously efficient yet wasteful productive apparatus that was efficient because it could produce limitless supplies of what it decided to produce, and wasteful because what it decided to produce was not based on what was most needed by society but on what was most profitable to business.

What the New Deal did was to refurbish middle-class America, which had taken a dizzying fall in the depression, to restore jobs to half the jobless, and to give just enough to the lowest classes (a layer of public housing, a minimum of social security) to create an aura of good will. Through it all, the New Dealers moved in an atmosphere thick with suggestions, but they accepted only enough of these to get the traditional social mechanism moving again, plus just enough more to give a taste of what a truly far-reaching reconstruction might be.

This harsh estimate of New Deal achievements derives from the belief that the historian discussing the past is always commenting—whether he realizes it or not—on the present; and that because he is part of a morally responsible public, his commentary should consider present needs at the expense, if necessary, of old attachments. It is fruitless today to debate "interpretations" of the New Deal. We can no longer vote for or against Roosevelt. We can only affect the world around us. And although this is the 1960's, not the 1930's, some among us live very high, and some live very low, and a chronic malaise of lost opportunities and wasted wealth pervades the economic air.

—Howard Zinn, ed., *New Deal Thought* (Indianapolis: Bobbs-Merrill, 1966), from editor's introduction, pp. xvi–xvii.

"Democracy is just a big fake," says Hitler when both Roosevelt and Willkie endorse aid to Britain.

Copyright Low all countries.

15

WORLD WAR II: THE DOCUMENTARY RECORD

INTRODUCTION

The scope of World War II is so vast that we cannot hope to cover more than a few points even of the American share in it. Probably no war in history has received such prompt and extensive treatment by historians and leading participants, and the general outlines of the diplomatic and military facts have been pretty well established for some time. The real uncertainties lie in the realms of motivations and "what might have been."

But there, also, we are in a realm so vast that no two editors could agree on which should be chosen for presentation in a limited space. Was it necessary for the United States to enter the war? And once it was in, why didn't it leave Germany and Japan powerful enough to balance Russia? Was Roosevelt wise in undermining colonialism? Did Roosevelt toll the Japanese into war? Did he lie to the American people? Was he fooled by the Russians at Teheran and Yalta? Or did he sell out to them? Could Roosevelt have preserved the Slavic nations from Russia? Who dominated coalition strategy? And who was right? Were high explosive and incendiary bombings of cities justified by the results, even aside from the terrible loss of human lives? Did Truman need to drop the Bomb? Was it wise to divide Germany into zones? Who made the blunder in failing to connect Berlin with the West by a ground route under Western control?

Under the circumstances it seems most feasible to offer a limited number of documents in this chapter, and then in the next chapter give certain interpretive essays on crucial aspects of the war.

CHURCHILL SPEAKS FOR BELEAGUERED BRITAIN

Even though large tracts of Europe and many old and famous states have fallen or may fall into the grip of the Gestapo and all the odious apparatus of Nazi rule, we shall not flag or fail. We shall go on to the end. We shall fight in France, we shall fight in the seas and oceans, we shall fight with growing confidence and growing strength in the air; we shall defend our Island, whatever the cost may be. We shall fight on the beaches, we shall fight on the landing-grounds, we shall fight in the fields and in the streets, we shall fight in the hills; we shall never surrender; and even if, which I do not for a moment believe, this Island or a large part of it were subjugated and starving, then our Empire beyond the seas, armed and guarded by the British Fleet, would carry on the struggle, until, in God's good time, the New World, with all its power and might, steps forth to the rescue and liberation of the Old.

—Winston Churchill, June 4, 1940, in a radio broadcast heard in the United States

What General Weygand called the Battle of France is over. I expect that the Battle of Britain is about to begin. Upon this battle depends the survival of Christian civilisation. . . . Hitler knows that he will have to break us in this Island or lose the war. If we can stand up to him, all Europe may be free and the life of the world may move forward into broad, sunlit uplands. But if we fail, then the whole world, including the United States, including all that we have known or cared for, will sink into the abyss of a new Dark Age, made more sinister, and perhaps more protracted, by the lights of perverted science. Let us therefore brace ourselves to our duties, and so bear ourselves that, if the British Empire and its Commonwealth last for a thousand years, men will still say: "This was their finest hour."

—Winston Churchill, June 18, 1940, addressing the House of Commons

RAPPROCHEMENT WITH LATIN AMERICA

North American aggressions had been so consistently explained as justified by aspects of the Monroe Doctrine that by the 1920's it had come to represent all that the Latin-American states hated. The United States began to turn away from the concept that it should force fiscal and moral responsibility on Latin America when in 1927 President Coolidge sent Dwight Morrow to negotiate with Mexico over the claims of American citizens to oil properties. The movement was accelerated under Hoover and F. D. Roosevelt. Here we propose to quote some of the more important highlights in that evolution.

(1) HOOVER INTRODUCES THE GOOD NEIGHBOR

[In his *Memoirs* (N.Y.: Macmillan, 1952), 2:210–215, Hoover described the goodwill tour he made of Latin America soon after his election to the Presidency. It was apparently at this time that he introduced the term *good neighbor*, and he gave the following as an example.]

I come to pay a call of friendship. In a sense I represent on this occasion the people of the United States extending a friendly greeting to our fellow democracies on the American continent. I would wish to symbolize the friendly visit of one *good neighbor* to another. In our daily life, *good neighbors* call upon each other as the evidence of solicitude for the common welfare and to learn of the circumstances and point of view of each, so that there may come both understanding and respect which are the cementing forces of all enduring society. This should be equally true amongst nations. We have a desire to maintain not only the cordial relations of governments with each other but the relations of *good neighbors*.

(2) MEMORANDUM ON THE MONROE DOCTRINE

[On December 17, 1928, Under Secretary of State J. Reuben Clark issued a memorandum defining the Monroe Doctrine and denying that the various popular interpretations and so-called corollaries were legitimately an extension of it. It was, of course, too late to undo the damage, but at least it cleared the way for multilateral agreements among the New World nations which sought the same end as the Monroe Doctrine. The memorandum was made public in 1930 under the above title.]

It is of first importance to have in mind that Monroe's declaration in its terms, relates solely to the relationships between European states on the one side, and, on the other side, the American continents, the Western Hemisphere, and the Latin American Governments which on December 2, 1823, had declared and maintained their independence which we had acknowledged.

It is of equal importance to note, on the other hand, that the declaration does not apply to purely inter-American relations.

Nor does the declaration purport to lay down any principles that are to govern the interrelationship of the states of this Western Hemisphere as among themselves.

The Doctrine states a case of United

States *vs.* Europe, not of United States *vs.* Latin America.

Such arrangements as the United States has made, for example, with Cuba, Santo Domingo, Haiti, and Nicaragua, are not within the Doctrine as it was announced by Monroe. They may be accounted for as the expression of a national policy which, like the Doctrine itself, originates in the necessities of security or self-preservation. . . .

In the normal case, the Latin American state against which aggression was aimed by a European power, would be the beneficiary of the Doctrine not its victim. This has been the history of its application. The Doctrine makes the United States a guarantor, in effect, of the independence of Latin American states, though without the obligations of a guarantor to those states, for the United States itself determines by its sovereign will when, where, and concerning what aggressions it will invoke the Doctrine, and by what measures, if any, it will apply a sanction. In none of these things has any other state any voice whatever. . . .

It is evident from the foregoing that the Monroe Doctrine is not an equivalent for "self-preservation"; and therefore the Monroe Doctrine need not, indeed should not, be invoked in order to cover situations challenging our self-preservation but not within the terms defined by Monroe's declaration. These other situations may be handled, and more wisely so, as matters affecting the national security and self-preservation of the United States as a great power. . . .

The so-called "Roosevelt corollary" was to the effect, as generally understood, that in case of financial or other difficulties in weak Latin American countries, the United States should attempt an adjustment thereof lest European Governments should intervene, and intervening should occupy territory—an act which would be contrary to the principles of the Monroe Doctrine. . . . It is not believed that this corollary is justified by the terms of the Monroe Doctrine, however much it may by justified by the application of the doctrine of self-preservation.

These various expressions and statements, as made in connection with the situations which gave rise to them, detract not a little from the scope popularly attached to the Monroe Doctrine, and they relieve that Doctrine of many of the criticisms which have been aimed against it.

Finally, it should not be overlooked that the United States declined the overtures of Great Britain in 1823 to make a joint declaration regarding the principles covered by the Monroe Doctrine, or to enter into a conventional arrangement regarding them. Instead this Government determined to make the declaration of high national policy on its own responsibility and in its own behalf. The Doctrine is thus purely unilateral. . . . It is our Doctrine, to be by us invoked and sustained, held in abeyance, or abandoned as our high international policy or vital national interests shall seem to us, and to us alone, to demand. . . .

Nor should another equally vital fact be lost sight of, that the United States has only been able to give this protection against designing European powers because of its known willingness and determination, if and whenever necessary, to expend its treasure and to sacrifice American life to maintain the principles of the Doctrine. So far as Latin America is concerned, the Doctrine is now, and always has been, not an instrument of violence and oppression, but an unbought, freely bestowed, and wholly effective guaranty of their freedom, independence, and territorial integrity against the imperialistic designs of Europe.

(3) THE NEW DEAL PROCLAIMS THE GOOD NEIGHBOR POLICY

F. D. Roosevelt's First Inaugural Address, March 4, 1933

In the field of world policy I would dedicate this Nation to the policy of the good neighbor—the neighbor who resolutely respects himself and because he does so, respects the rights of others—the neighbor who respects his obligations and respects the sanctity of his agreements in and with a world of neighbors.

If I read the temper of our people correctly, we now realize as we have never before, our interdependence on each other; that we cannot merely take, but we must give as well; that if we are to go forward we must move as a trained and loyal army willing to sacrifice for the good of a common discipline, because, without such discipline, no progress is made, no leadership becomes effective.

Hull's Address to the Montevideo Conference, Dec. 15, 1933, approving the resolution that "no state has the right to intervene in the internal or external affairs of another"

In its own forward-looking policy, the administration at Washington has pledged itself, as I have said, to the policy of the good neighbor. As President Roosevelt has defined the good neighbor, he "resolutely respects himself and, because he does so, respects the rights of others." We must think, we must speak, we must act this part.

I am safe in the statement that each of the American nations wholeheartedly supports this doctrine—that every nation alike earnestly favors the absolute independence, the unimpaired sovereignty, the perfect equality, and the political integrity of each nation large or small, as they similarly oppose aggression in every sense of the word. . . .

My Government is doing its utmost, with due regard to commitments made in the past, to end with all possible speed engagements which have been set up by previous circumstances. . . . The people of my country strongly feel that the so-called right of conquest must forever be banished from this hemisphere and, most of all, they shun and reject that so-called right for themselves. The New Deal indeed would be an empty boast if it did not mean that.

F. D. Roosevelt's Address to the Inter-American Conference in Buenos Aires, Dec. 1, 1936

In this determination to live at peace among ourselves we in the Americas make it at the same time clear that we stand shoulder to shoulder in our final determination that others who, driven by war madness or land hunger, might seek to commit acts of aggression against us will find a Hemisphere wholly prepared to consult together for our mutual safety and our mutual good. I repeat what I said in speaking before the Congress and the Supreme Court of Brazil: "Each one of us has learned the glories of independence. Let each one of us learn the glories of interdependence."

(4) THE PLATT AMENDMENT ABROGATED, May 1934

The United States of America and the Republic of Cuba . . . have agreed upon the following articles:

ARTICLE I. The Treaty of Relations which was concluded between the two contracting parties on May 22, 1903, shall cease to be in force, and is abrogated, from the date on which the present Treaty goes into effect. . . .

ARTICLE IV. If at any time in the future a situation should arise that appears to point to an outbreak of contagious disease in the territory of either of the contracting parties, either of the two Governments shall, for its own protection, and without its act being considered unfriendly, exercise freely and at its discretion the right to suspend communications between those of its ports that it may designate and all or part of the territory of the other party, and for the period that it may consider to be advisable. [The abrogation of the Platt Amendment treaty was followed by the abrogation of the other treaties of protection with other Caribbean nations.]

(5) THE DECLARATION OF LIMA, 1938

[The first step toward making the Monroe Doctrine multilateral was made at the Lima Conference, December 23, 1938, which met because of the looming threat of world war. Though the conference refused Hull's plea for regular consultation it adopted the following Declaration of Lima and a Declaration of American Principles.]

The Governments of the American States Declare:

First. That they reaffirm their continental solidarity and their purpose to collaborate in the maintenance of the principles upon which the said solidarity is based;

Second. That faithful to the above-mentioned principles and to their absolute sovereignty, they reaffirm their decision to maintain them and to defend against all foreign intervention or activity that may threaten them;

Third. And in case the peace, security or territorial integrity of any American republic is thus threatened by acts of any nature that may impair them, they proclaim their common concern and their determination to make effective their solidarity, coordinating their respective sovereign wills by means of the procedure of consultation, established by conventions in force and by declarations of the inter-American conferences, using the measures which in each case the circumstances may make advisable. It is understood that the Governments of the American Republics will act independently in their individual capacity, recognizing fully their juridical equality as sovereign states;

Fourth. That in order to facilitate the consultations established in this and other American peace instruments, the Ministers for Foreign Affairs of the American Republics, when deemed desirable and at the initiative of any one of them, will meet in their several capitals by rotation and without protocolary character. . . .

Fifth. This declaration shall be known as the "Declaration of Lima."

(6) THE DECLARATION OF HAVANA, 1940

[After war broke out a conference at Havana agreed by the Act of Havana, July 30, 1940, that to prevent war from reaching the hemisphere, foreign colonies could, in case of danger of seizure, be temporarily taken over by one or more American states. The Declaration of Havana, given below, took another step toward making the Monroe Doctrine multilateral.]

The Second Meeting of the Ministers of Foreign Affairs of the American Republics

That any attempt on the part of a non-American State against the integrity or inviolability of the territory, the sovereignty or the political independence of an American State shall be considered as an act of aggression against the States which sign this declaration.

In case acts of aggression are committed or should there be reason to believe that an act of aggression is being prepared by a non-American nation against the integrity or inviolability of the territory, the sovereign or the political independence of an American nation, the nations signatory to the present declaration will consult among themselves in order to agree upon the measure it may be advisable to take.

All the signatory nations, or two or more of them, according to circumstances, shall proceed to negotiate the necessary complementary agreements so as to organize cooperation for defense and the assistance that they shall lend each other in the event of aggressions such as those referred to in this declaration.

(7) THE ACT OF CHAPULTEPEC, 1945

[February and March, 1945, saw the Mexico City Conference of American nations "cooperating in the war effort"; the term was used to exclude Argentina which under Perón was warm toward the Axis. The Latin Americans had two purposes: to force the United States to take the lead in saving the United Nations from Russian domination; and to weld a hemisphere alliance so strong that it could settle its own problems and therefore give no excuse for United Nations' interference. The resultant Act of Chapultepec read in part as follows. It also recommended a permanent treaty to the same effect as the Act.]

The Governments Represented at the Inter-American Conference on War and Peace

Declare:

First. That all sovereign States are juridically equal amongst themselves.

Second. That every state has the right to the respect of its individuality and independence, on the part of the other members of the international community.

Third. That every attack of a State against the integrity or the inviolability of territory, or against the sovereignty or political independence of an American State, shall, conformably to Part III hereof, be considered as an act of aggression against the other States which sign this declaration. In any case invasion by armed forces of one State into the territory of another trespassing boundaries established by treaty and demarcated in accordance therewith shall constitute an act of aggression.

Fourth. That in case acts of aggression occur or there may be reasons to believe that an aggression is being prepared by any other State against the integrity and inviolability of territory, or against the sovereignty or political independence of an American State, the States signatory to this declaration will consult amongst themselves in order to agree upon measures it may be advisable to take.

Fifth. That during the war, and until the treaty recommended in Part II hereof is concluded, the signatories of this declaration recognize that such threats and acts of aggression as indicated in paragraphs Third and Fourth above constitute an interference with the war effort of the United Nations, calling for such procedures, within the scope of their constitutional powers of a general nature and for war, as may be found necessary. . . .

(8) THE RIO RECIPROCAL ASSISTANCE TREATY, 1947

[The Act of Chapultepec lasted only for the duration of the war, so a purpose of the Rio Conference of 1948 was to make the essentials of the Act permanent. The following treaty was adopted on September 2, 1947.]

In the name of their Peoples, the Governments represented at the Inter-American Conference for the Maintenance of Continental Peace and Security, desirous of consolidating and strengthening their relations of friendship and good neighborliness. . . . Conclude the following treaty, in order to assure peace, through adequate means, to provide for effective reciprocal assistance to meet armed attacks against any American State, and in order to deal with threats of aggression against any of them: . . .

Article 1. The High Contracting Parties formally condemn war and undertake in their international relations not to resort to the threat or the use of force in any manner inconsistent with the provisions of the Charter of the United Nations or of this Treaty.

Article 2. As a consequence of the principle set forth in the preceding Article, the High Contracting Parties undertake to submit every controversy which may arise between them to methods of peaceful settlement and to endeavor to settle any such controversy among themselves by means of the procedures in force in the Inter-American System before referring it to the General Assembly or the Security Council of the United Nations.

Article 3.

1. The High Contracting Parties agree that an armed attack by any State against an American State shall be considered as an attack against all the American States and, consequently, each one of the said Contracting Parties undertakes to assist in meeting the attack in the exercise of the inherent right of individual or collective self-defense recognized by Article 51 of the Charter of the United Nations.

2. On the request of the State or States directly attacked and until the decision of the Organ of Consultation of the Inter-American System, each one of the Contracting Parties may determine the immediate measures which it may individually take in fulfillment of the obligation contained in the preceding paragraph and in accordance with the principle of continental solidarity. The Organ of Consultation shall meet without delay for the purpose of examining those measures and agreeing upon the measures of a collective character that should be taken. . . .

Article 6. If the inviolability or the integrity of the territory or the sovereignty or political independence of any American State should be affected by an aggression which is not an armed attack or by an extra-continental or intra-continental conflict, or by any other fact or situation that might endanger the peace of America, the Organ of Consultation shall meet immediately in order to agree on the measures which must be taken in case of aggression to assist the victim of the aggression or, in any case, the measures which should be taken for the common defense and for the maintenance of the peace and security of the Continent.

Article 7. In the case of a conflict between two or more American States, without prejudice to the right of self-defense in conformity with Article 51 of the Charter of the United Nations, the High Contracting Parties, meeting in consultation shall call upon the contending States to suspend hostilities and restore matters to the *status quo ante bellum*, and shall take in addition all other necessary measures to reestablish or maintain inter-American peace and security and for the solution of the conflict by peaceful means. The rejection of the pacifying action will be considered in the determination of the aggressor and in the application of the measures which the consultative meeting may agree upon. . . .

Article 9. In addition to other acts which the Organ of Consultation may characterize as aggression, the following shall be considered as such:

a. Unprovoked armed attack by a State against the territory, the people, or the land, sea or air forces of another State;

b. Invasion, by the armed forces of a State, of the territory of an American State, through the trespassing of boundaries demarcated in accordance with a treaty, judicial decision, or arbitral award, or, in the absence of frontiers thus demarcated, invasion affecting a region which is under the effective jurisdiction of another State.

STEPS GOING DOWN TO WAR

This nation will remain a neutral nation, but I cannot ask that every American remain neutral in thought as well. Even a neutral has a right to take account of facts. Even a neutral cannot be asked to close his mind or his conscience.

—FDR, Sept. 3, 1939

Limited national emergency proclaimed, Sept. 8, 1939

Repeal of arms embargo, November 1939. Cash-and-carry proviso restored, and U.S. ships forbidden to enter a specific danger zone near Europe.

[President Roosevelt told me] to keep Winston Churchill and the British Government patient while the American people assessed the issues which faced them. He further instructed me to make plain to the people of Great Britain that we believed in their cause.

—John G. Winant, who became U.S. ambassador to St. James's in February, 1940

We have the lesson before us over and over again—nations that were not ready and were unable to get ready found themselves overrun by the enemy. So-called impregnable fortifications no longer exist. A defense which allows an enemy to consolidate his approach without hindrance will lose. A defense which makes no effort to destroy the line of supplies and communications of the enemy will lose. An effective defense by its very nature requires the equipment to attack the aggressor on his route before he can establish strong bases within the territory of American vital interests.

—FDR, May 16, 1940, asking Congress for large-scale rearmament

On this tenth day of June, 1940, the hand that held the dagger [Italy] has struck it into the back of its neighbor [France]. . . . We will extend to the opponents of force the material resources of this nation and, at the same time, we will harness and speed up the use of those resources in order that we ourselves in the Americas may have equipment and training equal to the task of any emergency and every defense.

—FDR, June 10, 1940

Preliminary military discussions begin in London, August, 1940

Destroyers-for-bases trade announced, Sept. 3, 1940

Selective Service Act approved, Sept. 16, 1940

Embargo on petroleum and scrap steel to Japan, Sept. 26, 1940

Your boys are not going to be sent into any foreign wars.

—FDR, Oct. 30, 1940

If Great Britain goes down, the Axis powers will control the continents of Europe, Asia, Africa, Australia, and the high seas—and they will be in a position to bring enormous military and naval resources against this hemisphere. . . . [We] would be living at the point of a gun—a gun loaded with explosive bullets, economic as well as military.

—FDR, Dec. 29, 1940

British and American staff talks begin in Washington, January, 1941

The staff conference assumes that when the United States becomes engaged in war with Germany it will at the same time engage in war with Italy . . . and Japan. . . . Since Germany is the predominant member of the Axis powers, the Atlantic and European area is considered the decisive theatre. The principal United States effort will be exerted in that theatre, and operations in other theatres will be conducted in such a manner as to facilitate that effort.

—Report of staff conferences, March 1941

The President is determined that we shall win the war together. Make no mistake about that.

—Harry Hopkins, speaking to Churchill, January, 1941

Let us say to the democracies: "We Americans are vitally concerned in your defense of freedom. We are putting forth our energies, our resources and our organizing powers to give you the strength to regain and maintain a free world. We shall send you, in ever-increasing numbers, ships, planes, tanks, guns. That is our purpose and our pledge." . . . Such aid is not an act of war, even if a dictator should unilaterally proclaim it so to be. . . .

In the future days, which we seek to make secure, we look forward to a world founded upon four essential human freedoms.

The first is freedom of speech and expression everywhere in the world.

The second is freedom of every person to worship God in his own way everywhere in the world.

The third is freedom from want, which, translated into world terms, means economic understandings which will secure to every nation a healthy peacetime life for its inhabitants everywhere in the world.

The fourth is freedom from fear—which, translated into world terms, means a world-wide reduction of armaments to such a point and in such a thorough fashion that no nation will be in a position to commit an act of physical aggression against any neighbor—anywhere in the world.

That is no vision of a distant millennium. It is a definite basis for a kind of world attainable in our time and generation. That kind of world is the very antithesis of the so-called new order of tyranny which the dictators seek to create with the crash of a bomb.

To that new order we oppose the greater conception—the moral order. A good society is able to face schemes of world domination and foreign revolutions alike without fear.

> —FDR, Jan. 6, 1941, message to Congress asking for Lend-Lease legislation and setting forth the "Four Freedoms"

Convoys mean shooting, and shooting means war.

> —FDR, Jan. 21, 1941, denying that he intended to to use naval forces to convoy Lend-Lease materiél

Give us the tools and we will do the job.

> —Churchill, Feb. 9, 1941

Our country is going to be what our people have proclaimed it must be—the arsenal of democracy.

> —FDR, March 15, 1941

British, American, and Dutch representatives in Singapore hold talks on what to do in case of war with Japan, April, 1941

Naval "patrols" begin in North Atlantic, April, 1941, west of 26° longitude

He [Roosevelt] kept reverting to the fact that the forces in the Atlantic were merely going to be a patrol to watch for any aggression and report that to America. I answered there, with a smile on my face, saying: "But you are not going to report the presence of the German Fleet to the Americas. You are going to report it to the British Fleet." I wanted him to be honest with himself. To me it seems a clearly hostile act to the Germans, and I am prepared to take the responsibility of it. He seems to be trying to hide it into the character of a purely reconnaissance action, which it clearly is not.

—Secretary of War Henry Stimson, *Diary*, April 24, 1941

Unlimited national emergency declared, May 27, 1941

The war is approaching the brink of the Western Hemisphere itself. . . . The attack on the United States can begin with the domination of any base which menaces our security—north or south. . . . We have, accordingly, extended our patrol in North and South Atlantic waters.

—FDR, May 27, 1941

German and Italian consulates ordered closed, June, 1941

U.S. troops occupy Iceland, July, 1941

Japanese credits frozen, July, 1941

Argentia Conference, September, 1941

The President of the United States and the Prime Minister, Mr. Churchill, representing His Majesty's Government in the United Kingdom, being met together, deem it right to make known certain common principles in the national policies of their respective countries on which they base their hopes for a better future for the world.

—The Atlantic Charter, Argentia, N.F., Aug. 14, 1941

Rejection of Konoye's request for a conference with Roosevelt, October, 1941. Konoye's Cabinet fell and Tojo became premier.

"Shoot at sight" order given U.S. naval vessels in North Atlantic, September, 1941

These Nazi submarines and raiders are the rattlesnakes of the Atlantic.

—FDR, Sept. 11, 1941

Lend-Lease to Russia planned, September, 1941

Roosevelt proposes Anglo-American cooperation in developing A-Bomb Oct. 11, 1941

Merchant ships armed and authorized to enter war zones, November, 1941

German submarines attack U.S. destroyers *Kearney* and *Reuben James*, October, 1941

Hull gives ultimatum to Japan, Nov. 26, 1941

Japan attacks Pearl Harbor, Dec. 7, 1941

Yesterday, December 7, 1941—a date which will live in infamy—the United States was suddenly and deliberately attacked by naval and air forces of the Empire of Japan.

—FDR, Dec. 8, 1941

THE ATLANTIC CHARTER

[Drawn up at the Argentia Bay Conference between Roosevelt and Churchill, Aug. 14, 1941.]

The President of the United States of America and the Prime Minister, Mr. Churchill, representing His Majesty's Government in the United Kingdom, being met together, deem it right to make known certain common principles in the national policies of their respective countries on which they base their hopes for a better future for the world.

First, their countries seek no aggrandizement, territorial or other;

Second, they desire to see no territorial changes that do not accord with the freely expressed wishes of the peoples concerned;

Third, they respect the right of all peoples to choose the form of government under which they will live; and they wish to see sovereign rights and self-government restored to those who have been forcibly deprived of them;

Fourth, they will endeavor, with due re-
spect for their existing obligations, to further the enjoyment by all States, great or small, victor or vanquished, of access, on equal terms, to the trade and to the raw materials of the world which are needed for their economic prosperity;

Fifth, they desire to bring about the fullest collaboration between all nations in the economic field with the object of securing, for all, improved labor standards, economic adjustment and social security;

Sixth, after the final destruction of the Nazi tyranny, they hope to see established a peace which will afford to all nations the means of dwelling in safety within their own boundaries, and which will afford assurance that all the men in all the lands may live out their lives in freedom from fear and want;

Seventh, such a peace should enable all

men to traverse the high seas and oceans without hindrance;

Eighth, they believe that all of the nations of the world, for realistic as well as spiritual reasons, must come to the abandonment of the use of force. Since no future peace can be maintained if land, sea or air armaments continue to be employed by nations which threaten, or may threaten, aggression outside of their frontiers, they believe, pending the establishment of a wider and permanent system of general security, that the disarmaments of such nations is essential. They will likewise aid and encourage all other practicable measures which will lighten for peace-loving peoples the crushing burden of armaments.

THE OPEN DOOR LEADS TO WAR

The Lansing-Ishii Agreement of 1917 had acknowledged Japan's "special interest" in China, thus in effect acknowledging Japan's priority over other nations. Then in 1922 the agreement was quietly shelved in favor of a general commitment to the Open Door in the Nine-Power Pact—which, however, had no enforcement clause. Japan may or may not have intended to observe the pact, but many of its leaders were convinced that the only way to avoid smothering industrially was to obtain raw materials and markets—preferably by political annexation.

(1) THE TANAKA MEMORIAL, 1927

In 1929 the Chinese published the Tanaka Memorial, which they claimed had been written two years earlier by Japan's Prime Minister Tanaka and presented to the Emperor. It has been denounced as a forgery—and may well have been—but at any rate it accurately forecast the creation of what Japan later called her Greater East Asia Co-Prosperity Sphere. Japan had for centuries believed that it was destined to rule the world, and Tanaka outlined the steps necessary to attain that end. Certain parts of the Memorial follow.

The Three Eastern Provinces [of China] are politically the imperfect spot in the Far East. For the sake of self-protection as well as the protection of others, Japan cannot remove the difficulties in Eastern Asia unless she adopts the policy of "Blood and Iron." But in carrying out this policy we have to face the United States which has been turned against us by China's policy of fighting poison with poison. In the future if we want to control China, we must first crush the United States just as in the past we had to fight in the Russo-Japanese War. But in order to conquer China we must first conquer Manchuria and Mongolia. In order to conquer the world, we must first conquer China. If we succeed in conquering China the rest of the Asiatic countries and the South Sea Countries will fear us and surrender to us. Then the world will realize that Eastern Asia is ours and will not dare to violate our rights. This is the plan left to us by Emperor Meiji, the success of which is essential to our national existence.

The Nine-Power Treaty is entirely an expression of the spirit of commercial rivalry. It was the intention of England and America to crush our influence in China with their power of wealth. The proposed reduction of armaments is nothing but a means to limit our military strength, making it impossible for us to conquer the vast territory of China. On the other hand, China's sources of wealth will be entirely at their disposal. It is merely a scheme by which England and America may defeat our plans. And yet the Minseito made the Nine-Power Treaty the important thing and emphasized our TRADE rather than our RIGHTS in China. This is a mistaken policy —a policy of national suicide. England [and America have other resources] . . . but in Japan her food supply and raw materials decrease in proportion to her population. If we merely hope to develop trade, we shall eventually be defeated by England and America, who possess unsurpassable capitalistic power. In the end, we shall get nothing. A more dangerous factor is the fact that the people of China might some day wake up. . . .

After studying the present conditions and possibilities of our country, our best policy lies in the direction of taking positive steps to secure rights and privileges in Manchuria and Mongolia. These will enable us to develop our trade. This will not only forestall China's own industrial development, but also prevent the penetration of European Powers. This is the best policy possible! . . .

Having China's entire resources at our disposal we shall proceed to conquer India, the Archipelago, Asia Minor, Central Asia, and even Europe. But to get control of Manchuria and Mongolia is the first step if the Yamato race wishes to distinguish itself on Continental Asia. Final success belongs to the country having raw materials; the full growth of national strength belongs to the country having extensive territory. If we pursue a positive policy to enlarge our rights in Manchuria and China, all these prerequisites of a powerful nation will constitute no problem. Furthermore our surplus population of 700,000 each year will also be taken care of.

If we want to inaugurate a new policy and secure the permanent prosperity of our empire, a positive policy towards Manchuria and Mongolia is the only way. . . .

(2) THE STIMSON DOCTRINE, 1932

The worldwide depression dealt Japan a severe blow, and no doubt this hastened Japan's effort to annex Manchuria. A local incident at Mukden in September, 1931, afforded the excuse. The action was a patent violation of the Nine-Power Pact, but the League of Nations refused to act. Stimson, speaking for a Quaker President (Hoover) knew that force could not be used, so contented himself with words—the Stimson Doctrine of January 7, 1932.

Please deliver to the Foreign Office on behalf of your Government as soon as possible the following note:

"With the recent military operations about Chinchow, the last remaining administrative authority of the Government of the Chinese Republic in South Manchuria, as it existed prior to September 18th, 1931, has been destroyed. The American Government continues confident that the work of the neutral commission recently authorized by the Council of the League of Nations will facilitate an ultimate solution of the difficulties now existing between China and Japan. But in view of the present situation and of its own rights and obligations therein, the American Government deems it to be its duty to notify both the Imperial Japanese Government and the Government of the Chinese Republic that it cannot admit the legality of any situation *de facto* nor does it intend to recognize any treaty or agreement entered into between those Governments, or agents thereof, which may impair the treaty rights of the United States or its citizens in China, including those which relate to the sovereignty, the independence, or the territorial and administrative integrity of the Republic of China, or to the international policy relative to China, commonly known as the open door policy; and that it does not intend to recognize any situation, treaty or agreement which may be brought about by means contrary to the covenants and obligations of the Pact of Paris of August 27, 1928, to which Treaty both China and Japan, as well as the United States, are parties."

(3) HULL'S TEN-POINT DEMAND, Nov. 26, 1941

Japan's main invasion of China proper began in 1937 with a clash at the Marco Polo Bridge outside Peking. The Chinese communists had been driven out by the Nationalists, and under Mao Tse-tung had taken refuge in Yenan in the far northwest near the border of Inner Mongolia. Now the Nationalists under Chiang Kai-shek were forced to retreat far up the Yangtze to Chungking. Japan was never able to consolidate her control of much more than the rivers and railways. The United States now began to counter Japan by seeking ways to aid Chiang. The result was a long and acerbic diplomatic battle which reached a crisis in August, 1941, after the Japanese moved into southern Indochina. Premier Konoye wanted a meeting with Roosevelt in order to work out—at the very least—a *modus vivendi* which would stop the drift toward war. The stumbling block was China, which Hull insisted on protecting against any form of Japanese penetration, so he demanded that the terms of the agreement be set in advance. Konoye agreed, but Hull persuaded Roosevelt that the meeting would be useless since Konoye would be blocked by the militarists. When Japan persisted in seeking a *modus vivendi* Hull, on November 26, 1941, handed the following paper to Ambassador Nomura. Of course it had no chance of being accepted.

The Government of the United States and the Government of Japan propose to take steps as follows:

1. The Government of the United States and the Government of Japan will endeavor to conclude a multilateral non-aggression pact among the British Empire, China, Japan, the Netherlands, the Soviet Union, Thailand and the United States.

2. Both Governments will endeavor to conclude among the American, British, Chinese, Japanese, the Netherland and Thai Governments an agreement whereunder each of the Governments would pledge itself to respect the territorial integrity of French Indochina and, in the event that there should develop a threat to the territorial integrity of Indochina, to enter into immediate consultation with a view to taking such measures as may be deemed necessary and advisable to meet the threat in question. Such agreement would provide also that each of the Governments party to the agreement would not seek or accept preferential treatment in its trade or economic relations with Indochina and would use its influence to obtain for each of the signatories equality of treatment in trade and commerce with French Indochina.

3. The Government of Japan will withdraw all military, naval, air and police forces from China and from Indochina.

4. The Government of the United States and the Government of Japan will not support —militarily, politically, economically—any government or regime in China other than the National Government of the Republic of China with capital temporarily at Chungking.

5. Both Governments will give up all extraterritorial rights in China, including rights and interests in and with regard to international settlements and concessions, and rights under the Boxer Protocol of 1901.

Both Governments will endeavor to obtain the agreement of the British and other governments to give up extraterritorial rights in China, including rights in international settlements and in concessions and under the Boxer Protocol of 1901.

6. The Government of the United States and the Government of Japan will enter into negotiations for the conclusion between the United States and Japan of a trade agreement, based upon reciprocal most-favored-nation treatment and reduction of trade barriers by both countries, including an undertaking by the United States to bind raw silk on the free list.

7. The Government of the United States and the Government of Japan will, respectively, remove the freezing restrictions on Japanese funds in the United States and on American funds in Japan.

8. Both Governments will agree upon a plan for the stabilization of the dollar-yen rate, with the allocation of funds adequate for this purpose, half to be supplied by Japan and half by the United States.

9. Both Governments will agree that no agreement which either has concluded with any third power or powers shall be interpreted by it in such a way as to conflict with the fundamental purpose of this agreement, the establishment and preservation of peace throughout the Pacific area.

10. Both Governments will use their influence to cause other governments to adhere to and to give practical application to the basic political and economic principles set forth in this agreement.

(4) PEARL HARBOR DAY, December 7, 1941

A meeting between Hull and the two Japanese envoys set for 1 P.M. on December 7th was delayed until 2:20, so Hull was aware of the attack on Pearl Harbor when they met—and apparently the Japanese knew nothing about the project or the attack. The Japanese handed Hull a long and remarkable dispatch reviewing recent diplomatic contacts and complaining bitterly of American high-handedness, selfishness, and hypocrisy. Its thesis that the Open Door was merely an excuse to maintain a *status quo* detrimental to Japan was clearly expressed in the following paragraph.

It is impossible not to reach the conclusion that the American Government desires to maintain and strengthen, in coalition with Great Britain and other Powers, its dominant position it has hitherto occupied not only in China but in other areas of East Asia. It is a fact of history that the countries of East Asia for the past hundred years or more have been compelled to observe the *status quo* under the Anglo-American policy of imperialistic exploitation and to sacrifice themselves to the prosperity of the two nations. The Japanese Government cannot tolerate the perpetuation of such a situation since it directly runs counter to Japan's fundamental policy to enable all nations to enjoy each its proper place in the world.

[Hull's response follows]

After the Secretary had read two or three pages he asked the Ambassador whether this document was presented under instructions of the Japanese Government. The Ambassador replied that it was. The Secretary as soon as he had finished reading the document turned to the Japanese Ambassador and said,

"I must say that in all my conversations with you (the Japanese Ambassador) during the last nine months I have never uttered one word of untruth. This is borne out absolutely by the record. In all my fifty years of public service I have never seen a document that was more crowded with infamous falsehoods and distortions—infamous falsehoods and distortions on a scale so huge that I never imagined until today that any Government on this planet was capable of uttering them."

The Ambassador and Mr. Kurusu then took their leave without making any comment.

CONGRESS WEAKENS ON ISOLATION

[That the American people were turning away from isolation and that it was weakening in its old Congressional stronghold, was shown by the passage of the Fulbright Resolution in the House, September 21, 1943, and the Connally Resolution in the Senate, November 6, 1943. They are given below in order.]

RESOLVED by the House of Representatives (the Senate concurring), that the Congress hereby expresses itself as favoring the creation of appropriate international machinery with power adequate to establish and to maintain a just and lasting peace, among the nations of the world, and as favoring participation by the United States therein through its constitutional process.

RESOLVED, That the war against all our enemies be waged until complete victory is achieved.

That the United States cooperate with its comrades-in-arms in securing a just and honorable peace.

That the United States, acting through its constitutional processes, join free and sovereign nations in the establishment and maintenance of international authority with power to prevent aggression and to preserve the peace of the world.

That the Senate recognize the necessity of there being established at the earliest practicable date a general international organization, based on the principle of the sovereign equality of all peace-loving states, and open to membership by all such states, large and small, for the maintenance of international peace and security.

That, pursuant to the Constitution of the United States, any treaty made to effect the purpose of this resolution, on behalf of the Government of the United States with any other nation or any association of nations, shall be made only by and with the advice and consent of the Senate of the United States, provided two-thirds of the Senators present concur.

The Three Fates

From Richmond Times-Dispatch

16

WORLD WAR II: COMMENTARY

THE TWO FACES OF TOTALITARIANISM

[The naïve opinion held by many innocents that one form of totalitarianism is preferable to another was blasted by William H. Chamberlin, in his *America's Second Crusade* (Chicago: Regnery, 1950), pp. 25–39. Chamberlin was a journalist who had been able to study both communism and fascism on their home grounds.]

When World War I was at its height, it must have seemed probable that the victor would be either the Kaiser or the leaders of the western powers. But the true political winners from that terrific holocaust were three men who were little known, even in their own countries, when hostilities began.

There was a Russian revolutionary, living in obscure poverty in Zürich. There was an Italian radical socialist who turned ultranationalist during the war. There was a completely unknown German soldier, an Austrian by birth, who wept tears of bitter rage when he heard the news of defeat as he lay gassed in a hospital. The names of these men were Vladimir Ilyitch Lenin, Benito Mussolini, and

Adolf Hitler. . . . The war begat a new type of plebeian dictatorship, which may most conveniently be called totalitarianism.

There were certain differences between the two main forms of the totalitarian state, communism and fascism. Both owed their existence to the despair, brutalization, and discarding of old economic forms and moral restraints which were associated with the war. Along with this common origin these twin offspring of the First World War possessed a more important bond. Starting from differing philosophic bases, they developed truly remarkable similarities in practice. There is infinitely more in common between communism and fascism than there is between either system and liberal democracy.

The connection between war and revolution was most direct and obvious in Russia. . . . [There the downfall of the Tsar was followed by mutiny in the armies and a general social upheaval with which the weak liberal republic was unable to cope. In November, 1917, V. I. Lenin led the Bolshevik, later renamed the Communist party, in] a successful coup d'état against the crumbling Provisional Government. A republic of soviets was proclaimed, based on the principle of the dictatorship of the proletariat, or manual-working class, and dedicated to the ideal of world communist revolution.

The soviets were elected bodies of workers, soldiers, and to a smaller extent, of peasants, which sprang up in spontaneous, haphazard fashion all over the country after the Revolution. Delegates were elected in factories and military units and at first could be freely recalled.

After the Communists became entrenched in power, elections to the soviets became an empty formality. Supreme authority in every field was in the hands of the ruling Communist party. Lenin is said to have remarked, half jokingly, that there could be any number of parties in Russia—on one condition: the Communist party must be in power and all the other parties must be in jail. This was an excellent description of Soviet political practice.

The world had witnessed the birth of a new kind of state, based on the unlimited power of a single political party. This party regarded itself as an elite, required a period of probation for applicants for membership, and deliberately kept this membership restricted.

Events followed a different course in Italy. Yet the political result was similar in many respects. There had been a good deal of ferment and unrest in Italy after the war, with strikes, riots, stoppages of essential services. The Italian Communists and some of the Socialists dreamed of setting up a revolutionary dictatorship on the Soviet model.

But they were anticipated and defeated by an ex-Socialist, Benito Mussolini, who had become the evangel of another armed doctrine. This was fascism.

Communism was based on the economic teachings of Karl Marx, as interpreted by Lenin and by Lenin's successor, Josef Stalin. Fascism was a much more personal and eclectic type of theory, worked out by Mussolini after he had broken with socialism. Contrary to a general impression, Mussolini was not a conservative or an upholder of the *status quo*.

The type of state which gradually evolved in Italy after the Fascist March on Rome of October 29, 1922, was a break with Italy's political past. The Fascist order emphasized the supremacy of the state over the individual. It tried to solve the clash of interest between capital and labor by making the government supreme arbiter in economic disputes. Fascism organized, indoctrinated, and drilled the youth, praised the martial virtues, gave the workers an organized system of free entertainment, tried to dramatize every economic problem in terms of a struggle in which every citizen must be a soldier. Had there been no war, it is very unlikely that fascism, a creed which was alien to the easy-going and skeptical Italian temperament, would have conquered Italy. Many of Mussolini's closest associates were veterans who disliked socialism and communism, wanted some kind of social change, and were attracted by Mussolini's energetic personality and nationalist ideas. The Italian Leftists played into Mussolini's hands by plunging the country into a state of chronic disorder, not enough to make a revolution, but enough to reconcile many middle-class Italians to Mussolini's strong-arm methods of restoring order.

The gap between war and revolution was longest in Germany. . . . But the hurricane of the world economic crisis, following the lost war and the inflation, which had ruined the German middle class, paved the way for the third great European political upheaval. This was the rise to power of Adolf Hitler and his National Socialist, or Nazi, party. . . .

Hitler knew how to appeal to German instincts and prejudices. The ideal of the powerful state had always been popular. Hitler promised a "Third Reich," more glorious than the two which had existed earlier. Interpretations of history in terms of race have long possessed a wide appeal in Germany. Hitler vulgarized and popularized the teachings of Teutonic race theorists like the Germanized Englishman, Houston Stewart Chamberlain.

Anti-Semitism had been strengthened in Germany after the war by two developments. Many leaders of Communist and extreme leftist movements—Rosa Luxemburg, Leo Jogisches, Kurt Eisner, to name a few—were of Jewish origin. Many Jews of eastern Europe, fleeing from pogroms and unsettled conditions, had migrated into Germany. Some of these East-European Jews took an active part in the speculation which was rampant in Germany because of the unstable currency and the shortage of commodities. Of course these two groups, the political extremists and the speculators, had nothing whatever to do with each other. But Hitler exploited both in building up for his audiences a picture of the Jew as simultaneously a conscienceless exploiter and profiteer and a force for the subversion of national institutions. . . .

Nazism, like communism and fascism, was an ironical product of the war that was fought in the name of democracy. The hard core of Hitler's following was recruited among men who, in their hearts, had never been demobilized, who could never adjust themselves to civilian life. A great part of Hitler's appeal was to feelings associated with the lost war, the inflation, the economic hardships of the postwar period.

Communists and Fascists may be inclined to dispute the essential kinship of these two systems. But it would be difficult to deny that the following ten characteristics are very important, politically, economically, and morally. They may be listed as follows.

(1) The all-powerful and supposedly infallible leader. These three plebeian dictators—Hitler, the unknown soldier; Stalin, the son of a drunken cobbler, a hunted political rebel in Tsarist times; Mussolini, whose father was a radical village blacksmith—have reveled in clouds of sycophantic incense. . . .

The personal power of these modern dictators has been far greater than that of any crowned ruler of modern times. They have been subject to no check or limit in law or public opinion.

(2) The single ruling party. Under communism, fascism, and nazism only the single ruling party has been permitted to exist legally. Parliaments in the Soviet Union, Germany, and Italy became mere rubber stamps for the registration of the party decisions. Voting under totalitarian regimes is virtually unanimous and altogether meaningless. No voice of independent criticism is ever heard.

(3) Government by a combination of propaganda, terrorism, and flattery of the masses. All three dictatorships developed very powerful methods for molding the minds of the peoples under their rule. The Soviet, Nazi, and Fascist citizen ("subject" would be a more accurate word) has been enveloped in a cloud of state-directed propaganda. From the cradle to the grave the idea is drummed into his head, through the newspapers, the schools, the radio, that he is living in the best of all possible worlds, that his highest glory and happiness are to be found in serving the existing regime, that the "toiler," the "worker," the "peasant,"

by this very service becomes a peculiarly noble and exalted creature.

Open counterpropaganda and free discussion are impossible. . . . The citizen under totalitarianism enjoys not the slightest defense against the arbitrary violence of the state. He can be seized, held in prison indefinitely, sent to a concentration camp, tortured, killed—all without the publicity which would inspire in some resisters the spirit of martyrdom. More than that, his family is exposed to reprisals if he falls into disfavor. . . . Totalitarian secret police organizations habitually employ threats against relatives as a means of extorting confessions.

(4) Exaltation of militarism. "Every Soviet family, school, or political organization is in duty bound to instill in the Soviet youth from the earliest age those qualities necessary to the Red soldier: military spirit, *a love of war*, endurance, self-reliance and boundless loyalty." This statement appeared in *Komsomolskaya Pravda*, official organ of the Soviet Union of Communist Youth, on May 21, 1941. . . .

The names of Hitler and Mussolini will always be associated with glorification of war. Hitler wrote in *Mein Kampf*: "What the German people owes to the army may be summed up in one word, namely, everything." Drills, marches, and parades became second nature to the German and Italian youth.

(5) Full government control of labor power and of the national economy. In this field the original methods of the totalitarian regimes varied. But the end result was strikingly similar. Communism started out as a violent social revolution, expropriating all kinds of private property from which profit was derived and confiscating almost all private wealth.

After three decades it has evolved into a system under which a Communist managerial class, much better paid than the average Soviet citizen and with many perquisites of office, runs the state-owned factories, mines, railways, banks, and other enterprises, including the collective farms.

Under fascism and nazism, owners of property were usually not directly expropriated, except, in Germany, for racial reasons. But they were subjected to so many curbs and regulations, designed to combat unemployment, to increase military output, to make German and Italian industries self-sufficient, that the employer became little more than a managing director for the state or the ruling party. The scope of state ownership under nazism and fascism was extended, and state interference and regulation became almost unlimited.

Labor was organized, regimented, and propagandized in very similar fashion under all three regimes. All went in heavily for much publicized social benefits to workers, insurance schemes, vacations with pay, free sports and entertainments. All took away from the workers the right to form independent unions and to strike. . . .

(6) Widespread use of slave labor. This is a natural and logical consequence of the Communist-Fascist belief that the individual has no rights which the state is bound to respect. Nazi-imposed forced labor came to an end with the military collapse of Germany in 1945. Some six or seven million workers, the majority recruited under some degree of compulsion and segregated in special barracks for wartime labor, were in German territory at that time. The majority of these uprooted human beings were sent back to their native countries. But over a million preferred the bleak and precarious life of the DP camp to the prospect of living in the Soviet Union or in the postwar Communist states of Eastern Europe.

Slave labor in Russia began on a large scale when about a million families of kulaks, or richer peasants, were dispossessed in the drive for collective farming in 1929 and 1930. A large number of these kulaks, men, women, and children indiscriminately, were thrown into freight cars and shipped off to timber camps and new construction enterprises.

Other groups swelled the numbers of this huge forced-labor system. Among these were dissatisfied nationalists in the Ukraine and other non-Russian regions, Communists who had been purged, persons suspected of foreign contacts and of too-active religious sympathies. Later, slave laborers were recruited from other sources.

There were mass roundups and deportations from Eastern Poland and the Baltic states and other regions occupied by the Red Army. There were considerable numbers of German and Japanese war prisoners. Some minor Soviet republics (the Volga German, Crimean Tartar, Kalmyk, and some administrative districts in the Caucasus) were dissolved during the war because the people were not considered loyal to the Soviet regime. Many of their inhabitants were sent to forced-labor concentration camps.

So a vast network of slave-labor reservations, which no independent foreign investigator has ever been allowed to visit, mostly located in northern Russia and Siberia, developed under the direction of the political police. Serious students of the subject estimate that there may be eight or ten million human beings in the Soviet labor camps.

The conditions of the food, housing, and sanitation, and the excessive overwork are appallingly inhuman, according to the testimony of a number of individuals, Russians and foreigners, who have escaped or who have been released. Mortality is very high. The methods of punishment make Negro slavery in the United States before the Civil War seem almost humane.

(7) Hostility to religion. Dictatorships which set themselves above all restraints, which arrogate to themselves the privilege of trampling on all human rights, are inevitably hostile to any form of belief in a transcendent moral law with divine sanctions. . . . The Soviet Government has persecuted all forms of religion . . . and the price which the greatly weakened Orthodox Church pays for the greater tolerance which it has enjoyed since the war is complete subservience to the political demands of the state. . . .

Many churchmen, both Catholics and Protestants, were thrown into Nazi concentration camps. . . . A somewhat easier *modus vivendi* was worked out between church and state in Italy. . . .

Rube Goldberg, Copyright 1950 King Features Syndicate, Inc.

Great upside-down philosopher

(8) A primitive tribal form of chauvinist nationalism. Hitler and Mussolini made a national superiority complex the very basis of their creeds. The Nazi "master race" theory has repeatedly been denounced and parodied.

Soviet Communism preached and still preaches a doctrine of international revolution, to be accompanied by an abolition of racial and national distinctions. But Communist theory and Russian practice have become more and more divergent. Stalin, perhaps impressed by the successes of his rival dictators with their nationalist propaganda, has been cultivating a form of Russian "master race" delusion. This takes the form of announcing that some unknown or little-known Russian has anticipated almost every important discovery in natural science, exploration, and military development. Foreign literature, music, art, and science are systematically belittled merely because they are foreign and non-Communist in inspiration.

(9) The cultivation of fear, hatred, and suspicion of the outside world. . . . Privations which are the natural and inevitable result of "guns instead of butter" economic policies and of bureaucratic blundering are attributed to the wicked designs and conspiracies of foreign powers. The propaganda machines are adept in conjuring up demons to serve as scapegoats —Jews in Germany, for instance; Trotskyites, saboteurs, "grovelers before the West" in Russia.

Normal free contacts with foreign countries are discouraged and forbidden. This policy has been carried to its greatest extreme in Russia. . . .

Because Germany and Italy are in a less isolated geographical position, Hitler and Mussolini never imposed such a complete blackout on foreign contacts. But there was a constant attempt by Nazi and Fascist propagandists to cultivate a spirit of bellicose suspicion of foreigners as spies. Under all three dictatorships it was stock procedure to represent independent foreign journalists as malicious slanderers.

(10) Perhaps the most ominous common trait of the totalitarian creeds is an almost paranoid conviction of world-conquering mission. Belief that the Russian Revolution is only the first step toward a Communist revolution that will encompass the entire globe is the very essence of Lenin's and Stalin's teachings. . . .

Hitler's idea of Teutonic racial destiny is an equivalent of Stalin's and Lenin's faith in the messianic role of the proletariat and the international revolutionary Communist movement. Both Communism and Nazism created fifth columns (the Communist far more numerous and better organized) and thereby contributed one of the great divisive and subversive forces of modern times.

And Mussolini boasted that, "if every century has its peculiar doctrine, there are a thousand indications that fascism is that of the twentieth century."

An additional common trait of the Soviet and Nazi brands of totalitarianism is the capacity and willingness to commit atrocities (in the full sense of that much abused word) on a scale that makes the most ruthless and oppressive governments of the nineteenth century seem positively humanitarian. The Nazi slaughter of millions of Jews during the war would stand on a lonely pinnacle of state-inspired criminality if it were not for the much less publicized horrors which must be laid to the account of the Soviet regime.

First of these was the "liquidation of the kulaks as a class," officially decreed in March 1930. Under this procedure hundreds of thousands of peasant families whose only crime was that they were a little more prosperous than their neighbors were stripped of all their possessions and impressed into slave labor. There were no gas-chamber executions of kulaks, but many perished as a result of overwork, underfeeding, and maltreatment.

Second was the man-made famine in the Ukraine and the North Caucasus in 1932–33. This was not an unavoidable natural disaster. It was a deliberate reprisal inflicted by the government on the peasants because of their failure to work enthusiastically in the collective farms. Several million people perished in this famine.

Third was the establishment of a vast system of slave labor as a normal feature of the Soviet economy. This system is far more cruel than was serfdom in Russia before its abolition in 1861 or slavery in the United States before Abraham Lincoln issued the Emancipation Proclamation, just because it is completely dehumanized. . . .

A good deal of nonsense has been written about the Soviet regime as a riddle, a mystery, an enigma, and what not. But there is no secret about the underlying philosophy of Communism. The Communist International was surely the most open conspiracy to promote violent revolution ever organized. . . .

Before America's Second Crusade was launched two things were, or should have been, crystal clear. First, there was no moral or humanitarian reason to prefer Soviet conquest to Nazi or Japanese conquest. Second, from the cold-blooded standpoint of American political interest, one center of aggressive expansion in Moscow would not be more desirable than two centers in Berlin and Tokyo.

GEOPOLITICS

Now that nuclear bombs can be delivered by rockets to any point on earth the science of geopolitics no longer attracts much popular attention. As a matter of fact—so long as the balance of terror can be preserved—geopolitics as the study of the dynamic relationship between geography and politics still has validity. As such it is worth recalling its origins and its most prominent—even though erroneous—doctrine and the part it played in World War II.

The Allied victory in World War I seemed to the followers of Mahan the ultimate proof of their doctrine of sea power, but as early as 1904 the Scotsman Halford Mackinder had pointed out that the unity of the oceans meant nothing unless the dominant navy also possessed naval bases at strategic places on shore. Eurasia and Africa, he claimed, comprised the only continent—the World-Island—on a globe that was three-fourths water, while North America was only another island which could not long remain a dominant sea power. He suggested that the Russian-Siberian area was the Heartland of the World-Island and occupied a position destined to dominate the outer crescent of Japan, China, India, Africa, and Europe. With unexcelled resources and invulnerable interior lines of communication at its command, the power that ruled the Heartland would not only be safe from successful invasion but could build up overwhelming naval power and topple Britain, the United States, and Japan from their naval thrones. Mackinder warned that a revived Germany could seize the Heartland and use it as a base for the conquest of the world, and he saw the small buffer states of eastern Europe as a barrier behind which Russia could grow strong enough to resist this German push.

Hitler took Mackinder's warning as the Nazi blueprint. It was Karl Haushofer, a German soldier and scholar, who drew together the ideas of Mackinder and various German and Swedish geographers into the "science" which he called geopolitics. Geopolitics is acceptable as a study of dynamic political geography in an attempt to foretell and influence the course of history, but Haushofer meant far more than this. He was concerned with justifying German expansion by showing that it was based upon the immutable scientific laws of geopolitics, just as natural phenomena are based upon the immutable laws of Nature. To do this, he injected a touch of mysticism—based, of course, upon a German's supposed peculiar spiritual insight. Each state, he said, was a living geographical organism which must engage in a conscienceless struggle with other states for a geographical realm which would combine living space (*Lebensraum*), freedom of movement, and internal cohesion (that is, contiguity). The Heartland, and only the Heartland, offered all of these; so it must be enslaved by Germany by alliance, infiltration, or force. After that, armed with matchless resources and traveling on interior lines, Germany

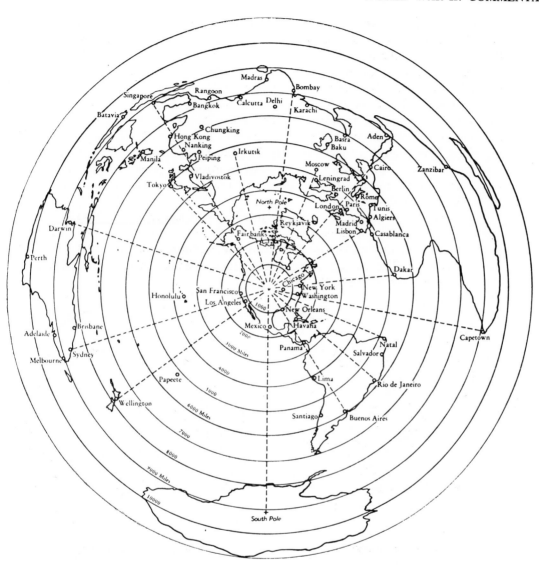

Courtesy Erwin Raisz and Global Press, Inc.

We are much closer to the Old World centers of power and population than people usually suppose.

could enslave the empires of the sea powers grouped in the crescent around the Heartland.

Haushofer's strangest mistake was that, in looking at the world through the eyes of Mercator, he regarded North America as a satellite island far apart from the World-Island. Actually if one looks down at a globe, say with the British Isles as the center, it becomes evident that the continents are grouped together about a new Mediterranean composed of the North Atlantic and the Arctic Ocean—bodies of water less formidable today than the old Mediterranean Sea was in the days of the Roman Empire. Europe is at the center of the global land mass geographically as well as historically—a fact that should be noted by those who believe that the Pacific will be the dominant area of the future. The advantages of the Heartland are not as clearly dominant as they seem on Mercator's projection. Haushofer thought of the Heartland as being protected on the north by the impenetrable Arctic while it forcibly extended its dominion over the periphery of the World-Island as did the nomad Mongol horsemen of the grasslands. But the situation is different now. The Mongols fell upon civilizations that were decadent and weakly organized. Now there is a chance that the Heartland will be balanced by the great population centers: Europe on the west, India on the south, possibly Japan or even China on the east, and North America on the north across Arctic floes which are no barrier in these days.

Germany failed to acquire the Heartland, but its defeat in World War II has left a resurgent Russia in indisputed control of the area. If German geopolitical doctrines are valid, nothing can prevent Russian domination of the world. But they may not be valid. The evidences presented on each side are controversial, and the decision will have to be left to the future.

LAND HEMISPHERE

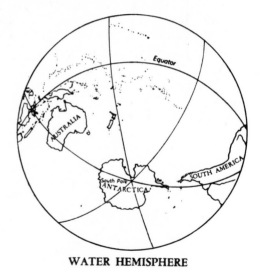

WATER HEMISPHERE

AMERICAN INTERVENTION: 1941

For a lively account of the argument between internationalists and isolationists—now called revisionists—over entry into World War II we turn to Wayne S. Cole's contribution *Interpreting and Teaching American History*, edited by William L. Cartwright and Richard L. Watson, and published by the National Council for the Social Studies, Washington, D.C., in 1961. Here we reprint only pages 286–295.

From 1933 to 1938 the American people and the Franklin D. Roosevelt administration were absorbed primarily with the task of cop-ing with the Great Depression. Most Americans and Congressmen were determined that the United States should never again become involved in "Europe's wars." This determination found expression in the enactment of a series of self-denying Neutrality Acts.

Just as Americans in the New Deal era were preoccupied with domestic matters, so, too, historians studying those years have dealt largely with domestic developments. The political studies and the histories of the New Deal that were analyzed in the preceding chapter contain much data relating directly or indirectly to foreign relations. But there is a striking dearth of specialized studies of the history of American foreign affairs in the New Deal era.

Edward O. Guerrant provided a useful survey of United States-Latin American policies in his book, *Roosevelt's Good Neighbor Policy*. Guerrant described the steps taken by the Roosevelt administration to win the friendship of the Latin American states and to secure their cooperation in protecting the security of the Western Hemisphere against the Axis threat. He concluded that the "United States has never had a foreign policy toward any area that was more successful than the Good Neighbor Policy was from 1933 to 1945."

Two useful accounts focused directly on American foreign affairs in the New Deal period that represent the two major schools of interpretation are Cordell Hull's *Memoirs* and *American Foreign Policy in the Making, 1932–1940*, by Charles A. Beard. These two works advance conflicting interpretations of American foreign policy during the New Deal.

Cordell Hull served as Secretary of State from the beginning of the Roosevelt administration in 1933 until 1944—longer than any other man in American history. His two-volume memoir is a detailed and valuable account of most major American diplomatic developments during the Roosevelt administration. In dealing with the New Deal years and the rise of the Axis challenge, Hull advanced the thesis that he and the President tried to preserve peace and security through internationalism, but that they were forced to move more slowly than they wished because of the isolationist

temper of the American people and Congress. Hull emphasized that "Congress was slower on many occasions than the Executive in seeing the dangers looming to world peace and in taking appropriate steps to meet them."

Critical of Roosevelt's foreign policies, Charles A. Beard was a pre-war "continentalist" and a prominent post-war "revisionist" historian. In *American Foreign Policy in the Making, 1932–1940*, Beard contended that, contrary to Hull's thesis, the Roosevelt administration's public foreign policy statements from 1932 to 1940 were not, for the most part, appeals for internationalism and collective security. Instead, Beard found that, except for the Quarantine Speech in 1937, the administration in public repeatedly spoke out in "isolationist" or non-interventionist terms.

Both "internationalists" and "revisionists" are well represented among the many books and articles on American foreign affairs in the months and years immediately preceding the Japanese attack on Pearl Harbor. Among the early internationalist accounts are *This Is Pearl*, by Walter Millis, and *Roosevelt from Munich to Pearl Harbor*, by Basil Rauch. Robert E. Sherwood used the files of Harry Hopkins as the basis for his Pulitzer-prize-winning *Roosevelt and Hopkins*, published in 1948. Herbert Feis's study of American relations with Japan, entitled *The Road to Pearl Harbor*, was based on more extensive research than earlier volumes on that subject. The culmination of the internationalist interpretation came with the publication in 1952 and 1953 of the two-volume work by William L. Langer and S. Everett Gleason under the general title of *The World Crisis and American Foreign Policy*. These volumes were based on unusually extensive research. The last book in the 1950's written from this same general point of view, and probably the most balanced in its judgments, is *The Passing of American Neutrality, 1937–1941*, by Donald F. Drummond, published in 1955. Though there are variations among these internationalist analyses, it is possible to suggest the main outlines of their interpretation.

Internationalist writers, looking back to the days before Pearl Harbor, viewed the Axis powers as extremely serious threats to American security and interests. They pointed to the strength and speed of the Axis forces which by the middle of 1940 had rolled over Austria, Czechoslovakia, Poland, Denmark, Norway, the Netherlands, Luxemburg, Belgium, and France. Britain alone was successfully resisting Nazi assaults on her home islands. Most authorities at the time expected the Soviet Union to fall quickly after Hitler's *Blitzkrieg* was turned against Russia on June 22, 1941. Axis successes in North Africa raised fears that control of that continent might prove a steppingstone to the Western Hemisphere. In the meantime, Japan took advantage of the European crises to step up her aggressive campaigns in Asia. According to the internationalist interpretation, the President hoped to prevent the United States from becoming involved in the hostilities—provided that could be accomplished without sacrificing American security, vital interests, and principles.

In general, internationalist writers followed the administration view that the defeat of Nazi Germany and Fascist Italy was esssential to American peace and security. Like the Roosevelt administration, most of these writers tended to rule out a negotiated peace as a possible acceptable alternative in Europe—particularly after the fall of France. President Roosevelt hoped that his policy of extending aid short of war to the victims of Axis aggression in Europe would prevent the defeat of Great Britain, contribute to the essential defeat of the Axis powers, and thereby enable the United States to maintain both its peace and its security. Among the many steps taken by the Roosevelt administration to aid the victims of aggression in Europe were repeal of the arms embargo, the destroyer deal, Lend-Lease, the Atlantic patrol system, the shoot-on-sight policy, arming of American merchant ships, and permitting the use of those ships to transport goods directly to England.

According to the internationalist inter-

pretation, Roosevelt and Hull wanted to prevent war between the United States and Japan—in part because such a war would interfere with the main task of defeating Hitler. They believed that the best way to preserve American peace and security in the Pacific was to take steps short of war to check Japanese aggression. Among American actions of this sort were the "moral embargo," the termination of the commercial treaty with Japan, various forms of aid to Chiang Kai-shek, keeping the American fleet at Pearl Harbor, and freezing Japanese assets in the United States. The United States was eager to seek a peaceful settlement with Japan—provided such a settlement would not jeopardize American security and principles, and provided it would not require the United States to abandon China, Britain, France, and the Netherlands in the Pacific. As it became increasingly apparent that compromise was impossible on terms acceptable to both countries, the Roosevelt administration tried to delay war to gain time for military preparations.

With regard to the European theater as well as the Pacific, there were distinct variations in the views of administration leaders before Pearl Harbor about implementing American policies and presenting them to the American people. Cordell Hull generally favored limiting action to steps short of war and he explained each step in terms of peace, security, and international morality. Henry L. Stimson, Frank Knox, and others were critical of this indirect and step-at-a-time approach. They early came to believe that aid short of war would not be sufficient to insure the defeat of the Axis and they urged the President to take more vigorous action against the aggressors. Stimson believed that the American people would support the President in a declaration of war even before Pearl Harbor. Though of a different temperament, President Roosevelt, like Hull, was fearful of arousing effective public opposition to his policies and adhered to the step-at-a-time, short-of-war approach.

Internationalist interpretations tend to reflect these variations in attitudes among pre-war interventionists. Feis treated Hull with considerable respect. Rauch's interpretation is similar to that advanced by Hull, though the hero in Rauch's book is definitely President Roosevelt. Millis and Sherwood generally believed that in view of conditions then existing, President Roosevelt's decisions and methods on foreign policy matters were wise and sound at most crucial points before Pearl Harbor. Langer and Gleason were sympathetic with the more direct and vigorous approach urged by Stimson—particularly as applied to the European theater. They believed that Roosevelt over-estimated the strength of the opposition to his policies.

Writers of the internationalist school found the fundamental causes for American involvement in the war in developments in other parts of the world—beyond the American power to control by 1941. They did not find the explanation within the United States —except in so far as non-interventionist opposition inhibited administration actions that might have prevented the war from beginning or from reaching such a critical stage. Nearly all internationalist historians were highly critical of the opponents of Roosevelt's foreign policies. They all denied that President Roosevelt wanted to get the United States into war. They were convinced that the Japanese attack on Pearl Harbor was a genuine surprise to the members of the Roosevelt administration. In so far as there was any American responsibility for the disaster at Pearl Harbor most internationalist writers blamed the military commanders in Hawaii—Admiral Husband E. Kimmel and General Walter C. Short. None of them believed that there were any alternatives available to President Roosevelt by 1940–1941 that could have prevented American involvement in World War II without sacrificing American security and principles.

Among the early revisionist volumes are *Pearl Harbor*, by George Morgenstern, *President Roosevelt and the Coming of the War, 1941*, by Charles A. Beard, and *America's Sec-*ond *Crusade*, by William Henry Chamberlin. Charles Callan Tansill, after extensive research, published his *Back Door to War* in 1952. Harry Elmer Barnes edited a volume called *Perpetual War for Perpetual Peace* that included essays written by most major revisionists.

In striking contrast to the internationalist interpretation, the revisionists minimized or rejected the idea that the Axis powers constituted a threat to American security. They pointed out that Hitler had no concrete plans for attacking the Western Hemisphere. They portrayed the Japanese attack on Pearl Harbor as an action provoked by American restrictions that threatened Japanese security and vital interests. In so far as revisionists conceded the reality of an Axis threat to the United States, they believed it was caused largely by American shortsighted and provocative policies. Like non-interventionists before Pearl Harbor, the revisionists maintained that the issue was not primarily security but instead was war or peace. And revisionists held that the United States Government had the power to choose for itself whether it would or would not enter the war. Thus, in contrast to internationalists, the revisionists found the explanation for American entry into World War II primarily within the United States rather than in the actions of nations in other parts of the world. In seeking the explanation within the United States, they focused their attention almost exclusively upon administration and military leaders—and particularly upon President Roosevelt.

Revisionists interpreted Roosevelt's steps to aid Britain short of war as actually steps *to* war. Opinions of revisionists varied on the question of whether Roosevelt deliberately meant these as steps to war. In any event, they contended, these actions did not provoke Hitler into war against the United States; and the shooting incidents that occurred in the Atlantic did not arouse American enthusiasm for entering the European war.

Instead, according to most revisionist writers, the Roosevelt administration got the

United States into war through the Asiatic "back door" by provoking Japanese attack on Pearl Harbor. This maneuver was accomplished by increasing pressures on Japan while refusing any compromise that the Japanese could accept. The decisive economic pressure in 1941 was exerted through the curtailment of oil shipments, and the key issue on which compromise proved impossible was China. The freezing of Japanese assets in the United States on July 26, 1941, accompanied by parallel action by the British and Dutch, cut Japan off from her essential oil supplies. The President rejected Premier Konoye's proposal for a personal meeting between the two leaders. Then, Secretary of State Hull, after objections from China and Britain, abandoned the idea of proposing a *modus vivendi*. Instead, on November 26, Hull submitted a ten-point program to Japan—including the demand that the Japanese withdraw from China and Indo-China. This proposal (which revisionists generally call an "ultimatum") was so extreme that Hull knew in advance that Japan would not accept it. According to most revisionists these and other actions by the Roosevelt administration (out of either design or blunder) provoked war with Japan. The United States confronted Japan with the alternatives of backing down or fighting. With oil reserves falling dangerously low, and believing that their vital interests and security were at stake, the Japanese chose to fight.

Through all of this, according to the revisionists, President Roosevelt deceived the American people concerning his policies and objectives in foreign affairs. Revisionists maintained that Roosevelt publicly committed his administration to a policy of peace while secretly leading the nation to war—a war that these writers considered contrary to national interests and contrary to the desires of 80 per cent of the American people. The most famous expression of this thesis is in Beard's last book and particularly in his final chapter.

Most revisionists insisted that administration and military leaders in Washington gave inadequate, ambiguous, and belated warnings to the commanders in Hawaii and withheld essential information from them. According to their contention, officials in Washington had sufficient information—including that obtained by breaking the Japanese secret diplomatic code—to anticipate an early Japanese attack. After Pearl Harbor, they say, the administration attempted unjustly to make General Short and Admiral Kimmel, the commanders in Hawaii, scapegoats for the tragedy. Instead of blaming the commanders in Hawaii, the revisionists placed the main responsibility upon civilian and military leaders in Washington—including Stimson, Knox, and particularly President Roosevelt. On this, as on other phases of the subject, some revisionists, including Beard and Current, wrote in more restrained and qualified terms than either Tansill or Barnes.

Finally, the revisionists insisted that the Roosevelt foreign policies failed to serve American national interests. If, as Roosevelt and Hull contended, American aid to the victims of aggression was designed to keep America out of war, these policies obviously failed. If the Roosevelt policies were designed to protect American security, they were, according to revisionists, of questionable success. By helping to crush Germany and Japan the United States removed two major barriers to Soviet expansion and created power vacuums and chaos that contributed to the rise of the Soviet Union to world power and to the resultant explosive cold war situation. China, which was considered too vital to compromise in 1941, fell into Communist hands—in part, some revisionists said, because of Roosevelt's policies before and during World War II. Revisionists maintained in general that American involvement left the United States less secure, more burdened by debts and taxes, more laden with the necessity of maintaining huge armed forces than ever before in American history.

An excellent recent revisionist study is Paul W. Schroeder's *The Axis Alliance and Japanese-American Relations, 1941.* Schroeder's interpretation differs at many points from that of most revisionists. For example, he rejected the Tansill-Barnes idea that Roosevelt deliberately provoked war with Japan, and he probably would reject the non-interventionist approach toward the European war. Schroeder wrote from the "realist" point of view expressed earlier by Hans Morgenthau and George Kennan. Schroeder contended that United States policies toward Japan underwent an important shift in July, 1941. He wrote:

> Until July . . . the United States consistently sought to attain two limited objectives in the Far East, those of splitting the Axis and of stopping Japan's advance southward. Both aims were in accordance with America's broad strategic interests; both were reasonable, attainable goals. Through a combination of favorable circumstances and forceful American action, the United States reached the position where the achievement of these two goals was within sight. At this very moment, on the verge of a major diplomatic victory, the United States abandoned her original goals and concentrated on a third, the liberation of China. This last aim was not in accord with American strategic interests, was not a limited objective, and, most important, was completely incapable of being achieved by peaceful means and doubtful of attainment even by war. Through her single-minded pursuit of this unattainable goal, the United States forfeited the diplomatic victory which she had already virtually won.

Schroeder believed that "American policy from the end of July to December was a grave mistake." He did not, however, place the blame primarily on President Roosevelt. Instead, Schroeder was particularly critical of Secretary Hull and also suggested that the responsibility for our policies was "shared by the whole nation, with causes that were deeply organic. Behind it was not sinister design or warlike intent, but a sincere and uncompromising adherence to moral principles and liberal doctrines." Schroeder believed that in 1941 there "existed the possibility of a *modus vivendi*, an agreement settling some issues and leaving others in abeyance." He concluded that such "an agreement, limited and temporary in nature, would have involved no sacrifice of principle for either nation, yet would have removed the immediate danger of war.

OPPOSITION TO ENTERING WAR

I remember vividly the days before April, 1917, when a country that did not want to go to war was tricked and bullied and persuaded into doing so. . . . I feel, as I watch the motion picture of events unreeling on the screen of time, that I have seen it all before. This is where I came in.

—Bruce Bliven, 1938

We should concentrate our attention on tilling our own garden. . . . Tilling it properly doubtless involves many drastic changes in capitalism as historically practiced. Well, with all due respect to the enterprise and virtues of capitalism, I never regarded that "system" as sacred, unchanging, and unchangeable.

—Charles Austin Beard, 1940

When your boy is dying on some battlefield in Europe—or maybe in Martinique—and he's crying, "Mother! Mother!—don't blame Franklin D. Roosevelt because he sent your boy to war—blame YOURSELF, because YOU sent Franklin D. Roosevelt back to the White House!

—Republican spot exhortation on the radio
during the Presidential Campaign of 1940

We stand today at the crossroads. So far as is given ordinary mortals to see, both roads which stretch ahead of us are fraught with danger. But if we take one road —the road for which the bill before us is a signpost—what lies ahead is clearly obvious. Down that road lies involvement in Europe's wars, eventual commitments to help bring order out of chaos in all the world, the shouldering of a back-breaking debt for all our people, possibly if not probably, death in some foreign land for the flower of our young men, the end of democracy and civil liberties, certainly, not only for the duration but perhaps for generations until our war-torn economy will be able once again to feed our people.

—Senator Robert A. Taft of Ohio, arguing
against the Lend-Lease Bill in 1941

Well, so now it's all morals and no economics, and we all rally behind the leader. And just which Roosevelt do we rally around—the Roosevelt who is going to keep us out of war by Lend-Lease or the Roosevelt who knows full well that Lend-Lease is the sure path to war?

—Charles Austin Beard, 1941

He [Roosevelt] lied the American people into war because he could not lead them into it.

—Clare Boothe Luce

PEARL HARBOR: WARNING AND DECISION

[Roberta Wohlstetter in *Pearl Harbor: Warning and Decision* (Stanford University Press, 1962) has given what is likely to prove to be the definitive analysis of the circumstances leading up to the Pearl Harbor disaster. In her concluding chapter she summarizes the intelligence available to the armed services and the State Department, including the famous decoding of Japanese diplomatic radio signals by Operation MAGIC. She also warns that the intelligence information from the various sources was uncoordinated among the various agencies of the U.S. government—as also were the actions the agencies contemplated. However, it seemed that the Japanese were moving into the British and Dutch areas of Southeast Asia and the East Indies, and perhaps also into the Philippines and Guam. Also, the attack was expected within a week. Here we give the closing and summary pages of the book, 387–398.]

The crucial question then, . . . is, If we could enumerate accurately the British and Dutch targets and give credence to a Japanese attack against them either on November 30 or December 7, why were we not expecting a specific danger to *ourselves?* And by the word "expecting," we mean expecting in the sense of taking specific alert actions to meet the contingencies of attack by land, sea, or air.

There are several answers to this question that have become apparent in the course of this study. First of all, it is much easier *after* the event to sort the relevant from the irrelevant signals. After the event, of course, a signal is always crystal clear; we can now see what disaster it was signaling, since the disaster has occurred. But before the event it is obscure and pregnant with conflicting meanings. It comes to the observer embedded in an atmosphere of "noise," i.e., in the company of all sorts of information that is useless and irrelevant for predicting the particular disaster. . . .

In short, we failed to anticipate Pearl Harbor not for want of the relevant materials, but because of a plethora of irrelevant ones. Much of the appearance of wanton neglect that emerged in various investigations of the disaster resulted from the unconscious suppression of vast congeries of signs pointing in every direction except Pearl Harbor. It was difficult later to recall these signs since they had led nowhere. Signals that are characterized today as absolutely unequivocal warnings of surprise air attack on Pearl Harbor become, on analysis in the context of December, 1941, not merely ambiguous but occasionally inconsistent with such an attack. . . .

There is a difference, then, between having a signal available somewhere in the heap of irrelevancies, and perceiving it as a warning; and there is also a difference between perceiving it as a warning, and acting or getting action on it. These distinctions, simple as they are, illuminate the obscurity shrouding this moment in history. . . .

For every signal that came into the information net in 1941 there were usually several plausible alternative explanations, and it is not surprising that our observers and analysts were inclined to select the explanations that fitted the popular hypotheses. They sometimes set down new contradictory evidence side by side with existing hypotheses, and they also sometimes held two contradictory beliefs at the same time. We have seen this happen in G-2 estimates for the fall of 1941. Apparently human beings have a stubborn attachment to old beliefs and an equally stubborn resistance to new material that will upset them.

Besides the tendency to select whatever was in accord with one's expectations, there were many other blocks to perception that prevented our analysts from making the correct interpretation. We have just mentioned the masses of conflicting evidence that supported alternative and equally reasonable hypotheses. This is the phenomenon of noise in which a signal is embedded. Even at its normal level, noise presents problems in distraction; but in addition to the natural clatter of useless information and competing signals, in 1941 a number of factors combined to raise the usual noise level. First of all, it had been raised, especially in Honolulu, by the background of previous alert situations and false alarms. Earlier alerts, as we have seen, had centered attention on local sabotage and on signals supporting the hypothesis of a probable Japanese attack on Russia. Second, in both Honolulu and Washington, individual reactions to danger had been numbed, or at least dulled, by the continuous international tension.

A third factor that served to increase the natural noise level was the positive effort made by the enemy to keep the relevant signals quiet. The Japanese security system was an important and successful block to perception. It was able to keep the strictest cloak of secrecy around the Pearl Harbor attack and to limit knowledge only to those closely associated with the details of military and naval planning. In the Japanese Cabinet only the Navy Minister and the Army Minister (who was also Prime Minister) knew of the plan before the task force left its final port of departure.

In addition to keeping certain signals quiet, the enemy tried to create noise, and sent false signals into our information system by carrying on elaborate "spoofs." False radio traffic made us believe that certain ships were maneuvering near the mainland of Japan. The Japanese also sent to individual commanders false war plans for Chinese targets, which were changed only at the last moment to bring them into line with the Southeastern movement.

A fifth barrier to accurate perception was the fact that the relevant signals were subject to change, often very sudden change. This was true even of the so-called static intelligence, which included data on capabilities and the composition of military forces. In the case of our 1941 estimates of the infeasibility of torpedo attacks in the shallow waters of Pearl Harbor, or the underestimation of the range and performance of the Japanese Zero, the changes happened too quickly to appear in an intelligence estimate.

Sixth, our own security system sometimes prevented the communication of signals. It confronted our officers with the problem of trying to keep information from the enemy without keeping it from each other, and, as in the case of MAGIC, they were not always successful. As we have seen, only a very few key individuals saw these secret messages, and they saw them only briefly. They had no opportunity or time to make a critical review of the material, and each one assumed that others who had seen it would arrive at identical interpretations. Exactly who those "others" were was not quite clear to any recipient. Admiral Stark, for example, thought Admiral Kimmel was reading all of MAGIC. Those who were not on the list of recipients, but who had learned somehow of the existence of the decodes, were sure that they contained military as well as diplomatic information and believed that the contents were much fuller and more precise than they actually were. The effect of carefully limiting the reading and discussion of MAGIC,

which was certainly necessary to safeguard the secret of our knowledge of the code, was thus to reduce this group of signals to the point where they were scarcely heard.

To these barriers of noise and security we must add the fact that the necessarily precarious character of intelligence information and predictions was reflected in the wording of instructions to take action. The warning messages were somewhat vague and ambiguous. Enemy moves are often subject to reversal on short notice, and this was true for the Japanese. They had plans for canceling their attacks on American possessions in the Pacific up to 24 hours before the time set for attack. A full alert in the Hawaiian Islands, for example, was one condition that might have caused the Pearl Harbor task force to return to Japan on December 5 or 6. The fact that intelligence predictions must be based on moves that are almost always reversible makes understandable the reluctance of the intelligence analyst to make bold assertions. Even if he is willing to risk his reputation on a firm prediction of attack at a definite time and place, no commander will in turn lightly risk the penalties and costs of a full alert. In December, 1941, a full alert required shooting down any unidentified aircraft sighted over the Hawaiian Islands. Yet this might have been interpreted by Japan as the first overt act. At least that was one consideration that influenced General Short to order his lowest degree of alert. While the cautious phrasing in the messages to the theater is certainly understandable, it nevertheless constituted another block on the road to perception. The sentences in the final theater warnings—"A surprise aggressive move in any direction is a possibility" and "Japanese future action unpredictable but hostile action possible at any moment"—could scarcely have been expected to inform the theater commanders of any change in their strategic situation.

Last but not least we must also mention the blocks to perception and communication inherent in any large bureaucratic organization, and those that stemmed from intraservice and interservice rivalries. The most glaring example of rivalry in the Pearl Harbor case was that between Naval War Plans and Naval Intelligence. A general prejudice against intellectuals and specialists, not confined to the military but unfortunately widely held in America, also made it difficult for intelligence experts to be heard. McCollum, Bratton, Sadtler, and a few others who felt that the signal picture was ominous enough to warrant more urgent warnings had no power to influence decision. The Far Eastern code analysts, for example, were believed to be too immersed in the "Oriental point of view." Low budgets for American Intelligence departments reflected the low prestige of this activity, whereas in England, Germany, and Japan, 1941 budgets reached a height that was regarded by the American Congress as quite beyond reason.

In view of all these limitations to perception and communication, is the fact of surprise at Pearl Harbor, then, really so surprising? Even with these limitations explicitly recognized, there remains the step between perception and action. Let us assume that the first hurdle has been crossed: An available signal has been perceived as an indication of imminent danger. Then how do we resolve the next questions: What specific danger is the signal trying to communicate, and what specific action or preparation should follow?

On November 27, General MacArthur had received a war warning very similar to the one received by General Short in Honolulu. MacArthur's response had been promptly translated into orders designed to protect his bombers from possible air attack from Formosan land bases. But the orders were carried out very slowly. By December 8, Philippine time, only half of the bombers ordered to the south had left the Manila area, and reconnaissance over Formosa had not been undertaken. There was no sense of urgency in preparing for a Japanese air attack, partly because our intelligence estimates had calculated that the Japanese aircraft did not have sufficient range to bomb Manila from Formosa.

The information that Pearl Harbor had been attacked arrived at Manila early in the morning of December 8, giving the Philippine forces some 9 or 10 hours to prepare for an attack. But did an air attack on Pearl Harbor necessarily mean that the Japanese would strike from the air at the Philippines? Did they have enough equipment to mount both air attacks successfully? Would they come from Formosa or from carriers? Intelligence had indicated that they would have to come from carriers, yet the carriers were evidently off Hawaii. MacArthur's headquarters also pointed out that there had been no formal declaration of war against Japan by the United States. Therefore approval could not be granted for a counterattack on Formosan bases. Furthermore there were technical disagreements among airmen as to whether a counterattack should be mounted without advance· photographic reconnaissance. While Brereton was arranging permission to undertake photographic reconnaissance, there was further disagreement about what to do with the aircraft in the meantime. Should they be sent aloft or should they be dispersed to avoid destruction in case the Japanese reached the airfields? When the Japanese bombers arrived shortly after noon, they found all the American aircraft wingtip to wingtip on the ground. Even the signal of an actual attack on Pearl Harbor was not an unambiguous signal of an attack on the Philippines, and it did not make clear what response was best.

The history of Pearl Harbor has an interest exceeding by far any tale of an isolated catastrophe that might have been the result of negligence or stupidity or treachery, however lurid. For we have found the roots of this surprise in circumstances that affected honest, dedicated, and intelligent men. The possibility of such surprise at any time lies in the conditions of human perception and stems from uncertainties so basic that they are not likely to be eliminated, though they might be reduced.

It is only to be expected that the relevant signals, so clearly audible after an event, will be partially obscured before the event by surrounding noise. Even past diligence constructs its own background of noise, in the form of false alarms, which make less likely an alarm when the real thing arrives: the old story of "cry wolf" has a permanent relevance. A totalitarian aggressor can draw a tight curtain of secrecy about his actions and thus muffle the signals of attack. The Western democracies must interpret such signals responsibly and and cautiously, for the process of commitment to war, except *in extremis,* is hedged about by the requirements of consultation. The precautions of secrecy, which are necessary even in a democracy to keep open privileged sources of information, may hamper the use of that information or may slow its transmission to those who have the power of decision. Moreover, human attention is directed by beliefs as to what is likely to occur, and one cannot always listen for the right sounds. An all-out thermonuclear attack on a Western power would be an unprecedented event, and some little time (which might be vital) would surely have to pass before that power's allies could understand the nature of the event and take appropriate action.

There is a good deal of evidence, some of it quantitative, that in conditions of great uncertainty people tend to predict that events that they want to happen actually will happen. Wishfulness in conditions of uncertainty is natural and is hard to banish simply by exhortation—or by wishing. Further, the uncertainty of strategic warning is intrinsic, since an enemy decision to attack might be reversed or the direction of the attack changed; and a defensive action can be taken only at some cost. (For example, at Pearl Harbor, flying a 360-degree reconnaissance would have meant sacrificing training, would have interrupted the high-priority shipment program to the Philippines, and would have exhausted crews and worn out equipment within a few weeks.) In general, an extraordinary state of alert that brings about a peak in readiness must be followed by a trough at a later date. In some cases the cost of the defensive actions is hard to estimate and their relevance is uncertain. Therefore the choice of action in response to strategic warning must also be uncertain. Finally, the balance of technical and military factors that might make an attack infeasible at one time can change swiftly and without notice to make it feasible at another. In our day such balances are changing with unprecedented speed.

ROOSEVELT AND CHURCHILL

It would be an exaggeration to say that Roosevelt and Churchill became chums. . . . They established an easy intimacy, a joking informality and a moratorium on pomposity and cant—and also a degree of frankness in intercourse which, if not quite complete, was remarkably close to it. But neither of them ever forgot for one instant what he was and represented or what the other was and represented. Actually, their relationship was maintained to the end on the highest professional level.

—Robert E. Sherwood, *Roosevelt and Hopkins* (N.Y.: Harper, 1948), p. 363

The Anglo-American success depended at bottom on the fact that the British Government *had* to agree with the Americans, and, realizing their position, yielded gracefully before the dispute had gone so far as to disturb day-to-day administrative co-ordination between the two Governments. The British voice was heard on all critical occasions, and sometimes it modified the Americans' decisions; but there was always an ultimate authority whose decision was binding. When the leaders of the American Government . . . said yes or no, action was undertaken accordingly; but the British yes and no was always subject to review. This did not result from a voluntary abdication on Churchill's part. He simply recognized that, if he insisted upon a course of action distasteful to the United States Government, the Americans could always afford, however reluctantly, to quarrel openly with him, and then bring economic pressure to bear against which no British Government could stand.

—W. H. McNeill, *America, Britain, and Russia*
(London: Oxford, 1953), p. 756

YALTA IN RETROSPECT

A center of bitter controversy has been the agreements made at Yalta in February, 1945, among Churchill, Roosevelt, and Stalin, dealing mainly with postwar problems. For a temperate summation we turn to Forrest C. Pogue, "Yalta in Retrospect," in John L. Snell, ed., *The Meaning of Yalta* (Louisiana State University Press, 1956), pp. 193–208.

In the five years between the end of World War II and the beginning of war in Korea, American distrust and fear of Soviet Russia increased as the Chinese Communists mastered all of continental China, Communist parties made election gains in France and Italy, and the U.S.S.R. imposed an "Iron Curtain" over most of central and eastern Europe. Greece, Turkey, and Iran were threatened and the western sector of Berlin was menaced with starvation by a Soviet blockade. Russian benediction was given to the North Korean attack in 1950 and to the later Chinese entry into the battle against the United Nations forces. The calling up of American troops for service in Korea intensified the sense of betrayal and frustration which had been created by the earlier aggression. To all Americans it was a forcible and sickening reminder that the war against totalitarianism had merely reached the intermission period in 1945, not the final curtain. Realization that years of war had brought only the briefest of respites from conflict created a mass anger which reached the point of hysteria when it was found that the Russians had the secret of that monstrous invention and "ultimate" weapon, the A-bomb.

Suspicion grew rapidly in the atmosphere of fear and anger and defeat, generated in the years 1945–50. When Whittaker Chambers, self-confessed former Russian agent, produced papers allegedly given him by Alger Hiss, a respected State Department official who had been at Dumbarton Oaks, at Yalta, and at San Francisco, it seemed that the Soviet plot ran everywhere. Political maneuvers for partisan advantage became intertwined with security measures. Liberals, who suspected that the Hiss case was a contemporary parallel of the "Dreyfus affair" intended to destroy the remaining architects of the New Deal and Fair Deal as well as to catch Communists, undertook to defend Hiss on the assumption that he could not be guilty because he *must* not be. When he was convicted of perjury, they were rendered speechless and virtually powerless for a season. The indictment or conviction of other officials increased the fear of the American public. When it was found that a number of atomic scientists, as Communists, or in the name of world science, or with a cosmic naïveté about the best means to keep the peace of the world, had handed over secrets to the Russians, it seemed that no one could be trusted.

It was in this period of unbridled suspicion that the Yalta conference commitments, known by 1946 to be more numerous than originally supposed, were wrenched out of historical perspective and blamed for most of the evils in world politics since February, 1945. As a result, Yalta's historical significance has been confused, its decisions exaggerated, and its effect on the course of subsequent events distorted. Above all, the historical context in which Yalta occurred was overlooked. Forgotten was the fact that the Soviet Union had borne the main brunt of the German attack in 1941 and 1942, while Britain and the United States were trying to hold on in the Pacific and were gathering their forces for a return to Europe. Forgotten were wartime fears in the West that Russia might succumb or that she might decide to let the western Allies and Germany fight a costly war of attrition. Forgotten also was the fact that in the years 1942–45 coordination of Anglo-American and Russian pressure against Germany had brought victory in Europe. As a result of this forgetfulness, all Soviet gains at Yalta seemed uncalled for or part of a conspiracy to aid Russia. Yalta became a symbol for betrayal and a shibboleth for the opponents of Roosevelt and of international co-operation.

Each year after 1945 thus brought increased demands for "the whole truth" about Yalta. The defeat of Chiang Kai-shek focused attention on the part the Yalta Far Eastern concessions supposedly played in his downfall. The beginning of the war in Korea raised the question of whether or not Yalta had been responsible for Communist influence in that country. The recall of MacArthur led his supporters to assert that his advice, had it been sought in 1945, would have prevented concessions to the Russians. The year 1955 saw the publication by the State Department of docu-

ments on the Crimea conference. These were followed by Department of Defense releases. Neither set of documents backed the thesis of "betrayal and sellout" presented so often in the halls of Congress and during the political campaigns of 1952.

The State Department and military advisers who drew up the briefing papers and memoranda for President Roosevelt's use at Yalta and the officials who accompanied him to the conference did not mislead him into making wrongful concessions to the Russians. On nearly every concession made at the Crimea conference State Department advisers were more anti-Russian than Roosevelt or Churchill. . . .

Yet, concessions were made to the Russians at Yalta, and the most significant thus far have been those concerning the Far East. For a variety of reasons these Far East concessions have given rise to the most pronounced denunciations of the Yalta conference. Among these reasons are the following: (1) attacks against Yalta by a coalition of proponents of Chiang Kai-shek, opponents of Roosevelt and Marshall, and the champions of MacArthur, (2) an uninformed assumption that it was Yalta that caused the downfall of Chiang Kai-shek, (3) a general prejudice against "secret diplomacy" among the American people and the fact that the agreements were reached privately by Roosevelt and Stalin, (4) the weakening of American and Japanese defenses which the concessions represented, and (5) a conviction that Roosevelt had no moral right to grant Chinese territory to the Russians. . . . The fact that the agreement was quickly reached regarding territory belonging to neither of the conferees is hard to reconcile with Wilsonian ideals of "open covenants openly arrived at" and with the spirit of the Atlantic Charter and the Cairo Declaration.

But the suggestion that Roosevelt's promise to seek Chiang Kai-shek's agreement to concessions in the Far East brought the downfall of Nationalist China has been effectively denied by Harriman and Bohlen, and is not borne out by the facts of twentieth-century Chinese development. The willingness of Chiang to carry out these concessions in return for Russian recognition of his government has already been noted. Arguments that the United States did not properly back Chiang Kai-shek against Mao Tse-tung and that Marshall and his advisers weakened the Nationalists in insisting on compromises with the Chinese Communists should not be charged against the negotiators at Yalta, whatever their foundation in fact. Actually, in 1945 the Generalissimo thought he had a good arrangement with Stalin and for a time after the war his armies seemed to be strongly situated in parts of northern China. Overextension of supply lines, failure to get firm possession of the liberated territory, overconfidence, poor leadership, inflation, refusal to reform Kuomintang corruption, failure to satisfy the land hunger of the Chinese peasant, and, above all, the failure of Stalin to keep his promises to Chiang Kai-shek are the chief explanations for the Nationalist debacle of 1946–50. Strategically, the grant of the Kuriles and southern Sakhalin to a potential enemy of the United States was unsound. In case of a future war between the United States and the U.S.S.R. the American position would be definitely weakened. But few Americans thought of such a war in 1945.

The moral aspects of the concessions have worried liberal supporters of Roosevelt and angered his opponents. . . . The 1945 grant of concessions which the czar's representatives had once won from a defenseless China smacked of a return to the breakup of China. In the disillusionment which came after 1946 many people forgot that the territory Russia gained in 1945 had not been in China's control since 1905. Within a few weeks after the war ended, the Russians held the various ports and possessions which had been promised them, without the Nationalists ever being in contact with the territory involved. Later, Stalin returned part of these areas to the technical control of the Chinese Communists, who in turn made concessions to the Russians.

Despite these extenuating arguments, and the explanations presented earlier, there is no real defense on *moral* grounds of the Far Eastern concessions to the Soviet Union. It is the one point at which Roosevelt openly went back to the type of arrangement which he and other western leaders had previously condemned. Morality and reality were in conflict; reality won. Defenders of the Far Eastern concessions can only justify them in terms of (1) the need of Russian aid against Japan to shorten the war in the Far East and save American lives, or (2) the need to prolong wartime co-operation with the U.S.S.R. into the postwar era.

Many critics of the Yalta conference have insisted that Russian participation was not needed. One group points to possession of the A-bomb and overwhelming naval and air superiority in the Pacific to prove that the United States at the beginning of February, 1945, needed no assistance to defeat Japan. . . . [Nevertheless, at that time] military planners forecast that the war against Japan would likely last eighteen months after the defeat of Germany, with possible casualties, according to Secretary of War Stimson, of at least 500,000 and possibly as many as a million men. The first months of the 1945 campaigns had produced constantly mounting totals of dead and wounded.

In the spring General MacArthur himself favored Russian action in support of his offensives against the Japanese home islands. This notwithstanding, in October, 1955, General MacArthur declared that he was not consulted about concessions to the Russians and that he considered them fantastic. This argument is irrelevant. Had [Roosevelt] refused to seek Soviet aid against Japan, he would almost certainly have been criticized by military commanders in 1945 instead of after his death. . . .

But the western Allies need not have promised the Russians anything, say the critics; Stalin would have fought Japan without concessions. Without Russian documents, one cannot say positively what the Soviet Union would have done. Stalin had made a deal with an enemy in 1939; in 1945, he might conceivably have remained true to his 1941 treaty of neutrality with Japan, or even have converted it into a pact of alliance, if the Japanese had offered him concessions which he could not obtain from China with American help. Various roads were open to Stalin in the spring and summer of 1945. He might have made a deal with Japan in return for concessions in Manchuria and Korea; he might have remained neutral in the Far East until the United States suffered heavy casualties and then entered at peak strength into the Pacific war. Either of these policies would have enabled the Red Army to dominate Europe, while the United States and Britain withdrew their forces from Germany and Italy to the Pacific. Finally, Stalin might have attacked Japan without any agreement regarding the future terms of peace.

In view of the Russian ability to take what they wanted in 1945 without Allied agreement, in view of the additional aid the Allies needed in Europe and the Pacific, and in view of what Chiang Kai-shek was willing to give in August, 1945, for what he thought to be recognition by the Soviet government, one must conclude that the Far Eastern concessions at Yalta did not seem excessive in February, 1945. Even today it is difficult to avoid the conclusion that if Stalin had not received them from Roosevelt and Churchill he would have sought them—or even greater gains—from someone else or have taken them without Allied or Chinese consent. The terms of the Yalta agreements concerning the Far East were in the nature of a Roosevelt-Stalin contract and constituted not only concessions to Stalin but also restraining limitations. It was not Roosevelt's fault that Stalin later broke the contract. . . .

Churchill was aware that a responsible leader cannot escape the consequences of his acts. To mobilize the full support of the British and American people for war against Germany and Japan, he and Roosevelt had encouraged strong feelings against the aggressors. In order to maximize the war effort against the Axis

states, Roosevelt and Churchill had often followed the rule of expediency in their dealings with the Soviet Union and other associated powers. Both leaders, perhaps mindful of the sneers of critics in the twenties at Wilson's World War I idealism, had tended to make their pleas at the level of self-preservation. Public demands for stern justice had been both acknowledged and spurred by the 1943 demand, which was never withdrawn, for unconditional surrender. . . .

Criticism of the actions of the Big Three at Yalta thus becomes in part an indictment of long-established Western assumptions about popular democracy. Roosevelt and Churchill were restricted in their actions at Yalta by the patterns of thought and action which their people demanded and which they themselves had laid down. As practical political leaders, they dared not go too far beyond what their followers would accept. . . .

The meaning of Yalta cannot be grasped unless the conditions under which the conference leaders worked are remembered. In February, 1945, the Allied peoples generally agreed that Germany and Japan must be severely punished and cured of aggressive tendencies. Agreement was widespread that Germany and Japan must be effectively disarmed and their heavy industries restricted in order to prevent them from making war in the future. The western powers generally acknowledged that the U.S.S.R. had suffered terribly in the war and should receive compensation from the common enemies. Thoughts of the postwar era were pervaded by a desire to counterbalance the power of Germany and Japan by the force of the "world policemen" who had co-operated to win the war. Roosevelt certainly hoped, and probably believed until the last weeks before his death, that he could sit down at a table with Stalin and Churchill and work out solutions to the problems of the world. The Big Three tended, as a result, to give smaller states little opportunity to shape their own futures. The President strongly believed that Soviet expansive tendencies would be allayed when

Arizona Republic

The Three Musketeers

Soviet Union might become the center of opposition to the West unless bound as closely as possible to its wartime allies.

All these factors powerfully asserted themselves when the Big Three met in the Crimean palace of the czar in February, 1945. But yet another factor loomed large in the conference at Yalta. The disintegration of Germany meant that the force which had dominated central Europe since 1938 was gone and that its place in central-eastern Europe would be taken by the Soviet Union. A disarmed Italy and a weakened France could not be expected to balance the enormous power of the Red Army. Britain, seriously drained of her capital wealth by the heavy exactions of the war and lacking the manpower reserves to challenge a potential enemy of Russia's strength, could not hope to redress the balance of Europe as she had for two centuries. The people of the United States viewed their exertions in Europe as temporary and hoped for their early termination; they were in no state of psychological readiness to take up Britain's traditional role. The approaching defeat of Japan threatened to create a power vacuum in the Far East like that which Hitler's defeat would leave in Europe. Thus concessions at Yalta inevitably reflected the powerful position of the Soviet Union in Europe and its potential power in the Far East. Personal diplomacy at Yalta came to grips with the basic realities of a new balance of power in the world at large, and the freedom of action of the individual statesman was greatly restricted by these impersonal forces. Therein lies the overriding fact about the conference; without its comprehension, the meaning of Yalta is sure to be missed.

Several courses were open to the western leaders at Yalta in dealing with the new set of power relationships. It was possible to make minimum concessions to Stalin and hope for Russian co-operation and goodwill; it was possible to break off discussions at the first sign of demands which would ratify the new power relationships or create a greater imbalance in world politics than already existed; and it was

the U.S.S.R. won security on its European and Asian frontiers.

Other assumptions likewise encouraged Roosevelt to overestimate the possibilities of postwar co-operation with the Soviet Union. Knowledge that Russia had been severely damaged in the early years of the war with Germany led him to surmise that the U.S.S.R. might require a generation to recover. Some Washington officials believed that the Soviet Union would be dependent upon postwar economic aid for her recovery, and that for this reason Stalin could be counted upon to maintain good relations with the United States. In short, one must remember both the war-born opportunism and the hopes and fears of 1945: concessions which would shorten the war and save lives would be acceptable to the people of the West; the formation of a workable United Nations organization held hope for the correction of any basic errors which might have been made in the various peace arrangements; and, more realistically, it was feared that the

possible to state certain moral positions in indignant and ringing Wilsonian phrases. Roosevelt and Churchill selected the first course, believing and hoping that it would bring victory and at the same time save the peace. They gained something by forcing the Russians to put their promises on record; but they could not make Stalin keep his word. The United States and Great Britain have at least the moral right and, technically, the legal right to use Soviet violations as the basis for repudiation of Allied concessions at Yalta, for it was the Soviet breach of contract that started the "Cold War."

After 1952 Eisenhower and Dulles faced the same alternatives which confronted Roosevelt and Stettinius in 1945: the Russians must be lived with, or they must be fought. There were elements of kinship between Roosevelt's belief that he could achieve real peace by sitting down with Churchill and Stalin and Eisenhower's attempt in 1955 to settle world problems in conferences at "the summit." And there were even clearer similarities between the "spirit of Geneva" of 1955 and the spirit of Yalta a decade earlier. Both were predicated upon the necessity of co-existence and both assumed a mutual desire for co-operation. In 1955, as in 1945, American efforts to co-operate "bumped, very hard indeed, against the great stone face of Communism." Thus the Geneva conferences of 1955 may in another day be as violently and as generally attacked as Yalta was assailed after 1946. If so, the result will be neither sound history nor wise politics.

The vitality of a democratic society certainly demands constant and well-informed criticism of leadership. But neither the free world nor the United States can be made strong by irrational denunciations of its leaders and cries of treason which grow out of frustration and fear. It was from these manifestations of national immaturity that the myth of the Yalta "betrayal" arose. The western world justifiably looks today to the United States for rational leadership and an infusion of confidence, not for mass hysteria and symptoms of a national inferiority complex. The country which constantly tears at its vitals and heedlessly destroys the reputations of its loyal public servants cannot give the sane and courageous guidance so desperately needed to calm the fears and solve the problems of a troubled world. In its reflections on Yalta, as in its conduct in world affairs, the United States can scarcely do better than adopt for its guidance the words of Washington: "Let us raise a standard to which the wise and honest can repair."

Long, *Minneapolis* Tribune

What did we do this time?

17

THE COLD WAR
IN THE WEST

INTRODUCTION

The problem of covering American foreign relations in the postwar period yields in complexity and sheer volume only to that of World War II itself. The United States and the other democracies have faced a global dilemma from which no early escape seems possible. Our opponents feel free to use subversion to fasten their hold on both old and new nations, and boldly undertake to force the democracies to spend their substance and pour out their blood in continual warfare.

Democracy, if it is true to its ideals, cannot resort to the same tactics of force and subversion. Democracies worry about their violations of their standards abroad, and feel guilty because they do not enforce equal justice at home. Communists are concerned about neither, but follow Lenin's advice to "resort to all sorts of cunning, schemes, and strategems, to employ illegal methods, to evade and conceal the truth." They accept his dictum that "morality is that which serves to destroy the old exploiting society."

America also faced another dilemma—the dilemma of power. It was to learn that as the most powerful nation in the world it was not only saddled with the task of leadership, but that this task could never be performed to the satisfaction of on-lookers. Essentially, the postwar history of American foreign relations has been the attempt to escape the dilemma of power by finding a multilateral means of defending freedom. The means used have frequently been awkward or arbitrary, and the results have been mixed.

Nevertheless, it seems likely that Truman will be remembered as a great President because he grasped the nettle firmly with a series of remarkable actions intended to gain time—time for Russia to mellow. These actions were the Truman Doctrine, which shored up the strength of Greece and Turkey; the Marshall Plan, which restored the productive capacity and the courage of Western Europe and initiated the drive to unite its economy; the North Atlantic Treaty; the Point Four Program; and the firm resistance to communism by the Berlin airlift and then by the Korean War. Some of these were ventures into fields of international cooperation never before attempted.

Americans, newly come to world politics, had naïvely expected some measure of gratitude. Instead, they were deluged with complaints about their lack of tact and their aggressive use of power in war, diplomacy, and trade. The American economic expansion which accelerated so markedly in the 1920's was resumed after World War II. Backed by mass production's know-how and plentiful capital, it grew so enormously that it seriously alarmed even the democracies lest their economies become mere adjuncts to that of the United States.

De Gaulle led the anvil chorus. No doubt animated by personal pique and an inflated view of the significance of France as the rightful leader of the world, he announced that America's economic and military power was so overweening that it had become the world's prime menace. He acted accordingly. He refused to permit Britain to enter the Common Market on the ground that it would

Yardley, Baltimore Sun

In 1950 Moscow inspired the so-called Stockholm Peace Pledge, demanding the prohi-

serve as an American Trojan Horse, withdrew from NATO's military arrangements, and ordered American troops out of France. Furthermore, he even sought to find ways to tie the Soviets to Western Europe so that the two could act together to trim the eagle's feathers.

De Gaulle may have been an ill-mannered and ill-tempered old man, but he did have some cause for complaint. There can be no doubt that America's efforts to rally support were frequently inept and ill-directed, and we shall seek to find some of the reasons. But there also can be no doubt that even among those presumed to share the same interests the United States had to contend with a point-blank refusal to give anything but advice; the only exceptions were the English-speaking nations, and even they were niggling and halfhearted. The inevitable result was that normally such multilateral means as were found were little more than shams. It was much easier for the democracies to let America shoulder the responsibilities while they stood around and criticized. Not even in the Korean War did they give more than token help, nor did they ever stop trading with the enemy.

The remarkable thing is not that the United States has done so badly but that under the circumstances it has done so well. Regardless of massive waves of abuse and even hatred, it has cleaved to its purpose of protecting freedom—including, of course, its own—its only consolation being that the foreign leaders who abuse it in public very often retract in private. The question is, how long can this go on? Will the time yet come when military disaster or sheer disgust will cause a retreat to Fortress America, leaving the European democracies to shoulder their own burdens?

Only the future can tell. Meanwhile, the American strategy of playing for time seems to be paying off, at least in Russia. In the April, 1951, issue of *Foreign Affairs*, George Kennan pointed out that the time would come when Russian communism's

bition of the atom bomb. Symbol of the campaign was the "peace" dove, designed by Picasso. Yardley points out the contrast between Communist profession and practice.

rigid ideology would no longer be suitable to an increasingly complex economy, nor any longer be accepted by a society with a long and still-remembered history of cultural creativity and a fine liberal tradition. The United States adopted a policy of watchful waiting, and though it did not always conduct itself with patience and skill, there are signs that the day foretold is nearing. This does not mean that private enterprise will take over or that the government will become a liberal democracy. But there have been changes.

Without admitting it, Russia has begun to alter some of its rigid practices in industrial management, and even to cater to the consumer. The dreaded knock of the secret police on doors at night is now heard less often. The old creativity is rising to the surface. True, the words *democracy* and *coexistence* still do not have the same meanings in English and Russian, nor are they likely to in our century, even though the process of attrition has begun. But, as Kennan warns us, we cannot expect them to be like us. The Russians will still be Russians.

THE DOCUMENTARY RECORD IN THE WEST

It is the intention in this section to follow the course of American postwar foreign policy toward Europe, including the Soviet Union, by citing from documents wherever that is feasible. Obviously, not every detail can be recounted, and a certain amount of commentary will be necessary.

(1) "THE SOVIET UNION WAS NOT A TRADITIONAL NATIONAL STATE"

Arthur Schlesinger, Jr., in "Origins of the Cold War," *Foreign Affairs*, October, 1967, examined the subject and drew a parallel between Russia on one side, and on the other the totalitarian dynamism of Nazi Germany (and, in an omitted portion, the "doctrinaire closed society in the American South" before the Civil War). We quote from pages 46–47. Note how consistent this is with Kennan's analysis, which appears later in this chapter.

So the machinery of suspicion and counter-suspicion, action and counter-action, was set in motion. But, given relations among traditional national states, there was still no reason, even with all the postwar jostling, why this should not have remained a manageable situation. What made it unmanageable, what caused the rapid escalation of the Cold War and in another two years completed the division of Europe, was a set of considerations which this account has thus far excluded. . . .

But the great omission of the revisionists —and also the fundamental explanation of the speed with which the Cold War escalated—

lies precisely in the fact that the Soviet Union was *not* a traditional national state. This is where the "mirror image," invoked by some psychologists, falls down. For the Soviet Union was a phenomenon very different from America or Britain: it was a totalitarian state, endowed with an all-explanatory, all-consuming ideology, committed to the infallibility of government and party, still in a somewhat messianic mood, equating dissent with treason, and ruled by a dictator who, for all his quite extraordinary abilities, had his paranoid moments. . . .

Stalin and his associates, whatever Roosevelt or Truman did or failed to do, were bound to regard the United States as the enemy, not because of this deed or that, but because of the primordial fact that America was the leading capitalist power and thus, by Leninist syllogism, unappeasably hostile, driven by the logic of its system to oppose, encircle and destroy Soviet Russia. Nothing the United States could have done in 1944–45 would have abolished this mistrust, required and sanctified as it was by Marxist gospel—nothing short of the conversion of the United States into a Stalinist despotism; and even this would not have sufficed, as the experience by Jugoslavia and China soon showed, unless it were accompanied by total subservience to Moscow. So long as the United States remained a capitalist democracy, no American policy, given Moscow's theology, could hope to win basic Soviet confidence, and every American action was poisoned from the source. So long as the Soviet Union remained a messianic state, ideology compelled a steady expansion of communist power.

(2) THE TRUMAN DOCTRINE

When Britain announced that it could no longer bear the burden of the anticommunist struggle in Greece, President Truman appeared before Congress, March 12, 1947, and asked that it vote aid to Greece and Turkey. This was a move toward implementing the new policy of containing Russia.

At the present moment in world history nearly every nation must choose between alternative ways of life. The choice is too often not a free one. . . .

I believe that it must be the policy of the United States to support peoples who are resisting attempted subjugation by armed minorities or by outside pressures. . . . I believe that our help should be primarily through economic and financial aid, which is essential to economic stability and orderly political processes.

The world is not static and the status quo is not sacred. But we cannot allow changes in the status quo in violation of the charter of the United Nations by such methods as coercion, or by such subterfuges as political infiltration. In helping free and independent nations to maintain their freedom, the United States will be giving effect to the principles of the charter of the United Nations.

It is necessary only to glance at a map to realize that the survival and integrity of the Greek nation are of grave importance in a much wider situation. If Greece should fall under the control of an armed minority, the effect upon its neighbor, Turkey, would be immediate and serious. Confusion and disorder might well spread throughout the entire Middle East.

(3) THE MARSHALL PLAN

At the same time Europe, with blood drained and economic resources exhausted, was in danger of falling prey to the onslaught of internal communism. Secretary of State George C. Marshall proposed a sweeping program of rehabilitation in a speech at Harvard, June 5, 1947.

In considering the requirements for the rehabilitation of Europe the physical loss of life, the visible destruction of cities, factories, mines, and railroads was correctly estimated, but it has become obvious during recent months that this visible destruction was probably less serious than the dislocation of the entire fabric of European economy. For the past

10 years conditions have been highly abnormal. The feverish preparation for war and the more feverish maintenance of the war effort engulfed all aspects of national economies. Machinery has fallen into disrepair or is entirely obsolete. Under the arbitrary and destructive Nazi rule, virtually every possible enterprise was geared into the German war machine. . . . The breakdown of the business structure of Europe during the war was complete. . . . The modern system of the division of labor upon which the exchange of products is based is in danger of breaking down. . . .

The remedy lies in breaking the vicious circle and restoring the confidence of the European people in the economic future of their own countries and of Europe as a whole. The manufacturer and the farmer throughout wide areas must be able and willing to exchange their products for currencies the continuing value of which is not open to question.

Aside from the demoralizing effect on the world at large and the possibilities of disturbances arising as a result of the desperation of the people concerned, the consequences to the economy of the United States should be apparent to all. It is logical that the United States should do whatever it is able to do to assist in the return of normal economic health in the world, without which there can be no political stability and no assured peace. Our policy is directed not against any country or doctrine but against hunger, poverty, desperation, and chaos. Its purpose should be the revival of a working economy in the world so as to permit the emergence of political and social conditions in which free institutions can exist. Such assistance, I am convinced, must not be on a piecemeal basis as various crises develop. Any assistance that this Government may render in the future should provide a cure rather than a mere palliative. Any government that is willing to assist in the task of recovery will find full cooperation, I am sure, on the part of the United States Government. . . .

The initiative, I think, must come from Europe. The role of this country should consist of friendly aid in the drafting of a European program and of later support of such a program so far as it may be practical for us to do so. The program should be a joint one, agreed to by a number, if not all European nations.

(4) POINT FOUR

Rehabilitating Europe was not enough, and in Point 4 of his Inaugural Address, January 20, 1949, Truman proposed a program of aid to other nations to enable them to build up their economies and promote political stability.

Fourth, we must embark on a new bold policy for making the benefits of our scientific advances and industrial progress available for the improvement and growth of underdeveloped areas. . . . Our aim should be to help the free peoples of the world, through their own efforts, to produce more food, more clothing, more materials for housing and more mechanical power to lighten their burdens. . . . Only by helping the least fortunate of its members to help themselves can the human family achieve the decent, satisfying life that is the right of all people.

(5) THE NORTH ATLANTIC TREATY

Stalin's attempt to acquire West Berlin by choking off ground access was thwarted by the Berlin Air Lift, but communism did take over Czechoslovakia. As a result, the Western European states, Canada, and the United States signed the North Atlantic Treaty, April 4, 1949. (Late in 1950 the Korean War led to the formation of the NATO Army.)

The Parties to this Treaty . . . are resolved to unite their efforts for collective defense and for the preservation of peace and security.

They therefore agree to this North Atlantic Treaty: . . .

Art. 5. The Parties agree that an armed attack against one or more of them in Europe or North America shall be considered an attack against them all; and consequently they agree that, if such an armed attack occurs, each of them, in exercise of the right of individual or collective self-defense recognized by Article 51 of the Charter of the United Nations, will assist the Party or Parties so attacked by taking forthwith, individually and in concert with the other Parties, such action as it deems necessary, including the use of armed force, to restore and maintain the security of the North Atlantic area.

Any such armed attack and all measures taken as a result thereof shall immediately be reported to the Security Council. Such measures shall be terminated when the Security Council has taken the measures necessary to restore and maintain international peace and security. . . .

Art. 9. The Parties hereby establish a council, on which each of them shall be represented, to consider matters concerning the implementation of this Treaty. The council shall be so organized as to be able to meet promptly at any time. . . .

Art. 13. After the Treaty has been in force for twenty years, any Party may cease to be a party one year after its notice of denunciation has been given to the Government of the United States of America, which will inform the Governments of the other Parties of the deposit of each notice of denunciation.

(6) THE DULLES PRONOUNCEMENTS

When John Foster Dulles became Eisenhower's Secretary of State he proclaimed that the policy of neutrality by the emerging nations was immoral, and began implementing the policy of irritating verbalization which he had already outlined—see below—and which frightened the European allies lest it lead to war. ["A Policy of Boldness," *Life*, May 19, 1952, p. 151.]

Those who think only of Western Europe and of making it "impregnable"—without regard to the Near, Middle and Far East and Africa—are just as blind as those who think only of the United States and of making it "impregnable." Policies that do not defend freedom in Asia are fatally defective.

How do we defend it? Obviously, we cannot build a 20,000-mile Maginot Line or match the Red armies, man for man, gun for gun and tank for tank at any particular time or place their general staff selects. To attempt that would mean real strength nowhere and bankruptcy everywhere.

There is one solution and only one: that is

for the free world to develop the will and organize the means to retaliate instantly against open aggression by Red armies, so that, if it occurred anywhere, we could and would strike back where it hurts, by means of our choosing.

Today they [the Soviet satellites] live close to despair because the United States, the historic leader of the forces of freedom, seems dedicated to the negative policy of "containment" and "stalemate."

As a matter of fact, some highly competent work is being done, at one place or another, to promote liberation. Obviously such activities do not lend themselves to public exposition. But liberation from the yoke of Moscow will not occur for a very long time, and courage in neighboring lands will not be sustained, *unless the United States makes it publicly known that it wants and expects liberation to occur*. The mere statement of that wish and expectation would change, in an electrifying way, the mood of the captive peoples. It would put heavy new burdens on the jailers and create new opportunities for liberation.

[Speech before Council on Foreign Relations, Jan. 12, 1954]

The way to deter aggression is for the free community to be willing and able to respond vigorously at places and with means of its own choosing. . . . The basic decision was to depend primarily upon a great capacity to retaliate, instantly, by means and at places of our choosing.

["How Dulles Averted War," *Life*, Jan. 16, 1956, p. 78]

You have to take chances for peace. Just as you must take chances in war. . . . The ability to get to the verge without getting into the war is the necessary art. . . . If you try to run away from it, if you are scared to go to the brink, you are lost. We've had to look it square in the face—on the question of enlarging the Korean war [1953], on the question of getting into the Indo-China war [1954], on the question of Formosa [1955]. We walked to the brink and we looked it in the face. We took strong action.

(7) THE SUEZ WAR, 1956

Israel had won its independence in 1948, but was perpetually menaced by Arab incursions, and Egypt refused to let it use the Suez Canal and continually threatened war. Egypt's Nasser naturally desired to take over the Suez Canal from Britain, and Dulles pushed Britain into agreeing despite the plea that Nasser could not possibly run it efficiently (which, incidentally, proved to be wrong) and would use it as an instrument of national policy (which he did). Finally, even Dulles tired of Nasser's demands and fulminations and withdrew a promise to finance the Aswan dam. By this time Britain and France had lost faith in the United States and secretly planned to seize the Canal. Suddenly on October 29, 1956, Israeli forces dashed across the Egyptian border into the Sinai Desert, and a few days later Britain and France attacked the Canal. The Arabs promptly blocked the Canal and cut the pipelines from the Persian Gulf, thus shutting off Europe's oil supplies. At the moment Dulles was in the hospital, so Eisenhower took charge and joined with Russia and the United Nations in forcing all three to abandon their conquests. (During those very days Russian tanks were crushing the Hungarian patriot rising in Budapest.) The effect on Britain and France can be imagined; the British prime minister fell, and the decline of the French government began which led to de Gaulle's take-over in 1958. Official accounts have been chary of admitting how Eisenhower forced withdrawal, so we turn to the *U.S. News and World Report*, December 21, 1956, p. 35.

U.S. pressure began to make its big impact after oil and gasoline shortages developed throughout Europe, in mid-November, due to the closing of the Suez Canal. Britain and

France were forced to start tight gasoline rationing, and they tried to place big orders for oil with American companies.

However, the U.S. Government refused to permit additional oil to flow to Western Europe until Britain and France would agree to withdraw from Egypt. What's more, these Governments were told that they could not make any conditions in exchange for agreeing to withdraw.

Prime Minister Eden, hard pressed to obtain guarantees on the Suez Canal before ordering a withdrawal of British troops, asked President Eisenhower for a Big Three meeting. The White House approved, then rejected this request.

Britain and France held out for two weeks, but their economies suffered more with each day that passed. Finally, they gave in. Only then did the Eisenhower Administration give the go-ahead for big oil shipments to Europe.

Thus, it was the United States, and not the United Nations, that really forced the withdrawal from Egypt.

(8) THE EISENHOWER DOCTRINE

Arabs gave the credit to Russia for the outcome of the Suez War, and Nasser of Egypt sought to stir up revolutions in neighboring states in order to unite them under his sway. The prospect of revolution became so serious that in March, 1957, Congress adopted the following joint resolutions. (In July, 1958, Eisenhower landed troops in Lebanon to forestall a revolution; Russia, suffering from internal problems, did not intervene.)

Resolved by the Senate and House of Representatives of the United States of America in Congress assembled.

That the President be and hereby is authorized to cooperate with and assist any nation or group of nations in the general area of the Middle East desiring such assistance in the development of economic strength dedicated to the maintenance of national independence.

The President is authorized to undertake, in the general area of the Middle East, military assistance programs with any nation or group of nations of that area desiring such assistance.

Furthermore, the United States regards as vital to the national interest and world peace the preservation of the independence and integrity of the nations of the Middle East. To this end, if the President determines the necessity thereof, the United States is prepared to use armed forces to assist any such nation or group of such nations requesting assistance against armed aggression from any country controlled by international communism: *Provided*, That such employment shall be consonant with the treaty obligations of the United States and with the Constitution of the United States.

(9) KENNEDY PROPOSES THE ALLIANCE FOR PROGRESS

An integral part of communist strategy in the Cold War was the effort to establish a base of operations in Latin America from which propaganda, arms, and trained guerrilla leaders could be smuggled to the rest of the hemisphere. Castro's revolution in Cuba was originally a liberal movement, but once he was in power he purged the liberals and took his revolution into the communist camp; it is debatable whether a more cooperative attitude by the Eisenhower administration could have prevented the shift.

With Cuba as a base, communist terrorism was able to cause considerable disruption, notably in Bolivia, Colombia, Venezuela, Guatemala, and the Dominican Republic. Most serious was a revolution in the last-named country in 1965, but the Johnson Administration succeeded in rallying the Organization of American States to join in suppressing it by armed force. Long before this the quarrel between Russia and Red China had been reflected in communist divisions in Latin America. Castro favored the dynamic policy of China, but was handicapped by his complete dependence on Russia, a dependence which was deepened by the crises of 1961 and 1962, soon to be noted.

Kennedy's response to Castro's drive was the Alliance for Progress, a proposal of aid to Latin America, announced on March 13, 1961, parts of which follow. In the parts not reproduced, the United States promised to step up the Food-for-Peace program and expand the training of badly needed experts.

This was a brave beginning, but accomplishments thus far have been minimal. Social, economic, and political privilege were too deeply rooted to permit a crash program of reform to succeed. (It is worth noting here that the sweeping domestic reforms proposed by Kennedy and Johnson within the United States were whittled down by Congress at the behest of similar, though admittedly less powerful, interests.) In the long run, the cause of reform in Latin America would probably have been more effectively advanced if the United States had more honestly and earnestly carried out its promise in Section 5 to promote economic stability by assuring reasonable prices for Latin-American exports.

. . . *First*, I propose that the American Republics begin on a vast new Ten Year Plan for the Americas, a plan to transform the 1960's into a historic decade of democratic progress.

These 10 years will be the years of maximum progress—maximum effort, the years when the greatest obstacles must be overcome, the years when the need for assistance will be the greatest.

And if we are successful, if our effort is bold enough and determined enough, then the close of this decade will mark the beginning of a new era in the American experience. The living standards of every American family will be on the rise, basic education will be available to all, hunger will be a forgotten experience, the need for massive outside help will have passed, most nations will have entered a period of self-sustaining growth, and, although there will be still much to do, every American Republic will be the master of its own revolution and its own hope and progress.

Let me stress that only the most determined efforts of the American nations themselves can bring success to this effort. They,

and they alone, can mobilize their resources, enlist the energies of their people, and modify their social patterns so that all, and not just a privileged few, share in the fruits of growth. If this effort is made, then outside assistance will give a vital impetus to progress; without it, no amount of help will advance the welfare of the people.

Thus if the countries of Latin America are ready to do their part, and I am sure they are, then I believe the United States, for its part, should help provide resources of a scope and magnitude sufficient to make this bold development plan a success—just as we helped to provide, against equal odds nearly, the resources adequate to help rebuild the economies of Western Europe. For only an effort of towering dimensions can insure fulfillment of our plan for a decade of progress.

Secondly, I will shortly request a ministerial meeting of the Inter-American Economic and Social Council, a meeting at which we can begin the massive planning effort which will be at the heart of the Alliance for Progress.

For if our Alliance is to succeed, each

Latin nation must formulate long-range plans for its own development, plans which establish targets and priorities, insure monetary stability, establish the machinery for vital social change, stimulate private activity and initiative, and provide for a maximum national effort. These plans will be the foundation of our development effort, and the basis for the allocation of outside resources.

A greatly strengthened IA-ECOSOC, working with the Economic Commission for Latin America and the Inter-American Development Bank, can assemble the leading economists and experts of the hemisphere to help each country develop its own development plan—and provide a continuing review of economic progress in this hemisphere.

Third, I have this evening signed a request to the Congress for $500 million as a first step in fulfilling the Act of Bogotá. This is the first large-scale Inter-American effort, instituted by my predecessor President Eisenhower, to attack the social barriers which block economic progress. The money will be used to combat illiter-acy, improve the productivity and use of their land, wipe out disease, attack archaic tax and land tenure structures, provide educational opportunities, and offer a broad range of projects designed to make the benefits of increasing abundance available to all. We will begin to commit these funds as soon as they are appropriated.

Fourth, we must support all economic integration which is a genuine step toward larger markets and greater competitive opportunity. The fragmentation of Latin American economies is a serious barrier to industrial growth. Projects such as the Central American common market and free-trade areas in South America can help to remove these obstacles.

Fifth, the United States is ready to cooperate in serious, case-by-case examinations of commodity market problems. Frequent violent change in commodity prices seriously injures the economies of many Latin American countries, draining their resources and stultifying their growth. Together we must find practical methods of bringing an end to this pattern.

(10) KENNEDY PROPOSES THE PEACE CORPS

One of the most successful undertakings in recent years was the Peace Corps, proposed by President Kennedy in a message to Congress, March 20, 1961.

Throughout the world the people of the newly developing nations are struggling for economic and social progress which reflects their deepest desires. Our own freedom, and the future of freedom around the world, depend, in a very real sense, on their ability to build growing and independent nations where men can live in dignity, liberated from the bonds of hunger, ignorance, and poverty.

One of the greatest obstacles to the achievement of this goal is the lack of trained men and women with the skill to teach the young and assist in the operation of development projects—men and women with the capacity to cope with the demands of swiftly evolving economies, and with the dedication to put that capacity to work in the villages, the mountains, the towns, and the factories of dozens of struggling nations.

The vast task of economic development urgently requires skilled people to do the work of the society—to help teach in the schools, construct developing projects, demonstrate modern methods of sanitation in the villages, and perform a hundred other tasks calling for training and advanced knowledge.

To meet this urgent need for skilled manpower we are proposing the establishment of a Peace Corps—an organization which will recruit and train American volunteers, sending them abroad to work with the people of other nations.

This organization will differ from existing assistance programs in that its members will supplement technical advisers by offering the specific skills needed by developing nations if they are to put technical advice to work. They will help provide the skilled manpower necessary to carry out the development projects planned by the host governments, acting at a working level and serving at great personal sacrifice. There is little doubt that the number of those who wish to serve will be far greater than our capacity to absorb them. . . .

(11) KENNEDY SEEKS ESCAPE FROM COLD WAR DILEMMAS

The abortive Bay of Pigs invasion of Cuba in April, 1961, taught Kennedy the lesson that any policy dependent on force must have sufficient force to assure its success—otherwise the situation was only made worse. As a result, Kennedy quietly resolved to outwait the Castro regime, and meanwhile sought to free American foreign policy from the jaws of the vise in which it was being held—on one side the Soviet's nuclear threats, and on the other the simplistic American demand to uphold morality by quick and total victory. To do this, he had to convince the Russians that nuclear threats might actually lead to nuclear war, and also convince Americans that total victory meant total destruction; the Cuban Crisis of 1962 and the test-ban treaty were his two convincing arguments. He began his campaign of education in a speech at Seattle, November 17, 1961, in which he asked Americans to abandon their "either-or" attitude.

In short, we must face problems which do not lend themselves to easy, quick or permanent solutions. And we must face the fact that the United States is neither omnipotent nor omniscient, that we cannot always impose our will on the other 94 per cent of mankind, that we cannot right every wrong or reverse each adversity, and that therefore there cannot be an American solution for every world problem.

These burdens and frustrations are accepted by most Americans with maturity and understanding. . . . But there are others who cannot bear the burden of a long twilight struggle. They lack confidence in our long-run capacity to survive and succeed. They see communism as the wave of the future. And they want some quick and easy and cheap solution, now.

There are two groups of these frustrated citizens, far apart in their views yet very much alike in their approach. On the one hand are those who urge upon us what I regard to be the pathway to surrender—appeasing our enemies, compromising our honor, purchasing peace at any price, disavowing our aims, our friends, our obligations. If their view had prevailed, the world of free choice would be smaller today.

On the other hand are those who urge upon us what I regard to be the pathway to war—equating negotiations with appeasement and substituting rigidity for firmness. If their view had prevailed, we would be at war today, and in more places than one.

It is a curious fact that each of these extreme opposites resembles the other. Each believes that we have only two choices—appeasement or war, suicide or surrender, humiliation or holocaust, to be either Red or dead. Each side sees only hard and soft nations, hard and soft policies, hard and soft men. Each believes that any departure from its own course inevitably leads to the other—one group believes that any peaceful solution means appeasement; the other believes that any arms build-up means war.

One group regards everyone else as warmongers, the other regards everyone else as appeasers. Neither side admits its path will lead to disaster, but neither can tell us how or where to draw the line once we descend the slippery slopes of either appeasement or intervention.

In short, while both extremes profess to be the true realists, neither could be more unrealistic. While both claim to be doing the nation a service, they could do it no greater disservice. For this kind of talk, if believed, could inspire uncertainty among our allies when they must, above all, be united. It could inspire uncertainty among our allies when they must, above all, be confident. And even more dangerously, it could, if believed, inspire doubt among our adversaries when they must, above all, be convinced of our readiness to defend our vital interest.

The essential fact that both of these groups fail to grasp is that diplomacy and defense are not substitutes for one another. Either, alone, would fail. A willingness to resist force, unaccompanied by a willingness to talk, could provoke belligerence, while a willingness to talk, unaccompanied by a willingnes to resist force, could invite disaster.

But as long as we know precisely what comprises our vital interest and our long-range goals, we have nothing to fear from negotiations at the appropriate time, and nothing to gain by refusing them. At a time when a single clash could escalate overnight into a holocaust of mushroom clouds, a great power does not prove its firmness by leaving the task of exploring the other's intentions to sentries or those without full responsibility. Nor can ultimate weapons rightfully be employed, or the ultimate sacrifice rightfully demanded of our citizens, until every reasonable solution has been explored.

But, while we shall negotiate freely, we will never negotiate freedom. . . . Our answer to the classic question of Patrick Henry is still no. Life is not so dear and peace is not so precious "as to be purchased at the price of chains and slavery." And that is our answer, even though, for the first time since the ancient battles between Greek city-states, war entails the threat of total annihilation, of everything we know, of society itself. For to save mankind's future freedom, we must face up to any risk that is necessary. We will always seek peace, but we will never surrender.

(12) THE CUBAN CRISIS OF 1962

No doubt Khrushchev regarded Kennedy's turn in policy as a retreat, and so resolved to find a way to catch him off balance and force a continued retreat. The method he chose was to install missile bases in Cuba which would be capable of reaching both the United States and Latin America. American aerial reconnaissance revealed their presence in October, 1962, and on the 22nd Kennedy delivered the following radio and television address. When a week later Khrushchev backed down and removed the missiles, it was a turning point in the Cold War.

Neither the United States of America nor the world community of nations can tolerate deliberate deception and offensive threats on the part of any nation, large or small. We no longer live in a world where only the actual firing of weapons represents a sufficient challenge to a nation's security to constitute maximum peril.

Nuclear weapons are so destructive and ballistic missiles are so swift that any substantially increased possibility of their use or any sudden change in their deployment may well be regarded as a definite threat to peace.

For many years both the Soviet Union and the United States, recognizing this fact, have deployed strategic nuclear weapons with great care, never upsetting the precarious status quo which insured that these weapons would not be used in the absence of some vital challenge. . . .

But this secret, swift, extraordinary build-up of Communist missiles in an area well-known to have a special and historical relationship to the United States and the nations of the Western Hemisphere, in violation of Soviet assurances and in defiance of American and hemispheric policy—this sudden, clandestine decision to station strategic weapons for the first time outside of Soviet soil—is a deliberately provocative and unjustified change in the status quo which cannot be accepted by this country if our courage and our commitments are ever to be trusted again, by either friend or foe.

The nineteen thirties taught us a clear lesson. Aggressive conduct, if allowed to go unchecked and unchallenged, ultimately leads to war. . . .

Acting, therefore, in the defense of our own security and of the entire Western Hemisphere and under the authority entrusted to me by the Constitution as endorsed by the resolution of the Congress, I have directed that the following initial steps be taken immediately:

First, to halt this offensive build-up, a strict quarantine of all offensive military equipment under shipment to Cuba is being initiated. . . . This quarantine will be extended if needed to other types of cargo and carriers.

We are not at this time, however, denying the necessities of life as the Soviets attempted to do in their Berlin blockade of 1948.

Second, I have directed the continued and increased close surveillance of Cuba and its military build-up. . . .

I have directed the armed forces to prepare for any eventualities, and I trust that in the interests of both the Cuban people and the Soviet technicians at the sites, the hazards to all concerned of continuing this threat will be recognized.

Third, it shall be the policy of this nation to regard any nuclear missile launched from Cuba against any nation in the Western Hemisphere as an attack by the Soviet Union on the United States requiring a full retaliatory response upon the Soviet Union.

Fourth, as a necessary military precaution, I have reinforced our base at Guantanamo, evacuated today the dependents of our personnel there and ordered additional military units to be on a stand-by alert basis.

Fifth, we are calling tonight for an immediate meeting of the organization of consultation under the Organization of American States to consider this threat to hemispheric security and to invoke Articles 6 and 8 of the Rio Treaty in support of all necessary action. . . .

Our other allies around the world have also been alerted.

Sixth, under the Charter of the United Nations we are asking tonight that an emergency meeting of the Security Council be convoked without delay to take action against this latest Soviet threat to world peace.

Our resolution will call for the prompt dismantling and withdrawal of all offensive weapons in Cuba under the supervision of U. N. observers before the quarantine can be lifted.

Seventh, and finally, I call upon Chairman Khrushchev to halt and eliminate this clandestine, reckless and provocative threat to world peace and to stable relations between our two nations.

I call upon him further to abandon this course of world domination and to join in an historic effort to end the perilous arms race and to transform the history of man.

He has an opportunity now to move the world back from the abyss of destruction by returning to his Government's own words that it had no need to station missiles outside its own territory, and withdrawing these weapons from Cuba; by refraining from any action which will widen or deepen the present crisis, and then by participating in a search for peaceful and permanent solutions.

(13) THE NUCLEAR TEST BAN TREATY, 1963

Khrushchev was apparently convinced that nuclear threats might bring nuclear war. Kennedy now renewed his efforts to convince the American people that negotiation was the only way out. As a result, they accepted the Test Ban Treaty of July, 1963, which Kennedy announced to the nation on the 26th.

Yesterday a shaft of light cut into the darkness. Negotiations were concluded in Moscow on a treaty to ban all nuclear tests in the atmosphere, in outer space and underwater. For the first time, an agreement has been reached on bringing the forces of nuclear destruction under international control—a goal first sought in 1946 when Bernard Baruch presented a comprehensive control plan to the United Nations. . . .

The familiar contest between choice and coercion, the familiar places of danger and conflict, are still there, in Cuba, in Southeast Asia, in Berlin and all around the globe, still requiring all the strength and the vigilance that we can muster. Nothing could more greatly damage our cause than if we and our allies were to believe that peace has already been achieved and that our strength and unity were no longer required.

But now, for the first time in many years, the path of peace may be open. No one can be certain what the future will bring. No one can say whether the time has come for an easing of the struggle. But history and our own conscience will judge us more harshly if we do not now make every effort to test our hopes by action, and this is the place to begin. According to the ancient Chinese proverb, "A journey of a thousand miles must begin with a single step."

A DIVERSITY OF CHOICES

You can acquire respect but not affection. You are too big, too strong, and too rich to be loved.

—Prime Minister Lester Pearson of Canada,
explaining the facts of life to Americans

But once war is forced upon us, there is no other alternative than to apply every available means to bring it to a swift end. War's very object is victory—not prolonged indecision. In war, indeed, there can be no substitute for victory.

—General Douglas MacArthur, 1951

A blind faith in total victory can be fatal because it assumes that evil exists in the world only by sufferance, and that all it takes to destroy it is godlike power.

—Vermont Royster, A Pride of Prejudices, 1967

I believe we should defend every place from Communism. I believe we can. I believe we are able to. I have confidence in us. I don't believe we should write off anything and accept the defeat that is involved in it. . . . I don't admit that we can't hold Communism wherever it shows its head.

—General Douglas MacArthur, 1951

Could Americans define their existence without recourse to the expanding frontier that had formerly provided them with the private property they used to prove their existence? Could they, in short, define their existence and conceive grand ideas and great ideals without recourse to private property as the *sine qua non* of democracy, prosperity, and the general welfare? . . . It just may be that the Age of Corporation Capitalism has created the conditions that will enable Americans to answer the question in the affirmative. In any event, American corporations had produced in the atom bomb the most radical and subversive product in their entire history. For just as the bomb had fused the sand into glass at Los Alamos, so had it transformed the rights of private property into the responsibilities of social property. The world was no longer a series of frontiers, it was a community which would survive or perish by its own hand. If through its creation of the bomb the Age of Corporation Capitalism forced Americans to recognize that fact, then it would have fulfilled itself—and more.

—William Appleman Williams, *The Contours of American History* (N.Y.: Quadrangle, 1966), pp. 477–478

THE ORIGINS OF THE COLD WAR

The origins of the Cold War are still being argued, and the so-called revisionists insist that the responsibility lies with the United States. As they see it, the Soviets were ready to cooperate with the United States providing only that the latter would respect the *cordon sanitaire* of satellite states; unfortunately, the United States, driven by the logic of capitalism, refused to agree to sealing off an area into which it could not expand economically—an accusation similar to leftist criticism of Wilson's actions at Versailles.

Regardless of the validity of this thesis, the United States gave at the end of the war evidence that it distrusted the Soviet Union by refusing to continue lend-lease or to promise a thumping big postwar loan, and by seeking to erode the system of satellite states the Soviet was building between itself and Western Europe. Incidentally, there is here a certain irony when it is remembered that at that very time critics of Roosevelt and Truman were attacking them on the ground that they were selling our Western interests—an attack that by 1950 was to burgeon into McCarthyism.

George F. Kennan, an expert on Russia and Minister-Counselor in the U.S. Embassy in Moscow, examined Soviet psychology in a remarkable paper drawn up for the State Department in May, 1945, and forecast the Cold War. It is found in the appendix to his *Memoirs: 1925–1950* (Boston: Little, Brown, 1967), from which we reprint pages 543–546.

It can be seen that Russia will not have an easy time in maintaining the power which it has seized over other people in Eastern and Central Europe unless it receives both moral and material assistance from the West. It must therefore be Russian policy in the coming period to persuade the Western nations, and particularly the United States (1) to give its blessing to Russian domination of these areas by recognizing Russian puppet states as independent countries and dealing with them as such, thus collaborating with the Soviet government in maintaining the fiction by which these countries are ruled; and (2) to grant to Russia the extensive material support which would enable the Soviet government to make good the economic damages caused by its costly and uncompromising political program and to claim credit for bringing economic as well as political progress to the peoples in question.

If it seems at first sight remarkable that the Kremlin should hope to win the support of democratic peoples for purposes so contrary to Western democratic ideals, it should be remembered that the Russian views all currents of public sentiment as the sailor views the winds. He is convinced that even if he cannot sail directly against them he can at least use their power to tack in general directions contrary to that in which they blow. It would not appear to him impossible to exploit Western enthusiasm for democracy and national independence in order to further the interests of authoritarianism and international oppression. He knows, to use a classical expression, that "mankind is governed by names"; and he has no compunction in adopting to his own use any slogan which he finds appealing to those whom he wishes to influence.

Furthermore, in the particular case of the United States, the Kremlin is counting on certain psychological factors which it knows will work strongly in Russia's favor. It knows that the American public has been taught to believe:

(a) That collaboration with Russia, as we envisage it, is entirely possible;
(b) That it depends only on the establishment of the proper personal relationships of cordiality and confidence with Russian leaders; and
(c) That if the United States does not find means to assure this collaboration (again, as we envisage it), then the past war has been fought in vain, another war is inevitable, and civilization is faced with complete catastrophe.

The Kremlin knows that none of these propositions is sound. It knows that the Soviet government, due to the peculiar structure of its authority, is technically incapable of collaborating with other governments in the manner which Americans have in mind when they speak of collaboration. It knows that the Soviet secret police have no intention of permitting anything like the number of personal contacts between the two peoples that would be required to lead to a broad basis of personal confidence and collaboration. It knows that throughout eleven years of diplomatic relations between the two countries it has been the United States government in at least ninety-nine cases out of a hundred which has taken the initiative to try to establish relationships of confidence and cordiality; that these efforts have met almost invariably with suspicion, discourtesy, and rebuff; and that this will not, and cannot, be otherwise in the future. Finally, it knows that the type of intimate collaboration for which Americans yearn is by no means necessary for the future of world peace. It knows, as a body thoroughly versed in the realities of power, that all that is really required to assure stability among the present great powers for decades to come is the preservation of a reasonable balance of strength between them and a realistic understanding as to the mutual zones of vital interest.

But it is no concern of the Soviet government to disabuse the American public of prejudices highly favorable to Soviet interests. It is entirely agreeable to Moscow that Americans should be indulged in a series of illusions which lead them to put pressure on their government to accomplish the impossible and to go always one step further in pursuit of the illusive favor of the Soviet government. They observe with gratification that in this way a great people can be led, like an ever-hopeful suitor, to perform one act of ingratiation after the other without ever reaching the goal which would satisfy its ardor and allay its generosity. As long as these prejudices can be kept alive among large sections of the American public, the Kremlin will not give up the hope that the Western democracies may, for the time being, be used as the greatest and most powerful auxiliary instrument in the establishment of Russian power in Eastern and Central Europe.

It is this hope which lies behind all Russian action in the question of international security. Russia expects from an international security organization that it will effectively protect Russian dominion in this belt of puppet states. It expects the organization to enlist automatically the support of the Western democracies against any forces which might undertake the liberation of the peoples in question. In addition to this, it expects to be repaid immediately in the form of credits and economic assistance for its generosity in consenting to join an organization of this nature at all.

There are undoubtedly thoughtful people in the higher councils of the Soviet government who see the preposterousness of this program and the possibilities for its failure. But they apparently still represent the weaker voice in the councils of state. And why should it be otherwise? Others can always talk them down by pointing to the extraordinary record of patience and meekness which the Western Allies have thus far exhibited. They can point out that there has been no act of Russian power, however arbitrary, which has not evoked an approving echo and at least some attempt at defense on the part of a considerable portion of the American and British press. They can point to the unshakable confidence of Anglo-Saxons in meetings between individuals, and can argue that Russia has nothing to lose by trying out these policies, since if things at any time get hot all they have to do is allow another personal meeting with Western leaders and thus make a fresh start, with all forgotten. Finally, they can point again to the fact that "getting along with the Russians" is political capital of prime importance in both of the Anglo-Saxon countries and that no English or American politician can pass up any halfway adequate opportunity for claiming that he has been successful in gaining Russian confidence and committing the Russians to a more moderate course of action. In other words, they consider that Anglo-Saxon opinion can always be easily appeased in a pinch by a single generous gesture, or even in all probability by a few promising words, and that Western statesmen can always be depended upon to collaborate enthusiastically in this appeasement.

As long as a number of Stalin's leading advisors are able to use these arguments and to point to an unbroken record of success in reliance upon this line of thought the Soviet government will continue to proceed on the theory that with the Western countries anything is possible, and that there is no reason to fear that serious difficulty will be encountered either in reconciling the Western world to Russia's program of political expansion in Europe or even in obtaining Western assistance for the completion of that program.

Before its own people the Soviet government is committed to nothing with respect to the Western Allies. In its own unceasing press campaign against reactionary elements and "vestiges of fascism" abroad, it has carefully kept a door open through which it can retire at any moment into a position of defiant isolation. Through the puppet government system which it has employed for the domination of Eastern and Central Europe, it can always withdraw the battle lines of its political power without damage to its own prestige.

Should the Western world, contrary to all normal expectations, muster up the political manliness to deny to Russia either moral and material support for the consolidation of Russian power throughout Eastern and Central Europe, Russia would probably not be able to maintain its hold successfully for any length of time over *all* the territory over which it has today staked out a claim. In this case, the lines would have to be withdrawn *somewhat*. But if this occurred, the nuisance value of Soviet power in the Western countries and in the world at large would be exploited to the full. The agents of Soviet power might have to abandon certain districts where they now hold sway; but they would, to use Trotski's vivid phrase, "slam the door so that all Europe would shake." Every difficulty that could conceivably be created for the Western democracies by Communist parties and Communist claques would be used in this baring of the fangs; and the world would have cause to remember Molotov's warning at San Francisco that if the conference did not give Russia peace and security on her own terms, she would seek it and find it elsewhere.

Should the Western world stand firm through such a show of ill temper and should democracies prove able to take in their stride the worst efforts of the disciplined and unscrupulous minorities pledged to the service of the political interests of the Soviet Union in foreign countries, Moscow would have played its last real card. It would have no further means with which to assail the Western world. Further military advances in the west could only increase responsibilities already beyond the Russian capacity to meet. Moscow has no naval or air forces capable of challenging the sea or air lanes of the world.

But no one in Moscow believes that the Western world, once confronted with the life-size wolf of Soviet displeasure standing at the door and threatening to blow the house in, would be able to stand firm. And it is on this disbelief that Soviet global policy is based.

Kennan spoke of the coming Cold War—not yet given a name—as Russia's "last real card." In other words, Russia could not afford to go to war and, as it turned out, it did make a partial retreat as Kennan foretold by abandoning Greece, Trieste, and Jugoslavia. By 1947 the Iron Curtain and the Cold War had become realities, and Kennan, now back in Washington, was urging the policy of "containment" of Russia on the administration.

In addition to formal papers he had explained the policy in a paper composed for the private information of Secretary of the Navy Forrestal. When the editor of *Foreign Affairs* heard Kennan lecture on the subject he asked for an article and was given a copy of the paper. It was published in *Foreign Affairs*, July 1947 (pp. 566–582) under the title "The Sources of Soviet Conduct," and was attributed to "Mr. X." Kennan's authorship was not disclosed for some time. He has explained that he had no inkling of the attention the paper would draw, otherwise he would have handled the subject in more detail and certainly more clearly.

The policy, as Kennan first envisioned it, was diplomatic; he would leave the Russians alone in their sphere, refusing to aid them with their problems, or to collaborate with them in promoting "justice" and "democracy" simply because the words had different—almost contradictory—meanings in East and West. Though he did not believe that the Soviets would resort to war, they certainly would seek to take over countries by internal violence—as they did Czechoslovakia. His hope was that, confronted by a well-thought-out and firm Western opposition to extensions of Soviet power, the Russians would in a decade or two mellow to the point where they would be reasonable. Thus Kennan recognized the futility of political and diplomatic attacks on the Soviet sphere, but would have withheld aid. Critics of containment would not only have approved the existence of the sphere but have given the Soviets economic aid in consolidating it—just as Kennan had pointed out the Soviets expected. It was the American refusal to do this that was blamed by leftists for the Cold War—and that is invoked by the revisionists now.

Kennan began his essay by describing the Marxist ideology of the inevitable collapse of capitalism, and then called attention to the necessity of a dictatorship in Russia if communism was to remold the country in its image and to build up the industrial base essential to make it a world power. But when internal opposition had been crushed, and Russians had been converted to the new ideology, Stalin found it useful to preserve the "semi-myth of implacable foreign hostility," and this inevitably "shaped the actual machinery of Soviet power." We take up the narrative at this point.

This means that we are going to continue for a long time to find the Russians difficult to deal with. It does not mean that they should be considered as embarked upon a do-or-die program to overthrow our society by a given date. The theory of the inevitability of the eventual fall of capitalism has the fortunate connotation that there is no hurry about it. The forces of progress can take their time in preparing the final *coup de grâce*. Meanwhile, what is vital is that the "Socialist fatherland" —that oasis of power which has been already won for Socialism in the person of the Soviet Union—should be cherished and defended by all good Communists at home and abroad, its fortunes promoted, its enemies badgered and confounded. The promotion of premature, "adventuristic" revolutionary projects abroad which might embarrass Soviet power in any way would be an inexcusable, even a counter-revolutionary act. The cause of Socialism is the support and promotion of Soviet power, as defined in Moscow.

This brings us to the second of the concepts important to contemporary Soviet outlook. This is the infallibility of the Kremlin. The Soviet concept of power, which permits no focal points of organization outside the Party itself, requires that the Party leadership remain in theory the sole repository of truth. For if truth were to be found elsewhere, there would be justification for its expression in organized activity. But it is precisely that which

the Kremlin cannot and will not permit. . . .

On the principle of infallibility there rests the iron discipline of the Communist Party. In fact, the two concepts are mutually self-supporting. Perfect discipline requires recognition of infallibility. Infallibility requires the observance of discipline. And the two together go far to determine the behaviorism of the entire Soviet apparatus of power. But their effect cannot be understood unless a third factor be taken into account; namely, the fact that the leadership is at liberty to put forward for tactical purposes any particular thesis which it finds useful to the cause at any particular moment and to require the faithful and unquestioning acceptance of that thesis by the members of the movement as a whole. This means that truth is not a constant but is actually created, for all intents and purposes, by the Soviet leaders themselves. It may vary from week to week, from month to month. It is nothing absolute and immutable—nothing which flows from objective reality. It is only the most recent manifestation of the wisdom of those in whom the ultimate wisdom is supposed to reside, because they represent the logic of history. The accumulative effect of these factors is to give to the whole subordinate apparatus of Soviet power an unshakeable stubbornness and steadfastness in its orientation. This orientation can be changed at will by the Kremlin but by no other power. Once a given party line has been laid down on a given issue of current policy, the whole Soviet governmental machine, including the mechanism of diplomacy, moves inexorably along the prescribed path, like a persistent toy automobile wound up and headed in a given direction, stopping only when it meets with some unanswerable force.

The individuals who are the components of this machine are unamenable to argument or reason which comes to them from outside sources. Their whole training has taught them to mistrust and discount the glib persuasiveness of the outside world. Like the white dog before the phonograph, they hear only the "master's voice." And if they are to be called off from the purposes last dictated to them, it is the master who must call them off. Thus the foreign representative cannot hope that his words will make any impression on them. The most that he can hope is that they will be transmitted to those at the top, who are capable of changing the party line. But even those are not likely to be swayed by any normal logic in the words of the bourgeois representative. Since there can be no appeal to common purposes, there can be no appeal to common mental approaches. For this reason, facts speak louder than words to the ears of the Kremlin; and words carry the greatest weight when they have the ring of reflecting, or being backed up by, facts of unchallengeable validity.

But we have seen that the Kremlin is under no ideological compulsion to accomplish its purposes in a hurry. Like the Church, it is dealing in ideological concepts which are of long-term validity, and it can afford to be patient. It has no right to risk the existing achievements of the revolution for the sake of vain baubles of the future. The very teachings of Lenin himself require great caution and flexibility in the pursuit of Communist purposes. Again, these precepts are fortified by the lessons of Russian history: of centuries of obscure battles between nomadic forces over the stretches of a vast unfortified plain. Here caution, circumspection, flexibility and deception are the valuable qualities; and their value finds natural appreciation in the Russian or the oriental mind. Thus the Kremlin has no compunction about retreating in the face of superior force. And being under the compulsion of no timetable, it does not get panicky under the necessity for such retreat. Its political action is a fluid stream which moves constantly, wherever it is permitted to move, toward a given goal. Its main concern is to make sure that it has filled every nook and cranny available to it in the basin of world power. But if it finds unassailable barriers in its path, it accepts these philosophically and accommodates itself to them. The main thing is that there should always be pressure, increasing constant pressure, toward the desired goal. There is no trace of any feeling in Soviet psychology that that goal must be reached at any given time. . . .

In these circumstances it is clear that the main element of any United States policy toward the Soviet Union must be that of a long-term, patient but firm and vigilant containment of Russian expansive tendencies. It is important to note, however, that such a policy has nothing to do with outward histrionics: with threats or blustering or superfluous gestures of outward "toughness." While the Kremlin is basically flexible in its reaction to political realities, it is by no means unamenable to considerations of prestige. Like almost any other government, it can be placed by tactless and threatening gestures in a position where it cannot afford to yield even though this might be dictated by its sense of realism. The Russian leaders are keen judges of human psychology, and as such they are highly conscious that loss of temper and of self-control is never a source of strength in political affairs. They are quick to exploit such evidences of weakness. For these reasons, it is a *sine qua non* of successful dealing with Russia that the foreign government in question should remain at all times cool and collected and that its demands on Russian policy should be put forward in such a manner as to leave the way open for a compliance not too detrimental to Russian prestige. . . .

But if ideology convinces the rulers of

Russia that truth is on their side and that they can therefore afford to wait, those of us on whom that ideology has no claim are free to examine objectively the validity of that premise. The Soviet thesis not only implies complete lack of control by the West over its own economic destiny, it likewise assumes Russian unity, discipline and patience over an infinite period. Let us bring this apocalyptic vision down to earth, and suppose that the Western world finds the strength and resourcefulness to contain Soviet power over a period of ten to fifteen years. What does that spell for Russia itself?

[Here Mr. Kennan describes the exhaustion of the people and the destruction wrought in Russia by the war. These inevitably hamper the Soviets' ability to build up industry in a country where the population has little of the "general culture of production and technical self-respect" of the Western worker. Moreover, the regime faces other problems as a new generation rises which does not have the old revolutionary zeal and unity, and which could be rent by rivalries for power.]

The possibility remains (and in the opinion of this writer it is a strong one) that Soviet power, like the capitalist world of its conception, bears within it the seeds of its own decay, and that the sprouting of these seeds is well advanced. . . .

It is clear that the United States cannot expect in the foreseeable future to enjoy political intimacy with the Soviet regime. It must continue to regard the Soviet Union as a rival, not a partner, in the political arena. It must continue to expect that Soviet policies will reflect no abstract love of peace and stability, no real faith in the possibility of a permanent happy coexistence of the Socialist and capitalist worlds, but rather a cautious, persistent pressure toward the disruption and weakening of all rival influence and rival power.

Balanced against this are the fact that Russia, as opposed to the Western world in general, is still by far the weaker party, that Soviet policy is highly flexible, and that Soviet society may well contain deficiencies which will eventually weaken its own total potential. This would of itself warrant the United States entering with reasonable confidence upon a policy of firm containment, designed to confront the Russians with unalterable counter-force at every point where they show signs of encroaching upon the interests of a peaceful and stable world.

But in actuality the possibilities for American policy are by no means limited to holding the line and hoping for the best. It is entirely possible for the United States to influence by its actions the internal developments, both within Russia and throughout the international Communist movement, by which Russian policy is largely determined. This is not only a question of the modest measure of informational activity which this government can conduct in the Soviet Union and elsewhere, although that, too, is important. It is rather a question of the degree to which the United States can create among the peoples of the world generally the impression of a country which knows what it wants, which is coping successfully with the problems of its internal life and with the responsibilities of a World Power, and which has a spiritual vitality capable of holding its own among the major ideological currents of the time. To the extent that such an impression can be created and maintained, the aims of Russian Communism must appear sterile and quixotic, the hopes and enthusiasm of Moscow's supporters must wane, and added strain must be imposed on the Kremlin's foreign policies. For the palsied decrepitude of the capitalist world is the keystone of Communist philosophy. Even the failure of the United States to experience the early economic depression which the ravens of the Red Square have been predicting with such complacent confidence since hostilities ceased would have deep and important repercussions throughout the Communist world.

By the same token, exhibitions of indecision, disunity and internal disintegration within this country have an exhilarating effect on the whole Communist movement. At each evidence of these tendencies, a thrill of hope and excitement goes through the Communist world; a new jauntiness can be noted in the Moscow tread; now groups of foreign supporters climb on to what they can only view as the band wagon of international politics; and Russian pressure increases all along the line in international affairs.

It would be an exaggeration to say that American behavior unassisted and alone could exercise a power of life and death over the Communist movement and bring about the early fall of Soviet power in Russia. But the United States has it in its power to increase enormously the strains under which Soviet policy must operate, to force upon the Krem-

lin a far greater degree of moderation and circumspection than it has had to observe in recent years, and in this way to promote tendencies which must eventually find their outlet in either the break-up or the gradual mellowing of Soviet power. For no mystical, Messianic movement—and particularly not that of the Kremlin—can face frustration indefinitely without eventually adjusting itself in one way or another to the logic of that state of affairs.

Thus the decision will really fall in large measure in this country itself. The issue of Soviet-American relations is in essence a test of the over-all worth of the United States as a nation among nations. To avoid destruction the United States need only measure up to its own best traditions and prove itself worthy of preservation as a great nation.

One may well question that the origins of the Cold War will ever be stated to everyone's satisfaction. Certainly we cannot lay the blame all on one side. Kennan, himself, was appalled by the Truman Doctrine's sweeping promise to oppose communism wherever it appeared and by the reliance on military action, doubtless prompted by the Pentagon. The inevitable result, Kennan thought, would be an overextension which might well be disastrous. Unfortunately the "Mr. X" article, written before the announcement of the Truman Doctrine but published months later, had missed a golden opportunity to spell out the limited nature of Kennan's concept of containment; official policy was now set and the author could not publicly criticize it. Perhaps no one would have listened anyhow. Americans have long had a naïve belief that evil can be crushed by naked force, and therein lies the American share of responsibility for the Cold War; the Pentagon was merely echoing public sentiment.

Here we offer Kennan's comments on the Truman Doctrine (*Memoirs*, pp. 318–324), some of them current and some recent, but all appropriate to the present. He was paraphrasing and quoting from an address given to the War College in the spring of 1947.

. . . . People in Western Europe did not, by and large, want Communist control. But this did not mean that they would not trim their sails and even abet its coming if they gained the impression that it was inevitable. This was why the shock of a Communist success in Greece could not be risked.

In Western Europe, too, I added, it was not likely that Communist domination could

last indefinitely. But while it lasted, it could do great damage.

Because floodwaters must—by the laws of nature—some day subside is no reason that one should welcome them on his place. . . . We have no cause to assume that Europe as we know it—and as we need it—would never recover from the blow which even a brief period of Russian control would deal to her already weakened traditions and institutions. . . . The waves of Communist authority might some day recede but we could have no reason to expect that American prestige and influence could easily re-enter the territories thus liberated. . . .

I went on, then, to point out that if we were to leave Europe to the Communists, the resulting problem of security for the United States "might not be one of external security alone."

Remember that in abandoning Europe we would be abandoning not only the fountain-heads of most of our own culture and tradition; we would also be abandoning almost all the other areas in the world where progressive representative government is a working proposition. We would be placing ourselves in the position of a lonely country, culturally and politically. To maintain confidence in our own traditions and institutions we would henceforth have to whistle loudly in the dark. I am not sure that whistling could be loud enough to do the trick.

I know that there are many people—and probably some among you—who will reply indignantly that I am selling short the strength and soundness of our institutions—who will maintain that American democracy has nothing to fear from Europe's diseases and nothing to learn from Europe's experiences.

I wish I could believe that that were true. I wish I could believe that the human impulses which give rise to the nightmares of totalitarianism were ones which Providence had allocated only to other peoples and to which the American people had been graciously left immune. Unfortunately, I know that that is not true. After all, most of us are only Europeans once or twice removed; and some of us are less removed than that. There are openly totalitarian forces already working in our society. Do you think that they could fail to derive new confidence and new supporters from such a series of developments? And it is not even with these small existing groups of extremists that the real danger lies. The fact of

the matter is that there is a little bit of the totalitarian buried somewhere, way down deep, in each and every one of us. It is only the cheerful light of confidence and security which keeps this evil genius down at the usual helpless and invisible depth. If confidence and security were to disappear, don't think that he would not be waiting to take their place. Others may lull themselves to sleep with the pleasing assumption that the work of building freedom in this country was accomplished completely and for all time by our forefathers. I prefer to accept the word of a great European, the German poet, Goethe, that freedom is something that has to be reconquered every day. And in that never-ending process of reconquest, I would hate to see this country lose all its allies.

So much for the reasons for our limited intervention in Greece. Why, then, approving this action, did I take exception to the language of the President's message?

I took exception to it primarily because of the sweeping nature of the commitments which it implied. The heart of the message and the passage that has subsequently been most frequently quoted was this:

I believe it must be the policy of the United States to support free peoples who are resisting subjugation by armed minorities or by outside pressures.

I believe that we must assist free peoples to work out their own destinies in their own way.

This passage, and others as well, placed our aid to Greece in the framework of a universal policy rather than in that of a specific decision addressed to a specific set of circumstances. It implied that what we had decided to do in the case of Greece was something we would be prepared to do in the case of any other country, provided only that it was faced with the threat of "subjugation by armed minorities or by outside pressures."

It seemed to me highly uncertain that we

would invariably find it in our interests or within our means to extend assistance to countries that found themselves in this extremity. The mere fact of their being in such a plight was only one of the criteria that had to be taken into account in determining our action. The establishment of the existence of such a threat was only the beginning, not the end, of the process of decision. I listed, in my presentation to the War College, three specific considerations that had supported our decision to extend assistance to Greece:

A. The problem at hand is one within our economic, technical, and financial capabilities.

B. If we did not take such action, the resulting situation might redound very decidedly to the advantage of our political adversaries.

C. If, on the other hand, we do take the action in question, there is good reason to hope that the favorable consequences will carry far beyond the limits of Greece itself.

These considerations, I pointed out, did not necessarily apply to all other regions. I doubted, for example, that any of them would fully apply in the case of China: the first most definitely would not. But if this was the case, then why use language that suggested that all that was required was proof of the existence of a threat of "subjugation by armed minorities or by outside pressure"—that this was the sole criterion of our response?

Were I reacting today to the Truman Doctrine message, I would certainly have added to this list of specific requirements the willingness and ability of the threatened people to pick up and bear resolutely the overwhelming portion of the responsibility and effort in their own defense against both direct and indirect aggression—not just to sit back and hedge against the possibility that resistance might not be effective and leave the burden of the struggle to us. I would also take exception to the repeated suggestions, in the text of that message, that

what we were concerned to defend in Greece was the democratic quality of the country's institutions. We would find it necessary to give aid, over the ensuing years, to a number of regimes which could hardly qualify for it on the basis of their democratic character. It was unwise to suggest that this, too, was an essential criterion. But these omissions, the recognition of which does indeed reflect the promptings of hindsight, only reinforce the validity of the objections to the language of the message that suggested themselves at the time. . . .

Throughout the ensuing two decades the conduct of our foreign policy would continue to be bedeviled by people in our own government as well as in other governments who could not free themselves from the belief that all another country had to do, in order to qualify for American aid, was to demonstrate the existence of a Communist threat. Since almost no country was without a Communist minority, this assumption carried very far. And as time went on, the firmness of understanding for these distinctions on the part of our own public and governmental establishment appeared to grow weaker rather than stronger. In the 1960s so absolute would be the value attached, even by people within the government, to the mere existence of a Communist threat, that such a threat would be viewed as calling, in the case of Southeast Asia, for an American response on a tremendous scale, without serious regard even to those main criteria that most of us in 1947 would have thought it natural and essential to apply.

On many occasions, both before and after this Greek-Turkish episode, I have been struck by the congenial aversion of Americans to taking specific decisions on specific problems, and by their persistent urge to seek universal formulae or doctrines in which to clothe and justify particular actions. We obviously dislike to discriminate. We like to find some general governing norm to which, in each instance, appeal can be taken, so that individual decisions may be made not on their particular merits but automatically, depending on whether the circumstances do or do not seem to fit the norm. We like, by the same token, to attribute a universal significance to decisions we have already found it necessary, for limited and parochial reasons, to take. It was not enough for us, when circumstances forced us into World War I, to hold in view the specific reasons for our entry: our war effort had to be clothed in the form of an effort to make the *world* (nothing less) "safe for democracy." It was not enough for us, in World War II, that the Japanese attacked us at Pearl Harbor and that both Japanese and German governments declared war on us: we did not feel comfortable until we had wrapped our military effort in the wholly universalistic—and largely meaningless—generalities of the Atlantic Charter. Something of this same compulsion became apparent in the post-war period in the tendency of many Americans to divide the world neatly into Communist and "free world" components, to avoid recognition of specific differences among countries on either side, and to search for general formulas to govern our relations with the one or the other. I think, in this connection, of the periodic wrangling in Congress, in connection with the annual aid bills, over the question whether most-favored-nation treatment should be extended, or various forms of aid be granted, to "Communist" countries or to countries "forming part of the Communist conspiracy" or whatever general language one chose to employ— the idea being always to define a category of states and to compel the executive to behave in a uniform way with relation to all of them. Seldom does it seem to have occurred to many congressional figures that the best thing to do would be to let the President, or the Secretary of State, use his head.

To this day I am uncertain as to the origins of this persistent American urge to the universalization or generalization of decision. I suspect it to be a reflection of the extent to which we are a people given to government by laws rather than by executive discretion. Laws, too, are general norms, and Congress, accustomed to limiting executive discretion through the establishment of such norms in the internal field, obviously feels more comfortable when its powers with relation to foreign policy can be exercised in a similar way. Unable to control executive decisions on a day-to-day basis, many Congressmen and Senators feel, I suspect, a need for general determinations defining the latitude within which those decisions may be taken.

Whatever the origins of this tendency, it is an unfortunate one. It confuses public understanding of international issues more than it clarifies it. It shackles and distorts the process of decision-taking. It causes questions to be decided on the basis of criteria only partially relevant or not relevant at all. It tends to exclude at many points the discrimination of judgment and the prudence of language requisite to the successful conduct of the affairs of a great power.

Turning now to the formulation of the Marshall Plan, Kennan recounts some of the circumstances and warnings from his papers which are still of use. (See *Memoirs*, pp. 348–353). We open with an address delivered on June 18, 1947, to the War College.

I have a largish farm in Pennsylvania. The reason you never see me around here on weekends (or rather, the reason you would never see me around if *you* were here weekends) is that I am up there to look after that farm. The farm includes two hundred thirty-five acres, and a number of buildings. On every one of those acres, I have discovered, things are constantly happening. Weeds are growing. Gullies are forming. Fences are falling down. Paint is fading. Wood is rotting. Insects are burrowing. Nothing seems to be standing still. The days of the weekend, in theory days of rest, pass in a . . . succession of alarms and excursions. Here a bridge is collapsing. No sooner do you start to repair it than a neighbor comes to complain about a hedgerow which you haven't kept up—a half-mile away on the other side of the farm. At the very moment your daughter arrives to tell you that someone left the gate to the hog pasture open and the hogs are out. On the way to the hog pasture you discover that the beagle hound is happily liquidating one of the children's pet kittens. In burying the kitten you look up and notice that a whole section of the barn roof has been blown off, and needs instant repair. Somebody shouts pitifully from the bathroom window that the pump must have busted—there's no water in the house. At that moment a truck arrives with five tons of stone for the lane. And as you stand helplessly there, wondering which of these crises to attend to first, you notice the farmer's little boy standing silently before you with that maddening smile that is halfway a leer, and when you ask him what's up, he says triumphantly: "The bull's busted out and he's eating the strawberry bed."

That's the only way I know to tell you what policy planning is like. The world is a big world. It has at least two hundred thirty-five big acres on it. On each of these something is incessantly happening. A nimble and astute person, working furiously against time, may indeed succeed in getting himself to a point where he thinks that with respect to one of those two hundred thirty-five acres he is some three or four months ahead of events. . . . But by the time he has gotten his ideas down on paper, the three or four months have mysteriously shrunk to that many weeks. By the time he has gotten those ideas accepted by others, they have become days. And by the time others have translated those ideas into action, it develops that the thing you were planning for took place day before yesterday, and everyone wants to know why in hell you did not foresee it a long time ago.

But suppose, I went on, you decide that you must not be put off by the plethora of urgent demands—that you must take one particular part of this harried globe and concentrate on the exploration of it. We might assume, for example, that you were examining the plight of a friendly European country which had not been able to revive its economic life by its own resources in the wake of the war. You are confronted immediately with a babble of tongues and conflicting opinions:

You say: "This shouldn't be so difficult. Why don't we tell these people to draw up a plan for the reconstruction of their economic life and submit it to us and we'll see whether we can support it or not?"

That starts it off. Someone says: "That's no good. They are too tired to draw up a plan. We have to do it for them."

Someone else says: "Even if they do draw up a plan, they wouldn't have the internal economic discipline to carry it out. The Communists would spike it."

Someone else says: "Oh, it isn't the Communists who would spike it—it is the local business circles."

Then someone says: "Maybe what we need isn't a plan at all. Maybe we just haven't given them enough in the past. If we just give them more, things will work out all right."

Another then says: "That's probably true, but we've got to figure out how the money is going to be spent. Congress just won't pour money down any more ratholes."

Then somebody says: "That's right; we need a program. We've got to figure out just what's to be done with the money and make sure that it does the whole job this time."

To that someone else replies: "Ah, yes, but it would be a mistake for us to try to draw this program up all by ourselves. The Commies would just take potshots at it and the European government would shrug off the responsibility."

Then someone says: "That's absolutely right. The thing for us to do is to tell these Europeans to draw up a plan and submit it to us and we'll see whether we can support it or not."

And then you ask: "Didn't somebody say that before?" And we're off again. . . .

Great modern democracies are apparently incapable of dealing with the subtleties and contradictions of power relationships. You men have examined here the crucial decisions of the war. I should say that the greatest error of the war on our side was the failure to distinguish clearly the personality of our Russian allies and to recognize and to explain frankly to our peoples the real nature of our wartime association with them. This failure, this lack of preparation for the aftermath of war, has caused us to suffer since the termination of hostilities setbacks which come close to balancing out the gains of our military victory over Germany. . . .

[Here follow some recent comments on the Marshall Plan.]

Except in Korea and Japan, the needs of people in other areas differed in fundamental respects from those of Europe. In Europe, it was a case of releasing capacities for self-help that were already present. This was a short-term problem. Elsewhere, it was a matter not of releasing existing energies but of creating new ones. This was a long-term problem. For this, new organizational machinery would be necessary. Here, the need would be for some sort of instrumentality, near government but not entirely of it, through which technical know-how could be drawn from American industry and made available to other peoples.

Seen historically, from the perspective of two decades, this distinction between Europe's needs and those of other areas seems too obvious to be challenged. This was, however, not the case at the time. Throughout the period of preparation of the legislation making possible American aid to Europe's recovery, and for years thereafter, those of us who had had to do with the original Marshall Plan concept would be plagued with demands from the congressional side that we draw up or inspire similar programs for China, for the Middle East, or for Latin America. Congressman Walter Judd, of Minnesota, was particularly insistent that something of the same nature be attempted for China, and blamed the later demise of the Nationalist government there—I have no doubt—partly on our unwillingness to pursue this suggestion. Nothing that we could point to in the way of differences between the problems and situations of the two areas—neither the primitiveness of the existing industrial base in China, nor the unpromising nature of the political background, nor any of the other gaps that existed in China's ability to absorb and to use effectively outside financial capital—could shake his belief, and that of many other people, that the principles invoked to govern our relationship to Europe ought to have universalized validity. The congenital American aversion to regional approaches, and the yearning for universal ones, were too strong to be entirely overcome even by the success of the Marshall Plan—on the contrary, they were only stimulated by it.

The Cold War was now well under way, and Kennan and his moderate policy were brusquely and even contemptuously shoved aside, and in 1950 he began a long leave from service. He looked on the creation of NATO and its army as needless irritants and opposed Dulles's long roll of alliances which in effect bound the United States to military action without adequate control of the conditions which might lead to it. As he saw it, the communist seizure of Czechoslovakia, the Berlin blockade, and the Korean War were predictable Soviet defensive reactions to being fenced in by offensive military forces and treaties. The result was to ruin the chances of a general settlement which might have been effective if the West had confined itself to firm and consistent diplomatic measures. Viewed from the vantage of more than two decades he may have been right.

"The most remarkable thing about Soviet diplomacy is its suicidal capacity for creating the very things it fears the most."—James Reston, N.Y. *Times.*

THE BASIC FAULTS OF AMERICAN DIPLOMACY

[In a slim volume based on a series of lectures, George F. Kennan analyzed American diplomacy and pointed out the flaws which had made and would continue to make it ineffectual. Here we reprint a part of the concluding lecture. See *American Diplomacy: 1900–1950* (University of Chicago Press, 1951), pp. 93–103.]

. . . . I see the most serious fault of our past policy formulation to lie in something that I might call the legalistic-moralistic approach to international problems. This approach runs like a red skein through our foreign policy of the last fifty years. . . . It is the belief that it should be possible to suppress the chaotic and dangerous aspirations of governments in the international field by the acceptance of some system of legal rules and restraints. . . .

It is the essence of this belief that, instead of taking the awkward conflicts of national interest and dealing with them on their merits with a view to finding the solutions least unsettling to the stability of international life, it would be better to find some formal criteria of a juridical nature by which the permissible behavior of states could be defined. There would then be judicial entities competent to measure the actions of governments against these criteria and to decide when their behavior was acceptable and when unacceptable. Behind all this, of course, lies the American assumption that the things for which other peoples in this world are apt to contend are for the most part neither creditable nor important and might justly be expected to take second place behind the desirability of an orderly world, untroubled by international violence.

To the American mind, it is implausible that people should have positive aspirations, and ones that they regard as legitimate, more important to them than the peacefulness and orderliness of international life. From this standpoint, it is not apparent why other peoples should not join us in accepting the rules of the game in international politics, just as we accept such rules in the competition of sport in order that the game may not become too cruel and too destructive and may not assume an importance we did not mean it to have.

If they were to do this, the reasoning runs, then the troublesome and chaotic manifestations of the national ego could be contained and rendered either unsubstantial or subject to easy disposal by some method familiar and comprehensible to our American usage. Departing from this background, the mind of American statesmanship, stemming as it does in so large a part from the legal profession in our country, gropes with unfailing persistence for some institutional framework which would be capable of fulfilling this function.

I cannot undertake in this short lecture to deal exhaustively with this thesis or to point out all the elements of unsoundness which I feel it contains. But some of its more outstanding weaknesses are worthy of mention.

In the first place, the idea of the subordination of a large number of states to an international juridical regime, limiting their possibilities for aggression and injury to other states, implies that these are all states like our own, reasonably content with their international borders and status, at least to the extent that they would be willing to refrain from pressing for change without international agreement. Actually, this has generally been true only of a portion of international society. We tend to underestimate the violence of national maladjustments and discontents elsewhere in the world if we think that they would always appear to other people as less important than the preservation of the juridical tidiness of international life.

Second, while this concept is often associated with a revolt against nationalism, it is a curious thing that it actually tends to confer upon the concept of nationality and national sovereignty an absolute value it did not have before. The very principle of "one government, one vote," regardless of physical or political differences between states, glorifies the concept of national sovereignty and makes it the exclusive form of participation in international life. It envisages a world composed exclusively of sovereign national states with a full equality of status. In doing this, it ignores the tremendous variations in the firmness and soundness of national divisions: the fact that the origins of state borders and national personalities were in many instances fortuitous or at least poorly related to realities. It also ignores the law of change. The national state pattern is not, should not be, and cannot be a fixed and static thing. By nature, it is an unstable phenomenon in a constant state of change and flux. . . .

By the same token, the American concept of world law ignores those means of international offense—those means of the projection of power and coercion over other peoples—which by-pass institutional forms entirely or even exploit them against themselves: such things as ideological attack, intimidation, penetration, and disguised seizure of the institutional paraphernalia of national sovereignty. It ignores, in other words, the device of the puppet state and the set of techniques by which states can be converted into puppets with no formal violation of, or challenge to, the outward attributes of their sovereignty and their independence. . . .

It assumes that civil wars will remain civil and not grow into international wars. It assumes the ability of each people to solve its own internal political problems in a manner not provocative of its international environment. It assumes that each nation will always be able to construct a government qualified to speak for it and cast its vote in the international arena and that this government will be acceptable to the rest of the international community in this capacity. It assumes, in other words, that domestic issues will not become international issues and that the world community will not be put in the position of having to make choices between rival claimants for power within the confines of the individual state.

Finally, this legalistic approach to international relations is faulty in its assumptions concerning the possibility of sanctions against offenses and violations. In general, it looks to collective action to provide such sanction against the bad behavior of states. In doing so, it forgets the limitations on the effectiveness of military coalition. It forgets that, as a circle of military associates widens in any conceivable political-military venture, the theoretical total of available military strength may increase, but only at the cost of compactness and ease of control. And the wider a coalition becomes, the more difficult it becomes to retain political unity and general agreement on the purposes and effects of what is being done. . . .

These, then, are some of the theoretical deficiencies that appear to me to be inherent in the legalistic approach to international affairs. But there is a greater deficiency still that I should like to mention before I close. That is the inevitable association of legalistic ideas with moralistic ones: the carrying-over into the affairs of states of the concepts of right and wrong, the assumption that state behavior is a fit subject for moral judgment. Whoever says there is a law must of course be indignant against the lawbreaker and feel a moral superiority to him. And when such indignation spills over into military contest, it knows no bounds short of the reduction of the lawbreaker to the point of complete submissiveness—namely, unconditional surrender. It is a curious thing, but it is true, that the legalistic approach to world affairs, rooted as it unquestionably is in a desire to do away with war and violence, makes violence more enduring, more terrible, and more destructive to political stability than did the older motives of national interest. A war fought in the name of high

moral principle finds no early end short of some form of total domination.

In this way, we see that the legalistic approach to international problems is closely identified with the concept of total war and total victory, and the manifestations of the one spill over only too easily into the manifestations of the other. And the concept of total war is something we would all do well to think about a little in these troubled times. . . .

It was asserted not long ago by a prominent American that "war's very object is victory" and that "in war there can be no substitute for victory." Perhaps the confusion here lies in what is meant by the term "victory." Perhaps the term is actually misplaced. Perhaps there can be such a thing as "victory" in a battle, whereas in war there can be only the achievement or nonachievement of your objectives. In the old days, wartime objectives were generally limited and practical ones, and it was common to measure the success of your military operations by the extent to which they

Evans, *The Columbus* Dispatch

Alice in Wonderland

brought you closer to your objectives. But where your objectives are moral and ideological ones and run to changing the attitudes and traditions of an entire people or the personality of a regime, then victory is probably something not to be achieved entirely by military means or indeed in any short space of time at all; and perhaps that is the source of our confusion.

In any case, I am frank to say that I think there is no more dangerous delusion, none that has done us a greater disservice in the past or that threatens to do us a greater disservice in the future, than the concept of total victory. And I fear that it springs in large measure from the basic faults in the approach to international affairs which I have been discussing here. If we are to get away from it. . . . It will mean the emergence of a new attitude among us toward many things outside our borders that are irritating and unpleasant today—an attitude more like that of the doctor toward those physical phenomena in the human body that are neither pleasing nor fortunate—an attitude of detachment and soberness and readiness to reserve judgment. It will mean that we will have the modesty to admit that our own national interest is all that we are really capable of knowing and understanding—and the courage to recognize that if our own purposes and undertakings here at home are decent ones, unsullied by arrogance or hostility toward other people or delusions of superiority, then the pursuit of our national interest can never fail to be conducive to a better world. This concept is less ambitious and less inviting in its immediate prospects than those to which we have so often inclined, and less pleasing to our image of ourselves. To many it may seem to smack of cynicism and reaction. I cannot share these doubts. Whatever is realistic in concept, and founded in an endeavor to see both ourselves and others as we really are, cannot be illiberal.

A NORTH ATLANTIC PARTNERSHIP

[A key purpose of American postwar policy was to encourage the formation of a united Europe which could absorb the productive energies of Germany and act in partnership with the United States in defense of the free world. Though President de Gaulle of France dealt this hope a series of severe—perhaps fatal—blows, the United States has quietly held on. George W. Ball uttered one of the many expressions of hope in the following address in 1963. See *The United States and Europe: Policy in Evolution,* Department of State Publication 7518, European and British Commonwealth Series 65.]

It is generally recognized that the progress of Europe toward unity has been among the most constructive and promising achievements of the postwar period. Through the creation and development of the European Economic Community, Europe has moved a long way toward economic integration. That goal, however, is far from full attainment and many difficult problems remain.

The United States has consistently encouraged the nations of Europe toward greater unity. Both the legislative and executive branch of our Government have provided this encouragement—by word and by action. We regard greater European unity as essential primarily for political reasons—although, over the long run, the United States should also benefit economically from the contribution of the Common Market to a higher level of European economic activity.

A united Europe would eliminate the frictions and jealousies that have been the cause of so many past conflicts—conflicts that on two occasions have embroiled the whole world in catastrophe. Moreover, a unified Europe could effectively mobilize the common strength of the European people. It should thus be able to play the role of equal partner with the United States, carrying its full share of the common responsibilities imposed by history on the economically advanced peoples of the free world.

The basis for such a partnership is hard economic fact. In the North Atlantic world—Western Europe and North America—there is concentrated 90 per cent of all free-world industrial strength as well as the great bulk of the free world's technical skill and knowledge. This combined resource must be put to the defense and advancement of the free world.

Combined action is particularly important in four areas:

First, Europe and North America must join in a common defense against the aggressive ambitions of the Communist bloc. The defense of Europe is vital to the United States as well as to Europe itself. It is a costly task; the growth of European strength permits Europe to make an increasing contribution to it.

Second, the national economies of the nations comprising the great industrial complex of the North Atlantic are interdependent. This is becoming increasingly evident. A slowdown in growth rates in Europe could adversely affect our own growth rate, while an American recession would have serious repercussion in Europe. Our balance-of-payments deficit is, to a large extent, the mirror image of balance-of-payments surpluses of certain major European countries. If one nation or area adopts restrictive commercial policies, those policies will find reflection in compensatory or retaliatory actions by its trading partners.

The recognition of this economic interdependence has led us to seek new means to coordinate and harmonize our domestic economic policies. Substantial progress toward this end has been achieved through the Organization for Economic Cooperation and Develop-

ment (OECD). Much further progress is required.

Third, the major industrialized areas of the free world—the Atlantic nations—must commit large amounts of money, equipment, and skill to assist the less developed countries in raising their standards of living, if political stability is to be achieved and the dangers of subversion reduced. The effective utilization of free-world resources for this purpose requires a high degree of coordination of effort. We are beginning to achieve that coordination through the Development Assistance Committee of the OECD.

Fourth, if the resources of the free world are to be efficiently utilized, obstacles to the free flow of international trade must be reduced and trade expanded under conditions where the forces of comparative advantage can fully operate. This means that American goods must have greater access to the European markets while we must provide greater access for European goods to our own markets. Just as in other fields, benefits and obligations must be reciprocal.

During the past few years United States policy has been increasingly based on the belief that these common tasks could best be achieved by the pursuit of two parallel lines of action—the attainment by Europe of a greater unity so that the European nations may act on a widening subject matter through common institutions and the attainment of a high degree of Atlantic cooperation through institutional arrangements designed for that purpose. . . .

[The actions of France have] not changed the underlying facts that have dictated the need for greater European unity or effective Atlantic cooperation. We believe, also, that these facts are generally understood by the great body of European opinion.

They can be summarized briefly:

1. Europe cannot defend itself today by its own efforts; its defense rests heavily upon the overwhelming nuclear strength of the United States.

2. The nuclear defense of the free world is indivisible.

3. The great industrial economies of the North Atlantic countries are to a high degree interdependent.

4. To reap the full economic benefits of this interdependence requires a free flow of trade.

5. The urgent needs of the newly developed nations require effective common effort on the part of the major industrialized powers of the free world.

The existence of these facts, it seems to us, determines the broad policy lines that we intend to pursue.

First, we shall continue to encourage the development of European unity and to express the hope that arrangements may ultimately be made for the accession of Great Britain to full membership in the EEC. . . .

Second, we shall seek to advance the arrangements for close economic cooperation with Europe through the OECD. . . .

Third, we shall continue to work toward the strengthening of NATO and the development of adequate conventional forces in Europe.

Fourth, we intend to utilize to the fullest the powers granted to the President under the Trade Expansion Act in order to improve access to the European Common Market as well as other major world markets for products of U.S. farms and factories. . . .

Fifth, we propose to continue to develop techniques to improve the cooperation of the major industrialized powers in providing assistance to the less developed countries. . . .

DAY DREAMS OF A DIPLOMAT ON LATIN-AMERICAN "MYTHS"

Even the best disciplined diplomats must do a little day dreaming now and then. There must be at least one U.S. diplomat dealing with Latin America who dreams of abandoning all the cant about Pan-American solidarity and good neighborliness and expressing all the itching, uncomfortable truths. We can imagine him imagining himself getting up in front of his Latin opposite numbers . . . and delivering himself somewhat as follows:

"You know and I know that the whole idea of Pan-Americanism is pretty unreal, more unreal than the idea of Pan-Europeanism. You are Latins, we are not. All of your power put together would equal only a fraction of the North American power. We are tied to the whole world; your axis of interest runs to the United States and Europe. These are the accidents of history, climate and soil, so we have learned not to brag about it anymore, but don't expect us to feel guilty about it any more, either.

"We may live in the Western Hemisphere as you do, but we also live in the Northern Hemisphere, and it's in the Northern Hemisphere that the history that affects the whole world, and us immediately, happens to happen. That's why we have had to put our power and money into Europe first and maybe always will have to. . . . There are two Latin Americas from our point of view. There is the Latin America of the Caribbean and the Gulf of Mexico. . . . It is only in this region that the United States has ever indulged in military intervention. . . . [Farther south] the job is essentially up to you. . . .

"There is much anti-Yankeeism in your countries; there is no 'anti-Latin Americanism' in the United States. We understand why; we know that to be anti-

Yankee amounts to an intellectual and emotional necessity for men with pride in countries without power. You can find similar relationships all over the world. But you don't really fear the United States' knock on your door in the middle of the night; you fear Castro's knock.

"You know, even if your young students don't, that American business in Latin America is not a plundering operation; that it has added far more in this part of the world than it has subtracted, for the last several decades. You know that in some countries down here American firms pay higher wages than local firms. They also pay their taxes by the book which many of your businessmen consider naive.

"It is a myth that the United States prefers military regimes in Latin America to democratic regimes. . . . If the alternative to a serious Communist threat or anarchy is a military regime, of course we prefer the military. So do you, which is why you have had so many military regimes. They rise and fall, but communism is permanent; all choice is gone. And people are so constituted everywhere that they will prefer even the cruelest boss rule to anarchy. . . .

"You can't import free and stable political institutions. They grow out of the soil. They are related to a people's traditions and psychology. Some of your countries do not have this tradition and spirit, as we do not have your tradition and spirit of racial tolerance. In the personal sense, you are more democratic than we are, but not in the political sense. Your real problem for this era is the political problem; ours is the personal problem.

"This is all I have to say about it. It is all I will ever have to say as a diplomat. Tomorrow the State Department will accept my resignation with alacrity. Since I will be a private person I shall spend my remaining years down here where the arts of private living are so much more advanced than in my own frightfully busy country."

—Eric Sevareid, Nov. 7, 1965

CONFLICT AND MORAL JUDGMENT

[The following is by the perceptive British historical theorist, Herbert Butterfield, *Christianity and History* (N.Y.: Scribner's, 1950), pp. 88–92.]

It is not always easy to realise how in modern times we have come to adopt as our initial conception of a human being a pattern that would be more fitting for gods. A speaker once put forward the view that a person who was unable to write poetry was hardly a complete man; he did not extend the principle to the writing of music, but he had caught from the liberals a view of man which was beyond the range of mortals. Those who are scholars and philosophers too easily believe that the unlettered do not really taste life, or that people who are ignorant in some field of knowledge are less than men. Let us be clear: The whole human race together may compass a great range of knowledge, experience and capacities; but all these are terribly broken and splintered between all the individuals that go to compose the race; and all of us lack a multitude of those things which the liberal would regard as essential to a complete man or a completely rounded view of life.

The splintering, however, is much more serious and goes much deeper, for it even extends to our vision. Each of us is more or less restricted to a narrow vision, gravely conditioned by time, temperament and age, and by the platform on which we happen to be standing. The most friendly foreign offices, the most friendly historians belonging to different nationalities, find somewhere or other the place where they cannot enter into one another's points of view. The Marxists are right when they assume that a member of a certain social class, even if he is unselfish, is liable to be limited in his outlook by the fact that he sees things from the platform of that social class. We may think that we have a spacious vision, level and equal as it takes in wide horizons; but in reality each of us looks upon the world from a special peep-hole of his own. Where actual interests complicate a question and a certain amount of wishful thinking may give a bias to our minds, it is doubtful whether it is possible for any of us to survey a problem comprehensively. And it is certain that we fail to realize our incompetence in an art that is of the greatest importance for human relations— the simple art of putting ourselves in the other person's place.

The situation is still further complicated by a certain human predicament which we are too seldom conscious of, and which I can only call the predicament of Hobbesian fear— Hobbesian because it was subjected to particular analysis by the seventeenth-century philosopher, Thomas Hobbes. If you imagine yourself locked in a room with another person with whom you have often been on the most bitterly hostile terms in the past, and suppose that each of you has a pistol, you may find yourself in a predicament in which both of you would like to throw the pistols out of the window, yet it defeats the intelligence to find a way of doing it. If you throw yours out the first you rob the other man of the only reason he had for getting rid of his own, and for anything you know he may break the bargain. If both of you swear to throw the pistols out

together, you may feel that he may make the gesture of hurling his away, but in reality hold tight to it, while you, if you have done the honest thing, would then be at his mercy. You may even have an *arrière-pensée* that he may possibly be concealing a second pistol somewhere about his person. Both of you in fact may have an equal justification for suspecting one another, and both of you may be men who in all predicaments save this had appeared reasonably well-behaved and well-intentioned. You may both of you be utterly honest in your desire to be at peace and to put an end to the predicament, if only in order to enable you to get on with your business. If some great bully were to come into the room and try to take your pistols from you, then as likely as not you would both combine against him, you would find yourselves cherished allies, find yourselves for the time being as thick as thieves. Only, after you had eliminated this intruder, you would discover to your horrible surprise that you were back in the original predicament again.

In international affairs it is this situation of Hobbesian fear which, so far as I can see, has hitherto defeated all the endeavour of the human intellect. Not only may both sides feel utterly self-righteous, but where a great obstruction occurs—as over the question of toleration in the sixteenth century, and that of disarmament in the twentieth—both may feel utterly baffled and frustrated; and sometimes even allies fall to blaming one another, as on one occasion papers of all complexions in England, out of pure exasperation, blamed France for the failure of the Disarmament Conference. Though one side may have more justice than another in the particular occasion of a conflict, there is a sense in which war as such is in reality a judgment on all of us. The fundamental predicament would not exist if men in general were as righteous as the situation requires, and of course the fundamental predicament is itself so maddening and exasperating that men sometimes resort to desperate measures with an idea of cutting the Gordian knot.

Even if vested interests did not enter more directly into the problem of war, therefore, this situation of Hobbesian fear, as I have called it, would make it difficult for historiography in the long run to regard the great wars between nations or creeds as clear straight conflicts of right against wrong. We are right if we want to see our history in moral terms, but we are not permitted to erect the human drama into a great conflict between good and evil in this particular way. If there is a fundamental fight between good and evil in history, therefore, as I think there is, we must regard it as being waged not directly between Catholics and Protestants in the sixteenth century, or between Germans and Russians in the twentieth, but in a deeper realm for the most part out of reach of the technical historian. In reality the essential strategies in the war of good against evil are conducted within the intimate interior of personalities. And if Christianity fights in the world it does not (when Churches are in their right mind) wage war on actual flesh and blood. Like the spread of charity or of education and like most of the good things of the world, it carries on a campaign only in the sense that the leaven may be said to carry on a campaign when it seeks to leaven the whole lump.

For this reason the historian does not content himself with a simple picture of good men fighting bad, and he turns the crude melodrama that some people see in life into a more moving kind of tragedy. In the last resort he sees human history as a pilgrimage of all mankind, and human achievement as a grand co-operative endeavour, in which whigs and tories complement one another, both equally necessary to the picture. In the last resort even tories and socialists are to the historian only allies who happen to have fallen out with one another. In modern history this view is all the more necessary in that, owing to the complicated character of society, moral responsibility is so subtly diffused and so camouflaged and dispersed that the forces in a democracy may drive a government to war, or may perpetuate a grave abuse, and it yet may be impossible to pin the precise responsibility for this anywhere.

During the conflicts of actual life we may have neither the time nor the materials for the understanding of the enemy of the moment; and if a madman is attacking a child, one may have to take action against the madman very quickly, though one might be rather sorry for him in his turn afterwards. But once battles are over the human race becomes in a certain sense one again; and just as Christianity tries to bind it together in love, so the rôle of the technical historian is that of a reconciling mind that seeks to comprehend. Taking things retrospectively and recollecting in tranquillity, the historian works over the past to cover the conflicts with understanding, and explains the unlikenesses between men and makes us sensible of their terrible predicaments; until at the finish—when all is as remote as the tale of Troy —we are able at last perhaps to be a little sorry for everybody. And this is particularly the case since, as Lord Acton once pointed out, the people who are fighting in real life rarely have clear vision, even of the issues which brought them into conflict with one another. Poor things—they need the historian to follow upon their tracks sometimes in order to discover what the bother was really about.

Fischetti, NEA Service, Inc.

Kibitzer's Delight

THE ASIAN FRONT

INTRODUCTION

The imperial powers warned Roosevelt during World War II that his insistence on freeing the Asian colonies might well lead to the breakdown of order and afford an excellent opportunity for Red infiltration or conquest. They were right. The Arab states are turbulent and contentious, and agree on nothing but their hatred of the West and of Israel, which they regard as a Western puppet; the result is that they have invited Russia into the Mediterranean, an entry which it had tried in vain to obtain for centuries. India and Pakistan, glowering at each other, refuse to take seriously the menace on the north. China has fallen to the Reds. South Korea was saved only by a supreme effort, Indonesia barely escaped falling over the brink, and the fate of Southeast Asia is still in doubt.

It is easy enough to understand the resentments felt by Asians against whites, and perhaps even to understand why in some cases they were willing to damage themselves if it would thwart or humiliate their ci-devant oppressors. Still, once the British were gone the Asians remembered what was good about them, and French culture was still admired; apparently only the Dutch were completely unregretted. A significant factor in the freeing of the Asian nations had been insistent pressure by the United States, but the Asian verdict was that it was only trying to clear the way to impose its own neocolonial rule by means of economic controls.

There was a great deal of loose talk about how the United States had squandered its moral ascendancy in Asia. The truth is that it never had any—not even, perhaps especially not even, in the Philippines.

American policy in Asia has been basically the same as in Europe—that is, to gain time. Time was needed to enable the emerging states to build prosperity and stability. And since Russia's eastern frontier was in Asia there was the same necessity as in Europe to contain it. The crisis of this holding action was the Korean War, fought by Red China but which also was intended to serve Russia's purpose. The split between Russia and Red China will doubtless have many results, but the United States is still confronted by the task of containment and by the need to gain time for the emerging nations and, hopefully, for China to learn its limitations and to recognize the necessity of internal construction.

Most of the emerging nations welcome American capital because they need it for development, but fear it because they feel it may be colonialism in a new form. As they see their situation, their first order of business is to build up their economies and seek political stability. This means that they can neither afford to take sides in the cold war nor risk the give-and-take of democracy.

It is now by no means clear that economic aid to them is helpful. It was one thing to set up a Marshall Plan for Europe, which was already industrialized. It is quite another to give industrial trappings to a society that may have an ancient and honorable culture, but whose entire spirit is opposed to the disciplines of a machine economy. How much more difficult it is to industrialize a society that has barely emerged from the bush!

When our own society creaks and groans under the stresses of change it is obvious that industrialization—let alone democratization—may well disrupt the emerging state. The result, then, is likely to be dictatorship—or, alternatively, breakdown. Where the people have anything to say, they often resent foreign aid on the ground that it is disguised colonialism, and governments frequently find it necessary to play down American aid—and play up Russian or Chinese. Dictatorships presumably can ignore such popular resentments, at least to a limited extent, and can force their people to accept a measure of industrialization even though it violates the old ways of doing things.

It is often pointed out that regardless of its supposed neocolonialism America does exercise a kind of imperialism—the imperialism of attraction; Rome exercised much the same sort of attraction in the Mediterranean world. American culture may still be vilified by intellectuals, but its music and its art are now being studied and imitated, even by the Russians. Its gadgetry has set a worldwide standard, and in remote corners of the earth advertisers attract attention by the boast that their product is "two years ahead of America." Paradoxical as it may seem, says Max Lerner, "to be an American has become, along with Communism and in rivalry with it, a key pattern of action and values. So summary a conquest of the world's imagination, never before achieved without arms and colonization, is proof of an inner harmony between America and the modern spirit."

THE DOCUMENTARY RECORD IN ASIA

The United States had never had much of an economic stake in China, but for reasons hard to define had always been partial to that country. By World War I the growing power of Japan and its efforts to carve out preferred political and economic positions in China had made America uneasy about the security of its status as a Pacific power, and it had sought to use the Open Door policy to thwart Japan's ambitions. By 1941 Japan was convinced that the Open Door was merely a hypocritical pretense for preserving the *status quo*, and launched the attack on Pearl Harbor.

The United States was thus stuck with the support of a country still living under backward conditions, bitterly hostile to everything foreign, divided between warring "Nationalists" and communists, and with its rivers and railroads under Japanese control. Roosevelt sought to assure the Nationalists of a position as a world power, but Chiang Kai-shek, their leader, did not have the ability to unite his country and make the position more than a hollow sham. The only dynamic force in the country was communism, led by Mao Tse-tung. The United States was thus confronted by a dilemma: find a means of stabilizing the country or abandon it to the Reds.

It was quite apparent to perceptive observers that the United States was investing more in China than its own national interests warranted, but there was no way of letting go without suffering embarrassing consequences—not to mention political repercussions at home. This, in short, has been the problem ever since.

(1) "THE COMMUNISTS ARE IN CHINA TO STAY"

During the war the Nationalists and Communists did relatively little fighting but sought to prepare for the struggle ahead. John Paton Davies, a State Department expert in China, warned of the coming crisis and pointed out that the Reds were quietly taking over the rural areas between the Japanese lines. The following passages are from his reports of June, 1943, and November, 1944. These were primary counts against him during the McCarthy era and led to his dismissal from the State Department.

The reason for this phenomenal vitality [of the Communists] and strength is simple and fundamental. It is mass support, mass participation. The Communist governments and armies are the first governments and armies in modern Chinese history to have positive and widespread popular support. They have this support because the governments and armies are genuinely of the people. . . .

The Kuomintang and Chiang Kai-shek recognize that the Communists, with the popular support which they enjoy and their reputation for administrative reform and honesty, represent a challenge to the Central Government and its spoils system. The Generalissimo cannot admit the seemingly innocent demands of the Communists that their party be legalized and democratic processes be put into practice. To do so would probably mean the abdication of the Kuomintang and the provincial satraps.

The Communists, on the other hand, dare not accept the Central Government's invitation that they disband their armies and be absorbed in the national body politic. To do so would be to invite extinction.

This impasse will probably be resolved,

American and other foreign observers in Chungking agree, by an attempt by the Central Government to liquidate the Communists. This action may be expected to precipitate a civil war from which one of the two contending factions will emerge dominant. . . .

We may anticipate that Chiang Kai-shek will exert every effort and resort to every stratagem to involve us in active support of the Central Government. We will probably be told that if fresh American aid is not forthcoming all of China and eventually all of Asia will be swept by communism. It will be difficult for us to resist such appeals, especially in view of our moral commitments to continued assistance to China during the post-war period. . . .

Only if he is able to enlist foreign intervention on a scale equal to the Japanese invasion of China will Chiang probably be able to crush the Communists. But foreign intervention on such a scale would seem to be unlikely. Relying upon his dispirited shambling legions, his decadent corrupt bureaucracy, his sterile political moralisms and such nervous foreign support as he can muster, the Generalissimo may nevertheless plunge China into civil war. He cannot succeed, however, where the Japanese in more than seven years of determined striving have failed. The Communists are already too strong for him.

If the Generalissimo neither precipitates a civil war nor reaches an understanding with the Communists, he is still confronted with defeat. Chiang's feudal China can not long coexist alongside a modern dynamic popular government in North China.

The Communists are in China to stay. And China's destiny is not Chiang's but theirs.

In this unhappy dilemma, the United States should attempt to prevent the disaster of a civil war through adjustment of the new alignment of power in China by peaceful processes. The desirable means to this end is to encourage the reform and revitalization of the Kuomintang so that it may survive as a significant force in a coalition government. If this fails, we must limit our involvement with the Kuomintang and must commence some cooperation with the Communists, the force destined to control China, in an effort to influence them further into an independent position friendly to the United States.

(2) THE RED TRIUMPH IN CHINA

The State Department sought a way out of its dilemma by encouraging the liberals on both sides—and there were such—to form a united force which could govern China, and this was General Marshall's purpose in spending 1946 in China. He failed, for neither Chiang nor Mao would yield. Indeed, Chiang was so certain that he had the United States over a barrel and could dictate its all-out support, that he entered civil war with confidence. But by the end of 1949 he had been defeated on every front and had been forced to take refuge in Formosa (Taiwan). The following material is from Secretary of State Acheson's letter of transmittal which opened the State Department's "White Paper" on United States Relations with China, published in 1949. The order has been slightly changed for the sake of clarity.

When peace came the United States was confronted with three possible alternatives in China: (1) it could have pulled out lock, stock and barrel; (2) it could have intervened militarily on a major scale to assist the Nationalists to destroy the Communists; (3) it could, while assisting the Nationalists to assert their authority over as much of China as possible, endeavor to avoid a civil war by working for a compromise between the two sides.

The first alternative would, and I believe American public opinion at the time so felt, have represented an abandonment of our international responsibilities and of our traditional policy of friendship for China before we had made a determined effort to be of assistance. The second alternative policy, while it may look attractive theoretically and in retrospect, was wholly impracticable. . . . [The Communists] probably could have been dislodged only by American arms. It is obvious that the American people would not have sanctioned such a colossal commitment of our armies in 1945 or later. We therefore came to the third alternative policy whereunder we faced the facts of the situation and attempted to assist in working out a *modus vivendi* which would avert civil war but nevertheless preserve and even increase the influence of the National Government. . . .

[However, with the failure of General Marshall's mission the United States was faced by a choice between the second alternative and confining itself to giving the Nationalists every aid short of active military participation.] Such intervention would have required the expenditure of even greater sums than have been fruitlessly spent thus far, the command of Nationalist armies by American officers, and the probable participation of American armed forces—land, sea, and air—in the resulting war. Intervention of such a scope and magnitude would have been resented by the mass of the Chinese people, would have diametrically reversed our historic policy, and would have been condemned by the American people. . . .

The reasons for the failures of the Chinese National Government appear in some detail in the attached record. They do not stem from any inadequacy of American aid. Our military observers on the spot have reported that the Nationalist armies did not lose a single battle during the crucial year of 1948 through lack of arms or ammunition. The fact was that the decay which our observers had detected in Chungking early in the war had fatally sapped the powers of resistance of the Kuomintang.

Its leaders had proved incapable of meeting the crisis confronting them, its troops had lost the will to fight, and its Government had lost popular support. The Communists, on the other hand, through a ruthless discipline and fanatical zeal, attempted to sell themselves as guardians and liberators of the people. The Nationalist armies did not have to be defeated; they disintegrated. History has proved again and again that a regime without faith in itself and an army without morale cannot survive the test of battle. . . .

The unfortunate but inescapable fact is that the ominous result of the civil war in China was beyond the control of the government of the United States. Nothing that this country did or could have done within the reasonable limits of its capabilities could have changed that result; nothing that was left undone by this country has contributed to it. It was the product of internal Chinese forces, forces which this country tried to influence but could not. A decision was arrived at within China, if only a decision by default.

And now it is abundantly clear that we must face the situation as it exists in fact. We will not help the Chinese or ourselves by basing our policy on wishful thinking. . . .

In the immediate future, however, the implementation of our historic policy of friendship for China must be profoundly affected by current developments. It will necessarily be influenced by the degree to which the Chinese people come to recognize that the Communist regime serves not their interests but those of Soviet Russia and the manner in which, having become aware of the facts, they react to this foreign domination. One point, however, is clear. Should the Communist regime lend itself to the aims of Soviet Russian imperialism and attempt to engage in aggression against China's neighbors, we and the other members of the United Nations would be confronted by a situation violative of the principles of the United Nations Charter and threatening international peace and security.

(3) THE SECRETARY OF STATE DRAWS A LINE

Chiang had been disastrously defeated but now the United States began to build up his strength in Taiwan so that he could serve as a counter-irritant to Red China. Korea had been "temporarily" divided between Russia in the north and the United States in the south, and presently governments were established in each. In a speech on January 12, 1950, Secretary of State Acheson unnecessarily proclaimed that the United States did not regard South Korea as essential to the defense of its interests, but that it should rely on the United Nations. Following is part of his address:

What is the situation in regard to the military security of the Pacific area, and what is our policy in regard to it?

In the first place, the defeat and the disarmament of Japan has placed upon the United States the necessity of assuming the military defense of Japan so long as that is required, both in the interest of our security and in the interests of the security of the entire Pacific area and, in all honor, in the interest of Japanese security. . . .

The defensive perimeter runs along the Aleutians to Japan and then goes to the Ryukyus. We hold important defense positions in the Ryukyu Islands, and those we will continue to hold. . . .

The defensive perimeter runs from the Ryukyus to the Philippine Islands. Our relations, our defensive relations with the Philippines are contained in agreements between us. Those agreements are being loyally carried out and will be loyally carried out. Both peoples have learned by bitter experience the vital connections between our mutual defense requirements. We are in no doubt about that, and it is hardly necessary for me to say an attack on the Philippines could not and would not be tolerated by the United States. But I hasten to add that no one perceives the imminence of any such attack.

So far as the military security of other areas in the Pacific is concerned, it must be clear that no person can guarantee these areas against military attack. But it must also be clear that such a guarantee is hardly sensible or necessary within the realm of practical relationship.

Should such an attack occur—one hesitates to say where such an armed attack could come from—the initial reliance must be on the people attacked to resist it and then upon the commitments of the entire civilized world under the Charter of the United Nations which so far has not proved a weak reed to lean on by any people who are determined to protect their independence against outside aggression.

(4) THE KOREAN WAR

Acheson's speech may or may not have been the fatal tip-off to Stalin that he could pick up South Korea cheaply. At any rate, in June, 1950, heavily armed North Korean forces stormed across the frontier, brushing aside all resistance. Truman promptly ordered MacArthur to intervene with U.S. troops from Japan, and called on the UN Council for support. Since Russia was boycotting the Council, that body was able to give UN sponsorship of the resistance in Korea. It was not until three years later that a stalemate armistice was agreed upon, and even today the peace is uneasy. Following are Truman's statement of June 21 and the Council's resolution of the same date.

Statement by President Truman:

In Korea the Government forces, which were armed to prevent border raids and to preserve internal security, were attacked by invading forces from North Korea. The Security Council of the United Nations called upon the invading troops to cease hostilities and to withdraw to the 38th parallel. This they have not done, but on the contrary have pressed the attack. The Security Council called upon all members of the United Nations to render every assistance to the United Nations in the execution of this resolution. In these circumstances I have ordered United States air and sea forces to give the Korean Government troops cover and support.

The attack upon Korea makes it plain beyond all doubt that Communism has passed beyond the use of subversion to conquer independent nations and will now use armed invasion and war. It has defied the orders of the Security Council of the United Nations issued to preserve international peace and security. In these circumstances the occupation of Formosa by Communist forces would be a direct threat to the security of the Pacific area and to United States forces performing their lawful and necessary functions in that area.

Accordingly I have ordered the Seventh Fleet to prevent any attack on Formosa. As a corollary of this action I am calling upon the Chinese Government on Formosa to cease all air and sea operations against the mainland. The Seventh Fleet will see that this is done. The determination of the future status of Formosa must await the restoration of security in the Pacific, a peace settlement with Japan, or consideration by the United Nations.

I have also directed that United States Forces in the Philippines be strengthened and that military assistance to the Philippine Government be accelerated.

I have similarly directed acceleration in the furnishing of military assistance to the forces of France and the Associated States in Indo China and the dispatch of a military mission to provide close working relations with those forces.

The Security Council:

Having determined that the armed attack upon the Republic of Korea by forces from North Korea constitutes a breach of the peace,

Having called for an immediate cessation of hostilities, and

Having called upon the authorities of North Korea to withdraw forthwith their armed forces to the 38th parallel, and

Having noted from the report of the United Nations Commission for Korea that the authorities in North Korea have neither ceased hostilities nor withdrawn their armed forces to the 38th parallel and that urgent military measures are required to restore international peace and security, and

Having noted the appeal from the Republic of Korea to the United Nations for immediate and effective steps to secure peace and security,

Recommends that the Members of the United Nations furnish such assistance to the Republic of Korea as may be necessary to repel the armed attack and to restore international peace and security in the area.

Copyright Low all countries.

KOREAN WAR

'HONEST, MISTER, THERE'S NOBODY HERE BUT US KOREANS'

(5) THE DOMINO THEORY

The Chinese entry into the Korean War may have been because they believed their own propaganda about the United States, but it was also an attempt to pull a Russian chestnut out of the fire. Meanwhile, French rule in Indochina had been threatened by a savage rebellion of nationalist and communist elements called Viet Minh, under Ho Chi Min, and communist guerrillas held British Malaya in terror. The United States was supporting the French lavishly with material, but there was intense argument over whether to send in U.S. armed forces. In a press conference on April 7, 1954, President Eisenhower commented on the gravity of the situation in Southeast Asia, as reported in the *New York Times* the next day.

Question. Mr. President, would you mind commenting on the strategic importance of Indo-China to the free world? I think there has been across the country some lack of understanding on just what it means to us.

President Eisenhower. Mr. Eisenhower said that the question could be approached both specifically and generally. First of all, he said, there is the specific value of a locality in its production of materials that the world needs.

Then, he continued, there is the possibility that many human beings could pass under a dictatorship that is inimical to the free world; and, finally, there are broader considerations that might follow the "falling domino" principle.

If someone sets up a row of dominoes, and knocks over the first one, the President said, it is certain that the last one will go over very quickly. It would be the beginning of a disintegration that would have the most profound influences.

With respect to Indo-China's specific value, Mr. Eisenhower explained, this area produces two items that the world uses, tin and tungsten. They are very important, he said, and Indo-China also produces other materials, including rubber.

With respect to the possibility that more people might pass under a dictatorship, Mr. Eisenhower pointed out that Asia has already lost some 450 million of its peoples to the Communist dictatorship. He asserted that the U.S. simply can't afford greater losses.

The third possibility, said the President, is that the loss of Indo-China would set off the loss of Burma, of Thailand, of the Malay Peninsula and Indonesia. This would not only multiply the disadvantages the U.S. would suffer through loss of materials, or sources of materials, but it would involve millions and millions and millions of people, and would create a new geographical position, he said.

It would turn the so-called island defenses' chain of Japan, Formosa and the Philippines, Mr. Eisenhower said, and to the southward it would move in to threaten Australia and New Zealand.

In its economic aspects, the President added, it would take away that region that Japan must have as a trading area, or it would force Japan to turn toward China and Manchuria, or toward the Communist areas in order to live. The possible consequences of the loss to the free world are just incalculable, Mr. Eisenhower said.

(6) THE GENEVA AGREEMENTS, 1954

The United States did not go to the rescue of the French in Indochina and the fall of Dienbienphu led to French surrender while an international conference at Geneva looked on and "took note" in the "Final Declaration." The so-called

Geneva Agreements of July, 1954, were really articles worked out between the French and the rebels. The chief provision was that the states of Laos, Cambodia, and Vietnam were to become independent. The last-named was to be divided temporarily near the 17th parallel, and elections on reunion were to be held two years later; it was stated that this boundary was not political, but other statements in the voluminous articles made this uncertain. At any rate, the French had just set up a new government in the south under Premier Diem and he registered his protest and warned he would not abide by the provisions for an election. The following statements clarified the American attitude:

Declaration by the U.S. representative in Geneva, July 21, 1954

As I stated on July 18, my Government is not prepared to join in a declaration by the Conference such as is submitted. However, the United States makes this unilateral declaration of its position in these matters:

Declaration

The Government of the United States, being resolved to devote its efforts to the strengthening of peace in accordance with the principles and purposes of the United Nations, takes note of the agreements concluded at Geneva . . . [and] declares with regard to the aforesaid agreements and paragraphs that (i) it will refrain from the threat or the use of force to disturb them, in accordance with Article 2 (4) of the Charter of the United Nations dealing with the obligation of members to refrain in their international relations from the threat or use of force; and (ii) it would view any renewal of the aggression in violation of the aforesaid agreements with grave concern and as seriously threatening international peace and security.

In connection with the statement in the declaration concerning free elections in Viet-Nam my Government wishes to make clear its position which it has expressed in a declaration made in Washington on June 29, 1954, as follows:

In the case of nations now divided against their will, we shall continue to seek to achieve unity through free elections supervised by the United Nations to insure that they are conducted fairly.

With respect to the statement made by the representative of the State of Viet-Nam [South Vietnam], the United States reiterates its traditional position that peoples are entitled to determine their own future and that it will not join in an arrangement which would hinder this. Nothing in its declaration just made is intended to or does indicate any departure from this traditional position.

Statement by President Eisenhower, July 21, 1954

The United States has not been a belligerent in the war. The primary responsibility for the settlement in Indochina rested with those nations which participated in the fighting. Our role at Geneva has been at all times to try to be helpful where desired and to aid France and Cambodia, Laos, and Viet-Nam to obtain a just and honorable settlement which will take into account the needs of the interested people. Accordingly, the United States has not itself been party to or bound by the decisions taken by the Conference, but it is our hope that it will lead to the establishment of peace consistent with the rights and the needs of the countries concerned. The agreement contains features which we do not like, but a great deal depends on how they work in practice.

The United States is issuing at Geneva a statement to the effect that it is not prepared to join in the Conference declarations, but, as loyal members of the United Nations, we also say that, in compliance with the obligations and principles contained in Article 2 of the United Nations Charter, the United States will not use force to disturb the settlement. We also say that any renewal of Communist aggression would be viewed by us as a matter of grave concern.

(7) THE SOUTHEAST ASIA TREATY, 1954

The Geneva Agreements were a bitter blow to Dulles's program of containment, and he sought to recoup by the Southeast Asia Collective Defense Treaty, signed at Manila, September 8, 1954. The so-called Pacific Charter was an innocuous pledge signed by the participating nations, Australia, France, New Zealand, Pakistan, Thailand, Britain, and the U.S. Parts of the treaty follow.

ARTICLE III

The Parties undertake to strengthen their free institutions and to cooperate with one another in the further development of economic measures, including technical assistance, designed both to promote economic progress and social well-being and to further the individual and collective efforts of governments toward these ends.

ARTICLE IV

1. Each Party recognizes that aggression by means of armed attack in the treaty area against any of the Parties or against any State or territory which the Parties by unanimous agreement may hereafter designate, would endanger its own peace and safety, and agrees that it will in that event act to meet the common danger in accordance with its constitutional processes. Measures taken under this paragraph shall be immediately reported to the Security Council of the United Nations.

2. If, in the opinion of any of the Parties, the inviolability or the integrity of the territory or the sovereignty or political independence of any Party in the treaty area or of any other State or territory to which the provisions of paragraph 1 of this Article from time to time apply is threatened in any way other than by armed attack or is affected or threatened by any fact or situation which might endanger the peace of the area, the Parties shall consult immediately in order to agree on the measures which should be taken for the common defense.

3. It is understood that no action on the territory of any State designated by unanimous agreement under paragraph 1 of this Article or on any territory so designated shall be taken except at the invitation or with the consent of the government concerned. . . .

ARTICLE VIII

As used in this Treaty, the "treaty area" is the general area of Southeast Asia, including also the entire territories of the Asian Parties, and the general area of the Southwest Pacific not including the Pacific area north of 21 degrees 30 minutes north latitude. [The purpose of this provision was to exclude Taiwan.] . . .

PROTOCOL

Designation of states and territory as to which provisions of Article IV and Article III are to be applicable:

The Parties to the Southeast Asia Collective Defense Treaty unanimously designate for the purposes of Article IV of the Treaty the States of Cambodia and Laos and the free territory under the jurisdiction of the State of Vietnam. [The last referred to South Vietnam.]

(8) THE FORMOSA RESOLUTION, 1955

Nationalist China, though now located on Formosa, held certain islands (Quemoy and Matsu) close to the communist mainland, and these were subject to frequent shelling by the Reds. In January, 1955, the Reds seemed to be preparing an invasion of Formosa, and at Eisenhower's request Congress passed the following joint resolution. The invasion did not come, but when in 1958 another seemed imminent Eisenhower announced the placing of nuclear cannon on the offshore islands. Since Russia refused to match those nuclear weapons, the invasion could not be carried out.

Whereas the primary purpose of the United States, in its relations with all other nations, is to develop and sustain a just and enduring peace for all; and

Whereas certain territories in the West Pacific under the jurisdiction of the Republic of China are now under armed attack, and threats and declarations have been and are being made by the Chinese Communists that such armed attack is in aid of and in preparation for armed attack on Formosa and the Pescadores. . . .

Whereas the President of the United States on January 6, 1955, submitted to the Senate for its advice and consent to ratification a Mutual Defense Treaty between the United States of America and the Republic of China, which recognizes that an armed attack in the West Pacific area directed against territories, therein described, in the region of Formosa and the Pescadores, would be dangerous to the peace and safety of the parties to the treaty: Therefore be it

Resolved by the Senate and House of Representatives of the United States of America in Congress assembled, That the President of the United States be and he hereby is authorized to employ the Armed Forces of the United States as he deems necessary for the specific purpose of securing and protecting Formosa and the Pescadores against armed attack, this authority to include the securing and protection of such related positions and territories of that area now in friendly hands and the taking of such other measures as he judges to be required or appropriate in assuring the defense of Formosa and the Pescadores.

(9) SPLIT IN THE RED MONOLITH

China's historic role as the "Middle Kingdom" and its contempt for foreigners made it impatient of Russian advice (especially when it turned out to be right) and it was angered by Russia's refusal to have a nuclear showdown with the United States. When Russia withdrew economic support and called home the experts who were helping China to develop a nuclear capability, the breach became open and bitter. No doubt Russia was motivated by fear of China's rising power and China, in turn, wished to get back Mongolia and Siberia, to which it had long laid claim. But more immediate, perhaps, was the fact that Russia had reached the stage of development where it had much to lose in a nuclear conflict, while Mao considered a few hundred million lives well lost if the result was a world gained for communism. Each country now sought to impose its leadership on communists everywhere, even while in gingerly fashion they cooperated in furnishing the sinews of war to North Vietnam and the Viet Cong in the Vietnam War. Following is a statement of the Chinese case against Russia by Lin Piao (*Hsinhua* Chinese Communist Press Agency), September 2, 1965, as it appears in *Current*, October 1965, pp. 8–9.

"The Khrushchev revisionists have come to the rescue of U. S. imperialism just when it is most panic-stricken and helpless in its efforts to cope with the people's war. Working hand in glove with the U. S. imperialists, they are doing their utmost to spread all kinds of arguments against the people's war, and wherever they can, they are scheming to undermine it by overt or covert means.

"The fundamental reason why the Khrushchev revisionists are opposed to the people's war is that they have no faith in the masses and are afraid of U. S. imperialism, of war and revolution. . . . They submit to the nuclear blackmail of the U. S. imperialists and are afraid that, if the oppressed peoples and nations rise up to fight the people's wars or the people of Socialist countries repulse U. S. imperialist aggression, U. S. imperialism will become incensed, they themselves will become involved and their fond dream of Soviet-U. S. cooperation to dominate the world will be spoiled. . . .

"The Khrushchev revisionists insist that a nation without nuclear weapons is incapable of defeating an enemy with nuclear weapons, whatever methods of fighting it may adopt. . . . The Khrushchev revisionists assert that nuclear weapons and strategic rocket units are decisive while conventional forces are insignificant, and that a militia is just a heap of human flesh. . . .

"The Khrushchev revisionists maintain that a single spark in any part of the globe may touch off a world nuclear conflagration and bring destruction to mankind. If this were true, our planet would have been destroyed time and time again. . . .

"By contrast, those who have done their utmost to stamp out the 'sparks' of people's war have in fact encouraged U. S. imperialism in its aggressions and wars.

"The Khrushchev revisionists claim that if their general line of 'peaceful coexistence, peaceful transition and peaceful competition' is followed, the oppressed will be liberated and 'a world without weapons, without armed forces and without wars' will come into being. . . .

"The essence of the general line of the Khrushchev revisionists is nothing other than the demand that all the oppressed peoples and nations and all the countries that have won independence should lay down their arms and place themselves at the mercy of the U. S. imperialists and their lackeys who are armed to the teeth. . . .' "

(10) THE TONKIN BAY RESOLUTION, 1964

The American descent into the Vietnamese maelstrom is too complicated to follow here, but a significant milepost was passed with the passage by Congress of the Tonkin Bay Resolution, in August, 1964, in response to a brush between U.S. and North Vietnamese naval forces.

That the Congress approves and supports the determination of the President, as Commander in Chief, to take all necessary measures to repel any armed attack against the forces of the United States and to prevent further aggression.

The United States regards as vital to its national interest and to world peace the maintenance of international peace and security in southeast Asia. Consonant with the Constitution of the United States and the Charter of the United Nations and in accordance with its obligations under the Southeast Collective Defense Treaty, the United States is, therefore, prepared, as the President determines, to take all necessary steps, including the use of armed force, to assist any member or protocol state of the Southeast Asia Collective Defense Treaty requesting assistance in defense of its freedom.

(11) "WHY ARE WE IN VIETNAM?"

In the preceding chapter we gave George Kennan's analysis of the American penchant for judging foreign problems on a moral basis, and his accuracy has never been more amply illustrated than by the reaction to the Vietnam War. Opponents of the involvement never ceased to complain that the Johnson Administration would not clarify its reasons for the policy it pursued. This was, to say the least, disingenuous. The President and leading officials incessantly repeated their reasons, and so clearly that even he who ran might read—if he cared to. This is not to imply that the reasons were sound—only that they were clear.

Among the numerous explanations and defenses of American policy in Vietnam was the testimony of Secretary of State Dean Rusk before the Senate Foreign Relations Committee on February 18, 1966. The full record appears in *Hearings before the Committee on Foreign Relations*, U.S. Senate, 89th Cong., 2nd Sess., on S.2793, Part I, pp. 561–684. Here we give brief extracts from pp. 563–565 and 567–568, which express the administration's beliefs that the Vietnam War involved not only American commitments but American security.

Why are we in Vietnam? Certainly we are not there merely because we have power and like to use it. We do not regard ourselves as the policeman of the universe. We do not go around the world looking for quarrels in which we can intervene. Quite the contrary. We have recognized that, just as we are not gendarmes of the universe, neither are we the magistrate of the universe. If other governments, other institutions, or other regional organizations can find solutions to the quarrels which disturb this present scene, we are anxious to have this occur. But we are in Vietnam because the issues posed there are deeply intertwined with our own security and because the outcome of the struggle can profoundly affect the nature of the world in which we and our children will live. The situation we face in southeast Asia is obviously complex but, in my view, the underlying issues are relatively simple and are utterly fundamental. . . .

What are our world security interests involved in the struggle in Vietnam?

They cannot be seen clearly in terms of southeast Asia only or merely in terms of the events of the past few months. We must view the problem in perspective. We must recognize that what we are seeking to achieve in South Vietnam is part of a process that has continued

for a long time—a process of preventing the expansion and extension of Communist domination by the use of force against the weaker nations on the perimeter of Communist power.

This is the problem as it looks to us. Nor do the Communists themselves see the problem

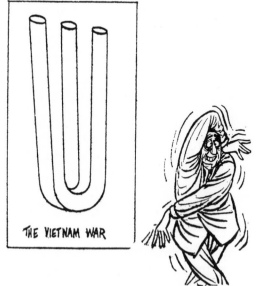

Interlandi, The Los Angeles Times © 1965

"The pattern as a whole is undecipherable; the brain becomes confused and the total effect is quite maddening!"

in isolation. They see the struggle in South Vietnam as part of a larger design for the steady extension of Communist power through force and threat. . . .

There may be differences within the Communist world about methods, and techniques, and leadership within the Communist world itself, but they share a common attachment to their "world revolution" and to its support through what they call wars of liberation.

So what we face in Vietnam is what we have faced on many occasions before—the need to check the extension of Communist power in order to maintain a reasonable stability in a precarious world.

That stability was achieved in the years after the war by the valor of free nations in defending the integrity of postwar territorial arrangements. And we have achieved a certain stability for the last decade and a half. It must not be overthrown now. . . .

In joining SEATO the United States took a solemn treaty engagement of far-reaching effect. Article IV, paragraph 1, provides that—

each party recognizes that aggression by means of armed attack . . . would endanger its own peace and safety, and agrees that it will in that event act to meet the common danger in accordance with its constitutional processes. . . .

The far-reaching implications of this commitment were well understood by this committee when it recommended, with only the late Senator Langer dissenting, that the Senate consent to the ratification of the treaty. The committee's report states, in its conclusion, that—

The committee is not impervious to the risks which this treaty entails. It fully appreciates that acceptance of these additional obligations commits the United States to a course of action over a vast expanse of the Pacific. Yet these risks are consistent with our own highest interests. There are greater hazards—the committee's conclusions stated

—in not advising a potential enemy of what he can expect of us, and in failing to disabuse him of assumptions which might lead to a miscalculation of our intentions.

Following this committee's recommendation, the Senate gave its advice and consent to the treaty by a vote of 82 to 1, the late Senator Langer voting against. All members of this distinguished committee who were then Senators voted for that treaty.

Our multilateral engagement under the SEATO Treaty had been reinforced and amplified by a series of bilateral commitments and assurances directly to the Government of South Vietnam.

On October 1, 1954, President Eisenhower wrote to President Diem offering, and I quote—

to assist the government of Vietnam in developing and maintaining a strong viable state, capable of resisting attempted subversion or aggression through military means.

In 1957, President Eisenhower and President Diem issued a joint statement which called attention to—

the large buildup of Vietnamese Communist military forces in North Vietnam—

and stated, and I quote:

Noting that the Republic of Vietnam is covered by article IV of the Southeast Asia Collective Defense Treaty, President Eisenhower and President Ngo Dinh Diem agreed that aggression or subversion threatening the political independence of the Republic of Vietnam would be considered as endangering peace and stability.

On August 2, 1961, President Kennedy declared that—

the United States is determined that the Republic of Vietnam shall not be lost to the Communists for lack of any support which the United States can render.

On December 14, 1961, President Kennedy wrote to President Diem, recalling the U.S. declaration made at the end of the Geneva Conference in 1954. The President once again stated that the United States was "prepared to help the Republic of Vietnam to protect its people and to preserve its independence." This commitment has been reaffirmed many times since.

The crux of the issue of involvement should have been the wisdom and/or effectiveness of the policy. There was a good case against it on these grounds. Temperate observers could and did argue that American interests in Southeast Asia were not worth the expenditure in blood and treasure, nor worth alienating our allies. They could argue that the war might lead to Chinese involvement and World War III, or alternatively that China's expansionism was spent, so Vietnam, even if it were communist, would not be an instrument of Red Chinese policy but rather a nationalist obstacle to its expansion. They could and did point out (as did Kennan himself) that containment had become too rigid and was attempting so much that the United States was overextended to the point that it might meet disaster; a trenchant expression of this thesis appears next in this chapter.

The most vocal opposition, however, came from the so-called New Left, which plunged into the fray with Garrisonian intransigence. Its advocates refused to debate the real issues of national interests, or, if they did, deliberately wrested the evidence to prove their view. Ordinarily they chose to invoke morality—always a shaky basis for action since interpretations of what is moral differ so widely. In this case they set up an absolute and demanded universal assent to it; dissent from it thus became immoral by definition.

A part of their method was to make vicious personal attacks; Johnson was regularly denounced as a war criminal and child murderer, and an off-Broadway play went so far as to accuse him of having been privy to Kennedy's assassination. (History *does* repeat itself: a similar accusation had been made a century earlier against another President Johnson.) Apparently the New Left was not communist, though it typically aimed its abuse only at the United States. It is impossible to convey the full viciousness of the propaganda without giving the subject more space than it deserves.

THE OTHER SIDE OF THE COIN

Socialist countries, no less than capitalist countries, are prepared to behave like the millionaire—to use millions to destroy the other "millionaire"—it is just as likely to be a socialist "millionaire." In other words, socialist wealth now tolerates poverty, which is an even more unforgiveable crime. . . . Don't forget that rich countries . . . may be found on either side of the division between the capitalist and socialist countries.

—President Julius Nyerere of Tanzania

We believe that foreign trade cannot, and should not, acknowledge frontiers or ideology. My government attributes the utmost importance to commercial relations with countries in the course of economic development, like Brazil. . . . The continuous increase of production in the Soviet economy permits us to accelerate the rhythm and volume of our exports.

—Nikolai Patolichev, 1966, justifying Russia's commercial
pact with Brazil signed over Castro's protest

Development is much more than a matter of encouraging economic growth within a given social structure. It is rather the *modernization* of that structure. . . . [If] the social psychology of these nations [changes] . . . I think it is likely to be . . . because some shock treatment like that of Communism has been administered to them. . . . Only a campaign of an intensity and singlemindedness that must approach the ludicrous and the unbearable offers the chance to ride roughshod over the resistance of the rich and the poor alike and to open the way for the forcible implantation of those modern attitudes and techniques without which there will be no escape from the misery of underdevelopment.

—Robert L. Heilbroner in *Commentary*, April, 1967

South Vietnam is the model of the national liberation movement in our time. . . . If the special warfare that the United States imperialists are testing in South Vietnam is overcome, that means that it can be defeated everywhere in the world.

—General Vo Nguyen Giap of North Vietnam

The central issue of the mid-twentieth century is how to sustain democracy and prosperity without imperial expansion and the conflicts it engenders. The reason is obvious: the sparks from those collisions now fall into a nuclear tinderbox.

—William Appleman Williams, *The Tragedy of
American Diplomacy* (1962), p. 303

The United States must abandon its ideological hostility to the public sector in the developing nations. In saying this, I do not intend to turn the free-enterprise myth topsy-turvy or argue that nationalization is some magic, painless way to modernization. For after recent events in countries like China and Cuba, this view can no longer be seriously maintained. There is no easy road out of underdevelopment, and one must talk pragmatically about some sort of international mixed economy. The Third World cannot simply put its faith in Adam Smith or any of his heirs; for the market mechanism is a cause of, rather than a solution to, its poverty.

—Michael Harrington, *Dissent*, Sept.–Oct., 1967

HOW FARES THE AMERICAN MISSION?

[The bitter contest in the United States over the Johnson Administration's policy in Vietnam has obscured the fact that practically everyone agrees that there should be intervention. The difference is that one side wants intervention by implementing political and social reforms; the other side wants the same things but holds that the basis must be laid by military action. Here we see two modern forms of the concept of American mission which has existed from the very founding of the American colonies. Our messianism pays little heed to the view—becoming daily more obvious—that neither persons nor nations can be saved. They can be *helped*, but they have to *save* themselves. Surely this was amply demonstrated by the Marshall Plan. We shall return to this problem in the concluding chapter, where we examine the failure of American intellectuals.

Here it is appropriate to introduce a perceptive analysis of the nature and result of this messianism, and some suggestions of what could happen. The article is "A Case against Interventionism" in *Dissent*, Sept.–Oct., 1967, pp. 546–556, and is by William Pfaff, foreign affairs columnist for *Commonweal*. Regardless of what happens in Vietnam, the analysis will be of continuing significance.]

The intervention of nations into the affairs of others is one of history's inevitabilities. Interests collide and interlock; states want to change the conduct of others. What is interesting—and perilously relevant—is why they do it, what means they use, and how far they are prepared to go.

In American policy today, the great controversy arises not so much from the fact that we are intervening abroad as from the scale and character of our interventions. In Vietnam, in Latin America, in Western Europe, an American political intervention was well established, supported by an American public consensus, and tolerated (or even welcomed) by the greater part of the international community, long before the present policy crisis. What seems to have gone wrong is that the United States has crossed a threshold of acceptable means. The objection is to the use of war as an instrument of intervention in Vietnam, large-scale military intervention in a Caribbean political crisis, the *kind* of pressures we have employed to attempt to isolate France and to affect West German policy. The judgment in these cases is that our methods are disproportionate to what reasonably can be expected to be achieved.

The objection is to excess—to a failure of political judgment and discrimination. It makes a sound argument, one of practicality rather than principle, and it probably is more persuasive for the omission. But there are two issues of principle involved in the present situation which are worth some attention for the light they throw on what may be expected from the future of this American world involvement.

The first concerns the morality of our means. . . . Behind much of the outcry against the American course in Vietnam is an instinctive (or historically conditioned) reaction against a casualness about violence, against an advertised "tough mindedness" about the established conventions of war and international law, which are literally demoralizing to international society.

The second issue of principle has to do with the rationale for American interventionism. The evolution of our foreign policy since the 1940's has not been wholly deliberate, and the commitment this country made to international "leadership" after 1945 was accompanied by much domestic controversy. . . . The Truman and Eisenhower administrations had to fight for [their] programs in Congress; and together the individual programs amounted to a reversal of a one-hundred-fifty-year-old American policy of isolationism.

The roots of isolationist policy lay very deep in the American consciousness—in the experience of physical isolation, of ocean barriers, but much more important, in the peculiar American historical experience of repudiation of Europe. . . . For the purpose of illuminating the interventionism of American policy today it is enough to say that the American historical experience conduced us to a view of the United States as a society morally different from and superior to the rest of the world, and to a view of other nations as politically unredeemed, waiting—as Woodrow Wilson put it—to "turn to America for those moral inspirations which lie at the basis of all freedom . . . [For America's] flag is the flag not only of America, but of humanity."

This strain of messianism in American political attitudes found gratification, but also a practical check in a foreign policy of isolationism. But when the events of the last two decades forced an American policy reversal, that messianism inevitably sought expression in the new policy. And indeed the appeal to messianism was one instrument by which the change was effected: the public was constantly told that ours was a "unique" challenge, a responsibility to create, in Secretary of State Dean Rusk's formulation, "A world free of aggression; a world which moves toward the rule of law . . . a world of better life for all mankind."

If such is the meaning and goal of American foreign policy, what compromises are plausible? And the practical obstacle to gaining this imposing objective is no mere nation or nations, but an ideology—a force which itself purports to be universal in relevance and morally inspired. The messianism of Lenin, looking beyond the borders of Russia to a world-wide class struggle, and of Mao Tse-tung, preaching the revolutionary unity of the "rural" peoples, today confronts the liberal messianism of America.

The Vietnamese intervention is hardly intelligible outside this intellectual framework which makes the political fate of a weak and remote society crucial to our own affairs. A justification may be argued in domino theories or indefensible analogies with Europe in the 1930's, or warnings that if we don't fight here we soon will have to fight . . . in Hawaii or California. Or it may be given a *Realpolitik* but question-begging statement which limits itself to arguments of past commitment or national prestige—we are there because we are there. Yet underlying all of this is a kind of universalism: we are threatened by world Communism, able to challenge "freedom" anywhere if it is not "taught a lesson"; or by Asian Communism, potentially the vehicle of all "rural" Afro-Asian discontent; or (as Mr. Rostow now puts it) by "romantic revolutionism" derived from 1789 and about to be given a final blow in Vietnam; or by multiple factors of poverty, racism, and human discontent which manifest themselves in Vietnamese Communism at this moment but will break out in some other violence elsewhere unless they are contained here and ultimately disarmed by energetic world-wide programs of social reform and political development.

The Left, often enough, is contemptuous of the former arguments but inclined to accept the last one. Much of the controversy in the United States over Vietnam is really an argument over method, not over assumptions or objectives. Liberals, after all, supported our early intervention on behalf of Ngo Dinh Diem. . . . That many of these same people now object to Mr. Johnson's militarization of the intervention does not change the fact that they wanted, got, and presumably still support, a vast American intervention, as such, into the affairs of Southeast Asia. They simply want it to be carried out through aid missions, political counsel, and the Peace Corps, rather than with combat troops. They want the same objectives Mr. Johnson wants, and share the same essential assumptions about America's responsibilities and role in Southeast Asia, but they want to do it all with clean hands. . . .

Contemporary interventionism—"globalism"—then is a democratic society's rejoinder to the transnational ideological challenge of communism. It flourishes on both left and right of the political spectrum because the old American sense of moral separateness and superiority disposes virtually all in this country to an interpretation of international politics as essentially a struggle of values—and to the historicism implicit in such a notion of universal struggle (a struggle which both we and the enemy assume to be to determine the character of "the next and higher stage of history"). The principal controversy is simply over the particular form which intervention should take—economic, social, educational, military?—and in fact American foreign policy in the last two decades has used all of these instrumentalities. For the CIA simultaneously to support leftist trade unionism abroad and sponsor rightist military cliques should not be surprising, for these merely are aspects of a general American effort, supported by nearly all the elements in our society, to bring about a world-wide "conversion" to the values we embrace. . . .

The Vietnamese war should then be understood as the end-point of a policy of sentimentality and intellectual complacency, rather than as an example of neocolonialism. Vietnam is the fulfillment of a kind of vulgar liberalism which assumes that the political experience and aspirations of all men everywhere are essentially identical with our own, and that the desire for peace, democratic government, and material welfare are the dominant ambitions of men everywhere. Corollary to this belief has been the conviction that when the conduct of peoples abroad contradicts these ambitions—which are our own, and should thus produce alignment with us—it must be the result of intimidation or evil, which must be fought, or deprivation, ignorance, or misunderstanding, which can and should be removed.

In Vietnam an American preoccupation with the freedom and well-being of other men, morally inspired but sentimental in its analysis of real possibilities, has converged with an American fear of Communism which naively exaggerates the unity, power and threat of the Communist movement. A serious foreign policy of containing Soviet power, and a decent national concern for the condition of our fellow men, have over two decades been allowed to

degenerate into a program that is messianic, intolerant, and intellectually unserious. The worst of America has proved stronger than the best, and the result is a war whose solution is not easily foreseen, conducted by a distracted and divided nation whose serious internal problems are ominously exacerbated by this war. The outcome of it all seems to me to include more disturbing possibilities than are ordinarily understood. And the prospect for a reform of policy, for a constructive or progressive remedy, seems to me rather bleak.

Let me deal first with what the outcome of present trends might be. The concern commonly expressed is that the war in Vietnam will grow bigger, that China or the Soviet Union might be provoked into counterintervention, and that major war or even nuclear war could result. . . .

More plausible is an enlargement of the war which simply deepens our commitment and increases American frustration and domestic controversy, producing a further hardening of government policy at the same time that it produces a further erosion of the government's confidence and assurance. Bad policy will be reinvested in and reinforced out of the unadmitted need to vindicate the human and moral investments already made.

The outcome, then, would undoubtedly be an eventual compromise—possibly under a Republican administration—which amounted to a disguised capitulation, not to the NLF so much as to the intractable realities of Vietnamese society. But while officially there would be neither victory nor defeat, it would be a self-defeat for the United States, and the domestic reaction could, I think, be very bitter, self-laceration accompanied by vengeful public controversy and a repudiation of the individuals, the party, the foreign policy advisers responsible for creating the conditions for this debacle.

I hardly think that in these circumstances public opinion would turn Left. I do not think it necessarily would turn Right, either, or at least toward the Right now politically recognizable as such, although a hardening of American attitudes, a deepening intolerance towards the world abroad, is plausible enough. There might, as one French critic has suggested, have to be an American "Algeria" in some such place as Brazil, before interventionism can die.

But the more likely turn in American attitudes is inward. Isolationism remains very close below the surface of both Left and Right in this country today. The interventionism of the Republican Right is simply a caricature of liberal interventionism, addicted to the language of military solutions and near-Manichean in its political simplifications; but the instinct of the Right remains conservative—resistant to ground wars on foreign soil, hoarding the peculiar treasure of Americanism. And the more benign interventionism of the rest, committed to a belief in the power of social and economic reform to dissolve conflict, expresses an American moral isolation—our innocence of that experience of civil devastation, betrayal, popular aggression, and mass political hysteria which has dominated the history of much of the world these last fifty years. . . .

What I suggest, then, can happen as a result of the Vietnamese war is a profound American disillusionment; and not with interventionism so much as with the possibilities of national action itself. Vietnam represents the fullest expression of the interventionist spirit; but our policies toward Europe and Latin America are also obsolete today, resisted by the most dynamic elements on both continents, and we show little interest in any policy changes except those which would reinforce the old ambitions and defend the old assumptions. A general collapse of American policy is not out of the question. The ensuing retreat could be an American popular retreat from internationalism, from liberalism as well, and a renewal of an intolerant American messianism that becomes wholly exclusivist, directed inwardly to national self-reassurance. There is precedent for this in other societies which have had an external mission repudiated by those whom they intended to save. For 16th-century Spain, frustration abroad resulted in an internal hypocrisy and decline which was undramatic in its progress but decisive in effect, a failure of confidence that eventually rendered Spain irrelevant to modern Europe. Nothing so dark need be predicted for the United States for the weight of the precedent to be felt.

There is another possible outcome. Interventionism could be persisted in and reasserted in collaboration with a Soviet Union whose own political messianism is today badly shaken. Russia clearly is in a period of political disorientation—or reorientation—today, an aftermath both of the excesses of Stalin and the failures of Stalin's successors. For a nation which defined itself as marking a new stage in man's social organization, the present condition of the Soviet Union and of its international bloc must prove deeply demoralizing—however well disguised the political truth may be by goulash and ballet. Proposals for Soviet-American collaboration to settle the war in Vietnam over the heads of the Vietnamese, to contain China, to contain nuclear proliferation and check the arms race, imply the possibility of collaboration to "contain" a good many other forces in the contemporary world whose collective effect is to reduce both Russia and the United States to the place of mere nations among nations. This, it seems to me, is a more plausible course for "convergence" between Soviet and American societies than any convergence in social democracy. But collaboration to protect one another's super-power status, however well rationalized it might be as preserving the peace or controlling arms, would amount to a neo-imperialism which genuinely deserves that epithet.

These are two outcomes which are plausible within the present course of American foreign policy. There are less bleak possibilities, the best probably being a series of half-failures of American policy—including a Vietnamese settlement on bad terms—which we refuse to acknowledge as failures. In this case the trend would be an enforced retreat from commitment but without the harsh decisions and sharp reactions of the first of the possibilities I have discussed. Yet even here the result is likely to be a creeping sense of American failure which obstructs domestic reform, a growing social stagnation.

But is this deep a pessimism warranted? In the immediate perspective I think that it is. The fact that our present foreign policy is under attack from as many different positions as it is today is a good sign. Yet beyond agreeing that we should get out of Vietnam, the New Left, the civil rights movement, the disestablished liberals, the literary Left, the neo-isolationists, the academic "realists," and the Robert Kennedy government-in-exile have little enough in common, and in some of these cases it is not at all clear that they understand what they should expect, or want, of a foreign policy. Yet clearly the more creative elements in American society reject what existing policy has come in practice to mean. . . . [They] are against Mr. Johnson's Vietnamese policy yet are committed to the same assumptions of universal crisis and universal goals which underlie that policy. They are no less ambitious in what they believe can and should be accomplished by an American foreign policy. Against them are the "neo-isolationists," presumably including all of those who believe that an increasingly intense and intolerant mission to the world has come to serve for America as an evasion of domestic realities and domestic accomplishment. But by definition this is an ill assorted group, drawn from the Left, Center, and Right of national politics, and an effective alliance is not easy to imagine. Yet if there is to be a turn away from interventionism the national political leadership will have to come from here.

Intellectual leadership remains the immediate problem because a new policy which does not deal with the established reality of American power and our inevitable involvement in the affairs of others would be fantasy; isolation is no longer an American policy option, even for neo-isolationists. Yet the existing community of foreign policy specialists and professionals is precisely that group most responsible for our present situation. The public has faithfully supported the foreign policies of the last three administrations as it accepts Mr. Johnson's leadership today, and the foreign policies of all these administrations have fairly faithfully reflected the counsel of the foreign policy establishment—in the universities, the foreign affairs institutes and policy centers, the government departments concerned with international relations. If sentimentality, messianism, an egregious lack of realism, have increasingly marked American conduct and resulted in the present crisis, this must ultimately be accounted the failure of an intellectual class. And this failure is a sobering one—for our world power and world involvement cannot be repealed.

It may be that the American historical experience all but precludes a sustained foreign policy of limited objectives and assumptions. . . . Such a policy is intrinsically defensive. Foreign policy is fundamentally a means by which the American nation is protected, and it is not an appropriate vehicle for the reform or revolution of foreign societies. The objection to the latter definition is, first of all, prudential —such is the course of ideological politics, unlimited in ambition and expedient in method. But it is also a practical argument. The fact is that nations and societies work out their own fates, and while outside powers can help them or crush them, true national successes (like national failures) result from the character of the society itself. Our power to help others in the matters that really count, in establishing decent and representative government, practicing humane social policies, achieving "development," is not very great: it necessarily is auxiliary to their own efforts and decisions, is warped by our own preoccupations, and is distorted by the very great problems of comprehending the character and rhythms of other cultures. (And the last is a matter in which the United States is notoriously weak.)

The values of American society are relevant to the world beyond America: to call for a limited foreign policy is not to discount the importance of the constitutional and social achievements of this country. It is, rather, to argue that these will not be promulgated by means of propaganda, military action, or—except minimally—by foreign aid and diplomacy. It is conventional today to warn about the limits of power, yet the warning seems hardly comprehended even by the government officials who issue it.

A new American policy cannot abandon a commitment to values and to moral influence in world affairs, but would be skeptical in its expectations and would understand that its primary obligation is to defend the international conditions which secure a civilized domestic society—for the United States, and by indirection for others. This means limiting conflicts, not enlarging them in the name of an ultimate banishment of conflict from the world. It means containing and isolating the disorders of international affairs, not inflating them and intervening in them on ideological—and ultimately historicist—arguments. It means strengthening the established institutions and conventions of international arbitration and legality, not breaking them. It means dealing with the ideological attacks of others in terms of what those states actually do and can do to harm us, rather than adding our own voice to the clamor of rhetoric and hysteria which embitters international relations.

Described as a policy of limit, this is perhaps better understood as an existential policy, dealing with international realities as they exist and with nations as they act—not as they conform to purported historical imperatives. Thus we must take seriously those who can hurt us or our friends—as we have been hard and prudent towards Russia since 1945. . . . Tolerance and patience are banal counsels—yet time steadily recasts the situations and ambitions of nations, and while this may be a matter for pessimism, it is also the ultimate argument for existential judgments. No doubt this makes up an unsatisfying prescription for America in its hour of world preeminence; and that is precisely our problem.

Yet history simply is not susceptible to solutions, any more than the essential anxieties and frustrations of individual life can be "solved." The personal analogy can be pursued. The nations that count in history are those which civilized themselves, establishing a standard of justice, and of social, intellectual, and artistic accomplishment. Here is permanent achievement, where the United States thus far has done not badly, but not so well as to earn that world leadership, which our foreign policy so insistently asserts. And the discrepancy between claim and achievement has grown disquietingly large, with a danger in this to others, but primarily to ourselves.

CHINA'S GRAND STRATEGY

[The following restatement of Red Chinese policy in the light of the Vietnam War was made by Marshal Lin Piao, Chinese Defense Minister. It appeared in *Hsinhua* (Chinese Communist Press Agency), September 2, 1965, and the version given here is from *Current*, October, 1965, pp. 32–35.]

"The seizure of power by armed force, the settlement of the issues by war, is the central task and the highest form of revolution. This Marxist-Leninist principle of revolution holds good universally, for China and for all other countries. . . .

"In the last analysis, whether one dares to

wage a tit-for-tat struggle against armed aggression and suppression by the imperialists and their lackeys, whether one dares to fight a people's war against them means whether one dares to embark on revolution. This is the most effective touchstone for distinguishing genuine from fake revolutionaries. . . .

"In view of the fact that some people were afflicted with the fear of the imperialists and reactionaries, Comrade Mao Tse-tung put forward his famous thesis that 'the imperialists and all reactionaries are paper tigers.' In appearance, the reactionaries are terrifying but in reality they are not so powerful. From a long-term point of view, it is not the reactionaries but the people who are really powerful.

"The history of the people's war in China and other countries provides conclusive evidence that the growth of the people's revolutionary forces from weak and small beginnings into strong and large forces is a universal law of development of the class struggle, a universal law of development of the people's war. A people's war inevitably meets with many difficulties, with ups and downs and setbacks in the course of its development, but no force can alter its general trend toward inevitable triumph.

"Comrade Mao Tse-tung points out that we must despise the enemy strategically and take full account of him tactically. To despise the enemy strategically is an elementary requirement for a revolutionary. Without the courage to despise the enemy and without daring to win, it will be simply impossible to make a revolution and wage a people's war, let alone to achieve victory. . . .

"It must be emphasized that Comrade Mao Tse-tung's theory of the establishment of rural revolutionary base areas and the encirclement of cities from the countryside is of outstanding and universal practical importance for the present revolutionary struggles of all the oppressed nations and peoples, and particularly for the revolutionary struggles of the oppressed nations and peoples in Asia, Africa and Latin America against imperialism and its lackeys. . . .

"In committing aggression against these countries, the imperialists usually begin by seizing the big cities and the main lines of communication, but they are unable to bring the vast countryside completely under their control. The countryside, and the countryside alone, can provide the broad areas in which the revolutionaries can maneuver freely. . . .

"Taking the entire globe, if North America and Western Europe can be called 'the cities of the world,' then Asia, Africa and Latin America constitute 'the rural areas of the world.'

"Since World War II, the proletarian revolutionary movement has for various reasons been temporarily held back in the North American and West European capitalist countries, while the people's revolutionary movement in Asia, Africa and Latin America has been growing vigorously. In a sense the contemporary world revolution also presents a picture of the encirclement of cities by the rural areas.

"The October Revolution [in Russia] opened up a new era in the revolution of the oppressed nations. The victory of the October Revolution built a bridge between the Socialist revolution of the proletariat of the West and the national-democratic revolution of the colonial and semi-colonial countries of the East. The Chinese revolution has successfully solved the problem of how to link up the national democratic with Socialist revolution in the colonial and semi-colonial countries.

"Comrade Mao Tse-tung has pointed out that, in the epoch since the October Revolution, anti-imperialist revolution in any colonial or semi-colonial country is no longer part of the old bourgeois, or capitalist world revolution, but is part of the new world revolution, the proletarian-Socialist world revolution. . . .

"There is no great wall between the two revolutionary stages. But the Socialist revolution is only possible after the completion of the national-democratic revolution. The more thorough the national-democratic revolution, the better the conditions for the Socialist revolution. . . .

"The Khrushchev revisionists are now actively preaching that Socialism can be built without the proletariat and without a Communist party. And they have cast the fundamental tenets of Marxism-Leninism to the four winds. The revisionists' purpose is solely to divert the oppressed nations from their struggle against imperialism and to sabotage their national-democratic revolution, all in the service of imperialism.

"The Chinese revolution provides a successful lesson for making a thoroughgoing national-democratic revolution under the leadership of the proletariat: it likewise provides a successful lesson for the timely transition from the national democratic revolution to the Socialist revolution under the leadership of the proletariat. . . .

"Since World War II, United States imperialism has stepped into the shoes of German, Japanese and Italian Fascism and has been trying to build a great American empire by dominating and enslaving the whole world. It is the most rabid aggressor in human history and the most ferocious common enemy of the people of the world.

"Every people or country in the world that wants revolution, independence and peace cannot but direct the spearhead of its struggle against U. S. imperialism. . . . The struggles waged by the different peoples against U. S. imperialism reinforce each other and merge into a worldwide tide of opposition to U. S. imperialism. The more successful the development of people's war in a given region, the larger the number of U. S. imperialist forces that can be pinned down and depleted there.

"When the U. S. aggressors are hard pressed in one place, they have no alternative but to loosen their grip on others. Therefore the conditions become more favorable for the people elsewhere to wage struggles against U. S. imperialism and its lackeys.

"Everything is divisible. And so is this colossus of U. S. imperialism. It can be split up and defeated. The peoples of Asia, Africa, Latin America and other regions can destroy it piece by piece, some striking at its head and others at its feet. That is why the greatest fear of U. S. imperialism is that people's wars will be launched in different parts of the world, and particularly in Asia, Africa and Latin America,

and why it regards people's wars as a mortal danger.

"U. S. imperialism relies solely on its nuclear weapons to intimidate people, but these weapons cannot save U. S. imperialism from its doom. Nuclear weapons cannot be used lightly. . . . The spiritual atom bomb that the revolutionary people possess is a far more powerful and useful weapon than the physical atom bomb.

"Vietnam is the most convincing example of a victim of aggression defeating U. S. imperialism by a people's war. The United States has made South Vietnam a testing ground for the suppression of people's war. It has carried on this experiment for many years, and everybody can now see that the U. S. aggressors are unable to cope with a people's war.

"The Khrushchev revisionists have come to the rescue of U. S. imperialism just when it is most panic-stricken and helpless in its efforts to cope with the people's war. . . . [They] maintain that a single spark in any part of the globe may touch off a world nuclear conflagration and bring destruction to mankind. If this were true, our planet would have been destroyed time and time again.

"There have been wars of national liberation throughout the 20 years since World War II. But has any single one of them developed into a world war? Isn't it true that the United States imperialists' plans for a world war have been upset precisely thanks to the wars of national liberation in Asia, Africa and Latin America? . . .

"Our attitude toward imperialist wars of aggression has always been clear-cut. First, we are against them, and secondly, we are not afraid of them. We will destroy whoever attacks us. As for revolutionary wars waged by the oppressed nations and peoples, so far from opposing them, we invariably give them firm support and active aid. It has been so in the past, it remains so in the present and, when we grow in strength as time goes on, we will give them still more support and aid in the future. . . .

"We are optimistic about the future of the world. We are confident that the people will bring to an end the epoch of wars in human history. Comrade Mao Tse-tung pointed out long ago that war, this monster, 'will be finally eliminated by the progress of human society. And in the not too distant future, too. But there is only one way to eliminate it and that is to oppose war with war, to oppose counterrevolutionary war with revolutionary war.'

"All peoples suffering from U. S. imperialist aggression, oppression and plunder, unite!"

THE THOUGHTS OF CHAIRMAN MAO

A revolution is not a dinner party, or writing an essay or painting a picture, or doing embroidery; it cannot be so refined, so leisurely and gentle, so temperate, kind, courteous, restrained and magnanimous. A revolution is an insurrection, an act of violence by which one class overthrows another.

The socialist system will eventually replace the capitalist system; this is an objective law independent of man's will.

Every Communist must grasp the truth, "Political power grows out of the barrel of a gun."

I have said that all the reputedly powerful reactionaries are merely paper tigers. The reason is that they are divorced from the people. Look! Was not Hitler a paper tiger? Was Hitler not overthrown? I also said that the tsar of Russia, the emperor of China and Japanese imperialism were all paper tigers. As we know, they were all overthrown. U.S. imperialism has not yet been overthrown and it has the atom bomb. I believe it also will be overthrown. It, too, is a paper tiger.

There are two winds in the world today, the East Wind and the West Wind. There is a Chinese saying, "Either the East Wind prevails over the West Wind or the West Wind prevails over the East Wind." I believe it is characteristic of the situation today that the East Wind is prevailing over the West Wind. That is to say, the forces of socialism have become overwhelmingly superior to the forces of imperialism.

People of the world, unite and defeat the U.S. aggressors and all their running dogs! People of the world, be courageous, dare to fight, defy difficulties and advance wave upon wave. Then the whole world will belong to the people. Monsters of all kinds shall be destroyed.

The atom bomb is a paper tiger which the U.S. reactionaries use to scare people. It looks terrible, but in fact it isn't. Of course, the atom bomb is a weapon of mass slaughter, but the outcome of a war is decided by the people, not by one or two new types of weapons.

We Communists are like seeds and the people are like the soil. Wherever we go, we must unite with the people, take root and blossom among them.

Many people think it impossible for guerrillas to exist for long in the enemy's rear. Such a belief reveals lack of comprehension of the relationship that should exist between the people and the troops. The former may be likened to water and the latter to the fish who inhabit it. How may it be said that these two cannot exist together? It is only undisciplined troops who make the people their enemies and who, like the fish out of its native element, cannot live.

—Quotations from Chairman Mao Tse-tung

CONTAINMENT OF CHINA WITHOUT ISOLATION

[The Vietnam War revived and embittered the argument over China. Would China patch up its differences with Russia? How far would it go in order to impose its hegemony on South and Southeast Asia? Would it enter the Vietnam War? To what extent did China's expansion menace the United States and the free world, and what could be done about it? Experts on China rather generally denied that it would embark on a career of widespread conquest unless it was clearly menaced, and they pled for an American policy of "containment without isolation." The Senate Foreign Relations Committee held a series of hearings, from which the following extract is given. It is by A. Doak Barnett, Director of the East Asian Institute at Columbia University.]

There is a need for basic changes in the over-all U.S. posture toward Communist China. For almost seventeen years, we have pursued a policy that might best be characterized as one aimed at containment and isolation of Communist China. In my view, the element of *containment*—using this term in a broad sense to include both military and non-military measures to block threats posed by China to its neighbors—has been . . ., in some respects at least, fairly successful. . . .

But the United States attempt to *isolate* Communist China has been, in my opinion, unwise and, in a fundamental sense, unsuccessful, and it cannot, I believe, provide a basis for a sound long-term policy that aims not only at containing and restraining Chinese power, but also at reducing tensions, exerting a moderating influence on Peking, broadening the areas on non-Communist agreement on issues relating to China, and slowly involving Com-

munist China in more normal patterns of international intercourse.

I strongly believe, therefore, that the time has come—even though the United States is now engaged in a bitter struggle in Vietnam—for our government to alter its posture toward Communist China and adopt a policy of containment but no isolation, a policy that would aim, on the one hand, at checking military or subversive threats and pressures emanating from Peking but, at the same time, would aim at maximum contacts with and maximum involvement of the Chinese Communists in the international community.

Such a policy would involve continued commitments to help non-Communist regimes combat Communist subversion and insurrection, as in Vietnam, and continued pledges to defend areas on China's periphery, including Taiwan. But it would involve changes in many other aspects of our policies. While continuing to fulfill our pledge to defend Taiwan against attack, we should clearly and explicitly acknowledge the Chinese Communist regime as the *de facto* government of the China mainland and state our desire to extend *de jure* recognition and exchange diplomatic representatives with Peking if and when it indicates that it would be prepared to reciprocate. We should press in every way we can to encourage nonofficial contacts. We should, instead of embargoing all trade with the China mainland, restrict only trade in strategic items and encourage American businessmen to explore other opportunities for trade contacts. And within the United Nations we should work for the acceptance of some formula which would provide seats for both Communist China and Nationalist China.

In taking these steps, we will have to do so in full recognition of the fact that Peking's initial reaction is almost certain to be negative and hostile and that any changes in our posture will create some new problems. But we should take them, nevertheless, because initiatives on our part are clearly required if we are to work, however slowly, toward the long-term goal of a more stable, less explosive situation in Asia and to explore the possibilities of trying to moderate Peking's policies. . . .

It is worth noting that to date there has been no extended period of peaceful relations between China and the Western world on the basis of reasonable equality. Before the mid-19th century, the Chinese held a superior position and attempted, unsuccessfully, to fit the Western powers into its traditional imperial system of relations with subordinate states. During the next hundred years, the Western powers held a superior position and attempted, also without great success, to fit China into the modern international system of relations. The still unresolved problem for the future is whether both China and the West can, in time, reach an acceptable peaceful accommodation within the modern nation-state system, on the basis of relationships in which the rights and obligations of both will be recognized. . . .

Peking's leaders now maintain that their experience provides a primary model for revolutions throughout the underdeveloped world. It is a model calling for the creation of Communist-led peasant armies, the establishment of so-called 'liberated areas' as basis for revolutionary struggle, the creation of broad anti-imperialist united fronts, and the overthrow of existing non-Communist regimes by violence. There is little doubt that the Chinese model has had, and will continue to have, an impact far beyond China's borders; revolutionary leaders in many parts of the world look to it for inspiration. We need, therefore, to understand it. . . .

We should not, however, magnify its significance. . . . The particular constellation of factors and forces which made it possible for Mao Tse-tung's strategy to succeed in China are not widely duplicated, and there are many reasons to believe that the Chinese model cannot be exported as easily as Mao and some of his colleagues have hoped. The available evidence also suggests that while the Chinese leaders would like to see their model widely emulated, their capacity to promote, and willingness and ability to support, Chinese-style revolutions elsewhere is definitely limited. . . .

It is equally important to note that, on the basis of available evidence and Communist China's performance to date, the Chinese Communists do not appear to think primarily in terms of spreading their influence through direct military and territorial expansion; they appear to recognize the limits to their capabilities for military action outside of China's borders; they have usually been quite realistic in assessing the power balance in concrete situations; they have generally been calculating and even cautious in avoiding military 'adventurism' and limiting their risks; they have tended to think in long-range terms about their most ambitious goals; and they have repeatedly been flexible and pragmatic. . . .

"For example, while Peking's leaders have sounded the trumpet for 'people's wars' wherever feasible and for the mobilization of the 'rural areas of the world' (the underdeveloped nations) against the 'cities of the world' (North America and Western Europe), at the same time they have called for closer links with many countries in the so-called 'intermediate zone'—including Japan and many Western countries—since their practical requirements, dictated by economic considerations, make it seem desirable to promote trade and other contacts with these nations. . . .

Recent events demonstrate, in short, that Peking's ability to manipulate or control even those situations where receptivity to Chinese influence has been greatest is severely limited. It remains to be seen whether Peking's leaders will grasp this fact and modify their policies as a result. Mao and some other top leaders may well resist doing so. But changes in Chinese policies are certainly within the realm of possibility—after Mao's death if not before. . . .

The Sino-Soviet dispute as it has evolved in recent years is clearly one of the most important developments in the international politics of the 1960's—just as the formation of the Sino-Soviet alliance was in the 1950's. There can be no doubt that the conflicts between Peking and Moscow now are very real, very bitter, and very deep. The dispute has involved basic clashes of national interests. . . .

In a fundamental sense the Sino-Soviet dispute has weakened Peking's international position, which has been to our advantage in many respects, since it imposes increased restraints on the Chinese Communist regime. But not all of the results of the dispute have been good from our point of view." It appears, for example, to have significantly reinforced Peking's tendency in recent years to maintain a highly militant posture.

In certain situations, Soviet interests and policies may run parallel to ours, as appears to be the case even in Vietnam today, to a very limited degree. But we cannot expect such parallelism to be dependable or believe that it will result—as some suggest—in a kind of Soviet-American anti-Chinese axis. Even when a degree of parallelism does exist, it cannot be expected to resolve all the difficult problems of dealing with the Chinese. . . .

What is required, it seems to me, to maximize the possibility of a desirable sort of shift in Peking's posture and policies, is a combination of two elements: developments in Vietnam as well as elsewhere that will help to convince the Chinese Communist leaders that excessive militancy is counter-productive, but at the same time indications in the general international environment, as they see it, that there are other reasonable and promising policy options—that they can see some possibility of expanding China's role in international affairs and achieving at least some of China's legitimate aspirations by moderate rather than militant means.

BUYING TIME IN SOUTHEAST ASIA

Late in 1967 a Conference on Asian Affairs was held by the Freedom House Public Affairs Institute of New York City, with fourteen leading Asian scholars and historians in attendance. The conference report called attention to the fact that Southeast Asia has ten nations with a total population of 250 million, and stressed that there would be disastrous results if the communists won in Vietnam, or even if the United States won a quick victory and got out. The following paragraphs are extracted from separate sections of the report.

This region may well hold the key to whether a political equilibrium for Asia as a whole can be achieved, a question which in turn affects the future of the entire world.

Conditions in Southeast Asia today, however, are not solely the product of internal developments. The decision of the United States to maintain a presence in this region has been of crucial importance. Every political leader within the area now recognizes that without that presence—economic, political, military—the political fate of the region as a whole would have been drastically different. To put the matter succinctly, the United States has bought time for some two hundred million people to develop, without their being ceaselessly confronted with combined external-internal Communist threats of growing proportions.

The time has come when we should encourage and expect Asian initiatives and leadership in all matters centrally involving the peoples of this area. To share, and sometimes to yield responsibility is a necessary means to the encouragement of Asian self-reliance, rationality and independence. Such politics do not in any sense constitute withdrawal. In some instances, indeed, they may bring more substantial commitments. Increasingly, however, a mutual responsibility must be sought in an atmosphere of multilateral partnership.

Our basic problem in foreign policy has not been an arrogance of power. Rather, it has been a continuing uncertainty as to how best to use the massive power at our disposal.

Justus, *The Minneapolis* Star
"Chickens coming home to roost."

19

THE POSTWAR YEARS: NEW PATTERNS IN POLITICS AND LAW

INTRODUCTION

The paralysis that overtook the New Deal after the fight over the Court-packing bill of 1937 continued in domestic affairs through the postwar period. Indeed, as we shall see presently, the internal contradictions of the political and Congressional systems had finally exacted their price, and Congress had become so ineffectual at doing anything but erecting obstacles to change that the lion's share of such power as there was had passed by default to the President and the Supreme Court.

On the other hand, the tremendous dynamism of the New Deal had made great changes. Americans now lived under a semiwelfare state, and it was grudgingly being extended by a snail-like Congress. Warfare and almost continual crises in foreign relations had made the President a more powerful ruler than Louis XIV ever dreamed of being. The dying struggles of the New Deal had transformed the Supreme Court into an institution responsive to the popular will as never before —running far ahead of the public will, as some would have it. Some historians have posited a thirty-year interval between reform waves; the interval since the New Deal had almost passed by 1964, and for a moment before war engulfed the nation again it looked as though the belief might be warranted. But the Great Society proved to be abortive and the problems it had hoped to cure only festered and became more alarming.

In the midst of a society which apparently is being deprived of its old means of social and political adjustment to changing times, the Supreme Court has emerged as a guiding influence. After the Court-packing battle of 1937 it was presumed that the Supreme Court would decline in significance; instead, it has increased. It has assumed the right to arbitrate between government power and private right in such matters as religion, segregation, criminal procedure, and the apportionment of legislative districts. The conservative defense of private property by the substantive due process of law (which we examined in Chapter 6) has been displaced in the Supreme Court by a new hospitality to social legislation both by Congress and the states. Indeed, in default of social legislation, the Supreme Court is finding ways of forcing change by making the Bill of Rights mandatory on the states. It has rejected "dual federalism"—the doctrine that the states and the federal government are each sovereign within mutually exclusive spheres—and has specifically affirmed that the nation is supreme. So great has the power of the Supreme Court become that, ironically, once again it is under attack for "subverting" the Constitution.

THE SLOW PROGRESS OF NEGRO RIGHTS

United Press International Photo

(1) PRESIDENT TRUMAN ASKS FOR CIVIL RIGHTS LEGISLATION, 1948

In his Message to Congress of February 2, 1948, President Truman pointed out that if the world was to trust American leadership, then the United States must assure freedom and equality at home.

The protection of civil rights is the duty of every government which derives its powers from the consent of the people. This is equally true of local, State, and National Governments. There is much that the States can and should do at this time to extend their protection of civil rights. Wherever the law-enforcement measures of State and local governments are inadequate to discharge this primary function of government, these measures should be strengthened and improved.

The Federal Government has a clear duty to see that constitutional guaranties of individual liberties and of equal protection under the laws are not denied or abridged anywhere in our Union. That duty is shared by all three branches of the Government, but it can be fulfilled only if the Congress enacts modern, comprehensive civil-rights laws, adequate to the needs of the day, and demonstrating our continuing faith in the free way of life.

I recommend, therefore, that the Congress enact legislation at this session directed toward the following specific objectives:

1. Establishing a permanent Commission on Civil Rights, a Joint Congressional Committee on Civil Rights, and a Civil Rights Division in the Department of Justice.

2. Strengthening existing civil-rights statutes.

3. Providing Federal protection against lynching.

4. Protecting more adequately the right to vote.

5. Establishing a Fair Employment Practice Commission to prevent unfair discrimination in employment.

6. Prohibiting discrimination in interstate transportation facilities.

7. Providing home rule and suffrage in Presidential elections for the residents of the District of Columbia.

8. Providing statehood for Hawaii and Alaska and a greater measure of self-government for our island possessions.

9. Equalizing the opportunities for residents of the United States to become naturalized citizens.

10. Settling the evacuation claims of Japanese-Americans. . . .

During the recent war and in the years since its close we have made much progress toward equality of opportunity in our armed services without regard to race, color, religion, or national origin. I have instructed the Secretary of Defense to take steps to have the remaining instances of discrimination in the armed services eliminated as rapidly as possible. The personnel policies and practices of all the services in this regard will be made consistent. . . .

The position of the United States in the world today makes it especially urgent that we adopt these measures to secure for all our people their essential rights.

(2) DESEGREGATION OF PUBLIC SCHOOLS, 1954

On May 17, 1954, Chief Justice Warren delivered the historic opinion of the Supreme Court on *Brown et al. versus Board of Education of Topeka et al.* which declared unconstitutional segregation of the races in public schools.

In approaching this problem, we cannot turn the clock back to 1868 when the [Fourteenth] Amendment was adopted, or even to 1896 when *Plessy v. Ferguson* was written. We must consider public education in the light of its full development and its present place in American life throughout the Nation. Only in

this way can it be determined if segregation in public schools deprives these plaintiffs of the equal protection of the laws.

Today, education is perhaps the most important function of state and local governments. Compulsory school attendance laws and the great expenditures for education both demonstrate our recognition of the importance of education to our democratic society. It is required in the performance of our most basic public responsibilities, even service in the armed forces. It is the very foundation of good citizenship. Today it is a principal instrument in awakening the child to cultural values, in preparing him for later professional training, and in helping him to adjust normally to his environment. In these days it is doubtful that any child may reasonably be expected to succeed in life if he is denied the opportunity of an education. Such an opportunity where the state has undertaken to provide it, is a right which must be made available to all on equal terms.

We come then to the question presented: Does segregation of children in public schools solely on the basis of race, even though the physical facilities and other "tangible" factors may be equal, deprive the children of the mi-

nority group of equal educational opportunities? We believe that it does.

The effect of this separation on their educational opportunities was well stated by a finding in the Kansas case by a court which nevertheless felt compelled to rule against the Negro plaintiffs:

"Segregation of white and colored children in public schools has a detrimental effect upon the colored children. The impact is greater when it has the sanction of the law; for the policy of separating the races is usually interpreted as denoting the inferiority of the Negro group. A sense of inferiority affects the motivation of a child to learn. Segregation with the sanction of law, therefore has a tendency to [retard] the educational and mental development of Negro children and to deprive them of some of the benefits they would receive in a racial[ly] integrated school system."

(3) PRESIDENT KENNEDY ASKS FOR CIVIL RIGHTS LEGISLATION, 1963

On June 11, 1963, in a public address President Kennedy asked that Congress mark the centennial of emancipation by passing legislation to assure Negroes the same rights enjoyed by white citizens.

One hundred years of delay have passed since President Lincoln freed the slaves, yet their heirs, their grandsons, are not fully free. They are not yet freed from the bonds of injustice. They are not yet freed from social and economic oppression, and this nation, for all its hopes and all its boasts, will not be fully free until all its citizens are free. . . .

We preach freedom around the world, and we mean it, and we cherish our freedom here at home; but are we to say to the world and, much more importantly, to each other that this is a land of the free except for the Negroes; that we have no second-class citizens except Negroes; that we have no class or caste system, no ghettos, no master race except with respect to Negroes? . . .

It is not enough to pin the blame on

others, to say this is a problem of one section of the country or another, or deplore the facts that we face. A great change is at hand, and our task, our obligation, is to make that revolution, that change, peaceful and constructive for all.

Those who do nothing are inviting shame as well as violence. Those who act boldly are recognizing right as well as reality.

Next week I shall ask the Congress of the United States to act, to make a commitment it has not fully made in this century to the proposition that race has no place in American life or law. The federal judiciary has upheld that proposition in a series of forthright cases. The Executive Branch has adopted that proposition in the conduct of its affairs, including the employment of federal personnel, the use of federal facilities and the sale of federally financed housing.

But there are other necessary measures which only the Congress can provide, and they must be provided at this session. The old code of equity law under which we live commands for every wrong a remedy, but in too many communities, in too many parts of the country, wrongs are inflicted on Negro citizens for which there are no remedies at law. Unless the Congress acts, their only remedy is in the street.

I am, therefore, asking the Congress to enact legislation giving all Americans the right to be served in facilities which are open to the public—hotels, restaurants, theaters, retail stores and similar establishments. . . .

I am also asking Congress to authorize the federal government to participate more fully in lawsuits designed to end segregation in public education.

My fellow Americans, this is a problem which faces us all, in every city of the North as well as the South. Today there are Negroes unemployed, two or three times as many compared to whites, inadequate in education, moving into the large cities, unable to find work, young people particularly out of work, without hope, denied equal rights, denied the opportunity to eat at a restaurant or lunch counter or go to a movie theater, denied the right to a decent education, denied the right to attend a state university even though qualified. It seems to me that these are matters which concern us all, not merely Presidents or Congressmen or Governors, but every citizen of the United States.

This is one country. It has become one country because all of us and all the people who came here had an equal chance to develop their talents.

(4) THE CIVIL RIGHTS ACT OF 1964

Congress held back on enacting the requested legislation, and it was not until after Kennedy's death that President Johnson managed to force it through. The bill was too long to reproduce here, so the following précis is taken from *The New York Times* of June 20, 1964.

Title I—Voting. Prohibits registrars from applying different standards to white and Negro voting applicants and from disqualifying applicants because of inconsequential errors on their forms. Requires that literacy tests be in writing, except under special arrangements for blind persons, and that any applicant desiring one be given a copy of the questions and his answers. Makes a sixth-grade education a rebuttable presumption of literacy. Allows the Attorney General or defendant state officials in any voting suit to request trial by a three-judge Federal Court.

Title II—Public Accommodations. Prohibits discrimination or refusal of service on account of race in hotels, motels, restaurants, gasoline stations and places of amusement if

their operations affect interstate commerce or if their discrimination "is supported by state action." Permits the Attorney General to enforce the title by suit in the Federal courts [of three judges] if he believes that any person or group is engaging in a "pattern or practice of resistance" to the rights declared by the title. . . .

Title III—Public Facilities. Requires that Negroes have equal access to, and treatment in, publicly owned or operated facilities such as parks, stadiums and swimming pools. Authorizes the Attorney General to sue for enforcement of these rights if private citizens are unable to sue effectively.

Title IV—Public Schools. Empowers the Attorney General to bring school desegregation suits under the same conditions as in Title III. Authorizes technical and financial aid to school districts to assist in desegregation. . . .

Title V—Civil Rights Commission. Extends the life of the Civil Rights Commission until Jan. 31, 1968.

Title VI—Federal Aid. Provides that no person shall be subjected to racial discrimination in any program receiving Federal aid. Directs Federal agencies to take steps against discrimination, including—as a last resort, and after hearings—withholding of Federal funds from state or local agencies that discriminate.

Title VII—Employment. Bans discrimination by employers or unions with 100 or more employees or members the first year the act is effective, reducing over four years to 25 or more. Establishes a commission to investigate alleged discrimination and use persuasion to end it. Authorizes the Attorney General to sue if he believes any person or group is engaged in a "pattern or practice" of resistance to the title, and to ask for trial by a three-judge court. . . .

Title VIII—Statistics. Directs the Census Bureau to compile statistics of registration and voting by race in areas of the country designated by the Civil Rights Commission. This might be used to enforce the long-forgotten provision of the 14th Amendment that states that discriminate in voting shall lose seats in the House of Representatives.

Title IX—Courts. Permits appellate review of decisions by Federal District judges to send back to the state courts criminal defendants who have attempted to remove their cases on the ground that their civil rights would be denied in state trials. Permits the Attorney General to intervene in suits filed by private persons complaining that they have been denied the equal protection of the laws.

Title X—Conciliation. Establishes a Community Relations Service in the Commerce Department to help conciliate racial disputes. . . .

Title XI—Miscellaneous. Guarantees jury trials for criminal contempt under any part of the act but Title I. . . . Provides that the statute shall not invalidate state laws with consistent purposes, and that it shall not impair any existing powers of Federal officials.

EISENHOWER'S FAREWELL WARNING

Crises there will continue to be. In meeting them, whether foreign or domestic, great or small, there is a recurring temptation to feel that some spectacular and costly action could become the miraculous solution to all current difficulties. A huge increase in newer elements of our defense; development of unrealistic programs to cure every ill in agriculture; a dramatic expansion in basic and applied research —these and many other possibilities, each possibly promising in itself, may be suggested as the only way to the road we wish to travel.

But each proposal must be weighed in the light of a broader consideration: the need to maintain balance in and among national programs—balance between the private and the public economy, balance between cost and hoped for advantage—balance between the clearly necessary and the comfortably desirable; balance between our essential requirements as a nation and the duties imposed by the nation upon the individual; balance between actions of the moment and the national welfare of the future. Good judgment seeks balance and progress; lack of it eventually finds imbalance and frustration.

The record of many decades stands as proof that our people and their government have, in the main, understood these truths and have responded to them well, in the face of stress and threat. But threats, new in kind or degree, constantly arise. I mention two only.

A vital element in keeping the peace is our military establishment. Our arms must be mighty, ready for instant action, so that no potential aggressor may be tempted to risk his own destruction. . . .

This conjunction of an immense military establishment and a large arms industry is new in the American experience. The total influence—economic, political, even spiritual—is felt in every city, every State house, every office of the Federal government. We recognize the imperative need for this development. Yet we must not fail to comprehend its grave implications. Our toil, resources and livelihood are all involved; so is the very structure of our society.

In the councils of government, we must guard against the acquisition of unwarranted influence, whether sought or unsought, by the military-industrial complex. The potential for the disastrous rise of misplaced power exists and will persist.

We must never let the weight of this combination endanger our liberties or democratic processes. We should take nothing for granted. Only an alert and knowledgeable citizenry can compel the proper meshing of the huge industrial and military machinery of defense with our peaceful methods and goals so that security and liberty may prosper together. . . .

Another factor in maintaining balance involves the element of time. As we peer into society's future, we—you and I, and our government—must avoid the impulse to live only for today, plundering, for our own ease and convenience, the precious resources of tomorrow. We cannot mortgage the material assets of our grandchildren without risking the loss also of their political and spiritual heritage. We want democracy to survive for all generations to come, not to become the insolvent phantom of tomorrow.

—Radio and television address,
January 17, 1961

JOHN F. KENNEDY SPEAKS

Address of September 12, 1960, before the Houston Ministerial Association:

Because I am a Catholic, and no Catholic has ever been elected President, the real issues in this campaign have been obscured—perhaps deliberately in some quarters less responsible than this. So it is apparently necessary for me to state once again—not what kind of church I believe in, for that should be important only to me, but what kind of America I believe in.

I believe in an America where the separation of church and state is absolute—where no Catholic prelate would tell the President (should he be a Catholic) how to act and no Protestant minister would tell his parishioners for whom to vote—where no church or church school is granted any public funds or political preference—and where no man is denied public office merely because his religion differs from the President who might appoint him or the people who might elect him.

I believe in an America that is officially neither Catholic, Protestant nor Jewish—where no public official either requests or accepts instructions on public policy from the Pope, the National Council of Churches or any other ecclesiastical source—where no religious body seeks to impose its will directly or indirectly upon the general populace or the public acts of its officials—and where religious liberty is so indivisible that an act against one church is treated as an act against all. . . .

Finally, I believe in an America where religious intolerance will someday end—where all men and all churches are treated as equal—where every man has the same right to attend or not attend the church of his choice—where there is no Catholic vote, no anti-Catholic vote, no bloc voting of any kind—and where Catholics, Protestants and Jews, both the lay and the pastoral level, will refrain from those attitudes of disdain and division which have so often marred their works in the past, and promote instead the American ideal of brotherhood.

That is the kind of America in which I believe. And it represents the kind of Presidency in which I believe—a great office that must be neither humbled by making it the instrument of any religious group, nor tarnished by arbitrarily withholding it, its occupancy, from the members of any religious group. I believe in a President whose views on religion are his own private affair, neither imposed upon him by the nation or imposed by the nation upon him as a condition to holding that office. . . .

I ask you tonight to follow in that tradition, to judge me on the basis of fourteen years in the Congress—on my declared stands against an ambassador to the Vatican, against unconstitutional aid to parochial schools, and against any boycott of the public schools (which I attended myself)—instead of judging me on the basis of these pamphlets and publications we have all seen that carefully select quotations out of context from the statements of Catholic Church leaders, usually in other countries, frequently in other centuries, and rarely relevant to any situation here—and always omitting, of course, that statement of the American bishops in 1948 which strongly endorsed church-state separation.

I do not consider these other quotations binding upon my public acts—why should you? But let me say, with respect to other countries, that I am wholly opposed to the state being used by any religious group, Catholic or Protestant, to compel, prohibit or persecute the free exercise of any other religion. And that goes for any persecution at any time, by anyone, in any country. . . .

I am not the Catholic candidate for President. I am the Democratic Party's candidate for President, who happens also to be Catholic.

I do not speak for my church on public matters—and the church does not speak for me.

Whatever issue may come before me as President, if I should be elected—on birth control, divorce, censorship, gambling, or any other subject—I will make my decision in accordance with these views, in accordance with what my conscience tells me to be in the national interest, and without regard to outside religious pressure or dictate. And no power or threat of punishment could cause me to decide otherwise.

But if the time should ever come—and I do not concede any conflict to be remotely possible—when my office would require me to either violate my conscience, or violate the national interest, then I would resign the office, and I hope any other conscientious public servant would do likewise.

But I do not intend to apologize for these views to my critics of either Catholic or Protestant faith, nor do I intend to disavow either my views or my church in order to win this election. If I should lose on the real issues, I shall return to my seat in the Senate, satisfied that I tried my best and was fairly judged.

But if this election is decided on the basis that 40,000,000 Americans lost their chance of being President on the day they were baptized, then it is the whole nation that will be the loser in the eyes of Catholics and non-Catholics around the world, in the eyes of history, and in the eyes of our own people.

Inaugural Address, January 21, 1961

We observe today not a victory of party but a celebration of freedom—symbolizing an end as well as a beginning—signifying renewal as well as change. For I have sworn before you and Almighty God the same solemn oath our forebears prescribed nearly a century and three-quarters ago.

The world is very different now. For man holds in his mortal hands the power to abolish all forms of human poverty and all forms of human life. And yet the same revolutionary beliefs for which our forebears fought are still at issue around the globe—the belief that the rights of man come not from the generosity of the state but from the hand of God.

We dare not forget today that we are the

heirs of that first revolution. Let the word go forth from this time and place, to friend and foe alike, that the torch has been passed to a new generation of Americans—born in this century, tempered by war, disciplined by a hard and bitter peace, proud of our ancient heritage—and unwilling to witness or permit the slow undoing of those human rights to which this nation has always been committed, and to which we are committed today at home and around the world.

Let every nation know, whether it wishes us well or ill, that we shall pay any price, bear any burden, meet any hardship, support any friend, oppose any foe to assure the survival and the success of liberty.

This much we pledge—and more.

To those old allies whose cultural and spiritual origins we share, we pledge the loyalty of faithful friends. . . .

To those new states whom we welcome to the ranks of the free, we pledge our word that one form of colonial control shall not have passed away merely to be replaced by a far more iron tyranny.

Finally, to those nations who would make themselves our adversary, we offer not a pledge but a request: that both sides begin anew the quest for peace, before the dark powers of destruction unleashed by science engulf all humanity in planned or accidental self-destruction. . . .

So let us begin anew—remembering on both sides that civility is not a sign of weakness, and sincerity is always subject to proof. Let us never negotiate out of fear. But let us never fear to negotiate. . . .

And if a beachhead of co-operation may push back the jungle of suspicion, let both sides join in creating a new endeavor, not a new balance of power, but a new world of law, where the strong are just and the weak secure and the peace preserved.

All this will not be finished in the first one hundred days. Nor will it be finished in the first one thousand days, nor in the life of this administration, nor even perhaps in our lifetime on this planet. But let us begin. . . .

Now the trumpet summons us again—not as a call to bear arms, though arms we need—not as a call to battle, though embattled we are—but a call to bear the burden of a long twilight struggle, year in and year out, "rejoicing in hope, patient in tribulation"—a struggle against the common enemies of man: tyranny, poverty, disease, and war itself.

Can we forge against these enemies a grand and global alliance, North and South, East and West, that can assure a more fruitful life for all mankind? Will you join in that historic effort?

In the long history of the world, only a few generations have been granted the role of defending freedom in its hour of maximum danger. I do not shrink from this responsibility —I welcome it. I do not believe that any of us would exchange places with any other people or any other generation. The energy, the faith, the devotion which we bring to this endeavor will light our country and all who serve it—and the glow from that fire can truly light the world.

And so, my fellow Americans: ask not what your country can do for you—ask what you can do for your country.

My fellow citizens of the world: ask not what America will do for you, but what together we can do for the freedom of man.

Finally, whether you are citizens of America or citizens of the world, ask of us here the same high standards of strength and sacrifice which we ask of you. With a good conscience our only sure reward, with history the final judge of our deeds, let us go forth to lead the land we love, asking His blessing and His help, but knowing that here on earth God's work must truly be our own.

PRESIDENT JOHNSON PROPOSES THAT AMERICA BUILD THE GREAT SOCIETY

[In an address at the University of Michigan on May 22, 1964, President Johnson launched the theme of the Campaign of 1964—The Great Society. It was to be a concerted attack on all the ills that afflicted America.]

I have come today from the turmoil of your Capitol to the tranquility of your campus to speak about the future of our country. The purpose of protecting the life of our Nation and preserving the liberty of our citizens is to pursue the happiness of our people. Our success in that pursuit is the test of our success as a nation. For a century we labored to settle and to subdue a continent. For half a century, we called upon unbounded invention and untiring industry to create an order of plenty for all of our people. The challenge of the next half century is whether we have the wisdom to use that wealth to enrich and elevate our national life, and to advance the quality of our American civilization.

Your imagination, your initiative and your indignation will determine whether we build a society where progress is the servant of our needs, or a society where old values and new visions are buried under unbridled growth. For in your time we have the opportunity to move not only toward the rich society and the powerful society, but upward to the Great Society. . . .

So I want to talk to you today about three places where we begin to build the Great Society—in our cities, in our countryside, and in our classrooms. . . .

It is harder and harder to live the good life in American cities today. The catalogue of ills is long: There is the decay of the centers and the despoiling of the suburbs. There is not enough housing for our people or transportation for our traffic. Open land is vanishing and old landmarks are violated. Worst of all, expansion is eroding the precious and time honored values of community with neighbors and communion with nature. The loss of these values breeds loneliness and boredom and in-difference. Our society will never be great until our cities are great. Today the frontier of imagination and innovation is inside those cities, and not beyond their borders. New experiments are already going on. It will be the task of your generation to make the American city a place where future generations will come, not only to live but to live the good life. . . .

A second place where we begin to build the Great Society is in our countryside. We have always prided ourselves on being not only America the strong and America the free, but America the beautiful. Today that beauty is in danger. The water we drink, the food we eat, the very air that we breathe, are threatened with pollution. Our parks are overcrowded. Our seashores overburdened. Green fields and dense forests are disappearing.

A few years ago we were greatly concerned about the Ugly American. Today we must act to prevent an Ugly America.

For once the battle is lost, once our natural splendor is destroyed, it can never be recaptured. And once man can no longer walk with beauty or wonder at nature, his spirit will wither and his sustenance be wasted.

A third place to build the Great Society is in the classrooms of America. There your childrens' lives will be shaped. Our society will not be great until every young mind is set free to scan the farthest reaches of thought and imagination. We are still far from that goal. . . . In many places, classrooms are overcrowded and curricula are outdated. Most of our qualified teachers are underpaid, and many of our paid teachers are unqualified. So we must give every child a place to sit and a teacher to learn from. Poverty must not be a bar to learning, and learning must offer an escape from poverty.

But more classrooms and more teachers

are not enough. We must seek an educational system which grows in excellence as it grows in size. This means better training for our teachers. It means preparing youth to enjoy their hours of leisure as well as their hours of labor. It means exploring new techniques of teaching, to find new ways to stimulate the love of learning and the capacity for creation.

These are three of the central issues of the Great Society. While our government has many programs directed at those issues, I do not pretend that we have the full answer to those problems. But I do promise this: We are going to assemble the best thought and the broadest knowledge from all over the world to find those answers for America. I intend to establish working groups to prepare a series of White House conferences and meetings on the cities, on natural beauty, on the quality of education, and on other emerging challenges. And from these meetings and from this inspiration and from these studies we will begin to set our course toward the Great Society.

The solution to these problems does not rest on a massive program in Washington, nor can it rely solely on the strained resources of local authority. They require us to create new concepts of cooperation, a creative federalism, between the national capitol and the leaders of local communities. . . .

Within your lifetime powerful forces, already loosed, will take us toward a way of life beyond the realm of our experience, almost beyond the bounds of our imagination. For better or for worse, your generation has been appointed by history to deal with those problems and to lead America toward a new age. You have the chance never before afforded to any people in any age. You can help build a society where the demands of morality, and the needs of the spirit, can be realized in the life of the Nation. So will you join in the battle to give every citizen the full equality which God enjoins and the law requires, whatever his belief, or race, or the color of his skin? Will you join in the battle to give every citizen an escape from the crushing weight of poverty? Will you join in the battle to make it possible for all nations to live in enduring peace as neighbors and not as mortal enemies? Will you join in the battle to build the Great Society, to prove that our material progress is only the foundation on which we will build a richer life of mind and spirit?

"THE QUEST FOR A CONSERVATIVE GRAIL"

[In recent years an earnest search for a definition of conservatism has been pursued by such writers as Russell Kirk, Clinton Rossiter, Barry Goldwater, and William Buckley. On the other hand, such men as Louis Hartz, Arthur M. Schlesinger, Jr., John Galbraith, and Peter Viereck have joined battle in defense of liberalism. John P. Roche, who might be called a nostalgic conservative and a practicing liberal, finds that the two flow together into one vast stream. He examined the matter in a short and pithy article, "I'm Sick of Conservatism: It's Irrelevant to Today's America" in *The New Leader*, August 22, 1955, pp. 6–7. Note that Professor Roche is not referring to the extremists often called radical reactionaries.]

The more I read of the literature of Conservatism, the more I become convinced that the whole controversy is an outgrowth of the failure of the participants adequately to define their major premises. To be precise, there are loose in the land two contradictory definitions of "Conservatism." Mixed up together, they supply a heady brew, but if they are isolated —and each author is forced to stick consistently to one or the other—the hallucinations vanish and the "Conservatism" they invigorate is revealed as meaningless in the American context.

The first definition explains Conservatism in terms of content, as a body of doctrine, a set of beliefs. To be an authentic Conservative, one must buy the package. Although commentators differ as to the contents of the Conservative program, it is probably safe to say that they would all agree that in order to ascertain the content of Conservatism one must turn to History. Following the trail blazed by Edmund Burke, these writers would assert that a society is an organism which moves through time slowly developing certain unique and precious characteristics. It is the task of the Conservative to defend these institutions, so slowly nurtured by countless generations—"the little platoons," in Burke's phrase—against the radical who seeks to undo with one blow the collective achievements of the past. Each generation, then, does not live in isolation, but has debts to the past and responsibilities to the future. The great social heresy, from this viewpoint, is the Jeffersonian concept of—to use Daniel Boorstein's phrase—the "sovereignty of the present generation."

If this is a fair summary of Burke's Conservative philosophy, as I think it is, the American who accepts it is put in an impossible position—*he must be a liberal*. As Louis Hartz has put it somewhere, "In America, Burke is Jefferson." To say this is not to play with paradox; unless one perversely distorts American history, it is clear that the dominant strains in the collective achievement that is the American past are experimentalism, equality and individual freedom. There are no sunny enclosures nor feudal fairylands in which the American would-be Conservative can frolic. . . .

In the nations of Europe or Asia, Conservatives can find footholds, can defend special privileges, caste prerogatives and an *ancièn régime*. But in the United States, unless he chooses to take up the cudgels on behalf of George III and the Stamp Tax, the Conservative can find no place to brace his lever. It is probably this unique situation, this flowing together of the Conservative and Liberal tributaries into one vast stream, that accounts for the absence, since the Colonial period, of significant American political thought. While Americans have had bitter political struggles, and have once taken up arms against each other, these dissensions fade into insignificance when compared with the vast body of shared assumptions which we simply take for granted. It should not be overlooked that both sides in the Civil War believed that they were fighting for the *true* principles of the Republic.

It is probably a dim recognition of this paradox, of the disheartening fact that, in the United States, the Burkean road leads into the camp of the enemy, that supplies Russell Kirk with his characteristic tone of desperate evangelism. But in his passionate quest for a foothold from which to crush the "social engineers," while he wanders far and wide through the gloomier figures of nineteenth century British thought, Kirk neglects what must be for Americans the crucial historical point: that probably never in the history of human achievement have any "social engineers" been as successful as the few men who met under the gavel of George Washington in 1787 to draft the Federal Constitution. *E. Pluribus Unum* was, after all, the boast of successful experimenters as well as the motto of the new Republic. Thus it is Abraham Lincoln, the pragmatic idealist, the bold experimenter, not Brooks Adams, the cynical New Englander of whom Kirk makes so much, who stands in the mainstream of American politics. And if Lincoln be dubbed a Conservative, it can only be for his noble defense of the Liberal tradition.

So much for the first definition which makes of Conservatism a body of doctrine. The second definition, which is far more sophisticated, takes a different tack: the Conservative is not distinctive for *what* he believes, but for *how* he believes and acts. A dogma is rejected for a psychology. Conservatism thus becomes a psychological set, a frame of reference, characterized by caution, respect for tradition and, above all, by an urbane skepticism about the efficacy of change. This view may spring from an uncomplex pessimism, or from a theology of a Niebuhrian cast which emphasizes the imperfectibility of man and the doggedness of Original Sin.

It is this approach which Clinton Rossiter has employed in his stimulating book *Conservatism in America*, which, despite a misleading title, is well worth careful reading. What Rossiter is really writing about, I submit, is not Conservatism in America, but the civilized tradition in America—a vastly different subject. What Rossiter advocates throughout, if one skips his occasional, and dubious, efforts to coin Conservative dogma, is what is commonly called the Liberal tradition. A practical consequence of reading his book would be to vote for Adlai Stevenson and Clifford Case and against those of the extremes who wish sudden radical changes in the American social, economic, or political system. *Conservatism in America* is, in effect, an exhortation to Americans to adhere to high standards of decency and to abjure the passionate enthusiast's moral and historical short-cuts.

But, while I have deep intellectual and emotional ties with this viewpoint, as Conservatism it simply will not wash. What has been established here is a subjective criterion of Conservatism which defies political objectivization. To be precise, a person holding this outlook may be a trade-unionist defending his union against radical insurgents; he may be a Thomas Jefferson reacting to the shattering of his humanitarian ideals by the French Terror; he may be a businessman asserting the rights of the small entrepreneur against the vices of monopoly. In short, if what unites Conservatives is a way of looking at life, rather than a platform, it is both futile and illogical to try to create a Conservative "program." The Conservative under these conditions can no more establish a catechism than can the Quaker, whose fundamental religious belief centers on the inspired intuition of the individual. I recently asked a French Socialist to define socialism, and he replied: "Socialism is being nice to people." Those who follow Rossiter come in the end to the identical, and the identically meaningless, definition of Conservatism.

In conclusion, while the quest for a Conservative Grail has flexed the muscles of our intellectual gymnasts, the semantic game seems hardly worth the candle. The hard rules of logic demand that spokesmen for an alleged American Conservatism define their term with precision. Yet, if they accept Burkean historicism, they find themselves embracing Thomas Jefferson and the Bill of Rights, while a psychological definition results in no objective program, but simply in an affirmation of human decency. Finally, there is a cosmic irony about all these efforts at definition, for if there is one thing that the Conservative—however defined—traditionally abhors, it is intellectual precision. As a Conservative Member of Parliament recently announced when asked to be precise about his views, "If I could define my views with precision, I wouldn't be a Conservative."

POLITICAL ROMANTICISM AND CONSERVATISM

[Hans J. Morgenthau, political scientist of the University of Chicago, has offered a valuable distinction between political romanticism and conservatism in his analysis of the Republican stance in 1964. As Morgenthau saw it, Goldwater was heading a coalition of Republican romantics and segregationist conservatives. See "Goldwater—The Romantic Regression" in *Commentary*, September 1964, as quoted in *Current*, October 1964, pp. 6–8.]

"The political romantic is the obverse of the political reformer. He is, as it were, a back-ward-looking reformer. . . . The reformer endeavors to bridge the gap between reality and a moral and rational ideal not yet achieved by transforming reality in the light of that ideal. The political romantic carries within himself the picture of a glorious past, fancied or real or both, of a golden age once achieved by ancestral virtue and despoiled by contemporary vice, of a political paradise once possessed and now lost. This picture provides the romantic with the standards for political judgment, the goals for political action, the arguments and imagery of political rhetoric. The past was great and simple; the present is complexity, decline, and decadence; the future will be great and simple again by being like the past. For the political romantic the ideal does not exist, as it does for the reformer, in the rational and moral imagination, to be realized *de novo* by hazardous and precarious effort. Rather it exists in the historic recollection of a state once attained and that is hence attainable again with relative ease and without undue risks merely by doing what was done before. For the political romantic, then, progress is tantamount to restoration.

"Political romanticism is not identical with conservatism. Romanticism is certainly a powerful disposition in American politics; so too, is a conservatism of *philosophy* and *method*. A conservatism of *purpose*, however, is not. The neglect of this dual distinction between romanticism and conservatism, and between the two different kinds of conservatism, has caused considerable confusion. Thus Goldwater calls himself a conservative and is actually a romantic who has recently turned conservative only by force of circumstance and in a partial sense through having become the champion of the segregationists. . . .

"A conservatism of *philosophy* and *method* is intrinsic to the American political tradition. *The Federalist* is its greatest literary monument; Alexander Hamilton is its greatest theoretician, John Quincy Adams and Abraham Lincoln are in different ways its greatest practitioners. This kind of conservatism holds that the imperfections of the world as seen from the rational point of view are the result of forces inherent in human nature. To improve the

world, one must work with these forces, not against them. The world being by nature made up of conflicting interests, abstract principles can never be fully realized; they can at best be approximated through the ever-temporary balancing of interests and the ever-precarious settlement of conflicts. This kind of conservatism, then, sees in a system of checks and balances a universal principle for all pluralist societies. It appeals to historic precedent rather than abstract doctrine and aims at the realization of the lesser evil rather than of the absolute good.

"The conservative view of the *purposes* of politics, on the other hand, endows the *status quo* with a special dignity and seeks to maintain and improve it. This kind of conservatism has its natural political environment in Europe; it has no place in the American tradition of politics. Europe, in contrast to America, has known classes, determined by heredity or otherwise sharply and permanently defined in composition and social status, which have had a legitimate stake in defending the *status quo*. But for the defense of what *status quo* could the American conservative have fought? The great majority of Americans—as opposed to the states of the Confederacy and other special interests, such as the contemporary concentrations of private power—have never experienced a *status quo* to whose preservation they could have devoted themselves. For America has been committed to a purpose in the eyes of which the *status quo* has always been but a steppingstone to a new achievement, a new *status quo* to be left behind by yet another new achievement. The very dynamics of American society are thus incompatible with a conservative position regarding the *purposes* of politics.

The great issues of American politics concern not the preservation of the present, but the creation of the future. American politics does not set the past and present against the future; rather it sets one kind of future against another kind of future. While, in philosophy and method, conservatism is the most potent single influence in American politics, the purposes of our politics from the very beginning have been unique and revolutionary, not only within narrowly political terms, but also in the more general sense of being oblivious to tradition. Thus—with certain temporary exceptions —the political programs of both our major parties have favored changes in the domestic *status quo*; for only with such a program could they have hoped to appeal to the voters. We have had no conservative political party because the number of conservative voters has never been sufficient to support one on the national scale. We have only had conservative minorities, which have been limited to trying, through obstruction and subterfuge, to prevent change or at least to slow it up.

IS AMERICAN PARTY POLITICS OBSOLETE?

[Ever since the heyday of the New Deal the phenomenon of Congressional lag has been more and more evident, until alarmists actually have come to fear that it portends a breakdown of democracy and the entry of a Caesar. The only important exceptions to the rule of lag have been caused by the crises of war and in one case by the manipulation of a master politician—President Johnson—and then only for a brief period in 1964 and 1965.

James MacGregor Burns, Williams College political scientist, examined the phenomenon in a remarkable book *The Deadlock of Democracy* (Englewood Cliffs, N.J.: Prentice-Hall, 1963) and proposed some remedies. Here we reprint the abstract published in *Current*, March 1963, pp. 51–56. Some things have changed since the book was published: Lyndon Johnson, a devoted leader of the Democratic Congressional Party, reached the Presidency by chance; the Supreme Court in a series of decisions has forced the states to redraw their legislative and Congressional districts into more equally populated areas, though the effect is not yet evident; and there have been some advances toward civil rights for Negroes. However, Burns's analysis is still sound.]

By and large, Madisonian theory much more than Jeffersonian practice has dominated the strategy of American politics. This emphasis has resulted in a *four-party system* in American politics, where both the Democratic and Republican parties are split into what I call *"Congressional"* and *"Presidential"* parties. The former are parochially oriented and draw their power, support, and perspectives from relatively small, local interests. They are the Madisonian minority factions. The latter are nationally oriented, and draw their power, support, and perspectives from large national interests. They are the diverse Jeffersonian majorities.

The base of the Congressional system is the one-party district, as established and protected by the state legislatures. It is hard to grasp the extent of noncompetition in Congressional elections. Almost half of the House seats never change party hands. Another quarter, roughly, switch only on rare occasions. Aside from great sweeps, about 150 Republican seats and about the same number of Democratic seats never switch to the other party. Reasonably competitive districts number about 125 out of a total of 435. To a lesser degree, the same is true of Senate seats.

These safe seats are only partly accidental in origin. The drawing of election districts is in the hands of state legislatures. Most state legislatures are controlled year after year and decade after decade by the same party, and legislators naturally carve up the districts to benefit their own party. Note the difference between this kind of manipulation and the shenanigans of gerrymandering. A state legislature can make every Congressional district approximately equal in population—and hence absolve itself of the charge of gerrymandering—and at the same time carve up the state with such expertness that some districts remain, or become, hopelessly noncompetitive. . . .

"A man in a safe district often finds himself . . . representing a constituency quite different from the state as a whole. . . . Hence it may be hard for such Congressmen to 'go statewide'; most of them hesitate to risk a safe seat for the arduous and risky job of appealing to the independents and moderates who might hold the balance of power in a statewide contest.

"So the Congressman from a safe seat usually follows the easy alternative: he stays put. He placates the dominant social forces in the district; 'protects' his district against hostile outside forces; does a great many individual favors; lobbies for benefits for the district; . . . and comfortably overwhelms the opposition party's candidate—if there is one. . . . His main commitment politically is to the status quo. . . .

"And he remains invincibly local. By remaining in the orbit of his Congressional area, he stays politically in the orbit of his party's local candidates and officeholders. Thus he operates in a world of political localism, for the electoral and other political forces in the area are largely activated by other local candidates. Hence the Congressman, though a national officeholder, is almost as locally oriented as the district attorney or county commissioner, and almost as much beyond the reach of influence by the President or the national party. And this is one more reason he achieves his key aim: unbroken longevity in office.

"Longevity in office—this is the crucial nexus between the man in the safe rural district and the Congressional party in Washington. The mechanism is well known—the rule of seniority, which promotes Congressmen up the committee ladder toward the chairmanship in

accordance with this unbroken tenure on the committee. . . .

From: *The Herblock Book* (Beacon Press).

"It's a hell of a way to run a railroad."

Thus the leaders of the Congressional party are the men who have climbed the seniority ladders and therefore represent the safe, local, and usually rural districts. They have interlocking and overlapping power on the more important committees out of all proportion to the populations they represent, and the proportion becomes further distorted if we consider the importance of the committees rather than merely their numbers. They control the machinery of Congress, the committees, the caucus and conference, the promotion system, the movement of legislation, procedure on the floor. They operate through a small coterie composed always of committee chairmen and sometimes of the elected leaders. Above all, they control the legislative fiscal machinery.

"Helping to unite the Congressional party is a common ideology. . . . This ideology is intrinsically negative; that is, it is hostile to major governmental trends in the twentieth century, although it offers grudging acceptance of welfare programs and other measures that have won wide support among voters. But on one matter the Congressional party ideologists are most articulate and positive—defense of the Congressional party system. States' rights, local elections, restricted franchise, minority rights, rural over-representation, checks and balances, Congressional power, the danger of majority or 'mass' rule, judicial review (at least in the old days), powerful committees, the seniority system, the filibuster—in short, the Madisonian system in all its ramifications—arouse their stout support. . . .

The head of the Presidential party is the President. He sets its policies, confirms its ideology, appoints its leaders, and carries its hopes in the quadrennial crisis of the Presidential election. If the election is lost, things are very different. There is no office around which the party can be organized, no office to lead it, discipline it, reward it. Defeated at the polls, the Presidential party becomes apathetic and disorganized. The national chairman, as the executor of the defeated candidate's political estate, is powerless and must yield to the Congressional party. . . .

Of that section of the whole party that we call the Presidential party, the President is undisputed leader. The President runs his party through a small political staff in the White House and through the chairman of the party's national committee. That chairman, like his own aides, is chosen by him and remains in office only as long as the President wishes. Other leaders of the President's party also remain at his sufferance: Cabinet members, top agency chiefs, and hundreds of administrative aides and operatives in the higher echelons of the Administration. These officials often appear to be nonpolitical but in the final test they will support the Presidential party.

The career lines in the Presidential party are significantly different from those in the Congressional. The traditional path to the Presidency has been through a big-state governorship, the party organization around which is likely to be fairly parallel with the Presidential

party organization in that state. Few governors, on the other hand, rise to high places in the Congressional party. Few Senators have become President in the past century, but we now know that it was not Senators in general but Senators who were committed members of the Congressional party that were ineligible for Presidential party leadership. As if realizing this, John Kennedy moved steadily out of the orbit of the Congressional party into that of the Presidential during his years in the Senate. It was Lyndon Johnson's failure to do this, and Robert Taft's similar failure earlier, that fatally handicapped them in their quest for the nomination.

The institutional bulwark of the Presidential party is the national party convention, which was originally set up to move the Presidential nomination out of the control of the Congressional party. By and large it has done just that [despite some recent exceptions. . . . Moreover,] the Presidential party has the electoral college, which favors the urban masses and therefore a national orientation.

Thus the Presidential party emerges as the champion of national principles. They are primarily for world government, the abolition of war, altruistic relations with the outside world, academic fiscal policy, redistribution of wealth, brotherhood, majority rule, progress, welfare for the underprivileged, science and the scientific attitude, and civil liberties. The Congressional party is not so much against these principles as they are primarily for others: small group discussions, deference to highly prestiged and presumably wiser citizens, and an anti-quixotic concern for the "hard realities" and potential costs of Presidential proposals. The Congressional and Presidential parties diverge into two very different and opposed ways of life, and the clash between them produces four-party politics in America.

The consequence of the four-party system is that American political leaders, in order to govern, must manage multi-party coalitions as the French did, for example, before de Gaulle. Coalition government is notoriously unable to generate strong and steady political power. To act, American leaders have had to gain the concurrence not simply of a majority of the voters, but of majorities of different sets of voters organized around leaders in mutually checking and foot-dragging sectors of government. The price of this has been enfeebled policy.

Hence as a nation we have lost control of our politics. We cannot solve unemployment problems. We cannot deliver on national platforms. . . .

"We lack popular control of the policy-making process. Our splintered parties set up barriers between the people and their national government rather than simplifying the alternatives, clarifying competing party doctrines, and allowing the victorious majority to govern. . . . We can choose bold and creative national leaders without giving them the means to make their leadership effective. Hence we diminish a democracy's most essential and priceless commodity—the leadership of men who are willing to move ahead to meet emerging problems, but who are also sensitive to the rights of the opposition and subject to the results of a free and competitive election.

What can we do to improve the situation? We need a new kind of bipartisanship. The two Presidential parties should join forces to work out the rules of the game. The Presidential parties must overcome the arrangements that thwart political competition. The overcoming of the Congressional parties requires the curbing of the institutional buttresses of their power: the seniority system, the other minority devices such as Rules Committee veto and the filibuster, malapportionment and one-party districts.

As far as possible the President and his party majorities in the Congress should be elected by substantially the same electoral groupings, for the sake of clarity of policy, unity in government, and responsibility to the majority. To do this the parties must pay a price: they cannot be all things to all men. In some states a nationally oriented party might

not be able to win; but it could still field candidates who would stage vigorous campaigns, put over the message of the national party and build toward the day when they would have a fighting opportunity.

The national government should control national elections. It is ridiculous that a man who moves to Alabama or Mississippi must wait two years before he can vote for Presidential candidates he has observed for years. It is tragic that state control of Senatorial and Congressional elections helps Congressional leaders to keep their constituencies small, noncompetitive, and exclusive. The national parties must build grass-roots memberships which are oriented to the *national* party's tradition, doctrine, and policy.

The Presidential and Congressional parties must be merged organizationally. For example, national offices like President, Senator, and Representative ought to be placed together on the ballot and separate from candidates for state and local offices, so that voters could choose national officers on national criteria and local officers on local criteria.

The parties and their candidates should be financed on a mass, popular, systematic basis. It is better that a lot of people give a little than that a few give a lot. A large dues-paying membership of the national party should help, and there should be legal restrictions on the total amount of money that one man (or family) can contribute.

In actual Constitutional reform, there are a number of possibilities. Representatives should be elected to a four-year term, to coincide with Presidential terms. The two-year term is an anachronism, and the off-year elections form one of the bases of the Congressional party system. Parliamentary democracies in other lands find such arrangements satisfactory.

Though it might be virtually impossible to do so at this time, the Senate's tenure should be shortened to four years for similar reasons. In addition, the Twenty-second Amendment should be repealed. Most political scientists and most Presidents believe that it makes a lame duck of a second-term President.

Finally, the Electoral College should be changed, though any change should be considered in light of its effect on four-party politics. Perhaps if the Congressional parties gave up their gerrymandered and one-party districts, the Presidential parties would yield their own gerrymandering in the Electoral College.

I list these proposals in a mixed spirit of conviction and skepticism. But unless we adopt them, we will be unable to define our national purpose and mobilize our strength to move vigorously against the problems that beset us at home and abroad, or to exploit the enormous possibilities of urban man and world man in the last third of the twentieth century.

SHOULD CONGRESS CEASE TO LEGISLATE?

[A further examination of Congressional lag is made by Samuel P. Huntington of Harvard University in "Congressional Responses to the Twentieth Century," his contribution to D. B. Truman, ed., *The Congress and America's Future* (Englewood Cliffs, N.J.: Prentice-Hall, 1965). The portion given here is an adaptation taken from *Current*, October 1965, pp. 39–42.]

[Congress has insulated itself from the new political forces which social change has generated, and so] has continued to be a collection of local interests at precisely the time when our problems have grown increasingly *national*. But "how can national institutions be represented in a locally-elected legislature? In the absence of an easy answer to this question, the administration has tended to emerge as the natural point of access to the government for these national organizations and the place where their interests and viewpoints are brought into the policy-making process. In effect, the American system of government is moving toward a three-way system of representation. Particular territorial interests are represented in Congress; particular functional interests are represented in the administration; and the national interest is represented territorially and functionally in the Presidency."

If the external affiliations of Congress should have become more national, so its internal power structure should have grown more centralized. "Instead, the dominant tendency has been toward the dispersion of power. This leaves Congress only partially equipped to deal with the problems of modern society.

"The complex modern environment re-

quires in social and political institutions *both* a high degree of specialization and a high degree of centralized authority to coordinate and to integrate the activities of the specialized units. Specialization of function and centralization of authority have been the dominant trends of 20th-century institutional development. Congress, however, has adjusted only halfway. Through its committees and subcommittees it has provided effectively for specialization, much more effectively, indeed, than the national legislature of any other country. But it has failed to combine increasing specialization of function with increasing centralization of authority. Instead the central leadership in Congress has been weakened, and as a result Congress lacks the central authority to integrate its specialized bodies. . . .

In a bureaucracy, specialized units compete with each other for the support of less specialized officials. In Congress, however, reciprocity among specialists replaces coordination by generalists. When a committee bill comes to the floor, the non-specialists in that subject acquiesce in its passage with the unspoken but complete understanding that they will receive similar treatment. . . . Reciprocity thus substitutes for centralization and confirms the diffusion of power among the committees. . . .

"The insulation of Congress from external social forces and the dispersion of power within Congress have stimulated significant changes in the functions of Congress. The Congressional role in legislation has largely been reduced to delay and amendment; Congressional activity in overseeing administration has expanded and diversified. . . . Since 1933 . . . the initiative in formulating legislation, in assigning legislative priorities, in arousing support for legislation, and in determining the final content of the legislation enacted has clearly shifted to the executive branch. All three elements of the executive branch—President, administration, and bureaucracy—have gained legislative functions at the expense of Congress. . . .

"The decline in the legislative role of Congress has been accompanied by an increase in its administrative role. The modern state differs from the liberal state of the 18th and 19th centuries in terms of the greater control it exercises over society and the increase in the size, functions, and importance of its bureaucracy. Needed in the modern state are means to control, check, supplement, stimulate, and ameliorate this bureaucracy. The institutions and techniques available for this task vary from country to country: the Scandinavian countries have their *Ombudsmen*; Communist countries use party bureaucracy to check state bureaucracy. In the United States, Congress has come to play a major, if not the major, role in this regard. Indeed, many of the innovations in Congress in recent years have strengthened its control over the administrative processes of the executive branch." As George B. Galloway has remarked, not legislation but the control of administration is becoming the primary function of the modern Congress.

"In performing these activities, Congress is acting where it is most competent to act: it is dealing with particulars, not general policies. Unlike legislating, these concerns are perfectly compatible with the current patterns of insulation and dispersion. Committee specialization and committee power enhance rather than detract from the effectiveness of the committees as administrative overseers. In addition, as the great organized interests of society come to be represented more directly in the bureaucracy and administration, the role of Congress as representative of individual citizens becomes all the more important. The congressman more often serves their interests by representing them in the administrative process than in the legislative process. . . .

"Insulation has made Congress unwilling to initiate laws. Dispersion has made Congress unable to aggregate individual bills into a coherent legislative program. Constituent service and administrative overseeing have eaten into the time and energy which congressmen give legislative matters. Congress is thus left in its legislative dilemma where the assertion of power is almost equivalent to the obstruction of action. . . .

"The resumption by Congress of an active, positive role in the legislative process would require a drastic restructuring of power relationships, including reversal of the tendencies toward insulation, dispersion, and oversight. Fundamental 'reforms' would thus be required." For example, it might be possible to weaken [Congressional insulation by promoting mobility between Congress and the administration. . . . This] would bring about drastic changes in American politics, not the least of which would be a great increase in the attractiveness of running for Congress. Opening up this possibility, however, depends upon the modification of seniority, and that, in turn, depends upon the centralization of power in Congress. . . .

"A politically easier, although psychologically more difficult, way out of Congress's dilemma involves not the reversal but the intensification of the recent trends of Congressional evolution. Congress is in a legislative dilemma because opinion conceives of it as a legislature. If it gave up the effort to play even a delaying role in the legislative process, it could, quite conceivably, play a much more positive and influential role in the political system as a whole. Representative assemblies have not always been legislatures. They had their origins in medieval times as courts and as councils. . . . Representative assemblies acquired their legislative functions in the 17th and 18th centuries; there is no necessary reason why liberty, democracy, or constitutional government depends upon their exercising those functions in the 20th century. Legislation has become much too complex politically to be effectively handled by a representative assembly.

"The primary work of legislation must be done, and increasingly is being done, by the three 'houses' of the executive branch: the bureaucracy, the administration, and the President. . . .

"The redefinition of Congress's functions away from legislation would involve, in the first instance, a restriction of the power of Congress to delay indefinitely Presidential legislative requests. Constitutionally, Congress would still retain its authority to approve legislation. Practically, Congress could . . . bind itself to approve or disapprove urgent Presidential proposals within a time limit of, say, three or six months. . . . Congress would also, of course, continue to amend and to vote freely on 'non-urgent' executive requests.

"Explicit acceptance of the idea that legislation was not its primary function would, in large part, simply be recognition of the direction which change has already been taking. It would legitimize and expand the functions of constituent service and administrative oversight which, in practice, already constitute the principal work of most congressmen. Increasingly isolated as it is from the dominant social forces in society, Congress would capitalize on its position as the representative of the unorganized interests of individuals. It would become a proponent of popular demands against the bureaucracy rather than the opponent of popular demands for legislation. It would thus continue to play a major although different role in the constitutional system of checks and balances."

THE SUPREME COURT AS KEEPER OF THE NATIONAL CONSCIENCE

[From the examination of the failures of President and Congress we turn to the courts. Robert F. Kennedy remarked that "when people criticize the courts for invading spheres of action which supposedly belong to other parts of our constitutional system, they often overlook the fact that the courts must act precisely because the other organs of government have failed to fulfill their own responsibilities." In his article, "Historic Change in the Supreme Court," in *The New York Times Magazine*, June 17, 1962, Anthony Lewis explored the change in the attitudes and actions of the Supreme Court and found that it was particularly active in three fields: criminal procedure, segregation, and legislative apportionment. He then suggested some generalizations.]

One constant . . . was the ethical element. In intervening in behalf of the abused criminal suspect, the Negro, the citizen disenfranchised by malapportionment, the Supreme Court has been responding to what it deemed to be a moral demand—a demand of the national conscience. Moreover, the national conscience had found no way to express itself except through the Supreme Court. The Court moved in only when the rest of our governmental system was stymied, when there was no other practical way out of the moral dilemma.

The conclusion is that the Supreme Court has tended in recent years to act as the instrument of national moral values that have not been able to find other governmental expression. If the Court has changed, it is because we have changed.

The unhappy recent history of the world has rearranged Americans' hierarchy of values, and so it should be no great surprise that the Supreme Court emphasizes interests different from those of the past. We are more concerned, now, about abuse of official authority, mistreatment of racial minorities and sabotage of democracy than we are about the state powers in a federal system.

This is not to say that everyone agrees on moral goals, much less ones that are judicially attainable. The nine justices cannot be expected to march in happy unanimity toward a legal heaven whose definition all applaud.

Only in the field of race relations—where, ironically, public reaction has been the most divisive—have the justices been regularly in agreement. They have apparently found the moral imperative more obvious. But even here it seems doubtful that unanimity can long be preserved as the Court reaches the difficult questions of how to distinguish "private" from "public" discrimination.

Outside the racial area the Court has been deeply divided. Justice Frankfurter has been the principal spokesman for the view that the Court should be hesitant to impose its moral ideal in a complex political structure. He, . . . of course, is not alone in his doubts about an expansive role for the Supreme Court as keeper of the national conscience. Most of today's critics of the Court are disaffected only because they dislike some particular result—say, the outlawing of school segregation. But there are some who, like Justice Frankfurter, have deeper and more general philosophical objections.

One is that judges are not necessarily competent to make broad moral judgments. Law school trains a man to work his way through conflicting principles in construing a contract or a statute. But does it equip Supreme Court justices, or the lower court judges who must

carry out their decisions, to pass judgment on great social questions such as race relations and legislative districting, where there are few guidelines—few easily defined principles?

Even more strongly pressed is the thesis that reliance on the courts to cure society's ills saps the strength of democracy. The late Judge Learned Hand put it most colorfully when he said that he did not care to be ruled by "a bevy of Platonic guardians."

The more citizens rely on the courts, it is argued, the less will they fight issues out where they ought to be fought out in a democracy—in the political forum. . . .

Those who believe in the moral role that the Supreme Court has increasingly come to play would not deny the difficulty of the job it gives to judges. But they make the point that it is a duty compelled by a written Constitution and its amendments deliberately chose to use phrases such as "due process" and "equal protection"—phrases that express no more than moral ideals, that must be given content by each generation. It is our judges who have been designated to supply that content, and their sources of inspiration must be national values.

Justice Frankfurter, for all his concern about judicial power, sees no escape from a judge's duty to give the Constitution concrete meaning. "It must be an impersonal judgment," he once wrote. "It must rest on fundamental presuppositions rooted in history to which widespread acceptance may fairly be attributed. . . . But in the end judgment cannot be escaped."

Another time, Justice Frankfurter spoke of the Supreme Court's right to enshrine in the Constitution "those liberties of the individual which history has attested as the indispensable conditions of an open against a closed society" —in short, deep-rooted national ideals of liberty. . . .

This is a sprawling country divided by regional and other animosities, with an unhappy tradition of corrupt and partisan officials, especially on the local level. It has a national legislature too often driven by sectional interests, and in any case too busy, to spend much time bringing local action into harmony with national ideals.

It is a country, also, that has always looked to its courts for moral inspiration. It has looked especially to the Supreme Court, whose very remoteness and freedom from sectional and political pressures have made Americans value it as a forum for the defense of human liberty.

The Court has not been a Platonic dictator and could never successfully be that. When it has tried to stand against the tide of history, as in the Nineteen Thirties, it has failed. Its great success has been as a moral goad to the political process—when it has urged politicians to do what they have avoided doing but knew in their hearts they should, as in race relations and apportionment.

There is every indication that the Supreme Court more and more sees its constitutional function in those terms. Slowly but perceptibly, with occasional retreats but with the overall direction clear, the Court is taking up the role of conscience to the country.

ORDER OR LIBERTY: A PROBLEM OF PRIORITIES

[Another view of the origin and nature of the split in the post-New Deal Supreme Court is given by a Yale Law School professor, Fred Rodell, in "Crux of the Court Hullabaloo," *The New York Times Magazine*, May 29, 1960. There has been considerable complaint that the Court's majority, in defending individual rights, has not only wrested the meaning of the Constitution but has seriously impeded law enforcement. The problem of which should come first—order or liberty—was a primary aspect of the battle between Hamilton and Jefferson, and though the leaders of the factions here described pass on, the philosophical difference between them is so sharp that the division is likely to continue.]

What is the proper role of the court, what should it do or not do, when the act of some other government body—state or Federal, legislative or executive—is challenged as plainly violating part of the Bill of Rights or its supplement, the Fourteenth Amendment?

On this key question, the court's division —the line-up of the justices—is not nearly so clear-cut as when Holmes and Brandeis and Stone and, later, Cardozo were regularly dissenting against the stubborn economic conservatism of their brethren earlier in the century. What is clear is only that Justice Frankfurter today captains one team, commonly if clumsily known as "advocates of judicial self-restraint," while Justices Black and Douglas co-captain the other team, dubbed "judicial activists"; that Black and Douglas almost always have Warren and Brennan with them; and that Frankfurter usually signs up the other four. Despite the occasional shifting of sides by this justice or that, the Frankfurter team tends to win the close ones.

And despite the shifting, the basic battle can be bitter. When the venerable Judge Learned Hand—who, though not on the Supreme Court, has long been a coach and a comfort to the Frankfurter contingent—once dismissed the First Amendment's guarantees of freedom of speech and press as "no more than admonitions of moderation," Justice Douglas retorted: "The idea that they are no more than that has done more to undermine liberty in this country than any other single force." . . .

What does it all add up to—this deep doctrinal division within the court—and whence did it arise? Though its philosophical sources stretch back through at least 2,000 years of political theory, its present explosiveness began to sputter soon after the clash between Old

Court and New Deal twenty-odd years ago.

There is not a man on the Court today, nor for many years past, who does not agree that the Nine Old Men were wrong to strike down social laws, in the name of the Constitution, and thus make themselves the country's economic overlords. But *why* was the Old Court wrong? Precisely how did the reigning justices abuse or stray from their proper judicial role? Here is the rub whose friction has split the current court—with results not unlike the splitting of an atom.

The Frankfurter faction feels that the Nine Old Men were wrong to substitute their collective judgment for that of other Government officers, especially for that of Congress, on any type of issue, under the aegis of any constitutional clause. This belief in judicial self-restraint, though all-inclusive, is not absolute; it will pay more deference to an Act of Congress—or a law passed by any legislature— than to the ruling of a regulatory agency or a local policeman's order.

But its strong slant is toward judicial hands-off whenever some other branch of government has acted—save when such action may create conflict within the Federal system; then the court should step in as a sort of impartial chairman or arbiter to keep order among our fifty-one separate sovereigns.

Most crucially, the Frankfurter view makes no distinction whatever between two different realms or reaches of Government action; with impeccable logic, it insists that the court should no more interfere where personal liberties may be infringed than where claimed economic rights are at stake.

The Black-Douglas view exalts this precise distinction. It sees the Old Court's error more narrowly—in the type of laws that were vetoed (all of them economic) and in the fuzzy imprecision of the Constitution's due-process and interstate-commerce clauses which the Old Court used to cut those laws down.

Unbothered by charges from the Frankfurter camp of illogic or inconsistency, the so-called judicial activists defend the distinction they make between personal liberties and economic rights on two major grounds: first, the semantic absoluteness of most of the Bill of Rights' guarantees, such as the First Amendment's flat and unqualified "Congress shall make no law . . ."; second, a deep conviction, born of both reason and emotion, that—regardless of syllogistic consistency about judicial review—this nation puts, or should put a higher premium on individual dignities and freedoms than on material matters like the getting and keeping of money, and that the court should honor that preference under the Constitution.

To support this conviction, the Black-Douglas group rhetorically asks: Why have a written Constitution (save to set up the sheer mechanics of government) in a republic devoted to law by majority rule? Why have a written Bill of Rights—if not to protect *against* majority rule, and against executive excesses, too, the minimum democratic decencies that dictatorships view with scorn, from the First Amendment freedoms of speech and religion and press and assembly to the guarantees of fair treatment and trial for every accused person, be he charged with kidnapping or communism? And, most crucially, who better than the courts can be counted on to stand up against lynch-minded law-makers or overeager officers or public pressures when the Bill of Rights is invoked on behalf of unpopular, or even despised, minority groups or nonconforming people?

In partial reply to this last question—and, of course, in support of their stand—the Black-Douglas group quotes James Madison, proposing the Bill of Rights to the first Congress:

"If they [the Bill of Rights amendments] are incorporated into the Constitution, independent tribunals of justice will consider themselves in a peculiar manner the guardians of those rights; they will be an impenetrable bulwark against every assumption of power in the legislative or executive; they will be naturally led to resist every encroachment upon rights expressly stipulated for in the Constitution by the declaration of rights."

The Frankfurter contingent also looks, but with a contrary slant, to constitutional theory and history. Their creed can be roughly summarized as: Leave law-making to legislatures and law-enforcing to executive officers, Bill of Rights or no; our job as judges is to interpret and apply laws, not to force any part of the Constitution down other governmental throats.

This attitude, while abstractly stressing a rather rigid separation of powers, in practice leaves the legislature supreme—as in constitutionless England. . . . As Douglas recently put it in dissent against a Frankfurter holding, "We [here] forsake much of our constitutional heritage and move closer to the British scheme."

Implicit, too, in the Frankfurter philosophy of judicial self-restraint is a strong re-luctance maybe to embroil the court, even to uphold civil liberties, in the sort of trouble the Nine Old Men encountered [in the 1930's] by bucking the popular will in the name of the Constitution. . . .

Justice Frankfurter often uses, in defense of his philosophy, the phrase "ordered liberty" —a phrase he borrowed from the late Justice Cardozo. Self-contradictory on its face, the phrase is even more so when applied to a specific case or issue; for then the noun and the adjective must clash. And here perhaps is the very crux of the current Supreme Court split. For no one supposed the Frankfurter faction does not believe in liberty, or the Black-Douglass bloc does not believe in order. It is when a choice must be made between them that Frankfurter chooses order; Black and Douglas choose liberty.

THE HIGHER LAW

[The threat by totalitarianism to the existence of democracy has promoted a bitter attack by the exponents of natural law upon the organic and pragmatic interpretation of law introduced by Holmes. The attack is based on the claim that once pragmatic relativism is admitted there is no halting place short of the all-powerful totalitarian state. Natural law has found champions not only among sincere believers in revealed religion but also among many who are concerned with blocking the progress of the "sociological jurisprudence" which arose from pragmatism. (See the Commager exposition of Roscoe Pound in Chapter 8.) Here we present certain highlights from "The Higher Law," an address delivered by Harold R. McKinnon of the San Francisco Bar, and taken from *Vital Speeches*, December 1, 1946. (13: 101–106).]

It is a paradox that at a time when this country is beset with many fears, the most fearful thing of all is something of which the country is generally unaware. It is the fact that while this country is traditionally democratic, the prevailing teaching of its political and legal philosophers is essentially anti-democratic and totalitarian.

This is so because this teaching denies three essential elements of democracy and thereby affirms three essential elements of totalitarianism. It denies that there is a moral law which is inherent in human nature and which is therefore immutable and to which all man-made laws to be valid must conform. It denies that by virtue of this law man possesses certain rights which are inherent and inalienable and therefore superior to the authority of the state. It denies that the purpose of government is to secure these inherent and inalienable rights. It asserts that because there are no immutable principles of human conduct, there is no ultimate standard of justice and the lawmaker is responsible to nothing but his own unfettered will. It asserts that since there are no natural rights, all man's rights come to him from the state, and what the state grants, the state may take away. It asserts that since man possesses no natural, inherent rights, the purpose of government is not to secure such rights but rather the purpose of man is to serve the state.

This teaching nullifies the Declaration of Independence, the preamble of the Constitution and the Bill of Rights. It nullifies twenty-five hundred years of progress in political and legal theory and re-enacts in the present age some of the worst political and legal errors of ancient times. It is indistinguishable, in its origin and its logical effect, from philosophies which characterized lands against which we have just fought the bloodiest war in history. . . .

In view of this situation, we may well take heed of the warning of Montesquieu, that the beginning of a nation's decadence is when it loses sight of the principles upon which it is founded.

In our case, what are those principles? They are the principles of the natural law. Volumes could be written upon the subject, but I must content myself with a very brief statement.

The basic element of the doctrine is, that by virtue of his nature, man has an awareness of right and wrong. It is not something communicated to him by his fellowman, but rather it is something inherent in him as a rational being, and because of that fact it is called the natural law. Since it is a part of his nature, it comes from the Author of his nature, namely from God. It is not the result of a process of reasoning; rather it is an initiative awareness of moral obligation. It is something written upon the tablet of his conscience by his Creator. Because it is a principle of human nature, it governs all men at all places and at all times and is essentially immutable. It applies to man both in his private and his social conduct. In respect of his social conduct, its first principle is, *seek the common good,* or, the same thing analytically expressed, *do good to others, harm no one and render to each his own.*

Now, of course, these principles are far too general to serve as criteria for either moral or legal justice. The reason is that they constitute the most general principles of law. Actually, they prescribe the ends of justice; what is needed to make them effective is the means, because action follows upon a choice of means. The first of these means are precepts which are necessarily drawn from these first principles and which have been called the *jus gentium* or law of nations because they can be known to all men of normal conscience and are generally recognized throughout the world. . . . [These precepts, in turn, are further refined by man-made rules which] are laws in the lawyer's sense and the judge's sense, the positive instrumentalities with which they deal.

Here, then, is the structure of the household of the law, a three-story edifice of principles, precepts and rules. The significant point is that rules, to be valid, must be based upon these underlying precepts and principles, for if they are not they will sooner or later become the instruments of tyranny rather than of justice.

This doctrine has had a long and illustrious history. The basic concept is found in the writings of ancient times, and in one way or another it has been recognized ever since by philosophers and poets, statesmen and lawyers, kings and saints. . . . [In America] it permeated the writings of the Founding Fathers . . . while from the pen of Jefferson it received classic and, let us hope immortal, expression in the famous preamble to the Declaration that all men are created equal and that they are endowed by their Creator with certain inalienable rights and that the purpose of government is to secure these rights. Akin to this great expression in the Declaration is the equally beautiful and powerful statement of Hamilton: "The sacred rights of mankind are not to be rummaged for among old records or musty parchments. They are written, as with a sunbeam, in the whole volume of human nature, by the hand of Divinity itself, and can never be erased or obscured by mortal power." It was this great concept which was given body and visibility by incorporation into our Bill of Rights, especially in the due process clause whereby the life, liberty and property of every least man in the land was brought within its protecting arms.

And now, after a century and a half of our national life, it still lives in the expressions of those who see in this principle the bulwark of our liberty and the source of our nation's strength. . . .

This . . . is our birthright. This is what is at stake in America today. And in this matter we are in the most unyielding dilemma. For if there is no higher law, there is no basis for saying that any man-made law is unjust, and if an act of Congress, benign in purpose and content and enacted within the limits of the Constitution, is called a law, by the same token the most vicious enactment of the late Nazi government must be called a law; and in such case, the ultimate reason for things, as Justice

Holmes himself conceded, is force. If there is no natural law, there are no natural rights; and if there are no natural rights, the Bill of Rights is a delusion, and everything which a man possesses—his life, his liberty and his property —are held by sufferance of government, and in that case it is inevitable that government will some day find it expedient to take away what is held by a title such as that. And if there are no eternal truths, if everything changes, everything, then we may not complain when the standard of citizenship changes from freedom to servility and when democracy relapses into tyranny.

What has preserved America from this teaching so far? My own answer is this. I think it is a carry-over of the early American tradition. We had a good start in theory of state and of law, but the theorists have reversed themselves, and we are now living in the declining momentum of the original theory.

How long can our tradition resist this teaching? Who can say? But this much is plain, that he who obtains control over men's minds will in the end master their institutions.

BLACK IS BEAUTIFUL

AND ITS SO BEAUTIFUL TO BE BLACK

Southern Christian Leadership Council

20

PATTERNS OF SOCIAL AND ECONOMIC CHANGE

THE TEN COMMITMENTS

[John W. Gardner, former Secretary of Health, Education, and Welfare, has set forth the ten problems that face America at home—though, of course, they also bear on our relations with other nations. His article appears under the title "The Ten Commitments" in *The Saturday Review*, July 1, 1967, pp. 39–40.]

Anyone giving thought to the tasks facing science and technology may find it useful to have in mind the problems our society faces in the years immediately ahead. Thoughtful people with time on their hands can make up their own lists; for those without time, here's mine.

Let's begin with the problem of building *an enduring peace*. It is far the most critical problem facing our nation and the world. The task is not to abolish tensions among nations, which is quite impossible, but to hold those tensions within safe bounds. This requires appropriate institutional arrangements, such as the United Nations. It requires efforts to extend the rule of law in international affairs. And it requires a base of mutual understanding. It is not necessary that all nations love one another or even that they trust one another completely. But it is necessary that they understand and tolerate one another to the point that their differences can be resolved in a just, orderly, nonviolent way.

Le Pelley in The Christian Science Monitor © TCSPS
"But are you old enough to mean it?"

I'm not going to attempt to list these problems in any order of importance, but since we began with peace, I'll list next the related problem of *the developing nations*. The combination of poverty and rising expectations that exists among half the world's population today is as volatile and threatening in its own way as the bomb. If bridges to peace are to be built among nations, the widening economic and social chasm that divides the world today is going to have to be narrowed.

Third is the problem of *population control*. Throughout the world there is a growing awareness of the gravity of unbridled population growth and the urgency of doing something about it. Today there are about 3.3 billion people in the world. By the year 2000 it is predicted that there will be 7.5 billion, most of them hungry. And, as Harrison Brown has said, "Hungry people are combustible."

The fourth problem on my list is *equal opportunity*. There isn't anything Americans have cared about more deeply throughout their history. Today, racial discrimination is the chief barrier to equality of opportunity, and is unquestionably our number one domestic problem. But the racial front is not the only one on which we are struggling to provide equality of opportunity, or equal access to the benefits of American life. There are other massive barriers to individual fulfillment—poverty, illness, ignorance, physical and mental handicaps. Our goal today is breathtaking in scope, but easy to describe. We don't want *anyone* hurt or handicapped or shut out from the life of the society by circumstances that can be prevented.

The fifth problem is closely related to the fourth. We must redouble our efforts to create *an educational system that will provide the maximum individual fulfillment for each American*. In the slums of our great cities today boys and girls who could easily be brought to the full use of their powers are left stunted, inarticulate, and angry. We need an educational system that will lift them. The complexity of our society has created spectacular requirements for educated talent. We need schools that will nurture that talent, that will awaken the spark of curiosity and eagerness to learn, that will develop individuals capable of defending their individuality in a highly organized society.

Sixth, we must bring *new life to our cities*. The city is the heart and brain of an industrial society. Yet today our cities are plagued with every conceivable ill—apathy, crime, poverty, racial conflict, slum housing, polluted air and water, inferior schools and hospitals, and hopelessly snarled transportation. The flight of industry and middle-class residents to the suburbs has left the city shorn not only of needed tax revenues, but of part of its leadership. We are going to have to do more than build bridges between the inner city and its opulent periphery. We need a totally new concept of metropolitan organization.

Seventh is the problem of our *natural environment*. We can't avoid some alteration of the natural world we live in. But man, even industrial man, is a part of nature, and must find some limit to the headlong destruction and fouling of the natural environment. How much fouled air can we breathe? How much filth can we spew into our rivers and lakes? How much bleakness and ugliness can we tolerate?

Eighth is the *reshaping of government*, the age-old problem of how best to organize ourselves to accomplish our shared purposes. We have indulged ourselves far too long in the luxury of supposing that everything in this country must change and develop except our governmental structure and processes.

Until state and local governments revamp their antiquated procedures and develop the strength to carry the heavy burdens that have been thrust upon them; until Congress faces up to the requirements of reorganization; until the Executive branch carries considerably further its present efforts to streamline its departmental structure and create mutually respecting partnerships with state, local, and nongovernmental agencies; until all these steps are underway we shall continue to be hobbled in the race with change.

My ninth problem concerns *economic growth*. Since the 1930s we have made impressive gains in stabilizing and managing the economy. Because of what we now know about the sources of economic growth we can envisage the elimination of poverty, the rebuilding of our cities, wise use of our natural resources, and more imaginative use of human skills. To the extent that we sustain a high rate of economic growth, all our other problems will be easier.

The final item on my agenda is the *rela-*

tionship of the individual to society. Everything that we do, all that we achieve, must finally be measured in terms of its effect on the individual. We set out to create a society in which the individual could flourish. But our highly organized society carries its own threats to individuality.

We can avert that threat. We can't escape size and complexity today, but we can design our institutions so that they serve the individual as well as the system. Our goal should be a society designed for people; and if we want it badly enough, we can have it.

One striking feature of our situation today is that we are creating new problems as we go along. Some of the most interesting of the new problems stem from scientific and technical advances. Consider the problems posed by some of the new mind-affecting drugs. Consider the economic, ethical, and social problems posed by the possibility of artificial organs, or weather control, or the control of genetic processes.

Our capacity to create new problems as rapidly as we solve the old has implications for the kind of society we shall have to design. We shall need a society that is sufficiently honest and open-minded to recognize its problems, sufficiently creative to conceive new solutions, and sufficiently purposeful to put those solutions into effect. It should be, in short, a self-renewing society, ready to improvise solutions to problems it won't recognize until tomorrow. The vitality of our science and technology will have a good deal to do with whether we achieve that kind of society.

THE NEGRO REVOLUTION

The movement for integration of Negroes into American life reached a climax in the "Freedom Movement" of the early 1960's when blacks and whites joined in numerous "sit-ins" and protest marches. In 1964 President Johnson managed to jam through a reluctant Congress a civil rights bill which may or may not solve the problems it was intended to meet. Then the tide of racial cooperation ebbed as Negroes took sole charge of their own movement, denounced integration, and lifted the banner of a "black nationalism" to be attained through "black power."

Whatever the reasons, a series of riots broke out in the Negro ghettos, the most serious of which gutted a large section of Watts in Los Angeles (1965) and an even larger section of Detroit (1967). Unlike the traditional pattern of clash between races these riots (with the exception of some sniping) were directed to the destruction of the Negroes' own homes, and the destruction of stores and other businesses run by white men which it was said had been exploiting Negroes. The common pattern, so far as one could be found, was that they rose suddenly from incidents in which white policemen were charged with brutality.

The Negro Revolution has only begun, and no man can foretell its course. The moderate Negro groups, to whom is credited much of the progress hitherto made by Negroes, are being crowded out of the spectrum by impatient young men who proclaim their loss of faith in white liberals and charge that all American whites are racist either openly or quietly. These young men have given up the Martin Luther King technique of demonstration marches and are organizing open campaigns of riot, arson, and looting which could conceivably lead to bloody war between the races. It is worth recalling in this connection that a democracy rarely remedies a bad situation until it is called to public attention by forcible, even bloody, means. But if this happens, whites had best blame their own unreasonable refusal to live up to the claims and promises of America.

Here we offer three selections which attempt to describe the situation and the thinking that lies behind it.

(1) BLACK AND WHITE TOGETHER?

The following is part of a paper circulated within the Student Nonviolent Coordinating Committee, and published in *The New York Times*, August 5, 1966. The version given here is from *Current*, October 1966, pp. 6–8.

"If we are to proceed toward true liberation, we must cut ourselves off from white people. We must form our own institutions, credit unions, co-ops, political parties, write our own histories. . . . These facts do not mean that whites cannot help. They can participate on a voluntary basis . . . but in no way can they participate on a policy-making level. The charge may be made that we are 'racists,' but whites who are sensitive to our problems will realize that we must determine our own destiny. . . .

"We propose that our organization (S.N. C.C.) should be black-staffed, black-controlled and black-financed. . . . If we continue to rely upon white financial support we will find ourselves entwined in the tentacles of the white power complex that controls this country. It is also important that a black organization (devoid of cultism) be projected to our people so that it can be demonstrated that such organizations are viable. . . . Previous solutions to black problems in this country have been made in the interests of those whites dealing with these problems and not in the best interests of black people in this country. Whites can only subvert our true search and struggle for self-determination, self-identification, and liberation in this country. Re-evaluation of the white and black roles must NOW take place so that whites no longer designate roles that black people play but rather black people define white people's roles.

"Too long have we allowed white people to interpret the importance and meaning of the cultural aspects of our society. We have allowed them to tell us what was good about our Afro-American music, art and literature. How many black critics do we have on the 'jazz' scene? How can a white person who is not a part of the black psyche (except in the oppressor's role) interpret the meaning of the blues to us who are manifestations of the songs themselves? . . .

"Another concern is how does the white radical view the black community and how does he view the poor white community in terms of organizing. So far, we have found that most white radicals have sought to escape the horrible reality of America by going into the black community and attempting to organize black people while neglecting the organization of their own people's racist communities. . . . We feel that S.N.C.C. and the civil rights movement in general is in many aspects similar to the anticolonial situations in the African and Asian countries. We have the whites in the movement corresponding to the white civil servants and missionaries in the colonial countries who have worked with the colonial people for a long period of time and have developed a paternalistic attitude toward them. The reality of the colonial people taking over their own lives and controlling their own destiny must be faced. Having to move aside and letting this natural process of growth and development take place must be faced. . . . The move by the black militants and S.N.C.C. in this direction should be viewed as a turn toward self-determination. . . .

"Any re-evaluation that we must make will, for the most part, deal with identification. Who are black people, what are black people; what is their relationship to America and the world?"

(2) WHAT WE WANT

The angriest of the angry young men in the Black Power movement is Stokely Carmichael, born in the West Indies, who rose meteorically in the Student Nonviolent Coordinating Committee and led it away from its original policy of nonviolence. His "What We Want" was published in *The New York Review of Books*, September 22, 1966, and is reproduced here from the version in *Current*, October 1966, pp. 8–11.

"Black Americans have two problems: they are poor and they are black. . . . Almost from its beginning, S.N.C.C. sought to address itself to both conditions with a program aimed at winning political power for impoverished Southern blacks. . . . We had to work for power, because this country does not function by morality, love, and nonviolence. . . .

"[When a man] and his family must endure—as hundreds of Alabamians have endured—loss of job, eviction, starvation, and sometimes death, for political activity, he may also need a gun and S.N.C.C. reaffirms the right of black men everywhere to defend themselves when threatened or attacked. As for initiating the use of violence, we hope that such programs as ours will make that unnecessary; but it is not for us to tell black communities whether they can or cannot use any particular form of action to resolve their problems. Responsibility for the use of violence by black men, whether in self defense or initiated by them, lies with the white community. . . .

"In such areas as Lowndes County, Ala., where black men have a majority, they will attempt to use it to exercise [political] control. . . . Where Negroes lack a majority, black power means proper representation and sharing of control. It means the creation of power bases from which black people can work to change statewide or nationwide patterns of oppression through pressure from strength—instead of weakness. Politically, black power . . . does not mean merely putting black faces into office. A man or woman who is black and from the slums cannot be automatically expected to speak to the needs of black people. Most of the black politicians we see around the country today are not what S.N.C.C. means by black power. . . .

"In Lowndes County, 86 white families own 90 per cent of the land. What are black people in that county going to do for jobs, where are they going to get money? There must be reallocation of land, of money. Ultimately, the economic foundations of this country must be shaken if black people are to control their lives. . . .

"For racism to die, a totally different America must be born. This is what the white society does not wish to face; this is why that society prefers to talk about integration. But integration speaks not at all to the problem of poverty, only to the problem of blackness. Integration today means the man who 'makes it,' leaving his black brothers behind in the ghetto as fast as his new sports car will take him. It has no relevance to the Harlem wino or to the cotton-picker making three dollars a day. . . .

"Integration, moreover, speaks to the problem of blackness in a despicable way. As a goal, it has been based on complete acceptance of the fact that in order to have a decent house or education, blacks must move into a white neighborhood or send their children to a white school. This reinforces, among both black and white, the idea that 'white' is automatically better and 'black' is by definition inferior. . . . [Integration] allows the nation to focus on a handful of Southern children who get into white schools, at great price, and to ignore the 94 per cent who are left behind in unimproved all-black schools. . . .

"To most whites, black power seems to mean that the Mau Mau are coming to the suburbs at night. . . . Articles appear about plots to 'get Whitey,' creating an atmosphere in which 'law and order must be maintained.' Once again, responsibility is shifted from the oppressor to the oppressed. Other whites chide,

'Don't forget—you're only 10 per cent of the population; if you get too smart, we'll wipe you out.' If they are liberals, they complain, 'what about me?—don't you want my help any more?' These are people supposedly concerned about black Americans, but today they think first of themselves, of their feelings of rejection. Or they admonish, 'you can't get anywhere without coalitions,' when there is in fact no group at present with whom to form a coalition in which blacks will not be absorbed and betrayed. Or they accuse us of 'polarizing the races' by our calls for black unity, when the true responsibility for polarization lies with whites who will not accept their responsibility as the majority power for making the democratic process work. . . .

"From birth, black people are told a set of lies about themselves. . . . It takes time to become free of the lies and their shaming effect on black minds. It takes time to reject the most important lie: that black people inherently can't do the same things white people can do, unless white people help them.

"The need for psychological equality is the reason why S.N.C.C. today believes that blacks must organize in the black community. Only black people can convey the revolutionary idea that black people are able to do things themselves. Only they can help create in the community an aroused and continuing black consciousness that will provide the basis for political strength. . . .

One of the most disturbing things about almost all white supporters of the movement has been that they are afraid to go into their own communities—which is where the racism exists—and work to get rid of it. They want to run from Berkeley to tell us what to do in Mississippi; let them look instead at Berkeley. They admonish blacks to be nonviolent; let them preach nonviolence in the white community. They come to teach me Negro history; let them go to the suburbs and open up freedom schools for whites. Let them work to stop America's racist foreign policy; let them press this government to cease supporting the economy of South Africa. . . .

"It is purely academic today to talk about bringing poor blacks and whites together, but the job of creating a poor-white power bloc must be attempted. The main responsibility for it falls upon whites. Black and white can work together in the white community where possible; it is not possible, however, to go into a poor Southern town and talk about integration. Poor whites everywhere are becoming more hostile—not less—partly because they see the nation's attention focussed on black poverty and nobody coming to them. Too many young middle-class Americans, like some sort of Pepsi generation, have wanted to come alive through the black community; they've wanted to be where the action is—and the action has been in the black community. . . .

"Our vision is not merely of a society in which all black men have enough to buy the good things of life. When we urge that black money go into black pockets, we mean the communal pocket. We want to see money go back into the community and used to benefit it. We want to see the cooperative concept applied in business and banking. We want to see black ghetto residents demand that an exploiting storekeeper sell them, at minimal cost, a building or a shop that they will own and improve cooperatively; they can back their demand with a rent strike, or a boycott, and a community so unified behind them that no one else will move into the building or buy at the store. The society we seek to build among black people, then, is not a capitalist one. It is a society in which the spirit of community and humanistic love prevail. The word love is suspect; black expectations of what it might produce have been betrayed too often. But those were expectations of a response from the white community, which failed us. The love we seek to encourage is within the black community. . . .

"As for white America, perhaps it can stop crying out against 'black supremacy,' 'black nationalism,' 'racism in reverse,' and begin facing reality. The reality is that this nation, from top to bottom, is racist; that racism is not primarily a problem of 'human relations' but of an exploitation maintained—either actively or through silence—by the society as a whole."

(3) THE TIDE IS TURNING

James J. Kilpatrick, former editor of the *Richmond News Leader* and author of the column *A Conservative View,* has analyzed opinion in South and North. See his column of September 3, 1965. Perhaps, after all, at least in this instance in the South, state-ways do change folkways, contrary to Sumner's dictum.

It is a fascinating experience, known to every man who ever lived by the water, to sit beside a shore and watch the turning of a tide. Mariners need no charts to sense that pregnant moment when a full tide stops and ebb begins. The river may seem the same, but the pull and thrust have changed.

Tides of public opinion are much trickier to read; their suns and moons are not so fixed —but the metaphor holds. And a word of prophecy may be ventured: A great many signs suggest that two tides are changing all at once, one North, one South, in the gulf of attitudes and opinions that contains the "Negro Revolution." Old currents shift; new flows and ebbs begin.

The changing attitudes of the South are more significant, perhaps, than those outside the South. They are quieter, and they have been longer coming; they reach more deeply into the totality of men's lives, and they hold a promise of tranquility ahead.

We are witnessing in Dixie this autumn, for the first time since Brown v. Board of Education—indeed, for the first time in 300 years —a certain sense of acceptance that holds prodigious meaning for white and Negro alike.

The mood should not be misunderstood. Nothing suggests that the white South has cheerfully embraced "integration." Neither is there any weary sense of surrender to Federal money or defeat by Federal law. It is more like a change in the wind or a drop in the temperature; a mist rises; and the Negro is seen differently now.

The word is "acceptance," the acceptance of change, the acknowledgement at last that things are no longer the same, that they never will be the same again. This fall, most of the South has hung up the shield that said "Never."

The portents of this critical hour can be seen most clearly in the country schools, where desegregation enters as quietly as a cloud that casts its shadow on a cotton patch. Shadows can be lived with, and clouds can be lived with; these hold no ominous threat of violent storm.

Equally significant omens may be seen in Southern cities, in the indifference that now accompanies desegregated restaurants, movies, hotels, chambers of commerce, professional societies. Most of all, the turning of a tide can be sensed in a subtleness of attitude—toward the Negro, toward the Klan, toward a thousand old patterns of relationship.

Mind you, this is not to say that vast new tides of amity have now come rushing in. The South is not done with racial trouble. Here and there, dumb brutes will shoot unarmed seminarians; hooded bullies will ride by night a few years longer; beneath a surface of acceptance, a legacy of rejection will remain.

It is to suggest merely that a point has been reached between flow and ebb. The segregationist politician is done for, and appeals to race—and nothing more—no longer find receptive ears.

Outside the South, this autumn also sees a changing mood, far more abrupt, much easier to read. The sacking of Los Angeles marked high water in the long-suffering tolerance of the American people for the criminal excesses of a Negro minority. A great deal of the mollycoddling, the paternalism, the soupy sentimentality, went up with the smoke that billowed over Watts. In recent years, the tendency has been to gush over the Negro, to condone, to explain, to rationalize, to put up with wanton trespass and flagrant contempt for the rights of others.

This misguided benevolence is vanishing in a rush of heady foam. From East to West, a timid and inarticulate public suddenly is giving voice to wrath and indignation much too long suppressed. The mood of the country is no longer to pamper the insolent demonstrator, lying supine upon the sidewalk; the mood is to kick him in the ribs. All at once, the maligned police have acquired new sympathy and respect. . . .

As in the South, one finds as yet no tide, but merely a turning point. The potent political power of the Negro bloc has scarcely been diminished. Professional apologists and mawkish bleeding-hearts will continue to exert an influential force. But the Northern politician who appeals in the name of "civil rights," and nothing else, is as dead in most districts as the old-line segregationist down South. . . .

Both tides carry hope—for human dignity, for law and order, for a new discrimination of merit, not of race. Slow and steady, or fast and angry, the waters change; and the task of all of us, white and Negro, is to harness the tides and make them work.

THE OTHER AMERICA: THE CULTURE OF POVERTY

[Michael Harrington, a Catholic and a socialist, wrote *The Other America: Poverty in the United States* (N.Y.: Macmillan, 1962), which forcibly called the attention of Americans to the existence of poverty, both among Negroes and whites. Relying on government statistics he estimated that there were somewhere between 40 million and 50 million citizens living in poverty—which on a rough estimate means less than $3,000 for a family of four. They are, for the most part invisible simply because they live in parts of the cities and rural areas to which the average middle-class person rarely goes. Even the housing projects of which cities are so proud cure nothing—they simply squeeze the poor into the surviving slum. The old and the sick do not move out of their neighborhoods, and the young meet the public eye only when they are caught in crime or engage in riots. And the poor no longer can turn to the political boss, their ever-present help in time of trouble, for he has gone the way of the old city machine. Here we take up Harrington's introductory chapter at page 7 and follow through to page 17. It will be seen that poverty is not merely a state of society but also a state of mind—an idea, "a culture, an institution, a way of life."]

That the poor are invisible is one of the most important things about them. They are not simply neglected and forgotten as in the old rhetoric of reform; what is much worse, they are not seen. . . . That is a shocking fact. But there is a second basic irony of poverty that is equally important: if one is to make the mistake of being born poor, he should choose a time when the majority of the people are miserable too.

J. K. Galbraith develops this idea in *The Affluent Society*, and in doing so defines the "newness" of the kind of poverty in contemporary America. The old poverty, Galbraith notes, was general. It was the condition of life of an entire society, or at least of that huge majority who were without special skills or the luck of birth. When the entire economy advanced, a good many of these people gained higher standards of living. Unlike the poor today, the majority poor of a generation ago were an immediate (if cynical) concern of political leaders. The old slums of the immigrants had the votes; they provided the basis for labor organizations; their very numbers could be a powerful force in political conflict. At the same time the new technology required higher skills, more education, and stimulated an upward movement for millions.

Perhaps the most dramatic case of the power of the majority poor took place in the 1930's. The Congress of Industrial Organizations literally organized millions in a matter of years. A labor movement that had been declining and confined to a thin stratum of the highly skilled suddenly embraced masses of men and women in basic industry. At the same time this acted as a pressure upon the Government, and the New Deal codified some of the social gains in laws like the Wagner Act. The result was not a basic transformation of the American system, but it did transform the lives of an entire section of the population.

In the thirties one of the reasons for these advances was that misery was general. There was no need then to write books about unemployment and poverty. That was the decisive social experience of the entire society, and the apple sellers even invaded Wall Street. There was political sympathy from middle-class reformers; there were an élan and spirit that grew out of a deep crisis.

Some of those who advanced in the thirties did so because they had unique and individual personal talents. But for the great mass, it was a question of being at the right point in the economy at the right time in history, and utilizing that position for common struggle. . . . As a group, the other Americans who stayed behind were not originally composed primarily of individual failures. Rather, they were victims of an impersonal process that selected some for progress and discriminated against others.

Out of the thirties came the welfare state. Its creation had been stimulated by mass impoverishment and misery, yet it helped the poor least of all. Laws like unemployment compensation, the Wagner Act, the various farm programs, all these were designed for the middle third in the cities, for the organized workers, and for the upper third in the country, for the big market farmers. If a man works in an extremely low-paying job, he may not even be covered by social security or other welfare programs. If he receives unemployment compensation, the payment is scaled down according to his low earnings.

One of the major laws that was designed to cover everyone, rich and poor, was social security. But even here the other Americans suffered discrimination. Over the years social security payments have not even provided a subsistence level of life. The middle third have been able to supplement the Federal pension through private plans negotiated by unions, through joining medical insurance schemes like Blue Cross, and so on. The poor have not been able to do so. They lead a bitter life, and then have to pay for that fact in old age.

Indeed, the paradox that the welfare state benefits those least who need help most is but a single instance of a persistent irony in the other America. Even when the money finally trickles down, even when a school is built in a poor neighborhood, for instance, the poor are still deprived. Their entire environment, their life, their values, do not prepare them to take advantage of the new opportunity. The parents are anxious for the children to go to work; the pupils are pent up, waiting for the moment when their education has complied with the law.

Today's poor, in short, missed the political and social gains of the thirties. They are, as Galbraith rightly points out, the first minority poor in history, the first poor not to be seen, the first poor whom the politicians could leave alone.

The first step toward the new poverty was taken when millions of people proved immune to progress. When that happened, the failure was not individual and personal, but a social

product. But once the historic accident takes place, it begins to become a personal fate.

The new poor of the other America saw the rest of society move ahead. They went on living in depressed areas, and often they tended to become depressed human beings. In some of the West Virginia towns, for instance, an entire community will become shabby and defeated. The young and the adventurous go to the city, leaving behind those who cannot move and those who lack the will to do so. The entire area becomes permeated with failure, and that is one more reason the big corporations shy away.

Indeed, one of the most important things about the new poverty is that it cannot be defined in simple, statistical terms. Throughout this book a crucial term is used: aspiration. If a group has internal vitality, a will—if it has aspiration—it may live in dilapidated housing, it may eat an inadequate diet, and it may suffer poverty, but it is not impoverished. So it was

Herblock, *The Washington* Post

"They've been going together for quite a while."

in those ethnic slums of the immigrants that played such a dramatic role in the unfolding of the American dream. The people found themselves in slums, but they were not slum dwellers.

But the new poverty is constructed so as to destroy aspiration; it is a system designed to be impervious to hope. The other America does not contain the adventurous seeking a new life and land. It is populated by the failures, by those driven from the land and bewildered by the city, by old people suddenly confronted with the torments of loneliness and poverty, and by minorities facing a wall of prejudice.

In the past, when poverty was general in the unskilled and semiskilled work force, the poor were all mixed together. The bright and the dull, those who were going to escape into the great society and those who were to stay behind, all of them lived on the same street. When the middle third rose, this community was destroyed. And the entire invisible land of the other Americans became a ghetto, a modern poor farm for the rejects of society and of the economy.

It is a blow to reform and the political hopes of the poor that the middle class no longer understands that poverty exists. But, perhaps more important, the poor are losing their links with the great world. If statistics and sociology can measure a feeling as delicate as loneliness (and some of the attempts to do so will be cited later on), the other America is becoming increasingly populated by those who do not belong to anybody or anything. They are no longer participants in an ethnic culture from the old country; they are less and less religious; they do not belong to unions or clubs. They are not seen, and because of that they themselves cannot see. Their horizon has become more and more restricted; they see one another, and that means they see little reason to hope. . . .

Finally, one might summarize the newness of contemporary poverty by saying: These are the people who are immune to progress. But

then the facts are even more cruel. The other Americans are the victims of the very inventions and machines that have provided a higher living standard for the rest of the society. They are upside-down in the economy, and for them greater productivity often means worse jobs; agricultural advance becomes hunger.

In the optimistic theory, technology is an undisguised blessing. A general increase in productivity, the argument goes, generates a higher standard of living for the whole people. And indeed, this has been true for the middle and upper thirds of American society, the people who made such striking gains in the last two decades. . . .

But the poor, if they were given to theory, might argue the exact opposite. They might say: Progress is misery.

As the society became more technological, more skilled, those who learn to work the machines, who get the expanding education, move up. Those who miss out at the very start find themselves at a new disadvantage. . . . Those who lack a high-school education tend to be condemned to the economic underworld —to low-paying service industries, to backward factories, to sweeping and janitorial duties. . . . The very rise in productivity that created more money and better working conditions for the rest of the society can be a menace to the poor.

But then this technological revolution might have an even more disastrous consequence: it could increase the ranks of the poor as well as intensify the disabilities of poverty. At this point it is too early to make any final judgment, yet there are obvious danger signals. There are millions of Americans who live just the other side of poverty. When a recession comes, they are pushed onto the relief rolls. (Welfare payments in New York respond almost immediately to any economic decline.) If automation continues to inflict more and more penalties on the unskilled and the semiskilled, it could have the impact of permanently increasing the population of the other America.

Even more explosive is the possibility that people who participated in the gains of the thirties and the forties will be pulled back down into poverty. Today the mass-production industries where unionization made such a difference are contracting. Jobs are being destroyed. In the process, workers who had achieved a certain level of wages, who had won working conditions in the shop, are suddenly confronted with impoverishment. This is particularly true for anyone over forty years of age and for members of minority groups. Once their job is abolished, their chances of ever getting similar work are very slim. . . .

Poverty in the 1960's is invisible and it is new, and both these factors make it more tenacious. It is more isolated and politically powerless than ever before. It is laced with ironies, not the least of which is that many of the poor view progress upside-down, as a menace and a threat to their lives. And if the nation does not measure up to the challenge of automation, poverty in the 1960's might be on the increase. . . .

There are, one must assume, citizens of the other America who choose impoverishment out of fear of work (though, writing it down, I really do not believe it). But the real explanation of why the poor are where they are is that they made the mistake of being born to the wrong parents, in the wrong section of the country, in the wrong industry, or in the wrong racial or ethnic group. Once that mistake has been made, they could have been paragons of will and morality, but most of them would never even have had a chance to get out of the other America.

There are two important ways of saying this: The poor are caught in a vicious circle; or, The poor live in a culture of poverty. . . . The individual cannot usually break out of this vicious circle. Neither can the group, for it lacks the social energy and political strength to turn its misery into a cause. Only the larger society, with its help and resources, can really make it possible for these people to help themselves. Yet those who could make the difference too often refuse to act because of their ignorant, smug moralisms. They view the effects of

poverty—above all, the warping of the will and spirit that is a consequence of being poor—as choices. Understanding the vicious circle is an important step in breaking down this prejudice.

There is an even richer way of describing this same, general idea: Poverty in the United States is a culture, an institution, a way of life.

There is a famous anecdote about Ernest Hemingway and F. Scott Fitzgerald. Fitzgerald is reported to have remarked to Hemingway, "The rich are different." And Hemingway replied, "Yes, they have money." Fitzgerald had much the better of the exchange. He understood that being rich was not a simple fact, like a large bank account, but a way of looking at reality, a series of attitudes, a special type of life. If this is true of the rich, it is ten times truer of the poor. Everything about them, from the condition of their teeth to the way in which they love, is suffused and permeated by the fact of their poverty. And this is sometimes a hard idea for a Hemingway-like middle-class America to comprehend.

The family structure of the poor, for instance, is different from that of the rest of the society. There are more homes without a father, there are less marriages, more early pregnancy and, if Kinsey's statistical findings can be used, markedly different attitudes toward sex. As a result of this, to take but one consequence of the fact, hundreds of thousands, and perhaps millions, of children in the other America never know stability and "normal" affection.

Or perhaps the policeman is an even better example. For the middle class, the police protect property, give directions, and help old ladies. For the urban poor, the police are those who arrest you. In almost any slum there is a vast conspiracy against the forces of law and order. If someone approaches asking for a person, no one there will have heard of him, even if he lives next door. The outsider is "cop," bill collector, investigator (and, in the Negro ghetto, most dramatically, he is "the Man"). . . .

There is, in short, a language of the poor,

a psychology of the poor, a world view of the poor. To be impoverished is to be an internal alien, to grow up in a culture that is radically different from the one that dominates the society. The poor can be described statistically; they can be analyzed as a group. But they need a novelist as well as a sociologist if we are to see them. They need an American Dickens to record the smell and texture and quality of their lives. The cycles and trends, the massive forces, must be seen as affecting persons who talk and think differently.

WEAKNESS, TOO, CORRUPTS

It has been often said that power corrupts. But it is perhaps equally important to realize that weakness, too, corrupts. Power corrupts the few, while weakness corrupts the many. Hatred, malice, rudeness, intolerance, and suspicion are the fruits of weakness. The resentment of the weak does not spring from any injustice done to them but from the sense of their inadequacy and impotence. We cannot win the weak by sharing our wealth with them. They feel our generosity as oppression. St. Vincent de Paul cautioned his disciples to deport themselves so that the poor "will forgive you the bread you give them." But this requires, in both giver and receiver, a vivid awareness of a God who is the father of all, and a living mastery of the religious idiom which we of this day do not, and perhaps cannot, have in full measure. Nor can we win the weak by sharing our hope, pride, or even hatred with them. We are too far ahead materially and too different in our historical experience to serve as an object of identification. Our healing gift to the weak is the capacity for self-help. We must learn how to impart to them the technical, social, and political skills which would enable them to get bread, human dignity, freedom, and strength by their own efforts.

My hunch is that in mastering the art or the technique of helping the weak to help themselves we shall solve some of the critical problems which confront us, not only in our foreign relations, but also in our domestic affairs.

—Eric Hoffer, *The Ordeal of Change* (N.Y.: Harper and Row, 1952), pp. 12–13.

CAN WE ADJUST TO ABUNDANCE?

[The alarming picture of creeping poverty given in the previous selection was a stimulus to the further study of the effects of automation on society and the economy. Here we offer an article, "Abundance—Threat or Promise?" by Robert Theobald in *The Nation*, May 11, 1963, as abstracted in *Current*, July 1963, pp. 55–58. The subject is too great to be adequately covered in this brief compass, so the student should consult Clarkson Potter's *Free Men and Free Markets*, excerpts of which appeared in Mr. Theobald's article, and the series of abstracts under "Automation and Unemployment" in *Current* for April 1964. These are only a few of the growing bibliography of studies of automation and its effects. One fact that emerges is that unionization is no cure; indeed, unions are rapidly becoming obsolescent. Another emergent fact is that there is an almost universal opinion among those who study the subject that capitalism has become so technologically efficient that (as Joseph Schumpeter warned) it is no longer socially practicable, and so a substitute must be found for the market economy. This does not mean the adoption of socialism, for its theory is no better fitted to abundance; it means that something entirely new must be found.]

Automation is providing us with a productive system of effectively unlimited capacity. We are going to be able to produce more than enough goods to insure a standard of living compatible with the maintenance of dignity for everybody. But the efficiency of automation is a double-edged sword: it not only provides abundance, but it does so with an increasingly smaller labor force. Indeed, that is often the definition of "more efficient."

In agriculture, for example, we already produce large-scale surpluses with less than 10 per cent of the labor force, and most economists expect that we will shortly need no more than 5 per cent. Donald Michael has prophesied in his pamphlet, *Cybernation—the Silent Revolution* [see *Current*, November 1961, page 49], that in twenty years most of the routine blue-collar and white-collar tasks will be automated.

The fact that we are able to produce more and more goods and services with fewer and fewer people means that we are creating a growing army of the *permanently unemployable* in the midst of plenty. This means, as Michael Harrington has argued in his book, *The Other America*, that some 40 to 50 million Americans have been cut off from the mainstream of affluent America.

Furthermore, since the permanently unemployable do not have much purchasing power, total effective demand is depressed at precisely the time when supply and potential supply are rapidly increasing. This leads to a situation in which supply consistently outstrips demand. *The growing gap between supply and demand* and *the increasing polarization of our economy into affluence and poverty* constitute the major socio-economic problems of our time, and they are uniquely problems of abundance.

What are the responses to these problems, and what effect do they have?

When there is more supply than demand, prices and the rate of profits drop. Traditionally, producers attempt to increase demand by advertising, to decrease supply by monopoly or oligopoly, and to reduce costs by making their operations more efficient. Since the gap between supply and demand has usually been a local condition within a total context of scarcity, these measures have usually succeeded, in some degree. If they did not, there was a *temporary* dip in the business cycle until demand caught up with supply.

Under conditions of abundance, however, the gap is *not* temporary, and is in fact made worse by the traditional responses. The attempt to restrict supply has led to production at less than capacity, which increases unemployment, further reduces demand, and thereby widens the gap. At the same time, the attempt to reduce costs leads to increased automation, which further increases both potential supply and unemployment.

The attempt to increase demand, on the other hand, has led to an unparalleled increase in expenditures on all aspects of consumer seduction—advertising, packaging, research and development. The implications of such increased expenditures are sobering, to say the least.

The responses of labor unions have also been less than successful. Traditionally they strive for higher wages, more fringe benefits, and shorter hours. The producer has until now usually been able to pass the higher labor costs on to the consumer. But the coming of abundance has drastically limited the ability of producers and sellers to set their own prices in order to maintain profit levels. The only possible action, then, is to automate vigorously to reduce labor costs, regardless of the effect on unemployment rates, and irrespective of the fact that the increased capacity thereby provided is not used because there is too much capacity (potential supply) already.

This revolution is only beginning. Up to now, many companies have been prepared to cooperate with the unions in keeping any diminution in the labor force which might follow an increase in automation to a level which could be absorbed by natural attrition—retirements, deaths, etc. When this was not possible, many employers have been prepared to adopt some plan to protect their workless employes.

Such approaches can protect those already within the labor force, but they do nothing about future labor forces and those who are presently unemployed. In fact, they insure a continuing decrease in the quantity of *new* jobs precisely at the time when the number of entrants to the labor force will be almost twice as large in the Sixties as it was in the Fifties, which means that it will be necessary to *triple* the number of job openings merely to prevent the unemployment situation from worsening.

As the threat of permanent unemployment has grown more ominous, the unions have increasingly demanded a shorter work week with no reduction in pay. They have argued that this is necessary in order to spread the available work.

Unfortunately, such a change would set up secondary effects which could largely prevent the increase in employment it was designed to achieve. The most important negative effect would result from the fact that such a change would increase the cost of labor per hour, and this would tilt the balance further in favor of investment in automation, thus leading to a more rapid elimination of the labor force, an increase in the gap between effective demand and potential supply, and a further polarization of the economy.

Government responses have also missed the central issue. Perhaps the keystones of the government's approach have been the social security and unemployment insurance provisions. But the major flaw in both those schemes is that they are based on *previous* employment and will be of no help to those who have never been and never will be able to find work within the abundant economy.

Retraining is also an extremely short-sighted remedy. The goal of providing suitable employment for all those who seek it is far from fulfilled even after retraining. The plain fact is that there are just not enough jobs. Many retrained workers, as Walter Reuther has pointed out, are just unemployed workers with new skills.

Proposed tax reductions, since they do not in fact progressively redistribute income to any significant degree, will not work because they will not increase demand among low-income people.

The other fiscal measure usually proposed is a lowering of the rate of interest. But although this would probably stimulate the *internal* rate of growth, it would weaken the *external* position of the United States with regard to the balance of payments problem, and would probably lead to a devaluation of the dollar. Reliance on a high interest rate as a defense against devaluation, however, biases income distribution in favor of those who have capital and against those who live on wages and salaries, and thus further polarizes the economy and aggravates the problem.

Finally, government's role as a prime mover in research and development encourages more rapid technological advance, thus widening the gap and worsening the very situation it is trying so desperately to improve. Nowhere is this more evident than in agriculture, where research and development programs have been so successful that the gap between supply and demand has widened enormously and worked against other government programs to restrict supply. The irrationalities and absurdities of the agricultural situation are increasingly typical of the whole economy, except for the differences between actual and potential supply.

Thus we have seen that the traditional responses, born under conditions of scarcity, have become self-defeating under the new conditions of abundance.

Unfortunately, America has never really considered the potentials opened up by abundance: it has simply continued to *assume* that there is no other possibility but continued growth in supply. At the same time, however, the government has accepted the responsibility to make sure there are jobs for all those who want them, on the assumption that employment is the *only* way in which people *could* and *should* receive an income. Government, unions, and producers are all committed to both increased production and full employment. They fail to recognize that the policies they adopt are contradictory and that the combination of all of them is destroying the socio-economic values of Western civilization.

It is the futile attempt to keep the economy growing fast enough to provide jobs for all that harnesses man to the juggernaut of scientific and technological change.

I propose the establishment of new principles, guaranteeing incomes for everyone, specifically designed to break the link between jobs and income. These principles must necessarily be implemented by the government as the sole body concerned with every member of society and with the adequate functioning of the total socio-economic system.

The need is clear: the principle of an *economic floor* under each individual must be established. It would carry with it no implications of personal inadequacy or undeserved income. It would merely be as extension of the present social security system to a world in which conventional job availability will steadily decline.

Furthermore, since automation can also be expected to invade many white-collar occupations of the middle class, an additional plan must be devised to maintain its standard of living, thereby insuring the maintenance of social standards, initiative, and drive which the middle class provides.

The guaranteed income due from government should be an absolute constitutional right. If this right could be withdrawn under any circumstances, government would have the power to deprive the individual not only of the pursuit of happiness, but also of liberty and even, effectively, of life itself. This absolute right to a due-income would be a new principle in jurisprudence.

Such a plan would increase demand by increasing the income of those outside the abundant economy. The increased demand would in turn call forth the potential supply and would therefore further stimulate the economy. It would tend to close the gap between supply and demand, and it would be an effective countermeasure against the polarization of the economy since it would redistribute the abundance among everyone.

Furthermore, besides liberating individuals from the chains of economic deprivation, it would minimize government intervention in the free market, although it would not eliminate government participation in the total socio-economic system. Thus the plan would be compatible, as present measures are not, with the basic goals of Western societies to insure that each individual obtains sufficient resources to allow him freedom in his choice of actions and that these resources be distributed without government interference in the market system. The only method of preserving both free men and free markets is to recognize the need to divorce the productive function from the distributive function.

Such a plan, since it would replace a mosaic of measures currently employed, would not require any large increases in revenue; it would merely be a rearrangement of present income provisions. Furthermore, the resultant stimulation to the economy would generate a higher gross national product and would therefore increase tax revenues.

Once incomes have been raised to adequate levels, the whirling dervish economy could stop. We would no longer have to encourage production in order to furnish market-supported jobs. We would not have to interfere with the market in order to provide reasonable incomes for such groups as the farmers. We would not have to stimulate sales artificially in the frantic effort to employ surplus productive capacity. The market mechanism would be allowed to resume its traditional role.

At the same time, the level of production could be determined by desired levels of consumption, rather than the reverse. In general, we would have the power to determine economic policy on the basis of our *social goals*, rather than continue to be forced into social actions because of *economic necessities*.

Individually, when man is no longer tied to the market, the right to an income will provide the means to an unparalleled freedom, although it will of course not determine the use of those means. Discovery of the proper uses of freedom will then become the chief task of the twentieth century.

We will have, we have already, the ability to be the modern Greeks, with mechanical slaves taking the place of human toil—once we can find a way to use abundance.

I believe that nonmarket incomes is the way, but I do not claim that the answers proposed here are final. There is a lack of information on the subject of abundance, and many aspects of its socio-economic implications remain unexamined.

What I am presenting is an agenda for discussion, a discussion which I believe is urgent. The coming of abundance provides all the potential for a new and better society, but it can also destroy us quickly unless we use it intelligently.

THOUGHTS ON THE PRESENT CRISIS

Civilization is perhaps approaching one of those long winters that overtake it from time to time. Romantic Christendom—picturesque, passionate, unhappy episode—may be coming to an end. Such a catastrophe would be no reason for despair.

—George Santayana

If you ask me—as a historian, let us say—whether a country in the state this country is in today, with no highly developed sense of national purpose, with overwhelming accent of life on personal comfort and amusement, with a dearth of public services and a surfeit of privately sold gadgetry, with a chaotic transportation system, with its great urban areas being gradually disintegrated by the headlong switch to motor transportation, with an educational system where quality has been extensively sacrificed to quantity, and with insufficient social discipline even to keep its major industries functioning without grievous interruptions—if you ask me whether such a country has, over the long run, a good chance of competing with a purposeful, serious, and disciplined society such as that of the Soviet Union, I must say that the answer is 'NO'!

—George F. Kennan

What worried me was the prospect of a skilled and highly competent population living off the fat of the land without a sense of usefulness and worth. There is nothing more explosive than a skilled population condemned to inaction. Such a population is likely to become a hotbed of extremism and intolerance, and be receptive to any proselytizing ideology, however absurd and vicious, which promises vast action.

—Eric Hoffer

IS CRIME A PROOF OF NATIONAL DECADENCE?

[Max Lerner, in *America As a Civilization* (N.Y.: Simon and Schuster, 1957,) has probed American character and society in depth. His examination of crime and other social disorders leads to some rather startling conclusions. See pages 663–666.]

Americans are concerned and baffled about these phases of their society. Having found that many of their problems yield to technology and organization, they feel ordinarily that their way of life ought to move toward purpose and contain solutions. Yet in the norm-breaking and normless behavior we have discussed they find a spectacle to shake their belief in their own institutions. They see the social breakdowns as symptoms of the decadence and disintegration of American society as a whole. Things "fly apart at the center," reversing what Americans regard as the natural order: children grow up to become criminals, gangsters, gamblers, the face of innocence takes on the hideous mask of the narcotics addict, families are broken up by divorce, "nice girls" engage in promiscuous sex or even become professional prostitutes, the image of the clean-cut young businessman turns into that of the uncontrolled alcoholic or the compulsive homosexual, respectable citizens are revealed as white-collar criminals, and the basic activities of life are turned into rackets. Thus the Americans find the most cherished symbols of their society turned topsy-turvy.

Yet does disorganization always violate the essential spirit of the culture? Does it always mean the abnormal, pathological, anticultural? Actually the departure from norms may shed extraordinary light on the inner nature of the culture. In trying to explain why Americans are themselves deeply drawn to the gangster films which they know to be distortions of their urban life, one notes that a gangster is an American "cultural hero" in whom Americans recognize a symbol of the energy of their culture. Or take American criminologists, who stress the paradox of the "rationality" of the habitual criminal, in the sense that given his twisted antisocial premises, his acts flow logically from them. What they often ignore is a different kind of rationality: that the criminal takes seriously the barely concealed premises of the culture itself. He sees easy money being made and predacity practiced, knows that the rules are constantly broken, knows that there is an internal violence in the act of exploiting the market and ravishing the environment.

Thus the forms of American disorganization arise from the more naked drives within the culture itself, with the workaday masks stripped away that have hidden the sadism and ugliness which are part of the human condition and are to be found in every culture.

In every society forces are generated that are harmful to its functioning and in the end destroy it. It would be strange if this were not happening in America as well. But those who fix upon crime and rackets, divorce, prostitution, and alcoholism as proofs of American decadence and degeneration may be fixing upon the wrong symptoms of the wrong disease. Most of the phases of social pathology I have listed are the extreme applications of principles which, in lesser degree, may be healthy. The delinquent and the criminal, so greatly feared by Americans, are not so dangerous to the social fabric as they seem to be. The point about the gangster, the racketeer, and the syndicate operator—even the housebreaker and the burglar—is not that they scorn property but that they value it enough to be ruthless in seeking short cuts for making it their own. The adolescent delinquent, in turn, in the act of rebelling against family or school or community, may be seeking the cherishing love upon which the family and other primary groups must be based.

The principles by which American culture lives are those of freedom and acquisition, and —where the two meet—the freedom of acquisition. There are always a number of people who feel themselves left out of the operation of these principles, or who are too much in a hurry to wait, or who feel resentful because others seem to start with an unfair set of principles, and who therefore seek some equalizer. Since they feel at a strategic disadvantage in the competition of life, they feel justified in ignoring the usual inhibitions and in tearing down the accepted cement of social relations. Because they use a distorted version of the cultural energies to destroy social bonds and rip apart the cohesiveness of the society, they in effect pit the culture against the society.

One may deplore these dislocating energies, but they would seem to be an inherent part of a society in which the pace of life is set by freedom, competitiveness, and acquisitiveness, and they are part of the price the society pays for those informing principles. A society less free and less dynamic—one of tradition and status, or one of totally state-directed power— may escape some of these dislocations but be beset by others. The whole impulse of American culture is to raise hopes and claims in the individual and spur him on to fulfill the hopes and nail down the claims. At the same time it is too young a society to have developed the kind of inner discipline which—let us say, in England—can serve to inhibit the full sway of the impulse.

Take, for example, the extreme case of the narcotics "pusher," who is even willing to corrupt children and develop the narcotics habit in them in order to make customers for his product. He represents the principle of creating a market, inherent in the market economy. In the mid-1950s he was thriving in America mainly because the severely repressive Federal narcotics laws, with constant "crackdowns" by enforcement officials, kept increasing the danger of narcotics distribution and therefore the price and profits—without reaching at all the terrible sense of isolation which underlies the use of narcotics. But he is also an example of the desensitized man in whom the principle has run wild, like cells in a cancerous growth. Or consider the case of the racketeer, who on principle recoils from the notion of earning his bread by the sweat of his brow, but who invests great resourcefulness in applying *force majeure* at the most vulnerable points of business enterprise.

The racketeer is likely to come up from the slums, reaching for quick affluence by breaking the windows of the mansion of American success rather than by entering at the door. There are studies showing how the prominence of Jews, Irish, and Italians in urban crime has swung from one immigrant group to another as each has flooded into the United States, sought to orient itself in American society, and become assimilated to it. At the beginning they are dislocated from their old culture but have not absorbed anything of the new culture except its cruder aspects; they have demons within them to assert themselves in a challenging new environment, they have few inhibiting fences around them, and they are in a hurry. The violence with which intense slum youngsters imitate the values of the culture, even while distorting them, may be seen as their own form of flattery. What they do is legally and morally wrong, but instead of being a sign of the decay of American life it may be taken almost as a sign of its vitality.

One of the clues is the dynamism of rapid social change. Racketeering crops up mostly in the areas of new business enterprise which have not yet been reduced to order or become subject to tradition, and where economic change moves more rapidly. The most serious outcroppings of violence and crime come also at the times of greatest social change, involving a rapid migration of population, the shifting of industries, the contact and clash of subcultures, the improvement of living standards, and the opening of new perspectives for which people are not yet prepared.

As a case in point we may take the known fact of the prevalence of reefer-and-dope addiction in Negro areas. This is usually explained in terms of poverty, slum living, and broken families, yet it would be easy to show the lack of drug addiction among other ethnic groups where the same conditions apply. One may guess that the rapid movement of Negroes from a depressed status to the improved status and partial freedoms of today, with new jobs and new living standards, has led also to the breaking down of old goals, while the new ones are still vague and seem inaccessible. I have noted in an earlier section that the passion for equality feeds on itself, setting the goals ever higher and making the distance from them more embittering. Drug addiction thus becomes one of the expressions of the isolation and normlessness that are the by-product of social advance, achieved under nerve-wracking stress, bitterly paid for. Where rigid status is being broken up and class lines shifting, and where a sense of social hope persists, social disorders are the tribute which the unbalanced individual pays to the naked premises of the culture.

Their real danger lies not in the pathology of cultural values but in their denial. The delinquencies and moral breakdowns which flow from the sense that only power counts and all American life is a racket are less dangerous than those which flow from the sense that nothing counts—not even the rackets. The breakdowns of family life or of sexual morality, and the crimes against property, by threatening the foundations of the American social structure, evoke counterforces in turn which solidify the social structure in its own defense. A frontal attack tends to be met by a defense in depth. Yet the disorganization which flows from the desensitizing of men, and from a lack of belief in any values, is a threat to the idea of social structure itself.

21

OLD PROBLEMS AND NEW DEFINITIONS

INTRODUCTION

Practically nothing has remained untouched by the winds of change as we enter the last third of the twentieth century, and in this chapter we can glance at only a few of the new ways of thinking. New concepts in philosophy and physics have displaced the old, even though we use many of the old shibboleths. This new recognition of purposiveness has illuminated the role of process—and here Americans should be at home, for we have long represented America as process.

On the other hand, as always, there are objections to the triumph of the new, and all over the nation individuals and groups are seeking to restore the old ways or to find new ones which satisfy the human craving for an absolute. The various movements are diverse not only from each other but are divided by internal contradictions. These emergent forces may separate into left and right, or into intellectuals and anti-intellectuals, but it is possible to characterize at least some of them as rising out of the same basic discontent with the new day. At times they seem to reject the pragmatic democrat's method of compromise and demand the immediate imposition of their favorite moral order.

One side, imbued with absolute moral certainty, denounces the affluent life and champions a new form of isolation which denies the country's postwar role of containing communism and demands that Americans confine themselves to perfecting democracy at home. On the other extreme, and equally imbued with moral certainty, is a demand that the United States wash out the welfare state at home, find a quick nuclear cure for evil abroad, and return to its pristine purity and simplicity.

Morality is the key word, and in its defense anything goes, even violence. Any dissent is the essence of immorality. There is here an alarming resemblance to the preachments of Lenin and Joseph McCarthy that since their fight is morality personified it does not need to be carried on in conformity to the moral code: it has become in itself the moral code. The left, at least, denounces the "hypocrisy" of halfway reform movements such as the New Deal, and scoffs at the old belief that hypocrisy is a way station in the progress from vice to virtue. If we can believe their most articulate spokesmen—and this is by no means certain—both the New Left and the Rampageous Right would seem to be rejections of the twentieth century just as antebellum Southernism was a rejection of the nineteenth.

However that may be, no age has ever been able to turn back the clock to the "time that never was." The Rampageous Right—and this does not mean conservatism—is mindless, and perhaps all we can do is wait for it to pass away. As for the New Left, it also seems mindless, but perhaps its self-appointed spokesmen are doing it an injustice. Perhaps what it is groping for is a new phase of the familiar historical process which brings synthesis on a higher plane.

THE PURPOSEFUL UNIVERSE

[It has become a truism that the world that has been unfolded since the fission of the atom in 1938 would be unrecognizable to a scientist—let alone the man in the street—of 1900. This is true not only of physics, biology, meteorology, and perhaps other sciences which only specialists could name, but, most astounding of all, philosophy's view of the universe. Here we reprint Peter F. Drucker's "The New Philosophy Comes to Life," from *Harper's Magazine*, August 1957, pp. 36–40.]

It is indeed frightening how fast the obvious of yesteryear is turning incomprehensible. An intelligent and well-educated man of the first "modern" generation—that of Newton, Hobbes, and Locke—might still have been able to understand and to make himself understood up to World War II. But it is unlikely that he could still communicate with the world of today, only fifteen years later. . . .

But what matters most for us—the first "post-modern" generation—is the change in fundamentals. We still profess and teach the world view of the past three hundred years. But we no longer see it. We have as yet no name for our new way of looking at things— no tools, no method. But a world view comes first; it is the foundation for philosophical terms and technical vocabulary. And that new foundation is something we have acquired, all of a sudden, within the past fifteen or twenty years.

The world view of the past three hundred years can perhaps be summed up in a word as

"Cartesian." Few professional philosophers during these years have followed René Descartes, the early seventeenth-century Frenchman, in answering the major problems of systematic philosophy. Yet the modern age has taken its important cues from him. More than Galileo or Calvin, Hobbes, Locke, or Rousseau, far more even than Newton, Descartes influenced the minds of three centuries—what problems would appear important or even relevant, what would be the scope of men's vision, their assumptions about themselves and their universe, and above all, their concept of what was rational and plausible.

His was a twofold contribution. First he gave to the modern world its basic axiom about the intelligibility of the universe. The best known formulation is that in which the Académie Française, a generation after Descartes' death, defined "science" as "the certain and evident knowledge of things by their causes." Expressed less elegantly and less subtly, this says that "the whole is the sum of its parts"— the oversimplification that might be made by an ordinary man who is neither scientist nor philosopher.

Second, Descartes provided the method to make his axiom effective in organizing knowledge. Whatever the mathematical significance of his "Analytical Geometry," it established the new concept of a world unified in simple quantitative relations that could deal efficiently with motion and change, the flow of time, and even the invisible. The perfecting of this mathematics, and its widespread adoption as a universal symbolic language, made it possible for Lord Kelvin two hundred years later to re-assert the principles of Cartesianism by saying, "I know what I can measure."

The statement that the whole is equal to the sum of its parts also implies that the whole is determined by its parts, that the behavior of the whole is caused by the motion of the parts, and that there is no such thing as wholeness apart from the different sums, structures, and relationships of the parts. These statements are likely to sound obvious today since they have been taken for granted for so long, even though they were radical innovations when first propounded. But though most of us still respond to the familiarity of these assertions, there are no longer many scientists who would accept the definition of the Académie Française—at least not for what they call "science" in their own field. Virtually every one of our disciplines now relies on conceptions which are incompatible with the Cartesian axiom, and with the world view we once derived from it.

Biology shows this dramatically. Its tremendous development in the past fifty years has resulted directly from our applying the strict "Cartesian" methods to the study of the living organism. But the more "scientific" the biologist has become, the more he has tended to talk in terms such as "immunity" and "metabolism," "ecology" and "syndrome," "homeostasis" and "pattern"—each of them essentially an aesthetic term describing not so much a property of matter or quantity as of a harmonious order.

The psychologist talks about "*Gestalt*," "ego," "personality," or "behavior"—terms that could hardly be found in serious works before 1910. The social sciences talk about "culture," about "integration," or about the "informal group." The aesthetician talks about "form." These are all concepts of pattern or configuration. Whether one searches for the "drives in a personality, the complex of chemical, electrical, and mechanical actions in a metabolism, the specific rites and customs in a culture, or the particular colors, and shapes in a nonobjective painting—all can be understood, explained, or even identified only from their place in a pattern.

Similarly, we have a pattern at the center of our economic life, the business enterprise. "Automation" is merely an ugly word to describe as an entity a new view of the process of production. "Management" is a similar term. In government we talk about "administration" or "political process"; the economist talks about "national income," "productivity," or "economic growth" much as the theologian talks about "existence." Even the physical sciences and engineering, the most Cartesian of all our disciplines, talk about "systems" or—the most non-Cartesian term of all—about "quanta" in which, with one measurement, are expressed mass and energy, time and distance, all absorbed into a single entity.

The most striking change is perhaps to be found in our approach to the study of speech and language. Despite the anguished pleas of teachers and parents, we talk less and less about "grammar"—the study of *parts* of speech—and more and more about "communication." It is the *whole* of speech, including not only the words left unsaid but the atmosphere in which words are said and heard, that "communicates." One must not only know the whole of the "message," one must also be able to relate it to the pattern of behavior, personality, situation, and even culture with which it is surrounded.

All these terms are brand-new. Not one of them had any scientific standing fifty years ago in the vocabulary of scholars and scientists. And all of them are *qualitative*. Quantity does not characterize them; a "culture" is not defined by the number of people who belong to it, nor is a "business enterprise" defined by its size. Quantitative change matters in these configurations only when it becomes qualitative—when, in the words of the old Greek riddle, the grains of sand have become a sand-pile. This is not a continuous but a discontinuous event, a sudden jump over a qualitative threshold at which sounds turn into recognizable melody, words and motions into behavior, procedures into a management philosophy, or the atom of one element into that of another. And, finally, none of these configurations as such is measurable or capable of being expressed—except in the most distorted manner—through the traditional symbols of quantitative relationship.

None of these new concepts, let me emphasize, conforms to the axiom that the whole is the result of its parts. On the contrary, all conform to a new, and by no means as yet axiomatic, assertion that the parts exist in contemplation of, if not for the sake of, the whole.

Moreover, none of these new concepts has any causality to it. Einstein was thoroughly "modern" in saying that he could not accept the view that the Lord plays dice with the universe. But what Einstein was criticizing was the inability of the physicists—including himself—to visualize any other kind of order except causality; that is, our inability to free ourselves from our Cartesian blinders. Underlying the new ideas, including those of modern physics, is a unifying order, but it is not causality; it is purpose.

Each of these new concepts I have mentioned expresses a purposeful unit. One might even say, as a general "modern" principle, that the elements (for we no longer really talk of "parts") will be found to arrange themselves so as to serve the purpose of the whole. This, for instance, is the assumption that underlies the biologist's attempt to study and to understand organs and cells. It is this "arrangement in contemplation of the purpose of the whole" that we mean today when we speak of "order."

This universe of ours is again a universe ruled by purpose, as was the one that the Cartesian world view displaced three hundred years ago. But our idea of "purpose" is a very different one from that of the Middle Ages or Renaissance. Theirs lay outside of the material, social, and psychological universe, if not entirely outside of anything Man himself could be, could do, or could see. Our "purpose," by sharp contrast, is in the configurations themselves; it is not metaphysical but physical; it is not the purpose *of* the universe, but the purpose *in* the universe.

I read the other day a piece by a leading physicist in which he talked about the "characteristics of sub-atomic particles." A slip of the pen, to be sure; but a revealing one. Only a generation ago it would not have been possible for a physicist, no matter how slipshod, to write of anything but the "properties" of matter. For atomic particles to have "characteristics," the atom—if not matter and energy themselves—must have a "character"; and that means that matter must have a purposeful order within itself.

The new world view, in addition, involves the idea of *process*. Each of the new concepts involves growth, development, dynamism—and these are irreversible, whereas events in the Cartesian universe were as reversible as the symbols on either side of an equation. Never, except in fairy tales, does the grown man become a boy again, nor does lead change back to uranium, nor does a business enterprise return to family partnership. All these changes are irreversible because the process changes its own character; it is, in other words, self-generated change.

Only seventy-five years ago the last remnant of pre-Cartesian thinking, the idea of "spontaneous generation" of living beings, was finally laid to rest by Louis Pasteur. Now it comes back to us in the researches of biologists who look for clues to the origin of life in the laboratory "creation" of amino-acids. Now respectable mathematical physicists seriously talk about something even more grossly shocking to the Cartesian view: a theory of constant and spontaneous self-generation of matter in the form of new stars and new galaxies. And a leading biochemist, Sir Macfarlane Burnet, the Australian pioneer of virus research, recently defined a virus, as "not an individual organism in the ordinary sense of the term but something that could almost be called a stream of biological pattern."

In this new emphasis on "process" may well lie the greatest of all the departures of the new world view. For the Cartesian world was not only a mechanical one, in which all events were finitely determined; it was essentially a static one. Inertia, in the strict meaning of classical mechanics, was the assumed norm. It had been an accepted doctrine since Aristotle that the Unchangeable and Unchanging alone was real and alone was perfect. On this one point Descartes, otherwise so daring an innovator, was the strictest of traditionalists.

In fact it was the great achievement of the Cartesian view to make this traditional axiom usable. Motion so obviously exists; yet on the basis of inertia it cannot be explained and measured—as was first pointed out two thousand years ago in the famous "paradoxes" of Zeno, such as that of Achilles and the tortoise. Only "calculus"—together with Descartes' Analytical Geometry—could find a way out of the impass between the idea of inertia and the experience of motion. This it did by a most ingenious trick: by explaining and measuring motion as though it consisted of an infinite number of infinitely small but perfectly static "stills."

It is far from true that this "solved" Zeno's paradox, as the textbooks assert. But it could do what no one before had been able to do—assert the axiom of inertia and yet handle motion with growing assurance—and it could point to its success in actually analyzing, predicting, and controlling physical motion. Today, however, we are becoming all-too-painfully aware that the "solution" is inapplicable to true motion—that is, to growth and development, whether biological or economic, which cannot be explained away as a kind of optical illusion. We assume—and are increasingly aware that we assume—that growth, change, and development are the normal and the real, and that their absence is the abnormal—the imperfect, the decaying, and the dead.

Within the past twenty or thirty years these new concepts have become the reality of our work and world. They are "obvious" to us. Yet, though we take them increasingly for granted, we do not fully understand them. Though we talk glibly of "configuration," "purpose," and "process," we do not yet know what these terms express. We have abandoned the Cartesian world view; but we have not developed, so far, a new tool box of methods or a new axiom of meaning and inquiry. We have certainly not yet produced a new Descartes. As a result we are in an intellectual and artistic crisis.

True, there is a rapidly growing literature of the "new" philosophy. Though anticipations of it can be found in numerous thinkers—for example, in Whitehead, Bergson, Goethe, Leonardo, or Aristotle—the earliest to expound the new vision in our time was probably that astounding South African, Jan Christiaan Smuts, with his philosophy of "holism" twenty-five or thirty years ago. There are pronounced reflections of it in the work of two physicists, Lancelot Law Whyte, with *The Next Development in Man*, and Erwin Schroedinger, with his *What is Life?*, and one of its latest and most persuasive expressions is provided by the distinguished economist, Kenneth Boulding, in a small book called *The Image*. It is hardly an accident, moreover, that one of the contemporary philosophers who sells best in paperback editions is the late Ernst Cassirer; his books—though anything but "popularly" written; in fact, a veritable thicket of Teutonic abstractions—deal with patterns, configurations, and symbols of order as essential elements in Man's experience.

But the people working in a specific discipline are still in difficult straits. They see the new ideas everywhere around them; indeed, they often see little else. But whenever they want to do rigorous work, all they have to work with are methods based on the old world view, methods which are quite inappropriate to the new.

In the social sciences this shows itself in the glaring discrepancy between our talk of "culture," "personality," or "behavior" and our inability to produce much more than vast collections of empirical data about particular—and therefore largely meaningless—manifestations. In a discipline that is much closer to my own daily interest, the study of management, the situation is equally frustrating. The discipline only exists because we have a new conception of the business enterprise. All of us know and stress continually that the really important things are process-characteristics, such as the

"climate" of an organization, the development of people in it, or the planning of its features and purposes. But whenever we try to be "scientific," we are thrown back on mechanistic and static methods, such as work measurement of individual operations or, at best, organization rules and definitions. Or take the physicists: the more they discover about the various subatomic particles of matter, the more confused, complicated, and inconsistent become their general theories of the nature of matter, energy, and time.

As a result, the very disciplines that are advancing the fastest, in which therefore there is the most to learn, are rapidly becoming unteachable. There is no doubt that medicine, for instance, has made giant strides in this generation. But virtually every experienced teacher of medicine I know wonders whether the young medical-school graduate of today—the very one who gets "the best medical education the world has to offer"—is as well taught and as well prepared as his much more ignorant predecessor of thirty years ago. The reason is simple. Medical schools are still organized around the idea of disciplines as static bundles of knowledge. But, where a hundred years ago there were at best six or seven such "bundles," there are perhaps fifty today. Each has become in its own right a full-blown "science" which takes a lifetime to master—even to acquire a "smattering of ignorance" in any one of them takes more than the five years of medical training.

In addition we suffer the affliction, perhaps inevitable in a time of philosophical transition, of a maddening confusion of tongues among the various disciplines, and the consequent cheapening and erosion of language and style. Each discipline has its own language, its own terms, its own increasingly esoteric symbols. And whenever we try to re-establish unity all we can do is fall back on the outworn language of the Cartesian world which originally brought disunity upon us.

All of this, it should be firmly said, is not merely the "natural" result of advancing knowledge, as some academicians assert. The "natural" result should be, as it has always been, greater simplicity—greater ease of learning and teaching. If our knowledge becomes constantly more specialized, more complicated, rather than more general, then something essential is lacking—namely, a philosophical synthesis appropriate to the world we actually inhabit.

Yet we now can—as we could not a decade or two ago—foresee what shape the new integration will take, when and if it comes. We can see, first of all, what it will not be. The way out is not to repudiate the Cartesian world view but to overcome and encompass it. Modern physics may have given us cause to rediscover Aristotle on a new level of understanding, but it has not made us more appreciative of astrology. Modern biology and operations research have made us more conscious of the need to measure quality, value, and judgment; they have not made us repudiate strict proof, or abandon the quest for objective measurement.

Another negative prediction: in the coming synthesis, the Cartesian dualism between the universe of matter and the universe of mind will not be retained. This was certainly the most potent, as it was the most central, element in Descartes' own system; and for three hundred years it has paralyzed philosophy—if not all our thinking—by widening the split between "idealist" and "materialist," so that each has built ever-higher fences around his own little plot of reality. If there ever was a useful distinction here, it ceased to be meaningful the day the first experimenter discovered that by the very act of observing phenomena he affected them.

Today our task is to understand patterns of biological, social, or physical order in which mind and matter become meaningful precisely because they are reflections of a greater unity.

We can also say something affirmative. We need a discipline rather than a vision, a strict discipline of qualitative and irrevocable changes such as development, growth, or decay, and methods for anticipating such changes. We need a discipline, in other words, that explains events and phenomena in terms of their direction and future state rather than in terms of cause—a "calculus of potential," you might say, rather than one of "probability." We need a philosophy of purpose; a logic of quality, and ways of measuring qualitative change; and a methodology of potential and opportunity, of "turning points" and "critical factors," of risk and uncertainty, of constants and variations, "jump" and continuity. We need a dialectic of polarity, one in which unity and diversity are defined as simultaneous and necessary poles of the same essence.

This may sound like a big order, and one we are as yet far from able to fill. Yet we may have the new synthesis more nearly within our grasp than we think. In philosophy and science—perhaps even more in art—a "problem" begins to be solved the moment it can be defined, the moment the right questions are being asked, the moment the specifications are known which the answers must satisfy, the moment we know what we are looking for.

And that, in one after another of the areas of modern knowledge, we already know.

VIEWS OF AMERICA

America is a tune. It must be sung together.

—Gerald Stanley Lee, *Crowds*

What America has done is to change the entire concept of culture, the values of civilization. The new American culture is not Chartres or Versailles, but the organization of talent. The Americans organize intelligence so that it creates. They have an industrial and scientific strategy. That's real culture.

—Jean-Jacques Servan-Schreiber, Editor of *L'Express*,
Paris, in *Le Défi Américain* (1967)

The psychological error lay in our conception of the American as a self-important boaster, a shoddy manufacturer of shoddy goods and an unscrupulous over-reacher in business, whose word could not be trusted. Such Americans there certainly were, but there is the other type of American, who is conspicuously efficient in all industrial and technical undertakings, the American who builds the highest houses, produces most motor-cars, attains record economic output, who built the Panama Canal and whose spirit of enterprise knows no bounds.

—Ewald Hermann August Banse, *Germany Prepares for War* (1934)

Down the Hatch

As the American people become more prosperous, so they become more upset. We deduce this from U.S. Government statistics which show that while they made a great deal more money in 1951 than they made in the previous year, they also took a great deal more medicine—49 per cent more, to be exact. Their consumption of aspirin rose from 11 million pounds to 13 million; and their consumption of barbiturates from 639,000 pounds to 789,000.

This confirms the commonest European criticism of the New World. The Americans are rich, yes; but they do not know how to live. Their wealth only gives them headaches, their success only brings them insomnia. What the European critics fail to understand is that the Americans themselves clearly recognize, and cheerfully accept, this state of affairs. They would rather toss and turn on silk than sleep soundly on flannelette; they would rather have migraine in a custom-built convertible than be at ease in a street car. As between the curse of wealth and the blessings of poverty, the Americans unanimously and enthusiastically choose the former. (So, it might be noted, do the large number of Europeans who have migrated, or would dearly love to migrate, to the Land of Freedom, Plenty and Duodenal Ulcers.)

Whether the Americans or the Europeans are right, is something for sages to argue. We merely note that the great American headache has made a substantial contribution to freedom's cause in the last generation or so; and that if Western Europe is eating regularly, much of the credit belongs with men in Minneapolis and Mobile who haven't slept a wink for three nights hand-running. The Americans are not a happy people, to be sure; but as one of their own philosophers has remarked, what use is happiness? You can't buy money with it.

—*Toronto Globe and Mail*, August 7, 1952

AMERICA IS PROCESS

[John A. Kouwenhoven, whose description of the American vernacular we used in Volume I, wrote an article, "What's American about America," in *Harper's Magazine*, 213: 25–33 (July 1956), in which he examined a dozen undoubted American phenomena and looked for their common quality.]

For all the contrarieties, there remains something which I think we all feel to be distinctively American, some quality or characteristic underlying the polarities which . . . makes the American way of doing things differ more from any other nation's way than the ways of any two other Western nations differ from each other.

I am aware of the risks in generalizing. And yet it would be silly, I am convinced, to assert that there are not certain things which are more American than others. Take the New York City skyline, for example—that ragged man-made Sierra at the eastern edge of the continent. Clearly, in the minds of immigrants and returning travelers, in the iconography of the ad-men who use it as a backdrop for the bourbon and airplane luggage they are selling, in the eyes of poets and of military strategists, it is one of the prime American symbols.

Let me start, then, with the Manhattan skyline and list a few things which occur to me as distinctively American. Then, when we have the list, let us see what, if anything, these things have in common. Here are a dozen items to consider:

1. The Manhattan skyline
2. The gridiron town plan
3. The skyscraper
4. The Model-T Ford
5. Jazz
6. The Constitution
7. Mark Twain's writing
8. Whitman's *Leaves of Grass*
9. Comic strips
10. Soap operas
11. Assembly-line production
12. Chewing gum

Here we have a round dozen artifacts which are, it seems to me, recognizably American, not likely to have been produced elsewhere. . . .

Those engaged in discovering America often begin by discovering the Manhattan skyline, and here as well as elsewhere they discover apparently irreconcilable opposites. They notice at once that it doesn't make any sense, in human or aesthetic terms. It is the product of insane politics, greed, competitive ostentation, megalomania, the worship of false gods. Its products, in turn, are traffic jams, bad ventilation, noise, and all the other ills that metropolitan flesh is heir to. And the net result is, illogically enough, one of the most exaltedly beautiful things man has ever made.

Perhaps this paradoxical result will be less bewildering if we look for a moment at the formal and structural principles which are involved in the skyline. It may be helpful to consider the skyline as we might consider a lyric poem, or a novel, if we were trying to analyze its aesthetic quality.

Looked at in this way, it is clear that the total effect which we call "the Manhattan skyline" is made up of almost innumerable buildings, each in competition (for height, or glamor, or efficiency, or respectability) with all of the others. Each goes its own way, as it were, in a carnival of rugged architectural individualism. And yet—as witness the universal feeling of exaltation and aspiration which the skyline as a whole evokes—out of this irrational, unplanned, and often infuriating chaos, an unforeseen unity has evolved. No building ever built in New York was placed where it was, or shaped as it was, because it would contribute to the aesthetic effect of the skyline—lifting it here, giving it mass there, or lending a needed emphasis. Each was built, all those now under construction are being built, with no thought for their subordination to any over-all effect.

What, then, makes possible the fluid and everchanging unity which does, in fact, exist? Quite simply, there are two things, both simple in themselves, which do the job. If they were not simple, they would not work; but they are, and they do.

One is the gridiron pattern of the city's streets—the same basic pattern which accounts for Denver, Houston, Little Rock, Birmingham, and almost any American town you can name, and the same pattern which, in the form of square townships, sections, and quarter sections, was imposed by the Ordinance of 1785 on an almost continental scale. . . . It is this simple gridiron street pattern which, horizontally, controls the spacing and arrangement of the rectangular shafts which go to make up the skyline.

The other thing which holds the skyline's diversity together is the structural principle of the skyscraper. When we think of individual buildings, we tend to think of details of texture, color, and form, of surface ornamentation or the lack of it. But as elements in Manhattan's skyline, these things are of little consequence. What matters there is the vertical thrust, the motion upward; and that is the product of cage or skeleton, construction in steel—a system of construction which is, in effect, merely a three-dimensional variant of the gridiron street plan, extending vertically instead of horizontally.

The aesthetics of cage, or skeleton, construction have never been fully analyzed, nor am I equipped to analyze them. But as a lay observer, I am struck by fundamental differences between the effect created by height in the RCA building at Radio City, for example, and the effect created by height in Chartres cathedral or in Giotto's campanile. In both the latter (as in all the great architecture of the past) proportion and symmetry, the relation of height to width, are constituent to the effect. One can say of a Gothic cathedral, this tower is too high; of a Romanesque dome, this is top-heavy.

But the logic of cage construction requires no such climax. It has less to do with the inner logic of masonry forms than with that of the old Globe-Wernicke sectional bookcase, whose interchangeable units (with glass-flap fronts) anticipated by fifty years the modular unit systems of so-called modern furniture. Those bookcases were advertised in the 'nineties as "always complete but never finished"—a phrase which could with equal propriety have been applied to the Model-T Ford. Many of us remember with affection that admirably simple mechanism, forever susceptible to added gadgets or improved parts, each of which was interchangeable with what you already had.

Here, then, are the two things which serve to tie together the otherwise irrelevant components of the Manhattan skyline: the gridiron ground plan and the three-dimensional vertical grid of steel cage construction. And both of these are closely related to one another. Both are composed of simple and infinitely repeatable units.

It was the French architect, Le Corbusier, who described New York's architecture as "hot jazz in stone and steel." At first glance this may sound as if it were merely a slick updating of Schelling's "Architecture . . . is frozen music," but it is more than that if one thinks in terms of the structural principles we have been discussing and the structural principles of jazz.

Let me begin by making clear that I am using the term jazz in its broadest significant application. . . . There is no definition of jazz, academic or otherwise, which does not acknowledge that its essential ingredient is a particular kind of rhythm. Improvisation is also frequently mentioned as an essential; but even if it were true that jazz always involves improvisation, that would not distinguish it from a good deal of Western European music of the past. It is the distinctive rhythm which differentiates all types of jazz from all other music and which gives to all of its types a basic family resemblance.

It is not easy to define that distinctive rhythm. Winthrop Sargeant has described it as the product of two superimposed devices: syncopation and polyrhythm, both of which have the effect of constantly upsetting rhythmical expectations. André Hodeir, in his recent analysis of *Jazz: Its Evolution and Essence*, speaks of "an unending alternation" of syncopations and of notes played *on* the beat, which "gives rise to a kind of expectation that is one of jazz's subtlest effects."

As you can readily hear, if you listen to any jazz performance . . . the rhythmical effect depends upon there being a clearly defined basic rhythmic pattern which enforces the expectations which are to be upset. That basic pattern is the 4/4 or 2/4 beat which underlies all jazz. Hence the importance of the percussive instruments in jazz: the drums, the guitar or banjo, the bull fiddle, the piano. Hence too the insistent thump, thump, thump, thump which is so boring when you only half-hear jazz—either because you are too far away, across the lake or in the next room, or simply because you will not listen attentively. But hence also the delight, the subtle effects, which good jazz provides as the melodic phrases evade, anticipate, and return to, and then again evade the steady basic four-beat pulse which persists, implicitly or explicitly, throughout the performance.

In other words, the structure of a jazz performance is, like that of the New York skyline, a tension of cross-purposes. In jazz at its characteristic best, each player seems to be—and has the sense of being—on his own. Each goes his own way, inventing rhythmic and melodic patterns which, superficially, seem to have as little relevance to one another as the United Nations

building does to the Empire State. And yet the outcome is a dazzlingly precise creative unity.

In jazz that unity of effect is, of course, the result of the very thing which each of the players is flouting: namely, the basic 4/4 beat—that simple rhythmic gridiron of identical and infinitely extendible units which holds the performance together. As Louis Armstrong once wrote, you would expect that if every man in a band "had his own way and could play as he wanted, all you would get would be a lot of jumbled up, crazy noise." But, as he goes on to say, that does not happen, because the players know "by ear and sheer musical instinct" just when to leave the underlying pattern and when to get back on it.

What it adds up to, as I have argued elsewhere, is that jazz is the first art form to give full expression to Emerson's ideal of a union which is perfect only "when all the uniters are isolated." That Emerson's ideal is deeply rooted in our national experience need not be argued. Frederick Jackson Turner quotes a letter written by a frontier settler to friends back East, which in simple, unself-conscious words expresses the same reconciling of opposites. "It is a universal rule here," the frontiersman wrote, "to help one another, each one keeping an eye single to his own business."

One need only remember that the Constitution itself, by providing for a federation of separate units, became the infinitely extendible framework for the process of reconciling liberty and unity over vast areas and conflicting interests. Its seven brief articles, providing for checks and balances between interests, classes, and branches of the government establish, in effect, the underlying beat which gives momentum and direction to a political process which Richard Hofstadter has called "a harmonious system of mutual frustration"—a description which fits a jazz performance as well as it fits our politics.

The aesthetic effects of jazz, as Winthrop Sargeant long ago suggested, have as little to do with symmetry and proportion as have those of a skyscraper. Like the skyscraper, a jazz performance does not build to an organically required climax; it can simply cease. The "piece" which the musicians are playing may, and often does, have a rudimentary Aristotelian pattern of beginning, middle, and end; but jazz performance need not. In traditional Western European music, themes are developed. In jazz they are toyed with and dismantled. There is no inherent reason why the jazz performance should not continue for another 12 to 16 or 24 or 32 measures (for these are the rhythmic cages which in jazz correspond to the cages of a steel skeleton in architecture). As in the skyscraper, the aesthetic effect is one of motion, in this case horizontal rather than vertical.

Jazz rhythms create what can only be called momentum. When the rhythm of one voice (say the trumpet, off on a rhythmic and melodic excursion) lags behind the underlying beat, its four-beat measure carries over beyond the end of the underlying beat's measure into the succeeding one, which has already begun. Conversely, when the trumpet anticipates the beat, it starts a new measure before the steady underlying beat has ended one. And the result is an exhilarating forward motion which the jazz trumpeter Wingy Manone once described as "feeling an increase in tempo though you're still playing at the same tempo." Hence the importance in jazz of timing, and hence the delight and amusement of the so-called "break," in which the basic 4/4 beat ceases and a soloist goes off on a flight of rhythmic and melodic fancy which nevertheless comes back surprisingly and unerringly to encounter the beat precisely where it would have been if it had kept going.

Once the momentum is established, it can continue until—after an interval dictated by some such external factor as the conventional length of phonograph records or the endurance of dancers—it stops. And . . . it is likely to stop on an unresolved chord, so that harmonically as well as rhythmically everything is left up in the air. Even the various coda-like devices employed by jazz performers at dances, such as the corny old "without a shirt" phrase of

blessed memory, are harmonically unresolved. They are merely conventional ways of saying "we quit." . . .

The references to the rectangular grid pattern of cities and townships and to the Constitution should remind us that the underlying structural principles with which we are concerned are deeply embedded in our civilization. To shift the emphasis, therefore, let us look at item number 7 on our list: Mark Twain's writing.

Mark's writing was, of course, very largely the product of oral influences. He was a born storyteller, and he always insisted that the oral form of the humorous story was high art. Its essential tool (or weapon), he said, is the pause —which is to say, timing. "If the pause is too long the impressive point is passed," he wrote, "and the audience have had time to divine that a surprise is intended—and then you can't surprise them, of course." In other words, he saw the pause as a device for upsetting expectations, like the jazz "break."

Mark, as you know, was by no means a formal performist. In fact he took delight in being irreverent about literary form. . . . Even his greatest book, which is perhaps also the greatest book written on this continent—*Huckleberry Finn*—is troublesome. One can scarcely find a criticism of the book which does not object, for instance, to the final episodes, in which Tom rejoins Huck and they go through that burlesque business of "freeing" the old Negro Jim—who is, it turns out, already free. But, as T. S. Eliot was, I think, the first to observe, the real structure of *Huck Finn* has nothing to do with the traditional form of the novel—with exposition, climax, and resolution. Its structure is like that of the great river itself —without beginning and without end. Its structural units, or "cages," are the episodes of which it is composed. Its momentum is that of the tension between the river's steady flow and the eccentric superimposed rhythms of Huck's flights from, and near recapture by, the restricting forces of routine and convention.

It is not a novel of escape: if it were, it

would be Jim's novel, not Huck's. Huck is free at the start, and still free at the end. Looked at in this way, it is clear that *Huckleberry Finn* has as little need of a "conclusion" as has a skyscraper or a jazz performance. Questions of proportion and symmetry are as irrelevant to its structure as they are to the total effect of the New York skyline.

There is not room here for more than brief reference to the other "literary items on our list: Whitman's *Leaves of Grass*, comic strips, and soap opera. Perhaps it is enough to remind you that *Leaves of Grass* has discomfited many a critic by its lack of symmetry and proportion, and that Whitman himself insisted: "I round and finish little, if anything; and could not, consistently with my scheme." As for the words of true poems, Whitman said in the "Song of the Answerer"—

> They bring none to his or her terminus or to be content and full,
> Whom they take they take into space to behold the birth of stars, to learn one of the meanings,
> To launch off with absolute faith, to sweep through the ceaseless rings and never be quiet again.

Although this is not the place for a detailed analysis of Whitman's verse techniques, it is worth noting in passing how the rhythm of these lines reinforces their logical meaning. The basic rhythmical unit, throughout, is a three-beat phrase of which there are two in the first line (accents falling on *none, his* and *term . . . be, tent,* and *full*), three in the second and in the third. Superimposed upon the basic three-beat measure there is a flexible, nonmetricall rhythm of colloquial phrasing. That rhythm is controlled in part by the visual effect of the arrangement in long lines, to each of which the reader tends to give equal duration, and in part by the punctuation within the lines.

It is the tension between the flexible, superimposed rhythms of the rhetorical patterns and the basic three-beat measure of the underlying framework which unites with the imagery and the logical meaning of the words to give the passage its restless, sweeping movement. It is this tension, and other analogous aspects of the structure of *Leaves of Grass* which give to the book that "vista" which Whitman himself claimed for it. If I may apply to it T. S. Eliot's idea about *Huckleberry Finn*, the structure of the *Leaves* is open at the end. Its key poem may well be, as D. H. Lawrence believed, the "Song of the Open Road."

As for the comics and soap opera, they too —on their own frequently humdrum level— have devised structures which provide for no ultimate climax, which come to no end demanded by symmetry or proportion. In them both there is a shift in interest away from the "How does it come out?" of traditional story telling to "How are things going?" . . .

Here, I think, we are approaching the central quality which all the diverse items on our list have in common. That quality I would define as a concern with process rather than with product—or . . . a concern with the manner of handling experience or materials rather than with the experience or materials themselves. Emerson, a century ago, was fascinated by the way "becoming somewhat else is the perpetual game of nature." And this preoccupation with process is, of course, basic to modern science. "Matter" itself is no longer to be thought of as something fixed, but fluid and ever-changing. Similarly, modern economic theory has abandoned the "static equilibrium" analysis of the neo-classic economists, and in philosophy John Dewey's instrumentalism abandoned the classic philosophical interest in final causes for a scientific interest in the "mechanism of occurrences"—that is, process.

It is obvious, I think, that the American system of industrial mass production reflects this same focus of interest in its concern with production rather than products. And it is the mass-production system, *not* machinery, which has been America's contribution to industry.

In that system there is an emphasis different from that which was characteristic of handicraft production or even of machine manufacture. In both of these there was an almost total disregard of the means of production. The aristocratic ideal inevitably relegated interest in the means exclusively to anonymous peasants and slaves; what mattered to those who controlled and administered production was, quite simply, the finished product. In a mass-production system, on the other hand, it is the process of production itself which becomes the center of interest, rather than the product. . . .

This fascination with process has possessed Americans ever since Oliver Evans in 1785 created the first wholly automatic factory: a flour mill in Delaware in which mechanical conveyors—belt conveyors, bucket conveyors, screw conveyors—are interlinked with machines in a continuous process of production. But even if there were no other visible sign of the national preoccupation with process, it would be enough to point out that it was an American who invented chewing gum (1869) and that it is the Americans who have spread it— in all senses of the verb—throughout the world. An absolutely non-consumable confection, its sole appeal is the process of chewing it.

The apprehensions which many people feel about a civilization absorbed with process —about its mobility and wastefulness as well as about the "dehumanizing" effects of its jobs— derive, I suppose, from old habit and the persistence of values and tastes which were indigenous to a very different social and economic system. Whitman pointed out in *Democratic Vistas* more than eighty years ago that America was a stranger in her own house, that many of our social institutions, like our theories of literature and art, had been taken over almost without change from a culture which was not, like ours, the product of political democracy and the machine. Those institutions and theories, and the values implicit in them, are still around, though some (like collegiate gothic, of both the architectural and intellectual variety) are less widely admired than formerly.

Change, or the process of consecutive occurrences, is, we tend to feel, a bewildering and confusing and lonely thing. All of us, in some moods, feel the "preference for the stable over the precarious and uncompleted" which, as John Dewey recognized, tempts philosophers to posit their absolutes. We talk fondly of the need for roots—as if man were a vegetable, not an animal with legs whose distinction it is that he can move and "get on with it." We would do well to make ourselves more familiar with the idea that the process of development is universal, that it is "the form and order of nature." . . .

As an "organic system" man cannot, of course, expect to achieve stability or permanent harmony, though he can create (and in the great arts of the past, has created) the illusion of them. What he can achieve is a continuing development in response to his environment. The factor which gives vitality to all the component processes in the individual and in society is "not permanence but development." . . .

So, too, the past of those who live in the United States, like their future, is open-ended. It does not, like the past of most other people, extend downward into the soil out of which their immediate community or neighborhood has grown. It extends laterally backward across the plains, the mountains, or the sea to somewhere else, just as their future may at any moment lead them down the open road, the endless vistaed street.

Our history is the process of motion into and out of cities; of westering and the counterprocess of return; of motion up and down the social ladder—a long, complex, and sometimes terrifyingly rapid sequence of consecutive change. And it is this sequence, and the attitudes and habits and forms which it has bred, to which the term "America" really refers.

"America" is not a synonym for the United States. It is not an artifact. It is not a fixed and immutable ideal toward which citizens of this nation strive. It has not order or proportion, but neither is it chaos except as that is chaotic whose components no single mind can comprehend or control. America is process. And in so far as people have been "American"—as distinguished from being (as most of us, in at least some of our activities, have been) mere carriers of transplanted cultural traditions—the concern with process has been reflected in the work of their heads and hearts and hands.

THE INTELLECTUAL

Eggheads of the world unite—you have nothing to lose but your yolks!

—Adlai Stevenson

The intellectual is a man who carries a brief case.

—Jacques Barzun

The intellectual lives *for* ideas; the professional man lives *off* them.

—Richard Hofstadter

An intellectual is a person for whom thinking fulfills at once the function of work and play.

—Christopher Lasch

Pamper them, pet them, give them everything they want, but don't ever give them power.

—Eric Hoffer

Soul raping has become a feature of government by intellectuals. Euripides did not know the whole story when he said, "A slave is he who cannot speak his thoughts." We now know that a thousand times a slave is he who is not allowed to keep silent.

—Eric Hoffer

Wilson was a great man but he had one basic fault. He was willing to do anything for people except get off their backs and let them live their own lives. He would never let go until they forced him to and then it was too late. He never seemed to understand there's a big difference between trying to save people and trying to help them. With luck you can help 'em—but they always save themselves.

—Raymond Robins

The doctrinaire never thinks of the pencil sketch in terms of coercion. It is not intended to interfere with freedom; on the contrary, it is designed to secure it. Only the ill-intentioned, the selfish and perverse can complain that their freedom is violated. They are guilty of sabotage, refusing to be free, and misleading others. They cannot be given freedom to do their evil deeds, for they are at war with the pattern of freedom that continues to unfold itself till its full realization. Liberty can be restored only after this war has come to an end, only when the enemy has been eliminated and the people re-educated, that is to say, when there will be no longer any opposition. So long as there is opposition there can be no freedom.

—J. L. Talmon, *The Origins of Totalitarian Democracy*
(N.Y.: Praeger, 1960), p. 137

THE INTELLECTUAL AND HIS CRITICS

The intellectual is a man who both values ideas for their own sake, and marshals them in the pursuit of truth. This means that there are times when he becomes a critic of the *status quo* and brings on his own destruction—as, for example, did Socrates. Regardless of the criticisms that follow, let it be understood here that the intellectual has been the great fructifyer, for out of his thought processes has come civilization. This has never been more true than in this century, when we owe to him the giant steps which have brought in the affluent society and the space age, but, even more significantly, whatever hope there is of conquering the age-old problems which still afflict human kind.

Since ancient times the intellectual—what Coleridge called the "clerisy"—has served as a valuable and usually contented member of the Establishment whose functions ranged from shriving sinners and instructing the young to advising popes and chiding royalty. In modernized form this is still true. However, within the last two centuries or so a splinter group of intellectuals has tried to restrict the use of the name to itself and has proudly announced its "alienation" from the existing order. It has abandoned most of the old role of the clerisy and come to regard its mission as pointing out what is wrong with things as they are and indoctrinating young intellectuals into the singleminded performance of that mission.

The philosophes of the Enlightenment exalted reason as the infallible guide which would help man to get out of the maze formed by past institutions and superstitions. But presently they split into rationalists and romantics. Of course, ideas passed between the two and became inextricably mixed, producing intellectuals and anti-intellectuals on both sides—a neat paradox paralleled in modern existentialism. Robespierre may have exhibited such a contradiction, and the utopia he envisioned may have been an intellectual construct of a romantic ideal. At any rate, the mission of the intellectuals was now confirmed—to fight the existing order and bring utopia to the masses whether they liked it or not. There was about it a tinge of belief in that mystic tie between leader and people which was to descend from Rousseau to Hitler; only great characters like Jefferson and Lincoln have been able to steer clear of the "father knows best" complex.

Another crisis came in the 1890's in France when the intellectuals championed the cause of Dreyfus—and it was at that time that the word "intellectual" came into general use. One must sympathize with the stand of Zola and his confreres and censure the Establishment which gathered its force to repel them. But as a result the intellectuals promptly began to picture themselves as being unappreciated

—even as martyrs. The situation was encapsulated in 1927 by a French intellectual, Julien Benda, in *The Treason of the Intellectuals,* wherein he accused his fellow intellectuals of having abandoned their role as dispassionate and independent thinkers and mentors, and plunged into the stormy sea of partisan causes. Now they were devoting themselves to rationalizing such popular passions as democracy, nationalism, Marxism, and a galaxy of schemes for the moral regeneration of the world.

At this point, issues become royally confused. Benda asserted that William James's pragmatism had become the religion of the new order of intellectuals. The truth is that the pragmatists were inveterate critics of Benda's ideal of the thinker in the ivory tower, and can be rated as one of the various sorts of anti-intellectuals. What had happened, one may venture, was that the intellectuals Benda was criticizing were seeking to eat their cake and have it—to present their hopes and aims for moral regeneration as the products of pure, transcendental thought, and to force them on society. William James could not justly be accused of doing either.

As a matter of fact, anti-intellectual currents had sprung up as soon as the intellectuals announced their new mission. One current on the right was represented by Joseph de Maistre, who proclaimed that "nothing new is good and nothing good is new." Edmund Burke is more acceptable to the American mind, for our folk wisdom includes the adage, "Be not the first by whom the new is tried, nor yet the last to lay the old aside." Critics of the intellectuals include many other familiar names: Newman, Ruskin, Carlyle, Nietzsche, Marx, Sorel, and Pareto. The student will find them conveniently characterized in Edward M. Burns, *Ideas in Conflict* (1960); and in Crane Brinton, *Ideas and Men* (1950), to which we will presently turn.

Our concern is with the men and the terms "intellectual" and "anti-intellectual" on the American scene. There we find that both terms have become pejoratives. True, the lofting of Sputnik in 1957 led to the rehabilitation of the intellectuals, but this probably should be applied to the clerisy rather than to the man whose chief function is to find fault. In any case, anti-intellectualism has been, and remains, so strong in America that some effort should be made to clarify its meaning. It then becomes evident that the term has been used in a number of senses, some of them exclusive, some of them overlapping. No doubt there are other senses than those named here, but we shall concentrate on five.

(1) *The Pragmatists.* They are far from being opposed to the use of intellect, but they suspect the intellectual of being too narrowly trained, of having too little contact with realities. In this view the intellectual draws his ideas so fully from books that his opinions are not to be taken as reliable guides in meeting and solving practical problems in everyday life—let alone in politics, diplomacy, and finance, where expert knowledge, pragmatic experience, and common sense are essential to success. The absent-minded professor would be the image of the intellectual; also there is President Eisenhower's definition of an intellectual as "a man who takes more words than are necessary to tell more than he knows."

(2) *The McCarthyites.* Richard Hofstadter has written a perceptive book *Anti-Intellectualism in American Life* (N.Y.: Knopf, 1962) in which he first makes a number of salutary qualifications about the term, then settles down to a history

of the way in which anti-intellectualism has ranged from distrust and envy of the expert—often an intellectual—to McCarthyite attacks on intellectuals. These attacks arose basically from the fears and frustrations caused by the twentieth century's undermining of the old, secure values. The intellectual had played a part in these changes either as expert or as ideologue, and his helpless isolation from the community made him an easy scapegoat. The attack was not primarily against communists as such but against the income tax, the Supreme Court, the New Deal, foreigners that refused to turn from evil and adopt the American way of life, and—anticlimax—fluoride in the drinking water.

(3) *The Romantic.* Crane Brinton, in *Ideas and Men* (pp. 504–505), speaks of one sort of anti-intellectual as *praising* nonrationality, exalting it as "the really desirable human activity, the denigration of rationality. Such an attitude of dislike for rationality and love for nonrationality we prefer to call *romanticism*, the romanticism of Goethe's 'feeling is all.' . . . The modern lover of the nonrational, like many of the apologists for Nazism, goes far beyond these first romanticists, but the root of the concept is in romanticism."

(4) *The Existentialist.* There are, as might be expected, numerous varieties of existentialists. As Edward M. Burns notes in *Ideas in Conflict* (pp. 291 ff.), existentialism brings together romanticism, nihilism, skepticism, pragmatism, and even utopianism. It posits that man is alone and miserable in a vast and indifferent universe, but can at least make existence endurable by "involvement" in human affairs. Thus, though there are no eternal values on which man can rely, he can create his own values—"a kind of Promethean defiance and refusal to surrender to fear and despair as the supreme values of all." But here lies the paradox: existentialism, despite its anti-intellectualism, has become the philosophy of the most vocal group of young intellectuals. They have made their "Promethean defiance" a moral absolute which they are determined to force on the world as a means of salvation—quite in the pattern of the intellectual's view of his saving mission. One can speculate that these intellectuals are unaware that they are hung up on a paradox. To go a step further, if they would exclude their determination to save the world willy-nilly, it may be that they offer as much comfort as man can have outside of religious faith.

(5) *The Cautious Rationalist.* Finally, there is the anti-intellectualism which by no means opposes thought but regards the intellect as a weak instrument because it is subject to the pull-and-haul of emotions, prejudices, and instinctual drives. This anti-intellectual, therefore, makes it his business to seek out the rational aspects of human behavior and distinguish them from the nonrational. His view is that the intellectual sometimes puts too much confidence in his own rationality and so becomes obsessed by an idea. This is why intellect must be used with due caution. The obsession may be a moral slant, exemplary in itself, but which nevertheless colors the intellectual's approach to everything he does. Examples would be the writers of the Whig school of history. However, when the obsession is the aim to bring in the millennium the intellectual becomes as dangerous as the McCarthyite—indeed more so, for he has the zeal and dedication of a builder of new worlds, while the McCarthyite is merely against something. It is this type of intellectual with whom we can in certain respects class Robespierre, Calhoun, Wilson, Lenin, and, of course, some of the existentialist salvationists.

Here we turn to certain analyses which should cast light on the role of intellectuals and anti-intellectuals on the American scene.

FREUD AND ANTI-INTELLECTUALISM

[An excellent treatment of the fifth type of anti-intellectual described in the preceding section is found in Crane Brinton's *Ideas and Men* (N.Y.: Prentice-Hall, 1950), pp. 504–526. It is part of a larger treatment which brings in numerous European thinkers, but here we are concerned with Freud and his effect on American life. The type of anti-intellectualism described here antedated Freud, of course, but Freud helped to clarify the reasons for its attitude.]

Basically the anti-intellectual, in the sense we here use the term, does not regard the instrument of thought as *bad*, but among most men most of the time as *weak*. The romantic agrees with Thomas Hardy that "thought is a disease of the flesh"; the anti-intellectual notes merely that thought seems often at the mercy of appetites, passions, prejudices, habits, conditioned reflexes, and of a good deal else in human life that is not thinking. . . . We shall, however, attempt to use the term *anti-intellectual* without praise or blame, to describe the attempt to ascertain the place of rationality in actual human behavior.

Now the anti-intellectual tends to distrust a certain kind of abstract, deductive thinking about the Big Questions. . . . But the anti-intellectual, though in his opposition to the philosophy of the Enlightenment that universal education would overnight teach everybody to think correctly he often seemed to disparage the instrument of thought, *is in a sense a true heir of the Enlightenment*, is at bottom a believer in the power of thought to make man's life here on earth a better one. Freud himself, whom some tender-minded people quite wrongly regard as the apostle of deep, dark, instinctual self-indulgence, believed as firmly as any eighteenth-century *philosophe* in the power of the truth—scientific truth duly established— to promote good conduct on the part of the individual who had succeeded in learning the truth; but—and this is a difference of major importance—the *philosophe* thought that all

that stood between the individual and the learning of truth was a rotten shell of decayed institutions, the Catholic Church and the French monarchy; whereas Freud thought that not only a very strong set of institutions but also a strong set of personal habits and inclinations and a strong set of habits established in early infancy stood between the individual and the learning of the truth. Freud, even before his old age of exile and unhappiness, had no hopes that *many* men could win their way through to this sort of truth in a short time. . . .

The anti-intellectual insists that man is a complex creature whose behavior must be studied as far as possible without preconceptions concerning the goodness and badness of that behavior. Just as with the place of logical thinking in human life, so with the place of good behavior; the anti-intellectual does not deny the difference between good and bad, does not hesitate to prefer goodness to badness. What he does insist is that, to judge by the evidence to be obtained by observation of what men have done and are doing, there is a great deal of badness about and—this is the important thing—there seems to be no direct and simple causal relation between men's moral ideals and their actions. Therefore the anti-intellectual repeats Bacon's praise of Machiavelli, himself in many ways an early anti-intellectual: "We are much beholden to Machiavelli and others that wrote what men do, and not what they ought to do."

To sum up: Most anti-intellectuals accept,

by and large, the goals of order, happiness, individual freedom, and all the rest we associate with the Enlightenment, but they hold these goals as only imperfectly and only very slowly attainable on earth; and they believe the best way to attain them is not to preach that they must be attained, *not to pretend they have been attained* (a not uncommon claim among American educators, editors, and preachers with aspirations to mass audiences), but to work patiently at building up a true social science based on the long-tried methods of cumulative knowledge and to hope that this knowledge will be used by men to promote the good rather than the bad. . . .

We have already noted how such natural scientists as Newton and Darwin gave leads in the social sciences. In our own times the great leads have come from biology and psychology. Probably the two most commanding figures in this respect of influence on the social studies are Pavlov and Freud, both psychologists trained in physiology and the other biological sciences. Note that we are here considering, not the meaning of their professional studies within their own nowadays very specialized professions, but their influence on the much more general currents of thought among men of various training concerned with human affairs.

Pavlov's is the simpler case. What reached the outside world from the laboratories of this Russian scientist whose independence was respected by both Tsarist and Soviet governments was the well-known phrase "conditioned reflexes." Pavlov's dogs are as familiar as any laboratory animals have ever been. Most of us know how, after being repeatedly fed at a certain signal, such as a bell, they came to water at the mouth in anticipation of food at a mere signal. The natural—that is the untrained—response of watering at the mouth would ordinarily come only when the dog had actual food before him; Pavlov got the same response artificially by a signal that certainly didn't smell or look like food to the dog. The upshot was clear evidence that training (conditioning) could produce automatic responses in the animal that were essentially similar to the kind of automatic responses the animal is born with. Conditioned reflexes like watering at the mouth at a signal were the same as natural reflexes like watering at the mouth when a fine red beefsteak was held before the animal.

What this meant in broad lines for the social scientist is this: In a sense, eighteenth-century notions about the power of environment (training, education) of the kind Robert Owen expressed so clearly . . . were confirmed, in the sense that environment can be manipulated to give organisms new responses; but—and this is a bitter blow to eighteenth-century optimism—once such training has taken hold the organism has, so to speak, incorporated the results almost as if they had been the product of heredity, not environment, and further change becomes very difficult, in some instances impossible. Pavlov, after having trained some of his dogs, tried mixing his signals, frustrating and confusing the dogs by withholding food at the signal that had always produced food for them, and so on until he succeeded in producing symptoms of a kind close to what in human beings would be neurosis, or even psychosis. . . .

Freud is a much more complex figure than Pavlov—indeed one of the most complex figures in the intellectual history of the West. He was a scientist brought up in the simple craftsman's belief in a material universe from which the supernatural was ruled out, and with the scientist's contempt for all metaphysical ideas but the unavowed, positivist metaphysics of conventional modern science. His total work is a bewildering compound of natural science and rather pessimistic—almost Christian—metaphysics. In a book of this scope we cannot properly examine Freud's complexities; moreover, his work, like that of all great system-making thinkers, looks quite different to outsiders and to true believers. He has created a method of dealing with certain kinds of human disability usually thought of as mental—nervous breakdown, neurosis, and the like. This method is called psychoanalysis, and must be distinguished from conventional handling of mental disease, usually by physicians with special training as neurologists, which is called psychiatry. . . .

Freud gave leads to many in the study of human behavior who knew nothing, or very little, about psychoanalysis and its metaphysical superstructure. Our century is indeed a century in which psychology is the fashionable science, and in which the chatter of the educated makes use of psychological terms much as the habitués of the eighteenth-century salons chattered about the laws of physics and astronomy discovered by Newton. Many of these modern smooth coins of conversation were once sharply minted by Freud himself—libido, Oedipus complex, infantile sexuality, sublimation. Perhaps the smoothest coin of all—inferiority complex —was minted by a disciple, Adler, who later quarreled with the master and set up his own psychological shop.

Here, as has been our practice in this book, we are concerned rather with this phase of Freud's ideas as they circulated among the intellectual classes than with their professional significance in psychology and medicine. For this purpose, a very schematic outline of his basic ideas as of about 1920 should suffice. To Freud, what makes people go is a whole set of "drives" he first called *libido* and associated very closely with sexual desires and later called the *id*, and made a little less clearly sexual. The id in the human being is part of the unconscious; it wishes, pushes the individual into action. But the whole behavior of the human being involves two other parts of the human psyche, the *ego* and the *super-ego*. . . .

The *ego* is wholly—or almost wholly— part of a man's conscious mental life, but it is not pure logical activity; it is an umpire, or governor, the guardian of the interests of the organism as a whole and the arbitrator of conflicting desires rising out of the id into consciousness. Some of these desires, especially if they seem to the ego of the kind to discredit the person, are suppressed by the ego, but continue hard at work in the unconscious id; some

of them are "sublimated," turned from a sexual goal, for instance, into art or poetry or governing men. The *super-ego* involves some of the elements that go into the conditioned reflexes. In the super-ego the notions taught the individual about right and wrong, the "proper" way to behave, the "proper" ideas to hold, come to play on the individual's actions. In part, the super-ego is unconscious, its dictates inculcated from infancy on so that they do not go through the logical process, do not present him with problems of alternative action. The ego is like a somewhat un-Christian individual conscience; the super-ego is like a social or collective conscience working on and in the individual. The ego mediates between the id and the external world of material *reality*; the super-ego mediates between the id and the external world of ideals, of "higher things," which last Freud rather begrudgingly granted a kind of objective reality.

In a healthy individual the id, the ego, and the super-ego cooperate to keep him aware of the realities of his environment and to enable him to adjust his conduct in accord with these realities so that he is on the whole a happy man and a good citizen. In the neurotic individual desires balked by the negative of the ego or the super-ego are thereby driven back into the unconscious, where they continue to live and push on as desires must. They make the stuff of a man's dreams. They crop up in disguised (but not genuinely sublimated) form in all sorts of acts that are clearly not in the line of normal, sensible conduct—in obsessive fears, in withdrawal from ordinary responsibilities, in worrying and fretting, in all the great variety of conduct we nowadays label "neurotic." These balked desires are, be it noted, in the unconscious; the neurotic individual does not really know what he wants.

Freud's basic notions of therapy—and it is these that caused us to classify him as a child of the Enlightenment—can be summed up as an elaborate, difficult (and very expensive) way of teaching the patient to know what he really wants. More particularly, Freud held that the original repression, the original driving back into the id of certain desires, was the source of the evil, the *trauma* or wound inflicted in the individual's psyche. Usually, he thought, this trauma went back to infancy and was tied up with the fact that the infant's very early sexual desires are strongly disapproved in our culture, that both his ego and his super-ego are taught rather harshly that they must not allow such conduct. Even if there were no simple single incident of infancy that seemed the origin of a difficulty in later life, Freud believed that the very early years were always of major importance. But how could these forgotten things be dug up by the individual? Only by a long process of "free association," of letting the individual roam back in memory day after day, with the psychoanalyst at his side noting the tiny clues as they came into the flow of memories, and by aid from dreams, recent and recalled.

We cannot of course attempt a detailed account of Freud's methods of therapy. The point should be clear: Freud held that the individual was a bundle of confused thoughts and desires that could only with the greatest difficulty be brought to make sense; but that when after long investigation the analyst could show the individual just *why* he behaved as he did, then the individual would cease to behave badly, unprofitably for himself and for his fellows. Note particularly that Freud did *not* take the old, innocent, Rousseauistic position that since all the trouble came from the original suppression the way to avoid difficulty is to have everybody from infancy on follow all his desires, let the id dictate all his acts. Freud and the Freudians do indeed tend to be "permissive" in child training, tend to sympathize with the ideal of as much individual freedom in society as can be attained. Freud himself seems never to have liked the contents of most of our super-egos, the "higher things" of Western tradition. But the Freudians do not advocate an orgy of lust, they do not want man to be the slave of his cruder appetites, they are not—for the most part—antinomian cranks. They are trained physicians trying to be true to the standards of an exacting profession, trying to see men as they really are.

Freud's contribution to contemporary anti-intellectualism was very great. His work, taken with that of Pavlov and many other psychologists and physiologists, put great emphasis on the proportion of human actions in which the traditional instrument of thought—Aristotle's *phronesis*, Christian *ratio*, the reason of Locke and the Encyclopedists, even the illative sense of Newman—had no part, or little part. Action came to the anti-intellectual to be the result of automatic responses, natural or conditioned, of all sorts of unconscious drives and urges, of traditions, social habits, even theological and metaphysical principles made by early training and conditioning part of the individual's way of responding to the need to make a decision. To the anti-intellectual actual ratiocinative thought in an individual is to the rest of his living even less than the small part of the iceberg visible above water is to the whole mass of the iceberg. The *amount* of reasoning in human life, then, and not the *existence* of reasoning, is the point over which the anti-intellectual and those who oppose anti-intellectualism really differ. The tradition of American moral and political thinking is *not* anti-intellectual. The practice of a good deal of American politics, and of much of American life—advertising is a clear example—is anti-intellectual. . . .

Yet there is also a strain, clear ultimately in Freud, that emphasizes the possibility that ordinary men may learn the truth about themselves, a truth far more complex than the eighteenth-century view of man, and that once having learned it they can themselves make the necessary adjustments to this newly seen reality. Once men realize the really grave difficulties of thinking straight, they will, according to this more democratic view, be well on the road to straight thinking. . . .

Much of modern anti-intellectualism, unpalatable though it is to optimistic democratic taste, is actually widespread in Western culture today. . . . We have all heard about rationalization, propaganda, the ambiguities and other inadequacies of language; we are all reminded daily that to get ahead in this world you must exercise your skill in handling other people, you must deliberately win friends and influence people by arts other than logic. The experts in propaganda know that one of the factors they must reckon with is public awareness and distrust of propaganda, which the French call expressively—and cynically—*bourrage de crâne*, "brain-stuffing."

We are brought squarely up against the problem of the relation of anti-intellectualism to our democratic tradition, way of life, cosmology. Democracy as it ripened in the eighteenth century held out hope of rapid and thorough social change toward universal happiness on earth to be achieved by educating all men to use their natural reason—or at least by entrusting power to an enlightened group of political planners who could devise and run institutions under which all men would be happy. Anti-intellectualism maintains against these democratic beliefs the belief that men are not and cannot under the best educational system be guided by their reason, that the drives, habits, conditioned reflexes that mostly do guide them cannot be changed rapidly, that, in short, there is something in the nature of man that makes him and will continue to make him

behave in the immediate future not very differently from the way he has behaved in the past. These two sets of beliefs, the democratic and the anti-intellectual, seem mutually incompatible. . . .

We are back, of course, to the eternal contrast, the eternal tension, so strong in Western culture, between this world and the next, the real and the ideal, the practical and the desirable. The anti-intellectuals are pulling democracy over toward the first of these pairs. Yet to emphasize the facts of life, the "spotted reality," is not necessarily to adopt the conclusion that no improvement in actual conditions is possible. Indeed, in Western tradition the realists have more often been ethical meliorists, even optimists, than cynics. They rarely gloat with pleasure over the bad conditions they insist are there, are real. The real and the ideal are not, we have insisted throughout this book, by nature enemies. They belong together. It is only when they are divorced that each, pursued in neglect of the other, is a danger to society. One of the great questions we now face is whether good democrats can accept the reality the anti-intellectuals have brought to their attention without losing their belief in the possibility of improving that reality.

THOSE MATERIALISTIC AMERICANS

[In his *Conversations with Henry Brandon* (Boston: Houghton, Mifflin, 1968), pp. 64–65, the noted British political writer asked Margaret Mead, Columbia anthropologist, "What about the materialistic nature of the American?"]

MEAD: Perhaps I might start by quoting the comments of the natives of New Guinea that I went back to restudy in 1953—I studied them before in 1928 when they were real Stone Age savages . . . and the most possessive, acquisitive, competitive, materialistic group of savages that I had ever met among all the savages I know. They were exposed, during World War II, to about a million Americans. They said: 'We learned from the Americans that

material things don't matter, that the only thing in the world that matters is a single human being. You can spend any amount of material goods to save the life of a single human being—now we have learned this, we want to have the kind of society that is organized around human beings instead of around property and things.' If I quote this to an ordinary American audience, they have some idea what I'm talking about, but if I quote it to the professional intelligentsia, they gasp with amazement. The natives added: 'The reason that American do *not* value material things too highly is because they have so many of them.' There's been a great confusion between having many material things and being materialistic. Europeans feel that to prefer a bathtub to a garden is crass materialism. Americans don't set things up as between a bathtub and a garden, because a bathtub isn't a luxury in this country, it's a necessity. So from what I have seen and the discussions I have had in Europe— I think Americans are much *less* materialistic than Europeans, much less.

BRANDON: Still, the American economy really is built on persuading people to buy and buy more, and so you have a concentration here on acquiring material things rather than—

MEAD: Well now! How would you characterize other economies? What are they based on? Persuading people not to buy?

BRANDON: No, but the economy is not that dependent on whether everybody will own a washing machine or not.

MEAD: I know it isn't. And other countries have had rather serious production problems as a result, haven't they? Ours is an economy that is geared to a rising standard of living. We are geared to a notion that we could live better than we do—so no one settles down very comfortably and is satisfied with the way he lives. Whereas, of course, in many parts of Europe there are class-typed standards. If people reach them, they are contented and they don't want to go out to get more things.

THE RAMPAGEOUS RIGHT

[A political phenomenon well known in Europe but comparatively new to American life until around 1920 was the reactionary element that yearns to return to the purity and simplicity of the past—what Hans Morgenthau calls romantics and Alan Barth calls the rampageous right. Here we give Alan Barth's "Report on the Rampageous Right" from *The New York Times Magazine*, Nov. 26, 1961.]

Frustration, which produces tantrums in babies, can lead to equally irrational fits of rage in adults. Unhappily, the contemporary world is, in many respects, a frustrating one. It is rotating not only on its axis but on all its axioms as well. It is involved in profound change—in its international power relationships, in its economic organization, in its social arrangements. And so it confronts many Americans with inevitable alterations in ways of life they cherish and with insurmountable obstacles to ways in which they want their country to move. . . .

That there is a great deal of frustration in the land today is made evident by a proliferation of societies, leagues, committees, councils and crusades which propose to stop the clock —or to turn its hands back to some easier, earlier time when men could move more readily

and directly to achieve what they wanted. How to classify these groups politically raises a difficult problem in semantics.

They are commonly called "Rightist"—a term which connotes conservatism. But in sober truth there is nothing conservative about them. They are much more in a rage to destroy than a fervor to conserve. They tend, as Under Secretary of State Chester Bowles remarked of some of them just the other day, to be saying: "Stop the world I want to get off." Clearly, these "Rightists" have nothing in common with such conservatives as, say, Dwight D. Eisenhower or Herbert Hoover. . . .

Sometimes they are referred to as the "radical Right." But the fact is that there is nothing radical about them. They offer no novel solutions to the problems that plague them; indeed, they offer no solutions at all.

They are immensely discontented with things as they are and furiously impatient with almost everyone in public office who can in any way be held responsible for their frustrations. But it cannot be said that they hold any clearly stated objectives or have any specific program either in common or individually. They are fundamentally and temperamentally "aginners." And perhaps the commonest characteristic among them is anger. They can fairly be called, if nothing else, the Rampageous Right. . . .

But if they defy designation under any simple political label, it is nevertheless possible to find certain lowest common denominators of philosophic outlook which may help to describe them and to set them off from the parties and factions which engage in the traditional pulling and hauling, the compromising and accommodating that are customary in the American political process. Here are some of their identifying traits:

First, they tend to see complex problems simply and to define problems in terms of "either-or" choices. For example, Senator Thomas J. Dodd, addressing a huge rally in the Hollywood Bowl in October under the sponsorship of the Christian Anti-Communist Crusade, said: "The only alternative to total defeat in the struggle with communism is total victory."

Whatever the merits of this formulation as rhetoric, it suffers from the logical fallacy of the excluded middle. Obviously there are a number of possible alternatives. Total annihilation is one of them. So is continued stalemate. So is some sort of temporary accommodation conferring neither victory nor defeat upon either side but providing for reciprocal concessions which might relax tensions while allowing life to go on for a while longer on the planet.

The "either-or" solution is a formula for frustration. It pits what is unattainable against what is intolerable and precludes all rational and feasible middle courses. In international affairs it makes negotiation impossible and assures for any compromise, no matter what gains or advantages it may embrace, a taunt from the "Rightists" that it amounts to abject surrender. It is hard to escape a conclusion that the essential negativism of the "either-or" approach is designed to frustrate rather than forward any kind of agreement.

This "either-or" approach is adopted by the Right in regard to domestic as well as foreign affairs. It expresses itself in an insistence that there can be no middle ground between pure capitalism and complete communism. In Southern California, automobile bumpers abound with stickers reciting the slogan, "Socialism is Communism." To the people who like to see things so simplistically, blurring the vital distinctions that make free choice possible, socialism is an epithet applied indiscriminately to almost any form of collective endeavor. Thus, any governmentally operated insurance program to provide medical care for the elderly is denounced as Socialist. So are Federal aid to education, Federally financed scholarships for college students and Federal support of scientific research—although there appears to be nothing particularly Socialistic about the same activities when supported by state tax revenues. Public assistance for the indigent, public housing, the Tennessee Valley Authority, even the progressive income tax are all looked upon as satanically inspired deviations from capitalism. . . .

Southern segregationists have joined hands with the professional anti-Communists, ideologically as well as politically. Almost a full century after Abraham Lincoln proclaimed the emancipation of Negroes in the United States, segregationists can present only a solid wall of "massive resistance" to Negro demands for any of the fruits of emancipation. . . .

A second common denominator of the Rightist groups is that they subscribe wholeheartedly to the conspiratorial, or devil, theory of history and tend to attribute every frustration to betrayal by traitors. It is out-of-the question for them to acknowledge honest differences of opinion or to consider the possibility that problems may arise in foreign affairs either through some skillful action by the enemy or through innocent error by conscientious, though fallible, public officials at home.

They have no uncertainty, for example, as to why "we lost China"—as though it was ever "ours" to lose. China was lost to communism, these angry Rightists assert unhesitatingly, not by the Chinese but by traitorous Americans who gave it away out of fealty to the Communist conspiracy.

How did the United States get into so disadvantageous a situation in Berlin—an island in a Communist sea? Softness toward communism, or worse, at Yalta or Teheran or Potsdam, the Rightists answer with easy assurance. And what more proof of the proposition can be demanded than the fact that Alger Hiss committed perjury before the House Committee on Un-American Activities? . . .

The Communist conspiracy, to these fixed-focus interpreters, is omnipresent, and very nearly omnipotent. It permeates every American institution and intrudes its poisonous influence into every aspect of American life. . . .

The close consanguinity between the segregationist and the anti-Communist strains in the Rightist movement is illustrated by their common attack on the Supreme Court. To the segregationists, the Court's unanimous decision in 1954 that segregated public schools violate the Constitution affords, of itself, proof positive that the Justices were subverted by communism —the all-purpose explanation for every frustration.

The anti-Communists find the same proof in Court decisions upholding the constitutional rights of persons charged with Left-Wing leanings. Robert Welch found it possible, therefore, to say quite flatly that "Communist influences are now in almost complete control of our Federal Government" and that the Supreme Court of the United States "is one of the most important agencies of communism."

The third of the common denominators characterizing the Right-Wing groups is a deep distrust of democratic institutions and of the democratic process—a distrust, in short, of the people. The Rightist never regard *themselves* as gullible or susceptible to Communist subversion; but they appear to be convinced that all their countrymen are outright simpletons ripe for a shift of loyalty at any moment from the Capitol to the Kremlin. . . .

What is the strength of the extreme Right today? The number of its adherents cannot be determined with any accuracy; and, as has been observed with regard to the subversives on the extreme Left, numbers do not afford a satisfactory index to influence. A score or more of Rightist groups are now vying with one another for supremacy. . . .

Undoubtedly the extreme Right is going to exercise a powerful negative influence in the difficult and inevitably frustrating years immediately ahead. Its weight will be thrown against Federal aid to education, against medical care for the aged, against generosity to the indigent—against civil liberties in general; and in foreign affairs it will strive militantly to represent any concessions to the Russians or to the Chinese as treasonable, any consideration for this country's allies as craven and any squeamishness about extermination of the human race in an atomic holocaust as subversively sentimental.

Lacking any realistic affirmative program, however, the Right is unlikely to be able to grasp the reins of political power in the United States. Genuine conservatives devoted to the nation's traditions, values and institutions will be reluctant to identify themselves with the extremists or to make common sense with them.

THE NEW RADICALS

[A sympathetic study of the New Left has been written by Paul Jacobs and Saul Landau in *The New Radicals: A Report with Documents* (N.Y.: Random House,

1966). Here we reprint certain descriptive passages found on pp. 3–7 and 14, and a tentative concluding analysis on pp. 82–85.]

The Movement is a mélange of people, mostly young; organizations, mostly new; and ideals, mostly American. In 1960 and 1961 the Freedom Riders and Negro college students who sat in in the South were acting in the spirit of The Movement. Most of those who protested against President Kennedy's Cuban policy in 1962 were responding to the impulse of The Movement. That same impulse took them south for the Student Nonviolent Coordinating Committee (SNCC) in 1963, got them arrested in Sproul Hall at the University of California in 1964, and marched them to Washington in 1965 to demonstrate their opposition to the war. Movement youth can be found today in the San Joaquin Valley of California, helping striking farm workers; some will become organizers in the slum communities of Northern cities; others will try to change the university system in America.

These young people believe that they must make something happen, that they are part of a movement stirring just below the surface of life hitherto accepted all over the world. So they identify with the Zengakuren students whose snake-dance demonstrations prevented President Eisenhower from visiting Japan, and wince at the photos of the young rebel shot by a policeman in Santo Domingo. They empathize with the young Soviet poets who read their poetry at the statue of Mayakovsky in Moscow until the police break up the meeting.

How many people are in the American Movement? Certainly it is possible to count those who are members of the organizations within The Movement, but that would be to misunderstand one of the basic facts of its nature: The Movement is organizations plus unaffiliated supporters, who outnumber by the thousands, and perhaps even hundreds of thousands, those committed to specific groups. The Movement's basic strength rests on those unaffiliated reserves, who are just as much a part of it as the organization youth.

The leitmotifs that dominate The Movement extend far beyond politics. The Movement is much more than anti-Vietnam marches, civil rights demonstrations, and student sit-ins. To be in The Movement is to search for a psychic community, in which one's own identity can be defined, social and personal relationships based on love can be established and can grow, unfettered by the cramping pressures of the careers and life styles so characteristic of America today.

The Movement rejects the careers and life styles of the American liberal, too, for to The Movement it is the liberal way of life and frame of mind that represent the evil of America. Those in The Movement feel that modern American liberals have substituted empty rhetoric for significant content, obscured the principles of justice by administrative bureaucracy, sacrificed human values for efficiency, and hypocritically justified a brutal attempt to establish American hegemony over the world with sterile anti-Communism. The Movement sees the liberals righteously proclaiming faith in American democracy from their comfortable suburban homes or offices, while the United States Air Force drops napalm on villages and poisons the rice paddies.

So, those in The Movement see not only the openly authoritarian or totalitarian society as an enemy but the administered, bureaucratic, dehumanized, rhetorical-liberal one as well. They reject liberal authority. They were stirred, momentarily, by President Kennedy's call for a commitment to freedom, but were so disappointed by his actions in Cuba and Vietnam that they turned on him with bitterness. And the Johnson Administration's foreign policy reinforces their view that America flouts, in action, the traditions of freedom and justifies the use of military instruments associated with the Nazis.

The new movement is also a revolt against the postwar "over-developed society," with its large bureaucracies in government, corporations, trade unions, and universities. To those in The Movement the new technologies of automation and cybernation, with their computers and memory-bank machines, are instruments of alienation, depersonalizing human relations to a frightening degree. The brain machines and the translation of human qualities into holes punched into a card are viewed as devices that break down communication and destroy community in the interests of efficiency. Technology's emphasis on routine efficiency has created a set of values, rationalized by its supporters as representing "the facts of modern life." But The Movement sees these values as false, imposed on the whole society without "the consent of the governed." Even worse, the decision-making over which the governed no longer have control extends far beyond politics: in the technological order every aspect of the people's lives is under the control of administrators far removed from responsibility to the governed. And the elders of those in The Movement have exchanged their decision-making right for the comforts of American affluence. All that remains is nineteenth-century rhetoric about democracy and freedom, and technology has drained the words of their content.

In their personal life style, their aesthetic sense, many in The Movement reject affluence and its associated symbols. The ambition to escape from poverty is no spur to action in their lives, for many are children of America's post-Depression *nouveau* middle class. Their parents are the once-poor scholars who head rich academic institutes; the ex-union organizers who run their own large businesses; the former slum dwellers who develop segregated real-estate tracts; the families once on the WPA who live in suburbia—all those who have made it. But their parents' desire to own, to accumulate, to achieve the status and prestige which go with material wealth, are meaningless goals to the children. To them television is not a wonder but a commonplace, and they see the $5,000 a year their parents spend on the analyst

as too high a price to pay for the loss of human values.

The marvels of the space age are commonplace to them, too, and the voices to which they listen are not those of the orbiting astronauts exchanging banalities. They respond instead to the sense and sound of friendship and community, to the exultation they feel when thousands of people link hands and sing "We Shall Overcome." And to achieve that feeling of community, of life, they have been willing to sacrifice most middle-class comforts.

They are willing to do this, for until they enter The Movement their inability to affect the quality of their own lives disturbs them profoundly. Those of the upper middle class were trapped, protected to the point of coddling through their childhood and early teens, sated with *nouveau* affluence by the time they were twenty. They knew they could achieve a place in the society of their parents, but it was not a society in which they wanted a place; it offered little beyond physical comfort. They believed the ideals they were taught, and felt miserable when the ideals were exposed as empty words. Their awareness that Negroes and millions of poor have been left out of the society moved them to act rather than depend on the persuasion techniques advocated by their elders.

Many of them were born in the year of The Bomb, and so their history begins with the history of nuclear destruction. The twenties and even the thirties are almost prehistory to them, and the burning issues which agitated the older generation's radicals and liberals are devoid of meaning. Some know of the mid-fifties' McCarthyism and the House Un-American Activities Committee (HUAC), but the internecine wars of the thirties have little personal significance for them.

In some measure, too, the modes of extreme personal behavior adopted by this group —their permissive view of marijuana or hallucinogenics like LSD, their matter-of-fact acceptance of sexual freedom and their habitual profanity—are part of their search for identity. That search assumes a rejection of everything connected with their old identity and of the technological, bureaucratic values they see as dominant in American life. It is also possible that their difficulties in finding personal meaning in the routine politics of the civil rights struggle and their anguish in seeing the country carry out a foreign policy they believe to be totally bad force these young people into seeking meaning in experiences. They think the ivory-towered men of ideas have cheated them, lied to them, and that action and spontaneous experience will show them truth.

Above all, those in The Movement now restlessly seek to find a new politics and a new ideology that will permit them to link existential humanism with morally acceptable modes of achieving radical social change.

.   .   .   .

In their revulsion against the liberal intellectuals who were celebrating America and the end of ideology, the young activists rejected all ideology and traditional party politics, turning instead to where the action was, to SNCC, formed in 1960 by Negroes and whites, Southern and Northern. SNCC wasn't political; it was concerned with right and wrong, with people. The SNCC ideal of morality in action also provided the spur for the Students for a Democratic Society (SDS) and its community and campus programs: the decision to act was reinforced by the role of the liberal intellectuals in the 1961 Bay of Pigs episode and the 1962 missile crisis.

What began perhaps as a rebellion against affluence and liberal hypocrisy grew in a few years into a radical activism that protested injustice at the very core of the society. But when even this was tolerated by the structures that were under attack, some of the young radicals began to think about something beyond rebellion or radical protest. The Movement now is struggling to develop an ideology that will guide them toward building an organization that can compete for political power.

.   .   .   .

It is impossible to assess. The Movement's long-term accomplishments now, for it is too young, and too little is known about it, despite the enormous publicity it has received. Nevertheless, it is possible to judge its immediate impact on American life and make some predictions about its future.

Immediately, Negroes' civil rights in the South have been advanced because The Movement's active presence forced the government to move more quickly than it had planned. The American universities are changing for the better, because The Movement's direct actions, or the potential of such actions taking place, have made the universities uncomfortably aware of the students' presence on the campus. In the anti-poverty drive the emphasis upon participation by the poor is partially, at least, a response to pressures stimulated by The Movement. Finally, because of The Movement, issues of foreign policy are being debated, far more intensely and by far more people in America today than since our entrance into World War II.

Yet, important as these accomplishments are, The Movement's real significance centers around other issues. Ample proof exists, for example, that The Movement attracts some of the best young people in the country, contrary to the vulgar popular notion that those who are involved are only "beats," "kooks," and "potheads." It is true that representatives of all those types can be found in The Movement, but its core is made up of those young people most committed to the values of intellectual honesty and social action rooted in the best American tradition.

That these young people reject the affluent society which produced them is one of The Movement's most startling characteristics. This generation has not grown up in a depression world, as did the youthful radicals of the thirties. Their drive is not to go from rags to riches; they know about poverty only because they adopt it as a way of life and not because they were born into it. And their repudiation of the American value system is so serious that they have forced thoughtful elements in society to re-examine their own acceptance of America, to discover what it is in American life that is so unattractive, so distasteful as to make these young people turn their backs on it and call for a revolution to replace it.

The Movement's intransigent moral posture is having consequences, too: the willingness of the participants in The Movement to translate their moral view of politics into a personal morality of action has forced others, outside The Movement, to assess their own commitment to moral positions. And The Movement's presence on the American political scene has replaced the view that ideology is dead in American politics with a revived interest in developing a new one.

We believe that this search for an ideology is at the root of the dispute between the new radicals and the traditional left. Superficially, the dispute has focused on the tactical question of whether the civil rights movement should make an alliance with the trade unions and liberal political organizations, and here we share the new radicals' disagreement with that grouping. But the real issue is that the new radicals are searching for a theory that will combine their individual, existential view of politics with the ability to carry out mass activities. We think that search is a healthy one, one that should be encouraged.

The difficulties encountered by The Movement in developing this ideology are related to its break with the past. The old left still concentrates its intellectual and activist energy on making changes in America's political and economic system on bread-and-butter issues. To many in the Marxist left, foreign policy is still explained by the simplistic view of imperialism as the stage of monopoly-capitalism's need for commodity and capital markets. On the other hand, most of the democratic left sees no pattern or systematic policy developing from the basic needs of American capitalism. This group attributes the failures of American foreign policy to a lack of understanding of Communism's dynamics and appeals; it assumes that America is capable of supporting what it describes as democratic-socialist movements in less developed countries, but has not done so from ignorance or the ill-will of a few powerful people.

In our view, both groups are wrong, and we share The Movement's determination to concentrate its basic efforts on the inadequate quality of life offered by our society. Alienation at home and intervention abroad are only different aspects of the same basic quality that results from the needs of the American corporate system. We agree with The Movement's emphasis on foreign policy: the exporting of anti-Communism has pervaded the quality, the tone, the character of our domestic life. In the name of anti-Communism the United States government has supported corrupt and totalitarian regimes that jail all dissenters.

In its attempt to create an anti-Communist empire throughout the world, America is committed to a permanent defense of and military alliance with any regime willing to share her anti-Communism. The American economy and political system have become inextricably linked to the building of the anti-Communist empire. Thus, anti-Communism has become a structural need, translated into every level of life, from Communist villains in the comic strips and TV series to the perpetual existence of the international Communist threat as a pre-condition for the permanent war economy.

Of equal seriousness is the United States government's inability to recognize the legitimacy of national revolutionary movements. In Vietnam official American policy is based on the myth that the National Liberation Front are robots being manipulated and directed from North Vietnam and/or Communist China. We applaud The Movement's efforts to explode that myth and expose the real nature of American involvement in Southeast Asia: to prevent, at all costs, the accession to power of any government influenced by the Communists, as is the National Liberation Front, whether or not it has the support of the people in the country.

The Movement has made many Americans

uncomfortable, and has inspired some radicals and liberals to renew their political commitment in some form. The new radicals may not succeed in achieving the fundamental change in American society that they and we feel is necessary. Instead, perhaps, their role will be the radicalizing of two generations, who are not afraid to build a larger Movement, and who are able and willing to fight for political power. Unless Americans are awakened to action about the moral anguish they must feel, as citizens and human beings, for the victims of our society both here and abroad, then The Movement itself will become a victim of a post-industrial America, a society whose value system even George Orwell might not have imagined.

THE RAMPAGEOUS LEFT

The student revolt which has swept many countries on both sides of the Iron Curtain and even affected Red China has so many aspects that it is useless to try to name them at this stage. Some of the conditions to which most American students object are so obvious and disgraceful that thoughtful elders have long since pinpointed them and sought to change them—generally with limited success —and now welcome the concern shown by students.

These students comprise the vast majority of the country's 7,000,000 college and university enrollment. When they accuse their elders of being phonies and hypocrites it is because of a natural revulsion from the newly discovered existential sordidness of life. Not only is this healthy but it is useful, for every generation when it comes to power has an opportunity to change things—let us hope for the better. In other words, there is no more wrong with the overwhelming majority of today's youth than with any other generation of youths, and very likely not as much.

But there is something unusual about the small percentage of student extremists not included among the above, but who have become known generically as the New Left, or the New Radicals. For one thing, they have no power base, nor are they united in any except the most general way. They are committed, but not to any program—only to revolution for the sake of revolution. Fascists, communists, socialists, and democratic capitalists are all—in the lingo of youth—lumped together as squares. Young communists may at times find comradeship among them, if they are willing to play down Marx and Lenin.

On the other hand, when the actions of the democratic and communist powers are in question, the rampageous left tends to find excuses for the latter, doubtless because their revolutions were so recent and because their present actions are not so visible. The New Left has even managed to make heroes of Castro, Guevara, and Mao. In the case of Mao this may be because he has proclaimed a gospel of permanent revolution which fits in with the New Left's yearning for the irresponsibility of perpetual adolescence. Or perhaps it is because Mao has been frowned on by the Russian Establishment, for, paradoxically, the New Left often denounces both the communist and democratic establishments as equally repressive and equally abhorrent.

One aspect of left factionalism is not exactly new. Some students speak of participatory democracy, which seems to mean that everyone shall have a veto on decisions—a sort of present-day Polish parliament, or in the American context, a *reductio ad absurdum* of Calhoun's concurrent voice. Perhaps they could profit by a study of the old West African process of decision-making where everyone talks continuously until out of sheer weariness a consensus is reached.

Their commitment, it was said above, is to revolution, and this is regarded as the supreme act of morality. The danger, of course, lies in the fact that such Garrisonian rigidity may summon an opposite morality; since moralities cannot compromise the result may well be war—as in the Civil War. They have made it clear that they are privy to the truth, so anyone who rejects their view of morality is therefore wicked; even to question it is to stifle freedom of opinion. Moreover, they assert that in furthering their cause they have the right to resort to violence without being subject to the penalties of the law. This is something rather new. Hitherto dissenters have usually felt that the justice of their cause is proven and enhanced by their joyous acceptance of legal penalties. Democracy has accepted this technique as an indispensible route to publicizing the need for social change, and frequently has honored those who, like John Brown, willingly gave their lives to forward their cause.

Then there is the rejection of the old concept that he who would destroy an institution must offer something better—or at least some substitute. Now it is held that programs are not only hindrances to action but actually dangerous. One who asks about program gets lectures on the power of love and the purity of the poor. Probe insistently and fill in certain blanks and you can catch vague glimpses of an order in which there are no big governments, no big corporations, no powerful school boards, no armies, and no machines to gobble up natural resources and pollute air and water. But these visions are not consistent. Occasionally someone envisions a society in which every community's needs are fed into computers and magically provided. This utopia, as someone has put it, will be replete with "airlines carrying people all over the country to visit the great museums." However, little thought is given to such dreams. The supreme object must be to unhorse the Establishments all over the world, to remove controls. When that has been done, utopia will take over. This, at least, has a familiar ring, for it has certain resemblances to Rousseau and some anarchists.

Perhaps even more striking is its resemblance to the nihilist students in Turgenev's *Fathers and Sons* (1862). At first the nihilists served a valuable purpose in calling attention to the ills of Russia, but when they turned black anarchists and resorted to terror they alienated liberals. Tkatchev, a terrorist leader, demanded immediate overthrow of the old institutions; he scoffed at reform programs and held that once the old had been destroyed natural forces would attend to the reconstruction of society. The most illustrious victim of the terror was Czar Alexander II, who against tremendous odds had been striving to liberalize Russia's institutions. The result, understandably, was a reaction which set Russian progress back for a generation; then came the Revolution which set it back for at least another generation.

There is at least a superficial resemblance between Tkatchev and Herbert Marcuse, the spiritual father of the present-day program of revolutions without programs and the hero of the New Left. Marcuse (b. 1898) is a German refugee, an expert on Hegel, who teaches philosophy at the University of California at San Diego. Reared in the European atmosphere which accepts Hegel's dialectic as a fact of life, he sees existing society as thesis and posits antithesis as rising out of its inner contradictions; from their struggle emerges a synthesis which will quickly deteriorate into a rigid thesis, and the whole process has to be repeated. Thus Marcuse instinctively assumes that every society has its internal contradictions, and that until these are found it is impossible to understand the society. The search is analytical and scientific; the New Left has—quite in the American Transcendental tradition—added the moral factor. Not but what Europeans recognize the moral factor, but they are less likely than Americans to see a given war as a moral struggle, and more likely to see morality as an aspect of tragedy or of irony.

Let us enlarge on this point. Marcuse's pessimistic view of history, of course, sharply contrasts with the optimistic American view that problems have solutions. The basic European criticism of the United States is that it has never really known tragedy, and so cannot have a realistic concept of human existence. The American expects, at the very least, to see progress made during his lifetime; the European often continues to struggle but underneath the turmoil has reconciled himself to inevitable failure and rates endurance as his highest virtue. His heroes, then, are likely to be tragic figures, men who struggled against insuperable odds and became noble failures—such men as Socrates, Marcus Aurelius, Leonardo, Galileo, Tolstoy, and Czar Alexander II.

It must be admitted at once that Europe's criticism of the American world view is at least partially justified; we rarely see the tragic grandeur in the failures of men like Jefferson, The Adamses, Lincoln, Wilson, and Roosevelt, but tend to laud their successes. But still unanswered is history's question whether it is better to be a mature pessimist or an immature optimist. This is said in full knowledge of the fact that our optimism warps our vision of reality and obscures our recognition of our limitations. (Perhaps also it is responsible for our national surges of anger, as in 1898, and our fits of defeatism, as in 1968.) Nevertheless, in the American context there is a certain justification for optimism simply because many problems have been solved—or if not solved, successfully bought off at least temporarily, which is perhaps more than Europe has been able to do. This is not an American virtue—it is simply the result of American conditions, particularly of its great natural resources.

Few thoughtful persons try to refute the New Left's criticism that all too often we have delayed solutions and in so doing ensured that the problems will become worse. We need only to look at problems of transportation, taxation, air pollution, water pollution, erosion, and above all poverty and race. Still, it may be reasonably held that the past did as much toward their solution as could have been expected, given past knowledge. One flaw in the New Left philosophy is that in censures the past for not having acted in the full glare of our excellent hindsight.

However that may be, the New Left has shown a curious and inconsistent mixture of European respect for logic and American reliance on pragmatism, of existentialism and democracy, of pessimism and optimism, of Marcuse and Jefferson. It has taken Marcuse's external analysis of the American and world condition without comprehending his deep conviction that the process of continuous revolution rises from the nature of the dialectic, not from moral imperatives, emotional restlessness, or a Utopian search for perfection. Whatever else he may be, Marcuse is no Utopian. And he is as much the prisoner of his pessimistic dialectic as the American is of his historical optimism.

From this mixture of slogans and attitudes has emerged a world view which bears a superficial resemblance to Marcuse—superficial especially because he has conceded that change can be brought about in America without revolution. The New Left holds that modern technological civilization has become a massive complex of interlocked corporate, labor, military, political, bureaucratic, and even religious interests, which battens on waste, has economic and diplomatic necessities which lead to aggression abroad, and must, like a bicycle, keep spinning along lest it collapse. All in all, society has become the prey of totalitarian vested interests, whether communist or capitalist matters little.

Public acquiescence, continues the doctrine, has been purchased by a modern form of the bread and circuses with which politicians won the support of Rome's voters. The result has been to destroy what might be a fruitful conflict between ideologies and make a mockery of democracy—indeed of all ideology. The men who once pondered and rebelled are now bought off by honors, goods, and amusements. The apparatus of democratic change has been taken over in toto by the Establishment. Programs of reform and political campaigns in their support mean nothing; they merely persuade the gullible that they influence decisions and become instruments for "absolving" their "servitude." Even sexual permissiveness has a like function. So anesthetized is the individual to everything but the rationale of his servitude that he has become a One-Dimensional Man (the title Marcuse gave to his principal book). Liberalism thus becomes the agent of the totalitarian control exercised by the Establishment and the enemy of freedom. Inevitably, then, any program merely plays into the hands of the enemy, and the only way to win freedom is to devote all revolutionary forces to the single-minded destruction of the Establishment. The ultimate horror would be to adopt a program and have it taken over and put into effect by the Establishment.

And this, ironically, is what may happen, at least in part, for the country is showing a growing hospitality to governmental and educational decentralization, and to blotting out the poor by giving them some form of guaranteed income. Does this prove the validity of New Left doctrine? Hardly. The New Left has so completely ignored the demonstrable historical fact that programs, agitations, and elections *do* change conditions that it reads like something out of Alice in Wonderland—or, perhaps better, out of Kafka.

But it does offer one thing to a pampered and frustrated faction of the younger generation—action through rebellion against authority of any kind. The beauty of it is that it gives comfort alike to the embittered, the weak-willed, the moralist, and the demagogue by showing that justification for rebellion mounts in geometrical proportion to its destructiveness. Beyond a vague belief that there was a time when society was simple and men were happy, the past means nothing, and its vestiges must be destroyed; the future by some magic alchemy, will take care of itself. The movement, then, is quite in tune with the presentist current which has had such a powerful influence on our day.

There is a warning to both nascent nihilists and bigoted establishmentarians in Santayana's dictum that those who ignore history are doomed to repeat it.

AMERICAN INTELLECTUALS AND FOREIGN POLICY

There is this critical difference between the intellectual of today and the average cleric of yesteryear: the intellectual, lacking in other-worldly interests, is committed to the pursuit of temporal status, temporal influence and temporal power with a single-minded passion that used to be found only in the highest reaches of the Catholic Church. . . .

It is simply not possible to comprehend what is happening in the United States today unless one keeps the sociological condition and political ambitions of the intellectual class very much in the forefront of one's mind. What we are witnessing is no mere difference of opinion about foreign policy, or about Viet Nam. Such differences of opinion do exist, of course. Some of the most articulate critics believe that the United States has, through bureaucratic inertia and mental sloth, persisted in a foreign policy that, whatever its relevance to the immediate postwar years, is by now dangerously anachronistic. They insist that the United States has unthinkingly accepted world responsibilities which are beyond its resources and that, in any case, these responsibilities have only an illusory connection with the enduring national interest. These men may be right; or they may be wrong. But right or wrong, *this* debate is largely irrelevant to the convulsion that the American intellectual community is now going through—even though occasional references may be made to it, for credibility's sake. One does not accuse the President of the United States and the Secretary of State of being "war criminals" and "mass murderers" because they have erred in estimating the proper dimensions of the United States' overseas commitments. And it is precisely accusations of this kind that are inflaming passions on the campus, and which are more and more coming to characterize the "peace movement" as a whole.

What we are observing is a phenomenon that is far more complex in its origins and far-reaching in its implications. It involves, among other things, the highly problematic relationship of the modern intellectual to foreign affairs, the basic self-definition of the American intellectual, the tortured connections between American liberal ideology and the American imperial republic, and the role of the newly established academic classes in an affluent society. Above all, it raises the question of whether democratic societies can cope with the kinds of political pathologies that seem to be spontaneously generated by their very commitment to economic and social progress.

—Irving Kristol, "American Intellectuals and Foreign Policy,"
Foreign Affairs, July 1967, pp. 595–596

THE NOW GENERATION

[The United States has long been set apart from the remainder of Western Civilization by its obeisance to youth. What are some of the results? In its January 6, 1967, article on the Man of the Year, the editors of *Time Magazine* chose to examine Americans under 25, and in so doing to make some characterizations of youth everywhere. Excerpts follow.]

In the closing third of the 20th century, that generation looms larger than all the exponential promises of science or technology: it will soon be the majority in charge. In the U.S., citizens of 25 and under in 1966 nearly outnumbered their elders; by 1970, there will be 100 million Americans in that age bracket. In other big, highly industrialized nations, notably Russia and Canada, the young also constitute half the population. If the statistics imply change, the credentials of the younger generation guarantee it. Never have the young been so assertive or so articulate, so well educated or so worldly. Predictably, they are a highly independent breed, and—to adult eyes—their independence has made them highly unpredictable. This is not just a new generation, but a new kind of generation.

What makes the Man of the Year unique? Cushioned by unprecedented affluence and the welfare state, he has a sense of economic security unmatched in history. Granted an ever-lengthening adolescence and life-span, he no longer feels the cold pressures of hunger and mortality that drove Mozart to compose an entire canon before death at 35; yet he, too, can be creative.

Reared in a prolonged period of world peace, he has a unique sense of control over his own destiny—barring the prospect of a year's combat in a brush-fire war. Science and the knowledge explosion have armed him with more tools to choose his life pattern than he can always use: physical and intellectual mobility, personal and financial opportunity, a vista of change accelerating in every direction.

Untold adventure awaits him. He is the man who will land on the moon, cure cancer and the common cold, lay out blight-proof, smog-free cities, enrich the underdeveloped world and, no doubt, write finis to poverty and war.

For all his endowments and prospects, he remains a vociferous skeptic. Never have the young been left more completely to their own devices. No adult can or will tell them what earlier generations were told: this is God,

that is Good, this is Art, that is Not Done. Today's young man accepts none of the old start-on-the-bottom-rung formulas that directed his father's career, and is not even sure he wants to be A Success. He is one already.

In the omphalocentric process of self-construction and discovery, he stalks love like a wary hunter, but has no time or target—not even the mellowing Communists—for hate.

One thing is certain. From Bombay to Berkeley, Vinh Long to Volgograd, he has clearly signaled his determination to live according to his own lights and rights. His convictions and actions, once defined, will shape the course and character of nations.

This is a generation of dazzling diversity, encompassing an intellectual *élite sans pareil* and a firmament of showbiz stars, ski whizzes and sopranos, chemists and sky watchers. Its attitudes embrace every philosophy from Anarchy to Zen; simultaneously it adheres above all to the obverse side of the Puritan ethic—that hard work is good for its own sake. Both sensitive and sophisticated, it epitomizes more than any previous generation the definition of talent by Harvard Dropout Henry James as "the art of being completely whatever it was that one happened to be.". . .

Youth, of course, has always been a topic of indefatigable fascination to what was once regarded as its elders and betters. But today's young people are the most intensely discussed and dissected generation in history. . . . A compelling reason for adult *angst* is that the young seem curiously unappreciative of the society that supports them. "Don't trust anyone over 30," is one of their rallying cries. Another, "Tell it like it is," conveys an abiding mistrust of what they consider adult deviousness.

Sociologists and psephologists call them "alienated" or "uncommitted"; editorial writers decry their "noninvolvement." In fact, the young today are deeply involved in a competitive struggle for high grades, the college of their choice, a good graduate school, a satisfactory job—or, if need be, for survival in Viet Nam. Never have they been enmeshed so early or so earnestly in society. Yet they remain honestly curious and curiously honest. Far from "disaffiliated," they are more gregarious than any preceding generation. . . .

Indeed, despite his tolerance of quixotic causes and idiosyncratic roles, the Man of the Year reflects—more accurately than he might care to admit—many of the mainstream currents in society at large. In 1966, the young American became vociferously skeptical of the Great Society. Though he retains a strong emotional identification with the deprived and spurned citizens of his own and other societies, he recognizes that the civil rights revolution, in which he was an early hero at the barricades, has reached a stage at which his own involvement is no longer vital. . . .

Having little fear that they will ever lack material comforts for their own part, the young tend to dismiss as superficial and irrelevant their elders' success-oriented lives. "You waited," sniffs a young Californian. "We won't." Nonetheless, today's youth appears more deeply committed to the fundamental Western ethos—decency, tolerance, brotherhood—than almost any generation since the age of chivalry. If they have an ideology, it is idealism; if they have one ideal, it is pragmatism.

Theirs is an immediate philosophy, tailored to the immediacy of their lives. The young no longer feel that they are merely preparing for life; they are living it. . . . As Buell Gallagher, president of the City College of New York, sees it: "This generation has no utopia. Its idea is the Happening. Let it be concrete, let it be vivid, let it be personal. Let it be *now!*"

With its sense of immediacy, the New Generation couples a sense of values that is curiously compelling. It esteems inventiveness, eloquence, honesty, elegance and good looks—all qualities personified in the Now Generation's closest approximation of a hero, John F. Kennedy. "Heroism and villainy begin with fantasy," says Stephen Kates, 23, a brilliant concert cellist. "This generation has no fantasies."

In fact, as Harvard Sociologist Seymour

Lipset observes, they are "caught up in the myth that J. F. K. was a radical President, and would have done all sorts of things, bypassing the older generation." By contrast, the Now People almost universally mock Lyndon Johnson . . . for his "bluffs, come-on gimmicks and intellectual dishonesty.". . .

Because the nation endorsed the civil rights movement, America's youthful activists tasted victory in their pioneering cause. For the first time, commitment seemed to pay off, and a New Left was born: a grass-roots populist mélange of organizations and splinter groups that struck in all directions—antipoverty, anticensorship, anti-war, anti-establishment. Says C.C.N.Y.'s Gallagher, himself a target of agitation: "Unlike the rebels of the '30s, who knew where they were going, the New Lefter today rejects ideologies—he's issue-oriented, not ideology-oriented.". . .

[The older generation worries about the dangers of psychedelic trips, sexual permissiveness, folk rock, and the no-touch, dead-pan dances, and asks,] Can the Now People really take it? Can they endure all the abrasive relationships and anomalous demands—the psychological subway wheels—that the "real world" has to offer? Can they, as a first step, accommodate their own parents? "The generational gap is wider than I've ever seen it in my lifetime," says Harvard's David Riesman. Predicts Britain's Leslie Paul, whose autobiography gave the phrase "angry young man" to the world in 1951: "The relations of the generations may become the central social issue of the next 50 years, as the relations between the classes have been for the past half-century."

The questing, restless majority of the young may already be ahead of that issue. By the existential act of rejecting *cogito, ergo sum* for *sum, ergo sum*, they have taken on willy-nilly, a vast commitment toward a kindlier, more equitable society. The young often seem romantics in search of a cause, rebels without *raison d'être*. Yet in many ways they are markedly saner, more unselfish, less hag-ridden than their elders. . . .

Indeed, Viet Nam has given the young—protesters and participants alike—the opportunity to disprove the doom criers of the 1950's who warned that the next generation would turn out spineless and grey-flannel-souled. Henry David Thoreau would have felt at home with the young of the 60's; they are as appalled as he was at the thought of leading "lives of quiet desperation." Indeed, for the future, the generation now in command can take solace from its offspring's determination to do better.

They will have to. For better or for worse, the world today is committed to accelerating change: radical, wrenching, erosive of both traditions and old values. Its inheritors have grown up with rapid change, are better prepared to accommodate it than any in history, indeed embrace change as a virtue in itself. With his skeptical yet humanistic outlook, his disdain for fanatacism and his scorn for the spurious, the Man of the Year suggests that he will infuse the future with a new sense of morality, a transcendant and contemporary ethic that could infinitely enrich the "empty society."

INDEX